Project
Management
for
Executives

Project Management for Executives

HAROLD KERZNER, Ph.D.

Division of Business Administration
Baldwin-Wallace College
Berea, Ohio

VNR VAN NOSTRAND REINHOLD COMPANY
NEW YORK   CINCINNATI   TORONTO   LONDON   MELBOURNE

Van Nostrand Reinhold Company Regional Offices:
New York   Cincinnati

Van Nostrand Reinhold Company International Offices:
London   Toronto   Melbourne

Library of Congress Catalog Card Number: 81-10357
ISBN: 0-442-25920-4

Manufactured in the United States of America

Published by Van Nostrand Reinhold Company
135 West 50th Street, New York, N.Y. 10020

Published simultaneously in Canada by Van Nostrand Reinhold Ltd.

15 14 13 12 11 10 9 8 7 6 5 4 3 2 1

Library of Congress Cataloging in Publication Data

Kerzner, Harold.
    Project management for executives.

    Bibliography: p.
    Includes index.
    1. Industrial project management.   2. Executives.
I. Title.
HD69.P75K48   658.4'04   81-10357
ISBN 0-442-25920-4   AACR2

To

Blen D. Nance
Thiokol Corporation,
Wasatch Division

"The Project Manager's Project Manager"

Preface

To make better use of and to achieve greater control over resources, more and more executives are realizing the importance of adopting and implementing the project management approach. Today, project management has spread to almost every major industry in the world, on either a formal or informal basis. An integral aspect of project management is that it forces top-level executives to modify the way they work with lower-level personnel and other managers.

This book is addressed not only to top-level executives who must provide their continuous support for all projects, but also to those project managers, project team members, and functional managers who must interact with top-level management during the execution of a project. It could also be used in seminars or classes for business and engineering students at the graduate level. With both textual material and case studies, the book stresses real-world project management. The majority of the case studies are actual situations taken from the author's consulting practice and the seminars and lectures the author has conducted throughout the world.

Chapters 1 and 2 introduce the concept and describe what an executive has to know about project management. Chapter 3 deals with the various organizational forms that an executive can use to implement project management and considers the advantages and disadvantages of each. The selection, training, and appointment of project managers are discussed in Chapter 4, and a variety of methods for evaluating project management performance are given.

Chapter 5 describes the problems and procedures for planning, controlling, and directing a project. It is assumed that the reader of this chapter is familiar with PERT/CPM. The following case studies should be omitted if the reader does not have a background in PERT/CPM: Williams Construction, The MX Project, and Project Status.

Chapter 6 considers the types of problems that can occur during a project. Conflict identification and resolution are discussed in Chapter 7. Chapter 8 provides the reader with a series of checklist questions that can be used to help identify potential problem areas. Various graphical techniques that are available for presenting project status are explained in Chapter 9. For answers to the various exams, an instructors manual is available by writing to the author at Baldwin-Wallace College, Division of Business Administration, Berea, Ohio 44107.

The author wishes to express his deepest appreciation to: Dr. Neal Malicky, President and Dean Mark Collier for providing an environment conductive to intellectual exploration; Dr. Dieter E. Wassen, for his encouragement and support in keeping close contact with industry so that I might bring the real world into the classroom; and Wiltrud Cornish and Patricia Ray, for their skill in transforming hand-written pages into a well-edited, typed manuscript.

Harold Kerzner
Baldwin-Wallace College

Contents

Case Studies

5. Management Functions 320

Case Studies

6. The Project Environment: Problems and Pitfalls   **448**

Case Studies

7. Conflicts   **554**

Project
Management
for
Executives

1
Overview

1.0 INTRODUCTION

Executives are facing increasingly complex challenges in the 1980s. These challenges are the result of high escalation factors for salaries and raw materials, increased union demands, pressure from stockholders, and the possibility of long-term, high inflation accompanied by a mild recession and a lack of borrowing power with financial institutions. These environmental conditions have existed before, but not to the degree that they do today.

In the past, executives have attempted to ease the impact of these environmental conditions by embarking on massive cost-reduction programs. The usual results of these programs have been early retirement, layoffs, and a reduction in manpower through attrition. As jobs become vacant, executives pressure line managers to accomplish the same amount of work with fewer resources, either by improving efficiency or by upgrading performance requirements to a higher position on the learning curve. Because people costs are more inflationary than the cost of equipment or facilities, executives are funding more and more capital equipment projects in an attempt to increase or improve productivity without increasing labor.

Unfortunately, the modern executive is somewhat limited in how far he can go to reduce manpower without running a high risk to corporate profitability. Capital equipment projects are not always the answer. Thus, executives have been forced to look elsewhere for the solutions to their problems.

Almost all of today's executives are in agreement that the solution to the majority of corporate problems involves obtaining better control and use of existing corporate resources. Emphasis is being placed on looking internally rather than externally for the solution to these problems. As part of the attempt to achieve an internal solution, executives are taking a hard look at the ways corporate activities are being managed. Project management is one of the techniques now under consideration.

The project management approach is relatively modern. It is characterized by new methods of restructuring management and adapting special management

1

techniques, with the purpose of obtaining better control and use of existing resources. Twenty years ago project management was confined to the Department of Defense contractors and construction companies. Today, the concept behind project management is being applied in such diverse industries and organizations as defense, construction, pharmaceuticals, chemicals, banking, hospitals, accounting, advertising, law, state and local governments, and the United Nations.

The rapid rate of change in both technology and the marketplace has created enormous strains upon existing organizational forms. The traditional structure is highly bureaucratic and experience has shown that it cannot respond rapidly enough to a changing environment. Thus, the traditional structure must be replaced by project management, or other temporary management structures which are highly organic and can respond very rapidly as situations develop inside and outside the company.

Project management has long been discussed by corporate executives and academics as one of several workable possibilities for organizational forms of the future that could integrate complex efforts and reduce bureaucracy. The acceptance of project management has not been easy, however. Many executives are not willing to accept change and are inflexible when it comes to adapting to a different environment. The project management approach requires a departure from the traditional business organizational form which was basically vertical and which emphasized a strong superior-subordinate relationship.

1.1 UNDERSTANDING PROJECT MANAGEMENT

Project management can mean different things to different people. Quite often, executives misunderstand the concept because they have ongoing projects within their company and feel that they are using project management to control these activities. In such a case, the following might be considered as an appropriate definition:

- Project management is the art of creating the illusion that any outcome is the result of a series of predetermined, deliberate acts when, in fact, it was dumb luck.

Although this might be the way that some companies are running their projects, this is not project management. Project management is designed to make better use of existing resources by getting work to flow horizontally as well as vertically within the company. This approach does not really destroy the vertical, bureaucratic flow of work, but simply requires that line organizations talk to one another horizontally so work will be accomplished more smoothly throughout the organization. The vertical flow of work is still the responsibility of the line managers. The horizontal flow of work is the responsibility of the project managers, and their primary effort is to communicate and coordinate activities horizontally between the line organizations. The following would be an over-view definition of project management:

- Project management is the planning, organizing, directing, and controlling of company resources for a relatively short-term objective that has been established to complete specific goals and objectives. Furthermore, project management utilizes the systems approach to management by having functional personnel (the vertical hierarchy) assigned to a specific project (the horizontal hierarchy).

The above definition requires further comment. Classical management is usually considered to have five functions or principles:

- Planning
- Organizing
- Staffing
- Controlling
- Directing

You will notice that, in the above definition, the staffing function has been omitted. This was intentional, because the project manager does not staff the project. Staffing is a line responsibility. The project manager has the right to request specific resources, but the final decision of what resources will be committed rests with the line managers.

We should also comment on what is meant by a "relatively" short-term project. Not all industries have the same definition for a short-term project. In engineering, it might be a six-month or two-year project; in construction, three to five years; in nuclear components, ten years; and in insurance, two weeks.

Figure 1-1 is a pictorial representation of project management. The objective of the figure is to show that project management is designed to manage or control company resources on a given activity, within time, within cost, and within performance. Time, cost, and performance are the constraints on the project. If the project is to be accomplished for an outside customer, then the project has a fourth constraint: good customer relations. Executives should immediately realize that it is possible to manage a project internally within time, cost, and performance and then alienate the customer to such a degree that no further business will be forthcoming. Executives often select the project managers based upon who the customer is and what kind of customer relations will be necessary.

We have made reference to the fact that the project manager must control company resources within time, cost, and performance. Most companies have six resources:

- Money
- Manpower
- Equipment

Figure 1-1. Overview Of Project Management.

- Facilities
- Materials
- Information/Technology

Actually, the project manager does *not* control any of these resources directly, except perhaps money (i.e., the project budget).[1] Resources are controlled by the line managers, functional managers, or, as they are often called, resources managers. The project managers must therefore negotiate with the line managers for all project resources. When we say that a project manager controls project resources, we really mean that he controls those resources (that are temporarily loaned to him) *through the line managers.*

Classical management has often been defined as a process in which the manager does not necessarily perform things for himself, but accomplishes objectives through others in a group situation. This basic definition also applies to the project manager. In addition, a project manager must help himself. There is nobody to help him.

If an executive takes a close look at project management, he will see that the project manager actually works for the line managers, *not* vice versa. Many executives do not realize this. They have a tendency to put a halo around the head of the project manager and give him a bonus at project termination when, in fact, the credit should really go to the line managers who are continuously pressured

---

1. Here we are assuming that the line manager and project manager are not the same individual.

to make better use of their resources. The project manager is simply the agent through whom this is accomplished. So, why do some companies glorify the project management position?

To illustrate the necessity for the project manager, consider the time, cost, and performance constraints in Figure 1-1. Many functional managers, if left alone, would recognize only the performance constraint: "Just give me another $50,000 and two more months and I'll give you the ideal technology."

The project manager, as part of this communicating, coordinating, and integrating responsibilities, reminds the line managers that there are also time and cost constraints on the project. This is the starting point for better resource control.

Project managers depend on line managers. When the project manager gets in trouble, the only place he can go is to the line manager because additional resources are almost always required to alleviate the problems. When a line manager gets in trouble, he usually goes first to the project manager and requests either additional funding or some type of authorization.

To illustrate this working relationship between the project and line manager, consider the following situation:

Project Manager: (addressing the line manager) I have a serious problem. I'm looking at a $50,000 cost overrun on my project and I need your help. I'd like you to do the same amount of work that you are currently scheduled for, but in 3,000 less man-hours. Since your organization is burdened at $20/hour, this would more than compensate for the cost overrun.

Line Manager: Even if I could, why should I? You know that good line managers can always make work expand to meet budget. I'll look over my manpower curves and let you know tomorrow.

The Following Day . . .

Line Manager: I've looked over my manpower curves and I have enough work to keep my people employed. I'll give you back the 3,000 hours you need but remember, YOU OWE ME ONE!

Several Months Later . . .

Line Manager: I've just seen the planning for your new project that's supposed to start two months from now. You'll need two people from my department. There are two employees that I'd like to use on your project. Unfortunately, these two people are available now. If I don't pick these people up on your charge number right now, some other project might pick them up in the interim period and they won't be available when your project starts.

Project Manager: What you're saying is that you want me to let you sandbag against one of my charge numbers, knowing that I really don't need them.

Line Manager: That's right. I'll try to find other jobs (and charge numbers) for them to work on temporarily, so that your project won't be completely burdened. Remember, you owe me one.

Project Manager: O.K. I know that I owe you one, so I'll do this for you. Does this make us even?

Line Manager: Not at all! But you're going in the right direction.

When the project management/line management relationship begins to deteriorate, the project almost always suffers. Executives must promote a good working relationship between line and project management. One of the most common ways of destroying this relationship is by asking, "Who contributes to profits—the line or project manager?" Project managers feel that they control all project profits because they control the budget. The line managers, on the other hand, argue that they must staff with appropriately budgeted-for personnel, supply the resources at the desired time, and supervise the actual performance. Actually, both the vertical and horizontal lines contribute to profits. These types of conflicts can destroy the entire project management structure.

The previous examples should indicate to the executive that project management is more behavioral than quantitative. Effective project management requires an understanding of:

- Quantitative tools and techniques
- Organizational structures
- Organizational behavior

Most executives understand the quantitative tools for planning, scheduling, and controlling work. It is imperative that project managers understand totally the operations of each line organization. In addition, the project manager must understand his own job description, especially where his authority begins and ends. During an in-house seminar on engineering project management, the author asked one of the project engineers to provide a description of his job as a project engineer. During the discussion that followed, several project managers, and line managers, said that there was a great deal of overlapping between their job descriptions and that of the project engineer.

Organizational behavior is important because the functional employees at the interface position find themselves reporting to more than one boss—a line manager and one project manager for each project they are assigned to. Executives must provide proper training so functional employees can report effectively to multiple managers.

1.2 THE NEED FOR PROJECT MANAGEMENT

The growth of project management has come about more through necessity than through desire. The major reason for its slow growth can be attributed to the lack of acceptance of the new management techniques so necessary for its successful implementation. An inherent fear of the unknown acted as a deterrent for those managers wishing to change over.

Between the middle and late 1960s more and more executives began searching for new management techniques and organizational structures that could be quickly adapted to a changing environment. The table below identifies two major variables that executives consider with regard to organizational restructuring:

Type of Industry	Tasks	Environment
A	Simple	Dynamic
B	Simple	Static
C	Complex	Dynamic
D	Complex	Static

Almost all type C and most of type D industries have project management-related structures. The key variable appears to be task complexity. Companies that have complex tasks and that also operate in a dynamic environment find project management mandatory. Such industries would include aerospace, defense, construction, high-technology engineering, computers, and electronic instrumentation.

The moral here is that not all industries need project management and executives must determine whether there is an actual need before making a commitment. Several industries with simple tasks, whether in a static or dynamic environment, do not need project management. Manufacturing industries with slowly changing technology do not need project management, unless of course they have a requirement for several special projects, as capital equipment activities, that could interrupt the normal flow of work in the routine manufacturing operations.

1.3 PROJECT MANAGEMENT GROWTH

The slow growth rate and acceptance of project management were related to the fact that the limitations of project management were readily apparent, yet the advantages were not completely recognizable. Project management requires organizational restructuring. The question, of course, is "How much restructuring?" Executives have avoided the subject of project management for fear that "revolutionary" changes must be made to the organization. As will be seen later in Chapter 3, project management can be achieved with little departure from the existing traditional structure.

Project management restructuring permitted companies to:

- Accomplish tasks that could not be effectively handled by the traditional structure
- Accomplish one-time activities with minimum disruption of routine business

The second item implies that project management is a "temporary" management structure and therefore causes minimum organizational disruption. The major problems identified by those managers who endeavored to adapt to the new system all revolved about conflicts in authority and resources.

Three major problems were identified by Killian:[2]

- Project priorities and competition for talent may interrupt the stability of the organization and interfere with its long-range interests by upsetting the normal business of the functional organization.
- Long-range planning may suffer as the company gets more involved in meeting schedules and fulfilling the requirements of temporary projects.
- Shifting people from project to project may disrupt the training of new employees and specialists. This may hinder their growth and development within their fields of specialization.

Another major concern was the fact that project management required upper-level managers to relinquish some of their authority through delegation to the middle managers. In several situations, middle management soon became the power positions, even moreso than upper-level management.

Despite these limitations, there were several driving forces behind the project management approach. According to John Kenneth Galbraith, these forces stem from "the imperatives of technology." The six imperatives are:[3]

- The time span between project initiation and completion appears to be increasing.
- The capital committed to the project prior to the use of the end item appears to be increasing.
- As technology increases, the commitment of time and money appears to become inflexible.
- Technology requires more and more specialized manpower.
- The inevitable counterpart of specialization is organization.
- The above five "imperatives" identify the necessity for more effective planning, scheduling, and control.

As the driving forces overtook the restraining forces, project management began to mature. Executives began to realize that the approach was in the best interest of the company. Project management, if properly implemented, can make it easier for executives to overcome such internal and external obstacles as:

- Unstable economy
- Shortages

---

2. William P. Killian, "Project Management – Future Organizational Concepts," *Marquette Business Review,* 2: pp. 90-107, 1971.
3. John Kenneth Galbraith, *The New Industrial State,* The New American Library: New York, 1968, pp. 25-28.

- Soaring costs
- Increased complexity
- Heightened competition
- Technological changes
- Societal concerns
  - Consumerism
  - Ecology
  - Quality of work

Project management may not eliminate these problems, but may make it easier for the company to adapt to a changing environment.

If these obstacles are not controlled, the results can be:

- Decreased profits
- Increased manpower needs
- Cost overruns, schedule delays, and penalty payments occurring earlier and earlier
- An inability to cope with new technology
- R & D results too late to benefit existing product lines
- New products introduced into the marketplace too late
- Temptation to make hasty decisions that prove to be costly
- Management insisting on earlier and greater return on investment
- Greater difficulty in establishing on-target objectives in real time
- Problems in relating cost to technical performance and scheduling during the execution of the project

Project management became a necessity for many companies. They began to expand into multiple product lines, many of which were often dissimilar, and organizational complexities grew almost without bound. The reasons for this can be attributed to:

- Technology increasing at an astounding rate
- More money invested in R & D
- More information available
- Shortening of project life cycles

To satisfy the requirements imposed by the above four factors, management was "forced" into organizational restructuring; the traditional organizational form which had survived for so many decades was now found to be inadequate for integrating activities across functional "empires."

CASE STUDY: GOSHE CORPORATION

"I've called this meeting to try to find out why we're having a difficult time upgrading our EDP department to an MIS division," remarked Herb Banyon, executive vice-president of Goshe Corporation. "Last year we decided to give the EDP department a chance to show that they can contribute to corporate profits by removing the department from under the control of the finance division and establishing an MIS division. I keep getting reports stating that we're having major conflicts and personality clashes among the departments involved in these MIS projects and that we're one month to three months behind on almost all projects. If we don't resolve this problem right now, the MIS division will be demoted to a department and once again find itself under the jurisdiction of the finance director."

Background

In June 1977, Herb Banyon announced that Goshe Corporation would be giving salary increases amounting to an average of 7 percent companywide, but the EDP department would receive only 5.5 percent. The EDP department, especially the scientific programmers, were furious because this was the third straight year they had received below-average salary increases. The scientific programmers felt that they were performing engineering-type work and therefore should be paid according to the engineering pay scale.

The year before, the scientific programmers tried to convince management that engineering needed its own computer and that a separate computer programming department should be established within the engineering division. This suggestion had strong support from the engineering community because they could benefit by having complete control of their own computer. Unfortunately, management rejected the idea, fearing that competition and conflict would develop by having two data processing units, and that one centralized unit was the only workable solution.

As a result of management's decision to keep the EDP department intact and not give them a chance to demonstrate that they can and do contribute to profits, the EDP personnel created a closed shop environment and developed a very hostile attitude toward all other departments, even those within their own finance division.

The Meeting of the Minds

In January 1978, Banyon announced the organizational restructuring that would upgrade the EDP department. Al Grandy, the EDP department manager, was given a promotion to division manager, provided he could adequately manage the MIS project activities. By December 1978, it became apparent that something had to be done to remedy the deteriorating environment between the functional departments and the MIS personnel. Banyon called a meeting of all functional and divisional managers in the hope that some of the problems could be identified and worked out.

Banyon: For the past ten months I've watched you people arguing back and forth about the MIS problems, with both sides always giving me a line about how we'll work it out. Now, before it's too late, let's try to get at the root of the problem.

Cost Accounting Manager: The major problem, as I see it, is the lack of interpersonal skills employed by the MIS people. Our organization here is, or should I say has been up to now, purely traditional with each person reporting and working for and with the manager. Now we have horizontal projects in which the MIS project leaders must work with several functional managers, all of whom have different management styles, different personalities, and different dispositions. The MIS group just can't turn around in one or two weeks and develop these necessary skills. It takes time and training.

Training Manager: I agree with your comments. There are two types of situations which demand immediate personnel development training. The first situation involves personnel who are required to perform in an organizational structure that has gone from the relatively simple, pure structure to a complex, partial matrix structure. This is what has happened to us. The second situation involves the task changes from simple to complex.

If either situation existed by itself, there would usually be some slack time. But when both occur almost simultaneously, as is our case, immediate training should be undertaken. I told this to Grandy several times, but all he kept saying was that we don't have time now because we're loaded down with priority projects.

Grandy: I can see from the start that we're headed for a rake-Grandy-over-the-coals meeting. So, let me defend each accusation as it comes up. The day Banyon announced the organizational change, I was handed a list of fifteen MIS projects that had to be completed within unrealistic time schedules. I performed a manpower requirements projection and found that we were understaffed by 35 percent. Now, I understand the importance of training my people. But how am I supposed to release my people for these training sessions when I have been given specific instructions that each of these fifteen projects had a high priority? I can just see myself walking into your office, Herb, telling you that I want to utilize my people only half-time so that they can undergo professional development training.

Banyon: Somehow I feel that the buck just got passed back to me. Those schedules I gave you appeared totally realistic to me. I just can't imagine any simple computer program requiring more time than my original estimates. And had you come to me with a request for training, I would have checked with personnel and then probably would have given you the time to train your people.

Engineering Manager: I wish to make a comment or two about schedules. I'm not happy when an MIS guy walks into my office and tells me, or should I say demands, that certain resources be given to him so that he can meet a schedule or milestone date that I've had no decision in establishing. My people are just not going to become pawns in the power struggle for MIS supremacy. My people become very defensive if they're not permitted to participate in the planning activities and I have to agree with them.

Manufacturing Manager: The manufacturing division has a project with the MIS group for purchasing a hardware system that will satisfy our scheduling and material handling system requirements. My people wanted to be involved in the hardware selection process. Instead, the MIS group came to us with proposal in hand identifying a system that was not a practical extension of the state-of-the-art and did not fall within our cost and time constraints. We in manufacturing, being nice guys, modified our schedules to be compatible with the MIS project leader's proposal. We then tried to provide more detailed information for the MIS team so that . . . .

Grandy: Just a minute here! Your use of the word "we" is somewhat misleading. Project management is structured so that sufficient definition of work to be performed is available and a more uniform implementation can result. My people requested a lot of detailed information from your staff and were told to go do the work ourselves and find our own information. "After all," as one of your functional employees put it, "we're gonna pass all of the responsibility over to you guys in project management; you people can do it all."

Therefore, because my people had insufficient data, we both ended up creating a problem that was intensified by a lack of formal communication between the MIS group and the functional departments, as well as between the functional departments themselves. I hold functional management responsible for this problem because some of the managers did not seem to understand that they were responsible for the project work under their cognizance. Furthermore, I consider you, the manufacturing manager, as being remiss in your duties by not reviewing the performance of your personnel assigned to the project.

Manufacturing Manager: Your people designed a system that was far too complex for our needs. Your people consider this project as a chance for glory. It's going to take us ten years to grow into this complex system you've created.

Grandy: Let me make a few comments about our delays in the schedule. One of our projects was a six-month effort. After the third month, there was a new department manager assigned in the department that was to be the prime user of this project. We were then given a change in user requirements and incurred additional delays in waiting for new user authorization.

Of course, people problems always have an effect on schedules. One of my most experienced people became sick and had to be replaced by a rookie. In addition, I've tried to be a "good guy" by letting my people help out some of the functional managers when nonMIS problems occur. This other work ended up encroaching on staff time to a degree where it affected the schedules.

Even though the MIS group regulates computer activities, we have no control over computer downtime or slow turnabout time. Turnabout time is directly proportional to our priority lists, and we all know that these lists are established from above.

And last, we have to consider both company and project politics. All the MIS group wanted to do was to show that we can contribute to company profits. Top management consistently tries to give us unwanted direction and functional management tries to sabotage our project for fear that if we're successful, then it will be less money for their departments during promotion time.

Banyon: Well, I guess we've identified the major problem areas. The question remaining is, what are we going to do about it?

CASE STUDY: PROJECT MANAGEMENT AT HYTEN CORPORATION

On June 5, 1978, a meeting was held at Hyten between Bill Knapp, director of sales, and John Rich, director of engineering. The purpose of the meeting was to discuss the development of a new product for a special customer application. The requirements included a very difficult, tight-time schedule. The key to the success of the project would depend on timely completion of individual tasks by various departments.

Knapp: The business development department was established to provide co-ordination between departments, but they have not really helped. They just stick their nose in when things are going good and mess everything up. They have been out to see several customers, giving them information and delivery dates that we can't possibly meet.

Rich: I have several engineers who have MBA degrees and are pushing hard for better positions within engineering or management. They keep saying that formal project management is what we should have at Hyten. The informal approach we use just doesn't work all the time. But I'm not sure any type of project management will work in our division.

Knapp: Well, I wonder who business development will tap to coordinate this project. It would be better to get the manager from inside the organization instead of hiring someone from outside.

Company Background

Hyten Company was founded in 1922 as a manufacturer of automotive components. In the 1940s the company manufactured electronic components for the military. After the war, Hyten was incorporated and continued to prosper.

Hyten was one of the major component suppliers for the space program, but it did not allow itself to become specialized. When the space program declined, Hyten acquired other product lines including energy management, building products, and machine tools to complement their automotive components and electronics fields.

Hyten has been a leader in the development of new products and processes. Annual sales are in excess of $300 million. The Automotive Components Division is one of Hyten's rapidly expanding business areas.

The Automotive Components Division

The management of both the Automotive Components Division and the corporation itself is young and involved. Hyten has enjoyed a period of continuous growth over the past fifteen years as a result of careful planning and having the right people in the right positions at the right time. This is emphasized by the fact that within five years of joining Hyten, every major manager and division head has been promoted to more responsibility within the corporation. The management staff of the Automotive Components Division has an average age of forty and no one is over fifty. Most of the middle managers have MBA degrees and a few have doctorates. Currently, the automotive components division has three manufacturing plants at various locations throughout the country. Central offices and most of the nonproduction functions are located at the main plant. There has been some effort by past presidents to give each plant some level of purchasing, quality, manufacturing engineering and personnel functions.

Informal Project Management at Hyten Corporation

The Automotive Components Division of Hyten Corporation has an informal system of project management. It revolves around each department handling their own functional area of a given product development or project. Projects have been frequent enough that a sequence of operations has been developed to take a new product from concept to market. Each department knows its responsibilities and what it must contribute to a project.

A manager within the business development department assumes informal project coordination responsibility and calls periodic meetings of the department heads involved. These meetings keep everyone advised of work status, changes to the project, and any problem areas. Budgeting of the project is based on the cost analysis developed after the initial design, while funding is allocated to each functional department based on the degree of its involvement. Funding for the initial design phase is controlled through business development. The customer has very little control over the funding, manpower, or work to be done. The customer, however, dictates when the new product design must be available for integration into the vehicle design, and when the product must be available in production quantities.

The Business Development Department

The business development department, separate from marketing/sales, functions as a steering group for deciding which new products or customer requests are to be pursued and which are to be dropped. Factors that they consider in making these decisions are: (1) the company's long- and short-term business plans, (2) current sales forecasts, (3) economic and industry indicators, (4) profit potential, (5) internal capabilities (both volume and technology), and (6) what the customer is willing to pay versus estimated cost.

The duties of business development also include the coordination of a project or new product from initial design through market availability. In this capacity, they have no formal authority over either functional managers or functional employees. They act strictly on an informal basis to keep the project moving, give status reports, and report on potential problems. They are also responsible for the selection of the plant that will be used to manufacture the product.

The functions of business development were formerly handled as a joint-staff function where all the directors would periodically meet to formulate short-range plans and solve problems associated with new products. The department was formally organized three years ago by the then 38-year-old president in recognition of the need for project management within the automotive components division.

Manpower for the business development department was taken from both outside the company and from within the division. This was done to honor the corporation's commitment to hire people from the outside only after it was determined that there were no qualified people internally (an area that for years has been a sore spot to the younger managers and engineers).

When the business development department was organized, its level of authority and responsibility was limited. However, the department's authority and responsibility have subsequently expanded, although at a slow rate. This was done in deference to the functional managers who were concerned that project management would undermine their "empire."

Introduction of Formal Project Management at Hyten Corporation

On July 10, 1978, Wilbur Donley was hired to direct new product development efforts in the business development department. Prior to joining Hyten, he worked as project manager with a company that supplied aircraft hardware to the government. He had worked both as an assistant project manager and as a project manager for five years prior to joining Hyten.

Shortly after his arrival, he convinced upper management to examine the idea of expanding the business development group and giving them responsibility for formal project management. An outside consulting firm was hired to give an in-depth seminar on project management to all management and supervisory employees in the division.

Prior to the seminar, Donley talked to Frank Harrel, manager of quality and reliability and George Hub, manager of manufacturing engineering, about their problems and what they thought of project management.

Frank Harrel is thirty-seven years old, has a MBA degree, and has been with Hyten for five years. He was hired as an industrial engineer and three years ago was promoted to manager of quality and reliability. George Hub is forty-five years old and has been with Hyten for 12 years as manager of manufacturing engineering.

Donley: Well, Frank, what do you see as potential problems to the timely completion of projects within the automotive components division?

Harrel: The usual material movement problems we always have. We monitor all incoming materials in samples and production quantities, as well as in-process checking of production, and finished goods on a sampling basis. We then move to 100 percent inspection if any discrepancies are found. Marketing and manufacturing people don't realize how much time is required to obtain either internal or customer deviations. Our current manpower requires that schedules be juggled to accommodate 100 percent inspection levels on "hot items." We seem to be getting more and more items at the last minute that must be done on overtime.

Donley: What you are suggesting is a coordination of effort with marketing, purchasing, production scheduling, and the manufacturing function to allow your department to perform their routine work and still be able to accommodate a limited amount of high-level work on "hot" jobs.

Harrel: Precisely, but we have no formal contact with these people. More open lines of communication would be of benefit to everyone.

Donley: We are going to introduce a more formal type of project management than has been used in the past so that all departments who are involved will actively participate in the planning cycle of the project. That way, they will remain aware of how they affect the function of other departments and prevent overlapping of work. We should be able to stay on schedule and get better cooperation.

Harrel: Good, I'll be looking forward to the departure from the usual method of handling a new project. It should work much better and result in fewer problems.

Donley: How do you feel, George, about improving the coordination of work among various departments through a formal project manager?

Hub: Frankly, if it improves communication between departments, I'm all in favor of the change. Under our present system, I am asked to make estimates of cost and lead times to implement a new product. When the project begins, the product design group starts making changes that require new cost figures and lead times. These changes result in cost overrun and not meeting schedule dates. Typically, these changes continue right up to the production start date. Manufacturing appears to be the bad guy for not meeting the scheduled start date. We need someone to coordinate the work of various departments to prevent this continuous redoing of various jobs. We will at least have a chance to meet the schedule, reduce cost, and improve the attitude of my people.

Personnel Department's View of Project Management

After the seminar on project management, a discussion was held between Sue Lyons, director of personnel and Jason Finney, assistant director of personnel. The discussion was about changing the organizational structure from informal project management to formal project management.

Lyons: Changing over would not be easy. There are several matters to be taken under consideration.

Finney: I think we should stop going to outside sources for competent people to manage new projects that are established within business development. There are several competent people at Hyten who have MBAs in systems/project management. With that background and familiarity with company operations, it would be to the company's advantage if we selected personnel from within our organization.

Lyons: Problems will develop whether we choose someone from inside the company or from an outside source.

Finney: However, if the company continues to hire outsiders into business development to head new projects, competent people at Hyten are going to start filtering to places of new employment.

Lyons: You are right about the filtration. Whoever is chosen to be a project manager must have qualifications that will get the job done. He should not only know the technical aspect behind the project, but he should also be able to work with people and understand their needs. He has to show concern for team members and provide them with work challenge. Project managers must work in a dynamic environment. They must be able to live with change and provide necessary leadership to implement it. It is the project manager's responsibility to develop an atmosphere to allow people to adapt to the changing work environment.

In our department alone the changes to be made will be very crucial to the happiness of the employees and the success of projects. They must feel they are being given a square deal, especially in the evaluation procedure. Who will do the evaluation? Will the functional manager be solely responsible for the evaluation, when in fact he might never see the functional employee for the duration of a project? He could not possibly keep tabs on all his functional employees who are working on different projects.

Finney: Then the functional manager will have to ask the project managers for evaluation information.

Lyons: I can see that could result in many unwanted situations. To begin with, say the project manager and the functional manager don't see eye to eye on things. Granted, both should be at the same grade level and neither one has authority over the other. But let's say there is a situation where the two of them disagree about either direction or quality of work. That puts the functional employee in an awkward position. He will have a tendency to favor the individual who signs his promotion and evaluation form. This can influence the project manager into recommending an evaluation below par, regardless of how the functional employee performs. There is also the situation where the employee is on the project for only a couple of weeks. He spends most of his time working by himself and does not get a chance to know the project manager. The project manager gives the functional employee an average rating even though the employee has done an excellent job. This results from very little contact. Then, what do you do when the project manager allows personal feelings to influence his evaluation of the functional employee? If the project manager knows the functional employee personally, he might be tempted to give a strong or weak recommendation, regardless of performance.

Finney: You seem to be aware of many difficulties that project management might bring.

Lyons: I've been doing a lot of homework since I attended that seminar on project management. It was a good seminar and since there is not much written on the topic, I've been making a few phone calls to other colleagues for their opinions on project management.

Finney: What have you learned from these phone calls?

Lyons: There are several personnel problems involved. What do you do in this situation: The project manager makes an excellent recommendation to the functional manager. The functional employee is aware of the appraisal and feels he should be given an above-average pay increase to match the excellent job appraisal; but the functional manager fails to do so. One personnel manager from another company using project management ran into problems when the project manager gave an employee of one grade level the responsibilities of a higher grade level. The employee did an outstanding job taking on the responsibilities of a higher grade level and expected a large salary increase or a promotion.

Finney: Well, that's fair isn't it?

Lyons: Yes it seems fair enough, but that's not what happened. The functional manager gave an average evaluation and argued that the project manager had no business giving the functional employee added responsibility without first checking with him. So then what you have is a disgruntled employee ready to seek employment elsewhere. Also, there are some functional managers who will only give above-average pay increases to those employees who stay in his department and make him look good.

Finney: So how does this leave our organization with respect to implementing formal project management?

Lyons: Right now I can see several changes that would have to take place. The first major change would have to be in attitudes toward formal project management and hiring procedures. We do have project management here at Hyten, but on an informal basis. If we could administer it formally, I feel we could do the company a great service. If we seek project managers from within, we could save on time and money. I could devote more time and effort on wage and salary grades and job descriptions. We would need to revise our evaluation forms—presently they are not adequate. Maybe we should develop more than one evaluation form; one for the project manager to fill out and give to the functional manager, and a second form to be completed by the functional manager for submission to personnel.

Finney: That might cause a few problems. Should the project manager fill out his evaluation during or after project completion?

Lyons: It would have to be after project completion. That way the employee would not feel tempted to distrupt the project if he felt he was not fairly evaluated. For example, he could decide not to show up for a few days and those days of absence could be most crucial for timely project completion.

Finney: How will you handle evaluation of employees who work on several projects at the same time? This could be a problem if employees are really enthusiastic about one project more than another. They could do a terrific job on the project they are interested in and slack off on other projects. You could also have functional people working on departmental jobs who would charge to the project overhead. Don't we have exempt and nonexempt people charging to projects?

Lyons: See what I mean? We can't just jump into project management. There will have to be changes first.

Finney: I realize that, Sue, but we do have several MBA people working here at Hyten who have been exposed to project management. I think that if we start putting our heads together and take a systematic approach to this matter, we will be able to pull this project together nicely.

Lyons: Well, Jason, I'm glad to see that you are for formal project management. We will have to approach top management on the topic. I would like you to help coordinate an equitable way of evaluating our people and develop the appropriate evaluation forms.

Product Management as Seen By the Various Departments

The general manager arranged through the personnel department, to interview various managers on a confidential basis. The purpose of the interview was to evaluate the overall acceptance of the concept of formal project management. The answers to the question, "How will project management affect your department?" were as follows:

Frank Harrel, Quality and Reliability Manager

"Project management is the actual coordination of the resources of functional departments to achieve the time, cost, and performance goals of the project. As a consequence, personnel interfacing is an important component in the success of the project. In terms of quality control, it means less of the attitude of the structured workplace where quality is viewed as having the function of finding defects and, as a result, is looked upon as a hindrance to production. It means that the attitude toward quality control will change to one of interacting with other departments to minimize manufacturing problems. Project management reduces inefficiency in functional areas and induces cooperation. Both company and department goals can be achieved. It puts an end to the 'can't see the forest for the trees' syndrome."

Harold Grimes, Plant Manager

"I think that formal project management will give us more work than long-term benefits. History indicates that we hire more outside men for new positions than we promote from within. Who will be hired into these new project management jobs? We are experiencing a lot of backlash from people who are required to teach new people the ropes. In my opinion, we should assign inside MBA graduates with project management training to head up projects and not hire an outsider as a formal project manager. Our present system would work fine if inside people were made the new managers in the business development department."

Herman Hall, Director of MIS

"I have no objections to the implementation of formal project management in our company. I do not believe, however, that it will be possible to provide the reports needed by this management structure for several years. This is because most of my staff are deeply involved in current projects. We are now working on the installation of minicomputers and on-line terminals throughout the plant. These projects have been delayed by the late arrival of new equipment, employee sabotage, and various start-up problems. As a result of these problems, one group admits to being six months behind schedule, and the other group, although on schedule, is eighteen months from their scheduled completion date. The rest of the staff currently assigned to maintenance projects consists of two systems analysts who are nearing retirement and two relatively inexperienced programmers. So, as you can readily see, unless we break up the current project teams and let those projects fall further behind schedule, it will be difficult at this time to put together another project team.

"The second problem is that even if I could put together a staff for the project, it might take up to two years to complete an adequate information system. Problems arise from the fact that it will take time to design a system that will draw data from all the functional areas. This design work will have to be done before the actual programming and testing could be accomplished. Finally, there would be a debugging period, when we receive feedback from the user on any flaws in the system or enhancements that he needs. We could not provide computer support for an 'overnight' change to project management."

Bob Gustwell, Scheduling Manager

"I am happy with the idea of formal project management, but I do see some problems in implementing it. Some people around here like the way we do things now. It is a natural reaction for employees to fight against any changes in management style.

"But don't worry about the scheduling department—my people will like the change to formal project management. I see this form of management as a way to minimize if not eliminate schedule changes. Better planning on the part of both department and project managers will be required and the priorities will be set at corporate level. You can count on our support because I'm tired of being caught between production and sales."

John Rich, Director of Engineering

"It seems to me that project management will only mess things up. We now have a chain of command in our organization that works. This new matrix will only create problems. The engineering department, being very technical, just can't take direction from anyone outside the department. The project office will start to skimp on specifications just to save time and dollars. Our products are too technical to allow schedules and project costs to affect engineering results.

"Bringing in someone from the outside to be the project manager will make things worse. I feel that formal project management should not be implemented at Hyten. Engineering has always directed the projects and we should keep it that way. We shouldn't change a winning combination."

Fred Kuncl, Plant Engineering

"I've thought about the trade-offs involved in implementing formal project management at Hyten and feel that plant engineering cannot live with them. Our departmental activities are centered around highly unpredictable circumstances that sometimes involve rapidly changing priorities related to the production function. We in plant engineering must be able to respond quickly and appropriately to maintenance activities directly related to manufacturing activities. Plant engineering is also responsible for carrying out critical preventive maintenance and plant construction projects.

"Project management would hinder our activities because project management responsibilities would burden our manpower with additional tasks. I am against project management because I feel that it is not in the best interest of Hyten. Project management would weaken our department's functional specialization because it would require cross-utilization of resources, manpower, and negotiation for the services critical to plant engineering."

Bill Knapp, Director of Marketing

"I feel that the seminar on formal project management was a good one. Formal project management could benefit Hyten. Our organization needs to focus on more than one direction at all times. In order to be successful in today's market, we must concentrate on giving all our products sharp focus. Formal project management could be a good way of placing individual emphasis on each of the products of our company. Project management would be especially advantageous to us because of our highly diversified product lines. The organization needs to allocate resources to projects, products, and markets efficiently. We cannot afford to have expensive resources sitting idle. Cross-utilization and the consequent need for negotiation insures that resources are used efficiently and in the organization's best overall interest.

"We can't afford to continue to carry on informal project management in our business. We are so diversified that all of our products can't be treated alike. Each product has different needs. Besides, the nature of a team effort would strengthen our organization."

Stanley Grant, Comptroller

"In my opinion, formal project management can be profitably applied in our organization. Management should not, however, expect that project management would gain instant acceptance by the functional managers and functional employees including the finance department personnel.

"The implementation of formal project management in our organization would have an impact on our cost control system and internal control system, as well.

"In the area of cost control, project cost control techniques have to be formalized and installed. This would require the accounting staff to: (1) break comprehensive cost summaries into work packages, (2) prepare commitment reports for 'technical decision makers,' (3) approximate report data, and (4) concentrate talent on major problems and opportunities. In project management, cost commitments on a project are made when various functional departments such as engineering, manufacturing, and marketing make technical decisions to take some kind of action. Conventional accounting reports do not show the cost effects of these technical decisions until it is too late to reconsider. We would need to provide the project manager with cost commitment reports at each decision state to enable him to judge when costs are getting out of control. By giving him timely cost commitment reports, he could take needed corrective actions and be able to approximate the cost effect of each technical decision. All these would require additional personnel and expertise in our department.

"In addition, I feel that the implementation of formal project management would increase our responsibilities in the finance department. We would need to conduct project audits, prepare periodic comparisons of actual versus projected costs and actual versus programmed manpower allocations, update projection reports and funding schedules, and sponsor cost improvement programs.

"In the area of internal control, we will need to review and modify our existing internal control system to meet effectively our organization's goals related to project management. A careful and proper study and evaluation of existing internal control procedures should be conducted to determine the extent of the tests to which our internal auditing procedures are to be restricted. A thorough understanding of each project we undertake must be required at all times.

"I'm all in favor of formal project management, provided management would allocate more resources to our department so we could maintan the personnel necessary to meet the added duties, responsibilities, and expertise required."

After the interviews, Sue Lyons talked to Wilbur Donley about the possibility of adopting formal project management.

Lyons: You realize that regardless of how much support there is for formal project management, the general manager will probably not allow us to implement it for fear it will affect the performance of the Automotive Components Division.

CASE STUDY: COLONIAL COMPUTER CORPORATION[4]

"We have a unique situation here at Colonial," remarked Ed White, vice-president for engineering. "We have three divisions within throwing distance of one another, and each one operates differently. This poses a problem for us at corporate headquarters because career opportunities and administrative policies are different in each division.''

Colonial Computer Corporation (CCC) was a $3-billion-a-year corporation with worldwide operations encompassing just about every aspect of the computer field. The growth rate of CCC exceeded 13 percent per year for the last two years, primarily due to the advanced technology developed by their Eton Division (which produces tape and disk drives). Colonial is considered one of the "giants" in computer technology development and supplies a great deal of equipment to other computer manufacturers.

World headquarters for CCC is in Concord, Illinois, a large northwest suburb which has recently attracted new industries. In addition to corporate headquarters, there are three other divisions: the Eton Division, manufacturers of tape and disk drives; the Lampco Division, which is responsible for Department of Defense (DOD) contracts; and the Ridge Division, the primary research center for peripherals and terminals.

"Our major problems first began to surface during the early seventies," remarked Ed White. "When we structured our organization, we assumed that each division would operate as a separate entity without having to communicate with one another except through corporate headquarters. Therefore, we permitted each of our division vice-presidents and general managers to set up whatever organizational structure they wanted to get the work accomplished. Unfortunately, we hadn't considered the problem of coordinating efforts between sister divisions.

"The Lampco Division, formed in 1962, is the oldest. It produces about $500 million worth of revenue each year from DOD funding. Lampco utilizes a pure matrix structure. Our reason for permitting our divisions to operate independently was cost reporting. In the Lampco Division we must keep two sets of books; one for government use and one for internal control. It has taken us about five years or so to get used to this idea, but now we have it well under control.

"We have never had to lay people off in the Lampco Division. Yet, our engineers still feel that a reduction in DOD spending may cause massive layoffs here. Personally, I'm not worried. We've been through lean and fat times without having to let people go.

"The big problem with the Lampco Division is that because of the technology developed in some of our other divisons, Lampco subcontracts a good portion of the work out to our other divisions. Not that it can't be done there, but we do have outstanding R & D specialists in our other divisions.

"We have been somewhat limited in the salary structure we can provide to our engineers. Our engineers in the Lampco Division used to consider themselves as aerospace engineers, not computer engineers, and were thankful for employment and reasonable salaries. But now the Lampco engineers are com-

---

4. This case study is fictitious and was prepared by the author as a basis for class discussion rather than an illustration of either effective or ineffective handling of an administrative situation. Copyright © 1978 by Harold Kerzner.

municating more readily with our other divisions and think that the grass is greener in these other divisions. Frankly, they're right. We've tried to institute the same wage and salary program corporatewide, but came up with problems. Our engineers, especially the younger ones who have been with us five or six years, are looking for management positions. Almost all of our management positions in engineering are filled with people between thirty-five and forty years of age. This poses a problem because there's no place for these younger engineers to go. So, they seek employment elsewhere.

"We've recently developed a technical performance ladder that is comparable to our management ladder. At the top of the technical ladder we have our consultant grade. Here, our engineers can earn just about any salary, based of course on their performance. The consultant position came about because of a problem in our Eton Division. I would venture to say that in the entire computer world, the most difficult job is designing disk drives. These people are specialists in a world of their own. There are probably only twenty-five people in the world who possess this expertise. We have five of them here at Colonial. If one of our competitors would come in here and lure away just two of these guys, we would literally have to close down the Eton Division. So, we've developed a consultant category. Now, the word has spread and all of our engineers are applying for transfer to the Eton Division to become eligible for this new pay grade. In the Lampco Division alone I have had over fifty requests for transfer from engineers who now consider themselves as computer engineers. To make matters worse, the job market in computer technology is so good today that these people could easily leave us for more money elsewhere.

"We've been lucky in the Lampco Division. Most of our contracts are large and we can afford to maintain a project office staffed with three or four project engineers. These project engineers consider themselves managers, not engineers. Actually, they're right in doing so because theoretically they are engineering managers, not doers. Many of our people in Lampco are title-oriented and would prefer to be a project engineer as opposed to any other position. Good project engineers have been promoted, or laterally transferred, to project management so that we can pay them more. Actually, they do the same work.

"In our Eton Division we have a rather unusual project management structure. We're organized on a product form rather than a project form of management. The engineers are considered to be strictly support for the business development function and are not permitted to speak to the customers, except under special circumstances. Business development manages both the product lines and R & D projects going on at one time. The project leader is selected by the director of engineering and can be a functional manager of just a functional employee. The project leader reports to his normal supervisor. The project leader must also report informally to one of the business development managers who is also tracking the project. This poses a problem because when a conflict occurs, we sometimes have to take it up two or three levels before it can be resolved. Some conflicts have been so intense that they've had to be resolved at the corporate level.

"The Eton Division happens to be our biggest money-maker. We're turning out disk drives at an incredible rate and are backlogged with orders for at least six months. Many of our top R & D engineers are working in production support capacities because we cannot get qualified people fast enough. Furthermore, we have a yearly turnover rate in excess of 10 percent among our engineers below thirty years of age. We have several engineers who are earning more than the department managers. We have five consultant engineers who are earning more than the department managers. We also have four consultant engineers who are earning as much as division managers.

"We've had the greatest amount of problems in this division. Conflicts arise because of interdependencies and misunderstandings. Our product line managers are the only people permitted to see the customers. This alienates our engineering and manufacturing people who are often called upon to respond to customer requests.

"Planning is another major problem that we're trying to improve upon. We have trouble getting our functional managers to make commitments. Perhaps this is a result of our inability to develop a uniform procedure for starting up a program. We always argue about when to anchor down the work. Our new and younger employees want to anchor everything down at once, whereas the project managers say not to anchor down anything. We, therefore, operate at several levels.

"We can carry this problem one step further. How do we get an adequate set of objectives defined initially? We failed several times before because we couldn't get corporate agreement or understanding. We're trying to establish a policy for development of an architectural design document that will give good front-end definition.

"Generally we're O.K., if we're simply modifying an existing product line. But with new product lines we have a problem in convincing people, especially our old customers.

"The Ridge Division was originally developed to handle all corporate R & D activities. Unfortunately, our growth rate became so large, and diversified, that this became impractical. We, therefore, had to decentralize the R & D activities. This meant that each division could do its own R & D work. Corporate then had the responsibility for resolving conflicts, establishing priorities, and insuring that all divisions are well informed of the total R & D picture. Corporate must develop good communication channels between the divisions so that duplication of effort does not occur.

"Almost all of our technical specialists have advanced degrees in engineering disciplines. This poses a severe problem for us, especially since we have a totally traditional structure. When a new project comes up, the project is assigned to the functional department that has the most responsibility. One of the functional employees is then designated as the project manager. We realize that the new project manager has no authority to control resources that are assigned to other departments. Fortunately, our department managers realize this also, and usually put forth a concerted effort to provide whatever resources are needed. Most of the conflicts that do occur are resolved at the department manager level.

"When a project is completed, the project manager returns to his former position as an engineering member of a functional organization. We've been quite concerned about these people who go back and forth between project management and functional project engineering. This type of relationship is a must in our environment because our project managers must have a command of technology. We hold in-house seminars on project management to provide our people with training in management skills, cost control, planning, and scheduling. We feel that we've been successful in this regard. We are always afraid that if we begin to grow, we'll have to change our structure and throw the company into chaos. When we began to grow, corporate reassigned some of our R & D activities to other divisions. I often wonder what would have happened if this had not been done.

"For R & D projects that are funded out of house, we generally have no major management problems for our project managers or project engineers. For corporate-funded projects, however, life becomes more complex. We have a tough time deciding when to kill a project or to pour more money into it. Our project managers always argue that with just a little more corporate funding they can solve the world's greatest problems.

"From the point of view of R & D, our biggest problems are in 'grass roots' projects. Let me explain what I mean by this. An engineer comes up with an idea and wants some money to pursue it. Unfortunately, our division managers are not budgeted for 'seed monies' whenever an employee comes up with an idea for research or new product development. Each person much have a charge number to bill his time against. I know of no project manager who would permit someone to do independent research on a budgeted project.

"So, the engineer comes to us at corporate looking for seed money. Occasionally we provide up to $20,000 on a short-term basis. That $20,000 might last for three to four months if the engineer is lucky. Unfortunately, obtaining the money is only the beginning. If the engineer needs support from another department, he's not going to get it because his project is just an informal effort, whereas everything else is a clearly definable, well-established project. People are reluctant to attach themselves to a 'grass roots' effort because history has shown that the majority of them will be failures.

"The researcher now has the difficult job of trying to convince people to support his project, instead of those that are clearly defined and have established priorities. If the guy is persistent, however, he has a good chance of succeeding. If he does, he gets a good evaluation. But if he fails, he's at the mercy of his functional manager. If the functional manager felt that this guy could have been of more value to the company on a project basis, then he's likely to grade him down. But even with these risks, we still have several 'seed money' requests each month by employees looking for glory."

CASE STUDY: JACKSON INDUSTRIES

"I wish they had never invented computers," remarked Tom Ford, president of Jackson Industries. "The computer we got has been nothing but a thorn in our side for the past ten years. We have to resolve this problem now. I'm through watching our people fight with one another. We must find a solution to this problem."

In 1966, Jackson Industries decided to rent an IBM-360 computer, primarily to handle the large, repetitive tasks found in the accounting and finance functions of the organization. It was only fitting, therefore, that control of the computer came under the director of finance, Al Moody. For two years, operations went smoothly. In 1968, the computer department was reorganized in three sections; scientific computer programming, business computer programming, and systems programming. The reorganization was necessary because the computer department had grown into the fifth largest department, employing some thirty people, and was experiencing some severe problems working with other departments.

After the reorganization, Ralph Gregg, the computer department manager, made the following remarks in a memo distributed to all personnel:

"The computer department has found it increasingly difficult to work with engineering and operations functional departments that continue to permit their personnel to write and document their own computer programs. In order to maintain some degree of consistency, the computer department will now assume the responsibility for writing all computer programs. All requests should be directed to the department manager. My people are under explicit instructions that they are to provide absolutely no assistance to any functional personnel attempting to write their own programs without authorization from me. Company directives in this regard will be forthcoming."

The memo caused concern among the functional departments. If engineering wanted a computer program written, they would now have to submit a formal request and then have the person requesting the program spend a great deal of time explaining the problem to the scientific programmer assigned to this effort. The department managers were reluctant to have their people "waste time" in training the scientific programmers to be engineers. The computer department manager countered this argument by stating that once the programmer was fully familiar with the engineering problem, then the engineer's time could be spent more fruitfully on other activities until the computer program was ready for implementation.

The same problem generated more concern by department managers when they were involved in computer projects that required integration among several departments. Although Jackson Industries operated on a traditional structure, the new directive implied that the computer department would be responsible for managing all projects involving computer programming, even if they crossed into other departments. Many people looked upon this as an inefficient project management structure within the traditional organization.

In June, 1977 Al Moody and Ralph Gregg met to discuss the deterioration of working relationships between the computer department and other organizations.

Moody: I'm getting complaints from the engineering and operations departments that they can't get any priorities established on the work to be done in your group. What can we do about it?

Gregg: I set the priorities as I see fit, according to what's best for the company. Those guys in engineering and operations have absolutely no idea how long it takes to write, debug, and document a computer program. Then they keep feeding me this line about how their projects will slip if this computer program isn't ready on time. I've told them what problems I have and yet they still refuse to let me participate in the planning phase of their activities.

Moody: Well, you may have a valid gripe there. I'm more concerned about this closed shop you've developed for your department. You've built a little empire down there and it looks like your people are unionized where the rest of us are not. Furthermore, I've noticed that your people have their own informal organization and tend to avoid socializing with the other employees. We're supposed to be one big, happy family, you know. Can't you do something about that?

Gregg: The problem belongs to you and Tom Ford. For the last three years, the average salary increase for the entire company has been 7.5 percent and our department has averaged a mere 5 percent because you people upstairs do not feel we contribute anything to company profits. My scientific programmers feel that they're doing engineering work and that they're making the same contribution to profits as an engineer. Therefore, they should be on the engineering pay structure and receive an 8 percent salary increase.

Moody: You could have given your scientific programmers more money. You had a budget for salary increases, the same as everyone else.

Gregg: Sure I did. But my budget was less than everyone else's. I could have given the scientific people 7 percent and everyone else 3 percent. That would be an easy way to tell people that we think they should look for another job. My people do good work and do, in fact, contribute to profits. If Tom Ford doesn't change his impression of us, then I expect to lose some of my key people. Maybe you should tell him that.

Moody: Between you and me, all of your comments are correct. I agree with your concerns. But my hands are tied, as you know.

We are contemplating the installation of a management information system for all departments and especially for executive decision making. Tom is contemplating creating a new position, director of information services. This would move the computer out of a department under finance and up to the directorate level. I'm sure this would have an impact on yearly salary increases for your people.

The problem that we're facing involves the managing of projects under the new directorate. It looks like we'll have to create a project management organization just for this new directorate. Tom likes the traditional structure and wants to leave all other directorates intact. We know that this new directorate will have to integrate the new computer projects across multiple departments and divisions. Once we solve the organizational structure problem, we'll begin looking at implementation. Got any ideas about the organizational structure?

Gregg: You bet I do. Make me director and I'll see that the work gets done.

2
The Changing Environment

2.0 INTRODUCTION

A major reason for the increasing acceptance of the project management approach has been recognition that the traditional organizational structure is too inflexible in adapting to a changing environment. Project management is an outgrowth of systems management. Systems management has emerged as a means of unifying the entire organization toward common goals and objectives. Figure 2-1 shows why systems management is needed to organize and unify the individual "islands" of the company. Simply stated, general systems theory attempt to integrate and unify scientific information across many fields of knowledge. It is an approach to solving problems by looking at the total picture rather than through analyzing individual components.

A system is generally regarded as an ongoing entity whereas a project has a finite time duration. Unfortunately, many executives today do not recognize this close relationship between systems theory and project management.

2.1 DEFINITIONS: SYSTEMS, PROGRAMS, AND PROJECTS

Executives as well as practitioners appear to have a relatively poor definition of systems, programs, and projects. The exact definition of each depends upon the user's environment and ultimate goal. Because there can be situations where programs, projects, and systems have different organizational structures, executives should understand the basic definitions.

Military and government organizations were the first to attempt to define clearly the boundaries of systems, programs, and projects. Below are two such definitions for systems:

- Air Force
  A composite of equipment, skills, and techniques capable of performing and/or supporting an operational role. A complete system includes related

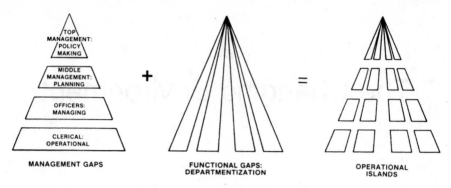

Figure 2-1. Why Are Systems Necessary?

facilities, equipment, material services, and personnel as a self-sufficient unit in its intended operational and/or support environment.

- NASA
  One of the principal functioning entities comprising the project hardware within a project or program. The meaning may vary to suit a particular project or program area. Ordinarily a "system" is the first major subdivision of project work, for example, spacecraft systems, launch vehicle systems.

Systems tend to imply an infinite lifetime, but with constant upgrading. Programs can be construed as the necessary, first-level elements of a system. Two representative definitions of programs are given below:

- Air Force
  The integrated, time-phased tasks necessary to accomplish a particular purpose.
- NASA
  A related series of undertakings that continue over a period of time (normally years), and are designed to accomplish a broad scientific or technical goal in the NASA long-range plan, for example, lunar and planetary exploration, manned spacecraft systems.

Programs can be regarded as subsystems. However, they are generally defined as time-phased efforts, whereas systems exist on a continuous basis. Projects are also time-phased efforts (much shorter than programs) and are the first level of breakdown of a program. A typical definition would be:

- NASA/Air Force
  A project is within a program as an undertaking with a scheduled beginning and end, and normally involves some primary purpose.

The government sector usually refers to its efforts as programs, headed by a program manager. Industries, on the other hand, prefer to call their efforts projects, headed by a project manager. The distinction is inconsequential because the same policies, procedures, and guidelines that regulate programs most often apply to projects also. For the remainder of this text, programs and projects will be discussed interchangeably. However, the executive should be aware that projects are normally the first-level subdivision of a program. This breakdown will be discussed in Chapter 5.

Once a group of tasks are selected and considered to be a project, the next step is to define the kinds of project units. There are four categories:

- Individual projects—short-duration projects normally assigned to a single individual who may be acting as both a project manager and functional manager.
- Staff projects—these are projects that can be accomplished by one organizational unit, a department, for example. A staff or task force is developed from each section involved. This works best if only one functional unit is involved.
- Special projects—very often special projects occur that require a certain primary function and/or authority to be assigned temporarily to other individuals or units. This works best for short-duration projects.
- Matrix of aggregate projects—these require input from a large number of functional units and usually control vast resources.

Each of these categories can require different responsibilities, job descriptions, policies, and procedures.

2.2 THE CHANGING ENVIRONMENT: ANALYSIS

Because current organizational structures are unable to accommodate the wide variety of interrelated tasks necessary for successful project completion, the need for project management has become apparent. It is usually first identified by those lower-level and middle managers who find it impossible to control their resources effectively for the diverse activities within their line organization. Quite often middle managers feel the impact of a changing environment more than upper-level executives.

Once the need for change is identified, middle management must convince upper-level management that such a change is actually warranted. If top-level executives cannot recognize the problems with resource control, then project management will not be adopted, at least formally. Informal acceptance, however, is another story.

In 1978, the author received a request from an automobile equipment manufacturer who was considering formal project management. The author was permitted to speak with several middle managers. The following comments were made:

- "Here at ABC Company (a division of XYZ Corporation), we have informal project management. By this, I mean that work flows the same as it would in formal project management except that the authority, responsibility, and accountability are implied rather than rigidly defined. We have been very successful with this structure, expecially when you consider that the components we sell cost 30 percent more than our competitors, and that our growth rate has been in excess of 12 percent each year for the past six years. The secret of our success has been our quality and our ability to meet schedule dates."
- "Our informal structure works well because our department managers do not hide problems. They aren't afraid to go into another department manager's office and talk about the problems they're having controlling resources. Our success is based upon the fact that *all* of our department managers do this. What's going to happen if we hire just one or two people who won't go along with this approach? Will we be forced to go to formalized project management?"
- "This division is a steppingstone to greatness in our corporation. It seems that all of the middle managers who come to this division get promoted either within the division, to higher management positions in other divisions, or to a higher position at corporate headquarters."

At this point, the author conducted two three-day seminars on engineering project management for seventy-five of the lower-, middle-, and upper-level managers. The seminar participants were asked whether or not they wanted to adopt formal project management. The following concerns were raised by the participants:

- "Will I have more or less power and/or authority?"
- "How will my salary be affected?"
- "Why should I permit a project manager to share the resources in my empire?"
- "Will I get top management visibility?"

Even with these concerns, the majority of the attendees felt that formalized project management would alleviate a lot of their present problems.

Although the middle levels of the organization, where resources are actually controlled on a day-to-day basis, felt positive about project management, convincing the top levels of management was another story. If you were the chief executive officer of this division, earning a salary in six figures, and looking at a growth rate of 12 percent per year for the last five years, would you "rock the boat" simply because your middle managers want project management?

This example highlights three major points:

- The final decision for the implementation of project management does (and will always) rest with executive management.
- Executives must be willing to listen when middle management identifies a crisis in controlling resources. This is where the need for project management should first appear.
- Executives are paid to look out for the long-range interests of the corporation and should not be swayed by near-term growth rate or profitability.

Today, ABC Company is still doing business the way it was done in the past— with informal project management. The company is a classic example of how informal project management can be made to work successfully. The author agrees with the company executives that, in this case, formal project management is not necessary.

William C. Goggin, board chairman and chief executive officer of Dow Corning, describes a situation in his corporation that was quite different from the one at ABC.[1]

Although Dow Corning was a healthy corporation in 1967, it showed difficulties that troubled many of us in top management. These symptoms were, and still are, common ones in U.S. business and have been described countless times in reports, audits, articles and speeches. Our symptoms took such forms as:

- Executives did not have adequate financial information and control of their operations. Marketing managers, for example, did not know how much it cost to produce a product. Prices and margins were set by division managers.
- Cumbersome communications channels existed between key functions, especially manufacturing and marketing.
- In the face of stiffening competition, the corporation remained too internalized in its thinking and organizational structure. It was insufficiently oriented to the outside world.
- Lack of communications between divisions not only created the antithesis of a corporate team effort but also was wasteful of a precious resource— people.
- Long-range corporate planning was sporadic and superficial; this was leading to overstaffing, duplicated effort and inefficiency.

Once the need for project management has been defined, the next logical question is, "How long a conversion period will be necessary before a company

---

1. William C. Goggin, "How the Multidimensional Structure Works at Dow Corning", *Harvard Business Review,* January-February, 54, 1974. Copyright © 1973 by the President and Fellows of Harvard College; all rights reserved.

can operate in a project management environment?" To answer this question we must first look at Figure 2-2. Technology, as expected, has the fastest rate of change, and the overall environment of a business must adapt to this rapidly changing technology.

In an ideal situation, the organizational structure of a company would immediately adapt to the changing environment. In a real situation, this will not be a smooth transition, but more like the erratic line shown in Figure 2-2. This erratic line is a trademark or characteristic of the traditional structure. Project management structures, however, can, and often do, adapt to a rapidly changing environment with a relatively smooth transition.

Even though an executive can change the organizational structure with the stroke of a pen, people are responsible for its implementation. However, it can be seen in Figure 2-2, that people have the slowest rate of change. Edicts, documents signed by executives, and training programs will not convince employees that a new organizational form will work. Employees will be convinced only after they see the new system in action, and this takes time.

As a ground rule, it often takes two to three years to convert from a traditional structure to a project management structure. The major reason for this is that in a traditional structure the line employee has one and only one boss; in a project management structure the employee reports vertically to his line

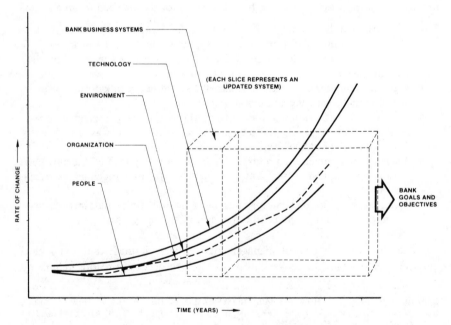

Figure 2-2. Systems In A Changing Environment.

manager and horizontally to every project manager on whose activities he is assigned, either temporarily or full time. Employees will perform in a new system because they are directed to do so, but will not have confidence in it or become dedicated until after they have been involved in several different projects and believe that they can effectively report to more than one boss.

When an employee is told that he will be working horizontally as well as vertically, his first concern is his take-home pay. Employees always question whether or not they can be evaluated fairly if they report to several managers during the same time period. One of the major reasons why project management fails is because top-level executives neglect to consider that any organizational change must be explained in terms of the wage and salary administration program.[2] This must be given *before* change is made. If change comes first, and employees are not convinced that they can be evaluated correctly, they may very likely try to sabotage the whole effort. From then on, it will probably be a difficult, if not impossible, task to rectify the situation. However, once the organizational employees accept project management and the procedure of reporting in two directions, the company can effectively and efficiently convert from one project management organizational form to another.

Not all companies need two to three years to convert to project management. The ABC Company described earlier would probably have very little trouble in converting because informal project management is well accepted. In the early sixties, TRW was forced to convert to a project management structure almost overnight. They were highly successful in this, mainly because of the loyalty and dedication of the employees. The TRW employees were willing to give the system a chance. Any organizational structure, no matter how bad, will work if the employees are willing to make it work. Yet other companies can spend three to five years trying to implement change and drastically fail. The literature describes many cases where project management has failed because:

- There was no need for project management.
- Employees were not informed about how project management should work.
- Executives did not select the appropriate projects or project managers for the first few projects.
- There was no attempt to explain the effect of the project management organizational form on the wage and salary administration program.
- Employees were not convinced that executives were in total support of the change.

Some companies (and executives) are forced into project management before they realize what has happened, and if recognition at the top levels of manage-

2. The mechanisms for employee evaluation in a project environment will be discussed further in section 4.10.

ment does not occur within a short time period thereafter, chaos seems inevitable. As an example, consider a highly traditional company that purchased a computer a few years ago. The company has five divisions: engineering, finance, manufacturing, marketing, and personnel. Not knowing where to put the computer, the chief executive officer created an electronic data processing (EDP) department and placed it under finance and accounting. The executive's rationale was that since the purpose for buying the computer was to eliminate repetitive tasks and the majority of these were in accounting and finance, that was where EDP belonged. The vice-president for accounting and finance might not be qualified to manage the EDP department but that seemed beside the point.

The EDP department has a staff of scientific and business computer programmers, and systems analysts. The scientific programmers spend almost all of their time working in the engineering division writing engineering programs; they must learn engineering in order to do this. In this company, the engineer does not consider himself to be a computer programmer, but does the computer programmer consider himself to be an engineer?

The company's policy is that merit and cost-of-living increases are given out in July of each year. This year the average salary increase will be 7 percent. However, the president wants the increase given according to merit, and not as a flat rate across the board. After long hours of deliberation, it was decided that engineering, manufacturing, and marketing would receive 8 percent raises and finance and personnel 5.5 percent.

After announcement of the salary increases, the scientific programmers began to complain because they feel they are doing engineering-type work and should therefore be paid according to the engineering pay scale. Management tried to resolve this problem by giving each division its own computer and personnel. However, this resulted in duplication of effort and inefficient use of personnel.

With the rapid advancements in computer technology of recent years, management realized the need for timely access to information for executive decision making. In a rather bold move, executives created a new division called management information systems (MIS). The MIS division now has full control of all computer operations and gives the EDP personnel the opportunity to show that they actually contribute to corporate profits.

Elevating the computer to the top levels of the organization was a significant step toward project management. Unfortunately, many executives did not fully realize what had happened. Because of the need for a rapid information retrieval system that can integrate data from a variety of line organizations, the MIS personnel soon found that they were working horizontally, not vertically. Today MIS packages cut across every division of the company. Thus, the emergence of the project management concept to handle a horizontal flow of work appeared on the scene.

With the emergence of data processing project management, executives were forced to find immediate answers to such questions as:

- Can we have project management strictly for data processing projects?
- Should the project manager be the programmer or the user?
- How much authority should be delegated to the project manager and will this delegated authority cause a shift in the organizational equilibrium?

The answers to these questions have not been and still are not easy to solve. Today, IBM provides its customers with the opportunity to hire IBM as the inhouse data processing project management team. This partially eliminates the necessity for establishing internal project management relationships that could easily become permanent.

In TRW Nelson Division,[3] data processing project management began with the MIS personnel acting as the project leaders. However, after two years, the company felt that the people best qualified to be the project leaders were the technical experts (i.e., users). Therefore, the MIS personnel now act as team members and resource personnel rather than as the project managers.

In Section 2.1 we provided definitions of the four different types of projects. Each of these projects can have its own organizational form and can operate concurrently with other active projects. This diversity of projects has contributed to the implementation of full project management in several industries.

J. Robert Fluor, chairman, chief executive officer and president of the Fluor Corporation commented on twenty years of operations in a project environment:[4]

The need for flexibility has become apparent since no two projects are ever alike from a project management point of view. There are always differences in technology; in the geographical locations; in the client approach; in the contract terms and conditions; in the schedule; in the financial approach to the project; and in a broad range of international factors, all of which require a different and flexible approach to managing each project.

We found the task force concept, with maximum authority and accountability resting with the project manager, to be the most effective means of realizing project objectives. And while basic project management principles do exist at Fluor, there is no single standard project organization or project procedure yet devised that can be rigidly applied to more than one project.

---

3. The TRW Nelson Division case study appears at the end of this chapter.
4. J. Robert Fluor, "Development of Project Managers", keynote address to the Project Management Institute, Ninth International Seminar Symposium, Chicago, Illinois, October 24, 1977.

Today, our company and others and their projects managers are being challenged as never before to achieve what earlier would have been classified as "unachievable" project objectives. Major projects often involve the resources of a large number of organizations located on different continents. The efforts of each must be directed and coordinated toward a common set of project objectives of quality performance, cost and time of completion as well as many other considerations.

As project management developed, some essential factors in its successful implementation were recognized. The major factor was the role of the project manager which became the focal point of integrative responsibility. This need for integrative responsibility was first identified in research and development activities:[5]

Recently, R & D technology has broken down the boundaries that used to exist between industries. Once-stable markets and distribution channels are now in a state of flux. The industrial environment is turbulent and increasingly hard to predict. Many complex facts about markets, production methods, costs and scientific potentials are related to investment decisions.

All of these factors have combined to produce a king-size managerial headache. There are just too many crucial decisions to have them all processed and resolved through regular line hierarchy at the top of the organization. They must be integrated in some other way.

Providing the project manager with integrative responsibility resulted in:

- Total accountability assumed by a single person
- Project rather than functional dedication
- A requirement for coordination across functional interfaces
- Proper utilization of integrated planning and control

Those executives who chose to accept project management soon found the advantages of the new technique:

- Easy adaptation to an ever changing environment
- Ability to handle a multidisciplinary activity within a specified period of time
- Horizontal as well as vertical work flow
- Better orientation toward customer problems
- Easier identification of activity responsibilities
- A multidisciplinary decision-making process

---

5. Paul R. Lawrence and Jay W. Lorsch, "New Management Job: The integrator," *Harvard Business Review,* November-December, 142, 1967. Copyright © 1967 by the President and Fellows of Harvard College; all rights reserved.

Executives must be cautious in implementing project management. If the new approach is not closely supervised during the implementation phase, it may create problems that have a direct bearing upon corporate profits. As an example, consider the effects and probable causes shown below:[6]

- Effects
  - Late completion of activities
  - Cost overruns
  - Substandard performance
  - High turnover in project staff
  - High turnover in functional staff
  - Two functional departments performing the same activities on one project
- Causes
  - Top management not recognizing this activity as a project
  - Too many projects going on at once
  - Impossible schedule commitments
  - No functional input into the planning phase
  - No one person responsible for the total project
  - Poor control of design changes
  - Poor control of customer changes
  - Poor understanding of the project manager's job
  - No integrated planning and control
  - Company resources are overcommitted
  - Unrealistic planning and scheduling
  - No project cost-accounting ability
  - Conflicting project priorities
  - Poorly organized project office
  - Wrong person assigned as the project manager

Many of these causes and effects can occur within any organizational structure. However, they are more pronounced with project management. Therefore, executives must exercise due caution and make sure that the implementation is correctly *planned* for.

2.3 DEFINING THE PROJECT MANAGER'S ROLE

The project manager is responsible for coordinating and integrating activities across multiple, functional lines. In order to do this, the project manager needs strong communicative and interpersonal skills, must become familiar with the operations of each line organization, and should have a general knowledge of the technology.

---

6. This has been adapted from Russell D. Archibald, *Managing High-Technology Programs and Projects,* New York: John Wiley, 1976, p. 10.

An executive with a computer manufacturer stated that his company was looking externally for project managers. When asked if the executive expected candidates to have a command of computer technology, the executive remarked: "You give me an individual who has good communicative skills and interpersonal skills and I'll give him a job. I can teach people the technology and give them technical experts to assist them in decision making. But I cannot teach somebody how to work with people."

The project manager's job is not an easy one. Managers may have increased authority and responsibility, but very little power. This lack of power can force them to "negotiate" with upper-level management as well as functional management for control of company resources, as shown in Figure 2-3. They may often be treated as outsiders by the formal organization. Yet, even with these problems and roadblocks, they have managed to survive. J. Robert Fluor has described the new responsibilities of project managers at Fluor Coporation:[7]

Project management continues to become more challenging and we think this trend will continue. This means we have to pay special attention to the development of project managers who are capable of coping with jobs that range from small to mega projects and with life spans of several months to ten years. At Fluor, a project manager must not only be able to manage the engineering, procurement and construction aspects of a project, he or she must also be able to manage aspects relating to finance, cost engineering, schedule, environmental considerations, regulatory agency requirements, inflation and cost escalations,

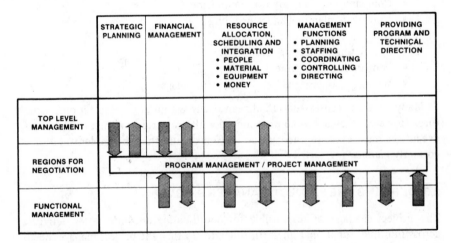

Figure 2-3. The Negotiation Activities Of Project Management.

7. J. Robert Fluor, "Development of Project Managers", keynote address to the Project Management Institute, Ninth International Seminar Symposium, Chicago, Illinois, October 24, 1977.

labor problems, public and client relations, employee relations and changing laws. That's primarily on the domestic side. On international projects, the list of additional functions and considerations adds totally different complications.

In the project environment, everything seems to revolve about the project manager. Although the project organization is a specialized, task-oriented entity, it cannot exist apart from the traditional structure of the organization. The project manager, therefore, must walk the fence between the two organizations. The term interface management is often used for this role that can be described as:[8]

- Managing human interrelationships in the project organization
- Maintaining the balance between technical and managerial project functions
- Coping with risk associated with project management
- Surviving organizational restraints

Organizational restraints have a tendency to develop into organizational conflict, often requiring that top management take an active role in conflict resolution by

- Setting a selection criteria for projects
- Establishing priorities among projects

To be effective as a project manager, an individual must have management as well as technical skills. Unfortunately, businessmen sometimes find it difficult to think as engineers, and engineers find it difficult at times to think as businessmen. Executives have found that it is usually easier to train engineers rather than businessmen to fill project management positions.

Because the engineers often consider their careers limited in the functional disciplines, they look toward project management and project engineering as career path opportunities. But becoming a manager entails learning about psychology, human behavior, organizational behavior, interpersonal relations, and communications. MBA programs have come to the rescue of individuals desiring the background to be effective project managers.

The average age of project managers in industry is between thirty-two and thirty-eight. There are three reasons for this:

- An individual often makes his most profitable contribution to society between thirty and forty. If individuals do not begin climbing the corporate ladder by the time they are forty, they may be severely limited in career growth.

---

8. David L. Wilemon and John P. Cicero, "The Project Manager—Anomalies and Ambiguities," *Academy of Management Journal,* September, 271, 1970.

- When is an individual most concerned about money? (All the time is not an acceptable answer!) It is not between the ages of twenty and thirty because to a person coming right out of college, any money looks good. It is not between the ages of forty and fifty because, by that time, individuals are fairly set in their ways and living styles. But between the ages of thirty and forty, the individual is thinking about financial security and the future.
- The younger individual in most cases is willing to take more risks than the older individual in order to meet the project objective. Furthermore, the individual is often willing to work long hours on overtime and weekends.

Actually, the age of the project manager varies from industry to industry. Data processing project managers are usually younger than the average because current knowledge of computer technology is a necessity. R & D project managers also fall into this category because of technology requirements. Manufacturing and construction project managers are often older because experience is so important.

In the past, executives motivated and retained qualified personnel primarily with financial incentives. Today other ways are being used. Some people are more title-oriented than money-oriented. For example, changing an individual's title sometimes motivates people to stay with the company simply because they want to put this new title on their resumé at a later date.

Another method, and by far the best, is work challenge. The project manager is actually a general manager and gets to know the total operation of the company. In fact, the project managers get to know more about the total operation of the company than do most executives. That is why project management is often used as a training ground to prepare future general managers who will be capable of filling top management positions. This is not a bad idea, provided that executives know the general management aspect is the result of experience in integrating work horizontally. Placing an individual into project management for the sole purpose of training a future general manager is not recommended.

2.4 THE PROJECT MANAGER AS THE PLANNING AGENT

The major responsibility of the project manager is planning. If project planning is performed correctly, then it is conceivable that the project manager will work himself out of a job because the project can run itself. This rarely happens, however. Few projects are ever completed without some conflict for the project manager to resolve.

In most cases, the project manager provides detailed definitions of the work to be accomplished, but the line managers (the true experts) do the detailed planning. Although project managers cannot control or assign line resources, they must make sure that they are adequate and scheduled to satisfy the needs of the project, not vice versa. As the architect of the project plan, the project manager must provide:

- Complete task definitions
- Resource requirement definitions
- Major timetable milestones
- Definition of end-item quality and reliability requirements
- The basis for performance measurement

These factors, if properly established, result in:

- Assurance that functional units will understand their total responsibility toward achieving project needs
- Assurance that problems resulting from scheduling and allocation of critical resources are known beforehand
- Early identification of problems that may jeopardize successful project completion so that effective corrective action can be taken to prevent or resolve the problems

Project managers are responsible for project administration and must therefore have the right to establish their own policies, procedures, rules, guidelines, and directives—provided these conform to overall company policy. Companies with mature project management structures usually have rather loose company guidelines so that project managers have some degree of flexibility in how to control their projects. However, there are certain administrative requirements project managers cannot establish. As an example, the project manager cannot make any promises to a functional employee concerning:

- Promotion
- Grade
- Salary
- Bonus
- Overtime
- Responsibility
- Future work assignments

These seven items can be administered by line managers only. However, the project manager can have indirect involvement by telling the line manager how well an employee is doing (and putting it in writing), requesting overtime because the project budget will permit it, and offering individuals the opportunity to perform work above their current pay grade. The latter can cause severe managerial headaches if coordination with the line manager does not take place because the individual will expect immediate rewards if he performs well.

The establishment of project administrative requirements is part of project planning. Executives must either work with the project managers at project initiation or act as resource persons. Improper project administrative planning can create a situation that requires:

- A continuous revision and/or establishment of company and/or project policies, procedures, and directives
- A continuous shifting in organizational responsibility and possible unnecessary restructuring
- A need for staff to acquire new knowledge and skills

If these situations occur simultaneously on several projects, there could be confusion throughout the organization.

2.5 PRODUCT VS PROJECT MANAGEMENT: A DEFINITION

For all practical purposes, there is no basic difference between program management and project management. But what about product management? Project management and product management are similar, with one major exception: the project manager focuses on the end date of his project, whereas the product manager is not willing to admit that his product line will ever end. The product manager wants his product to be as long-lived and profitable as possible. Even when the demand for the product diminishes, the product manager will always look for spin-offs to keep his product alive.

Figure 2-4 shows the relationship between project and product management. When the project is in the R & D phase, a project manager is involved. Once the product is developed and introduced into the marketplace, control is taken over by the product manager. In some situations, the project manager can become the product manager. Both product and project management can, and do, exist concurrently within companies.

Figure 2-4 identifies the fact that product management can operate horizontally as well as vertically. When a product is shown horizontally on the organizational chart, it implies that the product line is not big enough to control its own resources full time and therefore shares key functional personnel similar to project management. If the product line were large enough to control its own resources full time, it would be shown as a separate division or a vertical line on the organizational chart.

Also shown in Figure 2-4 is the remarkable fact that the project manager (or project engineer) is reporting to a marketing-type person. Should executives permit project managers and project engineers to report to a marketing-type individual even if the project entails a great amount of engineering? Many executives today would attest that the answer is "yes." The reason for this is that technically oriented project leaders get too involved with the technical details of the project and lose insight as to when and how to "kill" a project. Remember, most technical leaders have been trained in an academic rather than business

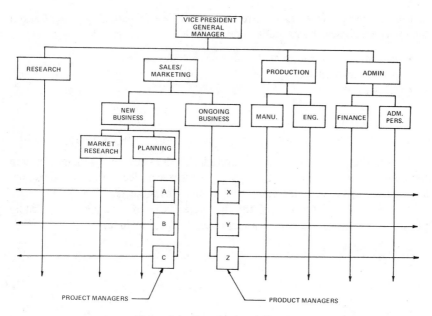

Figure 2-4. Organizational Chart.

environment. Their commitment to success often does not take into account such important parameters as return on investment, profitability, competition, and marketability.

To alleviate these problems, project managers and project engineers, especially on R & D-type projects, are now reporting to marketing so that marketing input will be included in all R & D decisions. Many executives have been forced into this position because of the high costs incurred during R & D, especially since, in case of a severe need to reduce costs, the R & D organization is usually the first to feel the pinch. Executives must exercise caution with regard to this structure where both product and project managers report to the marketing function. The marketing executive could become the focal point of the entire organization, with the capability of building a very large empire.

2.6 PROJECT LIFE CYCLES

Every program, project, or product has certain phases of development. A clear understanding of these phases permits managers and executives to better control total corporate resources in the achievement of desired goals. The phases of development are known as life cycle phases. However, the breakdown and terminology of these phases differ, depending upon whether we are discussing products or projects.

During the past few years, there has been at least a partial agreement about the life cycle phases of a product. They include:

- Research and Development
- Market Introduction
- Growth
- Maturity
- Deterioration
- Death

Today, there is no agreement among industries, or even companies within the same industry, about the life cycle phases of a project. This is understandable because of the complex nature and diversity of projects.

The theoretical definitions of the life cycle phases of a system, as defined by Cleland and King, can be applied to a project.[9] These include:

- Conceptual
- Definition
- Production
- Operational
- Divestment

The first phase is the conceptual phase and includes the preliminary evaluation of an idea. Table 2-1 defines the efforts attributed to this phase. Most

Table 2-1. Conceptual Phase.

- Determine existing needs or potential deficiencies of existing systems
- Establish system concepts that provide initial strategic guidance to overcome existing or potential deficiencies
- Determine initial technical, environmental, and economic feasibility and practicability of the system
- Examine alternative ways of accomplishing the system objectives
- Provide initial answers to the questions
  - What will the system cost?
  - When will the system be available?
  - What will the system do?
  - How will the system be integrated into existing systems?
- Identify the human and nonhuman resources required to support the system
- Select initial system designs which will satisfy the system objectives
- Determine initial system interfaces
- Establish a system organization

From *Systems Analysis and Project Management* by David I. Cleland and William Richard King. Copyright © 1968, 1975 by McGraw-Hill, Inc. Used with permission of McGraw-Hill Book Company, New York, p. 187.

9. Cleland, D. I., and King, W. R., *Systems Analysis and Project Management,* New York: McGraw-Hill, 1975, pp. 187-190.

important in this phase is a preliminary analysis of risk and the resulting impact on the time, cost, and performance requirements, together with the potential impact on company resources. The conceptual phase also includes a "first cut" at the feasibility of the effort.

The second phase is the definition phase and, as shown in Table 2-2, is mainly a refinement of the elements described under the conceptual phase. The definition phase requires a firm identification of the resources to be required together with the establishment of realistic time, cost, and performance parameters. This phase also includes the initial preparation of all documentation necessary to support the system. For a project based upon competitive bidding, the conceptual phase would include the decision of whether or not to bid, and the definition phase would include the development of the total bid package (i.e., time, schedule, cost, and performance).

Analyzing system costs during the conceptual and definition phases is not an easy task because of the amount of estimating involved. Most project or system costs can be broken down into operating (recurring) and implementation (nonrecurring) categories. The implementation costs include one-time expenses such as construction of a new facility, purchasing computer hardware, or detailed planning. Operating costs, on the other hand, include recurring expenses such as manpower. The operating costs may be reduced if personnel perform at a higher position on the learning curve. This identification of learning curve position is vitally important during the definition phase when firm cost positions must be established. Of course, it is not always possible to know what individuals will be available or how soon they can perform at a higher learning curve position.

Once the approximate total cost of the project is determined, a cost-benefit analysis should be conducted to determine if the estimated value of the information obtained from the system exceeds the costs of obtaining the information. This analysis is often included as part of a feasibility study. There are several

Table 2-2. Definition Phase.

- Firm identification of the human and nonhuman resources required
- Preparation of the final system performance requirements
- Preparation of the detailed plans required to support the system
- Determination of realistic cost, schedule, and performance requirements
- Identification of those areas of the system where high risk and uncertainty exist, and delineation of plans for further exploration of these areas
- Definition of intersystem and intrasystem interfaces
- Determination of necessary support subsystems
- Identification and initial preparation of the documents required to support the system, such as policies, procedures, job descriptions, budget and funding papers, letters, memoranda, etc.

From *Systems Analysis and Project Management* by David I. Cleland and William Richard King. Copyright © 1968, 1975 by McGraw-Hill, Inc. Used with permission of McGraw-Hill Book Company, New York, p. 188.

situations, such as in competitive bidding, where the feasibility study is actually the conceptual and definition phases. Because of the costs that can be incurred during these two phases, top management approval is almost always necessary before the initiation of such feasibility study.

The third phase is the production (or acquisition) phase and includes such items as those listed in Table 2-3. This phase is predominantly a testing and final standardization effort so operations can begin. Almost all documentation must be completed in this phase.

The fourth phase is the operational phase and, as shown in Table 2-4, integrates the project's product or services into the existing organization. If the project were developed for establishment of a marketable product, then this phase could include the product life cycle phases of market introduction, growth, maturity, and a portion of deterioration.

The final phase, as shown in Table 2-5, is divestment and includes the reallocation of resources. The question to be answered is, "Where should the resources be reassigned?" Consider a company that sells products on the open consumer market. As one product begins the deterioration and death phases of its life cycle (i.e., divestment phase of a system), then new products or projects must be established. Such a company would therefore require a continuous stream of projects in order to survive. In the ideal situation these new projects will be established at such a rate that total revenue will increase and company growth will be clearly visible.

The divestment phase evaluates the efforts on the total project and serves as input to the conceptual phases for new projects and systems. This final phase also has an impact on other ongoing projects with regard to priority identification.

The phases of a project and those of a product are compared in Figure 2-5. Notice that the life cycle phases of a product generally do not overlap, whereas the phases of a project can and often do overlap.

Table 2-3. Production Phase.

- Updating of detailed plans conceived and defined during the preceding phases
- Identification and management of the resources required to facilitate the production processes such as inventory, supplies, labor, funds, etc.
- Verification of system production specifications
- Beginning of production, construction, and installation
- Final preparation and dissemination of policy and procedural documents
- Performance of final testing to determine adequacy of the system to do the things it is intended to do
- Development of technical manuals and affiliated documentation describing how the system is intended to operate
- Development of plans to support the system during its operational phase

From *Systems Analysis and Project Management* by David I. Cleland and William Richard King. Copyright © 1968, 1975 by McGraw-Hill, Inc. Used with permission of McGraw-Hill Book Company, New York, p. 188.

Table 2-4. Operational Phase.

- Use of the system results by the intended user or customer
- Actual integration of the project's product or service into existing organizational systems
- Evaluation of the technical, social, and economic sufficiency of the project to meet actual operating conditions
- Provision of feedback to organizational planners concerned with developing new projects and systems
- Evaluation of the adequacy of supporting systems

From *Systems Analysis and Project Management* by David I. Cleland and William Richard King. Copyright © 1968, 1975 by McGraw-Hill, Inc. Used with permission of McGraw-Hill Book Company, New York, p. 189.

Table 2-6 identifies the various life cycle phases that are commonly used. Even in mature project management industries as construction, one could survey ten different construction companies and find ten different definitions for the life cycle phases.

The life cycle phases for computer programming, as listed in Table 2-6, are also shown in Figure 2-6 to illustrate how manpower resources can build up and decline during a project. In Figure 2-6, PMO is the present method of operations and PMO' will be the "new" present method of operations after conversion. This life cycle would probably be representative of a twelve-month activity. Most executives prefer short data processing life cycles because computer technology changes at a very rapid rate. An executive of a major utility commented that his company was having trouble determining how to terminate a computer programming project to improve customer service because by the time a package is ready for full implementation, an updated version appears on the scene. Should

Table 2-5. Divestment Phase.

- System phasedown
- Development of plans transferring responsibility to supporting organizations
- Divestment or transfer of resources to other systems
- Development of "lessons learned from system" for inclusion in qualitative-quantitative data base to include:
  - Assessment of image by the customer
  - Major problems encountered and their solutions
  - Technological advances
  - Advancements in knowledge relative to department strategic objectives
  - New or improved management techniques
  - Recommendations for future research and development
  - Recommendations for the management of future programs, including interfaces with associate contractors
  - Other major lessons learned during the course of the system

From *Systems Analysis and Project Management* by David I. Cleland and William Richard King. Copyright © 1968, 1975 by McGraw-Hill, Inc. Used with permission of McGraw-Hill Book Company, New York, p. 190.

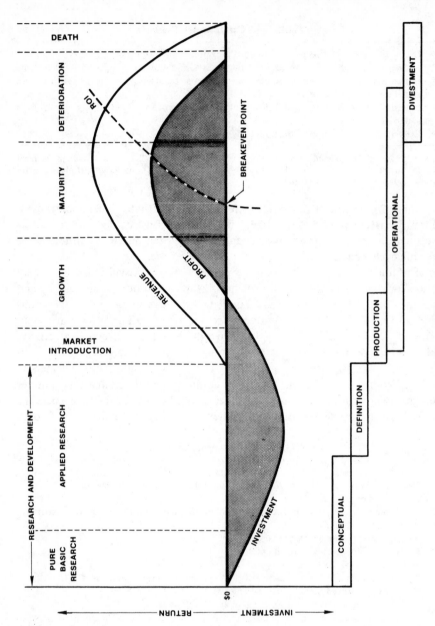

Figure 2-5. System/Product Life Cycles.

Table 2-6. Life Cycle Phase Definitions.

ENGINEERING	MANUFACTURING	CONSTRUCTION	COMPUTER PROGRAMMING
• Startup • Definition • Main • Termination	• Formation • Buildup • Production • Phase-out • Final Audit	• Planning, data gathering, and procedures • Studies and basic engineering • Major review • Detail engineering • Detail engineering/construction overlap • Construction testing and commissioning	• Conceptual • Planning • Definition and design • Implementation • Conversion

the original project be cancelled and a new project begun? The solution appears to be in establishing short data processing project life cycle phases, perhaps through segmented implementation.

As a final note, executives should realize that even within the same company, it is possible for different life cycle phase definitions to exist. This is because some projects are longer than others, more complex, or simply more difficult to manage.

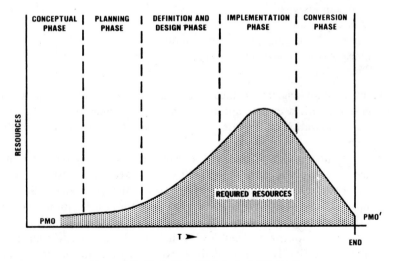

Figure 2-6. Definition Of A Project Life Cycle.

2.7 PROJECT MANAGEMENT: A VEIW FROM THE TOP

We have previously stated that project management should be viewed as a means of integrating work through more effective utilization of resources, not necessarily with the intent of creating future general managers. However, the fact that the project manager will mature at an accelerated rate causes some executives (and line managers) to feel threatened by the project manager, even though they still assert that project management is a necessary way of life. Executives must realize that not everyone in the organization will have the same view of project management. Line managers, line employees, executives, and even project managers can have differing views of what project management is all about. Below is a listing of the different ways that company personnel can view project management:

- A threat to established authority
- A source for future general managers
- A cause of unwanted change in ongoing procedures
- A means to an end
- A significant market for their services
- A way to build an empire
- A necessary evil to traditional management
- An opportunity for growth and advancement
- A better way to motivate people toward an objective
- A source of frustration in authority
- A way of introducing controlled changes
- An area of research
- A vehicle for introducing creativity
- A means of coordinating functional units
- A means of deep satisfaction
- A way of life

Executives must realize that their roles change in a project management environment. Executives cannot operate in the same manner as they did in the traditional organizational structure, and the expectations others have of them are different.[10]

There are three major changes in the way executives carry out their duties in a project management environment. First, the executives must rely heavily upon the project manager and line manager to run the day-to-day activities of the company. The executives must do what they are paid to do, namely look out for the long-range growth of the company through strategic planning and establishing administrative policies. Unless it is an emergency situation, executives will not be as involved in the daily activities of the company as they once were. Executive interference can destroy the project management environment.

---

10. These expectations will be described in more depth in Section 4-12.

Many executives now involved in project management claim that they are working sixty to seventy hours a week and blame the extra workload on project management. For the most part, this is their own fault because they put in forty hours per week on executive duties and thirty hours more by still trying to run the daily activities of the line groups. The cause is simple: executives refuse to give up control of the daily activities to the project and line managers. After all, it has taken them some thirty years to reach a top management position, and it shouldn't be surprising if delegating some of that authority and surrendering some control to thirty-year-old project and line managers is difficult.

Executive meddling isn't that bad as long as it occurs at the right time and place. For example, in the life cycle phases of Figure 2-6, executive input *is* expected during the conceptual and planning phases of a project. But after the project is planned, executives must have confidence in the ability of the project and line managers to execute and implement it, and should maintain only a monitoring posture except for conflict resolution, a shifting of priorities, or other such problems that require executive-level decisions.

A new executive management policy is developing in which executives will be paid year-end bonuses five years downstream based upon how well their strategic plan has been achieved, *not* upon the profitability of the last twelve months. When an executives realize that their bonuses are based upon short-term profits, they tend to neglect their primary function and meddle more in daily activities. If a company adopts this new management policy and executives separate themselves from daily activities, then who is in a better position than the line and project managers to take over daily operational control?

To summarize, executives interfere with project management because they:

- Are reluctant to delegate sufficient authority, accountability, and responsibility to the project managers
- Want a more active role in this "new" concept called project management
- Are unfamiliar with their new responsibilities and interface relationships in a project management environment

With project management a major change takes place in the chain of command. Executives are responsible for monitoring the environment; that is, those factors involving:

- Legal changes
- Social changes
- Economic changes
- Political changes
- Technological changes

If the executives are still the people who monitor the environment, then how do project managers know if and how any of the environmental conditions affect their projects, especially during the planning phase? Project managers *must* have the right to go to any level of management in the organization to obtain the information that is needed to plan, schedule, and control the project. Project managers cannot wait until the necessary information is filtered down through several layers of management to their level.

In ideal conditions, project managers will be at the same level as the individual with whom they negotiate for resources, that is, the department manager. If project managers have to meet with an executive to obtain the necessary information, then they should inform the intermediate levels (i.e., division managers and directors) of their intentions, at least as a courtesy, in case they wish to attend.

Another major change involves "tunnel vision." Most good project managers focus on their projects and exclude other concerns. They seem to see nothing except the end date of their projects and direct all their efforts toward making them successful. Project managers with this "tunnel vision" tend to divorce themselves from all other ongoing activities and from executive contact. Therefore, if environmental conditions change, executives may find it necessary to "force" the information down to the project managers.

Tunnel vision can be an element of dedication. However, it can also produce detrimental effects. Project managers with tunnel vision who are only concerned about their own projects can end up making decisions that are in the best interest of the project but may not be in the best interest of the company. As an example, a project manager on a low-priority project fights for the best functional manpower when, in fact, the best manpower should be assigned to higher-priority activities. If this can happen, then who should be used to provide a system of checks and balances to make sure that the project manager's decisions are in the best interest of the company? The first inclination is to say the executive. But this won't work because the executive should not be meddling in daily activities. The answer is the line managers. Line managers must make sure that project demands and decisions are in the best interest of the company. To do this, line managers must not be dedicated to any one project, but to all projects on an equal basis. Therefore, if at all possible, executives should not permit line managers to also act as project managers. They may decide to keep the best resources for their own project. Their project, therefore, may be a success, but at the expense of every other project that the line manager must supply resources to.

CASE STUDY: TRW NELSON
MIS AND MATERIALS MANAGEMENT SYSTEMS UPGRADE
A PROJECT—MANAGEMENT APPROACH[11]

Company Background

TRW Inc. was formed in 1957 by the merger of Thompson Products, Inc., a manufacturer of automobile and aircraft parts, and Ramo-Wooldridge Corpora-

---

11. Copyright © 1978 Bruce Galbreath. Reproduced by permission.

tion, a leader in advance planning for ballistic weapons systems and space technology. Today, the Cleveland-based, worldwide corporation has three major industry segments described generally as follows:

- Car and Truck includes a broad range of chassis, engine, and other components as original equipment and replacement parts for passenger cars, trucks, farm machinery, and other off-highway vehicles.
- Electronics and Space Systems includes four classes of products and services: electronic components; electronic systems, equipment, and services; computer-based and analytical services; and spacecraft design and manufacture.
- Industrial and Energy includes lines of basic industrial components such as fasteners, tools and bearings; energy-related products, such as pumps and valves, and aircraft products consisting primarily of jet engine components.

Industrial and Replacement (I & R) is an operating segment of TRW consisting of the Marlin-Rockwell Division, the Energy Products Group, Aftermarket Operations, the United Greenfield Divisions, and the United-Carr Divisions. TRW Nelson is a unit of United-Carr, manufacturing stud welding fasteners, stud welding systems, and cold-formed parts.

In 1975, management laid out new direction for TRW which Ruben F. Mettler (then president) stated would represent ". . . an even stronger commitment to quality of earnings and quality and strength of our balance sheet.

"Let me start with debt leverage. We have felt for years that we should manage the company to maintain a A rating on our debt securities. That has led us to operate with an approximate 40/60 debt/equity ratio as an upper limit on our leverage. We decided, for reasons that I'll describe later, that we want to reduce that leverage. We're moving towards a 30/70 target. We want to move beyond the A rating and toward the AA category.

"We're placing an added emphasis on return on assets employed. Our average return on assets employed has been roughly 10 percent during the past five years. Our new target is 15 percent. A combination of a 15 percent return on assets employed, and 30/70 leverage would result in a return on equity of 20 percent as compared with an average of about 14 percent in recent years. This higher return on equity is a key element of the new direction."[12]

A. William Reynolds, executive vice-president of I & R, defined the new direction for his units by noting that the debt/equity and ROAE goals required the I & R group, which accounted for 25 percent of TRW assets at that time, to improve its working capital ratio.

"To improve working capital ratios, we simply must improve our systems of control, especially in the areas of inventory and receivables management." Mr. Reynolds went on to point out that in most units of I & R, excellent customer service is the key element, the critical factor of competitive success. He also pointed out that ROAE levels of 15 percent are found only in larger, *leadership* companies. Again, he emphasized that excellence in customer service is obtained only with excellent systems of control.

---

12. From an address to institutional investors in Chicago in December, 1975 as quoted in the 1975 annual report.

A number of specific financial and operating goals evolved from this "new direction." In total, these became known as the "1980 Goals" stressing MIS and materials management systems with the objectives of commonality and excellence. In order to define excellence and assure movement toward common systems, Mr. Reynolds decided to draw on internal expertise. MIS and materials management advisory boards were formed from representatives of key units. These ongoing committees were charged with providing definition and guidance, and examining the materials and MIS plans of each unit to assure conformance and progress toward the stated goals.

Project Management Background

The problems facing Nelson management were two-folded. First, the TRW top management commitment to commonality and excellence of systems was unmistakable and Nelson was determined to be supportive. On the other hand, the concurrent drive for quality of earnings and return on assets employed meant that every expense, every job description, and every outlay was under careful scrutiny. The systems upgrade would, therefore, be accomplished without the addition of staff or consultive help.

Second, although Nelson management was receptive to the guidance coming from the divisional MIS and materials management committees, it was also concerned about maintaining the company's own priorities. Management felt it was entirely consistent to be fully supportive of corporate goals and, at the same time, approach the various tasks in the sequence that would allow Nelson the earliest payoffs in terms of better expense and asset management.

The approach to this problem of overhauling systems with the personnel available, personnel already fully committed to their functional duties, did not evolve overnight. However, project management, in the context of drawing on resources across the entire organization, was considered from the very start. This approach, which is highly structured and predominant in the construction and aerospace industries (TRW Systems, formerly Ramo Wooldridge Corporation, was a pioneer in project or program management), had been used less formally on occasion at Nelson, usually in the form of "task forces."

In 1970-71 such a transorganization team approach had been used on two occasions when unusually large contracts for Nelson equipment had been received from automotive customers. Similarly, in 1972, the project management approach had been applied to plan and coordinate the move of production facilities into a newly constructed plant. Likewise, an ad hoc group was set up in 1973 to investigate and recommend an approach to the company's long-range MIS hardware and staff needs.

Additionally, Nelson had, for a number of years, used product managers in its marketing effort. These managers would take charge of a product judged promising and coordinate its development across the functional areas of the company including market research, production planning, production, and sales.

The Evolution of an Approach

In 1975, TRW Nelson was in an unusually good position to address the challenges of MIS upgrade. Two years earlier, an experinced MIS manager had been hired and in early 1974 had supervised the transition from one generation of data processing equipment to the next. The balance of 1974 was spent updating existing applications, improving operating procedures, and extending know-how. By mid-1975, the company was prepared with both human and hardware resources to support a first-class MIS program.

At this point, an MIS steering committee was formed at the suggestion of the I & R MIS advisory board; it included the controller and managers from MIS, materials, manufacturing, and design engineering. The committee was charged with screening proposed MIS projects and requests for MIS services, and would assign priorities to projects based on payoffs claimed weighed against resource expenditure. Appeal was available through the vice-president of administration and, ultimately, the vice-president and general manager.

1975–The projects undertaken for the balance of 1975 were "upgrade" in nature, understandably finance and accounting oriented, and designed for eventual conversion to CRT input and inquiry. Among these projects were:

Order Entry and Billing
Accounts Payable
Accounts Receivable

Also conspicuous about these projects was the fact that they were led by MIS people.

1976–As 1976 unfolded, four facts became apparent:

1. "Management support" was evident by the sheer weight of commitment from divisional general managers on down, but as far as budget or direction was concerned. TRW Nelson would have to find the time, people, and expertise from their existing organization.
2. Selecting projects and establishing priorities were complicated tasks and critical to success.
3. How to approach, budget, and execute any given project (even what that project would eventually entail) could not always be readily determined.
4. User-leadership would be required for nonfinancial projects.

A typical 1976 project, however, was still outlined by the MIS manager and, with the exception of the MIP and order entry projects, was still assigned to the MIS manager or an MIS programmer-analyst for leadership. Projects for 1976 included:

Production Reporting (for factory incentive)
Materials-Inventory Control (redesign of inventory reporting system)
Materials-Inventory Control (MRP Phase I)

Accounting (consolidation of financial reporting)
Materials-Customer Service (customer order entry and inquiry—CRT)
Credit Department (tie-in, TRW National Credit Service)
Accounting (accounts payable to on-line CRT)
Accounting (payroll system update)
Materials-Inventory Control (surplus and obsolescence reporting)

1977—By August 1976, when 1977 plans were being finalized, another milestone had been reached. In addition to an MIS steering committee and better defined and structured projects, *user project leadership had become established at TRW Nelson.* Dependence was still heavy on the MIS manager for project structuring, but enthusiastic leadership was being received from the various functional departments. As an example, 1977 major projects and their leaders were as follows:

Project	*Project Leader*
Automated Purchasing System	Purchasing Manager
Capital Assets Perpetual Inventory	Production Engineer
MRP Phase II (1976 carryover)	Materials Manager
Elyria Plant On-Line CRT	Materials Manager
On Line Costing	Manager, Cost Department
Mechanization, Personnel Records	Supervisor, Personnel
On-Line Order Entry (1976 carryover)	Manager, Customer Service

Each of the above project leaders had served on previous committees and was an experienced manager. Also, each was in a position to benefit significantly from the successful integration of his project. For these reasons, the transition from MIS to functional leaders was not as difficult as had been envisioned.

The System Today

The following are projects completed in 1977:

SCHEDULED PROJECTS COMPLETED
   Capital Assets
   On-Line Order Entry
   Elyria On-Line
   Fastener Product Analysis
   Purchasing (Phase I and II)
   Material Requirements Planning (Phase II)
   Labor and Production Reporting Revision (Phase I)

NONSCHEDULED PROJECT COMPLETED
   Warehouse Effectiveness Report
   Standard Routing Revision (Fasteners)
   Surplus Sales Incentive Program
   West Coast Inventory Revision
   Bills of Material On-Line Inquiry
   Production Value Added Revision

That so many projects were successfully completed can be attributed, at least in part, to the project management approach as it has informally developed at TRW Nelson.

Table 2-7 is a list of projects planned for 1978. Total user involvement has evolved. Project identification and leadership has been entirely lifted from the MIS department (except where appropriate) and placed in the department where payoff is expected.

Figure 2-7 is a display of the project matrix, the overlay of 1978 projects on the TRW Nelson functional organization. It should be noted that the entire functional organization is not represented—only that portion involved in active projects.

Table 2-8 is a listing of projects planned for 1979 and beyond. These future projects will take on greater definition as the 1978 projects evolve. Also, comparing the 1978 and 1979 lists will reveal the transitory quality of the matrix. Table 2-8 is a "snapshot" of the interrelationships as they will exist going into 1978. This picture will alter as projects and project phases are completed until an entirely new matrix develops for 1979 and future years.

Project Management

Obviously, the development of a project approach was not without problems. At first, some people were uncomfortable operating outside of their functional areas with traditional lines of authority and responsibility. Others had difficulty working in groups. Slowly, however, the approach became accepted and then benefits began to accrue:

1. The general level of MIS awareness and expertise has been improved throughout the organization. Increased awareness is the foremost benefit of all—the key to success for the whole system. Instead of being handed a system and admonished to make it work, employees are sharing in the design, implementation, and debugging of *their own* systems.

Table 2-7. TRW Nelson: 1978 Projects.

SCHEDULED PROJECTS	PROJECT LEADER
A-100 Purchasing (Phase III)	Purchasing Manager
A-102 MRP (Phase III)	Supervisor, P & IC Equipment Products
A-103 Mechanization, Personnel	Supervisor, Personnel
A-107 Extend MIS Standards Worldwide	MIS Manager
A-108 Extend Material Management Standards Worldwide	Materials Manager
A-111 Warehouse Data Collection	Warehouse Coordinator/Customer Service Manager
A-112 On-Line Costing	Supervisor, Cost Department
A-114 Automated Financial Modeling	Controller
A-115 Labor and Production Reporting	Manufacturing Manager
A-117 Expanded Financial Reporting	Supervisor, Cost Department
A-119 Automated Production Order Entry	Supervisor, P & IC Fastener Products

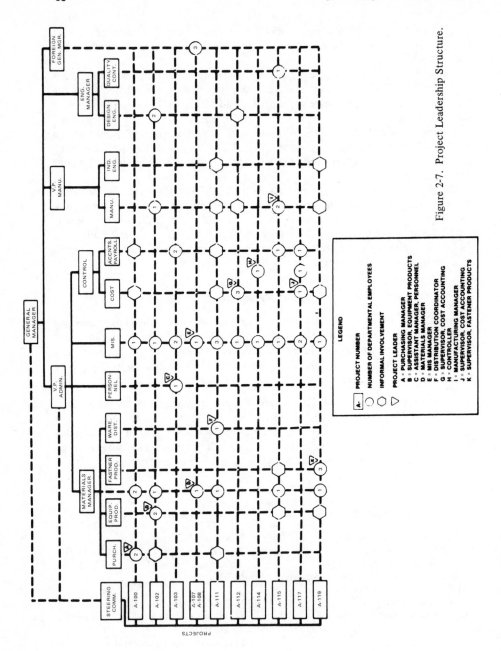

Figure 2-7. Project Leadership Structure.

Table 2-8. TRW Nelson: 1979-1980 Projects.

A-109 *New Surplus and Obsolete Inventory Reporting System*

An asset control project intended to replace an involved manual routine with an automated system. This system will allow immediate action decisions, reduce inventories, and facilitate the profitable disposal of surplus and obsolete items.

A-110 *Capacity Planning and Machine Center Loading*

This project will be a follow-up to MRP (A-102), labor reporting (A-115), and equipment routings (to be assigned) and will close the loop of manufacturing reporting and control systems. The system will provide further improvement of in the use of facilities and labor resources.

A-118 *Equipment Routing Revisions*

The entire line of equipment and accessories will be revised to conform to the present method used in the stud area. This will provide reports of production and performance-to-standard on a daily basis.

A-111 *Expansion of Warehouse Data Collection*

This project will be a continuation of the original project and will expand to include production reporting and purchasing information as required.

A-107 *Extension of MIS Standards to Profit Centers Outside the United States*

This project will be a continuous one of implementing proven systems installed at Lorain and at other locations outside of the United States. This will be accomplished by the cross-training of personnel at each location.

2. New systems are more readily accepted. People tend to be more receptive to change when they participate in it.
3. Membership on project teams and the resulting transorganizational relationships have gone far to reduce departmental provincialism. Informal lines of communication have been established and a higher degree of interdepartmental understanding achieved.
4. Project management is an excellent supplemental management training ground. For example, project A-119 (Figure 2-7 and Table 2-7) was assigned to a new production and inventory control supervisor. The objective of the project was an idea for a quick data processing payoff that he sold to the MIS steering committee. His project background was membership on the on-line order entry project completed in 1977. He is charged now with full project responsibility including design, planning, scheduling, obtaining and motivating human resources, debugging, and implementation. His instructions are to proceed entirely on his own, report regularly, and ask help when obstacles become insurmountable.
5. The project management approach offers opportunities. For the leaders, there is the opportunity to get the feel of management beyond their functional responsibilities. For all project members, there are opportuni-

ties for learning and individual visibility that would not be available otherwise.

6. Finally, the project-matrix approach has allowed TRW Nelson to deal with an immense task—the parameters of which are constantly changing—with a conventionally structured organization and without the expense and sometimes questionable results obtained from consultants.

CASE STUDY: PRODUCT MANAGEMENT AT UNITED BRANDS[13]

"They are the chosen few . . . the MBA Club. They're on the fastest track in the company."

"They're a bunch of young, bright, and terribly egotistical guys."

"It's the Momma's-chicken-soup syndrome. These guys *assume* they know how to do it best."

"What they call creative thinking would be called B.S. any other place."

"That department brings people in from the outside all the time; because they don't know their own business. They can't develop their own people; they promote them instead."

"They have charisma. They are always great personalities . . . a bunch of actors . . . a superior race. They're the prestigious group, the comers."

All these statements are about product managers. They were made by people in the various departments of the Butternut Division of United Brands, Inc. Only the last statement was made by a product manager.

The Development of Product Management at United Brands

Established in the late 1920s through the merger and acquisition of a number of independent packaged food producers, United Brands was one of the first multiproduct packaged food marketers in the United States. United Brands was also a pioneer in the use of the product management form of organization.

Originally, at United Brands, as in most companies, each function—production, research, marketing, and financial services—played a specialized role in the total operation of the company. The general manager of a divison coordinated the work of the functions in implementing the corporate strategy. However, as the number of products each division produced and sold increased, the job of coordination became increasingly complex. The product management type of organization was United Brand's response to this complexity in coordinating the functional departments in the development, production, and marketing of a large number of products.

---

13. Copyright © 1971 by the President and Fellows of Harvard College. Reproduced with permission. This case was prepared by Richard Marmer under the supervision of Jay W. Lorsch and Cyrus Gibson.

The product management organization was superimposed over the traditional functional organization, cutting across functional lines, as shown in the matrix below:

Functions

	Market Research	Sales	Production	Accounting and Control	Product Research
Product Group A					
Product Group B					
Product Group C					
Product Group D					
Product Group E					

Each product manager played a role similar to that of the division general manager, coordinating the work of people in the functional departments in implementing the strategy for the product (or products) for which he was responsible. An important difference, however, was that he had no structural authority over the people whose work he coordinated, as did the general manager. In fact, a product manager sometimes had to compete with other product managers for the services of the functional departments. For example, in the Butternut Division of United Brands, the same sales force handled all the products of all five product groups. In other departments, such as financial services and, to some extent, market research, employees were assigned to work with particular product groups, while at the same time working for their superiors within their functional departments.

In 1970, United Brands marketed a wide range of packaged food products in the United States through four operating divisions, each of which was treated as a relatively autonomous unit.

The Butternut Division

The Butternut Division of United Brands maintained its own production facilities, sales organization, product management section, marketing research group, research and development organization, raw food stuffs purchasing group, and personnel and controllership functions. (See organization chart and division headquarters floor plan, Figures 2-8 and 2-9.) Its products included peanut butter, jams and jellies, honey, and maple syrup.

According to Mr. Lee Edwards, Butternut's marketing manager, the Butternut Division had traditionally been United Brands' largest division and accounted for 37 percent of domestic sales.

However, although Butternut sales had continued to increase steadily over the past five years, their share of United Brands' total and domestic sales had decreased over the same period. This was due to a leveling off of the market for their group of products, United Brands' renewed acquisition program, and United Brands' increased activity in the institutional and international markets.

According to United Brands' 1970 annual report, the business of the Butternut Division will "remain a dependable and profitable business, but will account for a relatively smaller share of overall sales and earnings as other areas of the company grow more rapidly."

Product Management in the Butternut Division

According to Mr. Edwards, Butternut's marketing manager, the product manager's role was a key one in the operations of the division. Characterizing them as "little general managers," he described how the product managers were central to the planning and execution of marketing strategies:

"The product groups, with the advice of the various functional departments, formulate the marketing strategies and then pass them up the line of management for modification and/or concurrence. When agreement on the strategy is finally achieved, responsibility for the execution of the strategy rests with the product manager. This approach keeps senior management in control of policy and strategy, but it puts the burden of "managing" on the product manager. It also serves as a built-in manpower development program, as the product manager must constantly think up solutions to business problems and accomplish their successful execution."

The product manager's work in executing the product strategy could be divided into two broad categories:

1. The administration of trade discounts on current products.

Butternut management considered most of their products to be commodities in the packaged food business. Therefore, in terms of marketing expenditures, the division's marketing emphasis was on price competition. Three-fourths of the division's marketing expenditures were spent on trade deals.* Trade deals were

---

*Trade deals were promotional expenditures aimed at distributors and retailers, rather than directly at the customer. They included discounts of regular trade prices and allowances to retailers for running special newspaper advertising and retail coupon offers. These expenditures were often made with the intent that price reductions be passed on to the consumer. Sometimes trade discounts or dealer promotions required action by the retailer before the money was turned over; sometimes they did not. Trade deals did not include consumer promotions, such as sweepstakes contests, merchandise send-ins, etc.

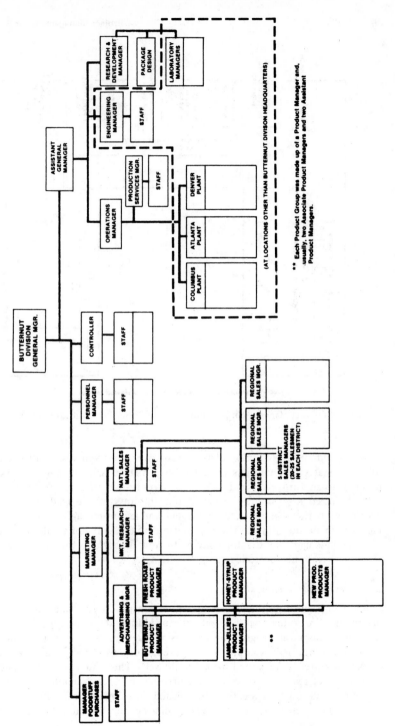

Figure 2-8. Product Management At United Brands (Butternut Division Organization Chart).

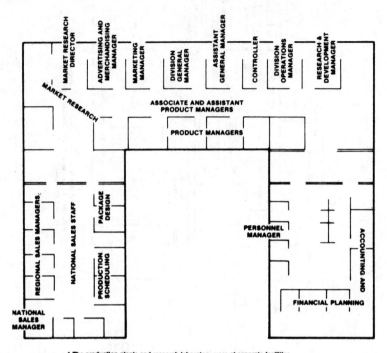

* The production plants and research laboratory were at separate facilities.

Figure 2-9. Product Management At United Brands (Floor Plan Of Butternut Division Headquarters).

administered on a district-by-district basis over the twenty sales districts. (The four regional sales managers each had five district sales managers working for them, who in turn each had twenty to twenty-five salesmen.) Managing trade deals required negotiating the types and amounts of the trade deals for each district with the regional sales managers and coordinating the volume requirements with production. In the negotiations with the regional sales manager, the product manager had the final say as to how and where the marketing money would be spent; he controlled the purse strings.

2. Managing advertising and product changes.

Introducing a new product, changing a current product, or changing its advertising required working together with the product research group, the market researchers, the product group's advertising agency, sales, and production. An extremely simplified example of the process follows. Product management and market research determined what could sell. This had to be reconciled with what product research could create and what production could produce within cost limits. Production was then established on a limited basis. Product management, market research, and the advertising agency then developed selling concepts and introduced them through the sales force to test-market the product. Test-market data were evaluated and decisions were made on a final strategy. The controller was involved in financial analysis throughout the complete process.

While this example is sequential, all the different functional departments were involved in the process at all points along the way to some degree. A large number of unforeseen problems would come up in coordinating the work of the functional departments. Much of the product manager's job involved getting these cross-functional conflicts resolved and getting decisions made, so that schedules and objectives could be met. The product group served as the focal point of most coordination and decision making.

When the case writer asked Mr. Edwards, the division marketing manager, the basis on which product managers were evaluated, he answered, "On how well they did their job." He was reluctant to be more specific, explaining that even though a product manager had met all the financial and market objectives of his product strategy, he could still be judged as performing poorly because of other circumstances, such as momentum in the product before his arrival, or his in-effectiveness in dealing with other people.

A successful product manager, he pointed out, must be able not only to co-ordinate the work of others, but must also be able to get good ideas from them and motivate them to carry out the decisions he ultimately makes, following the timetable he establishes.

The case writer discovered that product management in the Butternut Division had traditionally been the route to top management positions in the company. The chairman and the president of United Brands and twelve of the corporation's sixteen top nonproduction operating officers* were once product managers in the Butternut Division.

On the whole, people in the product management group were younger and more highly paid than their counterparts in the other departments of the division. Most of them had MBAs.

Product Management as Seen by the Other Departments

The case writer arranged to talk with people in each of the functional departments and with representatives of the advertising agency with whom the product managers came in contact. His intent was to find out what constituted "effective dealings" with each of the groups. The case writer asked these people two questions: (1) What are the basic conflicts between your department and product management? (2) In terms of helping you do your own job more effectively, what constitutes a good product manager and what constitutes a poor product manager?

Representative answers to the two questions appear below:

Question #1: *What are the basic conflicts between your department and product management?*

---

*Division managers, marketing managers, national sales managers, advertising and merchandising managers.

Advertising Agency
"The thing that's always bothered me about Butternut is that, while their business is so huge and the funds are there, they don't try *new* approaches to advertising. They spend too much time on the day-to-day operations, making sure the deals are effective, making sure they meet their monthly share objectives. Product management simply does not experiment enough."

Production
"Plants are basically big machines. Product management is constantly thinking of ways to market a product that don't fit those big machines, that require a significant amount of change. These machines don't like to get changed. So this basic plant wish—in an ideal world, to produce everything in a one-pound jar—is basically at odds with product management, which is trying to make up exotic things to sell, exotic ways to make products, and exotic ways to package it. The product management people seem to continually come up with new ideas that the plant cannot implement.

"Another conflict is the speed with which product management would like to react. Once they have an idea, our cycling times to get that idea from a drawing board into a package are usually far too long for product management; and they try their best to get us somehow to commit to a date that's unrealistic."

Market Research
"What keeps competent people in this department is the opportunity for being personally creative, the opportunity to develop new market research techniques. Too often product management gets in the way of that. They're constantly sending us out to put out brush fires—little projects, the same kinds of things all the time. What's worse is when they ignore your research results because they don't fit the product manager's preconceived conclusions."

Controllership
"Our main job is helping product managers project the results of their programs and then tracking what they've done and determining how successful it's been. They've got so many programs going at the same time—and these programs overlap—that it makes our job very difficult. And there's always something new and different that doesn't fit our ways of doing it. It's really a can of worms. But, then, that's what we're paid for. I shouldn't really complain about that.

"Product management has traditionally not paid close enough attention to profits and has emphasized market share. They have rationalized that they were buying future profits, but until recently they haven't tried to cash in on their past investment. That's beginning to change now. Mr. Parkes, the new division general manager, is putting increasing emphasis on the profitability of brand strategy, and the product managers are catching on. But it is still something of a problem."

Sales
"Some of the product managers are inexperienced. They don't really know what they're talking about. For the most part, they're trained to think about profits

and how to increase profits and spend the least amount of money. Or maybe it's the reverse—spend the least amount of money and, therefore, get more profits. Unfortunately it doesn't work out that way.

"Product management's job is to make sure the consumer wants our product. Sales' job is to make sure the products are there. That means sales has to know what is the best way to present it to the trade, which is the key in getting the product to the shelf.

"Every market is different. But our salesmen are in every market. So we know our customers' needs; we have accumulated knowledge about those markets. Given our intimate knowledge of each of these markets, we can recommend to the product management people how they should spend their promotion money. Sometimes they follow our recommendation; sometimes they won't. When they don't, then there's conflict."

"The major complaint in sales is that we don't handle the money. Product mangement has complete control of the purse strings. We try to get X amount of dollars from the product group for a program we feel will be beneficial to the division. They may not give it to us. And they have the final say."

Product Research
"The basic conflict is we can't make what they want as cheaply as they want it. And they don't want what we can make. Of course that's an overexaggeration. But the conflict is there."

"There's a tendency of the part of the product management people to theorize and postulate. They see themselves as being very creative. They'd much rather argue than go out and try to get the information to run the experiment. But they shouldn't be creative to the point that they neglect facts. There's too great a tendency, I think, for them not to get the facts."

Question #2: *In terms of helping you do your own job more effectively, what constitutes a good product manager and what constitutes a poor product manager?*

Advertising Agency
"Good product managers don't use me just for working up copy. They include me in the full range of marketing strategy formulation. That makes it very satisfying for me personally. It also insures that what we're thinking at the agency is in sync with what's brewing in the division. And, occasionally, I'm able to contribute something valuable that may have been overlooked by the product management people."

Production
"Good product managers understand the production function. So when we are unable to meet some of their timetables, they better understand the situation. They should be open-minded, willing to listen, and perhaps give some part of their time, or some importance, to production."

"Some product management people are honest and aboveboard. They tell you what they want, their reasons, and the impact on the compnay if they get it and if they don't get it. Others make you feel they're not really being honest with you. Their objective seems to be to make short-term heroes out of themselves at the expense of long-term gains. They are in such competition with each other that there's a lot of backbiting."

"Production people will do their best to get something for the people in product management if they know it's in the interests of the division or the corporation. But if they think it's just to make somebody look like a hero, they're not going to."

"A good product manager is willing to make a decision and stand by it."

Marketing Research

"The best product managers will ask the staff to make recommendations on how best to solve a problem. They will *not* tell them what test to use, what kind of sample, etc. Instead, they let the market researchers to do their job and make recommendations. Of course, they have the right to question the program—you know . . . 'Is this question really answered?' But they won't tell you what to do; they'll define the problem and then await your recommendations."

"A good product manager gives us the opportunity to be directly involved in the formulation of marketing strategy, the chance to make and defend our own recommendations."

"What I don't like in a product manager is indecisiveness. If I work out a program with a product manager, and he likes it and has bought it, I think he should support me in his recommendations to senior management. If there are points of conflict, he should be willing to let the market researcher into the discussion, where senior management is present, and let him defend it, too."

Controllership

"The person who fails as a product manager is the one who is not able to meet schedules and timetables."

"The good product managers are not only good at dictating, they're also good listeners."

Sales

"A good product manager has to have a good personality—almost a sales-type personality. He has to be able to come down like he has just stepped out of the shower, and given an amusing, enlightened presentation to the sales force. He's got to be an extrovert, to be able to project a good image.

"I have never seen a negative, or introverted, or nasty dispositioned product manager make it."

"A good product manager will come right out and tell it like it is. 'Here's how much I have. I'm sorry I can't give you more,' rather than, 'We feel this strategy would be better for you.' "

"My approach to them is, 'Tell me what your story is, and, if you dont't have the funds, I can sit down with my people and explain that to them.' But I can't tell my people we didn't get X promotion dollars because product management didn't think we were right. Because we know we were right!"

"You've got to have people to deal with who will act, who will make decisions, not the ones who think, 'If I don't do anything, it will go away.' "

"A good product manager can develop a strong point of view, articulate it correctly, and stand up to his superior with it."

Product Research
"The ineffective product managers tend to look down on people in the other departments—like 'you're my lackey.' "

"Product managers must be able to speak the languages of the people they deal with, which is quite different from technical research, operations, or financial people.

"They must have a basic desire to communicate with the different functions and be sympathetic to their needs as they relate to the total business. Not to cater to their gripes, but to really try to understand and appreciate the problems someone is trying to explain. They must be willing to give up valuable time to communicate to these people what they are trying to do and the reasons why."

Product Management as Seen by Subordinates of the Product Managers

Product managers also deal with their own subordinates. The case writer asked several junior members of the product management group what kind of product manager they preferred working for. Some of their answers appear below:

"A good product manager will give his subordinates new chances to develop their skills and new types of things to work on. I don't want to stay on one thing for too long after I've learned it. Then I'm just wasting time. I want to move on and up in the business. To do that I've got to learn all aspects of the business. A good product manager won't hold me back."

"A good boss will always be ready to help you out with a problem, but won't hover so closely over you that you can't grow through overcoming the difficulties of the problem yourself. He'll be there when you want him."

"He'll include me in on what's happening in the product group, beyond the particular project I'm working on, so I know where my work fits in."

Product Management as Seen by Product Managers

The case writer also asked two product managers to describe what they thought differentiated the successful product manager from a less successful one:

Product Manager #1:
"The most difficult part of the job is to get the uninvolved, the not-interested people, to be involved and interested in the business, like the production and

packaging people, the nine to five's, the people who see no future in their jobs.
A good product manager can do that.

"You have to understand what a person needs—a kick or a pat on the back.
Some fellows like to be loved. Others you have to lean on, get tough with,
threaten. It depends on the person. If you're sending pen and pencil sets to
retailers as a promotion gimmick, why not send some to staff, too?

"Let me give you an example—the purchaser in the production department.
If you don't get his attention, he could make you miss your target date. You
may have the best program, but without glass to pack the product in, you don't
have *any* program. And he is the guy who orders glass. He is the guy who can
make supply work extra hard for you. But he works for five product groups,
seven brands, and thirty different sizes. If he doesn't like you, you're in trouble.

"So it's a function of how you show your respect for him, and how you communicate with him, how you build up this rapport.

"If you need to get something done in three weeks, and the book says it takes
four to six weeks to get it done, but you know if he wants to help you he can
do it in three weeks, then it's that critical area of whether he's going to help
you that makes or breaks you, or makes you look good. That's why it's important to know how to deal with each person.

"There are other things too, of course. If people can't handle the complexity
of many things going at the same time, they'll never make it.

"Also, there are some who have great ideas, but can't sell them. They'll yield
right away when the boss gives them the pressure treatment, even if it's just to
test them. They don't last.

"There's another type that is extremely competent, but won't succeed because
they can't live within the system; they won't observe all the protocols, they
won't follow the procedures. If you want to succeed, you can step out of bounds
only once in a while, but not much, just sort of. You step on people's toes only
once in a while. You have to strike the right balance between independence
and compliance."

Product Manager #2:
"To become a product manager, you have to be smart, aggressive, and creative.
The smarter you are, the better. By aggressive, I'm referring to a people-oriented
agressiveness. To get ahead and succeed as a product manager, that agressiveness
must be attached to a commitment to get things done. Creativity is very important, but it's not necessary that the manager be the only one with new and
appropriate ideas. It's more important that he be able to recognize appropriate
creativity in others when he sees it. He should continually be running across
things others do with the reaction, 'Gee, I wish I'd though of that.' The important thing is that the fact that he didn't come up with it doesn't bother him—that
he is delighted to accept an idea someone else has."

"To get ahead as a product manager, a person has to have a commitment to
the results rather than to a particular technique or to a personality or to the
source of the ideas. He has to show aggressiveness and a toughness, a tenacity

that doesn't stop when somebody says 'No, you can't do it.' He'll try to figure out another way to do it."

"Another thing a person needs to get ahead in product management is the broadest view of the job possible—that means going beyond the requirements of the job. There are three kinds of people who start off in product management: (1) Those who just go through the motions, not wanting to do it. The job suffers. (2) Those who manage to do the job adequately, are committed to it, and want to do it well, so they can move on to something else more fun and exciting. (3) Those who do the job adequately and have the time—no, make the time—to do other things as well, things they think are important. They are the ones who go beyond their jobs. They are the ones who will succees in product management."

"Another important factor is what I call public relations (the cynic would probably call it politics). The fact that someone is using a great new idea in his work doesn't do any good unless the right people know about it. That is the job of the product manager. I am continually sending things up just to keep them posted about what people in my product group are doing that is good."

"Finally, a little humility goes a long way. That's trying to know as much as you possibly can without flaunting it. The person who says 'I've been in this business twenty years, so I ought to know more about it than you do'—that's categorically wrong. He knows more about his job, but I know more about how his job relates to what I'm trying to do—which is what he and I are sitting down to talk about."

"So his attitude is wrong, if that's his attitude. But making him see that does not move the ball ahead. Playing 'gotcha' is sometimes satisfying, but it doesn't help much."

CASE STUDY: PRODUCT MANAGEMENT AT COSTA PHARMACEUTICAL LABORATORIES

The pharmaceutical industry is considered to be one of the most competitive industries in business today. Numerous companies, both major and minor, compete to gain a share of the billions of dollars spent worldwide on health care services.

Costa Laboratories, headquartered in Chicago, Illinois, is one of the ten largest pharmaceutical houses in the world. The corporation consists of eight divisions employing more than 25,000 people and had sales of $1.5 billion in 1977.

The Pharmaceutical Products Division of Costa is the third largest division with sales of $250 million. Primary products of the division consist of anti-anxiety agents, anti-hypertensive agents for controlling blood pressure, anti-epileptic drugs, hematinics, and vitamins.

In June of 1978 the division underwent a reorganization that affected various marketing and promotional functions within the divison. Previously, the various functions of pricing, product management, advertising, market research, and sample promotion existed as separate service centers, with staff members reporting to their respective department heads. While the system worked efficiently in terms of each function, management felt it lacked one element for truly multidisciplined strategic planning: cohesion. The resources of each of these service departments were not always equally or immediately available to a particular business unit.

Inevitably, this tended to create problems because of competing priorities. With the budgets of each of the service centers under separate control, there were natural inhibitions on transferring or allocating resources across functional boundaries as needs arose. Simply stated, there was no common accountability for the activities or objectives of the various service units.

Thus, basic to the reorganization process was the formation of new business planning units called "strategic planning centers." The purpose of each center was to undertake and assume responsibility for the strategic business and promotional planning of an assigned group of products. The strategic planning center, utilizing the concept of zero-based budgeting, was designed to give each unit both authority and responsibility for allocation of resources to strategies and media that would best accomplish the unit's profit goal. It was the responsibility of the planning center to analyze the various strategies and develop action plans based on the current realities of the marketplace.

The reorganization of the key elements of the division also had the effect of broadening the authority and responsibility of the product manager, now referred to as a "business unit manager."

Under the previous system, the product manager lacked the authority to coordinate the activities of supporting departments in order to direct them toward the established objective of effective product promotion. Instead the manager was faced with a chain-of-command-type situation. The essential departments of market research, advertising, manufacturing, distribution, and sample promotion were reached only through their respective managers or vice-presidents, who weighted requests in terms of priorities and, most specifically, budget expenditures to complete the requested projects.

The previous system often led to such situations as: incomplete and late marketing research data due to communication problems over the type and amount needed; advertising that projected the wrong theme or used improper copy, creating regulatory problems with the Food and Drug Administration; manufacturing and distribution problems when a new product was sold to retailers by the sales force with no stock available in the distribution centers to be shipped to them; and the failure of drug samples to be sent out to the sales force for promotion to the medical community. Such situations combined with competing departmental priorities develop into a system that supported frustration, and the inability of departments to view an objective in comprehensive terms rather than in terms of specific departmental contributions to an objective.

The reorganization of the divisional structure was intended to broaden the authority of the product manager under the business unit concept.

Under the new concept, the organizational structure included the following persons within the strategic planning center:

1. Director of Strategic Planning
2. Business Unit Manager (Product Manager)

3. Promotion Manager
4. Pricing Assistant
5. Marketing Research Assistant
6. Medical Liaison
7. Manufacturing Liaison
8. Sales Liaison

Within this framework, the business unit manager reports to the director of strategic planning for all activities conducted within the unit itself. The unit or product manager coordinates the activities of advertising under the promotion manager, pricing under the pricing assistant, marketing research under the auspices of the market research assistant, medical under the director of the medical department, and contact with the sales department under a sales liaison. Because of the nature of Costa's products the manager must also be aware of the activities of the regulatory department.

Specifically, the relationship of the business unit manager to the various departments within the unit is as follows:

1. Pricing—Within the framework of pricing, the business unit manager has several duties. He is responsible for determining and updating factory costs of products; he must monitor profit margins and adjust retail prices when factory costs threaten to reduce the margin; he must monitor competitive product pricing so as to maintain near parity with highly competitive products; and he is responsible for segmentation of pricing between retail, wholesale, and government customers. The product manager not only works closely with the pricing assistant for the above requirements, but he also maintains active communication with pricing in competitive bidding situations. With the intense competition becoming keener daily, many large-volume pharmaceuticals are being put up for bid by hospital (nonprofit) and government customers. It is the role of the unit manager and the pricing assistant to accept or reject bids in the context of profit potential in terms of factory cost versus dollars realized from the bid, potential for retail sales as a result of a patient obtaining a refilled prescription on a drug that was first given in a hospital, etc. In addition, they must analyze when the drug was sold on bid, the type and size of the customer requesting the bid, and the status of competition in terms of who they are and what prices they are offering.

   Primary responsibility in pricing belongs to the pricing assistant, but all efforts are coordinated by the unit manager who accepts or rejects pricing recommendations. In turn, many decisions of a pricing nature (e.g., acceptance of a large-volume bid) have an effect on manufacturing, specifically product planning. Often these effects are changes in product forecasts and necessitate changes in product priorities. This requires involvement between the unit manager and manufacturing in order to reset those priorities.

   Normally, a business unit manager interacts with manufacturing only in terms of unit forecasts that control production schedules, product specifications and quality assurance, inventory control and production capacity questions. However, the manufacturing liaison also works closely with the unit manager to handle any sudden manufacturing problems, such as with equipment, that could significantly affect product throughput. The business manager provides essential manufacturing cost information when the unit manager begins to consider aspects of a new product or line extension.

2. Advertising—Within the framework of advertising, the unit manager works closely with the advertising promotion manager. The promotion manager is responsible for aspects of product promotion dealing with advertising, most often of the medical journal type, and the creation of sales aids used by the sales force. The promotion manager, often a creative artist, uses ideas suggested by the unit manager along with his own to create effective advertising that will convey a sales message to the medical community in an ethical and acceptable manner and reinforce the message communicated by the field sales force. In addition, the promotion manager creates sales aids or detail booklets, which contain medical product information, for use by the sales force with the medical community. Last, the promotion manager has the responsibility of coordinating the promotional budget with the business unit manager for all assigned products. Twice yearly the managers draw up and review promotional budgets to insure that proper expenditures are being carried out according to the promotional plan, and to readjust any factors of advertising, etc., that are not falling within the scope of the market plan. Final coordination and control of advertising and promotion rest with the business unit manager.

3. Marketing Research—To formulate, implement, and receive feedback from a marketing plan, the unit manager relies heavily on data obtained by market research. Foremost among the many duties that the business unit manager has is the maintenance and improvement of a product's share of market. The manager constantly strives for better methods to increase market share and relies heavily on market research for usable information. Market research uses a variety of tools, for example, surveys of physicians on a particular product. This type of information can allow the unit manager to judge the efficacy of a promotional theme in terms of physician recall from sales force calls and journal advertising. Market research can also describe competitive activity in terms of efficacy and depth of promotion as these relate to increases or decreases of sales force calls, sample mailings and regular mailings, along with an estimate of total dollars spent on each category.

Other areas essential to the unit manager and provided by market research include a statistical picture of the manager's product category, specifically the increase or decrease of a pharmaceutical category, for example, the antibiotic market. It also can portray how a particular product is faring against competition in terms of increase or decrease of market share, the number of new prescriptions written for a particular product, and the segmentation of a product category into retail and hospital markets.

Last, marketing research can provide valuable information to the unit manager when new products or line extensions are being considered. In early stages, a prime consideration for a new product is the state of the product category (increasing or decreasing) and the conclusion that a new product can gain a good share of market and be profitable. Marketing research can provide the essential information so the unit manager can make an informed decision.

4. Medical Department—All printed material of a promotional nature must be approved by the medical department for authenticity, accuracy, and compliance to FDA standards. Handling requests for documentation and information from the medical community on a variety of medical subjects is also the responsibility of the medical department. The business unit manager must have all promotional material approved by the medical department before it can be sent to the sales force. This material is reviewed for content accuracy under generally accepted medical guidelines enforced by the FDA. The medical department will either approve promotional materials or return them for restructuring with appropriate comments. In addition, the product manager relies on the medical department to handle complex medical questions from the medical community and often uses these as indications of physician interest in the promotional message. Last, the medical department and the product manager must work together closely during periods of clinical studies for a new product. The outcome of clinical studies can be the basis for either committing large sums of money to formulating a new product marketing plan or scrapping a potential product.

In the medical department the unit manager has the ability to coordinate efforts, but cannot exercise direct authority. The manager lacks in-depth medical knowledge and must accept the expert opinions of the physicians and scientists he is working with.

5. Regulatory affairs—For the safety of consumers, the FDA maintains rigid standards for all aspects of pharmaceutical company operations from manufacturing to sales. The regulatory department evaluates the accuracy of promotional materials, that is, advertising and sales force promotional aids. It reviews all such material and must give written approval before these can be released for general use. In addition, the department monitors the medical package inserts required for all drugs to insure correctness and adherence to FDA standards.

The involvement of the product manager with the regulatory department is not that extensive, but because strict compliance to FDA regulations is required, the manager must constantly be aware of the actions, if any, that regulatory is taking.

6. Sales—The unit manager's interaction with the sales department is crucial. Sales are the culmination of all efforts by the product manager and all other supportive departments. The sales effort determines if the fore-

casts for the success of a product are fulfilled. Product management and sales management can clash over promotional themes, sizes or samples, pricing, bids, stock situations, and promotional priorities, but they must reach some agreement or the product is a failure.

Basically the product manager must "sell" his promotional program to the managers of the sales department. Usually this involves discussion and compromise. But the final promotional effort must be supported by both product and sales management.

In dealing with the sales department, the product manager interacts with a variety of individuals. He works with a vice-president of sales, a director of sales, numerous regional and district managers, the salesmen themselves, and persons involved in sales training. The manager is truly one individual who must be able to motivate many. The old saying of "give us the tools to sell with" is in proper context here. The product manager does provide the tools to sell with—everything from promotional materials up to the design of sales samples. The manager needs feedback on programs from the sales department in order to alter ineffective programs, react quickly to competition, and maintain a consistency in materials and ideas. The result of all this effort by the product manager is successful programs that lead to sales increases.

It should be obvious that the role of the product manager is diverse. It is the manager's responsibility to formulate the market plans for products by drawing upon the skills and resources of supportive departments. The market plans serve as a baseline from which to formulate promotional ideas. The plans must take into account important areas such as the status of a particular pharmaceutical product category in terms of growth potential, competitive activity and methodology for coping with it, descriptions of key customers, the final promotional budget, a complete layout of planned promotional activities, and expected results based on short- and long-range forecasting.

The product manager also plays a key role in forecasting long- and short-range goals. Working with market research, manufacturing, and pricing, the manager is responsible for setting objectives both of a tactical and long-range nature. These objectives consist of forecasting gross dollar sales, percent share of market, unit sales, and percent of market served in relation to market share. These forecasts in turn are used for corporate long-range planning in terms of gross dollar sales, capital expenditure requests by manufacturing to meet demand for increased unit sales, and formulation of specific dollar budgets for use by various departments based on total percentages of sales.

One of the most important roles of the product manager is the creation of new product ideas. In a survey of the market, the manager often recognizes a need for a specific product. With supportive departments, the manager formulates preliminary information on market potential, competitive products, estimated gain of market share for a product based on price parity or price undercut, manufacturing costs with profit margin, new product requirements of the FDA, and time periods required to market the product.

Product managers bring together their own ideas and those of others into a cohesive, goal-oriented plan of action. They must maintain a clear view of objectives and must often clear away the confusion created by the meshing of efforts of unrelated departments. They must communicate the objective, clarify its purpose, and then motivate others to help them reach it. At all times, it will be the job of the manager to train individuals in various departments to work effectively toward an objective.

CASE STUDY: PROJECT FIRECRACKER

"Don, project management is the only way to handle this type of project. With forty million dollars at stake we can't afford not to use this approach."

"Listen, Jeff, your problem is you take seminars given by these ivory tower professors and you think you're an expert. I've been in this business for forty years and I know how to handle this job—and it isn't through project management."

History and Background

Jeff Pankoff, a registered professional engineer, came to work for National Incorporated after receiving a mechanical engineering degree. After he arrived at National he was assigned to the engineering department. Soon thereafter, Jeff realized that he needed to know more about statistics and he enrolled in the graduate school of a local university. When he was near completion of his masters of science, National transferred Jeff to one of its subsidiaries in Ireland to set up an engineering department. After a successful three years, Jeff returned to National's home office and was promoted to chief engineer. Jeff's department increased to eighty engineers and technicians. Spending a considerable time in administration, Jeff decided an MBA would be useful, so he enrolled in a program at a nearby university. At the time when this project began, Jeff was near the end of the MBA program.

National Corporation, a large international corporation with annual sales of about $600 million employs 8,000 people worldwide and is a specialty machine, component, and tool producer catering to the automotive and aircraft manufacturers. The company is over a hundred years old and has a successful and profitable record.

National is organized in divisions according to machine, component, and tool production facilities. Each division is operated as a profit center. (See Exhibit 2-1.) Jeff was assigned to the Tool Division.

National's Tool Division produces a broad line of regular tools as well as specials. Specials amounted to only about 10 percent of the regular business, but over the last five years had increased from 5 percent to the current 10 percent. Only specials that were similar to the regular tools were accepted as orders.

National sells all its products through about 3,000 industrial distributors located throughout the United States. In addition, National employs 200 sales representatives who work with the various distributors to provide product seminars.

Exhibit 2-1.

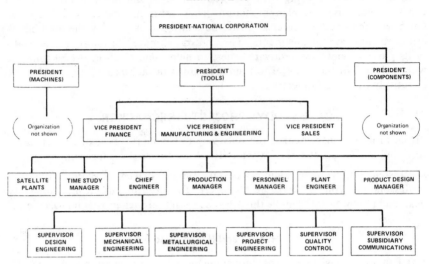

The traditional approach to project assignments is used. The engineering department, headed by Jeff, is basically responsible for the purchase of capital equipment and the selection of production methods used in the manufacture of the product. Project assignments to evaluate and purchase a new machine tool or to determine the production routing for a new product are assigned to the engineering department. Jeff assigns the project to the appropriate section, and, under the direction of a project engineer, the project is completed.

The project engineer works with all the departments reporting to the vice-president, including production, personnel, plant engineering, product design (the project engineer's link to sales), and time study. As an example of the working relationship, the project engineer selects the location of the new machine and devises instructions for its operation with production. With personnel the engineer establishes the job description for the new job as well as for the selection of people to work on the new machine. The project engineer works with plant engineering on the moving of the machine to the proper location and instructs plant engineering on the installation and services required (air, water, electricity, gas, etc.). It is very important that the project engineer work very closely with the product design department, which develops the design of the product to be sold. Many times the product designed is too ambitious an undertaking or cannot be economically produced. Interaction between departments is essential in working out such problems.

After the new machine is installed, an operator is selected and the machine is ready for production. Time study, with the project engineer's help, then establishes the incentive system for the job.

Often a customer requests certain tolerances that cannot be adhered to by manufacturing. In such a case, the project engineer contacts the product design department which contacts the sales department, which in turn contacts the customer. The communication process is then reversed and the project engineer gets an answer. Based upon the number of questions, the total process may take four to five weeks.

As the company is set up, the engineering department has no authority over time study, production, product design, etc. The only way that the project engineer can get these departments to make commitments is through persuasion or through the chief engineer, who could go to the vice-president of manufacturing and engineering. If the engineer is convincing, the vice-president will dictate to the appropriate manager what must be done.

Salaries in all departments of the company are a closely guarded secret. Only the vice-president, the appropriate department manager, and the individual know the exact salary. Don Wolinski, the vice-president of manufacturing and engineering, pointed out that this approach was the "professional way" and an essential aspect of smooth business operations.

The Ill-Fated Project

Jeff Pankoff, the chief engineer for National, flew to Southern California to one of National's (tool) plants. Ben Ehlke, manager of the Southern California plant (SCP), wanted to purchase a computer numerical controlled (CNC) machining center for $250,000. When the request came to Jeff for approval, he had many questions and wanted some face-to-face communication.

The Southern California plant supplied the aircraft industry and one airplane company provided 90 percent of SCP's sales. Jeff was mainly concerned about the sales projections used by Ehlke in the justification of the machining center. Ehlke pointed out that this was based on what the airplane company had told him they expected to buy over the next five years. Since this estimate was crucial to the justification, Jeff suggested that a meeting be arranged with the appropriate people at the airplane company to explore these projections. Since the local National sales representative was ill, the distributor salesman, Jack White, accompanied Jeff and Ben. While at the airplane company (APC), the chief tool buyer of APC, Tom Kelly, was informed that Jeff was there. Jeff received a message from the receptionist that Tom Kelly wanted to see Jeff before he left the building. After the sales projections were reviewed and Jeff was convinced that they were as accurate and as reliable as they possibly could be, he asked the receptionist to set up an appointment with Tom Kelly.

When Jeff walked into Kelly's office the fireworks began. He was greeted with, "What's wrong with National? They refused to quote on this special part. We sent them a print and asked National for their price and delivery, indicating it could turn into a sizable order. They turned me down flat saying that they were not tooled up for this business. Now I know that National is tops in the field and that National can provide this part. What's wrong with your sales department?"

All this came as a complete surprise to Jeff. The distributor salesman knew about it but never thought to mention it to him. Jeff looked at the part print and asked, "What kind of business are you talking about?" Kelly said, without batting an eye, "Forty million dollars per year."

Jeff realized that National had the expertise to produce the part and would require only one added machine (a special press costing $20,000) to have the total manufacturing capability. Jeff also realized he was in an awkward situation. The National sales representative was not there and he certainly could not speak for sales. However, a $40 million order could not be passed over lightly. Kelly indicated that he would like to see National get 90 percent of the order if they would only quote on the job. Jeff told Kelly that he would take the information back and discuss it with the vice-presidents of sales, manufacturing, and engineering and that most likely the sales vice-president would contact him next.

On the return flight, Jeff reviewed in his mind his meeting with Kelly. Why did Bob Jones, National's sales vice-president, refuse to quote? Did he know about the possible $40 million order? Although Jeff wasn't in sales, he decided that he would do whatever possible to land this order for National. That evening Jack White called from California. Jack said he had talked to Kelly after Jeff left and told Kelly that if anybody could make this project work, it would be Jeff Pankoff. Jeff suggested that Jack White call Bob Jones with future reports concerning this project.

The next morning, before Jeff had a chance to review his mail, Bob Jones came storming into his office. "Who do you think you are committing National to accept an order on your own without even a sales representative present? You know that all communication with a customer is through sales."

Jeff replied, "Let me explain what happened."

After Jeff's explanation, Jones said, "Jeff, I hear what you're saying, but no matter what the circumstances, all communications with any customer must go through proper channels."

Following the meeting with Jones, Jeff went to see Wolinski, his boss. He filled Wolinski in on what had happened. Then he said, "Don, I've given this project considerable thought. Jones is agreeable to quoting this job. However, if we follow our normal channels, we will experience too many time delays and problems. Through the various stages of this project, the customer will have many questions and changes, and will require continuous updating. Our current system will not allow this to happen. It will take work from all departments to implement this project and unless all departments work under the same priority system, we won't have a chance. What we need, Don, is project management. Without this approach where one man heads the project with authority from the top, we just can't make it work."

Wolinski looked out the window and said, "We have been successful for many years using our conventional approach to project work. I grant you that we have not had an order of this magnitude to worry about, but I see no reason why we should change even if the order were for 100 million dollars."

"Don, project management is the only way to handle this type of project. With forty million dollars at stake we can't afford not to use this approach."

"Listen Jeff, your problem is you take seminars given by these ivory tower professors and you think you're an expert. I've been in this business for forty years and I know how to handle this job—and it isn't through project management. I'll call a meeting of all concerned department managers so we can get started on quoting this job."

That afternoon, Jeff and the other five department managers were summoned to a meeting in Wolinski's office. Wolinski summarized the situation and informed the assembled group that Jeff would be responsible for the determination of the methods of manufacture and the associated manufacturing costs that would be used in the quotation. The method of manufacture, of course, would be based upon the design of the part provided by product design. Wolinski appointed Jeff and Waldo Novak, manager of product design, as co-heads of the project. He further advised that the normal channels of communication with sales through the product design manager would continue as usual on this project.

The project began. Jeff spent considerable time requesting clarification of the drawings submitted by the customer. All these communications went through Waldo. Before the manufacturing routing could be established for quotation purposes, questions concerning the drawing had to be answered. The customer was getting anxious to receive the quotation because their management had to select a supplier within eight weeks. One week was already lost due to communication delay. Wolinski decided that to speed up the quoting process he would send Jeff and Waldo along with Jones, the sales vice-president to see the customer. This meeting at APC helped clarify many questions. After Jeff returned, he began laying out the alternative routing for the parts. He assigned two of his most creative technicians and an engineer to run isolated tests on the various methods of manufacturing. From the results he would then finalize the routing that would be used for quoting. Two weeks of the eight were gone but Jeff was generally pleased until the phone rang. It was Waldo.

"Say Jeff, I think if we change the design on the back side of the part, it will add to its strength. In fact, I've assigned one of my men to review this and make this change and it looks good."

While this conversation was going on, Wolinski popped into Jeff's office and said that sales had promised that National would ship APC a test order of 100 pieces in two weeks. Jeff was irate. Product design was changing the product. Sales was promising delivery of a test order that no one could even describe yet.

Needless to say, the next few days were long and difficult. It took three days for Jeff and Waldo to resolve the design routing problem. Wolinski stayed in the background and would not make any position statement except he wanted everything "yesterday." By the end of the third week the design problem was resolved and the quotation was prepared and sent out to the customer. The quotation was acceptable to APC pending the performance of the 100 test parts.

At the start of the fourth week, Jeff, with the routing in hand, went to Charlie Henry, the production manager, and said he needed 100 parts by Friday. Charlie looked at the routing and said, "The best I can do is a two-week delivery."

After discussing the subject for an hour, the two men agreed to see Wolinski. Wolinski said he'd check with sales and attempt to get an extension of one week. Sales asked the distributor salesman to request an extension. Jack White was sure it would be okay so he replied to Bob Jones without checking that the added week was in fact acceptable.

The 100 pieces went out in three weeks rather than two. That meant the project was at the end of the sixth week and only two remained. Inspection received the test pieces on Monday of the seventh week and immediately reported them not to be in specification. Kelly was upset. He was counting heavily on National to provide these parts. Kelly had received four other quotations and test orders from National's competitors. The prices were similar and the test parts were to specification. However, National's parts, although out of specification, looked better than their competitors'. Kelly reminded Jones that the customer now had only nine days left before the contract would be let. That meant the 100 test parts had to be made in nine days. Jones immediately called Wolinski who agreed to talk to his people to try to accomplish this.

The tools were shipped in eleven days, two days after the customer had awarded orders to three of National's competitors. Kelly was disappointed in National's performance but told Jones that National would be considered for next year's contract, at least a part of it.

Jeff, hearing from Waldo that National lost the order, returned to his office, shut the door and thought of the hours, nearly round the clock, that were spent on this job. Hours that were wasted because of poor communications, non-uniform priorities, and because there was no project manager. "I wonder if Wolinski learned his lesson; probably not. This one cost the company at least six million dollars in profits, all because project management was not used." Jeff concluded that his work was really cut out for him. He decided that he must convince Wolinski and others of the advantages of using project management. Although Wolinski had attended a one-day seminar on project management two years ago, Jeff decided that one of his objectives during the coming year would be to get Wolinski to the point where he would, on his own, suggest becoming more knowledgeable concerning project management. Jeff's thought was that if the company was to continue to be profitable it must use project management.

The phone range, it was Wolinski. He said, "Jeff, do you have a moment to come down to my office? I'd like to talk about the possibility of using, on a trial basis, this project management concept you mentioned to me a few months ago."

3

Organizational Structures

3.0 INTRODUCTION

During the past ten years there has been a so-called hidden revolution in the introduction and development of new organizational structures. Management has come to realize that organizations must be dynamic in nature; that is, they must be capable of rapid restructuring should environmental conditions dictate. These environmental factors evolved from the increasing competitiveness of the market, changes in technology, and a requirement for better control of resources for multiproduct firms.

Much has been written about how to identify and interpret those signs which indicate that a new organizational form may be necessary. According to Grinnell and Apple, there are five general indications that the traditional structure may not be adequate for managing projects:[1]

- Management is satisfied with its technical skills, but projects are not meeting time, cost, and other project requirements.
- There is a high commitment to getting project work done, but great fluctuations in how well performance specifications are met.
- Highly talented specialists involved in the project feel exploited and misused.
- Particular technical groups or individuals constantly blame each other for failure to meet specifications or delivery dates.
- Projects are on time and to specifications, but groups and individuals aren't satisfied with the achievement.

Unfortunately many companies do not realize the necessity for organizational change until it is too late. Management continually looks externally (i.e., to the environment) for solutions to problems rather than internally. A typical example would be that new product costs are continually rising while the product

1. Grinnell, S.K., and Apple, H.P., "When Two Bosses are Better Than One," *Machine Design,* January 84-87, 1975.

life cycle may be decreasing. Should emphasis be placed on lowering costs or developing new products?

If we assume that an organizational system is composed of both human and nonhuman resources, then we must analyze the sociotechnical subsystem whenever organizational changes are being considered. The social system is represented by the organization's personnel and their group behavior. The technical system includes the technology, materials, and machines necessary to perform the required tasks.

Behavioralists contend that there is no one best structure to meet the challenges of tomorrow's organizations. The structure used, however, must be one that optimizes company performance by achieving a balance between the social and the technical requirements. According to Sadler:[2]

Since the relative influence of these (sociotechnical) factors change from situation to situation, there can be no such thing as an ideal structure making for effectiveness in organizations of all kinds, or even appropriate to a single type of organization at different stages in its development.

There are often real and important conflicts between the type of organizational structure called for if the tasks are to be achieved with minimum cost, and the structure that will be required if human beings are to have their needs satisfied. Considerable management judgement is called for when decisions are made as to the allocation of work activities to individuals and groups. High standardization of performance, high manpower utilization and other economic advantages associated with a high level of specialization and routinization of work have to be balanced against the possible effects of extreme specialization in lowering employee attitudes and motivation.

Even the simplest type of organizational change can induce major conflicts. The creation of a new position, the need for better planning, the lengthening or shortening of the span of control, the need for additional technology (knowledge), and centralization or decentralization can result in major changes in the sociotechnical subsystem. Argyris has defined five conditions that form the basis for organizational change requirements:[3]

These requirements . . . depend upon (1) continuous and open access between individuals and groups, (2) free, reliable communication, where (3) independence is the foundation for individual and departmental cohesiveness and (4) trust, risk-taking and helping each other is prevalent so that (5) conflict is identified

2. Sadler, Philip, "Designing and Organizational Structure," *Management International Review,* 11, 6: 1933, 1971.
3. Argyris, Chris, "Today's Problems With Tomorrow's Organizations," *The Journal of Management Studies,* February, 31-55, 1967.

and managed in such a way that the destructive win-lose stances with their accompanying polarization of views are minimized . . . . Unfortunately these conditions are difficult to create . . . . There is a tendency toward conformity, mistrust and lack of risk-taking among the peers that results in focusing upon individual survival, requiring the seeking out of the scarce rewards, identifying one's self with a successful venture (be a hero) and being careful to avoid being blamed for or identified with a failure, thereby becoming a "bum." All these adaptive behaviors tend to induce low interpersonal competence and can lead the organization, over the long-run, to become rigid, sticky, and less innovative, resulting in less than effective decisions with even less internal commitment to the decisions on the part of those involved.

Today, organizational restructuring is a compromise between the traditional (classical) and the behavioral schools of thought; management must consider the needs of the individuals as well as the needs of the company. After all, is the organization structured to manage people or to manage work?

There are a wide variety of organizational forms for restructuring management. The exact method depends upon the people in the organization, the company's product lines, and management's philosophy. A poorly restructured organization can sever communication channels that may have taken months or years to cultivate; cause a restructuring of the informal organization, thus creating new power, status, and political positions; and eliminate job satisfaction and motivational factors to such a degree that complete discontent is the result.

Sadler defines three tasks that must be considered because of the varied nature of organizations: control, integration, and external relations.[4] If the company's position is very sensitive to the environment, then management may be more concerned with the control task. For an organization with multiple products, each requiring a high degree of engineering and technology, the integration task can become primary. Finally, for situations with strong labor unions and repetitive tasks, external relations can predominate, especially in strong technological and scientific environments where strict government regulations must be adhered to.

In the sections that follow, a variety of organizational forms will be presented. Obviously, it is an impossible task to describe all possible organizational structures. Each of the organizational forms included is used to describe how the project management organization evolved from the classical theories of management. For each organizational form, advantages and disadvantages are listed in terms of both technology and social systems. Sadler has prepared a six-question checklist that explores a company's tasks, social climate, and relationship to the environment:[5]

4. Sadler, Philip, "Designing an Organizational Structure," *Management International Review*, 11, 6: 1933, 1971.
5. Ibid.

- To what extent does the task of organization call for close control if it is to be performed efficiently?
- What are the needs and attitudes of the people performing the tasks? What are the likely effects of control mechanisms on their motivation and performance?
- What are the natural social groupings with which people identify themselves? To what extent are satisfying social relationships important in relation to motivation and performance?
- What aspect of the organization's activities needs to be closely integrated if the overall task is to be achieved?
- What organizational measures can be developed which will provide an appropriate measure of control and integration of work activities, while at the same time meeting the needs of people and providing adequate motivation?
- What environmental changes are likely to affect the future trend of company operations? What organizational measures can be taken to insure that the enterprise responds to these effectively?

The answers to these questions are not easy. For the most part, they are a matter of the judgement exercised by organizational and behavioral managers.

3.1 ORGANIZATIONAL WORK FLOW

Organizations are continuously restructured to meet the demands imposed by the environment. Restructuring can produce a major change in the role of individuals both in the formal and informal organization. Many researchers believe that the greatest usefulness of behavioralists lies in their ability to help the informal organization adapt to changes and resolve the resulting conflicts. Unfortunately, behavioralists cannot be totally effective unless they have an input into the formal organization as well. Conflicts arise out of changes in the formal structure. Whatever organizational form is finally selected, formal channels must be developed so that each individual has a clear description of the authority, responsibility, and accountability necessary for the flow of work to proceed.

In the discussion of organizational structures, the following definitions will be used:

- *Authority* is the power granted to individuals (possibly by their position) so that they can make final decisions for others to follow.
- *Responsibility* is the obligation incurred by individuals in their roles in the formal organization in order to effectively perform assignments.
- *Accountability* is the state of being totally answerable for the satisfactory completion of a specific assignment.

Authority and responsibility can be delegated (downward) to lower levels in the organization. Accountability usually rests with the individual.

Yet, even with these clearly definable divisions of authority, responsibility, and accountability, establishing good interface relationships between the project and functional managers can take a great deal of time, especially during the conversion from a traditional to a project organizational form. Trust is the key to success here, and can overcome any problems in authority, responsibility, or accountability. When trust exists, the normal progression in the growth of the project-functional interface bond is as follows:

- Even though a problem exists, both the project and functional managers deny that any problem exists.
- When the problem finally surfaces, each manager blames the other.
- As trust develops, both managers readily admit responsibility for several of the problems.
- The project and functional managers meet face-to-face to work out the problem.
- The project and functional managers begin to formally and informally anticipate the problems that can occur.

For each of the organizational structures described in the following sections, advantages and disadvantages are listed. Many of the disadvantages stem from possible conflicts arising from problems in authority, responsibility, and accountability. The reader should identify these as such.

3.2 TRADITIONAL (CLASSICAL) ORGANIZATION

For more than two centuries the traditional management structure has survived. However, recent business developments, such as the rapid rate of change in technology and position in the marketplace, as well as increased stockholder demands, have created strains on the existing organizational forms. Fifty years ago companies could survive with only one or perhaps two product lines. The classical management organization, as shown in Figure 3-1, was found to be satisfactory for control and conflicts were at a minimum.[6]

However, as time progressed, companies found that survival depended upon multiple product lines (i.e., diversification) and vigorous integration of technology into the existing organization. As organizations grew and matured, managers found that company activities were not being integrated effectively, and that new conflicts were arising in the well-established formal and informal channels.

---

6. Many authors refer to classical organizations as pure functional organizations. This can be seen from Figure 3-1. Also note that the department level is below the division level. In some organizations these titles are reversed.

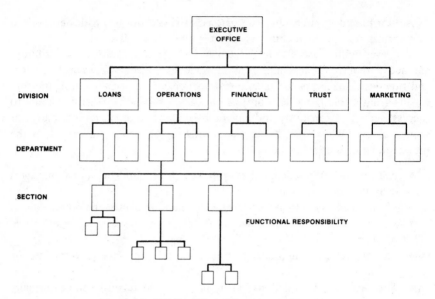

Figure 3-1. The Traditional Management Structure.

Managers began searching for more innovative organization forms that would alleviate the integration and conflict problems.

Before a valid comparison can be made with the newer forms, the advantages and disadvantages of the traditional structure must be shown. Table 3-1 lists the advantages of the traditional organization. As seen in Figure 3-1, the general manager has beneath him all of the functional entities necessary to either perform R & D or develop and manufacture a product. All activities are performed within the functional groups and are headed by a department (or, in some cases, a division) head. Each department maintains a strong concentration of technical expertise. Since all of the project must flow through the functional departments, each project can benefit from the most advanced technology, thus making this organizational form well suited for mass production. Functional managers can hire a wide variety of specialists and provide them with easily definable paths for career progression.

The functional managers maintain absolute control over the budget. They establish their own budgets, upon approval from above, and specify requirements for additional personnel. Because the functional manager has manpower flexibility and a broad base from which to work, most projects are normally completed within cost.

Both the formal and informal organizations are well established, and levels of authority and responsibility are clearly defined. Since each person reports to only one individual, communication channels are well structured. If a structure has this many advantages, they why are we looking for other structures?

Table 3-1. Advantages Of The Classical/Traditional Organization.

1. Easier budgeting and cost control.
2. Better technical control.
   A. Specialists can be grouped to share knowledge and responsibility.
   B. Personnel can be used on many different projects.
   C. All projects will benefit from the most advanced technology (better utilization of scarce personnel).
   D. Technology supervisors provide better control and supervision.
3. Provides flexibility in the use of manpower.
4. Provides broad manpower base to work with.
5. Provides continuity in the functional disciplines; policies, procedures, and lines of responsibility are more easily defined and understandable.
6. Readily admits mass-production activities within established specifications.
7. Provides good control over personnel since each employee has one and only one person to report to.
8. Communication channels are vertical and well established.
9. Quick reaction capability excels, but may be dependent upon the priorities of the functional managers.

For each advantage, there is almost always a corresponding disadvantage. Table 3-2 lists the disadvantages of the traditional structure. The majority of these are related to the fact that there is no strong central authority or individual responsible for the total project. As a result, integration of activities that cross functional lines become a difficult chore and top-level executives must get involved with the daily routine. Conflicts occur as each functional group struggles for power. The strongest functional group dominates the decision-making process. Functional managers tend to favor what is best for their functional group rather than what is best for the project. Many times, ideas will remain functionally oriented with very little regard for ongoing projects. In addition, the decision-making process is slow and tedious.

Table 3-2. Disadvantages Of The Traditional/Classical Organization.

1. No individual is directly responsible for the total project (i.e. no formal authority; committee solutions).
2. Does not provide the project-oriented emphasis necessary to accomplish the project tasks.
3. Coordination becomes complex and additional lead time is required for approval of decisions.
4. Decisions normally favor the strongest functional groups.
5. There is no customer focal point.
6. Response to customer needs is slow.
7. Difficulty in pinpointing responsibility; this is the result of little or no direct project reporting; very little project-oriented planning and no project authority.
8. Motivation and innovation are decreased.
9. Ideas tend to be functionally oriented with little regard for ongoing projects.

Because there exists no customer focal point, all communications must be channelled through upper-level management. Upper-level managers then act in a customer relations capacity and refer all complex problems down through the vertical chain of command to the functional managers. The response to the customer's needs therefore becomes a slow and aggravating process because the information must be filtered through several layers of management. If problem solving and coordination are required to cross functional lines, then additional lead time is required for the approval of decisions. All trade-off analysis must be accomplished through committees chaired by upper-level management.

Projects have a tendency to fall behind schedule in the classical organizational structure. Completing all projects and tasks on time, with a high degree of quality and efficient use of available resources, is all but impossible without continuous involvement of top-level management. Incredibly large lead times are required. Functional managers attend to those tasks that provide better benefits to themselves and their subordinates first. Priorities may be dictated by requirements of the informal as well as formal departmental structure.

3.3 DEVELOPING WORK INTEGRATION POSITIONS

As companies grew in size, more and more emphasis was placed upon multiple ongoing programs with high-technology requirements. Organizational pitfalls soon appeared, especially in the integration of the flow of work. As management discovered that the critical point in any program is the interface between functional units, the new theories of "interface management" developed.

Because of the interfacing problems, management began searching for innovative methods to coordinate the flow of work between functional units without modification to the existing organizational structure. This coordination was achieved through several integrating mechanisms:[7]

- Rules and procedures
- Planning processes
- Hierarchical referral
- Direct contact

By specifying and documenting management policies and procedures, management attempted to eliminate conflicts between functional departments. Management felt that, even though many of the projects were different, the actions required by the functional personnel were repetitive and predictable. The behavior of the individuals should therefore be easily integrated into the flow of

---

7. Galbraith, Jay R., "Matrix Organization Designs," *Business Horizons,* February, 29-40, 1971. Galbraith defines a fifth mechanism, liaison departments, which will be discussed later in this section.

work with minimum communication necessary between individuals or functional groups.

Another method for reducing conflicts and minimizing the need for communication was through detailed planning. Functional representation would be present at all planning, scheduling, and budget meetings. This method worked best for nonrepetitive tasks and projects.

In the traditional organization, one of the most important responsibilities of upper-level management was the resolution of conflicts through "hierarchical referral." The continuous conflicts and struggle for power between the functional units consistently required that upper-level personnel resolve those problems resulting from situations that were either nonroutine or unpredictable and for which no policies or procedures existed.

The fourth method is direct contact and interaction by the functional managers. The rules and procedures, as well as the planning process method, were designed to minimize ongoing communications between functional groups. The quantity of conflicts that executives had to resolve forced key personnel to spend a great percentage of their time as arbitrators, rather than as managers. To alleviate problems of hierarchical referral, upper-level management requested that all conflicts be resolved at the lowest possible levels. This required that functional managers meet face-to-face to resolve conflicts.

In many organizations, these new methods proved ineffective, primarily because there still existed a need for a focal point for the project to insure that all activities would be properly integrated.

When the need for project managers was acknowledged, the next logical question was where in the organization to place them. Executives preferred to keep project managers as low as possible in the organization. After all, if they reported to someone high up, they would have to be paid more and would pose a continuous threat to top management.

The first attempt to resolve this problem was to develop project leaders or coordinators within each functional department, as shown in Figure 3-2. Section-level personnel were temporarily assigned as project leaders and would return to their former positions at project termination. This is why the term "project leader" is used rather than project manager, because the word "manager" implies a permanent relationship. This proved effective for coordinating and integrating work within one department, provided that the correct project leader was selected. Some employees considered this position as an increase in power and status, and conflicts occurred about whether assignments should be based upon experience, seniority, or capability. Several employees wanted the title merely so they could use it on their resumés. Furthermore, the project leaders had almost no authority and section-level managers refused to take directions from them. Many section managers were afraid that if they did take direction, they were admitting that the project leaders were next in line for the department manager's position.

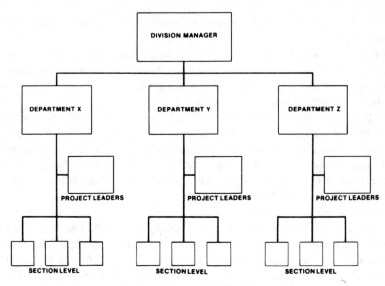

Figure 3-2. Departmental Project Management.

When the activities required efforts that crossed more than one functional boundary, say two or more sections or departments, conflicts arose. The project leader in one department did not have the authority to coordinate activities in any other department. Furthermore, the creation of this new position caused internal conflicts within each department.

Even though we have criticized this organizational form, it does not mean that it cannot work. Any organizational form (yes, *any* form) will work if the employees want it to work. As an example, a computer manufacturer has a midwestern division with three departments within it, as in Figure 3-2, and approximately fourteen people per department. When a project comes in, the division manager determines which department will handle most of the work. Let us say that the work load is 60 percent department X, 30 percent department Y, and 10 percent department Z. Since most of the effort is in department X, the project leader is selected from that department. When the project leader goes into the other two departments to get resources, he will almost always get the resources he wants. There are two reasons why this organizational form works here:

- The other department managers know that they may have to supply the project leader on the next activity.
- There are only three functional boundaries or departments involved (i.e., a small organization)

The next step in the evolution of project management was the task force concept. The rationale behind the task force concept was that integration could be achieved if each functional unit placed a representative on the task force. The group could then jointly solve problems as they occurred, provided that budget limitations were still adhered to. Theoretically, decisions could now be made at the lowest possible levels, thus expediting information and reducing, or even eliminating, delay time.

The task force was composed of both part-time and full-time personnel from each department involved. Daily meetings were held to review activities and discuss potential problems. Functional managers soon found that their task force employees were spending more time in unproductive meetings than performing functional activities. In addition, the nature of the task force position caused many individuals to shift membership within the informal organization. Many functional managers then placed nonqualified and inexperienced individuals on task forces. The result was that the group soon became ineffective because they either did not have the information necessary to make the decisions, or lacked the authority (delegated by the functional managers) to allocate resources and assign work.

Development of the task force concept was a giant step toward conflict resolution: work was being accomplished on time, schedules were being maintained, and costs were usually within budget. But integration and coordination were still problems because there were no specified authority relationships or individuals to oversee the entire project through completion. Many attempts were made to overcome this by placing various people in charge of the task force; functional managers, division heads, and even upper-level management had opportunities to direct task forces. However, without formal project authority relationships, task force members maintained loyalty to their functional organizations, and, when conflicts came about between the project and functional organization, the project always suffered.

Although the task force concept was a step in the right direction, the disadvantages strongly outweighed the advantages. A strength of the approach was that it could be established very rapidly and with very little paperwork. Integration, however, was complicated; work flow was difficult to control; and functional support was difficult to obtain, because it was almost always strictly controlled by the functional manager. In addition, task forces were found to be grossly ineffective on long-range projects.

The next step in the evolution of work integration was the establishment of liaison departments, particularly in engineering divisions that perform multiple projects involving a high level of technology (see Figure 3-3). The purpose of the liaison department was to handle transactions between functional units within the (engineering) division. The liaison personnel received their authority through the division head. The liaison department actually did not resolve conflicts, however; their prime function was to assure that all departments work toward the same requirements and goals. Liaison departments are still in existence

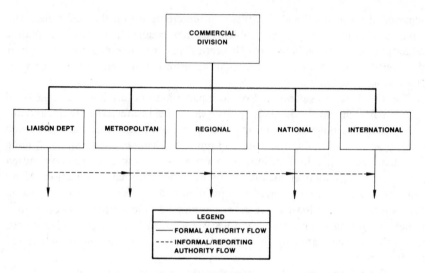

Figure 3-3. Engineering Division With Liaison Department.

in many large companies and typically handle engineering change and design problems.

Unfortunately, the liaison department is simply a scale-up of the project coordinator within the department. The authority given to the liaison department extends only to the outer boundaries of the division. If a conflict came about between the manufacturing and engineering divisions, for example, hierarchical referral would still be needed for resolution. Today, liaison departments are synonymous with project engineering and systems engineering departments.

3.4 LINE-STAFF ORGANIZATION

It soon became obvious that control of a project must be given to personnel whose first loyalty is directed toward the completion of the project. To do this, the project management position must be separated from any controlling influence of the functional managers. Figure 3-4 shows a typical line-staff organization.

Two possible situations can exist with this form of line-staff project control. In the first situation, the project manager serves only as the focal point for activity control, that is, a center for information. The prime responsibility of the project manager is to keep the division manager informed of the status of the project and to "harass" or attempt to "influence" managers into completing activities on time. As stated by Galbraith, "Since these men had no formal authority, they had to resort to their technical competence and their interpersonal skills in order to be effective."[8]

---

8. Galbraith, Jay, R., "Matrix Organization Designs," *Business Horizons,* February, 29-40, 1971.

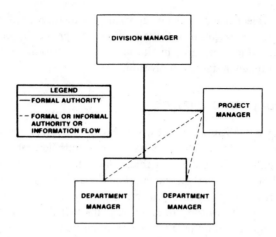

Figure 3-4. Line-Staff Organization.

The project manager maintained monitoring authority only, despite the fact that both he and the functional manager reported to the same individual. Both work assignments and merit reviews were made by the functional managers. Department managers refused to take direction from the project managers because this would seem like an admission that the project manager was next in line to be the division manager.

The amount of authority given to the project manager posed serious problems. Almost all upper-level and division managers were from the classical management schools and therefore maintained serious reservations about how much authority to relinquish. Many of these managers considered it a demotion if they had to give up any of their long-established powers.

The second situation involves the amount of authority given to the project manager. The project manager (using the authority vested in him by the division manager) can assign work to individuals in the functional organizations. The functional manager, however, still maintains the authority to perform merit reviews, but cannot enforce both professional and organizational standards in the completion of an activity. The individual performing the work is now caught in a web of authority relationships, and additional conflicts develop because functional managers are forced to share their authority with the project manager.

Although this second situation did occur during the early stages of matrix project management, it did not last because:

- Upper-level management was not ready to cope with the problems arising from shared authority.
- Upper-level management was reluctant to relinquish any of their power and authority to project managers.

- Line-staff project managers who reported to a division head did not have any authority or control over those portions of a project in other divisions; that is, the project manager in the engineering division could not direct activities in the manufacturing division.

3.5 PURE PRODUCT ORGANIZATION

The pure project organization, as shown in Figure 3-5, develops as a division within a division. As long as there exists a continuous flow of projects, work becomes stable and conflicts are at a minimum. The major advantage of this organizational flow is that one individual, the program manager, maintains complete line authority over the entire project. Not only does he assign work, but he also conducts merit reviews. Because each individual reports to only one person, strong communication channels develop and result in a very rapid reaction time. Long lead times became a thing of the past. Trade-off studies could be conducted as fast as time would permit without having to look at the impact on other projects (unless, of course, identical facilities or equipment were required). Functional managers were able to maintain qualified staffs for new product development without sharing personnel with other programs and projects.

The responsibilities attributed to the project manager were entirely new. First of all, his authority was now granted by the vice-president and general manager. The program manager handled all conflicts, both those within his organization and those involving other projects. Interface management was conducted at

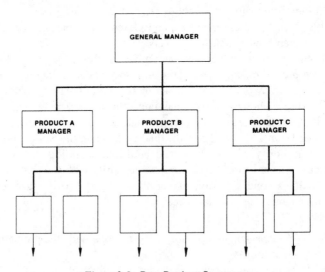

Figure 3-5. Pure Product Structure.

the program manager level. Upper-level management was now able to spend more time on executive decision making rather than conflict arbitration.

The major disadvantage with the pure project form is the cost of maintaining the organization. There is no chance for sharing an individual with another project in order to reduce costs. Personnel are usually attached to these projects long after they are needed, because once an employee is given up, the product manager might never be able to get him back. Motivating personnel becomes a problem. At project completion, functional personnel do not "have a home" to return to. Many organizations place these individuals into an overhead labor pool from which selection can be made during new project development. People still in the labor pool for a certain period of time may be laid off indefinitely. As each project comes to a close, people become uneasy and often strive to prove their worth to the company by overachieving, a condition which is only temporary. It is very difficult for management to convince key functional personnel that they do, in fact, have career opportunities in this type of organization.

In pure functional structures, technologies are well developed but project schedules often fall behind. In the pure project structure, the fast reaction time keeps activities on schedule, but technology suffers because without strong functional groups, which maintain interactive technical communication, the company's outlook for meeting the competition may be severely hampered. The engineering department for one project might not communicate with their counterpart on other projects and duplication of efforts can easily occur.

The last major disadvantage of this organizational form is the control of facilities and equipment. The conflict occurring most often is when two projects require use of the same piece of equipment or facilities at the same time. Hierarchical referral is required to alleviate this problem. Upper-level management can assign priorities to these projects. This is normally accomplished by defining certain projects as strategic, tactical, or operational, the same definitions usually given to plans.

Table 3-3 summarizes the advantages of this organizational form and Table 3-4 lists the disadvantages.

3.6 MATRIX ORGANIZATIONAL FORM

The matrix organizational form is an attempt to combine the advantages of the pure functional (traditional) structure and the product organizational structure and is ideally suited for companies, such as construction, that are "project-driven." Figure 3-6 shows a typical matrix structure. Each project manager reports directly to the vice-president and general manager. Since each project represents a potential profit center, the power and authority used by the project manager come directly from the general manager. The project manager has total responsibility and accountability for project success. The functional de-

Table 3-3. Advantages Of The Product Organizational Form.

1. Provides complete line authority over the project; that is, strong control through a single project authority.
2. The project participants work directly for the project manager. This creates a more profit-conscious environment. Unprofitable product lines are more easily identified and can be eliminated.
3. Strong communications channels.
4. Can maintain expertise on a given project without sharing key personnel.
5. Very rapid reaction time.
6. Personnel demonstrate loyalty to the project; better morale with product identification.
7. Development of a focal point for cut-of-company customer relations.
8. Flexibility in determining time (schedule), cost, and performance trade-offs.
9. Interface management becomes easier as a unit size is decreased.
10. Upper-level management maintains more free time for executive decision making.

partments, on the other hand, have functional responsibility to maintain technical excellence on the project. Each functional unit is headed by a department manager whose prime responsibility is to insure that a unified technical base is maintained and that all available information can be exchanged for each project. Department managers must also keep their people aware of the latest technical accomplishments in the industry.

Certain ground rules exist for matrix development:

*   Participants must spend full time on the project; this insures a degree of loyalty.
*   Horizontal as well as vertical channels must exist for making commitments.
*   There must be a quick and effective method for conflict resolution.
*   There must be communication channels and free access between managers.
*   All managers must have an input into the planning process.
*   Both horizontally and vertically oriented managers must be willing to negotiate for resources.
*   The horizontal line must be permitted to operate as a separate entity except for administrative purposes.

Table 3-4. Disadvantages Of The Product Organizational Form.

1. Cost of maintaining this form in a multiproduct company would be prohibitive due to duplication of efforts, facilities, and personnel; inefficient usage.
2. There exists a tendency to retain personnel on a project long after they are needed. Upper-level management must balance workloads as projects start up and are phased out.
3. Without strong functional groups, outlook for the future to improve company's capabilities for new programs would be hampered, that is, no perpetuation of technology.
4. Control of functional (i.e., organizational) specialists requires top-level coordination.
5. Lack of opportunities for technical interchange between projects.
6. Lack of career continuity and opportunities for project personnel.

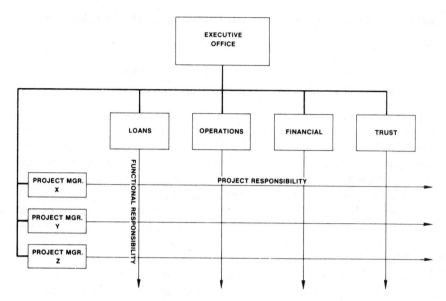

Figure 3-6. Pure Matrix Structure.

These ground rules simply state some of the ideal conditions that matrix structures should possess. Each ground rule brings with it advantages and disadvantages.

Before describing the advantages and disadvantages of this structure, the organization concepts must be introduced. The basis for the matrix approach is an attempt to create synergism through shared responsibility between project and functional management. Yet this is easier said than done. The following questions must be answered before successful operations of a matrix structure can be achieved.

- If each functional unit is responsible for one aspect of a project, and other parts are conducted elsewhere (possibly subcontracted to other companies), how can a synergistic environment be created?
- Who decides which element of a project is more important?
- How can a functional unit (operating in a vertical structure) answer questions and achieve project goals and objectives that are compatible with other projects?

The answers to these questions depend upon the mutual understanding between the project and functional managers. Since both individuals maintain some degree of authority, responsibility, and accountability on each project, they must continuously negotiate. Unfortunately, the program manager might only consider what is best for his project (disregarding all others), whereas the functional manager might consider his organization as being more important than each project.

In the matrix,

- There should be no disruption due to dual accountability.
- A difference in judgement should not delay work in progress.

In order to get the job done, project managers sometimes need adequate organizational status and authority. A corporate executive contends that the organizational chart shown in Figure 3-6 can be modified to show that the project managers have adequate organizational authority by placing the department manager boxes at the tip of the functional arrowheads. The executive further contends that, with this approach, the project managers appear to be higher in the organization than their departmental counterparts but are actually equal in status. Executives who prefer this method must exercise due caution because the line and project managers may not feel that there still exists an equality in the balance of power.

Problem solving in this type of environment is a fragmented and diffused process. The project manager acts as a unifying agent for project control of resources and technology. He must maintain open channels of communication between him and functional units as well as between functional units themselves so as to prevent suboptimization of individual projects. The problems of routine administration can and do become a cost-effective requirement.

In many situations, functional managers have the power and means of making a project manager look good, provided that they can be motivated enough to think in terms of what is best for the project. Unfortunately, this is not always accomplished. As stated by Mantell:[9]

There exists an inevitable tendency for hierarchically arrayed units to seek solutions and to identify problems in terms of scope of duties of particular units rather than looking beyond them. This phenomenon exists without regard for the competence of the executive concerned. It comes about because of authority delegation and functionalism.

This concept of "tunnel vision" can exist at all levels of management.

The project environment and functional environment cannot be separated; they must interact. The location of the project and functional unit interface is the focal point for all activities.

The functional manager controls departmental resources (i.e., people). This poses a problem in that, although the project manager maintains the maximum

---

9. Leroy H. Mantell, "The Systems Approach and Good Management," *Business Horizons*, October, 1972.

control (through the line managers) over all resources including cost and personnel, the functional manager must provide staff for the project's requirements. It is therefore inevitable that conflicts occur between functional and project managers.

These conflicts revolve about items such as project priority, manpower costs, and the assignment of functional personnel to the project manager. Each project manager will, of course, want the best functional operators assigned to his program. In addition to these problems, the accountability for profit and loss is much more difficult in a matrix organization than in a project organization. Projects managers have a tendency to blame overruns on functional managers, stating that the cost of the function was excessive. Whereas functional managers have a tendency to blame excessive costs on project managers with the argument that there were too many changes, more work required than defined initially and other such arguments.[10]

The individual placed at the interface position has two bosses: he must take direction from both the project manager and the functional manager. The merit review and hiring and firing responsibilities still rest with the department manager. Merit reviews are normally made by the functional manager after discussions with the program manager. The functional manager may not have the time necessary to continuously measure the progress of this individual. He must rely upon the word of the program manager for merit review and promotion. The interface members generally give loyalty to the person signing their merit review. This poses a problem, especially if conflicting orders are given by the functional and project managers. The simplest solution is for the individual at the interface to ask the functional and project managers to communicate with each other to resolve the problem. This type of situation poses a problem for project managers:

- How does a project manager motivate an individual working on a project (either part-time or full-time) so that his loyalties are with the project?
- How does a project manager convince an individual to perform work according to project direction and specifications when these requests may be in conflict with department policy, especially if the individual feels that his functional boss may not look upon him too favorably?

There are many advantages to matrix structures, as shown in Table 3-5. Functional units exist primarily as support for a project. Because of this, key people can be shared and costs can be minimized. People can be assigned to a variety of challenging problems. Each person, therefore, has a "home" after project

---

10. William P. Killian, "Project Management-Future Organizational Concepts," *Marquette Business Review*, 2: 90-107, 1971.

Table 3-5. Advantages Of A Pure Matrix Organizational Form.

1. The project manager maintains maximum project control over all resources, including cost and personnel.
2. Policies and procedures can be set up independently for each project, provided that they do not contradict company policies and procedures.
3. The project manager has the authority to commit company resources, provided that scheduling does not cause conflicts with each other projects.
4. Rapid responses are possible to changes, conflict resolution, and project needs.
5. The functional organizations exist primarily as support for the project.
6. Each person has a "home" after project completion. People are more susceptible to motivation and end-item identification. Each person can be shown a career path.
7. Because key people can be shared, program cost is minimized. People can work on a variety of problems: that is, better people control.
8. A strong technical base can be developed and much more time can be devoted to complex problem solving. Knowledge is available for all projects on an equal basis.
9. Conflicts are minimal, and those requiring hierarchical referral are more easily resolved.
10. Better balance between time, cost, and performance.

completion. Each person can be shown a career path in the company. People are more susceptible to motivation and end-item identification. Functional managers find it easier to develop and maintain a strong technical base and can therefore spend more time on complex problem solving. Knowledge can be shared for all projects.

The matrix structure can provide rapid response to changes, conflicts, and other project needs. Conflicts are normally minimal, but those requiring resolution are easily resolved using hierarchical referral.

This rapid response is a result of the project manager's authority to commit company resources, provided that scheduling conflicts with other projects can be eliminated. Furthermore, the project manager has the authority to independently establish his own project policies and procedures, provided that they do not conflict with company policies. This can do away with much red tape and permits a better balance between time, cost, and performance.

The matrix structure provides us with the best of two worlds: the traditional structure and the matrix structure. The advantages of the matrix structure eliminate almost all of the disadvantages of the traditional structure. The word "matrix" often brings fear into the hearts of executives because it implies radical change, or at least they think that it does. If we take a close look at Figure 3-6, we can see that the traditional structure is still there. The matrix is simply horizontal lines superimposed over the traditional structure. The horizontal lines will come and go as projects start up and terminate, but the traditional structure will remain forever.

Matrix structures are not without their disadvantages, as shown in Table 3-6. The main disadvantage of the matrix organization is that more administrative personnel are needed to develop policies and procedures, and therefore both

Table 3-6. Disadvantages Of A Pure Matrix Organizational Form.

1. Companywide, the organizational structure is not cost effective because more people than necessary are required, primarily administrative.
2. Each project organization operates independently. Care must be taken that duplication of efforts does not occur.
3. More effort and time is needed initially to define policies and procedures.
4. Functional managers may be biased according to their own set of priorities.
5. Although rapid response time is possible for individual problem resolution, matrix response time is slow, especially on fast-moving projects.
6. Balance of power between functional and project organizations must be watched.
7. Balance of time, cost, and performance must be monitored.

direct and indirect administrative costs will increase. Each project organization operates independently. This poses a problem in that duplication of effort can easily occur; for example, two projects might be developing the same cost accounting procedure or functional personnel may be doing similar R & D efforts on different projects. Both vertical and horizontal communication is a must in a project matrix organization.

Functional managers are only human and therefore may be biased according to their own set of priorities. Project managers, on the other hand, must realize that their project is not the only one, and that a proper balance is needed; this includes a balance of power between functional and project units as well as a proper balance between time, cost, and performance.

One of the advantages of the matrix is a rapid response time for problem resolution. This rapid response generally applies to slow-moving projects where problems occur within each functional unit. On fast-moving projects, the reaction time can become quite slow, especially if the problem spans more than one functional unit.

The matrix structure therefore becomes a compromise in an attempt to obtain the best of two worlds. In pure product management, technology suffered because there did not exist any single group for planning and integration. In the pure functional organization, time and schedule are sacrificed. Matrix project management is an attempt to obtain maximum technology and performance in a cost-effective manner and within time and schedule constraints.

We should note that with proper executive-level planning and control, all of the disadvantages can be eliminated. This is the only organizational form where this is possible. However, care must be taken with regard to the first disadvantage listed in Table 3-6. There is a natural tendency when going to a matrix to create more positions in executive management than are actually necessary in order to get better control, and this will drive up the overhead rates. This may be true in some companies, but there is a point where the matrix will become mature and less people will be required at the top levels of management. When executives wish to reduce cost, they normally begin *at the top* by combining positions when slots become vacant. This is a natural fallout of having mature project and line managers with less top-level interference.

In Section 2.4 we identified the necessity for the project manager to be able to establish his own policies, procedures, rules, and guidelines. Obviously, with personnel reporting in two directions and to multiple managers, conflicts over administration can easily occur. According to Shannon:[11]

When operating under a matrix management approach, it is obviously extremely important that the authority and responsibility of each manager be clearly defined, understood and accepted by both functional and program people. These relationships need to be spelled out in writing. It is essential that in the various operating policies, the specific authority of the program manager be clearly defined in terms of program direction, and that the authority of the functional executive be defined in terms of operational direction.

Most practitioners consider the matrix to be a two-dimensional system where each project represents a potential profit center and each functional department represents a cost center. (This interpretation can also create conflict because functional departments may feel that they no longer have an input into corporate profits.) For large corporations with multiple divisions, the matrix is no longer two-dimensional, but multidimensional.

William C. Goggin has described geographical area and space and time as the third and fourth dimension of the Dow Corning Matrix:[12]

Geographical areas — business development varied widely from area to area, and the profit-center and cost-center dimensions could not be carried out everywhere in the same manner. . . . Dow Corning area organizations are patterned after our major U.S. organizations. Although somewhat autonomous in their operation, they subscribe to the overall corporate objectives, operating guidelines, and planning criteria. During the annual planning cycle, for example, there is a mutual exchange of sales, expense, and profit projections between the functional and business managers headquartered in the United States and the area managers around the world.

Space and time — A fourth dimension of the organization denotes fluidity and movement through time . . . . The multi-dimensional organization is far from rigid; it is constantly changing. Unlike centralized or decentralized systems that are too often rooted deep in the past, the multi-dimensional organization is geared toward the future. Long-term planning is an inherent part of its operation.

11. Shannon, Robert, "Matrix Management Structures," *Industrial Engineering,* March, 27-28, 1972. Published and copyright 1972 by the American Institute of Industrial Engineers, Inc., Norcross, Georgia 30092.
12. William C. Goggin, "How the Multidimensional Structure Works at Dow Corning," *Harvard Business Review,* January-February, 56-57, 1974. Copyright © 1973 by the President and Fellows of Harvard College; all rights reserved.

Goggin then went on to describe the advantages that Dow Corning expected to gain from the multidimensional organization:

- Higher profit generation even in an industry (silicones) price-squeezed by competition. (Much of our favorable profit picture seems due to a better overall understanding and practice of expense controls throughout the company.)
- Increased competitive ability based on technological innovation and product quality without a sacrifice in profitability.
- Sound, fast decision making at all levels in the organization, facilitated by stratified but open channels of communications, and by a totally participative working environment.
- A healthy and effective balance of authority among the businesses, functions, and areas.
- Progress in developing short- and long-range planning with the support of all employees.
- Resource allocations that are proportional to expected results.
- More stimulating and effective on-the-job training.
- Accountability that is more closely related to responsibility and authority.
- Results that are visible and measurable.
- More top-management time for long-range planning and less need to become involved in day-to-day operations.

Obviously, the matrix structure is the most complex of all organizational forms. Careful consideration must be given as to where and how the matrix organization fits into the total organization. Grinnell and Apple define four situations where it is most practical to consider a matrix:[13]

- When complex, short-run products are the organization's primary output.
- When a complicated design calls for both innovation and timely completion.
- When several kinds of sophisticated skills are needed in designing, building, and testing the products—skills then need constant updating and development.
- When a rapidly changing marketplace calls for significant changes in products, perhaps between the time they are conceived and delivered.

3.7 MODIFICATION OF MATRIX STRUCTURES

The matrix can take many forms, but there are basically three common varieties. Each type represents a different degree of authority attributed to the program manager and indirectly identifies the relative size of the company. As an example,

---

13. Grinnell, S.K., and Apple, H.P., "When Two Bosses are Better Than One," *Machine Design*, January, 84-87, 1975.

in the matrix of Figure 3-6, all program managers report directly to the general manager. This type of arrangement works best for small companies that have a minimum number of projects, and assumes that the general manager has sufficient time to coordinate activities between his project managers. In this type of arrangement, all conflicts between projects are hierarchically referred to the general manager for resolution.

As companies grew in size and the number of projects, the general manager found it increasingly difficult to act as the focal point for all projects. A new position was created, that of director of programs or manager of programs or projects. This is shown in Figure 3-7. The director of programs was responsible for all program management. This freed the general manager from the daily routine of having to monitor all programs himself.

Beck has elaborated on the basic role of this new position, the manager of project managers (M.P.M.):[14]

The M.P.M. is a project manager, a people manager, a change manager and a systems manager. In general, one role cannot be considered more important than the other. The M.P.M. has responsibilities for managing the projects,

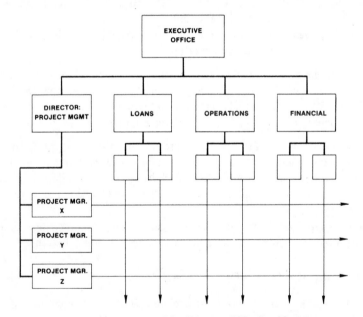

Figure 3-7. Development Of A Director Of Project Management.

---

14. Dale R. Beck, "The Role of the Manager of Project Managers," *Proceedings of the Ninth Annual International Seminar/Symposium on Project Management,* October 24-26, 1977 Chicago, Illinois, p. 141.

directing and leading people and the project management effort, and for planning for change in the organization. The Manager of Project Managers is a liaison between the Project Management Department and upper management as well as functional department management and acts as a systems manager when serving as a liaison.

Executives contend that an effective span of control is five to seven people. Does this apply to the director of project management as well? Consider a company that has fifteen projects going on at once. Three are over $5 million, seven are between $1 and $3 million, and five projects are under $700,000. Each project has a full-time project manager. Can all fifteen project managers report to the same person? The company solved this problem by creating a deputy director of project management. All projects over $1 million reported to the director and all projects under $1 million went to the deputy director. The director's rationale soon fell by the wayside when he found that the more severe problems that were occupying his time were occurring on the smaller dollar-volume projects. If the project manager is actually a general manager, then the director of project management should be able to supervise effectively more than seven project managers. The desired span of control, of course, will vary from company to company and must take into account:

- The demands imposed on the organization by task complexity
- Available technology
- The external environment
- The needs of the organizational membership

These variables influence the internal functioning of the company. Executives must realize that there is no one best way to organize under all conditions. This includes span of control.

As companies expand, it is inevitable that new and more complex conflicts arise. The control of the engineering functions poses such a problem.

- Should the project manager have ultimate responsibility for the engineering functions of a project, or should there be a deputy project manager who reports to the director of engineering and controls all technical activity?

Although there are pros and cons for both arrangements, the problem resolved itself in the company mentioned above when projects grew so large that the project manager became unable to handle both the project management and project engineering functions. Therefore, as shown in Figure 3-8, a chief project engineer was assigned to each project as deputy project manager, but remained functionally assigned to the director of engineering. The project manager was now responsible for time and cost considerations, whereas the project engineer

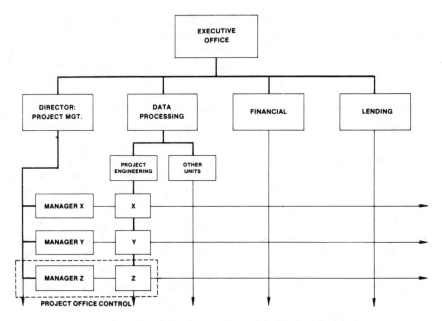

Figure 3-8. Placing Project Engineering In The Project Office.

was concerned with technical performance. The project engineer can be either "solid" vertically and "dotted" horizontally, or vice versa. There are also situations where the project engineer may be "solid" in both directions. This decision usually rests with the director of engineering. Of course, in a project where the project engineer would be needed on a part-time basis only, he would then be solid vertically and dotted horizontally.

This subdivision of functions is necessary in order to control large projects adequately. However, for small projects, say $100,000 or less, it is quite common on R & D projects for an engineer to serve as the project manager as well as the project engineer. Here, the project manager must have technical expertise, not merely understanding. Furthermore, this individual can still be attached to a functional engineering support unit other than project engineering. As an example, the mechanical engineering department receives a government contract for $75,000 to perform tests on a new material. The proposal is written by an engineer attached to this department. When the contract is awarded, this individual, although not in the project engineering department, can fulfill the role of project manager and project engineer while still reporting to the manager of the mechanical engineering department. This arrangement works best (and is cost-effective) for short-duration projects that cross a minimum number of functional units.

3.8 SELECTING THE ORGANIZATIONAL FORM

Project management has matured as an outgrowth of the need to develop and produce complex and/or large projects in the shortest possible time, within anticipated cost, with required reliability and performance, and (when applicable) to realize a profit. Based upon the realization that modern organizations have become so complex that traditional organizational structures and relationships no longer allow for effective management, how can executives determine which organizational form is best, especially since some projects last for only a few weeks or months while others may take years?

To answer such a question, we must first determine whether or not the necessary characteristics exist for warranting a project management organizational form. Generally speaking, the project management approach can be effectively applied to a one-time undertaking that is:[15]

- Definable in terms of a specific goal
- Infrequent, unique, or unfamiliar to the present organization
- Complex with respect to interdependence of detailed tasks
- Critical to the company

Once a group of tasks are selected and considered to be a project, the next step is to define the kinds of projects, described in Section 2.1. These include individual, staff, special, and matrix or aggregate projects.

Unfortunately, many companies do not have a clear definition of what a project is. As a result, large project teams are often constructed for small projects when they could be handled more quickly and effectively by some other structural form. All structural forms have their advantages and disadvantages, but the project management approach, even with its disadvantages, appears to be the best possible alternative.

Four fundamental parameters must be analyzed when considering implementation of a project organizational form:

- Integrating devices
- Authority structure
- Influence distribution
- Information system

Project management is a means of integrating all company efforts, especially research and development, by selecting an appropriate organizational form. Two questions arise when we think of designing the organization to facilitate the work of the integrators:[16]

---

15. John M. Stewart, "Making Project Management Work," *Business Horizons,* Fall, 54, 1965.
16. William P. Killian, "Project Management—Future Organizational Concepts," *Marquette Business Review* 2: 90-107, 1971.

- It is better to establish a formal integration department, or simply to set up integrating positions independent of one another?
- If individual integrating positions are set up, how should they be related to the larger structure?

Informal integration works best if, and only if, effective collaboration can be achieved between conflicting units. Without any clearly defined authority, the role of the integrator is simply to act as an exchange medium across the interface of two functional units. As the size of the organization increases, formal integration positions must exist, especially in situations where intense conflict can occur (e.g., research and development).

Not all organizations need a pure matrix structure to achieve this integration. Many problems can be solved simply through the scalar chain of command, depending upon the size of the organization and the nature of the project. The actual size of organizations needed to achieve project control can vary from one person to several thousand. The organizational structure needed for effective project control is governed by the desires of top management and project circumstances.

Unfortunately, integration and specialization appear to be diametrically opposed. As described by Davis:[17]

When organization is considered synonymous with structure, the dual needs of specialization and coordination are seen as inversely related, as opposite ends of a single variable, as the horns of a dilemma. Most managers speak of this dilemma in terms of the centralization-decentralization variable. Formulated in this manner, greater specialization leads to more difficulty in coordinating the differentiated units. This is why the (de)centralization pendulum is always swinging, and no ideal point can be found at which it can come to rest.

The division of labor in a hierarchical pyramid means that specialization must be defined either by function, by product, or by area. Firms must select one of these dimensions as primary and then subdivide the other two into subordinate units further down the pyramid. The appropriate choice for primary, secondary and tertiary dimensions is based largely upon the strategic needs of the enterprise.

Top management must decide upon the authority structure that will control the integration mechanism. The authority structure can range from pure functional authority (traditional management), to product authority (product management), and finally to dual authority (matrix management). This is shown in Figure 2-7. From a management point of view, organizational forms are often selected based upon how much authority top management wishes to delegate or surrender.

17. Stanley M. Davis, "Two Models of Organization: Unity of Command Versus Balance of Power," *Sloan Management Review,* Fall, 30, 1974. Reprinted by permission.

Integration of activities across functional boundaries can also be accomplished by influence. Influence includes such factors as participation in budget planning and approval, design changes, location and size of offices, salaries, and so on. Influence can also cut administrative red tape and develop a much more unified informal organization.

Information systems also play an important role. Previously we stated that one of the advantages of several project management structures is the ability to make both rapid and timely decisions with almost immediate response to environmental changes. Information systems are designed to get the right information to the right person at the right time in a cost-effective manner. Organizational functions must facilitate the flow of information through the management network.

Galbraith has described additional factors that can influence organizational selection. These factors are:[18]

- Diversity of product lines
- Rate of change of the product lines
- Interdependencies among subunits
- Level of technology
- Presence of economies of scale
- Organizational size

A diversity of product lines requires both top-level and functional managers to maintain knowledge in all areas. Diversity makes it more difficult for managers to make realistic estimates concerning resource allocations and the control of time, cost, schedules, and technology. The systems approach to management requires that sufficient information and alternatives be available so that effective trade-offs can be established. For diversity in a high-technology environment the organizational choice might, in fact, be a trade-off between the flow of work and the flow of information. Diversity tends toward strong product authority and control.

Many functional organizations consider themselves as companies within a company and pride themselves on their independence. This poses a severe problem in trying to develop a synergistic atmosphere. Successful project management requires that functional units recognize the interdependence that must exist in order for technology to be shared and schedule dates to be met. Interdependency is also required in order to develop strong communications channels as well as coordination.

The use of new technologies poses a serious problem in that technical expertise must be established in all specialties, including engineering, production,

---

18. Galbraith, Jay R., "Matrix Organization Designs," *Business Horizons,* February, 29-40, 1971.

material control, and safety. Maintaining technical expertise works best in strong functional disciplines, provided the information is not purchased outside the organization. The main problem, however, is how to communicate this expertise across functional lines. Independent R & D units can be established as opposed to integrating R & D into each functional department's routine efforts. Organizational control requirements are much more difficult in high-technology industries with ongoing research and development than with pure production groups.

The economies of scale and size can also affect organizational selection. The economies of scale are most often controlled by the amount of physical resources that a company has available. For example, a company with limited facilities and resources might find it impossible to compete with other companies on production or competitive bidding for larger dollar-volume products. Such a company must rely heavily on maintaining multiple projects (or products), each of low cost or volume, whereas a larger organization may need only three or four projects large enough to sustain the organization. The larger the economies of scale, the more the organization tends to favor pure functional management.

The size of the organization is important in that it can limit the amount of technical expertise in the econimies of scale. While size may have little effect on the organizational structure, it does have a severe impact on the economies of scale. Small companies, for example, cannot maintain large specialist staffs and therefore incur a larger cost for lost specialization and lost economies of scale.

The four factors described previously for organizational form selections together with the six alternatives of Galbraith can be regarded as universal in nature. Beyond these universal factors, we must look at the company in terms of its product, business base, and personnel. Goodman has defined a set of subfactors related to R & D groups:[19]

- Clear location of responsibility
- Ease and accuracy of communication
- Effective cost control
- Ability to provide good technical supervision
- Flexibility of staffing
- Importance to the company
- Quick reaction capability to sudden changes in the project
- Complexity of the project
- Size of the project with relation to other work in-house
- Form desired by customer
- Ability to provide a clear path for individual promotion

Goodman asked various managers to select from the above list and rank the factors from most important to least important in terms of how they would be

---

19. Goodman, Richard A., "Organizational Reference in Research and Development," *Human Relations,* 3, 4: 279-298, 1970.

considered in designing an organization. Both general management and project management personnel were queried. With one exception—the flexibility of staffing—the responses from both groups correlated to a coefficient of 0.811. Clear location of responsibility was seen as the most important factor, and a path for promotion the least important.

Middleton conducted a mail survey to aerospace firms in an attempt to determine how well the companies using project management met their objectives. Forty-seven responses were received. Tables 3-7 and 3-8 identify the results. Middleton stated: "In evaluating the results of the survey, it appears that a company taking the project organization approach can be reasonably certain that it will improve controls and customer (out-of-company) relations, but internal operations will be more complex."[20]

The way in which companies operate their project organization is bound to affect the organization, both during the operation of the project and after the project has been completed and personnel disbanded. The overall effects on the company must be looked at from a personnel and cost control standpoint. This will be accomplished, in depth, in later chapters. Although project management is growing, the creation of a project organization does not necessarily insure that an assigned objective will be accomplished successfully. Furthermore, weaknesses can develop in the areas of maintaining capability and structural changes.

Table 3-7. Major Company Advantages Of Project Management.

ADVANTAGES	PERCENT OF RESPONDENTS
• Better control of projects	92
• Better customer relations	80
• Shorter product development time	40
• Lower program costs	30
• Improved quality and reliability	26
• Higher profit margins	24
• Better control over program security	13

Other Benefits
- Better project visibility and focus on results
- Improved coordination among company divisions doing work on the project
- Higher morale and better mission orientation for employees working on the project
- Accelerated development of managers due to breadth of project responsibilities

20. C. J. Middleton, "How to Set Up a Project Organization," *Harvard Business Review,* March-April, 73-82, 1967. Copyright © 1967 by the President and Fellows of Harvard College; all rights reserved.

Table 3-8. Major Company Disadvantages Of Project Management.

DISADVANTAGES	PERCENT OF RESPONDENTS
• More complex internal operations	51
• Inconsistency in application of company policy	32
• Lower utilization of personnel	13
• Higher program costs	13
• More difficult to manage	13
• Lower profit margins	2

Other Disadvantages
• Tendency for functional groups to neglect their job and let the project organization do everything
• Too much shifting of personnel from project to project
• Duplication of functional skills in project organization.

From C.J. Middleton, "How to Set Up a Project Organization," *Harvard Business Review,* March-April, 73-82, 1967. Copyright © 1967 by the President and Fellows of Harvard College; all rights reserved.

Middleton has listed four undesirable results that can develop from the use of project organizations and can affect company capabilities:[21]

• Project priorities and competition for talent may interrupt the stability of the organization and interfere with its long-range interests by upsetting the traditional business of functional organizations.
• Long-range plans may suffer as the company gets more involved in meeting schedules and fulfilling the requirements of temporary projects.
• Shifting people from project to project may disrupt the training of employees and specialists, thereby hindering the growth and development within their fields of specialization.
• Lessons learned on one project may not be communicated to other projects.

An almost predictable result of using the project management approach is the increase in management positions. Killian describes the results of two surveys:[22]

One company compared its organization and management structure as it existed before it began forming project units with the structure that existed afterward. The number of departments had increased from 65 to 106, while total employment remained practically the same. The number of employees for every supervisor

21. C. J. Middleton, "How to Set Up a Project Organization," *Harvard Business Review,* March-April 1967. Copyright © 1967 by the President and Fellows of Harvard College; all rights reserved.
22. William P. Killian, "Project Management—Future Organizational Concepts," *Marquette Business Review,* 2: 90-107, 1971.

had dropped from 13.4 to 12.8. The company concluded that a major cause of this change was the project groups (see footnote 21 for reference article).

Another company uncovered proof of its conclusion when it counted the number of second-level and higher management positions. It found that it had 11 more vice-presidents and directors, 35 more managers, and 56 more second-level supervisors. Although the company attributed part of this growth to an upgrading of titles, the effect of the project organization was the creation of 60 more management positions.

Although the project organization is a specialized, task-oriented entity, it seldom, if ever, exists apart from the traditional structure of the organization.[23] All project management structures overlap the traditional structure. Furthermore, companies can have more than one project organizational form in existence at one time. A major steel producer, for example, has a matrix structure for R & D and a product structure elsewhere.

Accepting a project management structure is a giant step from which there may be no return. The company may have to create more management positions without changing the total employment levels. In addition, incorporation of a project organization is almost always accompanied by the upgrading of jobs. In any event, management must realize that whichever project management structure is selected, a dynamic state of equilibrium will be necessary.

3.9 LOCATION OF THE PROJECT MANAGER

Ideally, the project manager should be at the same organizational level as the person he must negotiate with for resources. However, there are good reasons for placing him elsewhere in the organization. According to Martin:[24]

Projects should be located wherever in the organization they can function most effectively. Several reasons for having the project manager report directly to a high level in the organization may be mentioned:

- The project manager is charged with getting results from the coordinated efforts of many functions. He should therefore report to the man who directs all those functions.
- The project manager must have adequate organizational status to do his job effectively.
- To get adequate and timely assistance in solving problems that inevitably appear in any important project, the project manager needs direct and specific access to an upper echelon of management.

23. Allen R. Janger, "Anatomy of the Project Organization," *Business Management Record,* November, 12-18, 1963.
24. Charles C. Martin, *Project Management: How to Make it Work,* New York, AMACOM, A Division of American Management Associations, 1976, p. 80.

- The customer, particularly in a competitive environment, will be favorably impressed if his project manager reports to a high organizational echelon.

Good reasons may also exist for having the project manager report to a lower echelon:

- It is organizationally and operationally inefficient to have too many projects, especially small ones, diverting senior executives from more vital concerns.
- Although giving a small project a high place in the organization may create the illusion of executive attention, its real result is to foster executive neglect of the project.
- Placing a junior project manager too high in the organization will alienate senior functional executives on whom he must rely for support.

3.10 SELLING TOP MANAGEMENT

The need for project management is usually first identified at the lower or middle management levels where resources are controlled on a day-to-day basis. Once the need for better resource control is identified, middle management has the task of having to convince top management that such a change is in the best interest of the company, regardless of the current profit picture.

Just because a top executive realizes the need for project management does not guarantee a ready acceptance of project management as a viable solution. Executives must overcome their personal fear of change. When an executive says that change is inevitable, the usual interpretation is that the organization must adapt to an everchanging environment in order to survive. Unfortunately, this inevitable change appears as new product development and lower level organizational restructuring rather than in changes at the top. Executives normally have a greater fear of change than lower and middle-level managers. Below are common concerns for executives:

- *Leadership Style*—"I have spent several years operating as I am now. I must be doing it correctly to get where I am now. I'm not sure that I will be successful if I have to start working differently, especially at my age. Why change?"
- *Authority*—"It has taken me thirty years to get where I am now. Why should I have to delegate much of my hard-earned authority to someone perhaps much lower in the organization? Authority belongs to those individuals who are the key decision-makers in the organization. Will I be blamed for a poor decision below me? Why change?"
- *Power*—"I have worked long and hard to develop my current power position within the company. Why should I let people below me become more powerful than I am? Why change?"
- *Control/Coordination*—"By virtue of my position, I currently coordinate lower-level activities and control organizational change. By delegating

these activities to lower-level personnel, project managers and functional managers will run the organization on a day-to-day basis. Why should I surrender my detail involvement in company activities? Why change?"

Obviously, it is not easy for executives to spend thirty years or so working their way up the traditional hierarchy and then consider changing their management approach. This is a major change in the way of doing business for many executives and must be approached with caution. Lower-level functional managers often have the job of convincing executives of the need for project management. Managers must realize that the executive's decision will require a great deal of thought.

Although an executive understands the concept of project management and is willing to consider change, there are still serious questions that must be asked and answered before the executives will consider implementation. Who should answer these questions? Many times executives will refrain from asking questions to lower-level managers and personnel because

- Executives do not want to make it appear as though they (lower-level personnel) have more of an understanding of project management than the executives do.
- Lower-level personnel may give answers which enhance their own positions in the organization but are not in the best interest of the company.

Outside consultants are usually called upon for impartial answers to these questions. Below are the most commonly asked questions by executives:

- *Can our people be part-time project managers?* This is one of the most frequently asked questions by executives. The argument here is that executives might be willing to implement project management if they feel that it can be accomplished without having to increase the manpower base of the organization. The answer to this question depends upon the nature of the projects, the size of the projects and the number of functional departments that the project cuts across.

The above question was asked by an executive of Minnesota Power and Light (MP & L). MP & L had implemented project management the previous year by the creation of a Project Administration Division. The purpose of the Project Administration Division was to manage the large, complex projects. This division was now managing three large projects, each with a full-time project manager. But what about some of these smaller projects which stayed within one or two functional areas? Could these projects, if necessary, be administered by part-time project managers who reported elsewhere?

Since project management is designed to cost-effectively utilize resources, executives must be willing to accept situations which cannot afford the luxury of full-time project managers. Even large, project-driven industries as construction and aerospace have the necessity for part-time project management, especially on in-house projects.

This should, by no means, imply to executives that anyone can be a part-time project manager. Part-time project managers should have the same attributes as their full-time counterparts. Many companies are solving this problem by maintaining full-time project managers who work part-time on several projects at once. On the surface this may appear as an ideal situation, but can become catastrophic if the priorities on these part-time projects are far apart.

• *Can functional employees act as part-time project managers?* Functional employees (and even functional managers) often make poor project managers because they have the tendency to overstress the technical details of a project and understress the administrative, scheduling and cost aspects of a project. If a functional employee can maintain the proper balance between the technical and administrative requirements of a project, then he or she may be a choice as a part-time project manager.

• *Is it better for functional employees to act as part-time assistant project managers or part-time project managers?* It is generally in the best interest of both the company and the project for the individual to act as an assistant project manager. If the individual acts as the project manager, and a project problem arises, then the project manager may tend to "bend" to the best interests of the functional manager rather than to the project. This would be expected because the functional manager controls the salary of the project manager. However, if the functional employee were an assistant project manager, then the functional employee could request that the project manager plead his case and thus avoid getting caught in the middle.

• *Which vice-president should be responsible for the project management function?* Project-driven organizations which have a continuous stream of projects usually have a full-time vice-president for project management. Small companies, on the other hand, may not wish to increase the overhead rate, but would rather assign overall project management responsibilities to one of their existing vice-presidents. The question, of course, is which one? That executive which will eventually supply the greatest amount of functional resources to all of the projects should also control the project managers because now there exists a common superior for the resolution of the majority of the conflicts. It is important that conflict resolutions should not have to involve several layers of management.

• *If we go to project management, must we increase resources, especially the number of project managers?* Initially, the number of employees should increase, primarily to fill the full-time project management positions. Executives then argue that this will drive up the overhead rate. Project managers usually are direct labor charges, and have a small impact on the overhead rate. The cost for the project managers should be more than compensated for by increased productivity and better utilization of resources. However, executives should not expect these results overnight. They are long-term benefits.

• *Is it true that the current industrial trend for a career path is from project manager to vice-president?* The project management position takes on a flavor of general management because the project manager is given a license to cut across all functional lines. Executives, especially in project-driven organizations as construction, are using project management as a training ground for future general managers. Some companies have even gone so far as to state that the only way to the top is through project management. This can create a frustrating situation for functional managers.

Most project managers believe that they are vice-presidents operating out of a project management position. Project managers view the organizational structure as being rotated ninety degrees to the right with the project managers sitting at the top of the organization and everyone else, including the president, reporting to them horizontally.

• *Can we give employees a rotation period of six to eighteen months in project management and then return them to functional positions where they should be more well-rounded individuals because they understand project management?* This situation can be disastrous. First, employees may not become dedicated to project management if they feel that the position is temporary, and the project may suffer. Second, after eighteen months in project management, the employees may find themselves technically obsolete and not worth their present salary to the functional department. Third, and most important, the employees may not want to leave the project management positions. People who get a taste of the power, authority, and responsibility in project management generally desire a project management career path. Employees should not be assigned to project management positions unless executives are willing to continue to assign these people to similar positions. The detrimental result could be a high turnover rate in good personnel.

• *How much control should a project manager have over costs and budgets?* Project managers must have complete control over projects costs and budgets. This, by no means, diminishes the power and authority of the vice-president for accounting and finance. It simply means that the project manager cannot be totally successful with project control over only partial resources.

• *How much authority should an executive delegate to the project manager?* Simply stated, executives should delegate sufficient authority to get the job done. Not all project managers are equal in authority. The amount of delegated authority depends upon such factors as project size, life cycle phase, duration, and the customer.

Some executives have found that they can obtain better control of resources by limiting the amount of delegated authority. For example, a project manager in Minnesota has the authority to negotiate for resources and monitor the project. However, all decisions must be made by the vice-president. In this case, the vice-president is controlling resources vertically through the functional managers and horizontally through the project managers. This lack of delegation of decision-making authority ultimately leads to executive meddling and can undermine a good organizational structure.

Executives should completely delineate exactly how much authority is delegated to a project manager, even if it must be documented. Executives must make sure the project managers do not overstep their bounds. In Company XYZ, the project managers continuously gave instructions to the manufacturing personnel as to how the job should be done. The vice-president for manufacturing built a brick wall around his line group and refused admittance to the project managers claiming that they continuously overstepped their bounds.

• *What should be the working relationships between executives and project managers?* Executives are responsible for strategic planning and policy formulation. Since each project (especially in project driven organizations) can have an impact in these two areas, there should be a close working relationship in the conceptual and planning stages of a project. However, once the project departs the planning phase, executives should let the project manager run the show and rely upon the structured feedback of information concerning project status. Of course, executives are expected to take a more active involvement if conflict resolution and priority setting are required.

• *What percentage of a total project budget should be available for project management/administrative support?* There is no correct answer to this question. Support could range from five to fifty percent depending upon the nature of the project and the customer project reporting requirements.

The following questions were asked by an executive at AT & T. The executive was concerned with those projects that involved the development of new methods, procedures, and ways of getting work done.

- There will be 50 projects going on at once. Project managers can report to any one in the organization. Some project managers will be handling multiple projects, each with a different priority. Can this work?
- What happens if a functional manager complains that pulling a good employee out of his department will leave a large gap?
- The first step in all projects is a cost/benefit analysis to see if the project is a feasible undertaking. Who will do this?
- How do we make sure that everyone knows what the priorities are?
- We have had an explosion of Operations Support Systems (the minicomputer era). How do we manage these projects? Do we use project management?

- How does management control the responsibilities that each person will have?
- How do we ensure effective and timely communications to all levels?
- How do we get top management committed to project management?
- We need an awful lot of front-end work (i.e., planning) on projects. We are living in a world of limited resources. We need commitments from our people. How do we get that?
- How do we resolve problems in which there is a lack of knowledge of project team members concerning their own role?
- How do we convince people to escalate problems, not bury them?
- How do we end a project especially if an improved technology occurs?

The executive has the final say in project management implementation and therefore becomes the architect in the design of the project team. The executive must anticipate the problems that can result from changing to a new organizational structure.

- *Differing roles, priorities and interests:* Not all people in the organization have the same view of project management. Executives may view project management as a way of doing business, a means to an end, a threat to established authority channels and a way of creating future general managers. Functional managers may view the project managers as power-hungry, egotistical individuals who are trying to get promoted ahead of the functional managers.

In converting to project management, there will be a shift in the balance of power; some people will become more powerful and others less powerful. As an example, cost accountants generally become more powerful because of their importance in controlling projects costs. The procurement function may view itself as being demoted if the project manager is given the charter to perform his own procurement.

There are always serious questions which must be answered. Sometimes these questions have to be answered either behind closed doors or subconsciously.

- "Will I become more or less powerful?"
- "Will I be delegated more or less authority?"
- "How will I be evaluated and by whom?"
- "I've spent ten years building up an empire in my functional group. Why should I permit a functional manager to share or even control my resources?"
- "Where can I be promoted to?"
- "Will somebody else now be establishing the priorities for my department resources?"

Until executives are willing to cope with these questions, project management implementation should not be attempted lest the executive risk a severe morale problem.

- *Role Ambiguities:* It is quite possible that during the first year or two of operations, there will be ambiguities in the roles of the employees. People tend to become unsure over their roles and responsibilities and duplication of effort can occur. Quite often, a given task could easily be accomplished by one of several departments. For example, consider a project in the R & D stage. Can R & D personnel perform their own quality control or must it be performed by the manufacturing/operations group? Usually, the project manager makes the final decision in a case as this. However, it is recommended that executives take an acting role in resolving these conflicts during project management implementation.

- *Organizing the Team:* The project team is composed of the project manager, the project office, and functional employees. The executive must take an active role in the selection of the project manager and the project office. Because of priorities, key personnel may be reassigned from one project office to another. Therefore, executive involvement is necessary for conflict resolution. Executives should not interfere in functional employee selection because the functional manager may feel that the executive is usurping the functional manager's authority. The project and functional managers should work out their differences at their own level and call in the executives only as a last resort.

The design of the project office, i.e., the number of employees and their qualifications, must be agreed upon by the executives and the project manager. A poor team organization can lead to catastrophic results. If at all possible, project managers and project office personnel should be given the right to refuse an assignment. There is no point in assigning people to key project positions unless these people are totally dedicated and committed to the task.

Project managers should be appointed based upon their maturity. Unfortunately, several companies equate maturity with thinning or grey hair. Age should not be a relevant factor. Construction project managers are in their fifties, as are capital equipment project managers. R & D project managers span the gamut between 25 to 60 and data processing project managers are usually employees in their twenties so they can grow with the technology.

Even if the project office is committed to the project, it can still fail because of poor functional employee dedication and commitment. Both the project and functional managers are responsible for this effort. Functional managers must be made aware of the fact that they themselves have "ownership" for part of work and cannot continuously expect the project office to "bail them out." Executives can make the motivation problem less acute by

- Taking an interest in each project on an equal basis.
- Making sure that all objectives are clearly definable and understandable.

If time permits, executives should make frequent appearances at project team meetings, or at least at the first meeting where questions over project objectives most commonly occur. The results can be disastrous if the executives, project manager and functional managers are all working toward different interpretations of the objectives. This is a common problem especially in data processing projects where user requirements and objectives can continuously change. This problem recently occured at Blue Cross.

• *Time Traps:* Whenever work flows concurrently in two directions, employees and managers alike get caught up in time traps, such as lack of self-control, activity traps, managing versus doing, people versus skill tasks, and ineffective communications. The last item, poor communications, creates a colossal managerial headache. If executives encourage too many meetings, time will not be utilized effectively. If executives encourage too few meetings, information may not be readily available and resource control may suffer. In addition, horizontal and vertical work flow creates an avalanche of paperwork. Executives should take an active interest in minimizing the flow of paperwork, developing a standard set of documents for controlling all projects, and determining which paperwork is actually necessary. Without executive involvement during implementation, paperwork can increase exponentially to a point where administrative costs exceed direct labor costs.

Recently, a divison of General Electric developed a task force to resolve this problem. All capital equipment projects in this manufacturing division of GE are now using the same three sheets of paper for planning, scheduling, and controlling projects.

The most difficult part of the implementation process is that the executive must take on a new role as to what is expected, what to expect of others, and when and how much meddling he should do. This new role means:

- Top management must delegate authority and responsibility to the project manager.
- Top management must delegate total cost control to the project manager.
- Top management must rely upon the project manager for total project planning and scheduling.
- Only the project managers must fully understand advanced scheduling techniques as PERT/CPM. This may require additional training. Functional managers may use other scheduling techniques for resource control.
- Top management must encourage functional managers to resolve problems and conflicts at the lowest organizational levels and not always run "upstairs."
- Top management must not consider functional departments as merely support groups for a project. Functional departments still control the company resources, and contrary to popular belief, the project managers actually work for the functional managers, not vice versa.

- Top management must provide sufficient training for functional employees on how to report and interact with multiple functional managers.
- Top management must take an interest in how project management should work.
- Top management must avoid infighting about who should control the project management function.
- Top management directly interfaces a project only during the idea development and planning phases of a project. Once the project is initiated, the executives should maintain a monitoring perspective via structured feedback from the project manager.
- Top management still establishes corporate direction and must make sure that the project managers fully understand this, especially in terms of project objectives.
- Top management must have confidence in the project managers and must be willing to give them projects which are both difficult as well as easy to perform.
- Top management must not meddle in a project simply because it is a new concept and the executive wishes to be involved.
- Top management must become familiar with its new role in a project management environment.
- Top management must try to control those variables which may be beyond the control of the project manager. These factors include such items as acting as a project sponsor and providing external communications with the customer, establishing joint venture relationships, providing internal support such as resolving conflicts and setting priorities, and providing on-going environmental intelligence.
- The first few projects should be "breakthrough" projects which have a high probability of success, and which can be easily tracked by executives. In addition, functional employees are more willing to accept project management if they see the system in action and leading to success.
- During implementation, employees do not expect executives to immediately surrender power and authority.

Decisions to implement project management must always be carefully considered. Sometimes a customer will make a project management structure part of the specifications for a contract. Executives must carefully analyze the capabilities of the organization before such an undertaking. If the project stays within one functional unit of the company, say a department, then it may be possible to implement departmental project management as long as either the project requires very little cross-functional involvement or the other department managers are willing to let the project managers enter their empires and negotiate for resources.

In another situation, the author interviewed the director of engineering services of a $1-billion corporation. As part of the interview, the director remarked:

- "All of our activities (or so-called projects if you wish) are loaded with up-front engineering. We have found in the past that time is the important parameter, not quality control or cost. Sometimes we rush into projects so fast that we have no choice but to cut corners and, of course, quality must suffer."

The director then wanted to know what organization form would solve this problem. But the important question was why the company rushed into projects in the first place. If the answer was that top management could not speed up their own approval process, then there might not be any organizational form that could alleviate the problem. Executives must not be quick to look toward project management for all solutions.

A large insurance company was considering the implementation of project management. Most projects were two weeks in duration with very few existing beyond one month. The insurance executive wanted to know whether or not a matrix would be practical. But for such short-duration projects, the matrix would not be cost-effective. The individual, task force, or special project format would be better and could be implemented within the traditional structure. Formal project management may not always be the best solution in every case.

Project management is designed to make effective and efficient use of resources. Some literature states that companies adopting project management find it easier and more cost-effective to underemploy and schedule overtime than to overemploy and either lay people off or drive up the overhead rate. This should not be the sole reason for implementing project management.

An Ohio-based utility company has what is commonly referred to as "fragmented" project management where each major division maintains project managers through staff positions and where each division manager establishes his own project priorities. The project managers occasionally have to integrate activities in divisions other than their own and each project involves several people. The company also has product managers operating out of a rather crude project (product) organizational structure. Recently, the product and project managers were competing for resources within the same department.

To complicate matters further, management put a freeze on hiring while approving 120 projects for the next year. This is forty projects more than last year. Unfortunately, there are not enough staff project managers available to handle these projects.

Staff personnel contend that the solution would be to establish a project management division under which there would be project and product management departments. The staff personnel feel that under this arrangement, better utilization of line personnel will be possible and that each project can run with fewer staff people, thus providing the opportunity for more projects without increasing manpower. In addition, priorities will be established companywide, rather than in a piecemeal fashion. In this situation, the author concurs with the staff personnel. Since project management already exists, even though it is fragmented, there should be no major obstacles standing in the way of implementation.

3.11 RESEARCH AND DEVELOPMENT PROJECT MANAGEMENT

One of the most difficult tasks in any organization is the management of R & D activities. These R & D activities are usually headed up by scientists, engineers, managers, employees, and even executives. All of these people, at one time or another, may act as R & D project managers. They start out with an idea and are asked to lay out a detailed schedule, cost summary, set of specifications and resource requirements such that the idea can become a reality. Unfortunately, this is easier said than done.

R & D personnel were probably the first true project managers. Unfortunately, very little training was available until the "vanguard" of modern project management occurred in the late 1950s within aerospace, defense, and construction companies. Even today, little project management training is provided for R & D personnel.

R & D personnel are technically trained perfectionists who believe that cost and time are unimportant when it comes to improving the state of the art. R & D personnel would rather crawl on their hands and knees and beg for more money and time rather than admit defeat on an R & D project. The more degrees an individual has, the greater the reluctance to accept defeat.

R & D personnel have been stereotyped and placed under more criticism than any other employees, even engineers. They are considered by some to be egocentric individuals sitting in small corners of laboratories. The R & D project managers avoid people contact whenever possible. Often, they cannot communicate well, write reports, or make presentations and seem illiterate except when it comes to complex graphs and equations. And yet they are consistently placed in charge of projects. In most project driven organizations, there is usually strong representation of former project managers in top echelons of management. How many senior corporate executives or CEOs do we have that came out of the R & D ranks? Could it be the result of this inappropriately applied stereotyping that has prevented R & D personnel from rising to the top?

Few people in an organization truly understand the R & D environment and the problems facing the R & D project manager. The R & D project manager is continually called upon to achieve an objective which even science fiction writers haven't thought of and which requires technology that hasn't been discovered yet. A detailed schedule is expected, with established milestones and predetermined costs set by some executive who may have trouble obtaining the necessary resources.

After a schedule is established, executives change the milestones because it affects their Christmas bonuses. And when the project finally gets on track, marketing pushes the end milestone to the left because they wish to have earlier introduction of the project into the marketplace in order to either beat or keep up with the competition.

The project manager therefore finds that work must be done in seclusion, avoiding meddling from executives, marketing, and manufacturing. The avoidance of the manufacturing group ultimately leads to the R & D project manager's downfall because it is often discovered too late that manufacturing cannot mass produce the item according to the R & D specifications. Who gets blamed? The R & D project manager, of course, who should have been communicating with everyone.

The R & D environment might very well be the most difficult and turbulent environment in which to manage a project. The remainder of this section will describe this problem in R & D project management in hopes that the readers will obtain more appreciation for those individuals who accept R & D project management as a career.

Scheduling activities for R & D projects is extremely difficult because of the previously mentioned problems. Many R & D people believe that if you know how long it will take to complete the objective, you do not need R & D. Most of these schedules are not detailed but are composed of major milestones where executives can decide whether or not additional money or resources should be committed. Some executives and R & D managers believe in the philosophy that

- I'll give you "so much time" to get an answer.

In R & D project management, failure is often construed as an acceptable answer.

There are two schools of thought on R & D scheduling, depending of course upon the type of project, the time duration, and resources required. The first school of thought involves the tight schedule. This may occur if the project is a one-person activity. R & D personnel are generally highly optimistic and believe that they can do anything. They, therefore, have the tendency to create rather tight, optimistic schedules. This type of optimism is actually a good trait. Where would we be without it? How many projects would be prematurely cancelled without optimistic R & D personnel?

Tight schedules occur mostly on limited resource projects. Project managers tend to avoid tight schedules if they feel that there exists a poor "window" in the functional organization for a timely commitment of resources. Another reason is that R & D personnel know that in times of crisis on manufacturing lines which are yielding immediate profits, they may lose their key functional project employees for perhaps an extended period of time.

Another school of thought is that R & D project management is not mechanical as other forms of project management and, therefore, all schedules must be loose. Scientists do not like or want tight structuring because they feel that they cannot be creative without having sufficient freedom to do their job. Many good results have been obtained from spin-offs and other activities where R & D project managers have deviated from predetermined schedules. Of course, too much freedom can prove to be disastrous because the individual might try to be overly creative and "reinvent the wheel."

This second school says that R & D project managers should not focus on limited objectives. Rather, the project manager should be able to realize that other possible objectives can be achieved with further exploration of some of the activities.

There are two special types of projects that are generally performed without any schedules. They are the "grass roots" project and the "bootleg" project. Both projects are simply ideas which, with one or two good data points, could become full-blown, well-funded activities. The major difference is that the grass roots project is normally funded with some sort of "seed" money whereas the bootleg project is accomplished in a piecemeal fashion on the sly. Employees charge their time to other activities while working on the bootleg R & D project.

Executives earn high salaries for their ability to perform long-range planning and policy formulation. In general, meddling in project management is common because the need to continuously reassess the priorities of the projects. In R & D, this problem of executive meddling becomes more pronounced because, in addition to the above-mentioned reasons, executives might still consider themselves to be technical specialists or might develop a sense of executive pride of ownership because this project was their idea. If an executive continuously provides technical advice, then it is entirely possible that an atmosphere of stifled creativity will occur. If the executive is considered to be the expert in the field, then everyone, including the R & D project manager, may let the executive do it all, and both the project as well as the executive's duties may suffer.

There is nothing wrong with an executive demonstrating pride of ownership for a project as long as possesiveness (i.e., "this project will be mine, all the way") and meddling are kept to a minimum. The R & D project manager should still be permitted to run the show with timely, structured feedback of information to the executive. If executives continuously meddle, then the R & D project manager may adopt a policy of "avoidance management" where executives are avoided unless problems arise.

In general project management, executives should actively interface with a project only during the conception and planning stages. The same holds true in R & D project management but with much more emphasis on the conceptual stage than the planning stage. The executive should work closely with the R & D project manager in defining the:

- Needs
- Requirements
- Objectives
- Success factors
- Realistic end date

The executive should then step out of the way and let the R & D project manager establish his own timetable. One cannot expect executive meddling to be entirely eliminated from R & D activities because each R & D activity could easily have a direct bearing upon the strategic planning that the executive must perform as part of the daily routine.

R & D activities have a direct bearing on the organization's strategic planning. Executives should therefore provide some sort of feedback to R & D managers. The following comments were made by an R & D project manager:

I know that there is planning going on now for activities which I will be doing three months from now. How should I plan for this? I don't have any formal or informal data on planning as yet. What should I tell my boss?

Executives should not try to understaff the R & D functions. Forcing personnel and project managers to work on too many projects at once can drastically reduce creativity. This does not imply that personnel should be used on only one project at a time. Most companies can not afford this luxury. However, the situation of multi-project project management should be carefully monitored.

As a final note, executives must be very careful as to how they wish to maintain control over the R & D project managers. Too much control can drastically reduce bootleg research and, in the long run, the company may suffer.

In most organizations, either R & D drives marketing or marketing drives R & D, with the latter being more common. Well-managed organizations should maintain a proper balance between marketing and R & D. Marketing-driven organizations can create havoc especially if marketing continuously requests information faster than R & D can deliver and if bootleg R & D is eliminated. In this case, all R & D activities must be approved by marketing. In some organizations, this funding comes out of the marketing budget.

In order to stimulate creativity, R & D should have control over at least a portion of its own budget. This is a necessity because not all R & D activities are designed to benefit marketing. Some activities are simply to improve technology or create a new way of doing business.

Marketing support, if needed, should be available to all R & D projects regardless of where they originate. An R & D project manager at a major food manufacturer made the following remarks:

A few years ago, one of our R & D people came up with an idea and I was assigned as the project manager. When the project was complete, we had developed a new product, ready for market introduction and testing. Unfortunately, R & D does not maintain funds for the market testing of a new product. The funds come out of marketing. Our marketing people either did not understand the product or placed it low on their priority list. We, in R & D, tried to talk to them. They were reluctant to test the new product because the project was our idea. Marketing lives in their own little world. To make a long story short, last year one of our competitors introduced the same product into the market place. Now, instead of being the leader, we are playing catch-up. I know R & D project managers are not trained in market testing, but what if marketing refuses to support R & D-conceived projects? What can we do?

Several organizations today have R & D project managers reporting directly to a new business group, business development group or marketing. Engineering-oriented R & D project managers continuously express displeasure with being evaluated for promotion by someone in marketing who really may not understand the technical difficulties in managing an R & D project. Yet, executives have valid arguments for this arrangement asserting that these high technology R & D project managers are so in love with their projects that they don't know how and when to cancel them. Marketing executives contend that projects should be cancelled when:

- Costs become excessive, causing product cost to be noncompetitive
- Return on investment will occur too late
- Competition is too stiff and not worth the risk

and other arguments. Of course, the question arises, "should marketing have a vote in the cancellation of each R & D project or only those that are marketing driven?" Some organizations cancel projects with a consensus from the project team.

R & D project management in small organizations is generally easier than similar functions in large organizations. In small companies, there usually exists a single group responsible for all R & D activities. In large companies, each division may have its own R & D function. The giant corporations try to encourage decentralized R & D departments under the supervision of a central research (or corporate research) group. The following problems were identified by a central research group project manager:

- "I have seen parallel projects going on at the same time."
- "We have a great duplication of effort because each division has their own R & D and Quality Control functions. We have a very poor passing of information between divisions."
- "Central research was originally developed to perform research functions which could not be effectively handled by the divisions. Although we are

supposed to be a service group, we still bill each division for the work we do for them. Some pay us and some don't. Last year, several divisions stopped using us because they felt that it was cheaper to do the work themselves. Now, we are funded entirely by corporate and have more work than we can handle. Everyone can think of work for us to do when it is free."

Priorities create colossal managerial headaches for the R & D project manager because each project is usually prioritized differently than all of the other projects. Functional managers must now supply resources according to two priority lists. Unfortunately, the R & D priority list is usually not given proper attention.

As an example of this, the Director of R & D of a Forture 25 Corporation made the following remarks:

Each of our operating divisions have their own R & D projects and priorities. Last year corporate R & D had a very high R & D project geared toward cost improvement in the manufacturing areas. Our priorities were based upon the short run requirements. Unfortunately, the operating divisions that had to supply resources to our project felt that the benefits would not be received until the long run and therefore placed support for our project low on their priority list.

Communication of priorities is often a problem in the R & D arena. Setting of priorities on the divisional level may not be passed down to the departmental level, and vice versa. We must have early feedback of priorities so that functional managers can make their own plans.

R & D project managers are no different from other project managers in that they are expected to have superior writing skills but actually do not. R & D project managers quickly become prolific writers if they feel they will receive recognition through their writings.

Most R & D projects begin with a project request form which includes a feasibility study and cost benefit analysis. The report can vary from five to fifty pages. The project manager must identify benefits that the company will receive if it allocates funds to this activity. In many non-R & D activities project managers are not required to perform such feasibility studies.

Because of a lack of professional writing skills, executives should try to reduce the number of interim reports since it can seriously detract from more important R & D functions. In addition, most interim reports are more marketing oriented than R & D oriented.

Many of today's companies have weekly or bimonthly status review meetings where each R & D project manager provides a five minute (or less) oral briefing on the status of his project, without getting involved in the technical details. Of course, at project completion or termination, a comprehensive written report is still be required.

R & D groups have one of the highest salaries ranges and are generally the first to establish a "dual ladder" system where employees can progress on a technical payscale to high salary positions without having to accept a position in management. In the R & D environment, it is quite common for some functional employees to be at a higher salary level than the R & D project manager or even their own functional managers. This technique is necessary in order to maintain a superior technical community and to select managers based upon their managerial expertise, not technical superiority. (The R & D group of a Fortune 25 corporation recently adopted a dual ladder system and found that it had created strange problems. Several scientists began fighting over the size of their office, type of desk, and who should have their own secretaries.)

The evaluation process of R & D personnel can be very difficult. R & D project managers can have either direct or indirect control over an employee's evaluation for promotion. Generally speaking, project managers, even R & D project managers, can make only recommendations to the functional managers, who in turn assess the validity of the recommendation and make the final assessment. Obviously, not all R & D projects are going to produce fruitful results. In such a case, should the employee be graded down because the project failed? This is a major concern to managers.

R & D project managers have no problem with self-motivation especially on one-person projects. But how does a project manager motivate project team members especially when you, the R & D project manager may have no say in the performance or evaluation? How do you get all of your employees to focus on the correct information? How do you motivate employees when their time is fragmented over several activities? How can you prevent employees from picking up bad habits which can lead to missed opportunities?

R & D project managers would rather try to motivate employees through work challenge and demonstrations of their own expertise. Most R & D project managers prefer not to use formal authority. One such project manager summed up his problems as follows:

I have only implied authority and cannot always force the project participants to perform my way. We have used task forces both effectively and ineffectively. We are always confronted with authority and priority problems when it comes to motivating people. Functional managers resent R & D project managers who continuously demonstrate their project authority. Our best results are obtained when the task force members visualize this project as part of their own goals.

Executives must take a hard look at how they are managing their R & D projects. In general, all R & D personnel are project managers and should be trained accordingly as any other project manager would be. If executives wish to develop an organization which will retain superior personnel and stimulate creativity and freedom, then executives must recognize the need for effective organizational communications and alleviate meddling by marketing and the executive level of the organization. R & D project managers are actually the architects of the conceptual phase of the corporation's long-range plans and their value to the organization appears to finally receiving recognition from management.

CASE STUDY: JONES AND SHEPHARD ACCOUNTANTS, INC.

By 1970, Jones and Shephard Accountants, Inc. (J&S) was ranked eighteenth in size by the American Association of Accountants. In order to compete with the larger firms, J&S formed an Information Services Division designed primarily for studies and analyses. By 1975, the Information Services Division (ISD) had fifteen employees.

In 1977, the ISD purchased three minicomputers. With this increased capacity, J&S expanded its services to help satisfy the needs of outside customers. By September 1978, the internal and external work loads had increased to a point where the ISD now employed over fifty people.

The director of the division was very disappointed in the way that activities were being handled. There was no single person assigned to push through a project and outside customers did not know who to call to get answers regarding project status. The director found that most of his time was being spent on day-to-day activities such as conflict resolution instead of strategic planning and policy formulation.

The biggest problems facing the director were the two continuous internal projects (called Project X and Project Y, for simplicity) which required month-end data collation and reporting. The director felt that these two projects were important enough to require a full-time project manager on each effort.

In October, 1978, corporate announced that the ISD director would be reassigned on February 1, 1979, and that the announcement of his replacement would not be made until the middle of January. The same week that the announcement was made, two individuals were hired from outside of the company to take charge of Project X and Project Y. Exhibit 3-1 shows the organizational structure of the ISD.

Within the next thirty days, rumors spread throughout the organization about who would become the new director. Most people felt that the position would be filled from within the division and that the most likely candidates would be the two new project managers. In addition, the associate director was due to retire in December, thus creating two openings.

On January 3, 1979 a confidential meeting was held between the ISD director and the systems manager.

ISD Director: "Corporate has approved my request to promote you to division director. Unfortunately, your job will not be an easy one. You're going to have

Exhibit 3-1. ISD Organizational Chart.

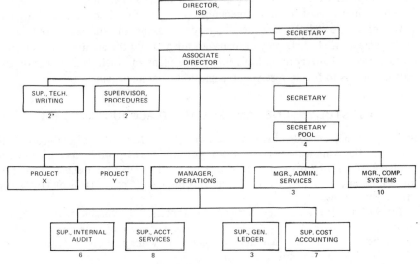

*DENOTES THE NUMBER OF ADDITIONAL FUNCTIONAL EMPLOYEES

to restructure the organization somehow so that our employees will not have as many conflicts as they are now faced with. My secretary is typing up a confidential memo for you explaining my observations on the problems within our division.

Remember, your promotion should be held in the strictest of confidence until the final announcement later this month. I'm telling you this now so that you can begin planning the restructuring. My memo should help you." (See Exhibit 3-2 for the memo.)

The systems manager read the memo and, after due consideration, decided that some form of matrix would be best. To help him structure the organization properly, an outside consultant was hired to help identify the potential problems with changing over to a matrix. The following problem areas were identified by the consultant:

1. The operations manager controls more than 50 percent of the people resources. You might want to break up his empire. This will have to be done very carefully.
2. The secretary pool is placed too high in the organization.
3. The supervisors who now report to the associate director will have to be reassigned lower in the organization if the associate director's position is abolished.
4. One of the major problem areas will be trying to convince corporate management that their change will be beneficial. You'll have to con-

EXHIBIT 3-2
CONFIDENTIAL MEMO

From: ISD Director
 To: Systems Manager
Date: January 3, 1979

Congratulations on your promotion to division director. I sincerely hope that your tenure will be productive both personally and for corporate. I have prepared a short list of the major obstacles that you will have to consider when you take over the controls.

1. Both Project X and Project Y managers are highly competent individuals. In the last four or five days, however, they have appeared to create more conflicts for us than we had previously. This could be my fault for not delegating them sufficient authority, or could be a result of the fact that several of our people consider these two individuals as prime candidates for my position. In addition, the operations manager does not like other managers coming into his "empire" and giving direction.
2. I'm not sure that we even need an associate director. That decision will be up to you.
3. Corporate has been very displeased with our inability to work with outside customers. You must consider this problem with any organizational structure you choose.
4. The corporate strategic plan for our division contains an increased emphasis on special, internal MIS projects. Corporate wants to limit our external activities for a while until we get our internal affairs in order.
5. I made the mistake of changing our organizational structure on a day-to-day basis. Perhaps it would have been better to design a structure that could satisfy advanced needs, especially one that we can grow into.

   vince them that this change can be accomplished without having to increase division manpower.
5. You might wish to set up a separate department or a separate project for customer relations.
6. Introducing your employees to the matrix will be a problem. Each employee will look at the change differently. Most people have the tendency of looking first at the shift in the balance of power—have I gained or have I lost power and status?

The Systems Manager evaluated the consultant's comments and then prepared a list of questions to ask the consultant at their next meeting.

1. What should the new organizational structure look like? Where should I put each person, specifically the managers?
2. When should I announce the new organizational change? Should it be at the same time as my appointment or at a later date?

3. Should I invite any of my people to provide input to the organizational restructuring? Can this be used as a technique to ease power plays?
4. Should I provide inside or outside seminars to train my people for the new organizational structure? If yes, how soon should they be held?

CASE STUDY: ACORN INDUSTRIES[25]

Prior to July of 1971, Acorn Industries was a relatively small midwestern corporation dealing with a single product line. The company dealt solely with commercial contracts and rarely, if ever, considered submitting proposals for government contracts. The corporation at that time functioned under a traditional form of organizational structure, although it did possess a somewhat decentralized managerial philosophy within each division. In 1968, upper management decided that the direction of the company must change. To compete with other manufacturers, the company initiated a strong acquisition program whereby smaller firms were bought out and brought into the organization. The company believed that an intensive acquisition program would solidify future growth and development, the acquisition of other companies would allow them to diversify into other fields, especially within the area of government contracts. However, the company did acknowledge one shortcoming that could possibly hurt their efforts: they never fully implemented any form of project management.

In July of 1971 the company was awarded a major defense contract after four years of research and development and intensive competition from a major defense organization. The company once again relied on their superior technological capabilities, combined with strong marketing efforts, to obtain the contract. According to Chris Banks, the current marketing manager at Acorn Industries, the successful proposal for the government contract was submitted solely through the efforts of the marketing division. Acorn's successful marketing strategy was based on three factors:

1. Know exactly what the customer wants.
2. Know exactly what the market will bear.
3. Know exactly what the competition is doing and where they are going.

The contract awarded in July of 1971 led to subsequent successful government contracts, and, in fact, eight more were awarded amounting to $80 million each. These contracts were to last anywhere from seven to ten years, taking the company into early 1981 before expiration would occur. Because of their extensive growth, especially within the area of government contracts as they pertained to weapon systems, the company was forced in 1972 to change general managers. An individual was brought in who had an extensive background in program management, and who previously had been involved in research and development.

---

25. This case study was prepared by Frank E. Ashcraft under the direction of Dr. Harold Kernzer as a basis for class discussion rather than to illustrate either effective or ineffective handling of an administrative situation.

Problems Facing the General Manager

The problems facing the new general manager were numerous. The company, prior to his arrival, was virtually a decentralized manufacturing organization. Each division within the company was somewhat autonomous, and the functional managers operated under a Key Management Incentive Program (K.M.I.P.). The previous general manager had left it up to each division manager to do what was required. Performance was measured against attainment of goals. If the annual objective was met under the K.M.I.P. program, each division manager could expect to receive a year-end bonus. These bonuses were computed on a percentage of the manager's base pay and were directly correlated to the ability to exceed the annual objective. Accordingly, future planning within each division was somewhat stagnant, and most managers did not concern themselves with any aspect of organizational growth other than what was required by the annual objective.

Because the company had previously dealt with a single product line and interacted solely with commercial contractors, little if any production planning had occurred. Interactions between research and development and the production and engineering departments were practically nonexistent. Research and development was either way behind or way ahead of the other departments at any particular time. Because of the effects of the K.M.I.P. program this aspect was likely to continue.

Change within the Organizational Structure

To compound the aforementioned problems the general manager faced the unique task of changing corporate philosophy. Previously, corporate management had been concerned with a single product with a short-term production cycle. Now, however, the corporation was faced with long-term government contracts, long cycles, and diversified products. Add to this the fact that the company had almost no individuals who operated under any aspect of program management, the tasks appeared insurmountable.

The goal of the new general manager during the period from 1972 to 1976 was to retain profitability and maximize return on investment. In order to do this, the general manager decided to maintain the company's commercial product line and operate at full capacity. This decision was made because the company was based on solid financial management and the commercial product line had been extremely profitable.

According to the general manager, Ken Hawks, "The concept of keeping both commercial and government contracts separate was a necessity. The commercial product line was highly competitive and maintained a good market share. If the adventure into weaponry failed, the company could always fall back on the commercial products. At any rate, the company at this time could not solely rely on the success of government contracts that were due to expire by 1981."

In 1976, Acorn reorganized its organizational structure and created a program management office under the direct auspices of the general manager. (See Exhibit 3-3).

Exhibit 3-3. 1976 Organizational Structure.

Expansion and Growth

In late 1976, Acorn initiated a major expansion and reorganization within its various divisions. In fact, during the period between 1976 and 1978 the government contracts resulted in the acquiring of three new companies and the acquisition of a fourth was being considered. As before, the expertise of the marketing department was heavily relied upon. Growth objectives for each division were set by corporate headquarters with the advice and feedback of the division managers. Up to 1976, Acorn's divisions did not have a program director. The program management functions for all divisions were performed by one program manager whose expertise was entirely within the commercial field. This particular program manager was concerned only with profitability and did not closely interact with the various customers. According to Mr. Banks, "The program manager's philosophy was to meet the *minimum* level of performance required by the contract. To attain this he required only adequate performance. As Acorn began to become more involved with government contracts, its position remained that given a choice between high technology and low reliability, the company would always select an acquisition with low technology and high reliability. If we remain somewhere in between, future government contracts should be assured."

At the time, Acorn established a Chicago office headed by a group executive. The office was mainly for monitoring government contracts. Concurrently, an office was established in Washington to monitor the trends within the Department of Defense and to further act as a lobbyist for government contracts. A director of marketing was appointed to interact with the program office on contract proposals. Prior to the establishment of a director of program management in 1977, the marketing division was responsible for contract proposals. Acorn believed that marketing would always, as in the past, set the tone for the company. However, in 1977 and then again in 1978, Acorn underwent further organizational changes (see Exhibits 3-4 and 3-5). A full-time director of program management was instituted, along with a program management office, with further subdivisions of project managers responsible for the various government contracts. It was at this time that Acorn realized the necessity of involving the program manager more extensively in contract proposals. One faction within corporate management wanted to keep marketing responsible for contract proposals. Another decided that a combination of the marketing input and the expertise of the program director must be utilized. According to Mr. Banks, "We began to realize that marketing no longer could exclude other factions within the organization when preparing contract proposals. As program management

Exhibit 3-4. 1977 Organizational Structure.

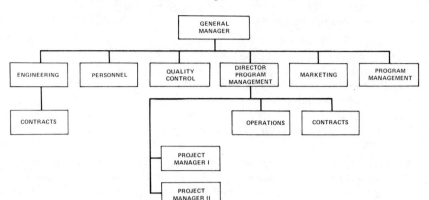

became a reality we realized that the project manager must be included in all phases of contract proposals."

Prior to 1976, the marketing department controlled most aspects of contract proposals. With the establishment of the program office, interactions between the marketing department and the program office began to increase.

Responsibilities of the Project Manager

In 1977 Acorn, for the first time, identified a director of program management. This individual reported directly to the general manager and had under his control:

1. The Project Managers
2. The Operations Group
3. The Contracts Group

Exhibit 3-5.

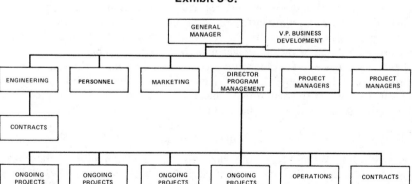

Under this reorganization the director of program management, along with the project managers, possessed greater responsibility relative to contract proposals. These new responsibilities included:

1. Research and development
2. Preparation of contract proposals
3. Interaction with marketing for submitting proposals
4. Responsibility for all government contracts:
   a. Trade-off analysis
   b. Cost analysis
5. Interface with engineering department to insure satisfaction of customer's desires

With the expansion of government contracts, Acorn is now faced with the problem of bringing in new talent to direct ongoing projects. The previous project manager had virtual autonomy over operations and maintained a singular philosophy. Under his tenure many bright individuals left Acorn because future growth and career patterns were questionable. Now that the company is diversifying into other product lines the need for young talent is crucial. Program management is still in the infancy stage.

Acorn's approach to selecting a project manager was dependent upon the size of the contract. If the particular contract was between two and three billion dollars the company would go with the most experienced individual. Smaller contracts would be assigned to whoever was available.

Interaction with Functional Departments

Since program management was relatively new, little data was available to the company to fully assess whether operations were successful. The project managers were required to negotiate with the functional departments for talent. This aspect has presented some problems because of the long-term cycle of most government contracts. Young talent within the organization saw involvement with projects as an opportunity to move up within the organization. Functional managers, on the other hand, apparently did not want to let go of young talent, and were extremely reluctant to lose any form of autonomy.

Performance of individuals assigned to projects was discussed between the project manager and the functional manager. Problems arose, however, due to length of projects. In some instances, if an individual had been assigned longer to the project manager than to the functional manager, the final evaluation of performance rested with the project manager. Further problems thus occurred when performance evaluations were submitted. In some instances adequate performance was rated high in order to maintain an individual within the project scheme. According to some project managers, this procedure was necessary because talented individuals were hard to find.

Current Status

In early 1978 Acorn began to realize that a production shortage relative to government contracts would possibly occur in late 1981 or early 1982. Acorn initiated a three-pronged attack in anticipation of this development.

1. Do what you do best.
2. Look for similiar product lines.
3. Look for products that do not require extensive R & D.

To achieve these objectives, each division within the corporation established its own separate marketing department. The prime objective was to seek more federal funds through successful contract proposals and use these funds to increase investment in R & D. The company had finally realized that the success of the corporation from 1972 to 1981 was primarily because of the selection of the proper general manager. However, this had been accomplished at the exclusion of proper control over R & D efforts. A more lasting problem still existed however: program management was still less developed than in most other corporations.

CASE STUDY: CONCRETE MASONRY CORPORATION[26]

Introduction

The Concrete Masonry Corporation (CMC), after being a leader in the industry for over twenty-five years, decided to get out of the prestressed concrete business. Although there had been a boom in residential construction in recent years, commercial work was on the decline. As a result, all the prestressed concrete manufacturers were going further afield to big jobs. In order to survive, CMC was forced to bid on jobs previously thought to be out of their geographical area. Survival depended upon staying competitive.

In 1975, the average selling price of a cubic foot of concrete was $8.35 and in 1977, the average selling price had declined to $6.85. As CMC was producing at a rate of a million cubic feet a year, not much mathematics was needed to calculate they were receiving one-and-a-half million dollars per year less than they had received a short two years before the same product.

Product management was used by CMC in a matrix organizational form. CMC's project manager had total responsibility from the design to the completion of the construction project. However, with the declining conditions of the market and the evolution that had drastically changed the character of the marketplace, CMC's previously successful approach was in question.

History

The Concrete Block Business

CMC started in the concrete block business in 1946. At the beginning, CMC became a leader in the marketplace because of: (1) advanced technology of manufacturing, and (2) an innovative delivery system. With modern equipment, specifically the flat pallet block machine, CMC was able to make blocks of different shapes without having to make major changes in the machinery. This change, along with the pioneering of the self-unloading boom truck which made

---

26. Copyright © 1978 by Harold Kerzner.

efficient, cost-saving delivery possible, contributed to the success of CMC's block business. Consequently, the block business success provided the capital needed for CMC to enter the prestressed concrete business.

The Prestressed Concrete Business

Prestressed concrete is made by casting concrete around steel cables that are stretched by hydraulic jacks. After the concrete hardens, the cables are released, thus compressing the concrete. Concrete is strongest when it is compressed. Steel is strongest when it is stretched, or in tension. In this way, CMC combined the two strongest qualities of the two materials.

Originally, the concrete block manufacturing business was a natural base from which to enter the prestressed concrete business; the very first prestressed concrete beams were made of a row of concrete block, prestressed by using high-tension-strength wires through the cores of the block. The wire was pulled at a high tension and the ends of the beams were grouted. After the grout held the wires or cables in place, the tension was released on the cables and resulted in compression on the bottom portion of the beams. Therefore, the force on the bottom of the beam would tend to counteract the downward weight put on the top of the beam. By this process, these prestressed concrete beams could cover three to four times the spans possible with conventional reinforced concrete.

In 1951, after many trips to Washington, D.C., and an excellent selling job by CMC's founder, T.L. Goudvis, CMC was able to land its first large-volume prestressed concrete project with the Corps of Engineers. The contract authorized the use of prestressed concrete beams, as described, with concrete block for the roof of warehouses in the large Air Force Depot complex being built in Shelby, Ohio. The buildings were a success and CMC immediately received prestige as a leader in the prestressed concrete business.

Wet-cast beams were developed next. For wet-cast beams, instead of concrete block, the cables were placed in long forms and pulled to the desired tension, after which concrete was poured in the forms to make beams. As a result of wet-cast beams, prestressed concrete was no longer dependent on concrete block.

At first, prestressed concrete was primarily for floors and roofs, but, in the early sixties, precasters became involved in more complicated structures. CMC started designing and making not only beams, but columns and whatever other components it took to put together a whole structure. Parking garages became a natural application for prestressed concrete structures. Eventually an entire building could be precast out of prestressed concrete. (See Exhibit 3-6).

Project Management

Constructing the entire building, as in the case of a parking garage, meant that jobs were becoming more complex with respect to interdependence of detailed task accomplishment. Accordingly, in 1967, project management was established at CMC. The functional departments did the work, but the project managers saw to it that the assigned projects were completed on schedule and within

Exhibit 3-6. Medwert Coliseum, Richfield, Ohio.

budget and specifications. A matrix organization, as illustrated in Exhibit 3-7, was adopted and used effectively by CMC. The concept of a matrix organization, as applied at CMC, entailed an organizational system designed as a "web of relationships" rather than a line and staff relationship for work performance.

Each project manager was assigned a number of personnel with the required qualifications from the functional departments for the duration of the project. Thus, the project organization was composed of the project manager and functional personnel groups. Although the project manager had the responsibility and accountability for the successful completion of the contract, he also had the delegated authority for work design, assignments of functional group personnel, and the determination of procedural relationships.

The most important functional area for the project manager was the engineering department, since prestressed concrete is a highly engineered product. A great deal of coordination and interaction was required between the project manager and the engineering department just to make certain that everything fit together and was structurally sound. A registered engineer did the design. The project manager's job was to see that the designing was done correctly and efficiently. Production schedules were made up by the project manager, subject to minor modifications by the plant. The project manager was also required to do all the coordination with the customer, architect, general contractor, and his own erection force. The project manager also had to have interaction with the distribution manager to be certain that the product designed could be shipped by trucks. Finally, there had to be interaction between the project manager and the sales department to determine that the product that he was making was what they had sold.

Exhibit 3-7. Matrix Organization Of Concrete Masonry Corporation.

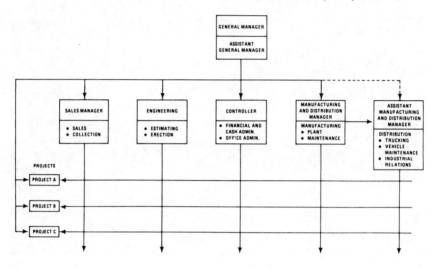

Estimating

Which Department?

At one time or another during CMC's history, the estimating function was assigned to nearly every functional area of the organization including sales, engineering, manufacturing, and administration. Determining which functional area estimating was to be under was a real problem for CMC. There was a short time when estimating was on its own, reporting directly to the general manager.

Assignment of this function to any one department carried with it some inherent problems, not peculiar to CMC, but simply related to human nature. For example, when the estimating was supervised in the sales department, estimated costs would tend to be low. In sales, the estimator knows his boss wants to be the low bidder on the job and therefore believes he is right when he says, "It is not going to take us ten days to cast this thing, we could run three at a time."

When estimating was performed by production, the estimate would tend to be high. This resulted because the estimator did not want his boss, the production manager, coming back to him and saying, "How come you estimated this thing at $5 a cubic foot and its costing us $6? It's not the cost of production that's wrong, it's the estimate."

W.S. Lasch, general manager of CMC, had this comment about estimating in a project management situation:

"It is very difficult to get accountability for estimating a project. When many of your projects are new ballgames, a lot of your information has to come from . . . well, let's just say there is a lot of art to it as well as science. You never can say with 100 percent certainty that costs were high because you could have just as easily said the estimate was too low.

"So, as a compromise, most of the time we had our estimating made by engineering. While it solved some problems, it also created others. Engineers would tend to be more fair; they would call the shots as they saw them. However, one problem was that they still had to answer to sales as far as their work load was concerned. For example, an engineer is in the middle of estimating a parking garage, a task which might take several days. All of a sudden, the sales department wants him to stop and estimate another job. The sales department had to be the one to really make that decision because they are the ones that know what the priorities are on the bidding. So even though the estimator was working in engineering, he was really answering to the sales manager as far as his work load was concerned."

Costing

Estimating was accomplished through a continual monitoring and comparison of actual versus planned performance, as shown below.

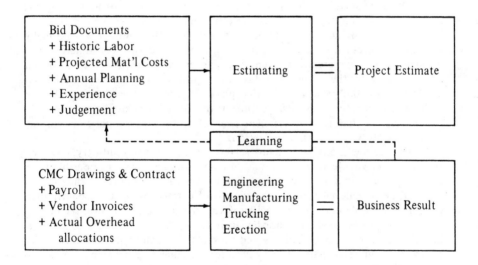

The actual costing process was not a problem for CMC. In recent years, CMC eliminated as much as possible the actual dollars and cents from the estimator's control. A great deal of the "drudge work" was done on the computer. The estimator, for example, would predict how much the prestressed concrete must span and how many cubic feet of concrete was needed. Once he had that information, he entered it in the computer. The computer would then come up with the cost. This became an effective method because the estimator would not be influenced by either sales or production personnel.

The Evolution of the Prestressed Concrete Marketplace

.During the twenty or more years since prestressing achieved wide acceptance in the construction industry, an evolution has been taking place that has drastically changed the character of the marketplace and thus greatly modified the role of the prestresser. Lasch had the following comments about these changes:

"In the early days, designers of buildings looked to prestressers for the expertise required to successfully incorporate the techniques and available prestressed products into their structures. A major thrust of our business in those days was to introduce design professionals, architects, and engineers to our fledgling industry and to assist them in making use of the many advantages that we could offer over other construction methods. These advantages included fire resistance, long spans, permanence, factory-controlled quality, speed of erection, aesthetic desirability, virtual elimination of maintenance costs, and, last but of prime importance, the fact that we were equipped to provide the expertise and coordination necessary to successfully integrate our product into the building. Many of our early jobs were bid from sketches. It was then up to our in-house experts, working closely with the owner's engineer and architect, to develop an appropriate, efficient structure that satisfied the aesthetic and functional requirements and maximized production and erection efficiency to provide maximum financial return to CMC. It should be noted that, although our contract was normally with the project's general contractor, most of our design coordination was through the owner's architect or engineer and, more often than not, it was our relationship with the owner and his design professional that determined our involvement in the project in the first place. It should be readily seen that, in such an environment, only organizations with a high degree of engineering background and a well-organized, efficient team of professionals could compete successfully. CMC was such an organization.

"There are few, if any, proprietary secrets in the prestressing industry, however, and it was inevitable that this would in later years be largely responsible for a dramatic change in the marketplace. The widepsread acceptance of the product that had been achieved through the success of companies like CMC contributed to increased availability of the technical knowledge and production techniques that design professionals had previously relied upon the producer to provide. In the later 1960s, some colleges and universities began to include prestressed concrete design as a part of their structural engineering programs. Organizations such as the Portalnd Cement Association offered seminars for architects and engineers to promote the prestressing concept. As a result, it is now common for architects and engineers to incorporate prestressed concrete products in bid drawings for their projects, detailing all connections, reinforcement, mix designs, etc. This obviously makes it possible for any organization capable of reading drawings and filling forms to bid on the project. We have found ourselves bidding against companies with a few molds in an open field and in several cases, a broker with no equipment or organization at all! The result of this, of course, is a market price so low as to prohibit the involvement of professional prestressing firms with the depth of organization described earlier."

Obtaining a Prestressed Concrete Job

The case writer believes the following example demonstrates the change in market conditions and best illustrates one of the reasons CMC decided not to remain in the prestressed concrete business. A large insurance company in Columbus, Ohio was planning a parking garage for 2,500 cars. CMC talked to the owner and owner's representative (a construction management firm) about using prestressed concrete in the design of their project rather than the poured-in-place concrete, steel, or whatever other options they had. Just by doing this, CMC had to give away some knowledge. You just cannot walk in and say, "Hey, how about using prestressed concrete?" You have to tell them what is going to be saved and how, because the architect has to make the drawings. Once CMC felt there was an open door, and that the architect and owner would possibly incorporate their product, then sales would consult engineering to come up with a proposal. A proposal in the early stages was simply to identify what the costs were going to be, and to show the owner and architect photographs or sketches of previous jobs. As time went by, CMC had to go into more detail and provide more and more information, including detailed drawings of several proposed layouts. CMC illustrated connection details, reinforcing details, and even computer design of some of the pieces for the parking garage. Receiving all this engineering information, the owner and the construction management firm became convinced that using this product was the most inexpensive way for them to go. In fact, CMC demonstrated to the insurance company that they could save over a million dollars over any other product. At this point, CMC had spent thousands of dollars to come up with the solution for the problem of designing the parking garage.

Months and years passed until the contract manager chose to seek bids from other precasters who up to this time had little or no investment in the project. CMC had made available an abundance of free-information which could be used by the competition. The competition only had to put the information together, make a material take-off, calculate the cost, and put a price on it. Without the costly depth of organization required to support the extensive promotional program conducted by CMC, the competiton could naturally bid the job lower.

Lasch felt that, as a result of present-day market conditions, there were only two ways that one survives in the prestressed concrete business.

"Face the fact that you are going to be subservient to a general contractor and that you are going to sell not your expertise but your function as a 'job shop' manufacturer producing concrete products according to someone else's drawings and specifications. If you do that then you no longer need, for example, an engineering department or a technically qualified sales organization. All you are going to do is look at drawings, have an estimator that can read the drawings, put a price tag on them, and give a bid. It is going to be a low bid because you have eliminated much of your overhead. We simply do not choose to be in business in this manner.

"The other way to be in the business is that you are not going to be subservient to a general contractor, or owner's architiect, or engineer. What you are going to do is to deal with owners or users. That way a general contractor may end up as a subcontractor to the prestresser. We might go out and build a parking garage or other structure and assume the role of developer or builder or even owner/ leaser. In that way, we would control the whole job. After all, in most cases the precast contract on a garage represents more than half the total cost. It could be argued with great justification that the conventional approach (i.e., precaster working for general contractor) could be compared to the tail wagging the dog.

"With complete control of design, aesthetics, and construction schedule, it would be possible to achieve maximum efficiency of design, plant usage, and field coordination which, when combined, would allow us to achieve the most important requirement—that of providing the eventual user with maximum value for a minimum investment. Unless this can be achieved, there would be no justification for being in business."

CASE STUDY: THE EASTLAND MALL BRANCH BANK PROJECT

The steering committee was to meet in fifteen minutes to discuss the fate of the Eastland Mall Project. Jack O'Boyle was conversing with the chief executive officer (CEO) of Third National Trust. "I don't know what the outcome of the meeting will be," lamented O'Boyle, senior vice-president of systems and programming. "I really thought Vince knew his stuff about project management. Maybe this banking industry really isn't suited to that approach."

"Let's not quit before the final count," responded Buzz Adams, CEO. "Let's wait to hear what Vince has to say at this meeting he called with the steering committee. It doesn't look to me like the Eastland Branch could possibly open on schedule, and I would tend to agree with you about project management. However, I've seen it work in New York's largest financial institutions. There has to be a good reason why it isn't working here. I say we let Vince make his presentation and then discuss some alternatives to get the branch open. Afterwards, we should all have a talk with the steering committee members about the future of project management here at Third National."

History

Vince Stewart had accepted a position with Third National Trust immediately after college graduation in 1972. With a bachelor's degree in operations research, he was assigned to the systems and programming department. He did commendable work on analysis and software for a series of check transportation studies. From 1974 to 1976, he was the system analyst in charge of software for Third National Trust's "Easy Money" automated teller machines.

Vince's experience in the programming department quickly showed him the advantages of project management in controlling a small staff in a task with limited scope and duration. As his experience and interest grew, he took part in several project management seminars given by local colleges and professional organizations. By 1977, not only was Vince convinced of the benefits of project management, he was also the leading proponent of project management throughout Third National Trust.

Third National Trust is located in a major midwestern city. After eighty-two years of existence, it had assets of $2.1 billion and had ninety-one branches serving the commercial interests and residential mortgage markets. Third National Trust is firmly established as one of the five dominant banks in its largely conservative area. Although it had experienced tremendous growth, Third National was falling behind in its use of state-of-the-art technology and services. In fact, several of the branches had experienced declines in mortgage loans, commercial loans, and time deposits. Several branches had been closed recently which further hurt Third National's image. In spring 1976, the board of directors appointed Buzz Adams as chief executive officer of Third National Trust.

Adams came to Third National from his position as senior vice-president of research for a New York bank. He was a firm believer in computer and communications technology as the answer to banks providing new services in an increasingly competitive financial market. His main thrust would be to increase the automation of services to Third National's customers and try to recover some of the sagging market.

Upon his arrival at Third National, Adams fired or reassigned over half of the 224 officers. At the senior-officer level, he moved the senior vice-president of marketing to planning, fired the senior vice-president of systems and programming, and brought with him, from New York, Jack O'Boyle as senior vice-president of systems and programming. He also brought along his own senior vice-president of marketing.

At his first officer's council meeting in the summer of 1976, Adams declared the need for an aggressive automation plan to provide new services using state-of-the-art technology. He announced project management as the means for maintaining a competitive posture. The first such project would be opening a branch at Eastland Mall. This would be Third National's first attempt at locating a branch within a large suburban shopping mall and would reverse the bank's policy of decreasing the number of branches over the past five years. The new branch would be designed around an "Easy Money" automated teller machine (ATM) for the convenience of evening and weekend shoppers. Adams appointed a steering committee to spearhead the Eastland Mall Branch Project. The committee consisted of: Jack O'Boyle, the vice-presidents of marketing, planning, branch banking, accounting, personnel, assistant legal counsel, and assistant vice-president of audit. Adams gave the project a completion date of Labor Day, 1978.

A Project Team Picks A Project Team

On September 6, 1976, the vice-president of branch banking scheduled the first meeting of the Eastland Mall Branch Project Steering Committee.

VP Branch Banking: Considering we're a half hour late in getting the meeting started, let's get down to business right away. Two years is a tight time frame for my people to convert a shoestore into a branch at Eastland Mall. Who's going to take the minutes of these meetings?

VP Planning: What is the project management approach Buzz Adams was talking about last week?

O'Boyle: Let me answer that one. In a systems approach a project manager takes all variables into account in order to attain a goal limited by time, cost, and performance. In order to coordinate the project's tasks, he heads a project office whose staff is drawn from a variety of functional areas.

VP Branch Banking: When you cut through all that jargon, it sounds like the implementation teams we've had for previous projects.

VP Planning: Jack, where do we go to hire this project manager?

O'Boyle: I've got a guy in my department named Vince Stewart who has great potential. He's had more experience than anyone else in the bank and has been pushing to apply project management outside the department. Also, his work on the "Easy Money" ATMs and transportation studies gives him a well-rounded background. It will help employee morale to promote from within. Besides, Buzz Adams asked me to keep him posted on the development of the project, so it will help to have my own man as manager.

VP Branch Banking: How can you say he's well-rounded? He's never stepped outside the programming department and doesn't have the foggiest idea of what it takes to start a branch. And look at his age! This is only his first job out of college. Frankly, I think one of my people should run the show as always.

O'Boyle: The PM's job is primarily one of coordinating tasks. I'm sure he'll acquire knowledge of the intricacies of branch banking by frequently tapping your wisdom. So unless there are any other objections, Vince Stewart will be the project manager for the project.

VP Accounting: How many hours per week will my man have to work at the project office?

VP Marketing: The only way project management worked for us in New York was to have project office staff committed full-time for the duration of the project.

VP Accounting: Well, if that's the way it's got to be, let's put somebody on the team from each of our departments, someone we can spare for two years.

O'Boyle: I can appreciate your view, but it may be more effective if Vince nominates the project office personnel, interviews them to insure that they want to join the team, and then obtains approval from this steering committee.

VP Planning: We're running a bank, not a picnic. We've all got a lot of projects brewing, so I agree that we ought to put on the team anyone we can spare for two years. You've ramrodded your boy on us for project manager, so to be fair let us determine who, if anybody, we can put on the project.

VP Audit: If I can add something, I think we should have some representatives from other departments.

VP Personnel: I'll take care of that. This may be a good area for training and weeding out the new hires who can't cut it.

After opening the folded slips of paper that were passed to the head of the table, the names of the project members were revealed: Jim Albert, senior programmer; Fred Clowser, assistant manager, West 54th branch; Dale Winters, assistant vice-president, branch management; Donald Kocurko, marketing analyst; Albert Pief, building department staff; and Roberta Jones, customer services department and head Teller.

VP Branch Banking: Now that we've got the project office put together, let's go to lunch. How about meeting the first Wednesday of each month at 11:00 AM to get a status report from the project manager?

The steering committee agreed to the scheduled meetings.

Project Manager's Status Report

Despite lack of cooperation from some functional departments, Vince Stewart worked hard at applying project management concepts to his project. Once the project got started, Vince found himself not only coordinating the project tasks but also performing them. On June 3, 1978, he presented his monthly status report to the steering committee.

VP Accounting: The officers have been invited to hear a luncheon address by Mike Blumenthal in about an hour, so let's make this a fast meeting. I see that the agenda, as always, starts with a PERT chart update and project cost variance reports. Those lines and circles on PERT don't mean any more to me today than they did two years ago. Adams wants this project done by Labor Day at any cost so let's skip the fancy charts and have Vince tell us what the problems are.

Vince Stewart: I came up with an idea to allow a customer to access both his checking and savings accounts with one ID number on the "Easy Money" ATM at the branches. In evenings or weekends when we are closed but the shopping mall is loaded with customers, a customer can access both accounts in the ATM located outside the branch. The only problem is that the software effort is running late.

Legal Counsel: You can't do that! If a husband and wife share a checking account, but the wife has her own savings account, you've put us in court over the woman's rights. When the husband can withdraw from the savings account, if his wife can't stop him, we are in trouble. You should have gotten an opinion from us before proceeding on that one.

VP Planning: You're devoting too much time to the ATM. Don Kocurko told me the ATM sign-up cards are getting a low response. If you are aware of the environment, you realize Eastland Mall is in an East European section of town where people want cash in the hand, not an ID number and a machine. Also, the other banks have high concentrations of time deposits and installment loan activity. That sort of business demands tellers, administrative assistants, and business hours. Frankly, I think we should deemphasize the ATM and consider longer office hours.

VP Branch Banking: Another thing, Stewart, I heard from the furniture dealer that you ordered red carpeting. You'd better learn a lesson in consistency if you want to survive in banking. Through the years, we've built a common sense of identity—an image—so all our branches seem the same to the customers. They have come to expect blue carpeting, and Eastland Mall will have blue carpeting. The other branches use separate ID numbers for separate accounts, and so will Eastland. You'd better realize that your job is to create a copy of our ninety-one other branches, not to confuse the public with your gimmicks.

O'Boyle: Hold on here, hold on! We asked Vince to give his status report on the branch project. We have all known of the plans for the Eastland Branch. Or should I say the reports have been available for your review. Now Vince has raised a deadline problem that we must consider. But first, may I suggest we all review the role of the project manager.

VP Accounting: That's a good idea, but I'm sorry to say we'll be late for the luncheon. Let's discuss it at next month's meeting.

A Political Roadblock

On the evening of June 28, 1978, a customer was robbed while making a withdrawal from American National Savings' "Instant Bank" ATM in the Eastland Mall. Mayor Roger Quincy of Columbia Heights called Vince Stewart the next day.

Mayor Quincy: I'm sorry, Vince, but you're not going to be able to have an ATM at your Eastland Mall Branch. I assume you've heard about the problem here the other night. Our city council wants to reconsider your request for the ATM in light of the safety of the citizens. But the safety is not the only issue, mind you. It is added to the list of problems we have had to grind through with Third National. We are still not satisfied with your answers to our questions on redlining. Our finance director and community development director are still concerned with your full compliance with the Community Reinvestment Act. I have had several citizen's groups in here on this thing, and after all this is an election year. I simply can't support you if everything is not satisfactory.

Stewart: But Mr. Mayor, please consider my position. I am counting on that ATM. I have a deadline of Labor Day and I am really under the gun.

Mayor Quincy: Don't start pushing me again, Stewart. We have already conceded several questionable conditions during your construction inspections. Right now we are only reconsidering the ATM—feel lucky you can open the branch at all. You know, my wife's civic pride bunch is still burned at me for allowing the lit-up 24-hour sign you are erecting.

Stewart: I only want to emphasize that the success of our branch depends on that ATM. We thought we had the approval of the Columbia Heights city council. We are a powerful bank in this area, and I don't think even you can stop us now.

No Way Out

On June 30, Jack O'Boyle met with the vice-president of branch banking.

O'Boyle: I need your help. Vince had a run-in with Mayor Quincy who is threatening us about the ATM.

VP Branch Banking: Now you come for help? When is that fool going to learn the ropes? I've had thirty-five years of branch banking, and I know how to deal with people like Quincy. That young guy goes charging off doing things on his own to get glory. When is he going to learn there are good reasons why this bank has an authority structure?

O'Boyle: Vince's job as PM was supposed to be to coordinate resources. Every time he's come to you, he gets tap dancing. If he didn't take matters into his own hands, this project would down the drain. You'd probably enjoy seeing this bank's first attempt at project management fail.

VP Branch Banking: Don't try to blame me. This is the first time you've discussed the project with me outside of the steering committee battles. Out here in the hinterlands, we don't get sucked up into change at your New York pace. I've always been suspicious of programmers and their toys. Remember you're the one who picked this ambitious kid Stewart who's using this project as his personal path to an assistant vice-president position. His gimmicks with ATM accounts and red carpeting may make him more visible to Adams, but he'll get burnt by us for sure.

O'Boyle: Vince approached me with a contingency plan today. On the unlikely chance that we can't have an ATM, he proposes we open the Eastland Mall Branch on Saturdays. What do you think?

VP Branch Banking: Impossible! We have to have consistency among our branches. If we open one on Saturdays, we have to open them all. Unless we allow everybody to write checks that will bounce, we'd have to open the Main Office so the branches could call in to verify account balances. Your computer programming guys don't realize what a radical change it is to staff on Saturday and modify your traditional hours. Even if we'd go that route, there's no way we could be open Saturdays by Labor Day for even only the Eastland Mall Branch. I credit Stewart for realizing shoppers have different hours from banks. But Saturdays are out of the question. We have to have the "Easy Money" ATM.

At this point, the secretary to the vice-president of branch banking entered the room with a note that read: "Mayor Quincy called threatening to withdraw Columbia Heights Tax collection funds from Third National, vowed never to do business with our Public Funds people and to rezone the mall to make ATMs illegal. Therefore, *NO* ATM at Eastland Mall Branch. Look into the possibility of having the branch open on Saturdays. Signed: Buzz Adams."

Jack O'Boyle picked up the phone and called Vince Stewart. He told Vince to prepare a plan for the July 3rd steering committee meeting. The plan would detail the resources necessary to implement Saturday openings instead of an ATM for the Eastland Mall Branch.

Project Office Showdown

Vince Stewart immediately called a meeting of the project office members.

Stewart: We've just been told that the ATM is out, and Eastland Mall Branch will be open on Saturdays. Adams still wants the project completed with the branch opening celebration scheduled for Labor Day. We're going to have to work around the clock to come up with a revised plan for the July 3rd steering committee meeting.

Marketing Analyst: My boss isn't going to appreciate us developing a plan without consulting him. He is the vice-president of planning.

Stewart: Don, you're in marketing and, even more, you're in this project office. I don't appreciate your squealing to your old boss. Now more than ever, success depends on teamwork.

Assistant Branch Manager: Speaking of teamwork, now is as good a time as any to announce that I've been traded from your team. My boss called to reassign me to the statewide branch banking project. He said to tell you he'd mail you a copy of the transfer form.

AVP Branch Management: Congratulations, Fred! It's nice to see someone will escape this sinking ship. I'm going to call upstairs after this meeting to see if my boss is loyal enough to his employees to save me too.

Stewart: Let's get in the team huddle and come up with a play to win this ball game. Let's start with my area. Jim, how much computer programming would it take to automate check verification to insure Saturday checks won't bounce?

Senior Programmer: I could program the teller's screens so they could key in the account number and have the account balance displayed. But it can't be done by Labor Day, and I don't feel like rushing to get it done. I've worked night and day developing your idea for separate accounts for the ATMs and now that's down the pipes. In the past year, I've spent practically every Saturday night with the computer. My kids don't remember who their father is. Now you tell me no ATMs, and you want me to save your act again. Before I do any more programming, I want the assignment in writing from Mr. Boyle.

Stewart: Don't worry, squad. Jim will come up with the programming when we need it. He always has in the past, and he won't let the team down this time either. Why don't we put together a PERT chart of tasks necessary for Saturday openings. Roberta, how much training do you think it would take for tellers to use the new screens? Before you answer, grab a piece of chalk and write the topics on the board as we discuss them so you can draw the PERT later.

Head Teller: Look, I've had it up to here with this secretarial stuff. I've felt all along that I was only hired because I'm black and a woman and as soon as he could he dumped me into this project to get me out of the way. I thought I joined this team to add a perspective from the teller staff—but all you've made me do is take notes and draw charts. Well no more! You want to talk about Saturdays and tellers and training, fine! You want notes and charts, do it yourself! I'm through being a token doing the token jobs.

Stewart: The steering committee assured me that each of you was specially chosen for the particular talents you could bring to this project.

Building Staff: That's a line, Vince, and you know it. I'm beginning to believe all of us were dumped here to get us out of the way upstairs. When I was up in building, I had two guys working with me, and I was the main consultant on all the electrical work. Now I hear in the last year they've hired two more people and the kid I was training has taken over all my calls.

AVP Branch Management: That may be true for you, Pief, but some of us are not throwaways. In fact, I'm getting more pressure than ever from the top. I'm expected to open Eastland Mall while at the same time working on contiguous county and statewide branching. And all that is added to my regional manager responsibilities. In the last year I've lost complete control of my managers and their plans. I was put on this project thinking I would only work part-time. I'm expected to do this and everything else too. I don't know when I've been home before 10 PM.

Stewart: All right—look, we've all got problems—somehow this project management concept never got completely off the ground. At least this isn't what I expected from the seminars.

AVP Branch Banking: I think that's your problem, college boy. You're trying to run this show from a textbook. You've never had any experience with a real project team. This is just the blind leading the blind.

Stewart: Nonetheless, we've all got a deadline and need a workable plan fast. Listen to my idea, and I'll tell you what I need to make it by Labor Day.

Head Teller: I guess you didn't hear me a minute ago. I've always thought a team meant working together. You've done nothing but tell us what to do for the last two years.

Building Staff: Roberta's right. And so was Mr. Burr (senior vice-president of branch banking). He said this project stuff would never work out, but O'Boyle wouldn't listen to him. I'm not surprised most of the managers wouldn't co-operate—they listened to Burr and knew he was right.

Stewart: Well what do you suggest?

Senior Programmer: We don't know—you're the quarterback. Call the next play. Only as I see it, there isn't a coach on the sideline to send it in.

Vince adjourned the project team meeting somewhat crestfallen. He decided that he needed to have a heart-to-heart talk with Jack O'Boyle and the steering committee.

Study Questions

1. What do you think was discussed with O'Boyle and the steering committee? What will be the outcome?
2. Did the steering committee fully comprehend the responsibilities and commitments of the project office? Explain.
3. Was Stewart the best man for project manager? Would the project have been successful with someone else?
4. Did Stewart have the full cooperation and support of his team? Support your answer.

CASE STUDY: MOHAWK NATIONAL BANK

"You're really going to have your work cut out for you, Randy," remarked Pat Coleman, vice-president for operations. "It's not going to be easy establishing a project management organizational structure on top of our traditional structure. We're going to have to absorb the lumps and bruises and literally 'force' the system to work."

Background

Between 1968 and 1978, Mohawk National matured into one of New York's largest full-service banks, employing a full-time staff of some 300 employees. Of the 300 employees, approximately 235 were located in the main offices in downtown New York.

Mohawk matured along with other banks in the establishment of computerized information processing and decision making. Mohawk leased the most up-to-date computer equipment in order to satisfy customer demands. By 1974, almost all departments were utilizing the computer.

By 1975, the bureaucracy of the traditional management structure was creating severe administrative problems. Mohawk's management had established many complex projects to be pursued, each one requiring the involvement of several departments. Each department manager was setting his own priorities for the work that had to be performed. The traditional organization was too weak structurally to handle problems that required integration across multiple departments. Work from department to department could not be tracked because there was no project manager who could act as focal point for the integration of work.

Understanding the Changeover Problem

It was a difficult decision for Mohawk National to consider a new organizational structure, such as a matrix. Randy Gardner, director of personnel, commented on the decision:

"Banks, in general, thrive on traditionalism and regimentation. When a person accepts a position in our bank, he or she understands the strict rules, policies, and procedures that have been established during the last thirty years.

"We know that it's not going to be easy. We've tried to anticipate the problems that we're going to have. I've spent a great deal of time with our VP of operations and two consultants trying to predict the actions of our employees.

"The first major problem we see is with our department managers. In most traditional organizations, the biggest functional department emerges as the strongest. In a matrix organization, or almost any other project form for that matter, there is a shift in the balance of power. Some managers become more important in their new roles and others not so important. We think our department managers are good workers and that they will be able to adapt.

"Our biggest concern is with the functional employees. Many of our functional people have been with us between twenty and thirty years. They're seasoned veterans. You just know that they're going to resist change. These people will fight us all the way. They won't accept the new system until they see it work. That'll be our biggest challenge: to convince the functional team members that the system will work."

Pat Coleman, the vice-president for operations, commented on the problems that he would be facing with the new structure:

"Under the new structure, all project managers will be reporting to me. To be truthful, I'm a little scared. This changeover is like a project in itself. As with any project, the beginning is the most important phase. If the project starts out on the right track, people might give it a chance. But if we have trouble, people will be quick to revert back to the old system. Our people hate change. We cannot wait one and a half to two years for people to get familiar with the new system. We have to hit them all at once and then go all out to convince them of the possibilities that can be achieved.

"This presents a problem in that the first group of project managers must be highly capable individuals with the ability to motivate the functional team members. I'm still not sure whether we should promote from within or hire from the outside. Hiring from the outside may cause severe problems in that our employees like to work with people they know and trust. Outside people may not know our people. If they make a mistake and aggravate our people, the system will be doomed to failure.

"Promoting from within is the only logical way to go, as long as we can find qualified personnel. I would prefer to take the qualified individuals and give them a lateral promotion to a project management position. These people would be on trial for about six months. If they perform well, they will be promoted and permanently assigned to project management. If they can't perform or have trouble enduring the pressure, they'll be returned to their former functional positions. I sure hope we don't have any inter- or intramatrix power struggles.

"Implementation of the new organizational form will require good communications channels. We must provide all of our people with complete and timely information. I plan on holding weekly meetings with all of the project and functional managers. Good communications channels must be established between all resource managers. These team meetings will give people a chance to see each other's mistakes. They should be able to resolve their own problems and conflicts. I'll be there if they need me. I do anticipate several conflicts because our functional managers are not going to be happy in the role of a support group for a project manager. That's the balance of power problem I mentioned previously.

"I have asked Randy Gardner to identify from within our ranks the four most likely individuals who would make good project managers and drive the projects to success. I expect Randy's report to be quite positive. His report will be available next week."

Two weeks later Randy Gardner presented his report to Pat Coleman and made the following observations:

"I have interviewed the four most competent employees who would be suitable for project management. The following results were found:

"Andrew Medina, department manager for cost accounting, stated that he would refuse a promotion to project management. He has been in cost accounting for twenty years and does not want to make a change into a new career field.

"Larry Foster, special assistant to the vice-president of commercial loans, stated that he enjoyed the people he was working with and was afraid that a new job in project management would cause him to lose his contacts with upper-level management. Larry considers his present position more powerful than any project management position.

"Chuck Folson, personal loan officer, stated that in the fifteen years he's been with Mohawk National, he has built up strong interpersonal ties with many members of the bank. He enjoys being an active member of the informal organization and does not believe in the applications of project management for our bank.

"Jane Pauley, assistant credit manager, stated that she would like the position, but would need time to study up on project management. She feels a little unsure about herself. She's worried about the cost of failure."

Now Pat Coleman had a problem. Should he look for other bank employees who might be suitable to staff the project management functions or should he look externally to other industries for consultants and experienced project managers?

CASE STUDY: FIRST SECURITY BANK OF CLEVELAND

The growth rate of First Security of Cleveland had caused several executives to do some serious thinking about whether the present organizational structure was adequate for future operations. The big question was whether the banking community could adapt to a project management structure.

Tom Hood had been the president of First Security for the past ten years. He had been a pioneer in bringing computer technology into the banking industry. Unfortunately, the size and complexity of the new computer projects created severe integration problems which the present traditional organization was unable to cope with. What was needed was a project manager who could drive the project to success and handle the integration of work across functional lines.

Tom Hood met with Ray Dallas, one of the bank's vice-presidents, to discuss possible organizational restructuring:

Hood: I've looked at the size and complexity of some twenty projects that First Security did last year. Over 50 percent of these projects required interaction between four or more departments.

Dallas: What's wrong with that? We're growing and our problems are likewise becoming more complex.

Hood: It's the other 50 percent that worry me. We can change our organizational structure to adapt to complex problem solving and integration. But what happens when we have a project and that stays in one functional department? Who's going to drive it home? I don't see how we can tell a functional manager that he's a support group in one organizational form and a project manager in the other, and have both organizational forms going on at the same time.

We can have either large, complex projects or small ones. The small ones will be the problem. They can exist in one department or be special projects assigned to one person or a task force team. This means that if we incorporate project management, we'll have to live with a variety of structures. This can become a bad situation. I'm not sure that our people will be able to adapt to this changing environment.

Dallas: I don't think it will be as bad as you make it. As long as we clearly define each person's authority and responsibility, we'll be all right. Other industries have done this successfully. Why can't we?

Hood: There are several questions that need answering. Should each project head be called a project manager, even if the project requires only one person? I can see our people suddenly becoming title-oriented. Should all project managers report to the same boss, even if one manager has thirty people working for him and the other manager has none? This could lead to power struggles. I want to avoid that because it can easily disrupt our organization.

Dallas: The problem you mentioned earlier concerns me. If we have a project that belongs in one functional department, the ideal solution is to let the department manager wear two hats, the second one being project manager. Disregarding for the moment the problem that this guy will have in determining priorities, whom should he report to as to the status of his work? Obviously, he can't report to the director of project management.

Hood: I think the solution must be that all project managers report to one person. Therefore, even if the project stays in one functional department, we'll still have to assign a project manager. Under project management organizational forms, functional managers become synonymous with resource managers. It is very dangerous to permit a resource manager to act also as a project manager. The resource manager might consider his project as being so important that he'll commit all of his best people to it and make it into success at the expense of all of the other projects. That would be like winning the battle but losing the war.

Dallas: You realize that we'll need to revamp our wage and salary administration program if we go to project management. Evaluating project managers might prove difficult. Regardless of what policies we establish, there are still going to be project managers who try to build empires thinking that their progress is dependent upon the number of people they control. Project management will definitely give some people the opportunity to build an empire. We'll have to watch that closely.

Hood: Ray, I'm a little worried that we might not be able to get good project managers. We can't compete with the salaries the project managers get in other industries such as engineering, construction, or computers. Project management cannot be successful unless we have good managers at the controls. What's your feeling on this?

Dallas: We'll have to promote from within. That's the only viable solution. If we try to make project management salaries overly attractive, we'll end up throwing the organization into chaos. We must maintain an adequate salary structure so that people feel that they have the same opportunities in both project management and the functional organization. Of course, we'll still have some people who will be more title-oriented than money-oriented. But at least each person will have the same opportunity for salary advancement.

Hood: See if you can get some information from our personnel people on how we could modify our salary structure and what salary levels we can pay our project managers. Also, check with other banks and see what they're paying their project managers. I don't want to go into this blind and then find out that we're setting the trend for project management salaries. Everyone would hate us. I'd rather be a follower than a leader in this regard.

CASE STUDY: MIS PROJECT MANAGEMENT AT FIRST NATIONAL BANK

During the last five years, First National Bank (FNB) has been one of the fastest-growing banks in the Midwest. The holding company of the bank has been actively involved in purchasing small banks throughout the state of Ohio. This expansion and the resulting increase of operations has been attended by considerable growth in numbers of employees and in the complexity of the organizational structure. In 5 years the staff of the bank has increased by 35 percent and total assets have grown by 70 percent. FNB management is eagerly looking forward to a change in the Ohio banking laws that will allow statewide branch banking.

ISD History

Data processing at FNB has grown at a much faster pace than the rest of the bank. The systems and programming staff grew from twelve in 1970 to over seventy-five during the first part of 1977. Because of several future projects, the staff is expected to increase by 50 percent during the next two years.

Prior to 1972, the information services department reported to the executive vice-president of the Consumer Banking and Operations Division. As a result, the first banking applications to be computerized were in the demand deposit, savings, and consumer credit banking areas. The computer was seen as a tool to speed up the processing of consumer transactions. Little effort was expended to meet the informational requirements of the rest of the bank. This caused a high-level conflict, since each major operating organization of the bank did not have equal access to systems and programming resources. The management of FNB became increasingly aware of the benefits that could accrue from a realignment of the bank's organization into one that would be better attuned to the total information requirements of the corporation.

In 1972 the Information Services Division (ISD) was created. ISD was removed from the Consumer Banking Operations Division to become a separate division reporting directly to the president. An organization chart depicting the Information Services Division is shown in Exhibit 3-8.

Priorities Committee

During 1972 the Priorities Committee was formed. It consists of the chief executive officer of each of the major operating organizations whose activities are directly affected by the need for new or revised information systems. The Priorities Committee was established to insure that the resources of systems and

Exhibit 3-8. Information Services Division Organization Chart.

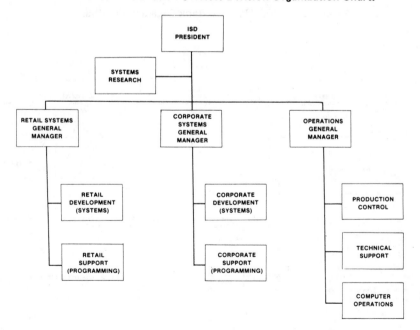

programming personnel and computer hardware would be used only on those information systems that can best be cost justified. Divisions represented on the committee are included in Exhibit 3-9.

The Priorities Committee meets monthly to reaffirm previously set priorities and rank new projects introduced since the last meeting. Bank policy states that the only way to obtain funds for an information development project is to submit a request to the Priorities Committee and have it approved and ranked in overall priority order for the bank. Placing potential projects in ranked sequence is done by the senior executives. The primary document used for Priorities Committee review is called the project proposal.

The Project Proposal Life Cycle

When a user department determines a need for the development or enhancement of an information system, it is required to prepare a draft containing a statement of the problem from its functional perspective. The problem statement is sent to the president of ISD who authorizes systems research (see Exhibit 3-8) to prepare an impact statement. This impact statement will include a general overview from ISD's perspective of:

- Project feasibility
- Project complexity
- Conformity with long-range ISD plans
- Estimated ISD resource commitment

Exhibit 3-9. First National Bank Organization Chart.

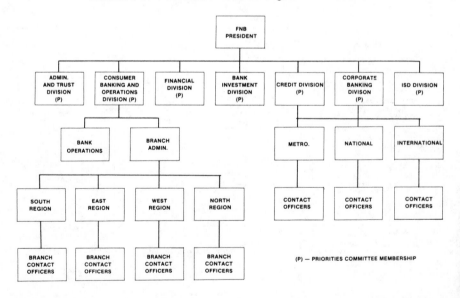

(P) — PRIORITIES COMMITTEE MEMBERSHIP

- Review of similar requests
- Unique characteristics/problems
- Broad estimate of total costs.

The problem and impact statements are then presented to the members of the Priorities Committee for their review. The proposals are preliminary in nature, but they permit the broad concept (with a very approximate cost attached to it) to be reviewed by the executive group to see if there is serious interest in pursuing the idea. If the interest level of the committee is low, then the idea is rejected. However, if the Priorities Committee feel the concept has merit, they authorize the systems research group of ISD to prepare a full-scale project proposal which contains:

- A detailed statement of the problem
- Identification of alternative solutions
- Impact of request on:
  - User division
  - ISD
  - Other operating divisions
- Estimated costs of solutions
- Schedule of approximate task duration
- Cost/benefit analysis of solutions
- Long-range implications
- Recommended course of action

After the project proposal is prepared by systems research, the user sponsor must review the proposal and appear at the next Priorities Committee meeting to speak in favor of the approval and priority level of the proposed work. The project proposal is evaluated by the committee and either dropped, tabled for further review, or assigned a priority relative to ongoing projects and available resources.

The final output of a Priorities Committee meeting is an updated list of project proposals in priority order with an accompanying milestone schedule that indicates the approximate time span required to implement each of the proposed projects.

The net result of this process is that the priority setting for systems development is done by a cross-section of executive management; it does not revert by default to data processing management. Priority setting, if done by data processing, can lead to misunderstanding and dissatisfaction by sponsors of the projects that did not get ranked high enough to be funded in the near future. The project proposal cycle at FNB is included in Exhibit 3-10. Once a project has risen to the top of the ranked priority list, it is assigned to the appropriate systems group for systems definition, system design and development, and system implementation.

The time spent by systems research in producing impact statements and project proposals is considered to be overhead by ISD. No systems research time is directly charged to the development of information systems.

Project Life Cycle

As noted before, the systems and programming staff of ISD has increased in
size rapidly and is expected to expand 50 percent during the next two years. As
a rule, most new employees have previous data processing experience and training in various systems methodologies. ISD management recently implemented a

Exhibit 3-10. The Project Proposal Cycle

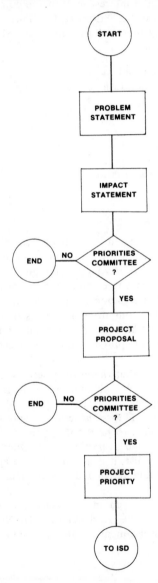

project management system which was dedicated to providing a uniform step-by-step methodology for the development of management information systems. All project work is covered by tasks that make up the information project development life cycle at FNB. The subphases used by ISD in the project life cycle are:

1. Systems Definition
   a. Project plan
   b. User requirements
   c. Systems definition
   d. Advisability study
2. Systems Design and Development
   a. Preliminary systems design
   b. Subsystems design
   c. Program design
   d. Programming and testing
3. System Implementation
   a. System implementation
   b. System test
   c. Production control turnover
   d. User training
   e. System acceptance

Project Estimating

The project management system contains a list of all normal tasks and subtasks (over 400) to be performed during the life cycle of a development project. The project manager must examine all the tasks to determine if they apply to his project. He must insert additional tasks if required and delete tasks that do not apply. The project manager next estimates the amount of time (in hours) to complete each task of each subphase of the project life cycle.

The estimating process of the project management system uses a "moving window" concept. ISD management feels that detailed cost estimating and time schedules are only meaningful for the next subphase of a project, where the visibility of the tasks to be performed is quite clear. Beyond that subphase, a more summary method of estimating is relied upon. As the project progresses, new segments of the project gain visibility. Detailed estimates are made for the next major portion of the project, and summary estimates are done beyond that until the end of the project.

Estimates are performed at five intervals during the project life cycle. When the project is first initiated, the funding is based on the original estimates, which are derived from the list of normal tasks and subtasks. At this time, the subphases through the advisability study are estimated in detail, and summary estimates are prepared for the rest of the tasks in the project. Once the project has progressed through the advisability study, the preliminary systems design is estimated in detail, and the balance of the project is estimated in a more summary fashion. Estimates are conducted in this manner until the systems implementation plan is completed and the scope of the remaining subphases of the project is known. This multiple estimating process is used because it is almost impossible at the beginning of many projects to be certain of what the magnitude of effort will be later on in the project life cycle.

Funding of Projects

The project plan is the official document for securing funding from the sponsor in the user organization. The project plan must be completed and approved by the project manager before activity can begin on the user requirements sub-phase (1b). An initial stage in developing a project plan includes the drawing of a network that identifies each of the tasks to be done in the appropriate sequence for their execution. The project plan must include a milestone schedule, a cost estimate, and a budget request. It is submitted to the appropriate general manager of systems and programming for review so that an understanding can be reached of how the estimates were prepared and why the costs and schedules are as shown. At this time the general manager can get an idea of the quantity of systems and programming resources required by the project. The general manager next sets up a meeting with the project manager and the user sponsor to review the project plan and obtain funding from the user organization.

The initial project funding is based on an estimate that includes a number of assumptions concerning the scope of the project. Once certain key milestones in the project have been achieved, the visibility on the balance of the project becomes much clearer and reestimates are performed. The reestimates may result in refunding if there has been a significant change in the project. The normal milestone refunding points are as follows:

1. After the advisability study (1d)
2. After the preliminary systems design (2a)
3. After the program design (2c)
4. After system implementation (3a)

The refunding process is similar to the initial funding with the exception that progress information is presented on the status of the work and reasons are given to explain deviations from project expenditure projections. A revised project plan is prepared for each milestone refunding meeting.

During the systems design and development stage, design freezes are issued by the project manager to users announcing that no additional changes will be accepted to the project beyond that point. The presence of these design freezes are outlined at the beginning of the project. Following the design freeze, no additional changes will be accepted unless the project is reestimated at a new level and approved by the user sponsor.

System Quality Reviews

The key element in insuring user involvement in the new system is the conducting of quality reviews. In the normal system cycles at FNB, there are ten quality reviews, seven of which are participated in jointly by users and data processing personnel, and three of which are technical reviews by data processing personnel only. An important side benefit of this review process is that users of a new system are forced to become involved in and are permitted to make a contribution to the systems design.

Each of the quality review points coincides with the end of a subphase in the project life cycle. The review must be held at the completion of one subphase to obtain authorization to begin work on the tasks of the next subphase of the project.

All tasks and subtasks assigned to members of the project team should end in some "deliverable" for the project documentation. The first step in conducting a quality review is to assemble the documentation produced during the subphase for distribution to the Quality Review Board. The Quality Review Board consists of between two and eight people who are appointed by the project manager with the approval of the project sponsor and the general manager of systems and programming. The minutes of the quality review meeting are written either to express "concurrence" with the subsystem quality or to recommend changes to the system that must be completed before the next subphase can be started. By this process the system is fine-tuned to the requirements of the members of the review group at the end of each subphase in the system. The members of the Quality Review Board charge their time to the project budget.

Quality review points and review board make-up are as follows:

Review	*Review Board*
User requirements	User oriented
Systems definition	User oriented
Advisability study	User oriented
Preliminary systems design	User oriented
Subsystems design	Users and D.P.
Program design	D.P.
Programming and testing	D.P.
System implementation	User oriented
System test	User oriented
Production control turnover	D.P.

To summarize, the quality review evaluates the quality of project subphase results, including design adequacy and proof of accomplishment in meeting project objectives. The review board authorizes work to progress based upon their detailed knowledge that all required tasks and subtasks of each suphase have been successfully completed and documented.

Project Team Staffing

Once a project has risen to the top of the priority list, the appropriate manager of systems development appoints a project manager from his staff of analysts. The project manager has a short time to review the project proposal created by systems research before developing a project plan. The project plan must be approved by the general manager of systems and programming and the user sponsor before the project can be funded and work started on the user requirements subphase.

The project manager is "free" to spend as much time as required in reviewing the project proposal and creating the project plan; however, his time is "charged" to the project at a rate of $26 per hour. The project manager must negotiate with his "supervisor," the manager of systems development, to obtain the required systems analysts for the project, starting with the user requirements subphase. The project manager must obtain programming resources from the manager of systems support. Schedule delays caused by a lack of systems or programming resources are to be communicated to the general manager by the project manager. All ISD personnel working on a project charge their time at a rate of $26 per hour. All computer time is billed at a rate of $64 per hour.

There are no user personnel on the project team; all team members are from ISD.

Corporate Data Base

John Hart had for several years seen the need to use the computer to support the corporate marketing effort of the bank. Despite the fact that the majority of the bank's profits were from corporate customers, most information systems effort was directed at speeding up transactions handling for small unprofitable accounts.

Mr. Hart had extensive experience in the Corporate Banking Division of the bank. He realized the need to consolidate information about corporate customers from many areas of the bank into one "corporate data base." From this information corporate banking services could be developed to not only better serve the corporate customers, but also to contribute heavily to the profit structure of the bank through repricing of services.

The absence of a corporate data base meant that no one individual knew what total banking services a corporate customer was using, because corporate services are provided by many banking departments. It was also impossible to determine how profitable a corporate customer was to the bank. Contact officers did not have regularly scheduled calls. They serviced corporate customers almost on a hit-and-miss basis. Unfortunately, many customers were "sold" on a service because they walked in the door and requested it. Mr. Hart felt that there was a vast market of untapped corporate customers in Ohio who would purchase services from the bank if they were contacted and "sold" in a professional manner. A corporate data base could be used to develop corporate profiles to help contact officers sell likely services to corporations.

Mr. Hart knew that data about corporate customers were being processed in many departments of the bank, but mainly in the following divisions.

- Corporate Banking
- Corporate Trust
- Consumer Banking

He also realized that much of the information was processed in manual systems, some was processed by time-sharing at various vendors, and other information was computerized in many internal information systems.

The upper management of FNB must have agreed with Mr. Hart because in December of 1976, the Corporate Marketing Division was formed with John Hart as its executive vice-president. Mr. Hart was due to retire within the year but was honored to be selected for the new position. He agreed to stay with the bank until "his" new system was "off the ground." He immediately composed a problem statement and sent it to the ISD. Systems research compiled a preliminary impact statement. At the next Priorities Committee meeting, a project proposal was authorized to be done by systems research.

The project proposal was completed by systems research in record time. Most information was obtained from Mr. Hart. He had been thinking about the systems requirements for years and possessed vast experience in almost all areas of the bank. Other user divisions and departments were often "too busy" when approached for information. A common reply to a request for information was "the project is John's baby; he knows what we need."

The project proposal as prepared by systems research recommended the following:

- Interfaces should be designed to extract information from existing computerized systems for the corporate data base (CDB).
- Time-sharing systems should be brought in-house to be interfaced with the CDB.
- Information should be collected from manual systems to be integrated into the CDB on a temporary basis.
- Manual systems should be consolidated and computerized, potentially causing a reorganization of some departments.
- Information analysis and flow for all departments and divisions having contact with corporate customers should be coordinated by the Corporate Marketing Division.
- All corporate data base analysis should be done by the Corporate Marketing Division staff, using either a user-controlled report writer or interactive inquiry.

The project proposal was presented at the next Priorities Committee meeting where it was approved and rated as the highest-priority MIS development project in the bank. Mr. Hart became the user sponsor for the CDB project.

The project proposal was sent to the manager of corporate development who appointed Jim Gunn as project manager from the staff of analysts in corporate development. Jim Gunn was the most experienced project manager available. His prior experience consisted of successful projects in the Financial Division of the bank.

Jim reviewed the project proposal and started to work on his project plan. He was aware that the corporate analyst group was presently understaffed but was assured by his manager, the manager of corporate development, that resources would be available for the user requirements subphase. He had many questions concerning the scope of the project and the interrelationship between the Corporate Marketing Division and the other users of corporate marketing data. But each meeting with Mr. Hart ended with the same comment: "This is a waste of time. I've already been over this with systems research. Let's get moving." Jim also was receiving pressure from the general manager to "hurry up" with the project plan. Jim therefore quickly prepared his project plan which included a general milestone schedule for subphase completion, a general cost estimate, and a request for funding. The project plan was reviewed by the general manager and signed by Mr. Hart.

Jim Gunn anticipated the need to have four analysts assigned to the project and went to his manager to see who was available. He was told that two junior analysts were available now and another analyst should be free next week. No senior analysts were available. Jim notified the general manager that the CDB schedule would probably be delayed because of a lack of resources, but received no response.

Jim assigned tasks to the members of the team and explained the assignments and the schedule. Since the project was understaffed, Jim assigned a heavy load of tasks to himself.

During the next two weeks the majority of the meetings set up to document user requirements were cancelled by the user departments. Jim notified Mr. Hart of the problem and was assured that steps would be taken to correct the problem. Future meetings with the users in the Consumer Banking and Corporate Banking Divisions became very hostile. Jim soon discovered that many individuals in these divisions did not see the need for the corporate data base. They resented spending their time in meetings documenting the CDB requirements. They were afraid that the CDB project would lead to a shift of many of their responsibilities and functions to the Corporate Marketing Division.

Mr. Hart was also unhappy. The CDB team was spending more time than was budgeted in documenting user requirements. If this trend continued, a revised budget would have to be submitted to the Priorities Committee for approval. He was also growing tired of ordering individuals in the user departments to keep appointments with the CDB team. Mr. Hart could not understand the resistance to his project.

Jim Gunn kept trying to obtain analysts for his project but was told by his manager that none were available. Jim explained that the quality of work done by the junior analysts was not "up to par" due to lack of experience. Jim complained that he could not adequately supervise the work quality because he was forced to complete many of the analysis tasks himself. He also noted that the quality review of the user requirements subphase was scheduled for next month, making it extremely critical that experienced analysts be assigned to the project. No new personnel were assigned to the project. Jim thought about contacting the general manager again to explain his need for more experienced analysts, but did not. He was due for a semi-yearly evaluation from his manager in two weeks.

Even though he knew the quality of the work was below standards, Jim was determined to get the project done on schedule with the resources available to him. He drove both himself and the team very hard during the next few weeks. The quality review of the user requirements subphase was held on schedule. Over 90 percent of the assigned tasks had to be redone before the Quality Review Board would sign-off on the review. Jim Gunn was "removed" as project manager.

Three senior analysts and a new project manager were assigned to the CDB project. The project received additional funding from the Priorities Committee. The user requirements subphase was completely redone despite vigorous protests from the Consumer Banking and Corporate Banking Divisions.

Within the next three months the following events happened:

- The new project manager resigned to accept a position with another firm.
- John Hart took early retirement.
- The CDB project was "tabled."

CASE STUDY: ON-LINE CONVERSION PROJECT

"I can't believe this! Before the project started, I knew exactly what my role was in the bank. Now, I don't even know if I am going to have a job or not. I worked hard on this project, and this is the thanks I get. Getting involved with this project is the biggest mistake I have ever made. I didn't even want this job to begin with. I'd sure like to tell them what they can do with their stupid project."

History

George Campbell has worked for State National Bank ever since he graduated from high school in 1957. He started as a teller, since he was not qualified for the management training program. During the years, he progressed to the position of head teller and eventually was promoted to the new accounts desk. George decided to attend college part-time at night and eventually earned his bachelor's degree.

George was placed in the management training program in 1962 and became a branch manager in 1966. George became known throughout the bank as a very meticulous worker. It was also known that he did not enjoy working with other people nor did he like responsibility.

State National Bank was one of the largest banks in Ohio. The parent bank (headquartered in Cleveland) employed about 2,000 people. The holding company, of which State National Bank was the lead bank, employed about 3,800 people throughout the state of Ohio. State National Bank started operations shortly before the Civil War and had always been very profitable.

State National Bank had always emphasized customer relations in all marketing and policy-making decisions. Management knew that the only real distinctions between the various branches was that of the staff make-up, since the branches all offered the same services. This policy was especially emphasized in the hiring decisions made in the employment office.

The bank had always used a traditional form of organizational structure, since it had proved successful. The sixty branches were responsible to branch administration located in the main office. Branch administration was responsible for decision making, staffing, and other needs of the branches. Each branch was considered to be its own profit center and was held responsible for any exceptions or losses that might occur. Exhibit 3-11 shows the organizational structure for the branch system.

Each branch consisted of a manager, one to three administrative personnel, a secretary, and from four to twelve tellers. The tellers worked various hours since they consisted of full-time, part-time, lunch-time, and Monday/Friday-only workers.

The competition between the various banks increased dramatically since the early 1970s. There were five major banks with over 230 branches in Cleveland in 1975. The market share of State National Bank had decreased slightly for the first time in 1975.

In addition, check-cashing losses and teller shortages had also reached an all-time high in 1975. The check-cashing losses and teller shortages had risen to over $250,000, as opposed to $175,000 in 1974. The branch system was being taken advantage of because of the delays in posting checks to a customer's account. An individual could cash a fraudulent check at one or more branches in one afternoon alone, and the bank would not be aware of this occurring until the next day.

Another problem was also a direct result of the check-cashing losses and teller shortages. Tellers overreacted and became too cautious when cashing checks. Customer complaints had been increasing due to the strict check-cashing policies and the longer waiting periods in line.

In January 1976, branch administration felt that they were forced to make a decision to overcome the problems. They decided at that time to approach senior management for funds to finance a complete conversion of all branches to an on-line computer system. Senior management decided to implement the on-line computer program as an attempt to increase their market share, reduce losses, and improve customer relations.

Establishing the Project Team

In February 1976, branch administration started the implementation of the on-line conversion by establishing a project team to plan the change. Branch administration decided to use a project management organizational structure for the conversion because of the uniqueness of the situation. Branch administration had heard many positive things about this form of management structure and decided to give it a try. The project team consisted of nine individuals:

One individual from the branch system
One individual from branch administration
One individual from the audit department
Two individuals from computer systems
One individual from the training department
One individual from the checking accounts department
One individual from the savings accounts department
One individual, the project leader, from branch operations and formerly from the branches

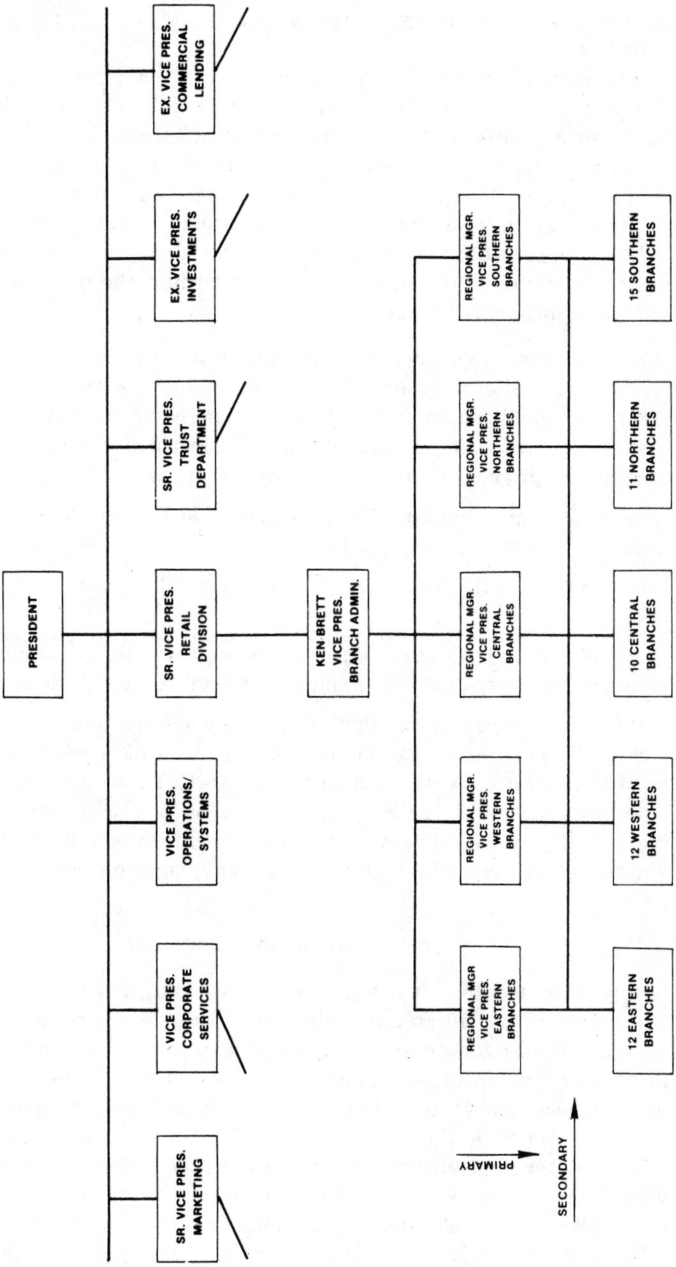

Exhibit 3-11.

PRESIDENT

SR. VICE PRES. MARKETING

VICE PRES. CORPORATE SERVICES

VICE PRES. OPERATIONS/ SYSTEMS

SR. VICE PRES. RETAIL DIVISION

SR. VICE PRES. TRUST DEPARTMENT

EX. VICE PRES. INVESTMENTS

EX. VICE PRES. COMMERCIAL LENDING

KEN BRETT VICE PRES. BRANCH ADMIN.

REGIONAL MGR VICE PRES. EASTERN BRANCHES

REGIONAL MGR. VICE PRES. WESTERN BRANCHES

REGIONAL MGR. VICE PRES. CENTRAL BRANCHES

REGIONAL MGR. VICE PRES. NORTHERN BRANCHES

REGIONAL MGR. VICE PRES. SOUTHERN BRANCHES

12 EASTERN BRANCHES

12 WESTERN BRANCHES

10 CENTRAL BRANCHES

11 NORTHERN BRANCHES

15 SOUTHERN BRANCHES

PRIMARY

SECONDARY

Exhibit 3-12 presents the organizational chart, titles, and locations of these individuals.

The project leader, George Campbell, had spent eight years in the branch system as a manager prior to this assignment in branch operations. George had asked for a transfer out of the branch system because of the extreme amount of pressure placed on him. George had spent the last two years updating branch operating procedures in compliance with departmental requests and other changes.

The selection of George Campbell as project leader was sudden and came as quite a surprise to him. The day after senior management had decided to implement the on-line program, George was called into the office of Ken Brett, vice-president in charge of branch administration.

Brett: George, as you may know, we have received approval to implement the on-line conversion program. We feel the on-line conversion has great potential for the branch system in the future. Because of the need to work with the branches, I feel that you are the most qualified person in this department to head up the project. What do you think about that?

Campbell: I am honored to be considered, but I don't know if I can handle that task.

Brett: Why is that? You were always successful in your management endeavors in the past.

Campbell: I'm afraid that I don't know anything about computers! I wouldn't even know how to plug one in, much less lead a group in the conversion process!

Brett: Don't worry about that. I'm sure you'll be able to pick up all of the technical aspects as you go along. In addition, I have selected a good group of people for you to work with in this project. They can help you consider all aspects of the change to make the conversion as easy as possible. Besides, you know that you can always come to me if you have any problems. Why don't you try it? I'm sure that you won't have any major problems.

Planning the Conversion

George accepted the challenge, because he really felt he had little choice. His first step was to plan an initial strategy meeting with his team workers. He also viewed this as a good opportunity to get to know the members better as he only knew two individuals, the branch manager and the training instructor. George had set the second Monday in February as the initial meeting date.

As the time for the meeting grew near, George was worried about what to discuss at the first meeting. He really did not have any information to discuss with the team members, nor did he have any ideas for the conceptual framework of the plan. George decided to just "play it by ear" for the first meeting.

At the first meeting, George was quite concerned since three of the team workers did not show up. He had the following conversation with Sam Lucas (audit department):

Campbell: Sam, why aren't you here for the meeting?

Exhibit 3-12.

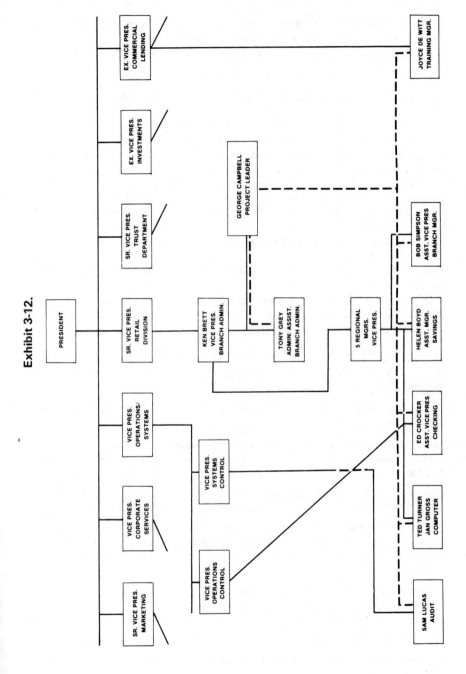

Lucas: I'm sorry Mr. Campbell, but I am simply too busy in my own depart-ment to attend any meeting for a project that I really don't have time to get involved with. Maybe I'll try to attend the next meeting.

Campbell: I understand. Please try to be at the next meeting.

George's conversation with the other two absent team works was similar in nature.

The meeting itself lasted only ten minutes, and no decisions were made. As a matter of fact, very little discussion took place at all. Since the meeting was going nowhere, George adjourned the meeting and set the next date for the be-ginning of March.

During the next few weeks, George spent a great deal of his time at the library researching the concept of project management. He learned of the importance of planning, the need to communicate, and the importance of motivating people. George made it a point to learn of the computer requirements of the checking and savings account departments so that the system would be practical and useful. He contacted various computer vendors to arrange for tours and demon-strations for the group. All in all, George spent a lot of time "doing his home-work."

As the time for the second meeting grew nearer, George made it a point to organize an agenda so that the meeting time could be best utilized. He then wrote a simple memo to his team workers as follows:

Subject: Organizational Meeting for On-Line Conversion Project

Message: Your attendance at this meeting would be appreciated. We have many items to discuss.

The day before the meeting, George received a phone call from Sam Lucas of the Audit Department.

Lucas: Mr. Campbell, I first wanted to call you in advance and tell you that I won't be able to make it tomorrow. My boss wants me to finish up a report for him first. After all, he's the one who pays my salary, not you!

Campbell: Sam, I really can't allow you to miss another meeting. I have a lot of material to present, and we should all get started in this project at once.

Lucas: What's the matter with you? Don't you understand? I have more im-portant things to do than to attend your silly meeting. Anyway, I probably wouldn't miss much if it is anything like the last meeting. I heard that it was a waste of time!

Campbell: I'm sorry that you feel that way. I wasn't very well organized at that time, and it probably was a waste of time. If you are not interested in working on the project, perhaps I can find someone who will want to participate.

Lucas: The project sounds interesting. It's just that, well . . . .

Campbell: What is the problem? Is the project creating a conflict between you and your boss?

Lucas: Yes. I can't serve two bosses. Anyway, I'm up for a promotion in this department soon, and I don't want to blow the opportunity. I hope you understand. It's nothing personal.

Campbell: I see the problem, and I'll arrange to get a replacement for you.

Later that afternoon, George arranged a meeting with Ken Brett. George wanted a meeting set up between themselves and the various functional department managers involved. George demanded that certain guidelines be established in order to get full participation of the team members. These guidelines included future promotions, responsibility, reporting relationships, evaluations, and many other factors. At the end of the meeting, Ken remarked: "When I selected you as project leader, I had no idea you would be this interested in details!"

Selecting a Vendor

Subsequent planning between George and the team members was done in great detail. Their initial goals were to select a vendor by July 1976, have the computer programs prepared by January 1977, and have the first branch converted to on-line by July 1977. The master plan and program schedules worked out were quite detailed in nature and seemed to include just about everything imaginable.

Meetings in April and May 1976 went smoothly, and George seemed to have the full cooperation of his team members. Tours in eight different cities were arranged with the vendors to see their computer equipment in action at other commercial banks. The team members developed a series of standardized questions to be asked at the various locations so that comparisons could be made. Since only the project leader and one other team member would visit all the locations, it was agreed by the group to rely heavily on their opinions and the results of their questionnaires.

All of the visits and demonstrations were finished by mid-June. The project team chose three vendors to ask for bids based on the data gathered by George and his assistant. After the bids were received, George summarized the data he collected with the bid amounts and prepared the following memo:

Subject: Analysis of Vendors
Message: The following memo includes the bids received and my general comments concerning the vendors.

IMB Co.—Bid:	$2,890,000
Comments:	Slowest response time of the three vendors. More accurate and less downtime with this equipment.
Zero Inc.—Bid:	$3,100,000
Comments:	Fastest response time. Able to handle more programs than the other equipment. Repairs could be a problem due to the location of the vendor.
Local Co., Inc.—Bid:	$1,800,000

Comments: Equipment is not as technically advanced as that of the
                         other vendors. Production of the equipment is irregular
                         due to a small demand. Vendor is located locally and
                         maintains a very satisfactory account relationship with
                         us.

After much discussion, the team decided to present senior management with
the following recommendations:

First choice: IMB Co.
Second choice: Zero Inc.
Third choice: Local Co., Inc.

The following morning, George was informed that senior management decided
to select Local Co., Inc. as the vendor because of the lower cost and the profitability of the account relationship. George was quite upset with the choice but
decided that the choice was made for "political," not practical reasons.

Teller Conversion Team

In July 1976, the team decided to recruit a teller conversion team that would
consist of twelve tellers. Initially, the teller conversion team would be used solely
to help prepare and test the training program. It was decided that they would
only consider applicants for the teller conversion team having three or more years
of experience. As an incentive, 5 percent premium pay plus mileage would be
offered to members of the team. The team workers felt that they would have no
difficulty in recruiting the conversion team.

The teller conversion team would spend two weeks with each branch prior
to on-line conversion. Each conversion member would train and assist the tellers
on an individual basis. Then, two days prior to the conversion, the branch tellers
would meet at the bank training center classroom. During this time, the tellers
would receive complete training for the on-line process. The conversion team
would cover for the tellers while they were out of the branch. Then, for two
weeks or more after the branch went on-line, a conversion staff member would
remain in the branch to give assistance.

By September 1976, there had been no applicants for the teller conversion
team. George Campbell was beginning to get worried. At the next group meeting, it was decided to lower the requirement for teller experience from three
years to six months and to increase the premium pay to 10 percent.

George also assigned the task of preparing the training manuals to Joyce DeWitt
of the training department and Tony Grey of branch administration. They were
expected to prepare two sets of training manuals: one set for the present employees and another more complete set for new employees. They were to have
the rough draft of these manuals completed by December 1976.

Meanwhile, problems were beginning to occur with obtaining the computers
and terminals from the vendor, Local Co., Inc. The vendor did not have a sufficient parts inventory on hand and could not manufacture the required number

of units needed. Even the possibility of receiving a single unit for testing before January 1977 seemed slim. George contacted the company on numerous occasions and stressed the need for a prototype in order to begin the program writing and conversion.

As of October, there were only six applicants for the teller conversion team. In reviewing the applications, George was disappointed in the performance records of the individuals as he felt they were far from adequate. George felt that the success of the entire program could be jeopardized if the make-up of this conversion team did not improve. After consulting Ken Brett regarding this matter, George was told not to worry about the conversion team.

At the meeting held in December 1976, George learned of the following developments:

First, Local Co., Inc. still had not delivered any equipment. This meant that work on the programming could never be completed as they had originally planned for January 1977.

Second, the manual writing had been a complete failure. The manuscript produced at this point was far from adequate. The team decided to hire outside educational consultants to write the manuals. This would mean a large expense. George became even more upset when he was told the manuals would take at least four months to complete.

Third, the team conversion members had nothing to do in regard to the project. The conversion team had left their orginal branches and replacements were found. Branch administration was assigning them to fill in as tellers at branches that needed additional staffing. Most of these branches were located in "bad" sections of town. Branch administration also decided that since the conversion team members were not involved in the project, they would not receive the premium pay. Many of the conversion members quit since the temporary branch assignments seemed to be permanent.

In February 1977, Local Co., Inc. had only delivered two computer terminals and the related accessories. Production of the other terminals was questionable as some of the components required for the assembly of terminals were now obsolete and unavailable. The computer programmers predicted that it would take at least six months to prepare the programs for the conversion, with the first branch conversion to occur some time in 1978 (originally scheduled for July 1977).

Meanwhile, three of the team workers asked to be dismissed from the project. They did not want to be involved any longer in a losing cause. George had to settle for replacements who knew nothing concerning the project since they had been employed for a short period of time with the bank.

In March, George received an urgent phone call asking him to report immediately to Ken Brett's office. Ken started in at once:

"What have you done to this project? The bank has given you full support and cooperation, and you stabbed us in the back! The project is nowhere even close to being completed. Your team workers are quitting, the teller conversion team no longer exists, and you have wasted a lot of time and money. Check cashing losses were over $200,000 for the last six months of 1976 alone! If you had met the goal, that wouldn't have happened! Senior management is upset with me and it's all your fault! What do you have to say for yourself?"

CASE STUDY: CANADIAN MARCONI COMPANY: AVIONICS DIVISION[27]

On April 5, 1968, the employees of the Commercial Products Division (CPD) of Canadian Marconi Company in Montreal, Quebec were advised that the division would undergo a significant organizational change. On May 21, the division was officially reorganized. Many divisional units were rearranged and incorporated into the operations of the Avionics and Telecommunications Departments which, with the Central Manufacturing Department, had constituted the three line departments of the Commercial Products Division. CPD also contained two staff departments: Quality and Reliability Assurance, and Finance. The reorganization left Avionics and Telecommunications as more self-sufficient organizations. Avionics incorporated into itself some purchasing, manufacturing, and quality-control functions.

In concert with this reorganization, Mr. K.C.M. Glegg, general manager of the Avionics Department, posted an extensive notice (see Exhibit 3-13) describing further changes Avionics would undergo as it converted to a program management type of matrix organization structure. (Figure 1 of Exhibit 3-13 illustrates the basic top management structure of the department as it became with the matrix conversion, and as it was essentially to remain for the next six years.)

Some two years after the conversion Avionics reorganized again, but still within the framework of the same matrix design. The program management concept, designed around aerospace contracts with defined tasks and of known duration, was replaced by a product management concept. Product managers were made responsible for the long-term concern of a particular product line, or sometimes, a technology. Program managers, whose responsibility was generally for one product on one or more contracts, reported to the product managers.

In 1969 Avionics became a division and Mr. Glegg its vice-president. The division expanded rapidly as the economy in general and the aerospace industry in particular enjoyed the tail end of a long economic boom. Mid-1970 sales reached a peak of $36 million and employees numbered in excess of 2,000. Before 1970 was over, Avionics had begun to respond to the economic downturn that battered the entire North American aerospace industry. By early 1973 Avionics' personnel were down to less than 700 and sales were on the order of $10-12 million.

However, the future was again hopeful. The conversion to product management had fostered the development of many new products. Some already appeared to be certain winners while others had attractive potential. More significantly, the product management form of matrix design had been fully con-

---

27. "Copyright © 1974 by the President and Fellows of Harvard College. Reproduced by permission. This case was prepared by Harvey F. Kolodny under the supervision of Paul R. Lawrence."

solidated within the division and had been instrumental in developing many competent product managers and program managers. Mr. Glegg felt that Avionics had the managerial wherewithal to take complete advantage of the opportunities which the new products promised.

With the anticipated growth, Avionics' management was once again having to come to grips with some of the organizational design questions that successful new matrix organization innovation engendered.

Predeterminants of Change

Mr. Glegg had joined Canadian Marconi in 1948 with a master's degree in electronic engineering from McGill University. He had worked his way up through the technical arm of the organization to become chief engineer of the Avionics Department. He was a significant inventor and innovator in basic frequency modulated continuous wave (FM-CW) Doppler radar technology, and had assisted in the development and championed the application of this technology. As a result of this success, the Canadian Aeronautics and Space Institute had, in 1964, awarded him the McCurdy Award for outstanding contributions in the scientific and engineering field of aeronautics and space.

Doppler radar technology was used in airborne navigation equipment to determine aircraft velocity and distance by bouncing microwave signals off the terrain and calculating the desired parameters from the "Doppler effect" of returning signals. A typical Doppler system was composed of several "black boxes" of electronic and electromechanical equipment including a microwave antenna slung under the airplane or helicopter. (Doppler systems in the Avionics product line had selling prices ranging between $20,000 and $80,000 per system.) The FM-CW technology gave Avionics a world leadership position in Doppler radar navigation equipment design and production. Mr. Glegg continued to emphasize the essential role of innovative research and development in the department's future. In this technological environment, engineers and R & D-type engineers in particular, were both dominant and very high status personnel.

As the department grew and Avionics' success with Doppler systems brought large increases in sales, Mr. Glegg's preoccupations became considerably more managerial than technical. He began to reassess some of his own thinking about organizations. The CPD organization appeared too weak, both structurally and managerially, to cope with the increasing complexity of his own department's activities. One outcome of his reassessment was a consolidation of essential activities from CPD into Avionics and another was a willingness to plunge into the relatively unknown complications of a full-fledged matrix organization.

During the three years prior to the reorganization, Mr. Glegg had carried out an extensive personal program of reading in managerial and organizational literature. He had come to believe that a matrix type of organization could really work. Matrix organization designs had started to make themselves quite evident in the aerospace industry by the mid-1960s. As a consequence of his familiarity with the aerospace environment, plus the managerial and organizational literature he had been digesting, matrix designs stood out as a clear alternative for Mr. Glegg.

However, it was the specific problems of the Avionics Department that gave him and his subordinate managers the impetus to move into the organizational directions that they did follow.

Mr. Glegg was finding it impossible to cope with the number of major decisions that had to be made. Six major programs and several minor ones were in different stages of design and/or production. All had different customers, sometimes in different countries. Every program's product, although they were all Doppler radar systems, was significantly different from every other one, particularly along a technology dimension. Nevertheless the programs had to share manufacturing facilities, major items of capital equipment and specialized functions. Mr. Glegg felt he had to find some way to force the whole decision process down to some level below his own. He described in some of his thinking:

"Despite all the difficulties that we found ourselves in at the time, many of us could see that if we could succeed in managing the place effectively, we could (a) get out of the difficulty and (b) get into a phase of our existence that would involve still more products and the necessity for still more decisions of the kind that were required. In a sense, I guess what I started looking for was a way of basically making the system nonlinear; a way of decoupling the number of decisions that I would have to make from the number of involvements of the division. Eventually one has to decouple the one nervous system from this linear attachment to all the involvements. And the way you do it, is to put another nervous system between you and it."

Mr. Glegg identified the uniqueness of the task as one of the key factors determining the particular approach taken to matrix design (see Exhibit 3-13). He felt that in Avionics' type of business the task could be isolated cleanly and relatively simply. More important, however, was his feeling that the concept of task isolation was something that could be understood by all the people in the division. After extensive discussion with his subordinates, it was clearly decided that a matrix organization structure should be the general form toward which Avionics must move.

Corporate Management Unfreezing. . .

Convincing himself and his subordinate managers was one task for Mr. Glegg. Convincing corporate management was quite another. At that time Avionics was still one of several departments of the Commercial Products Division and was quite thoroughly integrated into the division's structure. Corporate management had to be persuaded to allow Avionics to incorporate within itself those parts of the Commercial Products Division which were necessary to insure that a matrix design could function effectively within the Avionics Department. Mr. Glegg related how this process of corporate adaptation took place.

"First of all, I had to get an agreement from corporate management that would allow me to implement such a scheme. There was a tremendous amount of opposition. People opposed it because one person would be reporting to two people, and 'no man can serve two masters.' There were people on the accounting side of the house saying, 'It's going to cost too much.' Obviously it's a much more expensive way of managing than the straight functional approach.

"You could break down the objections they were presenting into two general classes. One of them was the sort of semiphilosophical reason based on common sense notions of management and people. Those, in the end, you could overcome simply by talking enough. The practical objections such as, 'But it's going to cost more,' were more difficult. I guess the way I ended up putting that one out of the way was to say, 'Look, what you're telling me is that I'm going to end up with a system that is overmanaged. Now if you ask me, I can tell you what the cost is of this overmanagement. But now I have to ask you a question. What is the cost of undermanaging? I can give you a bounded cost for the overmanagement. That is, I can count up the pieces and multiply them by salaries and I can tell you what the cost of overmanagement is. I can give you an absolute upper bound. Now you tell me, what are the costs of undermanagement? Are they $100,000 a year? Are they $1 million a year? What are they?'

"Well, at the time we had so many of these problems on our hands, which, quite apart from any other reasons for the difficulty, had at their core the problem of undermanagement, that it was easy for me to illustrate that the number was, first of all, unbounded and, in fact, potentially almost catastrophic for us, for a company of this kind. So I got a kind of grudging understanding that I could go ahead and implement this thing. But that it had better work or both it and I would go."

. . .and Unfreezing Everyone Else

With grudging acceptance from corporate management, Mr. Glegg then went about selling matrix to the rest of his organization. A series of meetings for middle managers answered some of the immediate questions and an extensive notice distributed throughout the department was designed to inform the rest of the department members of the intended changes (Exhibit 3-13 contains significant aspects of this notice). However, Mr. Glegg was aware that neither notices nor speeches were the real answer. The people would have to see the system function to have faith in it. He described how he believed the process of acceptance took place for many in the department.

"When you go from an extremely conventional functional arrangement to this matrix kind of an arrangement, you disturb some of the relationships of people; you disturb some of the things they had come to believe would never in their lives be disturbed. People go from being important to being relatively not so important, and vice versa. And so you find people who, for various reasons, don't really want to support the change.

"So this took a very long time to do. It took the better part of two years to work through enough of the cases, so to speak, so that you would at least remove questions about whether it could work. People still question whether it works for them, and if a change has caused them to lose something or other, then it might not seem like it is. But at least over two years, if the thing works in some objective way for most of the people, they do realize it can work."

Establishing the Program Manager's Boundaries

With corporate support of and commitment to a matrix form of management, Mr. Glegg and his immediate level of subordinate managers, the department group managers (see Figure 1 of Exhibit 3-13), faced the decisions about the detailed structure of the organization form toward which they were now moving. In many matrix organizations the program manager reports directly to the organization's head: the department general manager or divisional vice-president. Hence, the first of these decisions involved the level of reporting. Should the program managers report to Mr. Glegg or should there be a level between him and the program managers? While it was evident that Mr. Glegg could have coped with the number of program managers initially envisioned, it was also evident that as their number grew he would be unable to manage both them and the functions. Mr. Glegg commented:

"That is reason number one and it might turn out to be the basic reason. But there is another aspect I think should be emphasized. That is, the program manager is the first level in the organization at which integration really occurs. It is the first level at which the company's business is conducted whole. That means that when he is not available, either because he's sick or traveling or something, that it is not practical to go down in the organization to replace him. You have to go up. There must be some place in the organization to find someone with the time to pinch-hit for him for weeks at a time. You can't find it going down. You have to arrange the organization in such a way that there is always a kind of program manager pinchhitter available about him, namely, his group manager."

Mr. Glegg foresaw that there would still be occasions when both a program manager and his group manager would be away at the same time. In that event, he himself would be forced to manage the program for possibly a week or two. However, since two absences had to coincide before it became his problem, he felt that was a tolerable range of possibilities to accept. The occasions when it did occur would, in fact, get him close enough to the territory of a program manager's job to keep him aware of the job dimensions without shouldering him with the program's problems on a continuing basis.

"That's the reason program managers were separated from me by one organizational level. That's not without its problems. First of all there is the question of the image that this person generates outside when he talks about where he reports in the organization. For various reasons, people on the outside would be happier if the program manager said he reported to the VP. This would imply that they are managed in a way that they are expressly not intended to be man-

aged. It implies that if he were closer to me that I would manage him more
tightly. The fact is, he is there precisely so I don't have to manage him more
tightly.

"Another thing they will say is that since functional managers who report
directly to me are organizationally one level above program managers, that as
a result of this the program manager cannot approach the functional manager
and handle resource questions in a businesslike way. That again supports an assumption about interactions in the organization that are not factual. I make
certain that they're not. It's easier for me to cope with the problem of how it
works than the day-to-day working of it. So I am at very, very great pains, and
initially this was quite a difficult thing to do, to make certain that functional
managers understand that, in a sense, the program managers are their seniors.
They are senior in the sense that they are responsible for the business whole, and
no functional manager is.

"This is also reflected in their salaries. Program managers, as a group, generally earn more than functional managers. In fact, the only group managers who
earn more than program managers are the three group managers to whom program managers report."

Linked to the question of the program manager's organizational level was a
definition of the program manager's boundaries. How much would he control
and, as a consequence, whom would he control? What problems would this
create for the conventional career patterns and reward systems that had been
established not only in Avionics but throughout the Commercial Products Division and throughout the entire company? Mr. Glegg went on to discuss the outcome of the discussions he had conducted with the group managers.

"We had to decide on the extent to which a program manager would control his
facilities, his resources. That is, what would a program manager be? We decided
on an arrangement that took us far over on the side where the program manager
controls everything. I was looking for a way of really containing the decisions.
The more we thought about it, the group managers and myself, the more we
decided that the worst thing we could do in trying to implement this would be
to get ourselves into one of those crazy self-fulfilling prophecy things where you
begin by telling the guy you really don't think he can manage it so you don't
give him very much and he proves that really and truly you were right.

"There are some problems with this kind of an arrangement and let me just
touch on one serious problem that comes from this; the question of how the
people who are attached to this guy, on an essentially temporary basis, get their
progress review done. That's a hard, practical question. The way it was resolved
was through a decision that the employee's progress review would be done
jointly by the program manager and his functional shop. That is, eventually
the person's progress review would have to be agreed on by these two units of
the organization. This was to insure that where, for instance, the person had
become so embedded in the program that his functional boss was no longer

able to evaluate his performance, the program manager would make certain that this was taken care of. It would also accommodate the situation where, as is sometimes the case in some phases of the work, the coupling back to the functional shop still tends to be tight. It seemed to us that it would be important to make certain that the people who were reporting in a sense to two people, felt that the two people were indeed contributing to the assessment of their performance. The reason I go off in that direction is because when you suggest a system that makes the people become actively connected to the program and, are in fact managed day-to-day by the program, the question is always asked: 'Who says how the person's working?' "

Selecting Program Managers

Engineers dominated the Avionics Division. Mr. Glegg himself and six of the eleven group managers held formal engineering degrees. In addition to the very large numbers of engineers within the formal engineering groups, many of the marketing and applications personnel were engineers and a substantial number of the senior personnel in the production and manufacturing areas held engineering degrees. Any consideration of the characteristics needed to be a program manager under the proposed matrix design had to face this issue of professional background squarely. It was one of the dominant considerations for Mr. Glegg.

"The next sort of question had to do with the kind of person we would select for a program manager. Apart from the usual qualities one wants in people, we added the additional requirement that the person be an engineer. Immediately after one does that, of course, and more particularly, immediately after I do that, the process becomes suspect. There's always at least one rumor around the place that I don't think anybody can do anything unless he's an engineer. Which is only partly true. The reason for wanting an engineer in that job, for starting with an engineer, is that in all this kind of work the most serious problems have at their root some technicality or other. The object was not to get an engineer and turn him into a program manager so he could solve the problem. The real object of starting with an engineer was to make certain that there was someone who could understand the problem and assess how he should commit his resources to the solution of the problem."

In deciding to select engineers as program managers, Avionics opted for choosing individuals they felt could order the problems a program manager was bound to encounter. Programs are resource-limited operations and some priority assignments have to be made for the host of problems that inevitably arise. Only a program manager technically competent to understand the problems could make such an allocation.

"This has some inherent difficulties—this notion that what you're going to do is retread an engineer. One of the things you have to do is help him to suppress this tendency to want to become his own project engineer. You must sit down with the program managers and talk about these aspects and help them to resolve them. Basically, what you have to do is help the project manager resign himself to the fact that he's no longer going to be an engineer, although he's still going to have to use what he knows about engineering. In effect, what you have to do is help him resign himself to the fact he's now going to run a new kind of risk in life. He's going to run the risk of the generalist. I guess it's easier to do a job, in some respects, as a specialist than as a generalist. What you have to induce these people to do, and help get them to enjoy doing, is deemphasize one set of skills and use their energies to develop some other skills they may not have yet.

"Of all the problems we have had with the conversion of engineers into program managers, that has been the most serious of all—the problem of inducing the person to avoid the pitfall of ending up just being his own project engineer. However, when you finally get to the point where this changeover has occurred, well you can recognize it in the person quite quickly. You can begin to see the way he talks about it, the angles from which he talks about it. And the problems that now loom large for him. You can begin to see that he is, in fact, undergoing this conversion.

"I guess what we were really interested in was the extent to which the person had given some indication that he was prepared to try to learn the game. That more than anything else. If we could put the person in a position where he could largely control his fate, that this would allow the man to grow in some way that would suit himself, and very likely suit all of us. And that's almost exactly what happened."

From Program Management to Product Management

The year 1970 brought an end to North America's economic boom, and the aerospace industry was about the hardest hit of all. Avionics' dependence on programs with fixed termination dates left the division in a very vulnerable position. In some cases, follow-on contracts didn't come. In others, cancellations took place—cancellations that left a lot of contractual matters to resolve, but also left design and production areas with little or no work. Avionics needed a different type of business to insure its survival. It needed products that would endure. It needed applications that went beyond only one narrowly defined program. It also needed an organization structure that would support such a strategy. Avionics' response was to change the program management form of matrix to a product management form. Mr. Glegg explained the difference.

"The product manager's object in life is almost exactly the opposite of the program manager's. The object of the product manager is to take an opportunity that he has and extend it as far into the future as he possibly can. It is to start with whatever it is we elect to start him with, an idea, a product, someone else's product, and make of it whatever he can make of it. The idea is to make it as big, and as extensive, and as long-lived, and, of course, as profitable and productive as he can make it.

"The goal of the program manager is to take a task that is well defined with respect to schedule, cost, and function, and execute it. The goal of a product manager is to take a much more nebulous set of variables and somehow combine them into ongoing business in a much more indefinite kind of sense. A program is really a special case of a product. A program represents a kind of singularity in the product where the intensity of management it needs simply requires that you attach one nervous system to it exclusively."

Once again Mr. Glegg and the group managers worked their way through decisions similar to the ones they had encountered with the first move to program management. Some program would continue and others would develop as specific outputs of a particular product management organization. A technology developed under a product manager would create single products with specific applications that could be handled as programs. However, this meant that program managers, by reporting to product managers, who reported to group managers, would be still one level lower in the organization. Customers who previously worried about the fact that their program was two levels down from the divisional vice-president would now find their program three levels down. Nevertheless Avionics' management remained convinced that programs had to report into their own particular functional shops where the expertise associated with their respective technologies resided. They were determined to proceed in this fashion and face any consequences that might develop.

Product management was officially introduced into Avionics in the spring of 1970 when Mr. Glegg assembled all the division's managers and supervisors together to discuss the change. In a procedure similar to that used when program management was first introduced, a series of general meetings were called with some sixty to eighty managers and supervisors in attendance. The intended changes were explained and questions and answers exchanged. This time Mr. Glegg was calling extensively on the two years' experiences Avionics had with program management to support the decisions he and the group managers had made. Neither management literature nor industry practice were of much assistance in this reorganization.

"So far as I can tell from the literature, there's a lot of experience with the program management idea, with the fixed time, fixed money, fixed outcome situation. There is much less experience with the product manager, of the type we have tried putting into existence. What we're finding, however, is that it's an extremely powerful way of getting motivation into the system, because what the product manager has become, in our context, is a kind of minigeneral manager."

Modifying the Control System

To support his intention of having product managers able to make most of their own decisions at their own organizational level, Mr. Glegg insisted that the accounting system reflect the organization design as much as possible. With the appropriate cost information and with profit and loss data available to them, program and product managers could contain decisions at their own level and had need to approach the group manager level on financial matters only when major capital demands were being placed on the division.

Program or product reporting was broken out by total sales and further subdivided by main equipment, manufactured spares, resale spares, ancillary equipment, and support to provide program and product managers with as much visibility as possible. (Since some projects were mature and had minimal development costs while others incurred heavy development expenditures, this particular statement cut off reporting at the gross margin level to allow for comparative analysis of programs and product lines.) Within each subarea, program and product managers could also determine individual charges by cost centers that represented the different functional activities.

A parallel system recorded functional area costs. Every direct charging employee had to be accounted for by a "legitimate" charge number so that only overhead people in the function could remain unassigned to a particular program. As a consequence, slack personnel in the functional areas were quickly identified by their charges to program or product numbers.

Program projections of needs from the functional cost centers were estimated in order to determine the individual function's direct charging budgets. Overhead (supervision, secretarial, depreciation, administration, etc.) was loaded into the direct costs to determine a function rate (per cost center) which the programs or products could then challenge. Hence, while direct charging personnel could be identified immediately, overhead (or indirect) personnel were built into the rate charged and could only really be challenged at annual budget time by challenging the rate structure.

One difficulty of the matrix system, from an accounting viewpoint, was the sharing and allocation of joint costs or of savings from scale economies. Avionics handled the problem on an exception basis via special ledger accounts. However, the process did create an additional workload for the division's controller.

For example, all material purchases were burdened with an 18 percent MPE (material procurement expense) to cover material management activities (purchasing, inventory control, shipping, receiving, etc.) However, some programs might use high-cost items such as electronic memories costing $7000 each for which the 18 percent add-on seemed unfair. Consequently, a "high value rate" of 8 percent was established for items exceeding $500. Or, in another example, volume discounts on computers purchased for use within several different products were significant enough to encourage joint purchases. In this case, the controller maintained a special ledger account to purchase the items for the division as a whole and allow the division to benefit from the discounts.

Communication and Openness

In the early stages of matrix implementation, few people in the organization understood matrix concepts fully. Others understood them hardly at all. Believing that effective and open communication was central to successful matrix implementation, Mr. Glegg went about creating an atmosphere to support his beliefs.

"One of the things we decided to do as the key way of insuring that the matrix scheme would work was to insure that functional shops always had the best possible grasp of what the task side of the house was likely to want. It looked to me at the time to be vital that all of the resource pieces of the organization have the longest possible view of what the demands on them would be if they were to offer the most help to the people who were going to need the resources.

"In order to do this I decided that we would have meetings every Friday. The people who attend these meetings are group managers in charge of resource functions and the group managers in charge of task groups. All the group managers and myself talk about all the problems in the division. At this point in time, I would say, the meetings are about as open, frank, relaxed, and productive as one could hope to find in any industrial organization. I honestly believe that at this point we trust one another, and, maybe what's even more important, they trust one another."

Mr. Glegg felt that these meetings lay at the core of successful management of the matrix structure. It was a mechanism whereby every part of the organization could question every other part and come to a better understanding of each other's contribution. Initially the meetings were held every Friday with the group managers holding subsequent meetings with their subordinates on the following Monday. In time, some of the second-level meetings disappeared.

After approximately two years, one meeting a month was expanded to include program and product managers in addition to the group managers. With the variety of experiences that was developing among the product and program managers, it was felt that they could begin to learn much from each other's problems, successes, and failures. [Some two years later, this particular meeting was expanded to include the second-level functional managers (those below the functional group managers) and a function-by-function critique of each of the areas had commenced.] Mr. Glegg described the contributions gained from adding the product and program managers to this communication process.

"This allows me to listen to what's coming back from a level below me, from one level removed. But more important, it allows these people to hear from one another. It allows them to understand that they all have problems, that they all have troubles. That they have trouble isn't necessarily a reflection that they're new, good or bad, or any such thing. It allows them to build a kind of confidence in themselves, drawn from the fact that they can hear about other people's experience in similar sets of circumstances. They can learn what some of the elements of possible solution in their case might be by listening to what another person is doing.

"They really learn. A good illustration is someone like Jim Stephan, who is an excellent program manager, but who has what, on the face of it, might sound like a leftover misery to cope with, namely termination negotiations. The contract on his program was terminated and he has had to negotiate the termination phase of this work. This has turned out to be an extremely difficult thing to do because large sums of money are involved and good negotiation is vital. It's important for some of these other people to listen to some of the things he says are useful to do in the ongoing work, so that in a termination situation, they will know which negotiation position is best. I would say, in this instance, he is the best teacher we have in the house.

"I don't have regular meetings with product managers about product "things"—about their products in general. But when certain developments occur inside the product group, I often set up weekly meetings with them. These meetings are attended by people far down in the organization—manufacturing, product engineering, materials controls clerk, etc. There's no rule about whether these things will or will not occur. I use my own discretion with respect to the need for them. Generally, if the product manager is about to make resource demands, I need to know what he is doing in order to support him. The picture I get out of these meetings is a reasonably good one.

"I'm tending to get the impression that the communication propagation down through the product manager is more effective than through the functional shop. I believe that the close-knittedness of the organization on that side makes for easier communication than on the functional side where we've tended to disconnect the people, in a day-to-day sense, from the functional shop.

"The business of holding this clearly delicate "net" together is the most challenging part of what is now my work. The most powerful tool that one has in doing it, and it is really simple in a way, is openness. I don't have any secrets at all. Anything they want to know I'll tell them. Furthermore, it's easier for me to know things now, with a lot more activity going on, than it was even two years ago. I don't have to go after information. People come in and tell me things they think I should know. In fact, they'll come in and tell me things in the presence of whoever else is in the room, since we've no more secrets in the division.

"Generally, if someone thinks that there's something that you ought to know, regardless of what it is, he'll tell you. There's nothing that I can think of that anyone here would be afraid to come in and tell me. And to judge by some of the things they tell me, they must feel reasonably relaxed about it; including tremendous challenges, on occasion, with respect to various decisions and actions that they've taken, etc."

Maintaining the Product/Program vs Function Balance

As a final comment Mr. Glegg talked about the problems of trying to put the appropriate degree of importance on the product side vs the functional side; of achieving the "right" balance between the two sides of the organization.

"That was a very hard part of living with group managers early in the program. What I had to say to these people who report directly to me was that the people at the next level were, in a sense, organizationally more in control than they were. It was hard to do initially. The business of a functional manager deriving satisfaction from such a system is a very complicated one. To the extent that an operation like this one sees its outcome in terms of tasks, it's very difficult, at first, for a functional manager to identify with success in this way. It's difficult for him to find a way to achieve success because the organization is so structured that its main success indicator is attached to tasks and not the function.

"So he has to derive his pleasure in vicarious ways, and get his satisfaction 'sideways.' It turns out that they have learned to do that largely by identifying with me, because we sit here very often on Fridays and derive a great deal of satisfaction from the fact that these people are functioning effectively.

"At first it was a very, very difficult thing to do. And frustrating for them. This would often lead to impasses between program managers and functional managers since the functional manager would see his so-called prerogatives challenged. The program manager will come into the procurement shop, for instance, and say to Ken Winton, who is in charge of procurement, 'I don't like the way you're buying my stuff.' Needless to say he'll say, 'Look, I'm buying it better than you could.' And the program manager will say, 'Well, I'll show you. Just give me two people out of your shop and I'll attach them to the program and I'll buy it myself.'

"Well, we have gone from that unhappy state of affairs to the situation where today when we foresee that a program is going to develop a heavy procurement requirement, that long before it does this—perhaps two months before the time— we will sit down here on a Friday and anticipate that. We'll simply agree that what will happen is that Ken will go to the product manager or program manager and say, 'Look, for sure you're going to develop a need for a very heavy procurement operation. We can do it in a number of different ways. We can get a man, or two men, on your job, or I can keep them and try to do it for you here—over in the shop. How do you want it done?' We're that extreme. But there's been a lot of learning of this kind, learning of almost every imaginable kind. The functional managers stopped worrying about their prerogatives long ago. They see that the real satisfaction will come from allowing these people to perform in the most effective way.

"A sort of reciprocal thing has happened. The necessity for product managers to go bashing functional managers has largely disappeared. The system has become essentially supportive. And I think that we'll all live longer for it.

"It's now a real beauty to observe. You can see it doing some of these anticipatory things. Someone like Ken Kaysen can immediately sense the need for some kind of quality input of a certain kind that he should go talk to the fellow about and raise with him as a need that he can see he's going to have. And ask him how he can help him. The result of this is that one sees functional shops now receiving the most unbelievable bouquets from product managers and program managers. They derive satisfaction from this initiative.

"It's been a long time coming. But the average functional manager today knows now that he performs an important function. And he now knows how to perform it in order to be most useful."

An Unresolved Problem

Repair and overhaul were the primary activities in the Product Support and Programs Group. (See Figure 1 of Exhibit 3-13.) Support for mature products was and had always been one of the most lucrative parts of Avionics' business. During times of economic retrenchment, such as the one Avionics had just experienced and was still experiencing, these support activities provided a constant base of profitable revenue to the division and carried it through the troubled times. Since mature product support activity included the sale of basic equipment as well as the sale of spares and repair, overhaul, and maintenance activity, it could easily account for 50 percent of Avionics' volume during lean years. More significantly, that 50 percent of sales volume could represent at least 75 percent of the division's gross margin during that same period.

Customer training, the design of repair and maintenance manuals, the acquisition of spare equipment to support products no longer produced, and the design and construction of field-test equipment all lay within the area of responsibility of the Product Support organization. It was also responsible for the operation of the fixed wing and helicopter aircraft that the division owned and used for evaluation testing and final equipment calibration. The Product Support group numbered some seventy-five people, all of whom were technically trained except for secretarial staff and some stockroom clerks. Sixty of the seventy-five were direct charging employees, that is, assigned to specific work orders or programs. Two of the seventy-five were professional engineers.

Over the years the Product Support organization had developed a group of highly skilled technicians servicing Avionics' products in Japan, Southeast Asia, Europe, and throughout North America. They were supported with a spares and services organization in each geographic area. Most of the technicians were rotated through field assignments followed by extensive periods at the home plant to allow for familiarization with the division's new products. They usually became more experienced with the product details than even the design engineers who first developed the products. Their changing assignments allowed them to learn how to service different generations of Doppler equipment when assigned to geographic areas where several different customers and/or products were located.

With the reorganization to product management, Avionics faced a new structural question. If a program in a product organization neared the end of its life, moving into a predominantly repair and overhaul stage, should it remain in the product group? Was maintenance a product management function or was it better performed in a functional area specializing in product support? Mr. Glegg offered some thoughts on the problem:

"When we talked programs, there was always the understanding that at some point in time the program would eventually fade as an organizational entity. It was logical, at the time, to visualize another piece of the organization, which we called the mature Products and Support Group, inheriting these things; that is, inherit the long-lived support aspect and, in a sense, inherit the remains of the program. The things that you deliver, after they are in the hands of the customer, have not had all the problems removed. There are still questions for us to answer, questions of repair and overhaul, questions of modifications, either because the thing doesn't do exactly what it's supposed to do or the customer wants it to do something different. You have to have some way of responding to the customer's continuing needs for support of this thing.

"When it was clearly understood that the program was a sometime thing and it ended, it was clear that this piece of the organization should pick it up. There's a different question, however, with respect to a product. When you think of a product shop the question arises as to whether one should think of the product migrating into this shop as it matures. That's presently an open and unanswered question. Somewhere in all of this is a piece of thinking that we're going to have to do. It's conceivable that product managers are the best people to support the product. And they might be able to make a good case for that. However, there's also an argument that says, 'Look, when we go to support these things, it is better to use a common support organization.' I can already hear some of the rumblings about this, and we've started discussing it in a general sort of way, when we have the time. It's likely we will have to make a decision about it sometime soon.

EXHIBIT 3-13. CANADIAN MARCONI COMPANY: AVIONICS DIVISION

Background

As you are all doubtless aware, a notice from the divisional vice-president, Mr. W. Brayton issued on April 5, indicated that the division would undergo a significant organizational change. In particular, one object of the new organization would be to allow the Avionics Department to incorporate more fully into its own organization facilities such as manufacturing, purchasing and the like.

Since the release of Mr. Brayton's notice, the Avionics Department's senior management group have spent considerable time in working out the details of incorporating the additional facilities into the department. We have proceeded far enough to be able to agree with the other departments of the division (Telecommunications, Central Manufacturing, Quality Assurance, Finance) on May 21 as the date when we would formalize the new organization.

Object of this Note

The object of this note is to outline the organizational arrangements that have been devised by our management group as well as some of the underlying ideas. In areas where organizational detail is required to start functioning in the new configuration, this has been worked out and will either be given as a part of this note or will be available from a group manager on request. In some other areas the organizational detail is not required immediately and is not fully worked out but will be available within the next few weeks.

General Approach to Organization

The general approach to our organization is intended to reflect the following four features of the situation of the Avionics Department as it exists today and as it will doubtlessly exist for a considerable time in the future:

1. Most of our work can be viewed as being made up of large separable tasks having a unique character. This is our program acitivity and requires program management.

    By far the largest amount of the work we must perform can be regarded as separable tasks (such as IHAS Doppler, F-111D Doppler, NF-5 Nav System, ASN-64 Reliability Program, and so on) that are in some way unique. The tasks may have a singular quality because any of the following are special in some sense:

    a. The customer
    b. The equipment
    c. The schedule
    d. The contractual conditions
    e. The test requirements

    These separable tasks admit of a type of management known as "program management" in which the individual task, generally referred to as a "program," is assigned to a program manager for its accomplishment. This person breaks the main task into subtasks to which other people are assigned until a complete program team is evolved. The program manager integrates the activities in the subtasks in such a way as to accomplish the main task— the total of program objectives. We have been applying this type of management with increasing success over the last year and a half.

2. A relatively small fraction of our work cannot usefully be viewed as having a unique program character. This is usually initiation and follow-on activity and needs special provision for its management.

    Somewhere between 10 and 20 percent of our work is made up of a relatively large number of separable pieces which, because of limitations in size, complexity and so on, cannot usefully be viewed as individually having a program character.

    Activities of this type would be:

    a. Redesign of small areas of a product
    b. Updating of a manual
    c. Production of spares for a device for which there is no longer an active program
    d. Early study and experimental phases of new products

    Although these activities do not individually warrant program management, they require some type of organized management for which explicit provision must be made.

3. Most of our work can be demonstrated to require similar facilities. This is our facility or functional activity and requires facility or functional management.

Most of the work we must perform requires similar facilities for:

a. Selling
b. Design
c. Contracts
d. Manufacturing
e. Purchasing
f. Quality Control
g. Scheduling and Planning
h. Pricing

The total capacity required in any one facility far exceeds that for any one program or, initiation activity, or follow-on activity; thus it becomes useful to make each facility as effective as it can become *as a facility* and then make portions of these facilities available for integration into various activities *as the unique needs of the programs and initiation and follow-on activities determine.* This aspect of our work then gives rise to the need for "facility management" often referred to as "functional management" (management of functions, facilities) which is clearly complementary to "program management" or "task management," referred to previously. This is the "older" type of management scheme once employed exclusively prior to our use of program management and which we must continue in the first place to improve as an activity in itself and in the second place to augment with program management.

Details of Organization

Figure 1 shows the overall, essentially static, organization of the Avionics Department. To understand "how it works" it is necessary to combine with Figure 1 the typical program organization of Figure 2.

Using the foregoing discussion and nomenclature, the various groups can be classified into the following two categories:

1. Functional (Facility) Groups

Mechanical Design   Assembly and Components
Procurement   Marketing
Manufacturing Support   Quality Control

There would appear to be little necessity or likelihood of these groups having programs and hence program managers in them.

2. Functional and Program Groups

Products and Programs Group I
Products and Programs Group II
Product Support and Programs

These groups will tend to contain all the program activity and hence all the program managers. This is in addition to a certain amount of functional (facility) activity in each group.

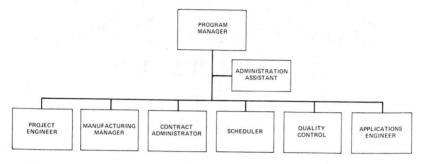

LIST OF PROGRAMS & SENIOR STAFF

PROGRAM	PROGRAM MGR.	REPORTS TO	PROJ./PROG. ENG.	MFG. MGR.	CONTRACT ADMIN.	SCHEDULER	OC	APPLIC. ENG.
IHAS	W. Denton	J. Haley	J. Stephan	D. Godot	K. Henry	R. Utter	R. Nolet	A. Brill
F111D	R. Rheaume	K.C.M. Glegg	H. Gordon	L. Zarley	C. Mousalis	A. Laurin	K. Kaysen	D. Colella
NF-5	H. Brinton	J. Haley	L. Heriot	A. Misen	R. Cohen	G. Peloquin	A. Clarke	A. Leyton
ASN-64	E. Sorrenta	T. Ronquist	Z. Giard	J. Allport	A. Morrison	D. Strean	C. Royal	A. Leyton
Simulator	G. Vanter	W. Ricci	G. Berg	J. Brown	H. Bishop	R. Tracy	L. Manet	D. Colella
APN-147	Not Assigned	Not Assigned	Not Assigned	Not Assigned	Not Assigned	Not Assigned	Not Assigned	Not Assigned

Figure 1. CPD Avionics Department.

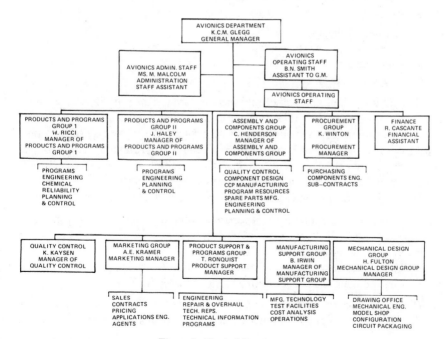

Figure 2. Typical Program.

4

Organizing and Staffing the Project Office and Team

4.0 INTRODUCTION

Successful project management, regardless of the organizational structure, is only as good as those individuals and leaders that are managing the key functions. Project management is not a one-person operation; it requires a group of individuals dedicated to the achievement of a specific goal. Project management includes:

- A project manager
- An assistant project manager
- A project (home) office
- A project team

Generally speaking, project office personnel are assigned full-time to the project and work out of the project office, whereas the project team members work out of the functional units and may spend only a small percentage of their time on this project. Normally, project office personnel report directly to the project manager. A project office generally is not required on small projects. There is also the situation where the project can be accomplished by just one person.

Before the staffing function begins, four basic questions are usually considered:

- What are the requirements necessary to become a successful project manager?
- Who should be a member of the project team?
- Who should be a member of the project office?
- What problems can occur during recruiting activities?

On the surface, these questions may not seem overly complex. But when we apply them to a project environment, which is defined as a "temporary" situation, and with the requirement of a constant stream of projects necessary for corporate growth, the staffing problems become overly complex. Conflicts and priority setting become a way of life during the staffing function.

4.1 THE STAFFING ENVIRONMENT

In order to fully understand the problems that occur during staffing, we must first investigate the characteristics of project management. The characteristics to be discussed include the project environment, the project management process, and the project manager.

There are two major problem areas under the project environment characteristics: personnel performance problems and personnel policy problems. Personnel performance poses difficulties for many individuals because the project environment is a change in the way of doing business. Individuals, regardless of how competent they are, find it difficult to continuously adapt to a changing situation in which they report to multiple managers. As a result, some people have come to resent change. Most individuals prefer a stable situation. Unfortunately, projects, by definition, are temporary assignments. There are many individuals who thrive on temporary assignments because it gives them a "chance for glory." These individuals are usually highly creative and enjoy challenging work. The challenge has greater importance than the cost of failure.

Unfortunately, there are situations where the line employee might consider the chance for glory as being more important than the project. For example, an employee pays no attention to the instructions of the project manager and performs the task his own way. When the project manager asks why, the employee asks, "Well, isn't my way better?" In this situation, all that the employee wants is to be recognized as an achiever and really does not care if the project is a success or failure. If the project fails, the employee still has a functional home to return to. Even the instructions of the line manager can be ignored if the individual wants that "one chance for glory" where he will be identified as an achiever with good ideas.

The second major performance problem lies in the project/functional interface where an individual suddenly finds himself reporting to two bosses; the functional manager and the project manager. If the functional manager and the project manager are in total agreement about the work to be accomplished, then performance at the interface may not be hampered. But if conflicting directions are received, then the individual at the interface, regardless of his capabilities and experience, may let his performance suffer because of his compromising position.

Personnel policy problems can create havoc in an organization, especially if the "grass is greener" in a project environment than in the functional environment. Functional organizations are normally governed by unit manning documents which specify grade and salary for the employees. Project offices, on the other hand, have no such regulations because, by definition, each project is different and therefore requires different structures. It is a fact, however, that opportunities for advancement are greater in the project office than in the functional organization. The functional organization may be regulated by a unit manning document, regardless of how well employees perform, whereas the project office promotes according to achievement. The difficulty here rests in the fact that one can distinguish between say grade 7, 8, 9, 10, and 11 employees, in a line organization, whereas for a project manager the distinction might appear only in the size of the project or the amount of responsibility. Bonuses for outstanding performance are easier to obtain in the project office than in the line organization. However, although bonuses may create the illusion of stimulating competition, the real result is creation of conflict and jealousy between the horizontal and vertical elements.

Many of the characteristics of the project management process have already been discussed. Project management is organized:

- To achieve a single set of objectives
- Through a single project of a finite lifetime
- That operates as a separate company entity except for administrative purposes.

Because each project is different, the project management process allows for each project to have its own policies, procedures, rules, and standards, providing that they fall within the broad company guidelines. Each project must be recognized as a project by top management so that the project manager has the delegated authority necessary to enforce the policies, procedures, rules, and standards.

Project management is successful only if the project manager and his team are totally dedicated to the successful completion of the project. This requires that each member of the project team and office has a good understanding of the fundamental project requirements. These include:

- Customer liaison
- Project direction
- Projection planning
- Project controlling
- Project evaluating
- Project reporting

Every member of the project office (and sometimes the project team) must have the ability to satisfy these requirements. Since these requirements cannot generally be fulfilled by single individuals, members of the project office, as well as functional representatives, must work together as a team. This teamwork concept is vital to the success of a project.

Ultimately, the person with the greatest influence during the staffing phase is the project manager. The personal attributes and abilities of project managers will either attract or deter highly desirable individuals. A project manager must like trouble. He or she must be capable of evaluating risk and uncertainty. Other basic characteristics include:

- Honesty and integrity
- Understanding of personnel problems
- Understanding of project technology
- Business management competence
  - Management principles
  - Communications
- Alertness and quickness
- Versatility
- Energy and toughness
- Decision-making ability

The project manager must exhibit honesty and integrity with his subordinates as well as line personnel, thus fostering an atmosphere of trust. He or she should not make unfulfilled or often impossible promises such as immediate promotions for everyone if a follow-on contract is received. Honesty, integrity, and an understanding of personnel problems can often eliminate any problems or conflicts which detract from the creation of a truly dedicated environment. Most project managers have "open door" policies for project as well as line personnel. On temporarily assigned activities, such as a project, managers cannot wait for personnel to iron out their own problems for the fear that time, cost, and performance requirements will not be satisfied. As an example, a line employee is having problems at home and it is beginning to affect his performance on your project. You talk to his line manager and are greeted with the statement, "Just give him a little time and he'll work out the problem himself." In this situation, the line manager may not recognize the time constraint on the project.

Project managers should have both business management and technical expertise. They must understand the fundamental principles of management, especially those involving the rapid development of temporary communication channels. Project managers *must* understand the technical implications associated with the problem since they are ultimately responsible for all decision making. They may have a staff of professionals to assist them. Many good technically oriented managers have failed because they get too involved with the technical side of the project rather than the management side. There are several strong arguments for having a project manager who has more than just an understanding of the technology. Technical expertise is ideal, but not always possible because the individual tends to become a generalist. This general understanding can become a major problem, as illustrated in the following example. A young woman

with a computer manufacturer is responsible for managing all projects involving
a specific product line. Marketing comes to her stating that they found a customer for the product line, but major modifications must be made. Since she only
has an understanding of technology, she meets with the true experts, the line
managers, who inform her that the modifications are impossible. She has the
authority to spend up to $1 million to make the modifications, but if the line
managers are correct, the $1 million will be wasted. She called a meeting between
engineering and marketing, but each held their ground and no final decision was
reached. She ultimately called a meeting between line managers and the vice-
president for engineering. The line managers held their ground with the vice-
president and the project was eventually rejected.

Because a project has a relatively short time duration, decision making must
be rapid and effective. Managers must be alert and quick in their ability to perceive "red flags" that can eventually lead to serious problems. They must demonstrate their versatility and toughness in order to keep subordinates dedicated
to goal accomplishment. Executives must realize that the project manager's
objectives during staffing are:

- Acquire the best available assets and try to improve them
- Provide a good working environment for all personnel
- Make sure that all resources are applied effectively and efficiently so that
  all constraints are met, if possible

4.2 SELECTING THE PROJECT MANAGER: AN EXECUTIVE DECISION

Probably the most difficult decision facing upper-level management is the selection of the project managers. Some managers work best on long-duration projects where decision making can be slow; others may thrive on short-duration
projects which can result in a constant pressure environment. Upper-level management must know the capabilities and shortcomings of their project managers.
A director was once asked whom he would choose for a key project manager
position: an individual who had been a project manager on previous programs
in which there were severe problems and cost overruns, or a new aggressive individual who may have the capability to be a good project manager but has never
had the opportunity. The director responded that he would go with the seasoned
veteran assuming that the previous mistakes would not be made again. The
argument here is that the project manager must learn from his own mistakes so
they would not be made again. The new individual is apt to make the same mistakes the veteran made. However, executives cannot always go with the seasoned
veterans without creating frustrating career path opportunities for the younger
personnel. Stewart has commented on this type of situation:[1]

---

1. John M. Stewart, "Making Project Management Work," *Business Horizons,* Fall, 63, 1965.

Though the project manager's previous experience is apt to have been confined to a single functional area of business, he must be able to function on the project as a kind of general manager in miniature. He must not only keep track of what is happening but also play the crucial role of advocate for the project. Even for a seasoned manager, this task is not likely to be easy. Hence, it is important to assign an individual whose administrative abilities and skill in personal relations have been convincingly demonstrated under fire.

Occasionally, an attempt is made to create specialized definitions for the project manager. As described by Shah:[2]

Like a physician, a project manager must be an expert diagnostician; he must guard his project from infection, detect symptoms, diagnose causes and prescribe cures for a multitude of afflictions.

The selection process for project managers is not an easy one. Five basic questions must be considered:

- What are the internal and external sources?
- How do we select?
- How do we provide career development in project management?
- How can we develop project management skills?
- How do we evaluate project management performance?

Project management cannot succeed unless a good project manager is at the controls. The selection process is an upper-level management responsibility because the project manager is delegated the authority of the general manager to cut across organizational lines in order to successfully accomplish the desired objectives. It is far more likely that project managers will succeed if it is obvious to the subordinates that the general manager has appointed them. Usually, a brief memo to the line managers will suffice. The major responsibilities of the project manager include:

- To produce the end item with the available resources and within the constraints of time, cost, and performance/technology
- To meet contractual profit objectives
- To make all required decisions whether they be for alternatives or termination
- To act as the customer (external) and upper-level and functional management (internal) communications focal point.

---

2. Ramesh P. Shah, "Cross Your Bridges Before You Come to Them," *Management Review*, December, 21, 1971.

- To "negotiate" with all functional disciplines for accomplishment of the necessary work packages within time, cost, and performance/technology
- To resolve all conflicts, if possible

If these responsibilities were applied to the total organization, they might reflect the job description of the general manager. This analogy between project and general managers is one of the reasons why future general managers are asked to perform functions that are implied, rather than spelled out in the job description. As an example, you are the project manager on a high-technology project. As the project winds down, an executive asks you to write a paper so that he can present it at a technical meeting in Tokyo, Japan. His name will appear first on the paper. Should this be a part of your job? As the author sees it, you really don't have much of a choice.

In order for project managers to fulfill their responsibilities successfully, they are constantly required to demonstrate their skills in interface, resource, and planning and control management. These implicit responsibilities are shown below:

- Interface Management
  - Product interfaces
    - Performance of parts or subsections
    - Physical connection of parts or subsections
  - Project interfaces
    - Customer
    - Management (functional and upper-level)
    - Change of responsibilities
    - Information flow
    - Material interfaces (inventory control)

- Resource Management
  - Time (schedule)
  - Manpower
  - Money
  - Facilities
  - Equipment
  - Material
  - Information/technology

- Planning and Control Management
  - Increase equipment utilization
  - Increase performance efficiency
  - Reduce risks
  - Identify alternatives to problems
  - Identify alternative resolutions to conflicts

Finding the man or woman with the right qualifications is not an easy task because the selection of project managers is based more on personal characteristics than on the job description. In Section 4.1 a brief outline of desired characteristics was presented. Russell Archibald defines a broader range of desired personal characteristics:[3]

- Flexibility and adaptability
- Preference for significant initiative and leadership
- Aggressiveness, confidence, persuasiveness, verbal fluency
- Ambition, activity, forcefulness
- Effectiveness as a communicator and integrator
- Broad scope of personal interests
- Poise, enthusiasm, imagination, spontaneity
- Able to balance technical solutions with time, cost, and human factors
- Well organized and disciplined
- A generalist rather than a specialist
- Able and willing to devote most of his time to planning and controlling
- Able to identify problems
- Willing to make decisions
- Able to maintain a proper balance in the use of time

The background for this ideal project manager would probably be doctorates in engineering, business, and psychology; experience with ten different companies in a variety of project office positions; and an age of about twenty-five. Good project managers in industry today would probably be lucky if they had 70 to 80 percent of these characteristics. The best project managers are willing and able to identify their own shortcomings.

The difficulty in staffing, especially for project managers or assistant project managers, is in determining what questions to ask during an interview to see if the individual has the necessary or desired characteristics. There are numerous situations where individuals are qualified to be promoted vertically, but not horizontally. An individual with poor communication skills and interpersonal skills can be promoted to a line management slot because of his technical expertise, but this same individual is not qualified for project management promotion.

Most executives have found that the best way to interview is by reading each element of the job description to the potential candidate. There are numerous individuals who want a career path in project management but are just totally unaware of what the project manager's duties actually are.

So far we have discussed the personal characteristics of the project manager. There are also job-related characteristics to consider, such as:

---

3. Russell D. Archibald, *Managing High-Technology Programs and Projects,* New York, Wiley, 1976, p. 55.

- Are feasibility and economic analyses necessary?
- Is complex technical expertise required? If so, is it within the individuals capabilities?
- If the individual is lacking expertise, will there be sufficient backup strength on the line organizations?
- Is this the company's or individual's first exposure to this type of project and/or client? If so, what are the risks to be considered?
- What is the priority for this project and what are the risks?
- Who must the project manager interface with, both inside and outside the organization?

Most good project managers generally know how to perform feasibility studies and cost/benefit analyses. Sometimes this capability can create organizational conflict. A major utility company begins each computer project with a feasibility study in which a cost/benefit analysis is performed. The project managers, all of whom report to a project management division, perform the study themselves without any direct functional support. The functional managers argue that the results are grossly inaccurate because the functional experts are not involved. The project manager, on the other hand, argues that they never have sufficient time or money to perform a complete analysis. This type of project requires executive attention. Some companies resolve this by having a special group simply to perform these types of analyses.

Most companies would prefer to find project managers from within. Unfortunately, this is easier said than done. The following remarks by Robert Fluor illustrate this point:[4]

On-the-job training is probably the most important aspect in the development of a project manager. This includes assignments to progressively more responsible positions in engineering and construction management and project management. It also includes rotational assignments in several engineering department disciplines, in construction, procurement, cost and scheduling, contract administration, and others . . . . We find there are great advantages to developing our project managers from within the company. There are good reasons for this:

- They know the corporate organization, policies, procedures, and the key people. This allows them to give us quality performance quicker.
- They have an established performance record which allows us to place them at the maximum level of responsibility and authority.
- Clients prefer a proven track record within the project manager's present organization.

---

4. J. Robert Fluor, "Development of Project Managers—Twenty Year's Study at Fluor," Keynote address to Project Management Institute Ninth International Seminar/Symposium, Chicago, Illinois, October 24, 1977.

There are also good reasons for recruiting from outside the company. A new project manager hired from the outside would be less likely to have strong informal ties to any one line organization, this would allow the manager to show impartiality on the project. Some companies further require that the individual spend an apprenticeship period of twelve to eighteen months in a line organization to find out how the company functions, to become acquainted with some of the people, and to understand the company's policies and procedures.

One of the most important but often least understood characteristics of good project managers is their ability to understand and know both themselves and their employees in terms of strengths and weaknesses. They must understand human behavior. Each manager must understand that in order for an employee to perform efficiently:

- They must know what they are supposed to do, preferably in terms of an end product.
- They must have a clear understanding of authority and its limits.
- They must know what their relationship with other people is.
- They should know what constitutes a job well done in terms of specific results.
- They should know when and what they are doing exceptionally well.
- They must be shown concrete evidence that there are just rewards for work well done and for work exceptionally well done.
- They should know where and when they are falling short.
- They must be made aware of what can and should be done to correct unsatisfactory results.
- They must feel that their superior has an interest in them as individuals.
- They must feel that their superior believes in them and is anxious for their success and progress.

4.3 SPECIAL CASES IN PROJECT MANAGER SELECTION

Thus far we have assumed that the project is large enough for a full-time project manager to be appointed. This is not always the case. There are four major problem areas in staffing projects:

- Part-time versus full-time assignments
- Several projects assigned to one project manager
- Projects assigned to functional managers
- The project manager role retained by the general manager

The first problem is generally related to the size of the project. If the project is small (in time duration or cost), the part-time project manager may be selected. Many executives have fallen into the trap of letting line personnel act as part-time project managers while still performing line functions. If the employee has a conflict between what is best for the project and what is best for his line organization, the project will suffer. It is only natural that the employee will favor the place the salary increases come from.

It is a common practice for one project manager to control several projects, especially if they are either related or similar. Problems come about when the projects have drastically different priorities. The low-priority efforts will be neglected.

If the project is a high-technology effort that requires specialization and can be performed by one department, then it is not unusual for the line manager to take on a dual role and act as project manager as well. This can be difficult to do, especially if the project manager is required to establish the priorities for the work under his supervision. The line manager may keep the best resources for the project, regardless of the priority. Then that project will be a success at the expense of every other project he must supply resources to.

Probably the worst situation is when the executive maintains the role of the project manager for a particular effort. The difficulty lies in the fact that the executive may not have the time necessary for total dedication to the achievement of the project. The executive cannot make effective decisions as a project manager while still discharging normal duties.

4.4 SELECTING THE WRONG PROJECT MANAGER

Even though executives know the personal characteristics and desired traits that project managers should possess, and even though job descriptions are often clearly defined, management still persists in selecting the wrong person. Below are several common situations where the wrong person was selected.

Maturity: Some executives consider grey hair and baldness to be sure indications of maturity. This is not the type of maturity needed for project management. Maturity in project management generally comes from exposure to several types of projects in a variety of project office positions. In aerospace and defense, it is possible for a project manager to manage the same type of project for ten years or more. When placed on a new project, the individual may try to force personnel and project requirements to adhere to the same policies and procedures that existed on the ten-year project. The project manager may know only one way of managing projects. Perhaps, in this case, the individual would best function as an assistant project manager on a new project.

Hard-nosed: Applying hard-nosed tactics to subordinates can be very demoralizing. Project managers must give people sufficient freedom to get the job done, without providing continuous supervision and direction. A line employee who is given "freedom" by his line manager, but suddenly finds himself closely supervised by the project manager, will be a very unhappy individual. Employees must be trained to understand that supervised pressure will occur in time of crisis. If the project manager provides continuous supervised pressure, then he may find it difficult to obtain a qualified staff for the next project.

Maturity in project management means maturity in dealing with people. Line managers, because of their ability to control an employee's salary, need only one leadership style and can force the employees to adapt. The project manager, on the other hand, cannot control salaries and must have a wide variety of leadership styles. The project manager must adapt a leadership style to the project employees, whereas the reverse is true in the line organization.

Availability: Executives should not assign individuals as project managers simply because of availability. People have a tendency to cringe when you suggest that project managers be switched halfway through a project. For example, Manager X is halfway through his project. Manager Y is waiting for an assignment. A new project comes up and the executive switches Managers X and Y. There are several reasons for this. The most important phase of a project is planning, and, if it is accomplished correctly, the project could be conceivably run itself. Therefore, Manager Y should be able to handle Manager X's project.

There are several other reasons why this switch may be necessary. The new project may be a higher priority and require a more experienced manager. Second, not all project managers are equal, especially when it comes to planning. When an executive finds a project manager who demonstrates extraordinary talents at planning, there is a natural tendency for the executive to want this project manager to plan all projects. An experienced project manager once commented to the author, "Once, just once, I'd like to be able to finish a project." There are other reasons for having someone take over a project in midstream. The director of project management calls you in to his office and tells you that one of your fellow project managers has had a heart attack midway through the project. You will be taking over his project which is well behind schedule and overrunning costs. The director of project management then "orders" you to complete the project within time and cost. How do you propose to do it? Perhaps the only viable solution to this problem is to step into a phone booth and begin taking off your clothes in order to expose the big "S" on your chest.

Technical Promotion: Executives quite often promote technical line managers without realizing the consequences. Technical specialists may not be able to divorce themselves from the technical side of the house and become project managers rather than project doers. There are also strong reasons for promoting technical specialists to project managers. These people often:

- Have better relationships with fellow researchers
- Can prevent duplication of effort
- Can foster teamwork

- Have progressed up through the technical ranks
- Are knowledgeable in many technical fields
- Understand the meaning of profitability and general management philosophy
- Are interested in training and teaching
- Understand how to work with perfectionists

As described by Taylor and Watling:[5]

It is often the case, therefore, that the Project Manager is more noted for his management technique expertise, his ability to "get on with people" than for his sheer technical prowess. However, it can be dangerous to minimize this latter talent when choosing Project Managers dependent upon project type and size. The Project Manager should preferably be an expert either in the field of the project task or a subject allied to it.

If an expert is selected, then the individual must learn how to use people effectively. As an example, a company (with $1 million in sales today) implemented project management with the adoption of a matrix, in 1972. The decision was made that the best technical experts would staff the project management slots. The technical experts then began usurping the authority of the line managers by giving continuous technical direction to the line people. Unfortunately, management felt that this was the way the system should operate. When an employee was assigned to a project, then the employee knew that the project manager would not stand behind him unless he followed the project manager's directions. Today, management is trying to clear up the problem of who is the true technical expert; the project managers or line managers.

Customer-oriented: Executives quite often place individuals as project managers simply to satisfy a customer request. Being able to communicate with the customer does not guarantee project success, however. If the project manager is simply a concession to the customer, then the executive must insist upon providing a strong supporting team. This is often an unavoidable situation and must be lived with.

New Exposure: Executives run the risk of project failure if an individual is appointed project manager simply for gaining exposure to project management. An executive of a utility company wanted to rotate his line personnel into project management for twelve to eighteen months and then return them to the line organization where they would be more well-rounded individuals and understand the working relationship between project management and line management

---

5. Taylor, W.J., and Watling, T.F., *Successful Project Management,* London, Business Books Limited, 1972, p. 32.

better. There are two major problems with this. First, the individual may become technically obsolete after eighteen months in project management. Second, and most important, individuals who get a taste of project management will generally not want to return to the line organization.

Company Exposure: Simply because individuals have worked in a variety of divisions does not guarantee that they would make good project managers. Working in a variety of divisions may indicate they couldn't hold a job in any one. If this is the case, you've found their true level of incompetency and will only maximize the damage they can do to the company by putting them into project management. Some executives contend that the best way to train a project manager is by rotation through the various functional disciplines for two weeks to a month in each organization. Other executives contend that this is useless because the individual cannot learn anything in such a short period of time.

Finally, there are three special points that should be considered:

- Individuals should not be promoted to project management simply because they are at the top of their pay grade.
- Project managers should be promoted and paid based upon performance, not upon the number of people supervised.
- It is not necessary for the project manager to be the highest ranking individual on the project team with the rationale that sufficient "clout" is needed.

4.5 THE ORGANIZATIONAL STAFFING PROCESS

Staffing the project organization can become a long and tedious effort, especially on large and complex engineering projects. Three major questions must be answered:

- What people resources are required?
- Where will the people come from?
- What type of project organizational structure will be best?

To determine the people resources required, the types of individuals (possibly job descriptions) must be decided upon, as well as how many individuals from each job category are necessary and when these individuals will be needed.

Consider the following situation: A project manager has an activity that requires three separate tasks, all performed within the same line organization. The line manager promises you the best available resources right now for the first task, but cannot make any commitments beyond that. The line manager may have only below-average workers available for the second and third tasks. However, the line manager is willing to make a deal with you. He can give you an employee who can do the work but will only give an average performance. However, if you accept the average employee, the line manager will guarantee that the employee will be available to you for all three tasks. How important is continuity to you? There is no clearly definable answer to this question. Some people will always want the best resources and are willing to fight for them, while others prefer continuity and dislike seeing new people coming and going. The author prefers continuity, provided that the assigned employee has the ability to do the up-front planning during the first task.

Sometimes, a project manager may have to make concessions to get the right people. For example, during the seventh, eighth, and ninth months of your project you need two individuals with special qualifications. The functional manager says that they will be available two months earlier and if you don't pick them up then, there will be no guarantee as to their availability during the seventh month. Obviously, the line manager is pressuring you, and you may have to give in. There is also the situation where the line manager says that he'll have to borrow people from another department in order to fulfill his commitments for your project. You may have to live with this situation, but be very careful; these employees will be working at a low level on the learning curve, and overtime will not necessarily resolve the problem. You must expect mistakes here.

Line managers often place new employees on projects so they can be upgraded. Project managers often resent this and immediately run to top management for help. If a line manager says that he can do the work with lower-level people, then the project manager *must* believe the line manager. After all, the line manager made the commitment to do the work, not the assigned employees, and it is the line manager's neck that is stuck out.

Mutual trust between project and line managers is crucial, especially during staffing sessions. Once a project manager has developed a good working relationship with an employee, the project manager would like to keep those individuals assigned to his activities. There is nothing wrong with a project manager requesting the same administrative and/or technical staff as before. Line managers realize this and are usually agree to it.

There must also be mutual trust between the project managers themselves. Project managers must work as a total team, recognize each other's needs, and be willing to make decisions that are in the best interest of the company.

Once the resources are defined, the next question must be whether staffing will be from within the existing organization or from outside sources such as new hires or consultants. Outside consultants are advisable if, and only if, internal manpower resources are being fully utilized on other programs, or if the company does not possess the required project skills. The answer to the last question should describe the organizational form that will be best for achievement of objectives. The form might be a matrix, product, or staff project management structure.

Not all companies permit a variety of project organizational forms to exist within the main company structure. Those that do, however, consider the basic tenets of classical management before making a decision. These include:

- How is labor specialized?
- What should the span of management be?
  - How much planning is required?
  - Are authority relationships delegated and understood?
  - Are there established performance standards?
  - What is the rate of change of the job requirements?
- Should we have a horizontal or vertical organization?
  - What are the economics?
  - What are the morale implications?
- Do we need a unity-of-command position?

As with any organization, the subordinates can make the superior look good in the performance of his duties. Unfortunately, the project environment is symbolized by temporary assignments in which the main effort put forth by the project manager is to motivate his (temporary) subordinates toward project dedication and to make them fully understand that:

- Teamwork is vital for success.
- Esprit de corps contributes to success.
- Conflicts can occur between project and functional ties.
- Communication is essential for success.
- Conflicting orders may be given by:
  - Project manager
  - Functional manager
  - Upper-level manager
- Unsuccessful performance may result in transfer or dismissal from the project as well as disciplinary action.

Previously we stated that a project operates as a separate entity but remains attached to the company through company administration policies and procedures. Although project managers can establish their own policies, procedures, and rules, the criteria for promotion must be based upon company standards. Therefore we can ask:

- What commitments can a project manager make to his prospective subordinates?
- What promises can a project manager make regarding an individual's assignment after termination?

The first question involves salary, grade, responsibility, evaluation for promotion, and bonus and overtime pay. There are many documented cases of project managers promising subordinates "the world" as a means of motivating them, when in fact the managers knew that these promises could not be kept.

The second question deals with the equity principle of job reassignment. According to Martin:[6]

After reassignment at the end of his tour on a project, a person should have the same prospects for the future that he would have had if he had performed equally well (or badly) in a normal assignment not connected with the project during the same period.

After promises on previous projects, a project manager will find it very difficult to get top-quality personnel to volunteer for another project. Even if top management orders key individuals to be assigned to his project, they will always be skeptical about any promises that he may make.

Selecting the project manager is only one-third of the staffing problem. Selecting the project office personnel and team members often can be a time-consuming chore. The project office consists of personnel who are usually assigned as full-time members of the project. The first step in selecting the project office staff requires that the project manager evaluate all potential candidates, regardless of whether or not they are now assigned to another project. This evaluation process should include active project team members, functional team members available for promotion or transfer, and outside applicants.

Upon completion of the evaluation process, the project manager meets with upper-level management. This coordination is required to assure that:

- All assignments fall within current policies on rank, salary, and promotion
- The individuals selected can work well with both the project manager (formal reporting) and upper-level management (informal reporting)
- The individuals selected have good working relationships with the functional personnel

Good project office personnel cannot be trained overnight. Good training is usually identified as experience with several types of projects. Project managers do not "train" project office members, primarily because time constraints do not often permit this luxury. Project office personnel must be self-disciplined, especially during the first few assignments.

The third and final step in the staffing of the project office is a meeting between the project manager, upper-level management, and the project manager on whose project the requested individuals are currently assigned. Project managers are very reluctant to give up qualfied personnel to the staff of other project offices. Unfortunately, this procedure is a way of life in a project environment. Upper-level management attends these meetings to represent to all negotiating

---

6. Charles C. Martin. *Project Management: How to Make it Work,* New York, AMACOM, A Division of American Management Associations, 1976, p. 41.

parties the fact that top management is concerned with maintaining the best possible mix of individuals from available resources and to help resolve staffing conflicts. Staffing from within is a negotiation process in which upper-level management establishes the ground rules and priorities.

The selected individuals are then notified of the anticipated change and asked about their opinions. If the individual has strong resentment to being transferred or reassigned, alternate personnel may be selected because projects cannot operate effectively under discontented managers. Upper-level managers, however, have the authority to direct changes regardless of the desires of the individuals concerned.

Most companies have both formal and informal guidelines for the recruiting and assigning of project personnel. Below are examples of such guidelines as defined by Charles Martin:[7]

- Unless some other condition is paramount, project recruiting policies should be as similar as possible to those normally used in the organization for assigning people to new jobs.
- Everyone should be given the same briefing about the project, its benefits, and any special policies related to it. For a sensitive project, this rule can be modified to permit different amounts of information to be given to different managerial levels, but at least everyone in the same general classification should get the same briefing. It should be complete and accurate.
- Any commitments made to members of the team about treatment at the end of the project should be approved in advance by general management. No other commitments should be made.
- Every individual selected for a project should be told why he or she was chosen.
- A similar degree of freedom should be granted all people, or at least all those within a given job category, in the matter of accepting or declining a project assignment.

This last one is a major consideration in the recruiting process: How much discretion is to be given to the employee concerning the proposed assignment? Several degrees of permissiveness appear possible:

- The project is explained and the individual is asked to join and given complete freedom to decline, no questions asked.
- The individual is told he will be assigned to the project. However, he is invited to bring forward any reservations he may have about joining. Any sensible reason he offers will excuse him from the assignment.

---

7. Charles C. Martin, *Project Management: How to Make it Work,* New York, AMACOM A Division of American Management Associations, 1976, p. 241.

- The individual is told he is assigned to the project. Only a significant personal or career preference is accepted as a reason for excusing him from joining the project.
- The individual is assigned to the project as he would be to any other work assignment. Only an emergency can excuse him from serving on the project team.

The recruitment process is not without difficulties. What is unfortunate, is that problems of recruiting and retaining good personnel are more difficult in a project organizational structure than in one which is purely traditional. Clayton Reeser identifies nine potential problems related to personnel that can exist in project organizations:[8]

- Personnel connected with project forms of organization suffer more anxieties about possible loss of employment than members of functional organizations
- Individuals temporarily assigned to matrix organizations are more frustrated by authority ambiguity than permanent members of functional organizations.
- Personnel connected with project forms of organization that are nearing their phase-out are more frustrated by what they perceive to be "make work" assignments than members of functional organizations.
- Personnel connected with project forms of organization feel more frustrated because of lack of formal procedures and role definitions than members of functional organizations.
- Personnel connected with project forms of organization worry more about being set back in their careers than members of functional organizations.
- Personnel connected with project forms of organization feel less loyal to their organization than members of functional organizations.
- Personnel connected with project forms of organization have more anxieties in feeling that there is no one concerned about their personal development than members of functional organizations.
- Permanent members of project forms of organization are more frustrated by multiple levels of management than members of functional organizations.

Grinnell and Apple have identified four additional major problems associated with staffing:[9]

- People trained in single line-of-command organizations find it hard to serve more than one boss.

8. Clayton Reeser, "Some Potential Human Problems of the Project Form of Organization," *Academy of Management Journal,* XII, 462-466, 1969.

9. Grinnell, S.K., and Apple, H.P., "When Two Bosses are Better than One," *Machine Design,* January, pp. 84-87, 1975.

- People may give lip service to teamwork, but not really know how to develop and maintain a good working team.
- Project and functional managers sometimes tend to compete rather than cooperate with each other.
- Individuals must learn to do more "managing" of themselves.

Project managers have the right to get people removed from their projects, especially for incompetence. However, although project managers can get project office people (who report to the project manager) removed directly, the removal of a line employee is an indirect process and must be accomplished through the line manager. The removal of the line employee should be made to look as if it were a transfer or else the project manager will be branded as an individual who gets people fired off his projects.

Executives must be ready to cope with the staffing problems that can occur in a project environment. C. Ray Gullett has summarized these major problems:[10]

- Staffing levels are more variable in a project environment.
- Performance evaluation is more complex and more subject to error in a matrix form of organization.
- Wage and salary grades are more difficult to maintain under a matrix form of organization. Job descriptions are often of less value.
- Training and development are more complex and at the same time more necessary under a project form of organization.
- Morale problems are potentially greater in a matrix organization.

4.6 THE PROJECT OFFICE

The project office is an organization developed to support the project manager in carrying out his duties. Project office personnel must have the same dedication towards the project as the project manager, and must have good working relationships with both the project and functional managers. The responsibilities of the project office include:

- Acting as the focal point of information for both in-house control and customer reporting
- Controlling time, cost, and performance to adhere to contractual requirements
- Insuring that all work required is documented and distributed to all key personnel
- Insuring that all work performed is both authorized and funded by contractual documentation

---

10. C. Ray Gullett, "Personnel Management in the Project Environment," *Personnel Administration/Public Personnel Review,* November – December, 17-22, 1972.

The major responsibility of the project manager and the project office personnel is the integration of work across the functional lines of the organization. Functional units, such as engineering, R & D, and manufacturing, together with extra-company subcontractors, must work toward the same specifications, designs, and even objectives. The lack of proper integration between these functional units is the most common cause of project failure. The team members must be dedicated to *all* activities required for project success, not just their own functional responsibilities. The problems resulting from lack of integration can best be solved by full-time membership and participation of project office personnel. Not all team members are part of the project office. Functional representatives, performing at the interface position, also act as integrators but at a closer position to where the work is finally accomplished, that is the line organization.

One of the biggest challenges facing project managers is determining the size of the project office. The optimal size is determined by a trade-off between the maximum number of members necessary to assure compliance with requirements and the minimum number for keeping the total administrative costs under control. Membership is determined by factors such as project size, internal support requirements, type of project (i.e., R & D, qualification, production), level of technical competency required, and customer support requirements. Membership size is also influenced by how strategic management views the project to be. There is a tendency to enlarge project offices if the project is considered strategic, especially if follow-on work is possible.

On large projects, and even on some smaller efforts, it is often impossible to achieve project success without permanently assigned personnel. The four major activities of the project office, shown below, indicate the need for using full-time people:

- Integration of activities
- In-house and out-of-house communicators
- Scheduling with risk and uncertainty
- Effective control

These four activities require continuous monitoring by trained project personnel. The training of good project office members may take weeks or even months, and can extend beyond the time allocated for a project. Because key personnel are always in demand, project managers should ask themselves and upper-level management one pivotal question when attempting to staff the project office:

- Are there any projects downstream that might cause me to lose key members of my team?

If the answer to this question is yes, then it might benefit the project to have the second- or third-choice person selected for the position or even to staff the position on a part-time basis. Another alternative, of course, would be to assign the key members to activities that are not so important and that can be readily performed by replacement personnel. This, however, is impractical because such personnel will not be employed efficiently.

Program managers would like nothing better than to have all of their key personnel assigned full-time for the duration of the program. Unfortunately, this is undesirable, if not impossible, for many projects because:[11]

- Skills required by the project vary considerably as the project matures through each of its life-cycle phases.
- Building up large permanently assigned project offices for each project inevitably causes duplication of certain skills (often those in short supply), carrying of people who are not needed on a full-time basis or for a long period, and personnel difficulties in reassignment.
- The project manager may be diverted from his primary task and become the project engineer, for example, in addition to his duties of supervision, administration, and dealing with the personnel problems of a large office rather than concentrating on managing all aspects of the project itself.
- Professionally trained people often prefer to work within a group devoted to their professional area, with permanent management having qualifications in the same field, rather than becoming isolated from their specialty peers by being assigned to a project staff.
- Projects are subject to sudden shifts in priority or even to cancellation, and full-time members of a project office are thus exposed to potentially serious threats to their job security; this often causes a reluctance on the part of some people to accept a project assignment.

All of these factors favor keeping the full-time project office as small as possible and dependent upon established functional departments and specialized staffs to the greatest extent possible for performance of the various tasks necessary to complete the project. The approach places great emphasis on the planning and control procedures used on the project. On the other hand, there are valid reasons for assigning particular people of various specialties to the project office. These specialties usually include:

- Systems analysis and engineering (or equivalent technical discipline) and product quality and configuration control, if the product requires such an effort
- Project planning, scheduling, control, and administrative support

Many times a project office is staffed by promotion of functional specialists. Unless careful examination of the individual qualifications is made, disaster can easily be forthcoming. This situation is quite common to engineering firms with a high percentage of technical employees.

---

11. Russell D. Archibald, *Managing High-Technology Programs and Projects,* New York, Wiley, 1976, p. 82.

In professional firms, personnel are generally promoted to management on the basis of their professional or technical competence rather than their managerial ability. While this practice may be unavoidable, it does tend to promote men with insufficient knowledge of management techniques and creates a frustrating environment for the professional down the line.[12]

With regard to the training needed by technicians who aspire to high positions in a world of increasing professionalism in management, more than half of the technically trained executives studied . . . wished that they had had "more training in the business skills traditionally associated with the management function." In fact, 75 percent admitted that there were gaps in their nontechnical education . . . . Essentially, the engineer whose stock in trade has always been "hard skills" will need to recognize the value of such "soft skills" as psychology, sociology, and so forth, and to make serious and sustained efforts to apply them to his current job.[13]

There is an unfortunate tendency today for executives to create an environment where line employees feel that the "grass is greener" in project management and project engineering than in the line organization. How should an executive handle a situation where line specialists continuously apply for transfer to project management? The solution being incorporated today is the development of a dual ladder system, as shown in Figure 4-1. There is a pay scale called "consultant." This particular company created the consultant position because:

- There were several technical specialists who were worth more money to the company but who refused to accept a management position to get it.
- Technical specialists could not be paid more money than line managers.

Promoting technical specialists to a management slot simply to give them more money can result in:

- Creating a poor line manager
- Turning a specialist into a generalist
- Leaving a large technical gap in the line organization

Line managers often argue that they cannot perform their managerial duties and control these "prima donnas" who earn more money and have a higher pay grade than the line managers. This is faulty reasoning. Every time the consultants do something well, it reflects upon the *entire* line organization, not merely upon themselves.

---

12. William P. Killian, "Project Management-Future Organizational Concept," *Marquette Business Review,* 1971, p. 90-107.
13. Richard A. Koplow, "From Engineer to Manager-And Back Again," *IEEE Transactions on Engineering Management,* EM-14, 2: 88-92, June, 1967.

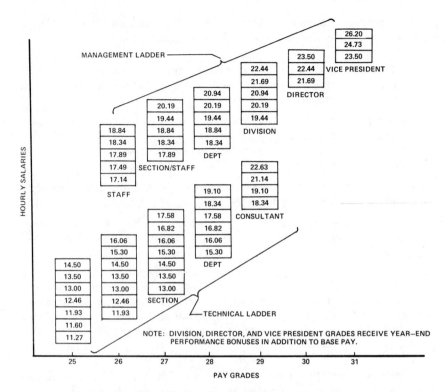

Figure 4-1. Exempt, Upper-level Pay Structure.

The concept of having functional employees with a higher pay grade than the line manager can also be applied to the horizontal project. It is possible for a junior project manager to suddenly find that the line managers have assigned the best available employees to his project and, as a result, they all have a higher pay grade than the project manager. It is also possible for assistant project managers (as project engineers) to have a higher pay grade than the project manager. Project management is designed to put together the best mix of people in order to achieve the objective. If this best mix requires that a grade 7 report to a grade 9 on a ("temporary") project, then so be it. Executives should not let salaries and pay grades stand in the way of constructing a good project organization.

Another major concern is the relationship that exists between project office personnel and functional managers. In many organizations, membership in the project office is considered to be more important than in the functional department. Functional members have a tendency to resent an individual who has just been promoted out of a functional department and into project management. Killian has described ways of resolving potential conflicts:[14]

It must be kept in mind that veteran functional managers cannot be expected to accept direction readily from some lesser executive who is suddenly labelled a Project Manager. Management can avoid this problem by:

- Selecting a man who already has a high position of responsibility or placing him high enough in the organization.
- Assigning him a title as important-sounding as those of functional managers.
- Supporting him in his dealings with functional managers.

If the Project Manager is expected to exercise project control over the functional departments, then he must report to the same level as the departments, or higher.

Executives can severely hinder project managers by limiting their authority to select and organize (when necessary) a project office and team. According to Cleland:[15]

His (project manager's) staff should be qualified to provide personal administrative and technical support. He should have sufficient authority to increase or decrease his staff as necessary throughout the life of the project. The authorization should include selective augmentation for varying periods of time from the supporting functional areas.

Sometimes, a situation occurs in the project office in which the assistant project manager does not fully understand the intentions of the project manager. As an example, an assistant project manager may become convinced that the project manager is making decisions that are in the best interest of the company. Unfortunately, what is in the best interest of the company is not in the best interest of the project. The cause of this problem was a communication breakdown in the project office.

Many executives have a misconception concerning the makeup and usefulness of the project office. People who work in the project office should be individuals whose first concern is project management, not the enhancement of their technical expertise. It is almost impossible for individuals to perform for any extended period of time in the project office without becoming cross-trained in a second or third project office function. As an example, the project manager for cost could acquire enough expertise to eventually act as the assistant to the assistant project manager for procurement. This technique of project office cross-training is an excellent mechanism for creating good project managers.

---

14. William P. Killian, "Project Management—Future Organizational Concept," *Marquette Business Review,* 1971, pp. 90-107.
15. David I. Cleland, "Why Project Management," *Business Horizons,* Winter, 85, 1964.

People who are placed in the project office should be individuals who are interested in making a career out of project management. These dedicated individuals must realize that there may not be bigger and better projects for them to manage downstream, and they may have to take a step backwards and manage a smaller project or simply be an assistant project manager. It is not uncommon for an individual to rotate back and forth between project management and assistant project management.

We have mentioned two important facts concerning the project management staffing process:

- The individual who aspires to become a project manager must be willing to give up technical expertise and become a generalist.
- Individuals can be qualified to be promoted vertically, but not horizontally.

Let us elaborate on these two points. Once an employee has demonstrated the necessary attributes to be a good project manager, there are three ways that the individual can become a project manager or part of the project office. The executive can:

- Promote the individual in salary and grade and transfer him into project management.
- Laterally transfer the individual into project management without any salary or grade increase. If, after three to six months, the employee demonstrates that he can perform, he will receive an appropriate salary and grade increase.
- Give the employee a small salary increase without any grade increase or a grade increase without any salary increase, with the stipulation that additional awards will be forthcoming after the observation period, assuming that the employee can handle the position.

Many executives believe in the philosophy that once an individual enters the world of project management, there are only two places to go: up in the organization or out the door. If an individual is given a promotion and pay increase and is placed into project management and fails, his salary may not be compatible with that of his previous line organization and now there is no place for him to go. Most executives, and employees, prefer the second method because it actually provides some protection for the employee. Of course, the employee might not want to return having been branded a failure in project management.

4.7 THE FUNCTIONAL TEAM

The project team consists of the project manager, the project office (whose members report directly to the project manager) and the functional or interface members (who must report both horizontally as well as vertically). Functional team members are often shown on organizational charts as being project office team members. This is normally done to satisfy customer requirements.

Upper-level management can have an input into the selection process for functional team members just as with project office membership. However, executives should not take an active role unless the project and functional managers cannot come to an agreement. If executives continuously step in and tell line managers how to staff a project, then the line managers will feel that the executives are usurping the line managers' authority and, of course, the project will suffer. Functional management must be represented at all staffing meetings. Functional staffing is directly dependent upon project requirements and must therefore include function management because:

- Functional managers generally have more expertise and can identify high-risk areas.
- Functional managers must develop a positive attitude toward project success. This is best achieved by inviting their participation in the early activities of the planning phase.

Functional team members are not always full-time. They can be a full-time or part-time for either the duration of the project or only specific phases.

The selection process for both the functional team member as well as the project office must include evaluation of any special requirements. The most common special requirements develop from:

- Changes in technical specifications
- Special customer requests
- Organizational restructuring because of deviations from existing policies

Each of these has a direct impact on whether an individual should be assigned to the project office or functional interface.

A typical project office may include between ten and thirty members, whereas the total project team may be in excess of a hundred people. Large staffs inherently create additional work and increase communication channel noise to such a degree that information reporting may become a slow process. Large staffs also create difficult problems with regard to customer relations.

For large projects, it is desirable to have a full-time functional representative from each major division or department assigned permanently to the project office. Such representation might include:

- Program management
- Project engineering
- Engineering operations
- Manufacturing operations
- Procurement

- Cost accounting
- Publications
- Marketing
- Sales

Under ideal conditions, each member of the project office would have a workable knowledge in all areas, with expertise in perhaps two or three. Unfortunately, this is almost never the case, except in the responsibilities of the project manager and project engineer as shown below:

PROJECT MANAGEMENT	PROJECT ENGINEERING
• Total project planning	• Total project planning
• Cost control	• Cost control
• Schedule control	• Schedule control
• System specifications	• System specifications
• Logistics support	• Logistics support
• Contract control	• Configuration control
• Report preparation and distribution	• Technical leadership support for fabrication, testing, and production
• Procurement	
• Identification of reliability and maintainability requirements	
• Staffing	
• Priority scheduling	
• Management information systems	

Above the dotted line the responsibilities are the same. This is a necessity because a good project manager must be his own chief engineer and, likewise, the chief engineer must make decisions as though he were the project manager. Below the dotted line are the major differences. Both the project manager and team members must understand fully the responsibilities and functions of each others team member so total integration can be achieved as rapidly and effectively as possible. On high-technology programs the chief project engineer assumes the role of deputy project manager. Project managers must understand the problems that the line managers have when selecting and assigning the project staff. Line managers tend to staff with people who understand the need for teamwork. Unfortunately, these people may simply be the average or below-average employees. As an example, a department manager hired a fifty-four-year old engineer who had two master's degrees in engineering disciplines. For the past thirty years, the individual was a true "loner," never having worked in a project management organization. How should the department manager handle this situation?

First, the department manager gave the individual an overload of work so that he would ask for help. Instead, the individual worked overtime, and did a good job. Next, the manager put the individual in charge of a line project and assigned two people to report to him. These two people were idle most of the time because the individual was still doing all the work himself (and quite well). The department manager did not want to lose this employee. Today, the employee is assigned only those tasks which he can do himself.

When employees are attached to a project, the project manager must identify the "star" employees. These are the employees who are vital for the success of the project and who can either make or break the project manager. Most of the time, "star" employees are found in the line organization, not the project office.

As a final point, we should discuss the responsibilities that the project manager can assign to an employee. Project managers can assign line employees added responsibilities within the scope of the project. If the added responsibilities can result in upgrading, then the project manager should consult with the line manager before such situations are initiated. Quite often, line managers (or even personnel representatives) send check people into the projects to verify that employees are performing at their proper pay grade. This is very important when working with blue-collar workers who, by union contractual agreements, must be paid at the grade level at which they are performing.

Also, project managers must be willing to surrender resources when they are no longer required. If the project manager constantly "cries wolf" in a situation where a problem really does not exist or is not as severe as the project manager makes it out to be, the line manager will simply pull away the resources (this is the line manager's right) and a deteriorating working relationship will result.

4.8 PART-TIME PROJECT MANAGEMENT

Not all companies need project management on a full-time basis. There are several industries, such as low-technology manufacturing, that operate most effectively in the traditional organizational structure. However, projects often come up, such as those involving capital equipment modifications, that can be accomplished either formally or informally using part-time project management.

With part-time project management, the individual reports to his own line manager, even if the project involves several line organizations. The individual must take care to avoid conflicts between the project and his line organization. If a project problem occurs, he will have to go to his line manager, and there is no guarantee that a decision will be made that is favorable for the project.

Part-time project management is not a career position as is full-time project management. The part-time project manager is selected because of his technical expertise and, after project termination, returns to his former position. If the project involves several line organizations, then it is often the responsibility of the line manager to coordinate the activities instead of the assistant project manager, mainly because the assistant project manager does not have the necessary authority or status to enter line organizations. Some companies modify this process by establishing a project administration office. A part-time project manager now reports informally (and horizontally) to the project administration office. The project administration office has the authority to cut across all line organizations and assists the project managers with conflict problems. This technique can prevent the line managers from getting too involved with projects. Even with the existence of a project administration office, part-time project management is accomplished informally.

4.9 THE PROJECT ORGANIZATIONAL CHART

One of the first requirements of the project startup phase is to develop the organizational chart for the project and to identify how it relates to the parent organizational structure. Figure 4-2 shows, in abbreviated form, the six major programs at Dalton Corporation. Our concern is with the Midas Program. Although the Midas Program may have the lowest priority of the six programs, it is placed at the top, and in bold face, to give the impression that it is the top priority. This type of representation usually makes the client or customer feel as though his program is considered important by the contractor.

The next step is to show the program office structure, as illustrated in Figure 4-3. Note that the chief of operations and the chief engineer have dual reporting responsibility; they report directly to the program manager and indirectly to the directors. Beneath the chief engineer, there are three positions. Although these positions appear as solid lines, they might actually be dotted lines. For example, Ed White might be working only part-time on the Midas Project but is still shown on the chart as a permanent program office member. Jean Flood, under contracts, might be spending only ten hours per week on the Midas Program.

If the function of two positions on the organizational chart takes place at different times, then both positions may be shown as manned by the same person. For example, Ed White may have his name under both engineering design and engineering testing if both activities are spaced sufficiently apart so he can perform them independently.

Most customers realize that the top-quality personnel may be shared with other programs and projects. Project manning charts, such as the one shown in

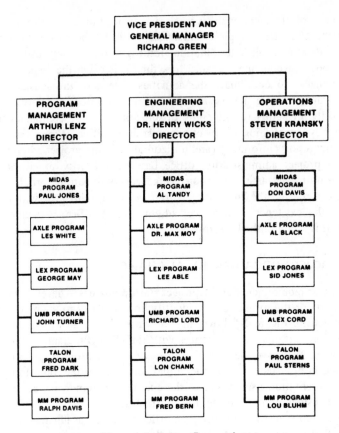

Figure 4-2. Dalton Corporation.

Figure 4-4, can be used for this purpose. These manning charts are also helpful in preparing the management volume for proposals.

4.10 REWARDS AND EVALUATION

When functional employees are assigned to a new project, their first concern is that their functional manager will be informed when they have performed well on their new assignment. A good project manager will make it immediately clear to all new functional employees that if they perform well in this effort, then he (the project manager) will inform the functional manager of their progress and achievements. This assumes that the functional manager is not providing close supervision over the functional employee and is, instead, passing on some of the responsibility to the project manager. This is quite common in project management organizational structures. Obviously, if the functional manager

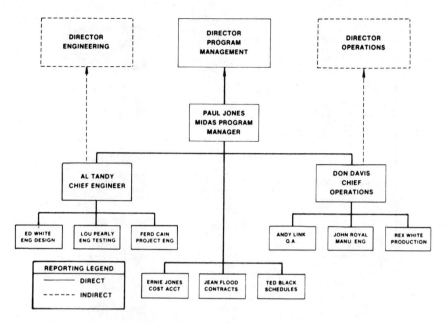

Figure 4-3. Midas Program Office.

has a small span of control and/or sufficient time to monitor closely the work of his subordinates, then the project manager's need for indirect reward power is minimal.

Many good projects as well as project management structures have failed because of the inability of the system to properly evaluate the functional employee's performance. This problem is, unfortunately, one of the most often overlooked trouble spots in project management.

In a project management structure, there are basically six ways that a functional employee can be evaluated on a project.

- *The project manager prepares a written, confidential evaluation and gives it to the functional manager.* The functional manager will evaluate the validity of the project manager's comment and prepare his own evaluation of the employee. The employee will be permitted to see only the evaluation form filled out by his immediate superior, the functional manager.
- *The project manager prepares a nonconfidential evaluation and gives it to the functional manager.* The functional manager prepares his own evaluation form and shows both evaluations to the functional employee. This is the technique preferred by most project and functional managers. However there are several major difficulties with this technique. If the functional employee is an average or below-average worker, and if this

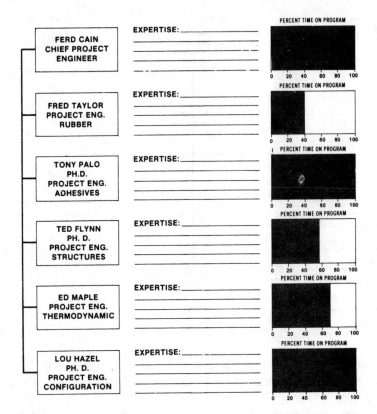

Figure 4-4. Project Engineering Department Manning For Midas Program.

employee is still to be assigned to this project after his evaluation, then the project manager might rate the employee as above average simply to prevent any sabotage or bad feelings downstream. In this situation, the functional manager might want a confidential evaluation instead, knowing that the functional employee will see both evaluation forms. Functional employees tend to blame the project manager if they receive a below-average merit increase, but give credit to the functional manager if the increase is above average. The best bet here is for the project manager to periodically inform the functional employees as to how well they are doing, and to give them an honest appraisal.

- *The project manager provides the functional manager with an oral evaluation of the employee's performance.* Although this technique is commonly used, most functional managers prefer documentation on employee progress.
- *The functional manager makes the entire evaluation without any input from the project manager.* In order for this technique to be effective, the

functional manager must have sufficient time to supervise each subordinate's performance on a continual basis. Unfortunately, most functional managers do not have this luxury because of their broad span of control.

- *The project manager makes the entire evaluation for the functional manager.* This technique can work if the functional employee spends 100 percent of his time on one project or if he is physically located at a remote site where he cannot be observed by his functional manager.
- *All project and functional managers jointly evaluate all project functional employees at the same time.* This technique may be limited to small companies with less than fifty or so employees, otherwise the evaluation process might be time-consuming for key personnel. A bad evaluation will be known by everyone.

In five of the six techniques, the project manager has either a direct or indirect input into the employee's evaluation process.

Since the majority of the project managers prefer written, nonconfidential evaluations, we must determine what the evaluation forms look like and when the functional employee will be evaluated. The indirect evaluation process will be time-consuming. This is of paramount importance on large projects where the project manager may have as many as 200 part-time functional employees assigned to his activities.

The evaluation forms can be filled out either when the employee is up for evaluation or after the project is completed. If the evaluation form is to be filled out when the employee is up for promotion or a merit increase, then the project manager should be willing to give an *honest* appraisal of the employee's performance. Of course, the project manager should not fill out the evaluation form if he has not had sufficient time to observe the employee at work.

The evaluation form can be filled out at the termination of the project. This, however, may produce a problem in that the project may end the month after the employee is up for promotion. The advantage of this technique is that the project manager may have been able to find sufficient time both to observe the employee in action and to see the output.

Figure 4-5 represents, in a rather humorous version, how project personnel perceive the evaluation form. Unfortunately, the evaluation process is very serious and can easily have a severe impact on an individual's career path with the company even though the final evaluation rests with the functional manager.

Figure 4-6 shows a simple type of evaluation form where the project manager identifies the box that best describes the employee's performance. The project manager may or may not make additional comments. This type of form is generally used whenever the employee is up for evaluation, provided that the project manager has had sufficient time to observe the employee's performance.

Figure 4-7 shows another typical form that can be used to evaluate an employee. In each category, the employee is rated on a scale from one to five. In

PERFORMANCE FACTORS	EXCELLENT (1 OUT OF 15)	VERY GOOD (3 OUT OF 15)	GOOD (8 OUT OF 15)	FAIR (2 OUT OF 15)	UNSATISFACTORY (1 OUT OF 15)
	FAR EXCEEDS JOB REQUIREMENTS	EXCEEDS JOB REQUIREMENTS	MEETS JOB REQUIREMENTS	NEEDS SOME IMPROVEMENT	DOES NOT MEET MINIMUM STANDARDS
QUALITY	LEAPS TALL BUILDINGS WITH A SINGLE BOUND	MUST TAKE RUNNING START TO LEAP OVER TALL BUILDING	CAN ONLY LEAP OVER A SHORT BUILDING OR MEDIUM ONE WITHOUT SPIRES	CRASHES INTO BUILDING	CANNOT RECOGNIZE BUILDINGS
TIMELINESS	IS FASTER THAN A SPEEDING BULLET	IS AS FAST AS A SPEEDING BULLET	NOT QUITE AS FAST AS A SPEEDING BULLET	WOULD YOU BELIEVE A SLOW BULLET?	WOUNDS HIMSELF WITH THE BULLET
INITIATIVE	IS STRONGER THAN A LOCOMOTIVE	IS STRONGER THAN A BULL ELEPHANT	IS STRONGER THAN A BULL	SHOOTS THE BULL	SMELLS LIKE A BULL
ADAPTABILITY	WALKS ON WATER CONSISTENTLY	WALKS ON WATER IN EMERGENCIES	WASHES WITH WATER	DRINKS WATER	PASSES WATER IN EMERGENCIES
COMMUNICATIONS	TALKS WITH GOD	TALKS WITH ANGELS	TALKS TO HIMSELF	ARGUES WITH HIMSELF	LOSES THE ARGUMENT WITH HIMSELF

Figure 4-5. Guide To Performance Appraisal.

order to minimize time and paper work, it is also possible to have a single evaluation form at project termination for evaluation of all employees. This is shown in Figure 4-8. As before, all employees are rated in each category on a scale of one to five. Totals are obtained to provide a relative comparison between employees.

Obviously, evaluation forms such as Figure 4-8 have severe limitations in that a one-to-one comparison of all project functional personnel is of little value if the employees are from different departments. How can a project engineer be compared against a cost accountant? If the project engineer receives a total score of forty and the cost accountant receives a score of thirty, does this mean that the project engineer is of more value or a better employee? Employees should have the right to "challenge" any item in the nonconfidential evaluation form.

Several companies are using this form by assigning coefficients of importance to each topic. For example, under a topic of technical judgment, the project engineer might have a coefficient of importance of 0.90 whereas the cost accountant's coefficient may be 0.25. These coefficients could be reversed for a

EMPLOYEE'S NAME		DATE	
PROJECT TITLE		JOB NUMBER	
EMPLOYEE ASSIGNMENT			
EMPLOYEE'S TOTAL TIME TO DATE ON PROJECT		EMPLOYEE'S REMAINING TIME ON PROJECT	

TECHNICAL JUDGEMENT:

☐ Quickly reaches sound conclusions ☐ Usually makes sound conclusions ☐ Marginal decision making ability ☐ Needs technical assistance ☐ Makes faulty conclusions

WORK PLANNING:

☐ Good planner ☐ Plans well with help ☐ Occasionally plans well ☐ Needs detailed instructions ☐ Cannot plan at all

COMMUNICATIONS:

☐ Always understands instructions ☐ Sometimes needs clarification ☐ Always needs clarifications ☐ Needs follow-up ☐ Needs constant instruction

ATTITUDE:

☐ Always job interested ☐ Shows interest most of the time ☐ Shows no job interest ☐ More interested in other activities ☐ Does not care about job

COOPERATION:

☐ Always enthusiastic ☐ Works well until job is completed ☐ Usually works well with others ☐ Works poorly with others ☐ Wants it done his/her way

WORK HABITS:

☐ Always project oriented ☐ Most often project oriented ☐ Usually consistent with requests ☐ Works poorly with others ☐ Always works alone

ADDITIONAL COMMENTS: _____

Figure 4-6. Project Work Assignment Appraisal.

topic on cost consciousness. Unfortunately, because such comparisons have questionable validity, this type of evaluation form is usually of a confidential nature.

Even though the project manager fills out an evaluation form, there is no guarantee that the functional manager will given any credibility to the project manager's evaluation. There are always situations where the project and functional managers disagree as to either quality or direction of work. This can easily alienate the project manager into recommending a poor evaluation regardless of how well the employee has performed. If the functional employee spends most of his time working by himself, then the project manager may give an average evaluation even if the employee's performance is superb. There is also the situa-

EMPLOYEE'S NAME						DATE
PROJECT TITLE						JOB NUMBER
EMPLOYEE ASSIGNMENT						
EMPLOYEE'S TOTAL TIME TO DATE ON PROJECT				EMPLOYEE'S REMAINING TIME ON PROJECT		

	EXCELLENT	ABOVE AVERAGE	AVERAGE	BELOW AVERAGE	INADEQUATE
TECHNICAL JUDGEMENT					
WORK PLANNING					
COMMUNICATIONS					
ATTITUDE					
COOPERATION					
WORK HABITS					
PROFIT CONTRIBUTION					

ADDITIONAL COMMENTS _____

Figure 4-7. Project Work Assignment Appraisal.

tion where the project manager knows the employee personally and may allow personal feelings to influence his decision.

Another problem exists in the situation where the project manager is a "generalist," say at a grade 7 level, and requests that the functional manager assign his best employee to the project. The functional manager agrees to the request and assigns his best employee, a grade 10. Now, how can a grade 7 generalist evaluate a grade 10 specialist? One solution to this problem is having the project manager evaluate the expert only in certain categories such as communications, work habits, and problem solving, but not in the area of his technical expertise. The functional manager might be the only person qualified to evaluate functional personnel on technical abilities and expertise.

As a final note, several people contend that functional employees should have some sort of indirect input into a project manager's evaluation. This raises rather interesting questions as to how far we can go with the indirect evaluation procedure.

From a top management perspective, the indirect evaluation process brings with it several headaches. Wage and salary administrators readily accept the

PROJECT TITLE		JOB NUMBER	
EMPLOYEE ASSIGNMENT		DATE	

CODE:

EXCELLENT = 5
ABOVE AVERAGE = 4
AVERAGE = 3
BELOW AVERAGE = 2
INADEQUATE = 1

NAMES	TECHNICAL JUDGEMENT	WORK PLANNING	COMMUNICATIONS	ATTITUDE	COOPERATION	WORK HABITS	PROFIT CONTRIBUTION	SELF MOTIVATION	TOTAL POINTS

Figure 4-8. Project Work Assignment Appraisal.

necessity for using different evaluation forms for white-collar and blue-collar workers. But now, we have a situation in which there can be more than one type of evaluation system for white-collar workers alone. Those employees that work in project-driven functional departments will be evaluated directly and indirectly, but based upon formal procedures. Employees that charge their time to overhead accounts and non-project-driven departments might simply be evaluated by a single, direct evaluation procedure.

Many wage and salary administrators contend that they cannot live with a white-collar system and therefore have tried to combine the direct and indirect evaluation forms into one, as shown in Figure 4-9. Some administrators have even gone so far as to adopt a single form companywide, regardless of whether an individual is a white- or blue-collar worker.

The design of the employee's evaluation form depends upon what evaluation method or procedure is being used. Generally speaking, there are nine methods available for evaluating personnel:

- Essay Appraisal
- Graphic Rating Scale

I. EMPLOYEE INFORMATION:

1. NAME_____ 2. DATE OF EVALUATION_____

3. JOB ASSIGNMENT_____ 4. DATE OF LAST EVALUATION_____

5. PAY GRADE_____

6. EMPLOYEE'S IMMEDIATE SUPERVISOR_____

7. SUPERVISOR'S LEVEL: ☐ SECTION ☐ DEPT. ☐ DIVISION ☐ EXECUTIVE

II. EVALUATOR'S INFORMATION:

1. EVALUATOR'S NAME_____

2. EVALUATOR'S LEVEL: ☐ SECTION ☐ DEPT. ☐ DIVISION ☐ EXECUTIVE

3. RATE THE EMPLOYEE ON THE FOLLOWING:

	EXCELLENT	VERY GOOD	GOOD	FAIR	POOR
ABILITY TO ASSUME RESPONSIBILITY					
WORKS WELL WITH OTHERS					
LOYAL ATTITUDE TOWARD COMPANY					
DOCUMENTS WORK WELL AND IS BOTH COST AND PROFIT CONSCIOUS					
RELIABILITY TO SEE JOB THROUGH					
ABILITY TO ACCEPT CRITICISM					
WILLINGNESS TO WORK OVERTIME					
PLANS JOB EXECUTION CAREFULLY					
TECHNICAL KNOWLEDGE					
COMMUNICATIVE SKILLS					
OVERALL RATING					

4. RATE THE EMPLOYEE IN COMPARISON TO HIS CONTEMPORARIES:

LOWER 10%	LOWER 25%	LOWER 40%	MIDWAY	UPPER 40%	UPPER 25%	UPPER 10%

5. RATE THE EMPLOYEE IN COMPARISON TO HIS CONTEMPORARIES:

SHOULD BE PROMOTED AT ONCE	PROMOTABLE NEXT YEAR	PROMOTABLE ALONG WITH CONTEMPORARIES	NEEDS TO MATURE IN GRADE	DEFINITELY NOT PROMOTABLE

Figure 4-9. Job Evaluation.

- Field Review
- Forced-Choice Review
- Critical Incident Appraisal
- Management by Objectives
- Work Standards Approach
- Ranking Methods
- Assessment Center

Descriptions of these methods can be found in almost any text on wage and salary administration. Which method is best suited for a project-driven organizational structure? To answer this question, we must analyze the characteristics of the organizational form as well as those of the personnel who must perform there. As an example, project management can be described as an arena of conflict. Which of the above evaluation procedures can best be used to evaluate an employee's ability to work and progress in an atmosphere of conflict? Figure 4-10 compares the above nine evaluation procedures against the six most common project conflicts. This type of analysis must be carried out for all variables and characteristics that describe the project management environment. Most com-

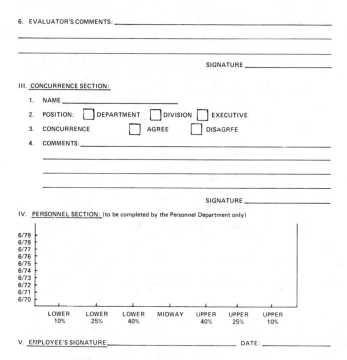

Figure 4-9. Job Evaluation. (Continued)

pensation managers would agree that the management by objectives (MBO) technique offers the greatest promise for a fair and equitable evaluation of all employees. Unfortunately, MBO implies that functional employees will have a say in establishing their own goals and objectives. This might not be the case. In project management, the project manager or functional manager might set the objectives and the functional employee is told that he has to live with it. Obviously, there will be advantages and disadvantages to whatever evaluation procedures are finally selected.

Having identified the problems with employee evaluation in a project environment, we can now summarize the results and attempt to predict the future. Project managers must have some sort of either direct or indirect input into an employee's evaluation. Without this, project managers may find it difficult to adequately motivate people on the horizontal line. The question is, of course, how this input should take place. Most wage and salary administrators appear to be pushing for a single procedure to evaluate all white-collar employees. At the same time, however, administrators recognize the necessity for an indirect input by the project manager and, therefore, are willing to let the project and functional managers (and possibly functional personnel) determine the exact method of input, which can be different for each employee and each project. This implies

	Essay Appraisal	Graphic Rating Scale	Field Review	Forced-Choice Review	Critical Incident Appraisal	Management By Objectives	Work Standards Approach	Ranking Methods	Assessment Center
Conflict over schedules	●	●		●	●		●	●	
Conflict over priorities	●	●		●	●		●	●	
Conflict over technical issues	●			●			●		
Conflict over administration	●	●	●	●			●	●	●
Personality conflict	●	●		●			●		
Conflict over cost	●		●	●	●		●	●	●

Circles define areas where evaluation technique may be difficult to implement.

Figure 4-10. Rating Evaluation Techniques Against Types Of Conflicts.

that the indirect input might be oral for one employee and written for another, with both employees reporting to the functional manager. Although this technique may seem confusing, it may be the only viable alternative for the future.

Sometimes, project management can create severe evaluation problems. As an example, Gary has been assigned as a part-time assistant project manager. He must function both as an assistant project manager and a functional employee. In addition, Gary reports both vertically to his functional manager and horizontally to a project manager. As part of his project responsibilities, Gary must integrate activities between his department and two other departments within his division. His responsibilities also include writing a nonconfidential performance evaluation for all functional employees from all three departments who are assigned to his project. Can Gary effectively and honestly evaluate functional employees in his own department, people with whom he will be working side-by-side when the project is over? The answer to this question is no; the project manager should come to the rescue. If Gary were the project manager instead of the assistant project manager, then the line manager should come to his rescue.

4.11 PROJECT MANAGEMENT EFFECTIVENESS[16]

Project managers interact continuously with upper-level management, perhaps more so than with functional managers. Not only the success of the project,

---

16. This section and section 4.12 have been adapted from *Seminar in Project Management Workbook,* copyright 1977 by Hans J. Thamhain. Reproduced by permission of Dr. Hans J. Thamhain.

but even the career path of the project manager can depend upon the working relationships and expectations established with upper-level management. There are four key variables in measuring the effectiveness of dealing with upper-level management. These variables are credibility, priority, accessibility, and visibility.

- CREDIBILITY:
  - Comes from the image of a sound decision maker.
  - Is normally based upon experience in a variety of assignments.
  - Is refueled by the manager and the status of his project.
  - Making success visible to others increases credibility.
  - Emphasize facts rather than opinions.
  - Give credit to others; they may return this favor.

- PRIORITY:
  - Sell the specific importance of the project to the objectives of the total organization.
  - Stress competitive aspect, if relevant.
  - Stress changes for success.
  - Secure testimonial support from others—functional departments, other managers, customers, independent sources.
  - Emphasize "spin-offs" that may result from projects.
  - Anticipate "priority problems."
  - Sell priority on a one-to-one basis.

- ACCESSIBILITY:
  - Accessibility involves the ability to directly communicate with top management.
  - Show that your proposals are good for the total organization, not just the project.
  - Weigh the facts carefully, explain the pros and cons.
  - Be logical and polished in your presentations.
  - Become personally known by members of top management.
  - Create a desire in the "customer" for your abilities and your project.
  - Make curiosity work for you.

- VISIBILITY:
  - Be aware of the amount of visibility you really need.
  - Make a good impact when presenting the project to top management.
  - Adopt a contrasting style of management when feasible and possible.
  - Use team members to help regulate the visibility you need.
  - Conduct timely "informational" meetings with those who count.
  - Use available publicity media.

4.12 EXPECTATIONS

In the project management environment, the project managers, team members, and upper-level managers each have expectations of how their relationships should be with the other parties. To illustrate this, top management expects project managers to:

- Assume total accountability for the success or failure to provide results
- Provide effective reports and information
- Provide minimum organizational disruption during the execution of a project
- Present recommendations, not just alternatives
- Have the capacity to handle most interpersonal problems
- Demonstrate a self-starting capacity
- Demonstrate growth with each assignment

At first glance, it may appear that these qualities are expected of all managers, not necessarily project managers. But this is not true. The first four items are different. The line managers are not accountable for total project success, just for that portion performed by their line organization. Line managers can be promoted on their technical ability, not necessarily on their ability to write effective reports. Line managers cannot disrupt an entire organization, but the project manager can. Line managers do not necessarily have to make decisions, just provide alternatives and recommendations.

Just as top management has expectations of project managers, project managers have certain expectations of top management. Project management expects top management to:

- Provide clearly defined decision channels
- Take actions on requests
- Facilitate interfacing with support departments
- Assist in conflict resolution
- Provide sufficient resources/charter
- Provide sufficient strategic/long-range information
- Provide feedback
- Give advice and stage-setting support
- Define expectations clearly
- Provide protection from political in-fighting
- Provide the opportunity for personal and professional growth

The project team also has expectations from their leader, the project manager. The project team expects the project manager to:

- Assist in the problem-solving process by coming up with ideas
- Provide proper direction and leadership
- Provide a relaxed environment
- Interact informally with team members
- Stimulate the group process
- Facilitate adoption of new members

- Reduce conflicts
- Defend the team against outside pressure
- Resist changes
- Act as the group spokesperson
- Provide representation with higher management

In order for a project team to provide high task efficiency and productivity, a project team should have certain traits and characteristics. Therefore, a project manager expects the project team to:

- Demonstrate membership self-development
- Demonstrate the potential for innovative and creative behavior
- Communicate effectively
- Be committed to the project
- Demonstrate the capacity for conflict resolution
- Be results oriented
- Be change oriented
- Interface effectively and with high morale

Team members want, in general, to fill certain primary needs. The project manager should understand these needs before demanding that the team live up to his expectations. Members of the project team need:

- A sense of belonging
- Interest in the work itself
- Respect for the work being done
- Protection from political in-fighting
- Job security and job continuity
- Potential for career growth

Project managers must remember that team members may not always be able to verbalize these needs, but they do exist nevertheless.

4.13 SPECIAL PROBLEMS

There are always special problems that influence the organizational staffing process. For example, the department shown in Figure 4-11 has a departmental matrix. All activities stay within the department. Project X and Project Y are managed by line employees who have been temporarily assigned to the projects, whereas Project Z is headed by supervisor B. The department's activities involve high-technology engineering as well as R & D.

The biggest problem facing the department managers is how to train their new employees. The training process requires nine to twelve months. The employees become familiar with the functioning of all three sections, and only after training is an employee assigned to one of the sections. Line managers

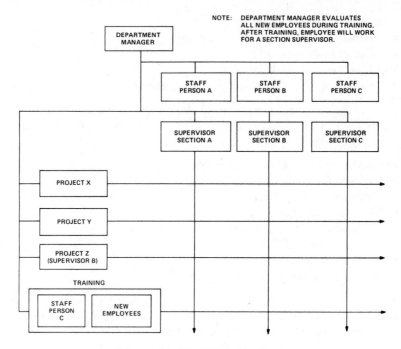

Figure 4-11. The Training Problem.

claim that they do not have sufficient time to supervise training. As a result, the department manager has found that staff person C is the most competent person to supervise training. A special departmental training project was set up, as shown in Figure 4-11.

At the end of six months, all new employees were up for their first perform-ance evaluation. The staff person signed the evaluation forms. Within forty-eight hours, the personnel department began screaming that only managers can sign evaluation forms, and since the staff person is not a manager, personnel cannot accept the evaluations. There are now four options available to the department manager:

- Request that the personnel department be disbanded
- Request personnel to change their procedures
- Speed up training and, before six months are up, assign the employees to one of the sections
- Continue as before, but the department manager will sign the evaluation forms after staff person C fills them out

The first two choices were found to be impossible, and the third was impracti-cal. The company is now using the fourth approach.

Figure 4-12 shows a utility company which has three full-time project managers controlling three projects, all of which cut across the central division. Unfortunately, the three full-time project managers cannot get sufficient resources from the central division because the line managers are also acting as divisional project managers and saving the best resources for their own projects, regardless of the priority.

The obvious solution to the problem is that the central division line managers not be permitted to wear two hats. Instead, one full-time project manager can be added to the left division to manage all three central division projects. It is usually best for all project managers to report to the same division for priority setting and conflict resolution.

Line managers have a tendency to feel demoted when they are suddenly told that they can no longer wear two hats. As an example, Mr. Adams is a department manager with thirty years of experience in the company. For the last several years, he has worn two hats and acted as both project manager and functional manager on a variety of projects. He is regarded as an expert in his field.

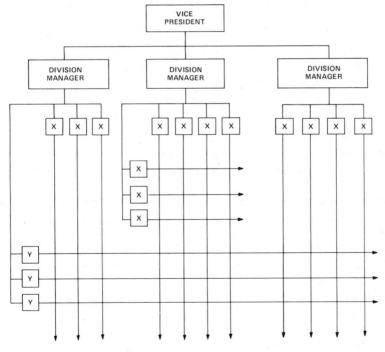

NOTE: X INDICATES FULL—TIME FUNCTIONAL MANAGERS
Y INDICATES FULL—TIME PROJECT MANAGERS

Figure 4-12. Utility Service Organization.

The company has decided to incorporate formal project management and has established a project management department. Mr. Bell, a thirty-year-old employee with three years experience with the company, has been assigned as the project manager. In order to staff his project, Bell has asked Adams that Mr. Cane (Bell's friend) be assigned to the project as the functional representative. Cane has been with the company for two years. Adams agrees to the request and informs Cane of his new assignment, closing with the remarks, "This project is yours all the way. I don't want to have anything to do with it. I'll be too busy with paperwork as a result of the new organizational structure. Just send me a memo once in a while telling me what's happening."

During the project kickoff meeting, it became obvious to everyone that the only person with the necessary expertise was Adams. Without his support, the time duration of the project could be expected to double.

The real problem here was that Adams wanted to feel important and needed, and was hoping that the project manager would come to him asking for his assistance. The project manager correctly analyzed the situation, but refused to ask for the line manager's help. Instead, the project manager asked an executive to step in and force the line manager to help. The line manager gave his help, but with great reluctance. Today, the line manager provides poor support to the projects that come across his line organization.

The last special problem to be discussed is the selling to top management. What can an individual or consultant say to an executive to sell him on the idea of project management? What areas will be stressed? What fears might the executives have? Below are the questions asked by the executives during a selling session. Why do you think these questions are being asked and what are your answers?

- Can our people be part-time project managers?
- Can part-time project managers report horizontally as well as vertically at the same time?
- Is it better for a functional employee who reports to a department manager to act as an assistant project manager or as the project manager?
- An employee is a part-time project manager for an effort that requires work to be integrated within three departments. When a project problem occurs, should the project manager go to his functional superior or to the project administration division?
- Which vice-president should be responsible for the project management function?
- If we go to project management, must we increase resources, especially the number of project managers?
- Is it true that the current industrial trend for a career path is from project manager to vice-president?

- Can we give employees a rotation period of six to eighteen months in project management and then return them to the functional departments where they should be more well-rounded individuals?
- How much control should a project manager have over costs and budgets?
- What role should a project manager have in strategic and operational planning?
- How much authority should an executive delegate to a project manager?
- What should the working relationship be between executives and project managers?
- What percentage of a total project budget should be available for project management and administrative support?

4.14 SMALL COMPANY PROJECT MANAGEMENT

Many people believe that project management will work the same in small companies as in large companies. Although some similarities do exist, such as the need for effective planning, scheduling, and controlling, there are major differences. They include:

- Project manager wears multiple hats (and can return to functional positions).
- Project manager handles multiple projects, each with a different priority.
- Project manager has limited resources.
- Project manager has shorter lines of communications.
- A project office might not exist.
- There is a greater need for interpersonal skills.
- There may be a greater risk with the failure of even one project.
- There might be tighter monetary controls but less sophisticated control techniques.
- Generally there exists more upper-level interference.
- Evaluation procedures for individuals are easier.
- Conflict resolution can become easier or more difficult and may be severely affected by the personalities of the conflicting parties.

It should be noted that project management in small companies can be much more difficult to implement because of the multiple roles that individuals must have.

CASE STUDY: WEBSTER INDUSTRIAL CONTROLS

Webster Industrial Controls (WIC) is a thirty-two-year-old company which manufactures quality industrial control systems for aerospace, defense, construction, electronics, and nuclear components. In 1975, WIC incorporated formal project management, by decree. On December 19, 1978, the author visited WIC (the name is fictitious) to ascertain some of the major problem areas affecting successful project management operations. Several of WIC's personnel were interviewed. All of the questions discussed revolved about three major areas of concern:

- What are the major problems with current WIC operations?
- What are the major weaknesses with the current organizational structure, the project managers, and the functional managers?
- What kind of training would you like to see developed here at WIC in order to help you perform your job better and to improve your working relationships with other project management personnel?

Below are the responses to these questions. They have been edited somewhat for conciseness.

Q. What are the major problems with current WIC operations?

A1. *Scheduling:* "Many people, both in project management and production, do not understand why we have such a terrible problem in scheduling activities. Sure, our people understand the necessity for getting the order out as fast as possible in order to meet customer requirements, but there are severe environmental factors. The government has tied our hands with requirements on qualified customer vendors."

A2. "Qualifying a vendor, means qualifying in terms of safety. This leads us to other questions. Does our vendor have design control? Has the vendor made these parts obsolete? How do we get vendor commitment? We spend $25-50K per product before we can call it qualified."

A3. "All vendors who have input also have changing situations. We have to write test procedure acceptance criteria, often under adverse conditions. If the control system is all right, then the point of release to manufacturing will be six months to a year. That's after three to four years in design. Also, how do we incorporate information on aging to show that the theoretical life of a nuclear control system is forty years? I wish I knew."

A1. *Priorities:* "There is lack of communication about how and why priorities can continuously shift. Manufacturing has the greatest concern. Priorities in manufacturing are related to the dollar value of the contract, usually through the marketing group and the project manager. Although there are several reasons for establishing a priority, the most common cause is with penalty or liquidated damages (i.e., failure to peform on a given date because the customer has people waiting to work and the equipment is not yet available)."

A2. "We have good channels to the upper levels of the organization for priority setting. But this doesn't resolve our problem. How do we keep people motivated with a shifting priority environment? Maybe we can't help it in our environment, but at least explaining the rationale to our people might ease some of the tension."

A1. *Conflicting Instructions to Manufacturing:* "This creates real havoc in our organization, and results from a lack of information, untimely information, wrong data, or incomplete engineering. The result is that manufacturing blames engineering, stating that it's engineering's fault (possibly because of incorrect drawings and wrong parts), and engineering blames manufacturing for making it wrong and not ordering the parts in time.

"When this occurs, we usually just get our heads together and hash it out. If penalty clauses are included as part of the contract, or any other clause that may require special attention, the usual result is weekly team meetings. Now time management becomes a problem. Perhaps there are better ways to handle this."

A2. "We have a very poor monitoring and control system. Not only are we tied down with too much paperwork, but the value of this paperwork always forces me to ask whether or not it is really necessary. Less than 50 percent of our orders go out without a final push. Here we are designing industrial control systems and we have no system that functions on its own.

"Fortunately we've been successful because we have an easy access to upper-level management. They usually get totally involved and try to give us immediate resolution."

A3. "Planning is poor, at best. Sometimes, marketing provides a very, very poor forecast and everyone has to live with it. This becomes a problem when our new project managers are at a low level on the learning curve. Manufacturing sometimes doesn't know the status of a piece of equipment until it physically appears in front of them".

A4. "We cannot control resources unless we have planning and know what's coming. I don't know what's coming until I see it on the floor. What happened to proper planning?"

Q. What are the major weaknesses with the current organizational structure, the project managers, and the functional managers?

A1. "I've been here several years and I have no idea about how project management is supposed to work. Who has what authority, responsibility, how, when . . . ?

A2. "Project managers cannot be successful unless they know the total picture, especially manufacturing operations. Perhaps they should spend some time there. Project engineers are not allowed to track activities in the production area. I'm not sure this is the way the project management system is supposed to work. There must be a better way to get total control of resources."

A3. "We have an extremely weak information system and poor feedback. Manufacturing does not want the project engineer in their domain in order to get feedback. They claim that the PM prevents people from working. The system shouldn't work this way. We have to get these people together to iron out their differences."

A4. "I've often wondered if there's a better way to control our paperwork, especially engineering change notices (ECNs). These ECNs are very,

very unmanageable. Who is responsible for chairing configuration management? What are the requirements? Nobody seems to know."

Q. What kind of training would you like to see developed here at WIC in order to help you perform your job better and to improve your working relationships with other project management personnel?

A1. "What is project management? I don't know. Why do the project engineers report to marketing, but have little authority in manufacturing? Is this the way the system should work?"

A2. "Section supervisors and group leaders now act as interface agents between department managers and project personnel. If they have to supervise more than five or six people, the system may break down. Is there a better way?"

A3. "Once a system is shipped, in effect, parts distribution becomes the customer interface. Aren't we therefore project managers? We should also be trained in project management."

A4. "Project management has a pecking order—not enough pull. Are there better ways of establishing authority and responsibility relationships?"

A5. "There is a lack of communications. Much information is not said or understood. How well do we listen? Perhaps people don't listen or just have a parochial view."

A6. "We must understand priorities and conflict resolution as well as why urgency is needed."

A7. "Interpersonal skills—from A to Z. Can this and attitude problems be taught or does it come with on-the-job training? How do we keep a cool head in stress situations? Can we teach professionalism and positive reaction?"

A8. "What is project management? I don't know. I lost track about two years ago. We've made too many changes and nobody knows what's going on."

A9. "I want to know the flow of paperwork. It's very difficult to become dedicated if you're kept in the dark."

A10. "The biggest problem is paperwork. We overcomplicate things by doing it serially instead of in parallel. Perhaps this is why we can't ship as fast as the customer would like."

A11. "Project managers are not technical specialists. Our project managers need formal training in project management. As far as I know, they've had none."

A12. "How can I do my job if I don't know who the players are?"

A13. "There is a logic to decisions, but people just don't listen. They build up roadblocks."

A14. "What is a cost-control system? The PM doesn't know where he stands costwise on a project? That shouldn't be. We need help."

A15. "Should our project managers be customer or cost oriented? When should we compromise? Most PMs are at the extremes. The best ones know when to give and take. Can this be learned?"

A16. "We in engineering are instructed to keep out of manufacturing. So, we have less information as to how manufacturing works."

A17. "PMs do not understand the operation of each department. That's a mistake in project management. Also, the PMs are very weak in planning and do not close the feedback loops. The result is scramble time. We need better planning and control of our resources. We need a cadet indoctrination program for ongoing people. Our people can read black and white, but not grey. They have strong tunnel vision. I'm not sure if this is good or bad."

A18. "We've had project management training programs in the past where everyone walked out saying that it was a fine program. Unfortunately, it was a failure because our people could not relate the information to their everyday job. Don't you make the same mistake."

CASE STUDY: GOVERNMENT PROJECT MANAGEMENT

A major government agency is organized to monitor government subcontractors as shown in Exhibit 4-1. Below are the vital characteristics of certain project office team members:

Project Manager: Directs all project activities and acts as the information focal point for the subcontractor.

Assistant Project Manager: Acts as chairman of the steering committee and interfaces with both in-house functional group and contractor.

Department Managers: Act as members of the steering committee for any projects which utilize their resources. These slots on the steering committee must be filled by the department managers themselves, not by functional employees.

Exhibit 4-1.

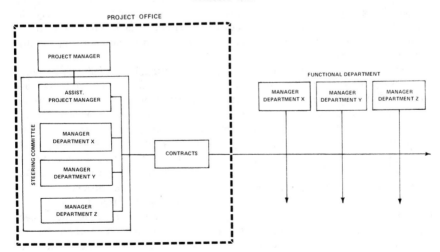

Contracts Officer: Authorizes all work directed by the project office to in-house functional groups and to the customer, and insures that all work requested is authorized by the contract. The contracts officer acts as the focal point for all contractor cost and contractual information.

1. Explain how this structure should work.
2. Explain how this structure actually works.
3. Can the project manager be a military type who is reassigned after a given tour of duty?
4. What are the advantages and disadvantages of this structure?
5. Could this be used in industry?

CASE STUDY: FALLS ENGINEERING

Falls Engineering is a $250-million chemical and material operation employing 900 people and located in New York. The plant has two distinct manufacturing product lines: industrial chemicals and computer materials. Both divisions are controlled by one plant manager, but direction, strategic planning, and priorities are established by corporate vice-presidents in Chicago. Each division has its own corporate vice-president, list of projects, list of priorities, and manpower control. The chemical division has been at this location for the past twenty years. The materials division is, you might say, the tenant in the landlord-tenant relationship with the materials division manager reporting dotted to the plant manager and solid to the corporate vice-president. (See Exhibit 4-2.)

The chemical division employed 3000 people in 1968. By 1973, there were only 600 employees. In 1974, the materials division was formed and located on the chemical division site with a landlord-tenant relationship. The materials division has grown from $50 million in 1975 to $120 million in 1979. Today, the materials division employs 350 people.

The chemical division has a much larger construction and facilities group compared to the materials division. However, for capital equipment projects, the materials group has to "rent" resources from the chemical group in order to get the projects accomplished. All projects are geared toward manufacturing because this is where the profits are.

All projects originate in construction or engineering, but usually are designed to support production. The engineering and construction departments have projects that span the entire organization directed by a project coordinator. The project coordinator is a line employee who is temporarily assigned to co-ordinate a project in his line organization in addition to performing his line responsibilities. Assignments are made by the division managers (who report to the plant manager) and are based upon technical expertise. The coordinators have monitoring authority only and are not noted for being good planners or negotiators. The coordinators report to their respective line managers.

Basically, a project can start in either division with the project coordinators. The coordinators draw up a large scope of work and submit it to the project engineering group who arrange for design contractors, depending upon the size of the project. Project engineering places it upon their design schedule accord-

Exhibit 4-2. Falls Engineering Organizational Chart.

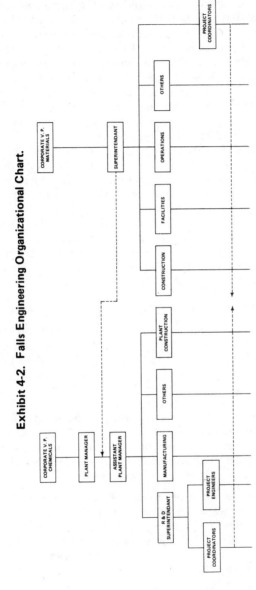

ing to priority and produces prints and specifications, and receives quotes. A construction cost estimate is then produced following 60-75 percent design completion. The estimate and project papers are prepared and the project is circulated through the plant and in Chicago for approval and authorization. Following authorization, the design is completed and materials ordered. Following design, the project is transferred to either of two plant construction groups for construction. The project coordinators then arrange for the work to be accomplished in their areas with minimum interference from manufacturing forces. In all cases, the coordinators act as project managers and must take the usual contraints of time, money and performance into account.

Falls Engineering has 300 projects listed for completion between 1980 and 1982. In the last two years, less than 10 percent of the projects were completed within time, cost, and performance constraints. Line managers find it increasingly difficult to make resource commitments because crises always seems to develop, including a number of fires.

Profits are made in manufacturing and everyone knows it. Whenever a manufacturing crisis occurs, line managers pull resources off the projects and, of course, the projects suffer. Project coordinators are trying, but with very little success, to put some slack onto the schedules to allow for contingencies.

The breakdown of the 300 plant projects is shown below:

NUMBER OF PROJECTS	$ RANGE
120	less than $50,000
80	$50,000-200,000
70	$250,000-750,000
20	$1-3 million
10	$4-8 million

Corporate realized the necessity for changing the organizational structure. A meeting was set up and between the plant manager, plant executives, and corporate executives to resolve these problems once and for all. The plant manager decided to survey his employees concerning their feelings about the present organizational structure. Below are their comments:

- "The projects we have the most trouble with are the small ones under $200,000. Can we use informal project management for the small ones and formal project management on the large ones?"
- "Why do we persist in using computer programming to control our resources. These sophisticated packages are useless because they do not account for firefighting."
- "Project coordinators need access to various levels of management, in both divisions."
- "Our line managers do not realize the necessity for effective planning of resources. Resources are assigned based upon emotions and not need."
- "Sometimes a line manager gives a commitment but the project coordinator cannot force him to keep it."

- "Line managers always find fault with project coordinators who try to develop detailed schedules themselves."
- "If we continuously have to 'crash' project time, doesn't that indicate poor planning?"
- "We need a career path in project coordination so that we can develop a body of good planners, communicators, and integrators."
- "I've seen project coordinators who have no interest in the job, cannot work with diverse functional disciplines, and cannot communicate. Yet, someone assigned them as a project coordinator."
- "Any organizational system we come up with has to be better than the one we have now."
- "Somebody has to have total accountability. Our people are working on projects and, at the same time, do not know the project status, the current cost, the risks, and the end date."
- "One of these days I'm going to kill an executive while he's meddling in my project."
- "Recently, management made changes requiring more paperwork for the project coordinators. How many hours a week do they expect me to work?"
- "I've yet to see any documentation describing the job description of the project coordinator."
- "I have absolutely no knowledge about who is assigned as the project coordinator until work has to be coordinated in my group. Somehow, I'm not sure that this is the way the system should work."
- "I know that we line managers are supposed to be flexible, but changing the priorities every week isn't exactly my idea of fun."
- "If the projects start out with poor planning, then management does not have the right to expect the line managers always to come to the rescue."
- "Why is it the line managers always get blamed for schedule delays, even if it's the result of poor planning up front?"
- "If management doesn't want to hire additional resources, then why should the line managers be made to suffer? Perhaps, we should cut out some of these useless projects. Sometimes I think management dreams up some of these projects simply to spend the allocated funds."
- "I have yet to see a project I felt had a realistic deadline."

After preparing alternatives and recommendations, as plant manager, try to do some role playing by putting yourself in the shoes of the corporate executives. Would you as a corporate executive approve the recommendation? Where does profitability, sales, return on investment, and so on enter in your decision?

CASE STUDY: WHITE MANUFACTURING

In 1975, White Manufacturing realized the necessity for project management in the manufacturing group. A three-man project management staff was formed. Although the staff was shown on the organizational chart as reporting to the manufacturing operations manager, they actually worked for the vice-president and had sufficient authority to integrate work across all departments and divisions. As in the past, the vice-president's position was filled by the manufacturing operations manager. Manufacturing operations was directed by the former manufacturing manager who came from manufacturing engineering. See Exhibit 4-3.

In 1978, the manufacturing manager created a matrix in the manufacturing department with the manufacturing engineers acting as departmental project managers. This benefited both the manufacturing manager and the group project managers since all information could be obtained from one source. Work was flowing very smoothly.

In January 1979, the manufacturing manager resigned his position effective March, and the manufacturing engineering manager began packing his bags ready to move up to the vacated position. In February, the vice-president announced that the position would be filled from outside. He said also that there would be an organizational restructuring and that the three project managers would now be staff to the manufacturing manager. When the three project managers confronted the manufacturing operations manager, he said, "We've hired the new man in at a very high salary. In order to justify this salary, we have to give him more responsibility."

On March 1, 1979, the new manager took over and immediately made the following declarations:

1. The project managers will never go "upstairs" without first going through him.
2. The departmental matrix will be dissolved and he (the department manager) will handle all of the integration.

How do you account for the actions of the new department manager? What would you do if you were one of the project managers?

Exhibit 4-3. White Manufacturing Organizational Structure.

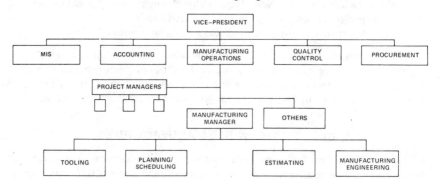

CASE STUDY: MARTIG CONSTRUCTION COMPANY

Martig Construction was a family-owned mechanical subcontractor business which had grown from $5 million in 1976 to $25 million in 1978. Although the gross profit had increased sharply, the profit as a percentage of sales declined drastically. The question was, "Why the decline?" The following observations were made:

1. Since Martig senior died in July of 1978, Martig junior has tried unsuccessfully to convince the family to let him sell the business. Martig junior, as company president, has taken an average of eight days of vacation per month for the past year. Although the project managers are supposed to report to Martig, they appear to be calling their own shots and are in a continuous struggle for power.

2. The estimating department consists of one man, John, who estimates all jobs. Martig wins one job in seven. Once a job is won, a project manager is selected and is told that he must perform the job within the proposal estimates. Project managers are not involved in proposal estimates. They are required, however, to provide feedback to the estimator so that standards can be updated. This very seldom happens because of the struggle for power. The project managers are afraid that the estimator might be next in line for executive promotion since he is a good friend of Martig.

3. The procurement function reports to Martig. Once the items are ordered, the project manager assumes procurement responsibility. Several times in the past, the project manager has been forced to spend hour after hour trying to overcome shortages or simply to track down raw materials. Most project managers estimate that approximately 35 percent of their time involves procurement.

4. Site superintendents believe they are the true project managers, or at least at the same level. The superintendents are very unhappy about not being involved in the procurement function and therefore look for ways to annoy the project managers. It appears that the more time the project manager spends at the site, the longer the work takes; the feedback of information to the home office is also distorted.

CASE STUDY: THE CARLSON PROJECT

"I sympathize with your problems, Frank," stated Joe McGee, manager of project managers. "You know as well as I do that I'm supposed to resolve conflicts and coordinate efforts among all projects. Staffing problems are your responsibility."

Frank: Royce Williams has a resumé that would choke a horse. I don't understand why he performs with a lazy, I-don't-care attitude. He has fifteen years of experience in a project organizational structure, with ten of those years being in project offices. He knows the work that has to be done.

McGee: I don't think that it has anything to do with you personally. This happens to some of our best workers sooner or later. You can't expect guys to give 120 percent all of the time. Royce is at the top of his pay grade, and, being an exempt employee, he doesn't get paid for overtime. He'll snap out of it sooner or later.

Frank: I have deadlines to meet on the Carlson Project. Fortunately, the Carlson Project is big enough so that I can maintain a full-time project office staff of eight employees, not counting myself.

I like to have all project office employees assigned full-time and qualified in two or three project office areas. It's a good thing that I have someone else checked out in Royce's area. But I just can't keep asking this other guy to do his own work and Royce's, too. This poor guy has been working sixty to seventy hours a week and Royce has been doing only forty. That seems unfair to me.

McGee: Look, Frank, I have the authority to fire him, but I'm not going to. It doesn't look good if we fire somebody because they won't work free overtime. Last year we had a case similar to this, where an employee refused to work on Monday and Wednesday evenings because it interfered with his MBA classes. Everyone knew he was going to resign the instant he finished his degree, and yet there was nothing that I could do.

Frank: There must be other alternatives for Royce Williams. I've talked to him as well as to other project office members. Royce's attitude doesn't appear to be demoralizing the other members, but it easily could in a short period of time.

McGee: We can reassign him to another project, as soon as one comes along. I'm not going to put him on my overhead budget. Your project can support him for the time being. You know, Frank, the grapevine will know the reason for his transfer. This might affect your ability to get qualified people to volunteer to work with you on future projects. Give Royce a little more time and see if you can work it out with him. What about Harlan Green from one of the functional groups?

Frank: Two months ago, we hired Gus Johnson, a man with ten years experience. For the first two weeks that he was assigned to my project, he got the work done ahead of schedule. His work was flawless. That was the main reason why I wanted him. I know him personally, and he's one great worker.

During weeks three and four, his work slowed down considerably. I chatted with him and he said that Harlan Green refused to work with him if he kept up that pace.

McGee: Did you ask him why?

Frank: Yes. First of all, you should know that for safety reasons, all men in that department must work in two- or three-men crews. Therefore, Gus was not allowed to work alone. Harlan did not want to change the standards of performance for fear that some of the other employees would be laid off.

By the end of the first week, nobody in the department would talk to Gus. As a matter of fact, they wouldn't even sit with him in the cafeteria. So, Gus had to either conform to the group or remain an outcast. I feel partially responsible for what has happened, since I'm the one who brought him here.

I know this has happened before, in the same department. I haven't had a chance to talk to the department manager as yet. I have an appointment to see him next week.

McGee: There are solutions to the problem, simple ones at that. But, again, it's not my responsibility. You can work it out with the department manager.

"Yeah," thought Frank. "But what if we can't agree?"

CASE STUDY: AMERICAN ELECTRONICS INTERNATIONAL

On February 13, 1976, American Electronics International (AEI) was awarded a $30-million contract for R & D and production qualification for an advanced type of guidance system. During an experimental program, funded by the same agency, AEI identified new materials with advanced capabilities, which could easily replace existing field units. The program was the Mask Project and would last thirty months and require the testing of fifteen units. The Mask Project was longer than any other project that AEI had ever encountered. AEI personnel were now concerned about what kind of staffing problems would be encountered.

Background

In June 1974, AEI won a one-year research project for new material development. Blen Carty was chosen as project manager. He had twenty-five years experience with the company in both project management and project engineering positions. During the past five years Blen had successfully performed as the project manager on R & D projects.

AEI used the matrix approach to structuring project management. Blen was well aware of the problems that can be encountered with this organizational form. When it became apparent that a follow-on contract would be available, Blen felt that functional managers would be reluctant to assign key personnel full-time to his project and lose their services for thirty months. Likewise, difficulties could be expected in staffing the project office.

During the proposal stage of the Mask Project, a meeting was held with Blen Carty, John Wallace, the director of project management, and Dr. Albert Runnels, the director of engineering. The purpose of the meeting was to satisfy a customer requirement that all key project members be identified in the management volume of the proposal.

Wallace: I'm a little reluctant to make any firm commitment. By the time your program gets off the ground, four of our other projects are terminating, as well as several new projects starting up. I think it's a little early to make firm selections.

Carty: But we have a proposal requirement. Thirty months is a long time to assign personnel for. We should consider this problem now.

Runnels: Let's put the names of our top people into the proposal. We'll add several Ph.D.s from our engineering community. That should beef up our management volume. As soon as we're notified of contract go-ahead we'll see who's available and make the necessary assignments. This is a common practice in the industry.

Completion of the Material Development Project

The material development program was a total success. From its inception, everything went smoothly. Blen staffed the project office with Richard Flag, a Ph.D. in engineering, to serve as project engineer. This was a risky move at first, because Richard had been a research scientist during his previous four years with the company. During the development project, however, Richard demonstrated that he could separate himself from R & D and perform the necessary functions of a project engineer assigned to the project office. Blen was pleased with the way that Richard controlled project costs and directed activities.

Richard had developed excellent working relations with development lab personnel and managers. Richard permitted lab personnel to work at their own rate of speed provided that schedule dates were kept. Richard spent ten minutes each week with each of the department managers informing them of the status of the project. The department managers liked this approach because they received first-hand (nonfiltered) information concerning the total picture, not necessarily on their own activities, and because they did not have to spend "wasted hours" in team meetings.

When it became evident that a follow-on contract might be available, Blen spent a large percentage of his time traveling to the customer, working out the details for future business. Richard then served as both project manager and project engineer.

The customer's project office was quite pleased with Richard's work. Information, both good and bad, was transmitted as soon as it became available. Nothing was hidden or disguised. Richard became familiar with all of the customer's project office personnel through the monthly technical interchange meetings.

At completion of the material development project, Blen and John decided to search for project office personnel and make recommendations to upper-level management. Blen wanted to keep Richard on board as chief project engineer. He would be assigned six engineers and would have to control all engineering activities within time, cost, and performance. Although this would be a new experience for him, Blen felt that he could easily handle it.

Unfortunately, the grapevine was saying that Larry Gilbert was going to be assigned as chief project engineer for the Mask Project.

Selection Problems

On November 15, Dr. Runnels and Blen Carty had a meeting to select the key members of the project team.

Runnels: Well Blen, the time has come to decide on your staff. I want to assign Larry Gilbert as chief engineer. He's a good man and has fifteen years experience. What are your feelings on that?

Carty: I was hoping to keep Richard Flag on. He has performed well, and the customer likes working with him.

Runnels: Richard does not have the experience necessary for that position. We can still assign him to Larry Gilbert and keep him in the project office.

Carty: I'd like to have Larry Gilbert working for Richard Flag, but I don't suppose that we'd ever get approval to have a grade 9 engineer working for a grade 7 engineer. Personally, I'm worried about Gilbert's ability to work with people. He has been so regimented in his ways that our people in the functional units have refused to work with him. He treats them like kids, always walking around with a big stick. One department manager said that if Gilbert becomes the boss, then it will probably result in cutting the umbilical cord between the project office and his department. His people refuse to work for a dictator. I have heard the same from other managers.

Runnels: Gilbert gets the job done. You'll have to teach him how to be a theory Y manager. You know, Blen, we don't have very many grade 9 engineering positions in this company. I think we should have a responsibility to our employees. I can't demote Gilbert into a lower slot. If I were to promote Flag, and the project gets cancelled, where would I reassign him? He can't go back to functional engineering. That would be a step down.

Carty: But Gilbert is so set in his ways. He's just totally inflexible. In addition, thirty months is a long time to maintain a project office. If he fails, we'll never be able to replace positions in time without totally upsetting the customer. There seem to be an awful lot of people volunteering to work on the Mask Project. Is there anyone else available?

Runnels: People always volunteer for long-duration projects because it gives them a feeling of security. This even occurs among our dedicated personnel. Unfortunately we have no other grade 9 engineers available. We could reassign one from another program, but I hate to do it. Our engineers like to carry a project through from start to finish. I think you had better spend some time with the functional managers making sure that you get good people.

Carty: I've tried that and I'm having trouble. The functional managers will not surrender their key people full-time for thirty months. One manager wants to assign two employees to our project so that they can get on-the-job training. I told him that this project is considered as "strategic" by our management and that we must have good people. The manager just laughed at me and walked away.

Runnels: You know, Blen, you can't have all top people. Our other projects must be manned. Also, if you were to use all seasoned veterans, the cost would exceed what we put into the proposal. You're just going to have to make do with what you can get. Prepare a list of the people you want and I'll see what I can do.

As Blen left the office, he wondered if Dr. Runnels would help him in obtaining key personnel.

1. Whose responsibility is it to staff the office?
2. What should be Blen Carty's role as well as that of Dr. Runnels?
3. Should Larry Gilbert be assigned?
4. How would you negotiate with the functional managers?

CASE STUDY: TRW SYSTEMS GROUP (A+B CONDENSED)[18,19]

History of TRW Inc. and TRW Systems Group

TRW Inc. was formed in 1957 by the merger of Thompson Products, Inc. and the Ramo-Wooldridge Corporation. Thompson Products, a Cleveland-based manufacturer of auto and aircraft parts, had provided $500,000 to help Simon Ramo and Dean Wooldridge get started in 1953.

Ramo-Wooldridge Corporation grew quickly by linking itself with the accelerating ICBM program sponsored by the Air Force. After winning the contract for the technical supervision of the ICBM program, R-W gradually expanded its capabilities to include advance planning for future ballistic weapons systems and space technology and by providing technical advice to the Air Force.

R-W was considered by some industry specialists to be a quasi-government agency. In fact, some of their competitors in the aerospace industry resented R-W's opportunities for auditing and examining their operations.

Because of this close relationship with the Air Force, R-W was prohibited from bidding on hardware contracts. This prevented them from competing for work on mainframes or on assemblies. In 1959, after the merger with Thompson, TRW decided that the hardware ban was too great a liability and moved to free the Systems Group from its limiting relationship with the Air Force.

The Air Force was reluctant to lose the valued services of the Systems Group. But they agreed to a solution which called for the creation by the Air Force of a nonprofit organization, the Aerospace Corporation, to take over the advance planning and broad technical assistance formerly given by the Systems Group. TRW agreed to recruit, from its own personnel, a group of top technicians to staff Aerospace, and in 1960, about 20 percent of Systems' professional people went over to Aerospace.

The Systems Group had to undergo a difficult transition from serving a single customer to a competitive organization. The change involved worrying about marketing, manufacturing, and dealing with different types of contracts. Previously, Systems had worked on a cost-plus-fixed-fee basis but now worked on

---

18. In its brief history this part of TRW, Inc. had had several names: The Guided Missiles Division of Ramo-Wooldridge, Ramo-Wooldridge Corporation, Space Technology Laboratories (S.T.L.) and most recently, TRW Systems Group. Frequently used abbreviations of TRW Systems Group are TRW Systems, and Systems Group.
19. Copyright © 1976 by the President and Fellows of Harvard College. Reproduced by permission. This case was prepared by Joseph Seher under the supervision of John Kotter.

incentive contracts rewarding performance and specified delivery dates, while penalizing failures.

Systems thrived in the new competitive arena (see Exhibit 4-4), winning a number of important contracts. Nested in the sunny, Southern California region at Redondo Beach, the Systems Group worked in a free and open atmosphere. According to an article in *Fortune*, Systems' competitive advantage was its professional personnel:[20]

S.T.L. is headed by 38-year-old Rube Mettler, who holds the title of president of the subsidiary. A Ph.D. from Caltech, he served with Hughes Aircraft, and was a consultant at the Pentagon before coming to Ramo-Wooldridge in 1955, where he made his mark directing the Thor program to completion in record time. Of his technical staff of 2,100, more than 35 percent hold advanced degrees, and despite their youth they average 11 years of experience per man: in other words, most of them have been in the space industry virtually since the space industry began. They are housed mostly in a group of 4 long, low buildings for research, engineering, and development in the campus-like Space Center at Redondo Beach. Some of them are occupied in the various labs for research in quantum physics, programming, and applied mathematics, inertial guidance and control, etc.; others simply sit in solitude in their offices and think, or mess around with formulas on the inevitable blackboard. But typically, the materialization of all this brainpower is accomplished in one medium-sized manufacturing building called FIT (Fabrication, Integration, and Testing), which has but 800 employees all told. FIT has a high bay area to accommodate its huge chamber for simulating space environment and other exotic testing equipment.

The Aerospace Industry

Observers have described the industry in which Systems competed as a large job-shop subject to frequent changes. An article titled "Survival in the Aerospace Industry" described it as follows:[21]

Because of rapid changes in technology, in customer requirements, and in competitive practices, product lines in the aerospace industry tend to be transitory.

Exhibit 4-4. TRW Systems Group (A and B Condensed)

Comparative Profile of TRW Systems Group

	JUNE 1960	FEB. 1963
Customers	8	42
Contracts	16	108
Total Personnel	3,860	6,000
Technical Staff	1,400	2,100
Annual Sales Rate	$63 million	$108 million

20. Fortune, LXVII, 2: 95, 1963.
21. T.C. Miller, Jr., and L.P. Kane, "Strategies for Survival in the Aerospace Industry," *Industrial Management Review*, Fall, 22-23, 1965.

The customers' needs are finite and discrete . . . . Although the aerospace industry as a whole has grown steadily during the last decade, the fluctuations of individual companies underscore the job-shop nature of defense work. Aerospace industry planners must be constantly aware of the possibility of cancellation or prolongation of large programs.

The rapid changes and temporary nature of the programs had several effects on companies within the industry. Sales and profits fluctuated with the number and size of contracts the company had; the level of activity in the company fluctuated, which meant hiring and later laying off large numbers of employees; and each plant went from full utilization of physical facilities to idle capacity.

The fluctuations resulted in a highly mobile work force which tended to follow the contracts, moving from a company that had finished a contract to one that was beginning a new contract. But the employees were highly trained and could find other jobs without difficulty. Miller and Kane pointed out that:[22]

The industry's ratios of technical employment to total employment and of technical employment to dollar volume of sales are higher than those in any other industry. Moreover, 30 percent of all persons privately employed in research and development are in the aerospace industry.

TRW Systems tried to minimize these fluctuations and their effects by limiting the size of a contract for which they might compete. They would rather have had ten $10-million contracts than one $100-million contract; also they had a policy of leasing a certain portion of their facilities in order to maintain flexibility in their physical plant.

In pursuing a conscious policy of growth, they competed for many contracts. By winning a reasonable number of these contracts, the company grew; and when one contract ran out, there were others always starting up. As a result, between 1953 and 1963 Systems did not have a single major layoff.

Another characteristic of the industry was the complexity of the products being produced. There were thousands of parts in a space rocket and they had to interrelate in numerous subtle ways. If one part didn't come up to specifications it might harm hundreds of others. Since the parts and systems were so interdependent, the people in the various groups, divisions, and companies who made and assembled the parts were also highly interdependent. These interdependencies created some organizational problems for the companies in the industry which forced them to develop a new type of organization called the matrix organization.

TRW Systems' Organization

Exhibit 4-5 shows an organization chart for TRW in 1963 with the various functional divisions and the offices for program management (the word project

---

22. Ibid., p. 20.

Exhibit 4-5. TRW Systems Group (A & B Condensed) Organizational Chart, 1963.

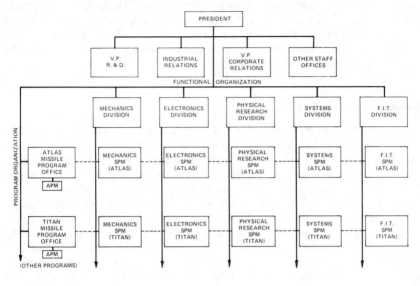

APM = ASSISTANT PROJECT MANAGER
SPM = SUBPROJECT MANAGER

is often used interchangeably for program). These different systems interrelated in what was called a matrix organization. The relationship between program offices and the functional divisions was a complex one, but can best be explained in a simple fashion by noting that instead of setting up, for example, a systems engineering group for the Atlas missile and another separate systems group for the Titan missile program, all the systems engineers were assigned organizationally to the Systems Division. This Systems Division was one of five technical divisions each staffed with MTS (Members Technical Staff) working in a particular functional area. The various program offices coordinated the work of all the functional groups working on their particular programs and, in addition, handled all relationships with the contracting customer. It will be noted that the program offices were, formally, on the same organizational level as the functional divisions.

The engineers in these functional divisions were formally responsible to the director of their division, but they might also have a "dotted line" responsibility to a program office. For example, an electrical engineer would be responsible to his manager in the Electronics Division even though he might spend all of his time working for the Atlas program office. While working on the program he would report to the Atlas program director through one of his assistants.

Functional Organization

Each functional division served as a technology center and focused on the disciplines and skills appropriate to its technology. Generally, a number of operations managers reported to the division manager, each of whom was in charge of a group of laboratories dealing with similar technologies. The laboratory directors who reported to the operation managers were each responsible for a number of functional departments which were organized around technical specialties. The engineers in these laboratory departments were the people who performed the actual work on program office projects.

Program Office Organization

A program manager maintained overall management responsibility for pulling together the various phases of a particular customer project. His office was the central location for all projectwide activities such as the project schedule, cost, and performance control, system planning, system engineering, system integration, and contract and major subcontract management. Assistant project managers were appointed for these activities as warranted by the size of the project.

The total project effort was divided into subprojects, each project being assigned to a specific functional organization according to the technical specialty involved. The manager of the functional organization appointed a subproject manager with the concurrence of the project manager. The subproject manager was assigned responsibility for the total subproject activity and was delegated management authority by the functional division management and by the assistant project manager to whom he reported operationally for the project. The subproject manager was a full-time member of the project organization, but he was not considered a member of the project office; he remained a member of his functional organization. He was accountable for performance in his functional specialty to the manager of his functional area, usually a laboratory manager. The functional manager was responsible for the performance evaluation of the subproject manager. The subproject manager thus represented both the program office and his functional area and was responsible for coordinating the work of his subproject with the engineers within the functional area. Normally each functional area was involved in work on several projects simultaneously. One manager defined the subproject manager's responsibility this way:

The subproject manager is a prime mover in this organization, and his job is a tough one. He is the person who brings the program office's requirements and the lab's resources together to produce a subsystem. He has to deal with the pressures and needs of both sides of the matrix and is responsible for bringing a subsystem together. He has to go to the functional department managers to get engineers to work on his project, but about all he can say is "Thanks for the work you've done on my subproject." His control of program office money is a source of power, however, since the functional managers need to fund their operations. The technical managers are strong people. They are not "yes" men; they have their own ideas about how things ought to be done. You do not want them to be "yes" men either. Otherwise you've lost the balance you need to make sure that technical performance is not sacrificed for cost and schedule expediencies which are of great importance to the program office. The functional managers also are interested in long-range applications of the work they are doing on a particular project.

This often puts the subproject manager in a real bind; he gets caught between conflicting desires. It is especially difficult because it is hard for him not to identify with the program office, since that's the focus of his interest. But he is paid by the lab and that is also where he must go to get his work done. If he is smart he will identify with his subsystem and not with either the program office or the lab. He must represent the best course for his subproject, which sometimes means fighting with the program office and the departments at different times during the life of the subproject. If he reacts too much to pressures from either side, it hurts his ability to be objective about his subproject, and people will immediately sense this.

The case writer asked Jim Dunlap, director of industrial relations, what happened when an engineer's two bosses disagreed on how he should spend his time. He replied:

The decisions of priority on where a man should spend his time are made by Rube Mettler because he is the only common boss. But, of course, you try to get them to resolve it at a lower level. You just have to learn to live with ambiguity. It's not a structured situation. It just can't be.

You have to understand the needs of Systems to understand why we need the matrix organization. There are some good reasons why we use a matrix. Because R & D-type programs are finite programs—you create them, they live, and then they die—they have to die or overhead is out of line. Also, there are several stages in any project. You don't necessarily need the same people on the project all the time. In fact you waste the creative people if they work until the end finishing it up. The matrix is flexible. We can shift creative people around and bring in the people who are needed at various stages in the project. The creative people in the functions are professionals and are leaders in their technical disciplines. So the functional relationship helps them to continue to improve their professional expertise. Also, there is a responsiveness to all kinds of crises that come up. You sometimes have thirty days to answer a proposal, so you can put together a team with guys from everywhere. We're used to temporary systems; that's the way we live.

Often an engineer will work on two or three projects at a time and he just emphasizes one more than others. He's part of two systems at the same time.

The key word in the matrix organization is interdependency. Matrix means multiple interdependencies. We're continually setting up temporary systems. For example, we set up a project manager for the Saturn project with twenty people under him. Then he would call on people in systems engineering to get things started on the project. Next he might call in people from the Electronics Division, and after they finish their work the project would go to FIT (Fabrication, Integration, and Testing) where it would be manufactured. So what's involved is a lot of people coming in and then leaving the project.

There is a large gap between authority and responsibility and we plan it that way. We give a man more responsibility than he has authority and the only way he can do his job is to collaborate with other people. The effect is that the system is flexible and adaptive, but it's hard to live with. An example of this is that the project manager has no authority over people working on the project from the functional areas. He can't decide on their pay, promotion, or even how much time they'll spend on his project as opposed to some other project. He has to work with the functional heads on these problems. We purposely set up this imbalance between authority and responsibility. We design a situation so that it's ambiguous. That way people have to collaborate and be flexible. You just can't rely on bureaucracy or power to solve your problems.

The case writer talked to a number of people in various positions at TRW Systems Group and their comments about the matrix could be summarized as follows:

It is difficult to work with because it's flexible and always changing, but it does work; and it's probably the only organization that could work here.

Nearly everyone the case writer talked with indicated that Systems Group was a "good place to work" and that they enjoyed the freedom they had. However, one critic of the system, a member of the administrative staff, presented his complaints about the system as follows:

People think this is a country club. It's a college campus atmosphere. Top management thinks everyone is mature and so they let them work as if they were on a college campus. They don't have rules to make people come to work on time or things like that. Do you know that 60-70 percent of the assigned parking spaces are empty at 8:30 a.m. Davis's group did a study of that—people are late. It's a good place to work for people who want complete freedom. But people abuse it. They don't come to work on time; they just do what they want around here. It's very democratic here. Nobody is telling you what to do and making all the decisions, but it can border on anarchy.

The management philosophy is that everybody will work harmoniously and you don't need a leader. But I think there has to be leadership, some one person who's responsible.

The case writer then asked the question: "Isn't the project engineer responsible?" The staff person replied:

The project engineer is a figurehead—in many cases he doesn't lead. I know one project engineer who provides no leadership at all. Besides, the matrix is constantly agitating. It's changing all the time, so it's just a bucket of worms. You never know where you stand. It's like ants on a log in a river and each one thinks he's steering—when none of them are. It's true that the top-level managers can make this philosophy work on their level. But we can't on our level. Let me give you an example. Mettler says he wants everything microfilmed, but he doesn't tell others to let me do it. I have responsibility but no authority in the form of a piece of paper or statement that I can do it. I just can't walk into some guy's empire and say I'm here to microfilm all of your papers. It's like an amoeba, always changing, so you never know where your limits are or what you can or can't do.

As a contrasting view, one of the laboratory heads felt that the lack of formal rules and procedures was one of the strengths of the organization. He commented as follows:

This is not a company characterized by a lot of crisp orders and formal procedures. Quite honestly, we operate pretty loosely as far as procedures are concerned. In fact, I came from a university environment, but I believe there's more freedom and looseness of atmosphere around here than there was on campus.

I think if you have pretty average people, you can have a very strict line type of organization and make it work, and maybe that's why we insist on being different. You see, I think you can also have a working organization with no strict lines of authority if you have broader gauged people in it. I like to think that the individuals in the company are extremely high caliber and I think there is some evidence to support that.

Another manager supported the matrix organization with the following comments:

The people around here are really committed to the job. They'll work twenty-four hours a day when it's necessary, and sometimes it's necessary. I was on a team working on a project proposal a few months ago and during the last week of the proposal there were people working here around the clock. We had the secretaries come in on different shifts and we just stayed here and worked. I think that Mettler makes this matrix organization work. It's a difficult job but people have faith that Mettler knows what he's doing so they work hard and it comes out all right.

Evolution of Career Development

In 1962, TRW Systems Group began a management development program called Career Development. Jim Dunlap, the director of industrial realtions, had responsibility for this program along with his other duties in industrial relations (see Exhibit 4-6).

Early History of Career Development (1957-1965)

"What are we doing about management development?" Simon Ramo was asked in 1957. Ramo replied: "We don't believe in management development. We

Exhibit 4-6. TRW Systems Group (A & B Condensed) Industrial Relations.

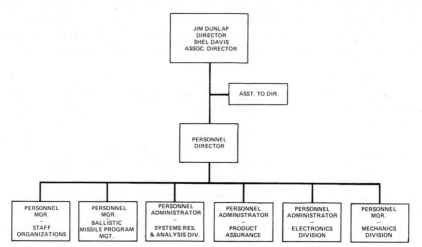

hire bright, intelligent people and we don't plan to insult their intelligence by giving them courses in courage."

In 1961, as Systems was trying to expand its customer base and cope with its new competitive environment, Rube Mettler became president. Mettler asked a consulting firm for advice on how best to make the transition to a competitive firm. "Systems needs men with experience in business management," the consultants said. "You will have to hire experienced top-level administrators from outside the firm. There aren't any here." Mettler agreed with them about needing top-level administrators. "But we'll develop our own people," Mettler added. Mettler confided in others that he feared that a manager with experience in another organization would have to unlearn a lot of bad habits before he could be successful at TRW.

Mettler put Dunlap in charge of the development program at TRW. Mettler made it clear to Dunlap that he wanted a task-oriented, dynamic development program to fit the special needs of the Systems Group.

Dunlap felt he needed assistance to implement the kind of program Mettler wanted. "The one thing I did was to entice Shel Davis to come into industrial relations," commented Dunlap. "He impressed me as a restless, dynamic, creative sort of guy." Davis had worked in a line position in one of TRW's other divisions.

With the help of an outside consultant, Dunlap and Davis began to design a development program. Early in 1962, forty top managers were interviewed about what they felt was needed. One manager characterized the feelings of the entire group: "We need skills in management. Every time a new project starts around here, it takes half of the project schedule just bringing people on board. If we could have a quicker startup, we'd finish these projects on time."

Dunlap, Davis, and the consultant went to work on a plan to fit these specific needs. Dunlap set up a two-day off-site meeting to discuss their plans and recommendations with some of the top managers. At the meeting, Dunlap and Davis talked about two relatively new applied behavioral science techniques called team development and T-groups[23] as ways of meeting the needs of managers. Dave Patterson was there and was impressed by this approach. Patterson was recently appointed head of a new project and asked for their assistance: "I have a new team and I'm ready to hold a team building meeting next week. Can you arrange it?"

Shel Davis, along with a consultant, held an off-site team development session for Patterson. After the meeting, Patterson's project group improved its working relationships with manufacturing. The success of this experiment became well known throughout the company. Mettler asked Patterson what effect the meeting had had. "It saved us six weeks on the program. About a million bucks," Patterson replied. This impressed people.

Late in 1962 Davis and Dunlap prepared a "white paper" on possible approaches in career development and sent it to the top seventy people. Most of the managers responded that TRW should improve its skills in three areas: communications and interpersonal skills, business management skills, and technical skills. Davis described the conversation he and Dunlap had with Mettler:

Jim and I talked with Mettler about the kind of program we wanted in the company and what we did and didn't want to do. As it turned out, we were in agreement with Mettler on almost every issue. For example, we decided not to make it a crash effort but to work at it and to take a lot of time making sure people understood what we wanted to do and that they supported it. We also decided to start at the top of the organization rather than at the bottom. During these discussions, they decided to call the training effort Career Development rather than organizational development or management development because Mettler didn't want to give the impression that they were going to concentrate on administrative training and neglect technical training.

Shortly after the white paper came out, Shel Davis and Jim Dunlap began to invite people to T-groups run by professionals outside of TRW. About twelve people took advantage of this opportunity between January and May of 1963. Ten of the twelve later reported that it was a "great experience." As a result, Mettler continued to support Dunlap and Davis, telling them, "Try things—if they work, continue them; if they don't , modify them, improve them, or drop them."

In April 1963, Davis and Dunlap decided to hold a team development meeting for the key people in industrial relations. The two men felt that once employees at the Systems group started going to T-groups that there would be a growing demand for "Career Development" activities which the IR group would be asked

---

23. *Team development* (or team building) refers to a development process designed to improve the performance and effectiveness of people who work together. *Laboratory T-groups* (training groups) is a form of experiential learning away from the normal environment. Using unstructured groups, participants attempt to increase their sensitivity to their own and others' behavior as well as factors that hinder group interaction and effectiveness.

to meet. The team development session, they felt, would help train the IR staff to meet this demand.

Dunlap and Davis next decided to run some T-groups themselves, within TRW. Dunlap argued for limiting this effort to twenty people. Davis wanted forty saying, "Let's go with it. Let's do too much too fast and then it will really have an effect on the organization. Otherwise it might not be noticed." Dunlap and Davis eventually decided to run four T-groups of ten people each.

The chain of events following that activity was later described by Frank Jasinski, who became director of career development in 1964:

After that things really started to move. There was a strong demand for T-group experience. But we didn't just want to send people through labs like we were turning out so many sausages. We wanted to free up the organization, to seed it with people who had been to T-groups. The T-groups were to be just the beginning of a continuing process.

This continuing process was in several stages and developed over the three-year period. Maybe I can describe it in terms of one manager and his work group. First, the manager volunteered to go to a T-group (we have kept the program on a voluntary basis). Before he went to the T-group, there was a pre-T-group session where the participants asked questions and got prepared for the T-group experience. Then they went through the T-group.

After the T-group, there were three or four sessions where the T-group participants got together to discuss the problems of applying the T-group values back home. After the manager had been through the T-group, some of the members of his work group could decide to go to a T-group. The next stage was when the manager and his group decided they wanted to undertake a team development process where they could work on improving intragroup relations, that is, how they could be more effective as a team.

Following a team development effort could be an interface meeting. This is the kind Alan East had. It seems Alan's department, product assurance, was having trouble getting along with a number of different departments in the organization. Alan felt if they were going to do their job well they had to be able to work effectively with these other groups. So he got three or four of his people together with the key people from five or six other departments and they worked on the interdepartmental relationship. Still another type of meeting that is similar is the intergroup meeting. If two groups just can't get along and are having difficulties, they may decide to hold an off-site meeting and try to work on the problems between them.

We also started doing some technical training and business management training. As with all of our training we try to make it organic: to meet the needs of the people and the organization. We tend to ask, 'What is the problem?' Specific skill training may not be the answer. For example, a manager calls us and says he wants his secretary to have a review course in shorthand because she is slipping in her ability to use it. Sharon might say, 'Let's talk about it; maybe her shorthand is slipping because she doesn't use it enough and maybe she wants more challenging work. Why don't I get together with you and your secretary and let's discuss it.' Sharon has held several meetings with bosses and their secretaries to improve boss-secretary relationships. When they understand each other better, the secretary is more willing to help her boss and she is also in a better position to do so.

Such a large increase in career development activities required a rapid buildup of uniquely trained personnel. This problem was met in part by the use of outside consultants. Systems Group was able to interest a number of the national leaders in T-group-type activities to act as consultants, to serve as T-group trainers, and to work with the divisions on team building activities. By December 1964, they had built up a staff of nine outside consultants. (This group consisted of senior professors at some of the largest business schools in the country and nationally recognized private consultants.)

In order for the program to work on a day-to-day basis, they felt a need to build a comparable internal staff. It was decided that the personnel manager in each division would not only be responsible for traditional personnel activities but would also be an internal consultant on career development activities. Lynn Stewart, one of the outside consultants working with the Systems Group, described how TRW obtained a group of trained personnel managers.

Systems Group needed to build some internal change agents, which meant expanding the industrial relations effort. It required the development of the skills of people in industrial relations, especially the personnel managers. They were able to retool some of the people in industrial relations by sending them to T-groups. Some were not able to make the transition. They were transferred or fired. All of this was done to provide a staff that could service the needs created when people returned from T-groups.

In December 1964, Jim Dunlap announced that he had been promoted to vice-president of human relations for TRW, Inc., and would be moving to Cleveland. He also announced that Shel Davis would succeed him as director of industrial relations. (Exhibit 4-7 presents an organization chart of industrial relations as of January 1965.)

A number of the personnel managers became concerned about the future of industrial relations. They knew Shel Davis had been very critical of the day-to-day personnel activities, and they wondered what changes he would make. One personnel manager expressed this feeling when he said of the December 28 meeting: "There were some undertones of a threat in Jim's leaving. We thought Shel might force us to work exclusively on career development and neglect our day-to-day personnel responsibilities."

By summer, 1966, however, most of the people in industrial relations felt that Shel Davis had adjusted to his role as director of industrial relations and was doing a good job of balancing the demands of career development and the day-to-day personnel activities.

Exhibit 4-7. TRW Systems Group (A & B Condensed) Industrial Relations.

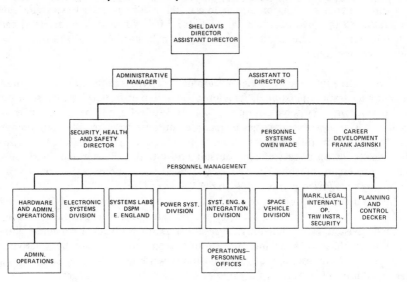

Exhibit 4-7. Industrial Relations Career Development. (Continued)

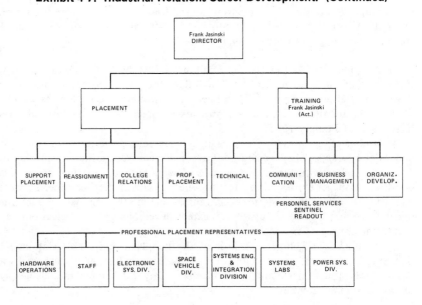

Exhibit 4-7. Industrial Relations Security–Health & Safety. (Continued)

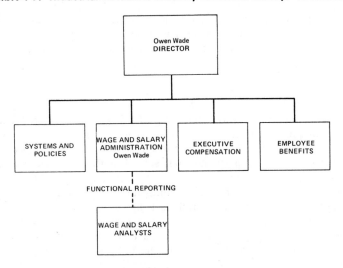

Exhibit 4-7. Industrial Relations Personnel Systems. (Continued)

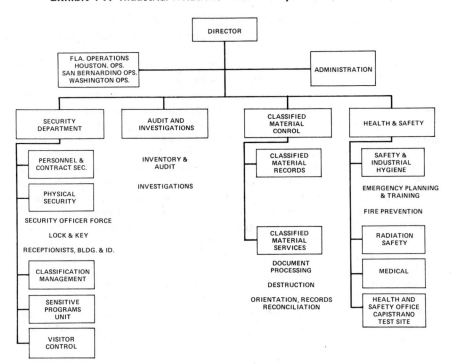

Career Development in 1966

By 1966, career development activities had greatly increased since their initiation in 1963 (see Exhibit 4-8). While T-groups continued to be used, the major effort of the department was in facilitating team building and intergroup labs.

Team Development

There were a number of different types of team development activities. One was an effort to get a new team started faster. TRW repeatedly created temporary teams to accomplish recurring tasks. The tasks were quite similar but the team membership changed considerably. One example was a team established to prepare a proposal to bid on a particular contract. More than a dozen organizations would contribute to the final product: the written proposal. On major proposals, the representatives from the administrative and nontechnical areas remained fairly constant. The technnical staff, however, varied with the task and usually was entirely new from proposal to proposal. This changing team membership required constant "bringing up to speed" of new members and repeated creation of a smoothly working unit. As the new team came together a team development session, usually off-site, helped to get the team working together sooner and would save time in the long run. A session would last one or two days and the participants would try to identify potential problems in working together and then begin to develop solutions for such problems. Lynn Stewart, an outside consultant, described a team development session for a launch team:

TRW has a matrix organization so that any one man is a member of many systems simultaneously. He has interfaces with many different groups. In addition, he is continually moving from one team to another, so they need team development to get the teams off to a fast start. On a launch team, for example, you have all kinds of people that come together for a short time. There are project directors, manufacturing people, the scientists who designed the experiments, and the men who launch the bird. You have to put all of those men together into a cohesive group in a short time. At launch time they can't be worrying about an organizational chart and how their respective roles change as preparation for the launch progresses. Their relationships do change over time, but they should work that through and discuss it beforehand, not when the bird is on the pad. The concept of the organization is that you have a lot of resources and you need to regroup them in different ways as customers and contracts change. You can speed up the regrouping process by holding team development sessions.

Another type of team development activity was one with an ongoing group. Typically the manager would come to the personnel manager in his division and express an interest in team development for his group. If both agreed it would be beneficial, they would begin to plan such a session. First, an effort would be made to identify an agenda for the one- or two-day off-site meetings. This would be developed in one of two ways. The personnel manager or the consul-

Exhibit 4-8. TRW Systems Group (A & B Condensed)
Career Development Activities 1963-1965

ACTIVITIES	1963		1964		1965	
	COURSES	ATTENDEES	COURSES	ATTENDEES	COURSES	ATTENDEES
Orientation	49	627	32	369	32	1,146
Colloquia	51	3,060	31	5,580	7	1,525
Invited Lectures	2	800	4	1,600	-	-
Evening Courses	12	261	17	438	16	651
Staff Education	-	767	-	1,066	-	1,166
Technical Courses	-	-	3	97	6	377
Internal Leadership Laboratories (T-groups)	1	45	4	104	4	151
External Leadership Laboratories (T-groups)	-	20	-	17	-	27
Team Development Meetings	-	-	4	76	44	671

tant could interview, on an individual basis, all the people who would be attending the session to identify problem areas on which they needed to work. He would then summarize the problems identified in his interviews and distribute this summary to the participants a day or two before the session was held. Another method sometimes used to develop an agenda was to get all of the participants together on-site for two or three hours several days before the off-site meeting. The participants would then be divided into subgroups and would identify problem areas to work on. At the extended off-site staff meeting, the intention was that the group would be task oriented, addressing itself to the question, "How can we improve the way our group works together?" They would look at how the group's process got in the way of the group's performance. The manager of the group would conduct the meeting but the personnel manager and an outside consultant would be there to help the group by observing and raising issues that the group should look at. There had been a number of similar team development sessions at TRW and the people involved felt that they had been worthwhile in that they had improved the group's effectiveness.

Another type of team development activity that was carried out on a continuous basis was the critiquing of the many meetings held in the organization. The case writer sat in on a staff meeting of the industrial relations department which was attended by the personnel managers and key people in the staff groups of personnel systems and career development. The purpose of the meeting was to plan the projects to be undertaken by personnel systems and career development throughout the remainder of the year. This included a discussion of what projects the personnel managers would like undertaken and a priority listing as to which were most important. Owen Wade, director of personnel systems, led the discussion during the first hour and one-half of the meeting while the group discussed projects for personnel systems. Frank Jasinski, director of career development, led the discussion in the last hour of the meeting in which projects for career development were discussed. Near the end of the meeting the following discussion took place:

Shel: We only have ten minutes left so we had better spend some time on a critique of the meeting. Does anyone have any comments?

Ed (Personnel Manager): We bit off more than we could chew here. We shouldn't have planned to do so much.

Don (Personnel Manager): I felt we just floated from 10:30 to 10:45. We got through with Frank and his subject and then nothing was done until the break.

Bob (Personnel Manager): Why didn't you make that observation at 10:30, Don, so we could do something about it? Do you feel intimidated about making a process observation?

Don: No. I felt like I was in the corner earlier. But not after making this observation. Besides, I did say earlier that we weren't doing anything and should move on, but I guess I didn't say it loud enough for people to hear me.

Ed: Don, that is the first time you've made a process observation in six months. I wish you'd make more of them.

Shel: I think Owen's presentation was very good because he had estimated the number of man-weeks of work required for each of the projects. Frank's presentation was less effective because his didn't have that.

Jasinski: I have a question on the manpower requirements. I spent seven or eight hours preparing for this meeting in setting priorities on all the projects we had listed and then it wasn't followed up in this meeting. [Two or three people echoed support for this statement.]

Bob: I thought we were asked to do too much in preparing for this meeting. It was just too detailed and too much work, so I rebelled and refused to do it.

Wade (Director of Personnel Systems): Well, from my point of view on the staff side of the fence, I feel pressured and as if I'm asked to do too much. The personnel managers have a very different set of rules. You don't plan as much as we have to and I think you should plan more.

One of the participants commented that a large number of the meetings at TRW were critiqued in a similar manner.

Intergroup and Interface Labs

As a result of the nature of the work at TRW and of the matrix organization, there was a great deal of interaction between the various groups in the organization. Sometimes this interaction was characterized by conflict; the career development staff began to work on ways to help groups deal with this conflict. One such effort, the first interface lab, developed out of an experience of Alan East, director of product assurance. Mr. East commented on his experience:

I came to product assurance from a technical organization so I knew very little of what product assurance was about. First, I tried to find out what our objectives were. I talked to our supervisors and I found there was a lack of morale. They thought they were second-class citizens. They were cowed by the domineering engineers and they felt inferior. I decided one of the problems was that people outside product assurance didn't understand us and the importance of our job. I concluded that that was easy to solve: we'd educate them. So, we set out to educate the company. We decided to call a meeting and we drew up an agenda. Then, as an afterthought, I went to see Shel Davis to see if he had some ideas on how to train people. But he just turned it around. He got me to see that rather than educating them, maybe we could find out how they really saw us and why. Well, we held an off-site meeting and we identified a lot of problems between product assurance and the other departments. After the meeting, we came back and started to work to correct those problems.

After East's successful interface meeting, the idea caught hold and similar meetings were held by other groups. Harold Nelson, the director of finance, held an interface meeting between four members of his department and a number of departments that had frequent contact with finance. The purpose of the meeting was to get feedback on how finance was seen by others in the organization. Commenting on the effectiveness of the meeting, Nelson added, "They were impressed that we were able to have a meeting, listen to their gripes about us and not be defensive. The impact of such meetings on individuals is tremendous. It causes people to change so these meetings are very productive."

Del Thomas, a participant in the interface meeting with finance, represented another department. Thomas observed that, prior to the meeting, his group felt Finance was too slow in evaluating requests and that Nelson and his subordinates ". . . were too meticulous, too much like accountants." Thomas felt the meeting improved the performance of finance:

I think Harold [Nelson] got what he was looking for, but he may have been surprised there were so many negative comments. I think there are indications that the meeting has improved things. First, Harold is easier to get ahold of now. Second, since the meeting, Harold brought in a new man to evaluate capital expenditures and he's doing a top job. He's helpful and he has speeded up the process. I think the atmosphere of the whole finance group is changing. They are starting to think more of 'we the company' and less of 'us and them.'

Evaluation of the Career Development Effort

Jim Dunlap, the vice-president for human relations, was asked to evaluate the effect of career development on TRW Systems. Dunlap pulled two studies from his desk drawer. The first, a report by a government official titled "Impulse for Openness," noted in its summary:

It is not our intention, nor certainly that of TRW Systems, to imply that either the company reorganization or the physical progress are results solely of the career development program, but it does appear that the program had a substantial impact on the success of the company. The data shown completes the picture of changes in the company during the period under discussion. Employment, at 6,000 in 1962 and over 11,000 in March 1966, will most likely double by the end of this year. Sales more than tripled between 1962 and 1965. Professional turnover decreased from 17.1% in 1962 to 6.9% in March 1966. The average for the aerospace industry in this area of California is approximately 20%.

Also, Dunlap revealed the results of a study by a professional organization to which many of Systems Group employees belong. It took a survey of all of its members, asking them to rank fifty-four firms in the aerospace industry on six different factors. The respondents ranked TRW Systems first in "desirability as an employer," seventh for "contribution to aerospace," and second in "salary."

Dunlap also added his personal comments on the efforts of the career development program:

It's very hard to make an evaluation of the program and say it has saved us X million dollars. But there are several indications that it has been effective. Turnover is down significantly and I've heard a lot of people say, 'I stayed at TRW because of the career development activities.' Some people make more definite claims for the program. Dave Patterson says our team development process saved us $500,000. Rube Mettler is convinced the program has improved our skills so that we've won some contracts we wouldn't have gotten otherwise. I believe it has improved our team performance. All of our proposal teams spend two days of team building before they start on the proposal. Every program starts with an off-site team development lab. They help build a team esprit de corps and it creates an openness so they are better able to solve problems.

A number of employees were willing to discuss their attitudes toward the career development program. Denis Brown, a member of the administrative staff, and a participant in the activities of career development, felt the program was valuable. Denis noted:

They took the OGO launch crew off-site and improved their effectiveness. Well, a launch is very tense and if one guy is hostile toward another it may mean a failure that can cost $20 million. I don't know how much they spent on career development, but say it's a quarter of a million dollars. If one man improves his relationship with another and it saves a launch and $20 million, you've made it back many times over. The company feels it is a good thing, and it has worked well, so they'll continue it.

Jim Whitman, a subproject manager, had high praise for career development. Whitman credited the program for making groups more effective in communicating and working with one another. Recounting his own experiences, Whitman added that the program led to better collaboration and working conditions between the design engineer and the fabrication engineer.

But other employees were less enthusiastic. John Ward, a member of a program office discussed his participation in career development activities. Ward felt that some of the off-site sessions were "rather grueling affairs, particularly when you are the center of attention." But Ward added that the session he attended was valuable.

In my opinion, the reason it was worthwhile is that under the pressure of work people cannot—I use the word cannot when I should say will not—take the time to sit down and discuss some very basic issues to get the air cleared. Even in a small group people tend to wear blinders. You think about your own problems because you have so many of them, so you tend to build up a fence to keep some of the other fellow's problems from getting through. He talks about them but you don't hear them; you don't get the significance of what he's trying to tell you. But if you go away with instructions that people are not to bother you unless it is really important, you create an environment where there is time to work out some of these things.

One member of the administrative staff, Dan Jackson, had very different views on career development. Jackson noted:

Idealistically, it's a good thing. If in the real world people lived that way, were open and sincere and could tell each other their feelings without getting hurt, it would be excellent. But people just aren't that way in the real world. The people who are enthusiastic about this, like Mettler, Hesse, and Davis, are at a level in the company where they can practice this. They're just dealing with other vice-presidents and top-level people. But down on my level it won't work. We've got to produce things down here and we can't just be nice to people all the time. We have to get some work done.

I think that the trainers at the lab live that way and that's all right, but they tend to be frustrated head-shrinkers. They want to be psychiatrists but they don't have the training—so they do sensitivity training. It's kind of like running a therapy group. I think the techniques they use are pretty good, like having one group inside talking and one group on the outside observing, but the people running it aren't trained well enough. They may be the best available, but they are not good enough. Frankly, I think these trainers are really just trying to find our their own problems, but they do it by getting mixed up in other people's problems.

Jackson continued, observing that participation in these activities was not completely voluntary:

Oh, it's voluntary, but you are kind of told you had better go. You aren't fired if you don't, but there's pressure put on you to go. One of our Ph.D.s walked out after two days at a T-group. I don't think it has hurt his career, but people know he took a walk. He just felt it was a sin, morally wrong, what was going on up there.

While Jackson seemed to express the most negative attitudes toward career development, there was a widely circulated story about a man who had suffered a nervous breakdown after attending a T-group. Jim Dunlap was asked to comment on the incident:

Yes, one person had a traumatic experience, or as they say, 'cracked up.' Very early in the program we decided that the people in personnel should go to a T-group so they'd understand what we were going to do. I asked this fellow if he'd like to go. He took it as an order and he went. But I was only asking him to go. If I'd known more about him, I wouldn't have asked him if he wanted to go. But I just saw him at work and he seemed to be getting along all right, although I knew that he didn't enjoy his job. He wanted to get into education. But I didn't know he was having troubles at home and that things weren't going very well for him in general. He was just kind of holding himself together as best he could. He went to the T-group and it caused him to start thinking about his situation and he fell apart; he had a nervous breakdown. After the T-group was over he came home, but he didn't come to work. He stayed home for a week or two. Finally, he decided he needed help and began to see a psychiatrist. Apparently that was just what he needed because he then decided to get that job in education which he liked very much. He seems to have solved his problems, so everything has turned out for the best. But it scared the hell out of us at the time.

CASE STUDY: TRW SYSTEMS GROUP (D)[24]

TRW Systems Group of Redondo Beach, California, was a successful supplier of systems and hardware in the aerospace industry. A major operating group of TRW Inc. which was headquartered in Cleveland, Ohio, TRW Systems Group employed nearly 17,000 people, many of whom were technical professionals.

This case will describe the history and organization of TRW Systems Group as it existed in the late summer of 1967, to provide background for the E and F cases of the series.

History of TRW Inc. and TRW Systems Group

TRW Inc. was a highly diversified company formed by the merger of two distinctly different companies—Thompson Products, a leading maker of auto and aircraft parts in Cleveland, Ohio; and Ramo-Wooldridge, an aerospace company founded by Caltech scientists Simon Ramo and Dean Wooldridge. In 1953 these two men left Hughes Aircraft Company and established their business with the Thompson Company's financial backing. Winning a contract for the systems engineering and technical direction of the Air Force's ICBM Program, Ramo-Wooldridge quickly became one of the most respected "think factories" in the United States. This contract established a special relationship that made Ramo-Wooldridge (R-W) the technical supervisor for all ICBM contracts.

During this period, a nucleus of highly competent people were attracted to R-W. In the words of one senior manager:

The leverage of our activities in the old systems engineering and technical direction business was great. With a few decisions, we had great influence in the aerospace industry. Because of this, we were able to attract the best people. Some of these people were put on assignments that were not really up to their capability because we put the very best man possible on every job. We had an extremely competent group and this is reflected in the character of the organization. If you put a fellow with a terrific background in a fairly moderate job, he's not about to be pushed around. So this strength of individuality showed up in the organizational structure. We started out with that core of individuals and they're still here.

R-W's merger with Thompson into TRW Inc. occurred in 1958. The two firms' amicable relations and complementary capabilities made the merger a natural evolution of their earlier relationship. TRW Systems Group was the successor to the Ramo-Wooldridge arm of the merger.

In 1959 TRW Systems decided to give up its privileged relationship with the Air Force's ICBM Program because its role as technical director precluded it from competing for Air Force contracts. The transition from a sheltered captive of the Air Force to an independent, competitive company was successfully com-

24. Copyright © 1968 by the President and Fellows of Harvard College. Reproduced by permission. This case was prepared by John J. Gabarro under the supervision of Jay W. Lorsch.

pleted by 1963. By 1967, TRW Systems was in some way engaged in 90 percent of the government's missile and space projects, including such diverse contracts as the Comsat communications satellites, NASA's Orbiting Geophysical Observatory, and engines for the Apollo Lunar Excursion Module. TRW Systems' strategy was to have as many small, diverse contracts relating to the same technology as possible to avoid dependence on one large contract, thus providing internal stability for the long run.

The "Matrix" Relationship

TRW's projects ranged from major space vehicle contracts and large subcontracts requiring integration of many capabilities, to small projects within a single discipline. Its functional capabilities included expertise in such varied specialties as guidance and control systems, digital systems, telecommunications, electronic detection, rocket propulsion systems, electrical power systems, and solar array batteries. In addition, TRW provided systems analysis in thermodynamics, space vehicle structures, and orbital and trajectory mathematics. A large hardware contract for a space vehicle would require the integration of all of these capabilities to produce the systems engineering and detailed vehicle design (called software) and the actual fabrication and testing of the vehicle (called hardware). Even small contracts required the coordination of different disciplines. Interdependency was inherent in virtually every project regardless of size.[25]

To handle these projects, TRW Systems had developed an organization which they described as a "matrix." On one side of the matrix were the project offices which directed and coordinated the projects and on the other side of the matrix were the functional departments which provided the manpower and technical resources needed by the project offices.

Typically, a project office had a small group of thirty to forty people assigned to it. These people were concerned with the planning, coordinating, and systems engineering of the project. The project office called on the functional departments in its division and other divisions to perform the actual design and other technical work. As a result, the engineers working on a project were not members of the project office, but rather of functionally specialized departments, even though they might work on a project for several months or longer. The reasons for this organization were described in the report of a working committee formed to study the TRW Systems organization:

TRW Systems is in the business of applying advanced technology. The hardware work that we do is awarded by our customers in bid packages that usually require the integration of hardware from several technical fields into a single end item. We have hundreds of these projects in operation at a time. The number of people assigned to them range from three or four to several hundred. Most of the projects are small—only a few fall in the "large hardware project" category we are mainly concerned with in this document.

---

25. The terms project and program were used interchangeably at TRW.

From the standpoint of personnel and physical resources, it is most efficient to organize by specialized groups of technologies. To stay competitive, these groups must be large enough to obtain and fully utilize expensive special equipment and highly specialized personnel. If each project had its own staff and equipment, duplication would result, resource utilization would be low, and the cost high; it might also be difficult to retain the highest caliber of technical specialists. Our customers get lowest cost and top performance in organization by specialty.

For these reasons, the company has been organized into units of technical and staff specialties. As the company grows, these units grow in size, but a specialty is normally not duplicated in another organization. Each customer's needs call for a different combination of these capabilities. [Hence] a way of matching these customer needs to the appropriate TRW organizational capabilities is necessary. The use of the project office and matrix organization allows TRW Systems Group to make this fit.

Project Management

The project manager was responsible for the technical effort through all phases of development. He was also responsible for the control of project schedules and costs and in a total sense the profit of the project. As project manager, he controlled the funds and was ultimately responsible for their expenditure.

The work of the project office was carried out with the aid of a staff and several assistant project managers (APMs), whose responsibilities varied with the needs of the specific contract. Certain of these APMs had "line responsibility" over one or more subprojects. These APMs were responsible for preparing the subsystem specifications and coordinating their design. Other APMs provided services for all of the subprojects. For example, the APM for planning and control was responsible for cost and schedule control, and PERT costing. In a sense he performed the functions of a local comptroller and master scheduler. The APM for systems engineering was responsible for formulating the project's systems requirements and making sure that everything was designed to fit together in the end. And the APM for product integrity was responsible for developing and implementing a reliability program for the entire project including all of its subprojects.

Subproject Management

The total project effort was divided into subprojects by the project office. A typical hardware subproject was in the $2 million to $4 million range, with an average manpower level of fifty people and a peak of over 100. The effort consisted of the analysis, design, development, and fabrication of perhaps four different assemblies comprising a subsystem. Typically, these assemblies were new designs and five to eight of each were produced over a two-year period.

Each hardware subproject was assigned to a specific functional organization. The manager of that functional organization appointed a subprogram manager

(SPM) with the concurrence of the project manager. The SPM was responsible for the total subproject and was delegated management authority by both the functional management and the APM to whom he reported operationally for the project. Normally he reported administratively to a laboratory or department manager in the functional organization.

The SPM worked full-time directing his subproject, but was not a member of the project office; he remained a member of his functional organization. He represented both the program office and functional management in his authority over the divisional people working on his subproject. He spoke for the project in such matters as scheduling personnel and facility assignments, expenditure of funds, customer requirements, and design interfaces. He also, however, represented the laboratory or division in such issues as technical approach, cost-effective scheduling, and on the impact of design changes. The project manager provided his evaluation of the SPM's performance to the SPM's functional manager for the SPM's salary review.

Work Packages

The SPM was responsible for proposing a "work breakdown structure" of his subproject for the project manager's approval. In this work breakdown structure the subproject effort was successively subdivided into work packages, work units, and tasks for schedule, cost, and performance control. Job numbers were assigned at each level.

The functional engineer or supervisor receiving project direction from the SPM was called the Work Package Manager (WPM). Below the level of the WPM, the work was managed within the functional structure but the project manager maintained project control through the APM-SPM-WPM chain. The work package was generally performed entirely within one functional department.

Functional Organization

TRW Systems was organized into five operating divisions; specifically, the Space Vehicles, Electronic Systems, Systems Laboratory, Power Systems, and Systems Engineering and Integration Divisions. Each of the divisions served as a technology center which focused on the disciplines and resources necessary to practice its technology. Although each division was organized differently, they shared a similar pattern or organization.

Reporting to the division general manager were several operations managers. These operations managers were each in charge of a group of laboratories which were engaged in similar technologies. Each laboratory included a number of functional departments which were organized around technical specialties. Most divisions had a fabrication or manufacturing operations group headed by an operations manager.

While a project could be conducted entirely within one or two divisions, work for projects that were too complex or large for one laboratory to handle, were organized into project offices reporting to the division manager or an operations manager for projects.

Functional Operations Managers

Functional operations managers were responsible for directing the activities of two or three laboratories dealing in "adjacent" technologies. The operations manager level of management was a relatively new development and the job was not yet defined in detail. His major concern was matching TRW's technical competence to developments in the changing aerospace environment. He also spent considerable time monitoring the administrative aspects of his organization's operations with respect to cost and schedule. His review of subprojects conducted within his operations area was limited to general proposals and plans. His influence and attention, however, were strongly felt when a subproject was in technical or cost-schedule problems.

The operations manager also played a strong role in determining the allocation of TRW's IR&D (Independent Research and Development) funds within his and other operational areas. IR&D funds were appropriated for use in research and development not directly associated with contract work, their purpose being to maintain TRW's technical capability by developing the state of the art.

Laboratories

The typical laboratory contained from 100 to 300 personnel and was engaged in anywhere from two to ten subprojects. The laboratory manager spent about half of his time reviewing the progress of these subprojects and reviewing new proposals. His main concerns also included the assignment of personnel and facilities to meet new demands on the laboratory or in anticipating impending problems. Many laboratory managers had an assistant who was in charge of the subprogram managers and responsible for monitoring the subproject work being performed in the lab. In other cases the subproject managers were responsible to department managers.

Departments

The number of departments in a laboratory might vary from two to six. A typical department could have from twenty-five to 100 people assigned to it, and most departments were divided into at least two sections. Few had more than five. Normally the departments were organized so that their activities were confined to a single technical specialty. The department manager was responsible for developing and maintaining the technical capabilities of his particular specialty.

Unlike the laboratory manager, the department manager might be involved in giving technical supervision of a detailed nature. He was responsible for the professional growth and personnel management of his people, as well as capital planning and other resource administration. The department manager had a small budget for the operation of his department, but had to rely mainly on project work and IR&D (to a much smaller degree) for funding the department's operation.

Section

A typical section contained between five and fifteen engineers or scientists and an equal number of support personnel. Sections differed widely in the number and type of project tasks they handled. The section head provided the day-to-day direction of his personnel, although larger sections were sometimes divided into groups with group leaders for this purpose. The number of project tasks in a single section might vary from one to ten. Sometimes the entire section was committed to a single unit or subsystem on an important project.

A Typical Large Hardware Project

An organizational chart of a typical large hardware project is shown in Exhibit 4-9. To the left of the dotted line is the project organization described in the early portion of this case showing the link between the PM and APM. To the right of the line is the functional organization with the operations manager, laboratory manager, and department managers described in the latter part of this case.

Exhibit 4-9. TRW Systems Group (D). Organization of a Typical Large Hardware Project Showing the APM-SPM-WPM Chain.

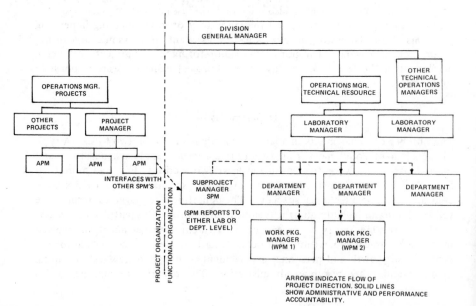

The SPM, although formally in the functional side of the matrix was, in reality, in the middle.

Because most projects went through a life cycle of several phases from their conception to their completion, both the size and the individual membership of the project team constantly shifted. For instance, the organizational structure changed significantly as task emphasis shifted from conceptual design to detailed design and production. Exhibit 4-10 shows four shifts in emphasis and the accompanying shifts in organization which took place during the life cycle of one such project.

The case writer talked to members of two project offices considered typical of medium to large hardware programs and to the functional people supporting these projects. One of the projects was the Vela Space Vehicle Program which was sponsored by the Space Vehicles Division although much of its work was being conducted in other divisions, especially the Electronic Systems Division. The second was the LMDE project (Lunar Module Descent Engine) which, unlike the Vela program, was almost entirely conducted within the Power Systems Division—its sponsoring division.

Building a Project Team

Mr. Gene Noneman, project manager of the Vela project, described how he put together a project team:

First I look at the project office's workload as a function of time so that no one person's workload peaks while the rest of the people in the organization have little to do. We want everyone busy with small peaks if possible.

Exhibit 4-10. TRW Systems Group (D). LMDE Project Office Organizations June 1966 to June 1967. June 1966—Development Phase.

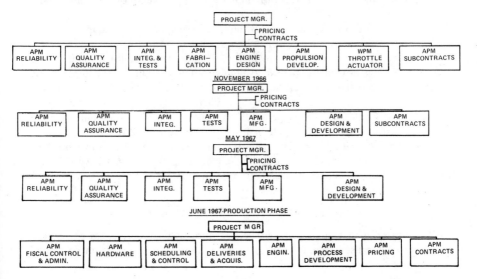

Then I take various cuts of how we could organize the project office. If a guy is overloaded on the first cut, I adjust and so forth. It is a "real-time" thing that you assess day by day even after you have made your basic organization.

The next step I take is to look at how I am going to split up the total work along the functional side of the matrix. What departments will be needed? What will have to be subcontracted?

In doing this there are overlaps. It's then a question of defining where one subproject begins and where one ends. Another question is how big should each subproject be? Do I need two subprojects to accomplish something or do I need one? This requires a lot of thought on our part and collaboration with the functional departments. We've tried to develop some criteria over the years for defining subprojects.

One criteria is the dollars that a subproject manager is going to have to look after. Second is the number of people within the company that his man is going to direct and monitor. The third criteria is the number of technical interfaces he has. How many technical people and how many discrete technical problems does he have to work with? The fourth factor is the management interfaces involved. How many functional departments is he going to have to interface with from a management point of view? A fifth key factor would be the number of subcontracts and the nature of the procurement. Is it easy to do or is it protracted, technically detailed, demanding subcontract work? And the sixth one is the nature of the total effort. Here's where risk comes in. Does the job border on basic research where you're dealing with factors that are not yet known, or is it more applied?

Generally, we go to the divisions with our requirements and our initial breakdown of the work within the program office, and probably some subsystems in mind, and say, 'Look, this is how I think it should be worked out—how does it look to you?' We have to compromise. I take the original cut because I know the requirements and interfaces, but then we sit down and work out the details with them.

When I go to the functional departments, I have specific people in mind that I'd like to have work for me—people who I know can do the job.

In the end we put together a team for every contract. A lot of times it's a question of their not having people available to help us. One of the department manager's concerns is who can he give me that I'll be happy with. I never ask for a hotshot to do a small project because I know they can't afford to give him to me and it wouldn't be a proper utilization of his time. If the company was shrinking instead of expanding, all this might be different. But now they aren't worried about keeping their men busy. Rather they are worried about who they can give to whom and when. Now their concern is, 'When can I have this guy back to put him on something else,' rather than 'I've got to keep this guy going.'

Internal Control System

TRW Systems management was concerned about the effectiveness of project cost control because of changes in the contracting environment from cost-plus-fixed-fee contracts to contracts with a fixed cost plus incentive fee based on performance, target cost, and schedule.

There was no single control system which applied to all projects in early 1967, although control personnel were working on developing a cost reporting system which would be flexible enough to apply in all situations. Many major project offices had developed their own cost control systems based on the perceived needs of the project.

The reporting systems used by the project offices were intended for use at the project office level. These systems were not intended nor detailed enough for use by the SPMs for their subprograms or by work package managers. SPMs and WPMs made their own control systems. The assistant project manager for project planning and control of the Vela project described subprogram control in the following way:

The reports we generate in this office are not intended for use by the SPMs in controlling their subprograms. They have to develop their own system to do this. We don't dictate formats—only the information that we need out of their reports. We try to leave it as flexible as possible so they can do the managing. All we want is the correct information so we know that they are not in trouble. We sit down with each SPM once a month or so, and if he is in trouble, at least once every two weeks. We've been putting pressure on the SPM to make sure he is using the tools that he has available to control his costs and schedule, and also that he is working at least one level greater in detail than we are here in the project office.

The assistant project manager for fiscal control on the LMDE project described how the cost control system used in that project was constructed and how it was related to the development of a management organization.

When the job is first estimated in a proposal, we establish a control matrix and a work breakdown structure. Across the top is the work breakdown structure which has all the work packages and work units and the major significant tasks. On the vertical axis we have the customer requirements. In this particular case our customer requires that we report to him the progress we were making by hardware line item, the throttle actuator, the injector, the nozzle extension, and so on. Essentially the customer imposes this kind of an axis on the matrix. Ultimately all this information goes into a data bank for estimating costs on new jobs.

CASE STUDY: TRW SYSTEMS GROUP (E)[26]

The extent to which relationships in the matrix should be defined and procedures standardized was a major organizational issue facing TRW Systems Group mana-

---

26. Copyright © 1968 by the President and Fellows of Harvard College. Reproduced by permission. This case was prepared by John J. Gabarro under the supervision of Jay W. Lorsch.

gers in the early summer of 1967. There were three principal reasons for this concern. Customers who did not understand the matrix relationships became uneasy with the project office's seeming lack of control over laboratory and shop resources. Second, TRW Systems meteoric growth from 2,000 to 14,000 employees in less than ten years caused some managers to worry that operating without rigidly defined organizational relationships would become difficult, especially since many new employees were accustomed to more traditional, structured organizations. Their inability to understand the organizational ambiguity led them to interpret it as confusion. The most significant factor, however, was the increasing number of large hardware projects being won by TRW. These projects required the control of tens of millions of dollars annually, and brought extremely complex interdependencies into the organization.

An APM's comment was typical of one point of view on this issue:

"There is no question that for utilizing talent, the matrix organization is superior to a strict project organization. However, in the matrix you end up with a large overlay of management—too much management structure. I see this as a problem every time we negotiate with the customer. We have to sell the program office, the SPMs, the SPM staff, the functional organization, and then all of the staff functions.

"We need more control because we're getting too big. You can't run a large hardware project with expenditures of millions of dollars a year in the same informal way that we have operated in the past. There is a strong need for more consistent definition of tasks and organizational units."

Other managers were less concerned about a need for clear definition and control, as was the manager who made this comment:

"I think you find more frustration with the matrix in the manufacturing and scheduling operations where people tend to be oriented to more traditional organizations. For example, I can think of an SPM who is a real 'heavy' in manufacturing and he is very unhappy here because he's been used to calling the shots and having people jump, or if there is a problem going up the ladder to get a definite answer.

"We have procedures, but procedures are guides. Procedures show people how things are done. But you can never write down on a piece of paper everything that makes a highly development-oriented organization like this go. Maybe you can do it at the post office department, but this isn't the post office."

Feeling About the Matrix

Although differences of opinion existed over the need for procedures, most TRW managers and engineers felt that the matrix was on balance a very satisfactory way of organizing, given TRW's resources and business. One department manager in the power systems division described its advantages:

"The matrix organization is of value when you reach the point where you don't need the specialist full time for a long period on any one given project. We have encouraged the matrix system because most of our projects are small and we need the flexibility."

Mr. Robert DiBono, a former APM in the Vela Project recently promoted to manager of another project, said he believed the matrix organization was fundamentally good. It allowed a man to do whatever he was best at all of the time, whether he was oriented towards systems work, management, or technical jobs:

"There is a complete spectrum of work available and you can't help but find a good fit. And the company can't help but get a good fit."

Mr. DiBono also felt that the matrix organization made poor unilateral decisions almost impossible, because so many people interfaced with the program manager. However,

"Some of the bad aspects are that it's really difficult to pinpoint responsibility and it's also hard to identify yourself with a specific accomplishment because there are so many other people involved in that accomplishment. Personal identity is sometimes hard for people in the program office to feel, so I would imagine that it is even harder for someone in a functional lab . . . .

"Stress is concentrated on those people who feel responsible. I can't say where most of the stress is in the organization. It's an individual thing. I think this goes along with the difficulty in pinpointing responsibility. You either feel responsible or you don't. The very nature of the matrix distributes stress over a number of people."

Richard Gress, liaison engineer from LMDE's customer, National Aircraft Company, saw the TRW matrix system this way:

"It's quite an unusual atmosphere here. I don't know what your impression is, but my first impression coming from an aircraft company four years ago was that nothing was being done here. But I found as I stayed here, that it's not that way at all. People accomplish a lot more. The key to their success is their ability to recognize a problem and to put all their effort toward solving it. If any of their jobs have problems, the first thing they do is find out what they can do to correct it. Not, what to do to *hide it*.

"We find in our exposure to other companies that lots of times the first thing they do is hide a problem so they can quietly solve it, and then tell us. They don't do that here. They'll tell you most things as soon as they known them."

Differences in the Orientations of the Functional and Project Organizations

Many managers felt that one inevitable characteristic of the matrix organization was the difference which existed between the orientation and objectives of the functional and project organizations.

The manager of a PSD design and development laboratory summed up the basic differences by explaining that the program office controlled the program by allocation of resources, by interpreting the often obscure customer requirements, and by the probing and testing of progress. The engineering organization, however, believed itself to be the "doer" organization and resented program office restraints on development activities.

A manager of another development department engaged in the LMDE Project explained that another difference in orientation was the tendency of engineers to produce a good technical product (sometimes at the cost of lengthening the schedule and exceeding the budget), while the project office "pulled too hard the other way." He commented,

"The engineers don't really understand the project implications nor are they interested in controlling the project. The project people don't really understand the technical implications of what they are doing, and often don't present technical things well enough to the customer nor screen the customer's unreasonable demands from getting into the work. So natural conflict begins to arise."

Mr. Lionel Hammet, whose laboratory was involved in the Vela Project, elaborated on these different concerns:

"Noneman (Vela Program manager) looks at the problem with the 2792 systems a little differently than I do.[27]

"I'm close to the numbers. I've talked to the experts in the area and I feel I have a much stronger feeling for what will happen than he has. He comes to me and he asks me, 'Well, have you talked to the experts?' and I say, 'Yes, I have talked to this fellow and that fellow, etc.' He says, 'Have you checked them, have you doublechecked what they said?'

"We are just as concerned as he is but in a more detailed way. We are concerned with a given location of the relay. I see the detailed analyses that are conducted and I know pretty much what the engineers are thinking. He's concerned because another program has had trouble with a component similar to the one we are using, and we've had some problems with it too. He's not concerned with the numbers we have to show him; he wants to see the box itself working. He wants to be able to shake the box up and see what happens to the relays. He wants to get maximum attention from the department managers, which you can't blame him for."

The comments of two managers who had served in both sides of the matrix summed up the differences between the project and functional organizations, and particularly emphasized the difference in personal satisfactions. Mr. John Wyman, a line manufacturing manager and a former APM, described his feelings:

---

27. The 2792 was a subsystem which had been having difficulties. A difference of opinion existed between the laboratory and the Vela Project office as to the source and extent of the problem.

"I have spent most of my life in line organizations, and I feel I have more control over my destiny there than I do in the project. Maybe it is a personal thing for me. For example, in the project office I had difficulty in getting the attention of people working on the project in the functional area. You're assigned men of varying capabilities from the functional areas to work for you. But whatever he's like you've got to depend on him to get the job done. If he's not performing, you can go to his boss. But your project is just one of many to his boss. And he's in a different organization than you, so you have little direct control there. If you keep hammering on his boss's door every day, the man himself will resent it and is not going to be effective."

A recently assigned APM described his point of view another way:

"I was in development engineering until the middle of March of this year, so I have been on the other side of the fence doing the design and development of the engine, and always complaining about those 'dirty guys over in the project office.' Now I'm in the project office. When you're sitting over in development engineering, you're trying to do a good technical job—an engineer likes to get a thing perfect. The guys in development and design engineering are not looking at it from a business standpoint. That is why you have a project office. Somebody has to make a profit for the company."

He went on to express his feeling that perhaps there was more satisfaction to be found in the functional organization, since the engineers found solutions to detailed technical problems themselves, while the project managers dealt with problems that had to be solved by others; the project manager's satisfaction seemed to be in getting the total job done within the schedule and the budget.

Project Office Involvement in Integrating Activities

The project office focused on directing and coordinating the project's work in the various departments. Thus, the working relationships between people in the project office and in the line and the handling of differences between them were of special interest to project office managers. Mr. DiBono, former Vela APM, described these concerns:

"How do you maintain a relationship with the guy in the functional department so that he gives you maximum creativity and his best efforts while also getting what is required for the project? It's an influence sort of thing. You never have direct control over your resources. You have to know how the other people operate and in many cases it is a completely individual relationship with each one of the men who work on your part of the project. You work it out by having some good healthy discussion with the SPMs and the key people in the functional departments. The people over whom you have control in the project office also have to interface outside and be influencers in the functional departments.

"The matrix organization is really an interlacing of personal relationships. For example, everyone who had worked with us on the last launch at the test site wanted to do a good job and people really put out. As a result you make a lot of personal arrangements with the people who work for you in the functional area. For example, company policy says that unless a man is sent to a test location for more than forty-five days he can't go on per diem or take his family. Well, when you have technicians who have been working fantastic overtime for you, much more than you can humanly expect, you do everything you can to let them take their families to Florida even though it's not strictly in accordance with company policy.

"But people have a devotion here to their work that you can't find anywhere else. For example, it's common on the test site for technicians, at the end of a fourteen-hour day, to leave the number of the bar or restaurant that they're going to after work in case a problem comes up and they're needed. And they are hourly people; they aren't salaried.

"But people have to feel that they're important to do this. They have to know you and trust you. Another part of establishing a good relationship is making sure that the line people in your project are recognized by their bosses for a good job. You help them look good in front of their bosses."

Mr. Robert Wilder, a younger APM in the Vela Program, described his job as "making sure that the right thing is being done at the right time." Since he was not able to work on technical problems in any great detail, Mr. Wilder explained that he had to rely on strong working relationships. He had initiated off-site meetings at the beginning of the design phase for his SPMs and some of the other APMs, and he felt that these sessions were important in helping people get to know each other. According to Wilder, at one such session Professor James Clarke of UCLA had explained the "arc of dissonance" concept:

"He explained that every person projects an arc of dissonance which is a measure of the inconsistency or incongruence that people see in him, mainly referring to his openness and honesty. His studies have shown that the most successful leaders have small arcs of dissonance. That made a lot of sense to me and since then I've tried to be as open as possible."

Mr. Wilder felt that team building was extremely important in an organization where so many people were dependent on each other. In his opinion coordination was essential to a successful project and, in addition, he noted, "You have to have trust and understanding to make this kind of organization work . . . if you don't have it you're dead."

Mr. Morris Adler, an SPM on the Vela Project in Wilder's area, also discussed the effect of team building on his subprogram's success:

"I attribute a lot of the success our subsystem has had to our relationship with the project office and my relationship with the people who worked on it. The project office started by having off-site meetings. Wilder actually initiated it with his SPMs and some of the APMs who were involved with us, and he chaired these meetings. We started by going to a restaurant where we had dinner and a couple of drinks and just talked to each other. But we did it under a different atmosphere. We weren't under the pressures of daily problems. The first session was more friendly than anything else—getting to know each other. In later sessions, however, we really grappled with some meaty problems. We dealt with relationships and problems directly, bringing a lot of things into the open. For example, we found out that there were a lot of problems within one of the functional areas and it helped me prevent similar things from occurring in my own area. It also helped the guys in that area clear up their own."

Adler was impressed enough by this experience to obtain funding for similar meetings with his own unit engineers:

"When we sat down, we got a lot of things squared away. It was an opportunity for everyone to talk about problems they were having by themselves and problems that others were causing. For example, when a design engineer wants to make a change, the production engineer screams at him because the change screws up his operation. Now, the production guy has a good feeling for what problems the design engineer has and vice versa, and they can talk to each other. This was all a very important part of making my people project oriented, and I think was behind our success.

"The thing I have to remember to appreciate team building is that no one works for me on a solid-line basis but my secretary."

Many other TRW personnel, both functional and program office, also stressed the importance of communication and trust in the reconciliation of differences in outlook between them. Mr. DiBono expressed his belief that no unresolvable differences in outlook existed between the specialists and the program office people; the specialists were extremely anxious to do a good job, and the key was simply to get both parties looking at the same problem. He had encountered difficulty only when the program office had failed to define the nature of problems to people in the functional area.

DiBono explained that many misunderstandings developed over documentation. As an example he explained that equipment specifications for orbital operations equipment had to be user-oriented, but design people would give design-oriented equipment specifications unless the exact need was communicated to them. Sometimes it was necessary to take a man out of the lab and up to the test site to achieve this understanding. He gave a further example:

"I had a case where I couldn't communicate to a group of design people what it was that I needed for equipment specs. I tried but it was obvious that I wasn't getting across. So I took the design information that was available and tried to translate it into operating specs myself. With this in hand, I went back to them and showed it to them. They said, 'Boy, that's pretty bad.' And they were right, it was pretty bad because it wasn't really detailed enough. But this gave them an opportunity to see what I wanted."

Some program office personnel, however, found the relationship with the functional areas frustrating. Mr. Wyman, for example, a former APM on the LMDE Program, described his feelings in the following way:

"The real problem we have in many of the divisions is that the work is left to the man down at machine, and his boss is in an office somewhere and doesn't know what is really going on. You are more or less at the mercy of that particular man. If you get one that you don't have rapport with, then you have to go work on his boss to get him moving, and frequently it is difficult to get a number of things done except under extreme pressure. This is because of the buddy system. A guy down there has a friend and he will put other people's work aside to help his buddy out."

Mr. Wyman stated that there were times in the course of a program when he was dependent on a whole department for assistance. He described a situation when Electronic Hardware Operations didn't have enough of a special wire in stock:

"This was critical to us, so we actually had people go over there and work with them to find out how much wire they really had and how we could steal a little bit here and there.

"When we first started into this, we had a very negative reaction. Then Anderson and I had the manager in charge of that department over for supper. We laid out our problem to him and told him why we needed his help and what it meant to the company, and what we were risking. There was a little lag in getting their cooperation while the desires of the lab supervisor filtered down to the lower levels. In other words they had to get interested in the things their boss was interested in, but we ended up getting a lot of cooperation, and everything turned out OK. That's the important thing in this business—how it ties together. It really is not so important what people think of you in the middle of all these things as it is what they think of you when you come to the end of it."

Subprogram Manager's Role

The SPM was a key person in the accomplishment of project work since he was responsible for managing the efforts of a major business subsystem of the project. Although he was in actuality a member of a functional area, and reported administratively to a laboratory or department manager, his full-time effort was directed toward his subprogram. Mr. Joe Kranz, an APM on the Vela Project who was formerly an SPM, described the SPM as "the one person in the functional area who can insure that costs and schedules are maintained for a part of the project." This job was difficult because an SPM represented both the project office and the functional organization, and their aims were often dissimilar. An SPM made many decisions affecting the project and its profitability, and it was essential that he balance the objectives of both organizations.

"The SPM's job is probably one of the most uncomfortable yet rewarding positions a man can have. I think it needs strengthening the most, with more support staffed to him. Let's face it, that's where the interfacing takes place between the line and the project office and in large programs that's where most of the technical direction takes place."

Mr. Kranz stated that although the project office and lab could put pressure on an SPM, both organizations "know that if you put too much pressure on that point, it will break down . . . especially because it has so much stress on it already." He categorized SPMs as two types: "the kind of guy who is strong technically and the kind of guy who isn't." Technically capable SPMs were received with respect and cooperation by the engineers, while the not-so-competent SPM was perceived as an outsider from the program office. Mr. Kranz felt that an SPM had to be competent technically in order to communicate with people about detailed technical problems. He talked about his own experiences:

"I think I had this respect as an SPM because when I decided to transfer to the project side of the house, the people in the laboratory didn't want me to go and tried to talk me into staying. It's hard to explain, but I felt that when I was an SPM my own position as a member of the laboratory was unchallenged because people accepted me and they realized that I was a capable guy and a pretty good engineer. I guess it was easier for me to look after the best interests of the program office because I didn't have to worry about my standing as a member of the laboratory."

An SPM for a fabrication subproject of the Vela Program attempted to describe the role he played as the intermediary between the project office and the functional area:

"I have asked our people to treat the project office like a customer, that is, honest and so forth, but discrete. I've encouraged contact between our working guys and the project office for information purposes. All other things and the technical direction come through me.

"One of the dangers of being in this job is that you identify too much with the project office. You can't become so identified with a project that you lose sight that the guy who is in trouble is in your department. It's possible to be so program-oriented that you're throwing stones at your own guys. You're the front-line representative of the program office but you're still getting paid by the lab manager . . . there is no question in my mind that he's my boss.

"I also have conflicts with other SPMs. It's easy for problems to develop when two projects are coming down the same assembly line. We're all TRW, so it's a question of figuring out who has the worst problem and helping each other. Sometimes I have problems working in another lab, and I have to make sure that we're getting the internal maanagement there that we need without my being there eight hours a day."

Mr. Adler, the SPM for an electronic subprogram, whose comments were introduced earlier, felt differently about the SPM's conflicting loyalties:

"The question of divided loyalties doesn't really come up very often. I feel responsibility for both the program office and the functional area. I won't carry people for the functional department for free on a project, for example. But, on the other hand, I won't push people for an early completion just to feel safe—especially when it means these people are going to be sitting around after it's done. I've found that if I'm objective with both sides and focus on the subprogram's needs I'm not squeezed. A good part of this is because my lab manager says, 'Your charter is to look out for your subprogram, period.'

"I'm sure there are several labs that have their SPMs more functionally oriented than we are and it's not because the SPM wants to be. It's because the lab manager wants him to be. If the lab manager wants an SPM to be functionally oriented first and foremost, you can say anything you want and write all the reports you want, they will be functionally oriented."

The frustrations and satisfactions of being an SPM were also described by Ray La Flamme, another SPM on the Vela Project. He said his satisfaction came from seeing his ideas develop into tangible accomplishment; from living with a minimum of information; and from combining technical work and management responsibility within a broad program pricture. Further, he noted:

"I get my greatest satisfaction when we're able to carry off the plan with a minimum of changes. My frustrations, they're legion: organization, personal relationships, misinformation on overruns, adapting to changes constantly in design plans, schedule, etc. But it has to be that way because that's the nature of the job. I enjoy this kind of excitement and going into meetings. It's part of the romance of the job.

"There are a lot of binds that an SPM can find himself in. The most typical one is when there is a difference of technical opinion between the project office and the functional department manager. I think my own position is harder because I'm on the department manager's staff, and not the lab manager's. I'm at a level where I can't quite get out of the detail stuff. It also makes it hard for me to interface with other department managers."

Another frustration described by SPMs was getting someone with management status to look at the work going on in the departments between crises, and occasionally during problem periods.

Many SPMs transferred into the project offices as assistant project managers after one or two assignments as an SPM. Joe Kranz had left the SPM's job primarily because he felt there was no recognition to be gained from doing project management-type work in a functional division, and the program office was the place to do this type of work. He felt that a tour as an SPM might be a good learning experience for a man who wanted to stay in the functional side of the house, but after more than one or two stints as an SPM a man would lose touch with the state of the art. Thus he became less effective both in the lab and as an SPM. Kranz concluded that there was little to be gained from remaining very long in the SPM's job.

Other TRW managers, however, did not all feel that the SPM's future career path was a problem. An APM stated that SPMs were an important source of program office people, since they were close to the program office as well as to their discipline, and their work was visible to many people.

Temporary Membership in the Project Offices

As the comments above suggest, one characteristic of a project office was that it had a finite life as an organization, ending when the project was completed. Managers other than SPMs also spoke about how this affected their outlook. One APM listed three alternative courses which could be followed after the closing of a project: (1) get follow-up work on the old project, (2) find a new customer for a new application of your old project, or (3) hunt for a new job. He stated that the company did not necessarily have a new job waiting at the end of a program but finding something had not been a problem. If a man had done a good job, finding the next job was easy since new program offices always looked for a man whose judgment and competence could be trusted. He commented:

"If we were starting a new program office, we'd look for people who we knew had the capability to do the job. If you can't find them directly, then you go to people whose judgment you can trust and ask them whom they would recommend.

"The company still works on the basis that a man's competence and personal reputation are very important. Competence and knowledge are a way in which a man can provide for the future and reduce the uncertainty of a career in the project side of the house."

This particular APM's predecessor had lost an opportunity outside of his project because he had been "indispensable"; the current APM intended to replace himself before the project ended in order to avoid this. He added, "Noneman (Vela Program manager) now requires that people brought into the project office have the capacity to grow into the APM job, but sometimes this requirement is overlooked because of the need for people."

APM Bob Wilder of the Vela Program commented that the issue of temporary membership was no problem because of TRW's continuing growth; no one felt threatened about job security. If the company were in a declining stage, however, he thought he might be worried and the program office would no longer be as attractive a place to work. He continued,

"I'd imagine that if I were not too sure about my present performance, I might be pretty worried. But I say to myself, I'm a pretty good guy and I'm valuable to TRW, things would have to be pretty bad for me to go, a lot of other people would go before me. My personal competence as a manager is very important to me, and I gain my sense of security by knowing that there is a fairly wide recognition of my competence.

"I will admit though that occasionally I think about TRW not yet having faced the aerospace cycle—big boom and bust—that most other outfits have. We're counting on our diversity and large number of small projects to prevent our ever facing one."

A third APM described the procedure of looking for another assignment after a project drew to a close:

"Around this place you look for a job; they don't look for you. Like everything else here it is unstructured. I don't really like the way it's done. You find another assignment by nosing around the company, seeing who has what. If I were looking for another assignment, I would tell all my friends I was available and Gene Noneman, the project manager, would also. I remember a guy who was about to phase out of a project. He started looking about a month before and just couldn't find anything, so he stayed on two months or so. This is really unusual. More often than not, a guy is needed on another project before he can leave the project he's working on."

This APM thought that people should not be kept in a program office too long because of the pressure: "You can't ever really relax." He suggested rotating people, perhaps to a functional area.

The Functional Manager's Views of the Functional-Program Relationship

The functional managers, like their program office counterparts, felt that most of the conflicts caused by different orientations were resolved. Dr. Drake, manager of a development department engaged in the LMDE program, explained that different orientations sometimes crystallized around situations where his organization felt more work should be done and the program office wanted them to stop. Such problems were only occasionally resolved by going up to the lab manager—program manager level. Dr. Drake thought that people higher in the organization tended to be more mature and broad-minded.

Drake explained that similar conflicts arose within the technical organization; for example, design engineers felt subjugated to development engineers in the same way that development engineers felt subjugated to program office people. In a period of significant technical problems, however, Drake felt that the project organization was at the mercy of the technical organization, and there had to be a feeling of trust and mutual purpose.

"There have been times when nobody has known clearly what to do, and where the pressures have been intense, budgets were exceeded, schedules slipped, problems became almost unbearable, personal workloads were high, tempers short, and clumsiness made everyone irritable. You literally get to the point where you may have some nervous breakdowns. The force of a few personalities becomes very important at that point. The same people are not quite so important when things are running smoothly.

"The matrix requires you to be aware of the individual you are dealing with in judging the way they present their case .... We have had problems when personalities are not well-balanced. It's a bad situation when one personality is much stronger than the other. The stronger begins to dictate, and the balance between line and project office is lost. We had a very strong development engineer in one area and his counterpart on the project side was weak. The development engineer was in control. No doubt about it. The project office in that situation was providing service, keeping the budget and documents straight and everybody worked for this development engineer. At exactly the same time there was another area where the project engineer was a very strong personality and the development engineer was not. The project was in absolute control there because it controls the funds to begin with."

In referring to the functional-project office relationship, another department manager, whose area was involved in the Vela Project, described the value he saw in the looseness of this relationship:

"Everything can't always be put on paper. We can't play the same game that a vendor plays with a customer. That's our strength. We don't live to the letter of the law. We meet the spirit and the intent. We're not subcontractors. We maintain a pretty flexible and loose relationship with the project office, but, at the same time, if I don't stay involved this relationship can cause some problems.

"One of the problems is that the department manager and section heads are not pulled into project work early enough when problems come up. The SPMs have interfaced pretty closely with the development engineer causing him to feel he's taking direction from the SPM. This has led to cases where the department manager or the section heads aren't involved until it gets really bad. In essence, the department managers are left out of the information loop until costs or problems are too big. This also results in under- or overdesign."

In speaking about their jobs, laboratory managers pointed out that they were generally involved in nontechnical problems (such as capital and manpower planning), rather than detailed technical problems. The exception was very major technical problems, in which they became deeply involved.

Mr. Hammet stated that there were a lot of frustrations involved in being a lab manager due to personalities and the nebulous nature of problems. But the satisfaction came from solving these same problems, and from being able to see people who were involved grow. He also felt that it was not true that functional personnel were dissatisfied because they could not work on a project from beginning to end:

"Everyone in the lab who's worked on a project gets satisfaction out of seeing a good launch. The manager of the Integration and Test Lab and I have worked out a pretty fluid relationship between our areas which enables us to transfer people so that they can follow the project through right to the launch. The surprising thing is that few of the designers ever want to do that. They would rather design. In many respects having a designer follow his project through to the launch would be good because the launch experience would have a good effect on his future design work. But, we've had few takers."

All the department managers and most of the SPMs reported to Mr. Hammet. He said that his SPMs were theoretically of equal organizational status as the department managers, but the department managers felt more important because they had the people needed by the SPMs. However, an SPM was in a very visible position and was therefore able to make or break himself, while the department manager's performance averaged out.

A development engineer working on the LMDE program discussed the functional project relationship in a manner which was typical of development and design engineers:

"One of the ways in which being an engineer here is different from other places is that you have technical responsibility and in effect no authority. We've had problems on the shut-off valve. They were technical problems which I, as a development engineer, felt needed correction. But the project office thought that it was satisfactory the way it was and that no changes were required. It's not so much the dollar that the project office is concerned with as schedules . . . .

"It's very difficult when you feel you have the responsibility, knowledge, and experience, but not the funds to authorize more work. You have to convince other people who are not familiar or experienced that it's necessary. Unfortunately, with valves, it's hard to justify them until you've had a series of failures and have actually stopped delivery of an engine. When this happens they sometimes look at you and say why didn't you push harder. It's happened here but they've always been man enough to accept the responsibility."

Assessing Priorities Between Programs

An important part of the functional manager's role was to assess the priorities between projects competing for resources. A manager of a design department in the Power System Division said that they never had enough people to do everything at once, and some jobs had to slide at the decision of the department manager. He said priorities were allocated by discussing jobs with the responsible people in the various programs, trying to establish which was most urgent; if no agreement could be reached, then someone up the line like a lab manager or operations manager might be approached.

Another department manager put it this way:

"When you really come down to it, the real job is to keep all your projects with passing grades. If one of them looks like it's heading for a D or an F you put more effort into it, regardless of whether you like that one better than you do another. If things are equal, I'll admit that I find all sorts of justifications to work on the things I like to work on, rather than on those I don't."

An APM on the LMDE project felt that the procedure used was satisfactory to the project office:

"Everyone in the project office thinks his is the highest-priority job, and that's, of course, what he should think. But you have to look at it from a company standpoint. Recently there was a case where we had a guy over in development engineering and we needed him to do some work on our program. However, they had him assigned to another spacecraft project because of a very difficult problem they were having. If he did not work on this one, it meant a large sum of money to the company. They were in some kind of a contractual situation, where if they did not start a certain test at a certain day, they would lose a lot of the fee. So the LMDE Program suffered a little bit.

"If there is a conflict, as in this case, it gets up to the project manager. He goes over and has a chat with the laboratory manager and they have a meeting of the minds about it. What means more to the company? We know that you want this man for your project, but we need him over here. So an agreement is generally worked out."

Control

As one indication of the concern for better control and better definition of jobs, TRW had in the planning stages a control system which was being designed specifically for controlling project-type work. As it had not been fully developed by August of 1967, a control system called a work breakdown structure was being used to control projects.

The APM for planning and control for the LMDE Project said that in the matrix system the difficulty of trying to collect costs accurately, promptly, and in enough detail to manage effectively arose because most department heads, section heads and engineers were working a number of projects simultaneously; they therefore had a lot of job numbers against which to charge their time and materials. For example:

"In the early days of LM, we had 250 charge numbers, for example, and about 650 'equivalent people' working on the program. We had as many as 2,000 individual people charging the program—some as little as half an hour a month. The part-time chargers, particularly, due to unfamiliarity with the program, tend to mischarge inadvertently.

"People don't realize that you're trying to segregate recurring and nonrecurring costs, or development activity from production activity. We have a control matrix that gives you all kinds of sophisticated information if it's properly used. But this sophistication has to be conveyed well to all the people charging the program.

"You find a subtle conflict of interest because the engineer has a natural desire to polish and improve the product to the ultimate degree. Maybe he's in the middle of a redesign, or maybe he isn't quite finished, so he'll work an extra hour, or day, or the rest of the week to do what he thinks is necessary from an engineering standpoint. You never know this because he continues to work on the program while charging another number. So you have an inherent inaccuracy in the data itself for that reason."

The APM explained that as the program progressed the work breakdown structures and matrix were revised, certain development numbers were closed, and production numbers opened. People tended, however, to keep using an old number because they remembered it. Inaccuracy was minimized by a high response system for collecting and reporting charges: each individual had a number, and where he worked had a cost center code identifying his division, laboratory, and department. It was possible to tell by the actual charge where and who the individual was; it was difficult, however, to know what was *not* being charged to a project although, presumably, charges made to another project would be detected by that project's APM.

A development engineer provided the viewpoint of some professionals at his level about the matter of controls:

"I'm somewhat of a maverick. I'm of the firm opinion that once you've got a contract you should throw the budget out the door, in effect, and do the job. Of course keep accounting records of how much it costs you. And the hell with what you estimated it was going to cost. That's water under the bridge. Your job once you have a contract is to do it as efficiently as possible and at a minimum of cost. And do it properly. If you're keeping the name for the company, you have to do a good job.

"The project office will very often come up and say we can't fix it because we don't have the money. This is a ridiculous statement. You have to fix it. Where they get the money is their problem. You ought to keep budget records because you have to know how much it costs and use that information to improve your estimate on the next contract.

"What sometimes happens when we run out of funds is that other phases of the program are charged, because this other phase might be overbudgeted and yours is underbudgeted. You end up with data that is not entirely accurate. We continue to underestimate, because we really don't know what it costs. The other facet of this is that most good development engineers work a lot of overtime for which they're not paid and which never shows up in accounting records. They work twice as much as actually shows up including nights and Saturdays.

"Moonlighting is standard practice for a conscientious engineer to solve a problem now so that when the problem hits he has a solution for it. You don't want to spend nights, Saturdays, and Sundays when it does hit because it affects your personal life and you don't do a good job solving problems that you didn't have the time to think about. When the problem comes up and you say, 'I happen to have the answer right here,' they're overjoyed. They don't say, 'How come you were working on that?' I think the answer would be somewhat embarrassing to them and very seldom do they go into that. They just take it, and usually give the engineer very little credit for it."

The APM for control in the Vela Project explained that a big problem in controlling costs was knowing when people were merely tracking costs. TRW's reputation for technical excellence at any cost affected cost control, in that individuals in the functional organization were not evaluated on management skills but on technical skills, that is, how good were the boxes that they built:

"I think customers realize that we are expensive. I think they know, though, that if they come here, it will be expensive but good—better than it could be done anywhere else."

He explained that this was a question of management philosophy and basic change in orientation had to come from the top on down. The president of TRW Systems was beginning to put more emphasis on cost management because of customer concern, however, and he felt that costs would become an item of greater importance to the organization.

Mr. Gene Noneman, the Vela Project manager, said that the subprogram plan was a very important tool in defining the tasks that had to be completed in establishing a cost and time schedule for control. The plan had to be made up by the SPM early in the program, and in such a way that it could be understood by everyone. The finished plan was sent to the APM, and Noneman said that this was how he knew that the SPM understood the requirements of the job, and that the people in his department and all the departments he interfaced with would understand the job.

As described in TRW Systems Group (D), the SPMs designed their own control systems and were only required to give key inputs to the program office. Mr. Ray La Flamme, an SPM in the Vela Program, felt that this and the work breakdown structure had a number of limitations:

"The program office is often naive in realizing how much it costs to do work in a shop. My own recognition and documentation of these added costs has not been adequate and for this reason we're 'overrun' on manpower and money. I find it very hard to keep up with the documentation.

"There's nothing that's set up in our cost control system with which you can document a change rapidly and efficiently. If I had it to do all over again, I'd attempt to develop a system whereby everyone realizes the impact of what they're doing to us.

"The other influence on controlling costs lies with the departments doing the work. If someone there doesn't feel responsible for meeting and beating cost where possible and preventing costly overdesign, you've had it."

Formalizing the Matrix Relationships

Many TRW managers stressed that formalizing and standardizing the matrix relationships and control system had to be considered in the context of the

TRW Systems organization and its distinct characteristics. Robert Anderson, operations manager for projects in the Power Systems Division, was one of the most articulate in making this point:

"I'd like to talk just a little bit about the character of the company because I think it influences the capability of this kind of system to work in a good way: This outfit is always *working the problem*. I have never seen anything like it. It just seems that this whole company is infused with the idea of working hard and making itself better.

"It is the most self-critical place you have ever seen, and as a result it is not stagnant. Everything is sort of continuously changing and there is always a little degree of fuzziness around. But they are all working, and not just on their own problems. A guy is just as likely to work on somebody else's problems. It is none of his business, but he's doing it anyway, presumably from pure motives. He is trying to help the other guy to do better. Organizational definitions are not really rigid.

"Every year they get a little more so. And many of us look at that with fear and trepidation and beat them down every now and then just for fun.

"But in this organization there is enough diversity and enough talent so that the organization sort of evolves as needs change. The good parts of the organization grow and prosper and the bad parts of the organization sort of don't.

"You could argue that it makes for empire building, but if the strong and needed parts survive it's a valid empire."

CASE STUDY: POWER CONTROLS: A DIVISION OF ABC PRODUCTS[28]

On June 16, 1976, Mr. Buford Bently returned from vacation. Mr. Bently had spent the previous three weeks fishing in Canada. As manager of the manufacturing department, he held a key position in Power Controls. Over the years, he had developed a reputation of being very conscientious and knowledgeable in the field of specialized machining techniques. These attributes had led to personal success as department manager for fifteen years, and had contributed greatly to the success of the division. Mr. Bently returned to work that morning and immediately wrote a letter of resignation to be effective June 30, 1976.

Division Background

The Power Controls Division of ABC Products was established in the late 1950s when it became evident that the energy situation in this country would require new sources of electrical power. The nuclear reactor seemed to be destined to replace coal and oil as the primary source of power in future years.

---

28. This case was prepared by Kenneth A. Paetsch and Spyridon B. Farmakidis under the supervision of Associate Professor Harold Kerzner, as the basis for class discussion rather than to illustrate either effective or ineffective handling of an administrative situation. Copyright © 1978 by Harold Kerzner.

Originally, a project team was established by ABC Products to design and develop major components for the Nuclear Reactor Program under the auspices of the Atomic Energy Commission (AEC). The team consisted of eight people headed by a project manager. The project was given top priority and key people from the departments of design, manufacturing, quality control, test and assembly and production control were assigned.

Corporate planning considered the ABC project as a key to the attainment of the expertise required to compete in the new and upcoming field of nuclear reactors. Of course, management understood the risks involved:

1. No one was sure how large a market existed.
2. No one was sure if nuclear reactors were economically feasible.

There appeared to be an unlimited opportunity in the commercial market if the product could be produced at a reasonable cost. Not only domestic energy development but foreign energy contracts as well as various Department of Defense projects existed. There was also a distinct possibility that reactors could be developed for use on ships and other forms of transportation.

To gain a technological advantage over its competitors, ABC higher-level management was willing to take the risk of a loss on the AEC project but insisted that their reputation as one of the top engineering companies in the country be maintained. In fact, management identified this project as offering ABC Products an excellent opportunity to enhance its reputation as the "Cadillac of the engineering companies."

Through a series of outstanding efforts by some young engineers, ABC was able to meet feasibility requirements and land three additional government contracts. By the early 1960s, about 100 more people were added to the group. Based on this and other government projections on the development of a large number of nuclear reactors to generate electricity, the decision was made to expand the program to a division status. The evolution of a matrix organization by product design seemed inevitable. The division status involved the development of a formal organization; this made it necessary to add functions such as accounting, personnel, and sales to the existing functions of design, manufacturing, quality control, and test and assembly. Furthermore, since the division's work was done on the basis of contracts with clients, each contract was a project within the division. Responsibility was vested in project leaders as shown in Exhibit 4-11. Exhibit 4-12 lists personnel by function and indicates which members lead the functional team of each project.

Product

A brief discussion of nuclear reactors in general aids in the understanding of the complexity, requirements, and application of the specific product. A nuclear power plant can be viewed as having three basic parts:

1. Heat source
2. Coolant and attendant path to transfer the heat
3. Energy conversion devices

Exhibit 4-11. Organization Chart Power Controls Division. ABC Products As Of June 30, 1976.

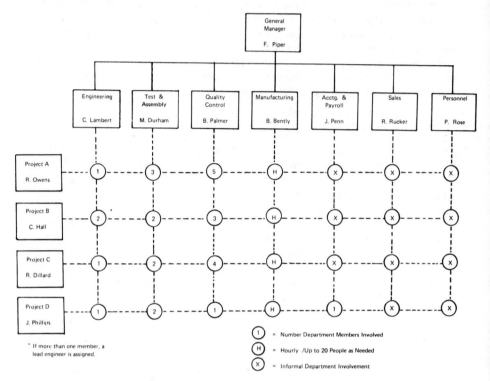

The heat source is the reactor core, water and piping systems are the coolant and path, and heat exchangers, steam generators, and electrical generators are the energy conversion devices.

Electric power is extracted from the reactor through atomic fission, or the splitting of an atomic nucleus by bombardment with neutrons, resulting in the release of enormous amounts of energy. The reactor core (heat source) and its coolant, usually water, are located in the reactor vessel; this primary coolant also is pumped through equipment outside the reactor vessel to act as (or provide heat to) the working fluid. Fission is continually going on, the level of activity depends on the position of numerous rods which slide into the core. These are the control rods, and the device that positions them is the control rod drive mechanism (CRDM). Power Controls manufactures a control rod drive mechanism.

There are various types of CRDMs—magnetic jacks, hydraulic drives, and roller nut drives. The specific type manufactured by Power Controls is of the roller nut type.

The roller nut drive is based on a unique anti-friction screw and nut combination. The control rod is coupled to a leadscrew (somewhat like a lock and key);

Exhibit 4-12. Personnel Chart Power Controls Division ABC Products As Of June 30, 1976.

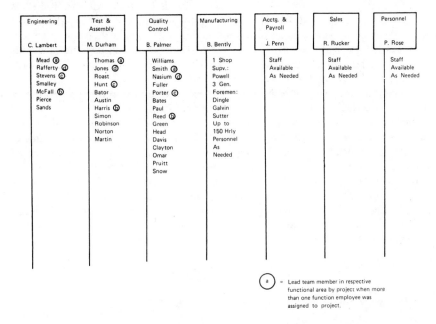

Engineering	Test & Assembly	Quality Control	Manufacturing	Acctg. & Payroll	Sales	Personnel
C. Lambert	M. Durham	B. Palmer	B. Bently	J. Penn	R. Rucker	P. Rose
Mead ⓐ	Thomas ⓐ	Williams	1 Shop	Staff	Staff	Staff
Rafferty ⓓ	Jones ⓓ	Smith ⓑ	Supv.:	Available	Available	Available
Stevens ⓒ	Roast	Nasium ⓓ	Powell	As Needed	As Needed	As Needed
Smalley	Hunt ⓒ	Fuller	3 Gen.			
McFall ⓑ	Bator	Porter ⓒ	Foremen:			
Pierce	Austin	Bates	Dingle			
Sands	Harris ⓑ	Paul	Galvin			
	Simon	Reed ⓓ	Sutter			
	Robinson	Green	Up to			
	Norton	Head	150 Hrly			
	Martin	Davis	Personnel			
		Clayton	As			
		Omar	Needed			
		Pruitt				
		Snow				

ⓐ = Lead team member in respective functional area by project when more than one function employee was assigned to project.

this prevents the leadscrew from rotating about its axis. The leadscrew is operated upon by a nut maintained at a constant elevation. Rotation of the nut raises or lowers the leadscrew. In the roller nut configuration, the nut does not contain fixed threads. Rather, it contains a set of four spools located around the screw at one elevation and mounted in an annular frame. The annular frame rotates about the leadscrew axis. Each spool in the annular frame is free to rotate on its own axis, which lies in a plane parallel to the leadscrew but which is canted by the amount of the screw helix angle. Each of these spools has circumferential lands on its outside diameter, to engage the threads of the leadscrew. When the annular frame (nut) is driven to rotate, the keyed leadscrew is lifted or lowered by the lands on the spools (or rollers). The linear motion of the leadscrew is transmitted to the control rod through a coupling.

The roller nut CRDM includes a section of pressure vessel in the shape of a deep thimble which extends above the roller nut. This section receives the upper end of the leadscrew as the control rod is drawn upward, out of the core. The control rod drive includes this thimble and the motor housing below it. Radially outward, the CRDM includes everything out to the seal which attaches the CRDM to the reactor head. The term "control rod drive" also covers electrical gear such as the stator and position indicator associated with the drive, both of which are outside the pressure boundary.

The basic function of the CRDM is, of course, to position the control rod within the core to make controlled power-level changes upon command. Additionally, total insertion of the control rod causes the reaction to cease; safety dictates that the mechanism provide for rapid and reliable total insertion. A basic requirement of the CRDM is long, trouble-free operation. ("Long" is defined as more than of ten years.) Typically, there are ten to eighty control rod devices in a reactor, usually so close together as to be difficult to maintain. Also the CRDM will typically, be welded to the reactor. Even if the facility is shut down, removing a CRDM for repair is a sizable undertaking. As a result, the importance of reliability can hardly be overstated.

Quality of design must provide the reliability called for in the technical specifications on CRDMs; these are among the most stringent in any industry. Conformance to these technical requirements is proved through administrative (quality control) specifications. These are also among the most stringent in any industry, and assurance of compliance to these specifications, which encompass the entire organization, is the responsibility of the quality control department. Any change or question relative to performance deviation must be concurred with by quality control or relayed through them to the customer quality control for their concurrence. (This situation results in great internal conflict between the quality control department and manufacturing department and/or the project management.)

Division Personnel

The following is a discussion of the key division personnel:

Manufacturing Manager

As can be seen from Exhibit 4-11, the manufacturing functional element was originally headed by Buford Bently. Buford was one of the original members of the project team when the control division was established in the early 1960s. He is a relatively young executive at the age of fifty-five and is recognized by the industry as an expert in machining techniques for nuclear products. He is active in various professional societies and often speaks at functions related to manufacturing operations.

He manages a very technical functional area that has complex machining and welding equipment needed to produce components for nuclear reactors. His very demanding personality was perfect in an environment that requires exacting specifications and high-quality output.

Assistants who worked for him often praised his excellent work habits; after working for him, they were usually transferred to other divisions taking with them the experience they had gained. Many manufacturing managers throughout the corporation had worked for him as an understudy at one time or another.

Although Control Products is a matrix organization and all the functional managers should be equal in authority and stature, the manufacturing function tends to be the first among equals, and the manufacturing manager traditionally replaces the general manager during his absence. It is also considered an automatic promotion from the head of the manufacturing function to general manager when that position becomes vacant.

Quality Control Manager

Mr. Palmer was the quality control manager and was considered an "expert" within his functional area of quality control and was recognized throughout the industry. He has written many papers on quality control and is an active member of the Executive Committee of the American Society of Quality Control.

The quality control functional area he manages is responsible for the quality of the product from the receipt of new material to shipment of the finished product. Quality control becomes involved with extensive contractual requirements and complicated control procedures which are outlined by the customer. An example of contract requirements would be:

Requires an effective and economical program in consonance with contractor's other administrative and technical programs. Based on consideration of technical and manufacturing aspects of production, all supplies and services in-plant or at any other source to be controlled at all points to assure conformance to contract. Program to provide for prevention and detection of discrepancies and positive corrective action. Objective evidence of quality to be readily available to government representative. Authority and responsibility of those (personnel) in charge of the design of the product, tests, production quality, to be clearly stated. *Program shall facilitate determinations of effects of quality deficiencies and quality on price.* Facilities and standards shall be effectively managed (drawings, engineering changes, measuring equipment necessary for required quality). Program shall include an effective control of purchased materials and subcontracted work. In-plant work shall be controlled completely. Program shall include effective execution of responsibilities shared jointly with the government or related to government functions (government property, government source inspection).

This type of requirement promoted the natural conflict between quality control and the manufacturing element of the division. Conflictive interpretation of extensive contractual requirements resulted. In line with corporate image and divisional philosophy of being the Cadillac of vendors, "gray areas" were always interpreted in favor of the customer (government).

Quality control was probably the second most influential functional area within the division; in certain instances, it was the most powerful area. As mentioned, competition was keen between quality control and manufacturing. Mr. Palmer was always highly concerned with his personnel. He was a "father image" to his subordinates and he developed a powerful sense of loyalty among his people. He always stressed high quality and his subordinates were committed to this type of philosophy.

Project C Manager

Mr. Ronald Dillard was assigned project manager of project C because of his exceptional engineering skills. He was a young man, in his late thirties, with bachelor's and master's degrees in mechanical engineering. This was a critical project and a man of his caliber was essential.

Mr. Dillard has been with the company for ten years. He started in the engineering department and rose quickly to assistant manager of that department. He developed the reputation of always meeting commitments relative to costs and scheduling. He is known as a very tough taskmaster, which led to personality conflicts—especially with the functional group leaders in his project team. Although he considered cost and scheduling as more important than performance, he did stress quality to its utmost. But this did not satisfy the quality control people involved in project C. They felt performance should be given preferential consideration above costs/scheduling. (This relates back to the quality control manager's influence on his subordinates.) Mr. Dillard consistently had to negotiate quality control specifications with the quality control functional manager (Mr. Palmer) and many times had to have the problem resolved by the general manager (Mr. Piper). Dillard's arguments were always related to saving time and costs, but Mr. Piper would usually side with quality control since he was committed to maintain the corporate reputation of a Cadillac organization.

Mr. Dillard supported those individuals who worked hard for him. Conversely, he had little patience with people who did not put out and would complain to the respective functional manager whenever one of his people did not perform satisfactorily.

Incidents

Concurrent with, and perhaps a contributing factor to, Mr. Bently's retirement was the apparent shift in management philosophy. Since the division was formed, management, both divisional and corporate, had always been willing to support "performance" whenever there was a conflict between it and "cost or schedule." This had caused Mr. Bently many problems over the years in his position as manufacturing manager; in the final analysis, however, he understood and supported this philosophy. Corporate and divisional management were no longer willing to support this position. (It is not known if Mr. Bently was truly aware of this situation when he retired. It is speculated, however, because of his contacts within the corporate structure of ABC that he was aware of management's changing attitude.) Managers of the functional departments and the program managers were informed by Mr. Piper on June 25 of this changing philosophy. The results of this information were felt by the customer in a very short period of time. Customer requests, in most cases, were met with responses such as, "Show me in the contract where this is stated as a requirement. . . ." and/or "That is an excellent idea, I'm sure if you would submit a Request for Bid on this modification we would surely respond."

Mr. Dillard, project manager of project C, seized upon this situation and forced the resolution of every conflict between himself and Mr. Palmer, quality control manager, to be resolved by Mr. Piper, general manager. Mr. Palmer knew the outcome before going to guidance. Time after time, Mr. Piper would support the time/cost position. It should not be thought that these were questions relevant to flagrant reductions in performance; usually "gray areas" which could be interpreted either in favor of the customer or Power Controls were involved.

In the past, these "gray areas" were always resolved in favor of the customer, with Power Controls incurring any additional cost or schedule delays.

Needless to say, it was only a matter of a couple of months before Mr. Palmer was asked to resign. The resignation was, however, from the manager's position only and not from the organization entirely. (His expertise, reputation, and excellent working relationship with the customers were still needed.) He was to resign and assume the duties of special assistant to a newly appointed quality control manager.

The naming of the new quality control manager was quite a surprise to many people—Mr. Dillard was chosen. The manufacturing manager's position was still open and "insiders" were predicting Mr. Dillard for that position. Along with this appointment, it was formally announced that Mr. Sands would serve as temporary manufacturing manager until a permanent manager was selected. (To many people in the organization the outcome was apparent. Mr. Dillard would eventually be the manufacturing manager but first the matter of quality control needed to be resolved.)

Mr. Dillard assumed the position of quality control manager on September 1, 1976. The department was reorganized on September 15. Until that time, the lead quality engineer for a specific project informally supervised the work of all other quality personnel assigned to the project. He was the contact between the project manager and the quality function. All matters related to quality were under his control including vendor contacts, in-house operations, customer requests, deviations reporting, inspection methods, etc. The reorganization diffused this power/control by creating two separate units in the department—one to handle operations within Power Controls and the other to handle matters with vendors or customers. The lead quality engineer designation remained but the separate "service" type operation for all projects when dealing outside of Power Controls reduced the power/control of the lead engineer. Mr. Porter was appointed to head this service operation.

Many personnel in quality control and assembly and test resented an "outsider" being named as quality control manager. They individually appealed to Mr. Piper that he reconsider his decision, but these objections were to no avail. No formal, organized objection to Mr. Dillard being quality control manager was ever made by the employees.

Almost systematically, through voluntary and involuntary retirement, resignation, and reassignment, the lead quality engineers were replaced. Promotion to these positions was not from within the quality department but usually from the engineering department. The personnel in quality who felt they were next in line for the lead positions were, needless to say, quite disappointed.

In September 1977, almost a year to the day that Mr. Dillard was assigned as quality control manager, he was further promoted to manufacturing manager. The reorganization continued, but now at the department manager level. Again, almost systematically, and occurring every two or three months, the heads of the various functional departments were replaced. The reorganization was completed in mid-1978 and the resulting organization is illustrated by Exhibit 4-13 and Exhibit 4-14.

Exhibit 4-13. Organization Chart Power Controls Division ABC Products As Of June 30, 1976.

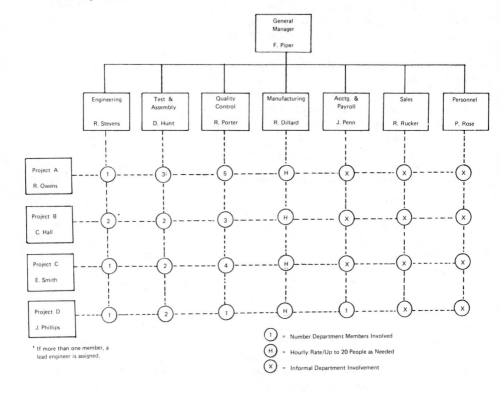

CASE STUDY: SKYLINE OIL COMPANY

In 1977, Skyline Oil Company decided to implement formal project management. Realizing that any new organizational structure must incorporate a compensation package, the wage and salary administrator prepared the following job description package.

Function

Acts as project leader, normally on medium-size projects, to originate, plan, coordinate and/or supervise complete engineering projects related to the design and operation of petroleum and chemical facilities. Accepts complete responsibility for cost, time, and quality control on assigned projects.

Scope

Manages under the administrative supervision of the manager of project manager. Receives little technical guidance on the technical aspects of the activity. This

Exhibit 4-14. Personnel Chart Power Controls Division. ABC Products As Of June 30, 1978.

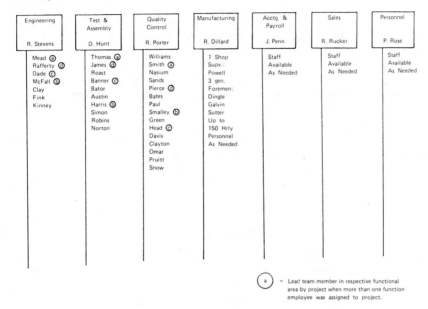

Engineering	Test & Assembly	Quality Control	Manufacturing	Acctg. & Payroll	Sales	Personnel
R. Stevens	D. Hunt	R. Porter	R. Dillard	J. Penn	R. Rucker	P. Rose
Mead ⓐ	Thomas ⓐ	Williams	1 Shop	Staff	Staff	Staff
Rafferty ⓑ	James ⓓ	Smith ⓐ	Supv.:	Available	Available	Available
Dade ⓒ	Roast	Nasium	Powell	As Needed	As Needed	As Needed
McFall ⓑ	Banner ⓒ	Sands	3 gen.			
Clay	Bator	Pierce ⓓ	Foremen:			
Fink	Austin	Bates	Dingle			
Kinney	Harris ⓑ	Paul	Galvin			
	Simon	Smalley ⓑ	Sutter			
	Robins	Green	Up to			
	Norton	Head ⓒ	150 Hrly			
		Davis	Personnel			
		Clayton	As Needed			
		Omar				
		Pruitt				
		Snow				

ⓐ = Lead team member in respective functional area by project when more than one function employee was assigned to project.

position is concerned with organizing, leading, and conducting engineering projects for the parent company, its subsidiaries, and its affiliates relating to new construction and revamp of facilities, plants, and other locations, within the money and schedule allowed, and at a minimum cost consistent with recognized safety practices. The project's size or complexity may require a task force group to complete; it may involve the use and technical direction of company or outside engineering, drafting, construction, and other needed personnel, from one to a dozen or so. Most projects would be of medium size, such as additional plant expansion facilities; but they may vary from a few thousand dollars to over one million, or may be a phase of a very large, multimillion dollar project.

Projects may include feasibility study, economic justification, design, engineering, installation, inspection, startup, and initial operational check and repairs or any part thereof as requested by sponsor. Project leader can either use own judgment regarding problems or consult with available specialists or consultants on certain phases of project. Projects include: refining or chemical process units; tank fields, including piping and pump systems and pipeline construction; office, laboratory, and shop buildings; unusual projects include construction of storage cavities underground by means of solutioning salt beds or mining in rock formations; some projects consist of a study and report with recommendations. A project leader is essentially a "general engineer," capable of handling a wide variety of work including detailed design and estimating if necessary; however, his main specialty is the ability to coordinate so that a project is completed successfully.

Contacts are maintained with all departments and levels required by project and with contractors, engineering firms, governmental agencies, equipment manufacturers, etc., as projects dictate.

The most complex problems are those which involve the planning, coordination and execution of many simultaneous functions within and outside the company so as to accomplish the project objective in the allocated time with the allocated funds. They involve judgments as to the precise nature of the technical problems to be resolved; the conceptual and definitive design of facilities that will resolve such problems; and the resolution of unforeseen problems.

Position requires a bachelor degree in engineering with a minimum of five years engineering experience. Must have the temperament and ability to be a supervisor and be able to conduct and lead groups of engineers, suppliers, etc., in technical discussions for expediting engineering assignments.

Assignments may involve work out-of-doors, long and irregular hours, being away from home for extended periods, where he is ranking company official in the area.

Primary Duties

1. Calls to the attention of management opportunities for profitable engineering projects.
2. Plans the engineering scope of a project in time and money, and secures necessary approval to proceed.
3. Discusses with sponsors and others, the nature of the problem and designs whatever facilities are necessary, sometimes with several alternative solutions.
4. Directs the technical efforts of others assigned to the project.
5. Estimates the investment and operating costs of such facilities and calculates the economic attractiveness.
6. Presents the results, conclusions, and appraisals to management for approval and for decision to proceed with facilities construction.
7. Instructs plant personnel on the proper use of such facilities.
8. Controls the expenditure of all project funds.
9. Reports status and progress of project regularly to project sponsor and to supervisors.
10. May request and follow up on laboratory or pilot plant studies for the development of data necessary for design, operation, and testing.
11. May take part in projects other than own, usually as a specialist, using background of education and experience in specialized area of engineering.
12. Keeps abreast of and advises on latest ideas, schemes, equipment in his field of interest. Attends professional meetings, contacts manufacturers and suppliers, and consults with other interested parties both within and outside the company.
13. May be required to adapt available equipment and methods to meet certain project requirements.

14. Maintains correct knowledge and adheres to engineering and company safety procedures, rules, and practices relating to a given project assignment.

Although most of the executives of Skyline Oil were favorably impressed with the job description, there was still a major hurdle which had to be overcome. Management wanted six different pay grades within the project management group, but did not know how to distinguish between the six pay grades using the job description for a project engineer.

5
Management Functions

5.0 INTRODUCTION

In the previous sections we stated that the project managers measure success by how well they can negotiate with both upper-level and functional management for the resources necessary to achieve the project objective. If, in addition, we consider the fact that the project manager may have a great deal of delegated authority but very little power, then the managerial skills required for successful performance may be drastically different than those of functional management counterparts.

The difficult aspect of the project management environment lies with the individuals at the project-functional interface who must report to two bosses. Functional managers and project managers, by virtue of their different authority levels and responsibilities, treat their people in different fashions depending upon their "management school" philosophies. There are generally five management schools as outlined below:

- The classical/traditional school: management is the process of getting things done (i.e., possibly achieving objectives) by working both with and through people operating in organized groups. Emphasis is placed upon the end item or objective, with little regard for the people involved.
- The empirical school: managerial capabilities can be developed by studying the experiences of other managers regardless of whether or not the situations are similar.
- The behavioral school: two classrooms are considered within this school. First, the human relations classroom in which the emphasis is on the interpersonal relationships between individuals and their work. The second classroom considers the social system of the individual. Management is considered to be a system of cultural relationships involving social change.

- The decision theory school: management is a rational approach to decision-making using a system of mathematical models and processes, such as operations research and management science.
- The management systems school: management is the development of a systems model, characterized by input, processing, and output, and directly identifies the flow of resources (money, equipment, facilities, personnel, information, and material) necessary to obtain some objective by either maximizing or minimizing some objective function. The management systems school also includes contingency theory which stresses that each situation is unique and must be optimized separately within the constraints of the system.

In a project environment, functional managers are generally practitioners of the first three schools of management, whereas project managers utilize the last two. This imposes hardships on both the project managers and functional representatives. The project manager must motivate functional representatives toward project dedication on the horizontal line using management system theory and quantitative tools, often with little regard for the employee. After all, the employee might be assigned for a very short-term effort, whereas the end item is the most important objective. The functional manager, however, expresses more of a concern for the individual needs of the employee using the traditional or behavioral schools of management.

Modern practitioners still tend to identify management responsibilities and skills in terms of the principles and functions developed in the early management schools, namely:

- Planning
- Organizing
- Staffing
- Controlling
- Directing

Although these management functions have generally been applied to traditional management structures, they have recently been redefined for temporary management positions. Their fundamental meanings are still the same but the applications are different.

Organizing and staffing has been discussed in Chapters 3 and 4. The remainder of this chapter will discuss the planning, controlling, and directing of functions, as applied to project management.

5.1 GENERAL PLANNING

The most important responsibilities of a project manager are planning integrating, and executing plans. Almost all projects, because of their relatively short duration and often prioritized control of resources, require formal, detailed planning. The integration of the planning activities is necessary because each functional unit may develop its own planning documentation with little regard for other functional units.

Planning, in general, can best be described as the function of selection the enterprise objectives and establishing the policies, procedures, and programs necessary for achieving them. Planning in a project environment may be described as establishing a predetermined course of action within a forecasted environment. The project sets the major milestones and the line managers hope that they can meet them. If the line manager cannot commit because the milestones are perceived as unrealistic, the project manager may have to develop alternatives, one of which may be to move the milestones. Upper-level management must become involved in the selection of alternatives during the planning stage. Planning is, of course, decision making since it involves choosing among alternatives. Planning is a required management function to facilitate the comprehension of complex problems involving interacting factors.

One of the objectives of project planning is to completely define all work required (possibly through the development of a documented project plan) so that it will be readily identifiable to each project participant. This is a necessity in a project environment because:

- If the task is well understood prior to being performed, much of the work can be preplanned.
- If the task is not understood, then during the actual task execution more knowledge is learned which, in turn, leads to changes in resource allocations, schedules, and priorities.
- The more uncertain the task, the greater the amount of information that must be processed in order to insure effective performance.

These three facets are important in a project environment because each project can be different, requiring a variety of different resources that has to be performed under time, cost, and performance constraints with little margins for error. Figure 5-1 identifies the type of project planning required to establish an effective monitoring and control system. The boxes in the upper portion of the curve represent the planning activities, and the lower portion identifies the "tracking" or monitoring of the planned activities.

Without proper planning, programs and projects can start off "behind the eight ball" because of poorly defined requirements during the initial planning phase. Below is a list of the typical consequences of poor planning:

- Project initiation
- Wild enthusiasm
- Disillusionment

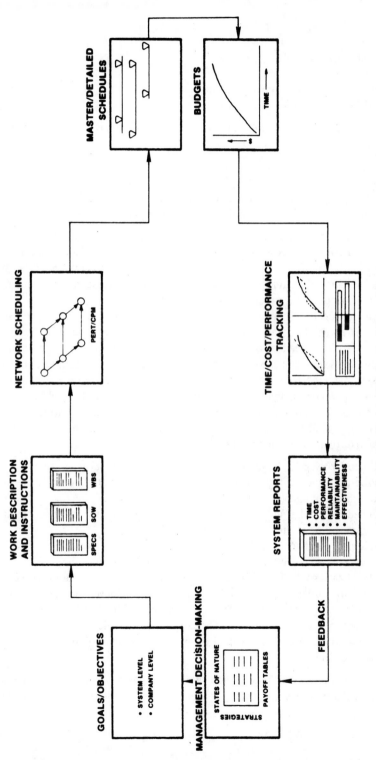

Figure 5-1. The Project Planning And Control System.

- Chaos
- Search for the guilty
- Punishment of the innocent
- Promotion of the nonparticipants
- Definition of the requirements

Obviously, the definition of the requirements should have been the first step. There are four basic reasons for project planning:

- Eliminate or reduce uncertainty
- Improve efficiency of the operation
- Obtain a better understanding of the objectives
- Provide a basis for monitoring and controlling work

There are involuntary and voluntary reasons for planning. Involuntary reasons can be internally mandatory functions of the organizational complexity and organizational lag in response time, or externally, correlated to environmental fluctuations, uncertainty, and discontinuity. The voluntary reasons for planning are attempts to secure efficient and effective operations.

Planning is decision making based upon futurity. It is a continuous process of making entrepreneurial decisions with an eye to the future, and methodically organizing the effort needed to carry out these dicisions. Furthermore, systematic planning allows an organization to set goals. The alternative to systematic planning is decision making based upon history. This generally results in reactive management leading to crisis management, conflict management, and fire fighting.

Planning is determining what needs to be done, by whom, and by when, in order to fulfill one's assigned responsibility. There are nine major steps which must be developed during the planning phase:

- Objective: a goal, target, or quota to be achieved by a certain time
- Program: the strategy to be followed and major actions to be taken in order to achieve or exceed objectives
- Schedule: a plan showing when individual or group activities or accomplishments will be started and/or completed
- Budget: planned expenditures required to achieve or exceed objectives
- Forecast: a projection of what will happen by a certain time
- Organization: design of the number and kinds of positions, along with corresponding duties and responsibilities, required to achieve or exceed objectives
- Policy: a general guide for decision making and individual actions
- Procedure: a detailed method for carrying out a policy
- Standard: a level of individual or group performance defined as adequate or acceptable

Several of these steps require additional comments. Forecasting what will happen may not be easy, especially if predictions of environmental reactions are required. For example, planning is customarily defined as either strategic, tactical, or operational. Strategic planning is generally five years or more, tactical can be one to five years, and operational is the here and now of six months to one year. Although most projects are operational, they can be considered as strategic especially if spin offs or follow-up work is promising. Forecasting also requires an understanding of strengths and weaknesses, as:

- Competitive situation
- Marketing
- Research and development
- Production
- Finance
- Personnel
- Management structure

If project planning is strictly operational, then these factors may be clearly definable. However, if strategic or long-range planning is necessary, then the future economic outlook can vary, say year to year, and replanning must be accomplished at regular intervals because the goals and objectives can change. (The procedure for this can be seen in Figure 5-1)

The last three factors, policies, procedures, and standards, can vary from project to project because of their uniqueness. Each project manager can establish project policies provided that they fall within the broad limits set forth by top management. Policies are predetermined general courses or guides based upon the following principles:[1]

- Subordinate policies are supplementary to superior policies
- Policies are based upon known principles in the operative areas
- Policies should be complementary for coordination
- Policies should be definable, understandable, and preferably in writing
- Policies should be both flexible and stable
- Policies should be reasonably comprehensive in scope

Project policies must often conform closely to company policies, and are usually similar in nature from project to project. Procedures, on the other hand, can be drastically different from project to project, even if the same activity is performed. For example, the signing off of manufacturing plans may require different signatures on two selected projects even though the same end item is being produced.

Planning varies at each level of the organization. At the "individual" level, planning is required so that cognitive simulation can be established before taking irrevocable actions. At the "working group or functional level," planning must include:

---

1. Edwin Flippo and Gary Munsinger, *Management,* 3rd ed., Boston, Allyn and Bacon, 1975, p. 83.

- agreement on purpose
- assignment and acceptance of individual responsibilities
- coordination of work activities
- increased commitment to group goals
- lateral communications

At the "organizational or project" level, planning must include:

- recognition and resolution of group conflict of goals
- assignment and acceptance of group responsibilities
- increased motivation and commitment to organizational goals
- vertical and lateral communications
- coordination of activities between groups

The logic of planning requires answers to several questions in order for the alternatives and constraints to be fully understood. A partial list of questions would include:

- Environmental Analysis
  - Where are we?
  - How and why did we get here?
- Setting Objectives
  - Is this where we want to be?
  - Where would we like to be? In a year? In five years?
- List Alternative Strategies
  - Where will we go if we continue as before?
  - Is that where we want to go?
  - How could we get to where we want to go?
- List Threats And Opportunities
  - What might prevent us from getting there?
  - What might help us to get there?
- Prepare Forecasts
  - Where are we capable of going?
  - What do we need to take us where we want to go?
- Select Strategy Portfolio
  - What is the best course for us to take?
  - What are the potential benefits?
  - What are the risks?
- Prepare Action Programs
  - What do we need to do?
  - When do we need to do it?
  - How will we do it?
  - Who will do it?
- Monitor And Control
  - Are we on course? If not, why?
  - What do we need to do to be on course?
  - Can we do it?

One of the most difficult activities in the project environment is to keep the planning on target. Below are typical procedures that can assist project managers during planning activities:

- Let functional managers do their own planning. Too often operators are operators, planners are planners, and never the twain shall meet.
- Establish goals before you plan. Otherwise short-term thinking takes over.
- Set goals for the planners. This will guard against the nonessentials and places your effort where there is pay off.
- Stay flexible. Use people to people contact and stress fast response.
- Keep a balanced outlook. Don't overreact and position yourself for an up-turn.
- Welcome top management participation. Top management has the capability to make or break a plan, and may just well be the single most important variable.
- Beware of future spending plans. This may eliminate the tendency to underestimate.
- Test the assumptions behind the forecasts. This is necessary because professionals are generally too optimistic. Do not depend solely upon one set of data.
- Don't focus on today's problems. Try to get away from crisis management and firefighting.
- Reward those who dispell illusions. Avoid the Persian messanger syndrome (i.e., behead the bearer of bad tidings.) Reward the first to come forth with bad news.

5.2 IDENTIFYING STRATEGIC PROJECT VARIABLES

For long-range or strategic projects, the project manager must continuously monitor the external environment in order to develop a well-structured program which can stand up under pressure. These environmental factors play an integral part in planning. The project manager must be able to identify and evaluate these strategic variables in terms of the future posture of the organization with regard to constraints on existing resources.

In the project environment, strategic project planning is performed at the horizontal hierarchy level, with final approval by upper-level management. There are three basic guidelines for strategic project planning:

- Strategic project planning is a job that should be performed by managers, not for them.
- It is extremely important that upper-level management maintain a close involvement with project teams, especially during the planning phase.
- Successful strategic planning must define the authority, responsibility, and roles of the strategic planning personnel.

For the project to be successful, all members of the horizontal team must be aware of those strategic variables which can influence the success or failure of the project plan. The analysis begins with the environment, subdivided as internal, external, and competitive, as shown below:

- Internal environment
  - Management skills
  - Resources
  - Wage and salary levels
  - Government freeze on jobs
  - Minority groups
  - Layoffs
  - Sales forecasts
- External Environment
  - Legal
  - Political
  - Social
  - Economic
  - Technological
- Competitive environment
  - Industry characteristics
  - Company requirements and goals
  - Competitive history
  - Present competitive activity
  - Competitive planning
    - Return on Investment
    - Market share
    - Size and variety of product lines
  - Competitive resources

Once the environmental variables are defined, the planning process continues with the following:

- Identification of company strengths and weaknesses
- Understanding personal values of top management
- Identification of opportunities
- Definition of product market
- Identification of competitive edge
- Establishment of goals, objectives, and standards
- Identification of resource deployment

Complete identification of all strategic variables is not easily obtainable at the program level. Internal, or operating variables are readily available to program personnel by virtue of the structure of the organization. The external variables are normally tracked under the perceptive eyes of top management. This presents a challenge for the organization of system. In most cases, those in the horizontal hierarchy of a program are more interested in the current operational plan and tend to become isolated from the environment after the program begins, losing insight into factors influencing the rapidly changing external variables in the process Proper identification of these strategic variables requires that communication channels be established between top management and the project office.

Top management support must be available for strategic planning variable identification such that effective decision making can occur at the program level. The participation of top management in this regard has not been easy to implement. Many top level officers consider this process a relinquishment of some of their powers and choose to retain strategic variable identification for the top levels of management.

The systems approach to management does not attempt to decrease top management's role in strategic decision making. The maturity, intellect, and wisdom of top management cannot be replaced. Ultimately, decision making will always rest at the upper levels of management, regardless of the organizational structure.

The identification and classification of the strategic variables are necessary to establish relative emphasis, priorities, and selectivity among the alternatives, to anticipate the unexpected, and to determine the restraints and limitations of the program. Universal classification systems are nonexistent because of the varied nature of organizations and projects. However, variables can be roughly categorized as internal and external, as shown in Table 5-1.

A survey of fifty companies was conducted to determine if lower-level and middle-management, as well as project managers, knew what variables in their own industry were considered by top management as important planning variables. The following results were obtained:[2]

- Top management considered fewer variables as being strategic than did middle managers.
- Middle-management and top management in systems-oriented companies had better agreement on strategic variable identification than did managers in nonsystems-oriented companies.
- Top executives within the same industry differed as to the identification of strategic variables, even within companies having almost identical business bases.
- Very little attempt was made by top management to quantify the risks involved with each strategic variable.

---

2. Harold Kerzner, "Survey of Strategic Planning Variables," unpublished report, Project/ Systems Management Research Institute, Baldwin-Wallace College, 1977.

Table 5-1. Strategic Planning Variables In The Tire Industry.

INTERNAL	*EXTERNAL*

• Operating
  • Product changes
  • Volume (economies of scale)
  • Wages vs. automation
  • R & D
	• Operating
	  • Customer requirements
	  • Capacity of plants
	  • Borrowing expenses
	  • Technological advances

• Legal
  • Product quality
  • Union and safety considerations
	• Legal
	  • OSHA noise levels
	  • Product liabilities
	  • Dot requirements

• Economic
  • Market indicators
  • Division of market
  • Production runs (timing)
  • Pricing/promotion policy
	• Economic
	  • Forecast of industry
	  • Inventory (on hand/dealers)
	  • Steel and chemical output
	  • Competition

• Sociopolitical
  • Allocation of resources
  • Raw material price/availability
  • Feasibility of exporting
  • Productivity levels
	• Sociopolitical
	  • Produce what is profitable
	  • Primarily third world
	  • Threat of imports
	  • Stability of free market

As an example of the differences between the project manager and upper-level management, consider the six strategic variables listed below which are characteristic of the machine tool industry.

- Business markets and business cycles
- Product characteristics
- Pricing and promotion policies
- Technology changes
- Labor force and available skills
- Customer organization restructuring

Both project managers and upper-level management agreed upon the first four variables. The last two were identified by upper-level management. Since many products are now made of material other than steel, the question arises as to the availability of qualified workers. This poses a problem in that many customers perform a make or buy analysis before contracting with machine tool companies. The machine tool companies surveyed felt that it was the responsibility of upper-level management to continuously communicate with all customers to ascertain if they are contemplating developing or enlarging their machine tool capabilities. Obviously, the decision of a prime customer to develop their own machine shop capabilities could have a severe impact on the contractor's growth potential, business base, and strategic planning philosophy.

5.3 PROJECT PLANNING

Successful project management, whether it be in response to an in-house project or a customer request, must utilize effective planning techniques. From a systems point of view, management must make effective utilization of resources. This effective utilization over several different types of projects requires a systematic plan in which the entire company is considered as one large network subdivided into smaller ones.

The first step in total program scheduling is understanding the project objectives. These goals may be to develop expertise in a given area, become competitive, modify an existing facility for later use, or simply to keep key personnel employed.

The objectives are generally not independent; they are all inter-related both implicitly and explicitly. Many times it is not possible to satisfy all objectives. At this point, management must prioritize the objectives as to which are strategic and which are not.

Once the objectives are clearly defined, four questions must be considered:

- What are the major elements of the work required to satisfy the objectives and how are these elements inter-related?
- Which functional divisions will assume responsibility for accomplishment of these objectives and the major element work requirements?
- Are the required corporate and organizational resources available?
- What are the information flow requirements for the project?

At what point does upper level management become involved? If the project is large and complex, then careful planning and analysis must be accomplished by both the direct and indirect labor-charging organizational units. The project organizational structure must be designed to fit the project; work plans and schedules must be established such that maximum allocation of resources can be made; resource costing and accounting systems must be developed; and a management information and reporting system must be established.

Effective total program planning cannot be accomplished unless all of the necessary information becomes available at project initiation. These information requirements are:

- The Statement of Work (SOW)
- The Project Specifications
- The Milestone Schedule
- The Work Breakdown Structure (WBS)

The statement of work (SOW) is a narrative description of the work to be accomplished. It includes the objectives of the project, a brief description of the work, the funding constraint if one exists, and the specifications and schedule. The schedule is a "gross" schedule and includes such items as the

- start date
- end date
- major milestones
- written reports (data items)

Written reports should always be identified so that if functional input is required, the functional manager will know to assign an individual who has writing skills. After all, it is no secret as to who would write the report if the line people did not.

The last major item is the Work Breakdown Structure. The WBS is the breaking down of the statement of work into smaller elements so that better visibility and control will be obtained.

5.4 WORK BREAKDOWN STRUCTURE

The successful accomplishment of both contract and corporate objectives requires a plan which defines all effort to be expended, assigns responsibility to a specially identified organizational element, and establishes schedules and budgets for the accomplishment of the work. The preparation of this plan is the responsibility of the Program Manager who is assisted by the Program Team assigned in accordance with Program Management System directives. The detailed planning is also established in accordance with Company Budgeting Policy before contractual efforts are initiated.

In planning a project, the project manager must structure the work into small elements that are:

- Manageable, in that specific authority and responsibility can be assigned
- Independent or with minimum interfacing with and dependence on other on-going elements
- Integratable so that the total package can be seen
- Measurable in terms of progress.

The first major step in the planning process is the development of the Work Breakdown Structure (WBS). The Work Breakdown Structure is the single most important element because it provides a common framework from which:

- The total program can be described as a summation of subdivided elements
- Planning can be performed
- Costs and budgets can be established
- Time, cost, and performance can be tracked
- Objectives can be linked to company resources in a logical manner

- Schedules and status reporting procedures can be established
- Network construction and control planning can be initiated
- The responsibility assignments for each element can be established.

The Work Breakdown Structure acts as a vehicle for breaking the work down into smaller elements, thus providing a greater probability that every major and minor activity will be accounted for. Although a variety of Work Breakdown Structures exist, the most common is the five-level indentured structure shown below:

Level	Description
1	Total Program
2	Project
3	Task
4	Subtask
5	Work Package

Level one is the total program and is composed of a set of projects. The summation of the activities and costs associated with each project must equal the total program. Each project, however, can be broken down into tasks, where the summation of all tasks equals the summation of all projects which, in turn, comprises the total program. The reason for this subdivision of effort is simply for ease of control. Program management therefore becomes synonomous with the integration of activities and the project manager acts as the integrator using the Work Breakdown Structure as the common framework.

The upper three levels of the WBS are normally specified by the customer (if part of an RFP/RFQ) as the summary levels for reporting purposes. The lower levels are generated by the contractor for in-house control. Each level serves a vital purpose; level 1 is generally used for the authorization and release of all work; budgets are prepared at level 2, and schedules are prepared at level 3. Certain characteristics can now be generalized for these levels:

- The top three levels of the WBS reflect integrated efforts and should not be related to one specific department. Effort required by departments or sections should be defined in subtasks and work packages.
- The summation of all elements in one level must be the sum of all work in the next lower level.
- Each element of work should be assigned to one and only one level of effort. For example, the construction of the foundation of a house should be included in one project (or task), not extended over two or three.
- The WBS must be accompanied by a description of the scope of effort required or else only those individuals who issue the WBS will have a complete understanding of what work has to be accomplished. It is common practice to reproduce the customer's Statement of Work as the description for the WBS.

In setting up the Work Breakdown Structure, tasks should

- Have clearly defined start and end dates
- Be usable as a communicative tool in which results can be compared with expectations.
- Be estimated on a "total" time duration, not when the task must start or end
- Be structured so that a minimum of project office control and documentation (i.e., forms) are necessary

Table 5-2 shows a simple Work Breakdown Structure with the associated numbering system follows the Work Breakdown Structure; the first number represents the total program (in this case, it is represented by 01); the second number represents the project, and the third number identifies the task. Therefore, number 01-03-00 represents project 3 or program 01 while 01-03-02 represents task 2 of project 3. This type of numbering system is not unique; each company may have its own system depending on how costs are to be controlled.

The preparation of the Work Breakdown Structure is not easy. The WBS is a communications tool, providing detailed information to different levels of management. If the WBS does not contain enough levels, then the integration of activities may prove difficult. If too many levels exist, then unproductive time will be incurred along with additional costs and paperwork. No attempt should be made to have the same number of levels for all projects, tasks, etc. Each major work element should be considered by itself. Remember, the Work Breakdown Structure establishes the number of required networks for cost control.

For many programs, the Work Breakdown Structure is established by the customer. If the contractor is required to develop a WBS, then certain guidelines must be considered: A partial list is identified below:

Table 5-2. Work Breakdown Structure For New Plant Construction And Start-up.

Program: New Plant Construction and Start-up	01-00-00
Project 1: Analytical Study	01-01-00
Task 1: Marketing/Production Study	01-01-01
Task 2: Cost Effectiveness Analysis	01-01-02
Project 2: Design and Layout	01-02-00
Task 1: Product Processing Sketches	01-02-01
Task 2: Product Processing Blueprints	01-02-02
Project 3: Installation	01-03-00
Task 1: Fabrication	01-03-01
Task 2: Set-up	01-03-02
Task 3: Testing and Run	01-03-03
Project 4: Program Support	01-04-00
Task 1: Management	01-04-01
Task 2: Purchasing Raw Materials	01-04-02

- The complexity and technical requirements of the program (i.e., the Statement of Work)
- The program cost
- The time span of the program
- The contractor's resource requirements
- The contractor's and customer's internal structure for management control and reporting
- The number of subcontracts

Applying these guidelines serves only to identify the complexity of the program. This data must then be subdivided and released, together with detailed information, to the different levels of the organization. The WBS should follow a specified criteria, because, although preparation of the WBS is performed by the program office, the actual work is performed by the doers, not the planners. Both the doers and the planners must be in agreement as to what is expected. A sample criteria listing for developing a Work Breakdown Structure is shown below:

- The WBS and work description should be easy to understand.
- All schedules should follow the WBS.
- No attempt should be made to arbitrarily subdivide work to the lowest possible level. The lowest level of work should not end up being a ridiculous cost in comparison to other efforts.
- Since scope of effort can change during a program, every effort should be made to maintain flexibility in the WBS.

From a cost control point of view, cost analysis down to the fifth level is advantageous. However, it should be noted that the cost required to prepare cost analysis data to each lower level may increase exponentially, especially if the customer requires data to be presented in a specified format which is not part of the company's standard operating procedures. The level five work packages are normally for in-house control only.

The WBS can be subdivided into subobjectives with finer divisions of effort as we go lower into the WBS. By defining subobjectives, we add greater understanding and, it is hoped, clarity of action for those individuals who will be required to complete the objectives. Whenever work is structured, understood, and easily identifiable and within the capabilities of the individuals, there will almost always exist a high degree of confidence that the objective can be reached.

Work Breakdown Structures can be used to structure work for reaching such objectives as lowering costs, reducing absenteeism, improving morale, and lowering scrap factors. The lowest subdivision now becomes an end item or subobjective, not necessarily a work package as described here. However, since we are describing project management, for the remainder of the text we will consider the lowest level as the work package.

5.5 ROLE OF THE EXECUTIVE IN PLANNING

Many project managers view the first critical step in planning as obtaining the support of top management, because once it becomes obvious to the functional managers that top management is expressing an interest in the project, they (the functional managers) are more likely to respond favorably to the project team's request for support partly to protect themselves.

Executives are also responsible for selecting the project manager, and the person chosen should have planning expertise. Not all technical specialists are good planners. As Rogers points out:[3]

The technical planners, whether they are engineers or systems analysts must be experts at designing the system, but seldom do they recognize the need to "put on another hat" when system design specifications are completed and design the project control or implementation plan. If this is not done, setting a project completion target date of a set of management checkpoint milestones is done by guesswork at best. Management will set the checkpoint milestones, and the technical planners will hope they can meet the schedule.

Executives must not arbitrarily set unrealistic milestones and then "force" line managers to fulfill them. Both project and line managers should try to adhere to unrealistic milestones but if a line manager says he cannot, executives should comply because the line manager is supposedly the expert. Sometimes, executives lose sight of what they are doing. As an example, a bank executive took the six-month completion date milestone and made it three months. The project and line managers rescheduled all of the other projects to reach this milestone. The executive then did the same thing on three other projects and again the project and line managers came to his rescue. The executive began to believe that the line people did not know how to estimate and that they probably loaded up every schedule with "fat." So, the executive changed the milestones on *all* of the other projects to what his "gut feeling" told him was realistic. The reader can imagine the chaos which followed.

Executives should interface with project and line personnel during the planning stage in order to define the requirements and establish reasonable deadlines. Executives must realize that creating an unreasonable deadline may require the reestablishment of priorities and, of course, changing priorities can push milestones forward.

---

3. Lloyd A. Rogers, "Guidelines for Project Management Teams," *Industrial Engineering,* December, 12, 1974. Published and copyright 1974 by the American Institute of Industrial Engineers, Inc., Norcross, Georgia 30092.

5.6 WHY DO PLANS FAIL?

No matter how hard we try, planning is not perfect and sometimes plans fail. Typical reasons why plans fail include

- Corporate goals not understood at the lower organizational levels
- Plans encompass too much in too little time
- Poor financial estimates
- Plans based upon insufficient data
- No attempt to systematize the planning process
- Planning performed by a planning group
- No one knows the ultimate objective
- No one knows the staffing requirements
- No one knows the major milestone dates, including written reports
- Project estimates are best guesses, and are not based upon standards or history
- Not enough time was given for proper estimating
- No one bothered to see if there would be personnel available with the necessary skills
- People are not working toward the same specifications
- People are consistently shuffled in and out of the project with little regard for schedule.

Why do these situations occur, and who should be blamed? If corporate goals are not understood, it is because corporate executives were negligent in providing the necessary strategic information and feedback. If a plan fails because of severe optimism, then the responsibility lies with both the project and line managers for not assessing risk. Project managers should ask the line managers if the estimates are optimistic or pessimistic, and expect an honest answer. Erroneous financial estimates are the responsibility of the line manager. If the project fails because of a poor definition of the requirements, then the project manager is totally at fault.

Project managers must be willing to accept failure. Sometimes, a situation occurs which can lead to failure, and the problem rests with either upper-level management or some other group. As an example, consider the major utility company with a planning group which budgets (with help of functional groups) and selects those projects to be completed within a given time period. A project manager on one of these projects discovered that the project should have started last month in order to meet the completion date. It is in cases like this that project managers will not become dedicated to projects unless they are active members during the planning and know what assumptions and constraints were considered in development of the plan.

Sometimes, the project manager is part of the planning group and as part of a feasibility study is asked to prepare, with the assistance of functional managers,

a schedule and cost summary for a project which will occur three years downstream, if the project is approved at all. Suppose that three years downstream the
project is approved. How does the project manager get functional managers to
accept the schedule and cost summary that they themselves prepared three years
before? It cannot be done because technology may have changed, people may be
working higher or lower on the learning curve, and salary and raw material escalation factors are inaccurate.

Sometimes project plans fail because simple details are forgotten or overlooked.
Examples of this might be:

- Neglecting to tell a line manager early enough that the prototype is not ready
  and that rescheduling is necessary.
- Neglecting to see if the line manager can provide additional employees for
  the next two weeks because it was possible six months ago.

Sometimes plans fail because the project manager "bites off more than he can
chew," and then something happens. Even if the project manager were effective
at doing a lot of the work overburdening is unnecessary. Many projects have failed
because the project manager was the only one who knew what was going on, and
then got sick.

5.7 STOPPING PROJECTS

There are always situations where projects have to be stopped. Below are several
reasons why:

- Final achievement of the objectives
- Poor initial planning and market prognosis
- A better alternative has been found
- A change in the company interest and strategy
- Allocated time has been exceeded
- Budgeted costs have been exceeded
- Key people have left the organization
- Personal whims of management
- Problem too complex for the resources available

Once the reasons for cancellation are defined, the next problem is how to go
about stopping the projects.

- Orderly planned termination
- The "hatchet" (withdrawal of funds and removal of personnel)
- Reassignment of people to higher priority
- Redirection of efforts toward different objectives
- Burying it or letting it die on the vine (i.e., not taking any official action)

There are three major problem areas to be considered in stopping projects:

- Worker morale
- Reassignment of personnel
- Adequate documentation and wrap up

Sometimes, executives do not realize the relationship between projects, and what happens if one is cancelled prematurely. As an example, the following remarks were made by an executive concerning data processing operations:

When 75% - 80% of the resource commitment is obtained, there is the point of no return and the benefits to be obtained from the project are anticipated. However, project costs, once forecast, are seldom adjusted during the project life cycle. Adjustments, when made, are normally to increase costs prior to or during conversion. Increases in cost are always in small increments and usually occur when the corporation is 'committed,' i.e., 75% -80% of the actual costs are expended, however, total actual costs are not known until the project is over . . .

Projects can and sometimes should be cancelled at any point in the project life cycle. Projects are seldom cancelled because costs exceed forecasts. More often, resources are drained from successful projects. The result of the action is the corporation as a whole becomes marginally successful in bringing all identified projects on line. One might assume individual projects can be analyzed to determine which projects are successful and which are unsuccessful. However, the corporate movement of resources makes the determination difficult without elaborate computer systems. For example, as Project A appears to be successful, resources are diverted to less successful Project B. The costs associated with Project A increase dramatically as all remaining activities become critical to Project A completion. Increasing costs for Project A are associated with overtime, traveling, etc. Costs for Project B are increasing at a straight time rate and more activities are being accomplished because more manpower can be expended. Often resources, particularly manpower working on Project B, are charged to Project A because the money is in the budget for Project A. The net result is Projects A and B overrun authorized budgets by about the same percentage. In the eyes of top corporate management, neither project team has done well nor have the teams performed poorly. This mediocrity in performance is often the goal of corporate project management technique.

5.8 DETAILED SCHEDULES AND CHARTS

The scheduling of activities is the first major requirement of the program office after program go ahead. The program office normally assumes full responsibility for activity scheduling if the activity is not too complex. For large programs, functional management input is required before scheduling can be completed. Depending on program size and contractual requirements, it is not unusual for the program office to maintain, at all times, a program staff member whose responsibility is that of a scheduler. This individual continuously develops and updates activity schedules to provide a means of tracking program work. The resulting information is then supplied to the program office personnel, functional management, team members and, last but not least, presented to the customer.

Activity scheduling is probably the single most important tool for determining how company resources should be integrated such that synergy will be produced. Activity schedules are invaluable for projecting time-phased resource utilization requirements as well as providing a basis for visually tracking performance. Most programs begin with the development of the schedules so that accurate cost estimates can be made. The schedules serve as master plans from which both the customer and management have an up-to-date picture of operations.

Certain guidelines should be followed in preparation of schedules, regardless of the projected use or complexity:

- All major events and dates must be clearly identified. If a Statement of Work is supplied by the customer, then those dates shown on the accompanying schedules must be included. If for any reason the customer's milestone dates cannot be met, then the customer should be notified immediately.
- The exact sequence of work should be defined through a network in which interrelationships between events can be identified.
- Schedules should be directly relatable to the Work Breakdown Structure. If the WBS is developed according to a specific sequence of work, then it becomes an easy task to identify work sequences in schedules using the same numbering system as in the WBS. The minimum requirement should be to show where and when all tasks start and finish.
- All schedules must identify the time constraints and, if possible, should identify those resources required for each event.

Although these four guidelines serve as reference for schedule preparation, they do not define how complex the schedules should be. Before preparing the schedules, three questions should be considered:

- How many events or activities should each network have?
- How much of a detailed technical breakdown should be included?
- Who is the intended audience for this schedule?

Most organizations develop multiple schedules: summary schedules for management and planners and detailed schedules for the doers and lower level control. The detailed schedules may be strictly for interdepartmental activities. Program management must approve all schedules down through the first three levels of the Work Breakdown Structure. For higher level schedules (i.e., detailed interdepartmental) program management may or may not request sign of approval.

The necessity for two schedules is clear. According to Martin,[4]

> In larger complicated projects, planning and status review by different echelons are facilitated by the use of detailed and summary networks. Higher levels of management can view the entire project and the interrelationships of major tasks without looking into the detail of the individual subtasks. Lower levels of management and supervision can examine their parts of the project in fine detail without being distracted by those parts of the project with which they have no interface.

One of the most difficult problems to identify in schedules is a hedge position. A hedge position is a situation in which the contractor may not be able to meet a customer's milestone date without incurring a risk, or may not be able to meet activity requirements following a milestone date because of contractual requirements. To illustrate a common hedge position, consider Example 5-1 below:

Example 5-1: Condor Corporation is currently working on a project which includes three phases: design, development, and qualification of a certain component. Contractual requirements with the customer specify that no components will be fabricated for the development phase until the design review meeting is held following the design phase. Condor has determined that if they do not begin component fabrication prior to the design review meeting, then the second and third phases will slip. Condor is willing to accept risk that should specifications be unacceptable during the design review meeting, the costs associated with pre-authorization of fabrication will be incurred. How should this be shown on a schedule? (The problems associated with performing unauthorized work are not being considered here.)

The solution to Example 5-1 is not an easy one. Condor must play an honest game and identify on the Master Production Schedule that component fabrication will begin early, at the contractor's risk. This should be followed up by a contractual letter in which both the customer and contractor understand the risks and implications.

Example 5-1 also brings up the question as to whether this hedge position could have been eliminated with proper planning. Hedge positions are notorious for occurring in research and development or design phases of a program. Condor's technical community, for example, may have anticipated that each component could be fabricated in one week based on certain raw materials. If new raw materials were required or a new fabrication process had to be developed, it is then possible that the new component fabrication time could increase from one week to two or three, thus creating an unanticipated hedge position.

---

4. Charles Martin, *Project Management: How to Make It Work,* New York, AMACOM, a division of American Management Associations, 1976, p. 137.

Detailed schedules are prepared for almost every activity. It is the responsibility of the program office to marry all of the detailed schedules into one master schedule to verify that all activities can be completed as planned. The preparation sequence for schedules (and also for program plans) is shown in Figure 5-2. The program office submits a request for detailed schedules to the functional managers. The request may be in the form of a planning work authorization document. The functional managers then prepare summary schedules, detailed schedules, and if time permits, interdepartmental schedules. Each functional manager then reviews his schedules with the program office. The program office, together with the functional program team members, integrate all of the plans and schedules and verify that all contractual dates can be met.

Before submitting the schedules to publications, rough drafts of each schedule and plan should be reviewed with the customer. This procedure accomplishes the following:

- Verifies that nothing has fallen through the crack.
- Prevents immediate revisions to a published document and can prevent embarassing moments.
- Minimizes production costs by reducing the number of early revisions.
- Shows customers early in the program that you welcome their help and input into the planning phase.

After the document is published, it should be distributed to all program office personnel, functional team members, functional management and the customer.

The exact method of preparing the schedules is usually up to the individual performing the activity. All schedules, however, must be approved by the program

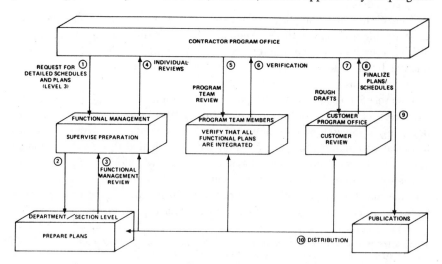

Figure 5-2. Preparation Sequence For Schedules And Program Plans.

office. The schedules are normally prepared in a manner that is suitable to both the customer and contractor in a manner that is easily understood by all. The schedules may then be used for in-house use as well as customer review meetings, in which case the contractor can "kill two birds with one stone" by tracking cost and performance on the original schedules. Examples of detailed schedules will be shown in Chapter 9.

In addition to the detailed schedules, the program office, with input provided by functional management, must develop organizational charts. The organizational charts provide information to all active participants of the project as to who has responsibility for each activity. Examples have previously been shown in Section 4.9. The organizational charts display the formal (and often informal) lines of communication.

The program office may also establish linear responsibility charts (LRCs). Regardless of the best attempts by management, many functions in an organization can overlap between more than one functional unit. Also, management might wish to have the responsibility for a certain activity given to a functional unit which normally would not have this responsibility. This is a common occurence on short duration programs where management desires to cut costs and red tape.

Care must be taken that project personnel do not forget the reason why the schedule was developed. The primary objective of detailed schedules is usually to coordinate activities into a master plan in order to complete the project with the:

- Best time
- Least cost
- Least risk

Of course, the objective can be constrained by:

- Calendar completion dates
- Cash or cash flow restrictions
- Limited resources
- Approvals

There are also secondary objectives of scheduling:

- Studying alternatives
- Developing an optimal schedule
- Using resources effectively
- Communicating
- Refining the estimating criteria
- Obtaining good project control
- Providing for easy revisions

5.9 PROGRAM PLAN

Fundamental to the success of any project is documented planning in the form of a program plan. In an ideal situation, the program office can present the functional manager with a copy of the program plan and simply say, "accomplish it." The concept of the program plan came under severe scrutiny during the 1960s when the Department of Defense required all contractors to submit detailed planning to such extremes that many organizations were wasting talented people by having them serve as writers instead of doers. Since then, because of the complexity of large programs, requirements imposed on the program plan have been eased.

For large and often complex programs, customers may require a program plan which documents all activities within the program. The program plan then serves as a guideline for the lifetime of the program and may be revised as often as once a month, depending upon the circumstances and the type of program. (i.e., research and development programs require more revisions to the program plan than manufacturing or construction programs.) The program plan provides the following framework:

- Eliminates conflicts between functional managers
- Eliminates conflicts between functional management and program management
- Provides a standard communicative tool throughout the lifetime of the program (It should be geared to the Work Breakdown Structure)
- Provides verification that the contractor understands the customer's objectives and requirements
- Provides a means for identifying inconsistencies in the planning phase
- Provides a means for early identification of problem areas and risks so that no "surprises occur downstream"
- Contains all of the schedules defined in Section 5.8 as a basis for progress analysis and reporting.

Development of a program plan can be time consuming and costly. The input requirements for the program plan depend on the size of the project and the integration of resources and activities. All levels of the organization participate. The upper levels provide summary information and the lower levels provide the details. The program plan, as with activity schedules, does not preclude departments from developing their own planning.

The program plan must identify how the company resources will be integrated. Finalization of the program is an iterative process similar to the sequence of events for schedule preparation as shown in Figure 5-2. Since the program plan must explain the events in Figure 5-2, additional iterations are required which can cause changes in a program. This can be seen in Figure 5-3.

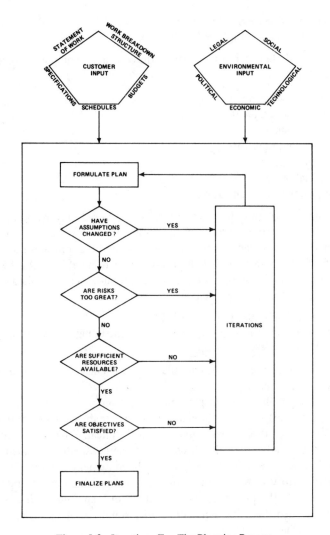

Figure 5-3. Iterations For The Planning Process.

The program plan is a standard from which performance can be measured, not only by the customer, but by program and functional management as well. The plan serves as a cookbook for the duration of the program by defining for all personnel identified with the program:

- What will be accomplished?
- How will it be accomplished?
- Where will it be accomplished?

- When will it be accomplished?
- Why will it be accomplished?

The answers to these questions force both the contractor and the customer to take a hard look at:

- Program Requirements
- Program Management
- Program Schedules
- Facility Requirements
- Logistic Support
- Financial Support
- Manpower and Organization

The program plan is more than just a set of instructions. It is an attempt to eliminate crisis by preventing anything from "falling through the crack." The plan is documented and approved by both the customer and the contractor to determine what data, if any, is missing and the probable resulting effect. As the program matures, the program plan is revised to account for new or missing data. The most common reasons for revising a plan are:

- "Crashing" activities to meet end dates
- Trade-off decisions involving manpower, scheduling, and performance
- Adjusting and leveling manpower requests

Maturity of a program usually implies that crisis will decrease. Unfortunately, this is not always the case.

The makeup of the program plan may vary from contractor to contractor.[5] Most program plans can be subdivided into four main sections: introduction, summary and conclusions, management, and technical. The complexity of the information is usually up to the discretion of the contractor provided that customer requirements, as may be specified in the Statement of Work, are satisfied.

The introductory section contains the definition of the program and the major parts involved. If the program follows another, or is an outgrowth of similar activities, this is identified together with a brief summary of the background and history behind the project.

The summary and conclusion section identifies the targets and objectives of the program and includes the necessary "lip service" on how successful the program will be and how all problems can be overcome. This section must also include the Program Master Schedule showing how all projects and activities are related. The total Program Master Schedule should include the following:

---

5. Cleland and King define 14 subsections for a program plan. This detail appears more applicable to the technical and management volumes of a proposal. They do, however, provide a more detailed picture than presented here. See Cleland and King, *Systems Analysis and Project Management*, New York, McGraw-Hill, 1975 pp. 371-380.

- An appropriate scheduling system (Bar Charts, Milestone Charts, Network, etc).
- A listing of activities at the project level or lower.
- The possible interrelationships between activities. This can be accomplished by logic networks, critical path networks or PERT networks.
- Activity time estimates. (This is a natural result of the item above.)

The summary and conclusion chapter is usually the second section in the program plan so that upper level customer management can have a complete overview of the program without having to search through the technical information.

The management section of the program plan contains procedures, charts, and schedules for the following:

- The assignment of key personnel to the program. This usually refers only to the program office personnel and team members, since under normal operations these will be the only individuals interfacing with customers.
- Manpower, planning, and training will be discussed to assure customers that qualified people will be available from the functional units.
- A Linear Responsibility Chart might also be included to identify to customers the authority relationships which will exist in the program.

Situations exist where the management section may be omitted from the proposal. For a follow-up program, the customer may not require this section if management's positions are unchanged. Management sections are also not required if the management information was previously provided in the proposal or if the customer and contractor have continuous business dealings.

The technical section may include as much as 75 to 90% of the program plan, especially if the effort includes research and development. The technical section may require constant updating as the program matures. The following items can be included as part of the technical section:

- A detailed breakdown of the charts and schedules used in the Program Master Schedule, possibly including schedule/cost estimates.
- A listing of the testing to be accomplished for each activity. (It is best to include the exact testing matrices.)
- Procedures for accomplishment of the testing. This might also include a description of the key elements in the operations or manufacturing plans as well as a listing of the facility and logistic requirements.
- Identification of materials and material specifications. (This might also include system specifications.)
- Although uncommon, some program plans attempt to identify the risks associated with specific technical requirements. This has the tendency to scare management personnel who are unfamiliar with the technical procedures and should therefore be omitted if at all possible.

The program plan, as used here, contains a description of all phases of the program. For many programs, especially large ones, detailed planning is required for all major events and activities. Table 5-3 identifies the type of individual plans that may be required in place of a (total) program plan. However, care must be taken in that too much paperwork can easily inhibit successful managment of a program.

The program plan, once agreed upon by the contractor and customer, is then used to provide program direction. This is shown in Figure 5-4. If the program plan is written clearly, then any functional manager or supervisor should be able to identify what is expected of them.

The program plan should be distributed to each member of the program team, all functional managers and supervisors interfacing with the program, and all key functional personnel. The program plan does not contain all of the answers, for if it did, there would be no need for a program office. The plan serves merely as a guide.

One final note need be mentioned concerning the legality of the program plan. The program plan may be specified contractually to satisfy certain requirements as identified in the customer's Statement of Work. The contractor retains the right as to how to accomplish this, unless of course, this is also identified in the SOW. If the Statement of Work specifies that quality assurance testing be accomplished on 15 end items off of the production line, then 15 is the minimum number that must be tested. The program plan may show that 25 items are to be tested. If the contractor develops cost overrun problems, he may wish to revert to the SOW and test only 15 items. Contractually, he may do this without informing the customer. In most cases, however, the customer is notified and the program is revised.

Table 5-3. Types Of Plans.

TYPE OF PLAN	DESCRIPTION
Budget	How much money is allocated to each event?
Configuration Management	How are technical changes made?
Facilities	What facilities resources are available?
Logistics Support	How will replacements be handled?
Management	How is the program office organized?
Manufacturing	What are the time-phase manufacturing events?
Procurement Plan	What are my sources? Should I make or buy? If vendors are not qualified, how shall I qualify them?
Quality Assurance	How will I guarantee specifications will be met?
Research/Development	What are the technical activities?
Scheduling	Are all critical dates accounted for?
Tooling	What are my time-phased tooling requirements?
Training	How will I maintain qualified personnel?
Transportation	How will goods and services be shipped?

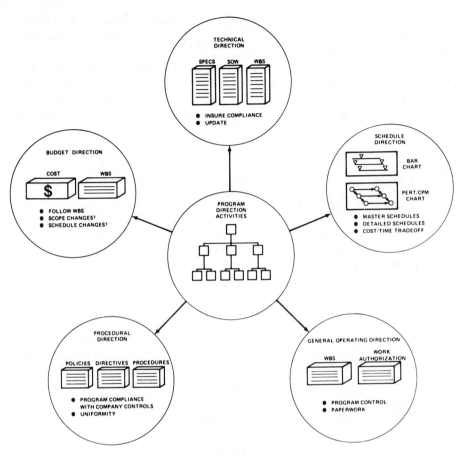

Figure 5-4. Program Direction Activities.

5.10 MANAGEMENT CONTROL

Because the planning phase provides the fundamental guidelines for the remainder of the project, careful management control must be established. In addition, since planning is an ongoing activity for a variety of different programs, management guidelines must be established on company-wide basis in order to achieve unity and coherence.

All functional organizations and individuals working directly or indirectly on a program are responsible for identifying, to the Program Manager, scheduling and planning problems which require corrective action during both the planning cycle and the operating cycle. The Program Manager bears the ultimate and final responsibility for identifying requirements for corrective actions. Management policies and directives are written specifically to assist the Program Manager in defining the requirements. Without clear definitions during the planning phase, many projects run off into a variety of directions.

Many companies establish planning and scheduling management policies for the project and functional managers, as well as a brief description of how they should interface. Table 5-4 identifies a typical management policy for planning and requirements, and Table 5-5 described scheduling management policies.

5.11 CONTROLLING

Controlling is a three-step process of measuring progress toward an objective, evaluating what remains to be done, and taking the necessary corrective action to achieve or exceed the objectives. These three steps are defined below:

1. Measuring: determining through formal and informal reports the degree to which progress toward objectives is being made
2. Evaluating: determining cause of and possible ways to act upon significant deviations from planned performance
3. Correcting: taking control action to correct an unfavorable trend or to take advantage of an unusually favorable trend

The project manager is responsible for insuring the accomplishment of group and organizational goals and objectives. To effect this, requires a thorough knowledge of standards, cost control policies, and procedures enabling a comparison between operating results and preestablished standards. The project manager must then take the necessary corrective actions. Later chapters will provide a more in-depth analysis of control, especially the cost control function.

In Chapter 1, we stated that project managers must understand organizational behavior in order to be effective, and must have strong interpersonal skills. This is especially important during the controlling function. As stated by Doering,[6]

The team leader's role is crucial. He is directly involved and must know the individual team member well, not only in terms of their technical capabilities but also in terms of how they function when addressing a problem as part of a group. The technical competence of a potential team member can usually be determined from information about previous assignments, but it is not so easy to predict and control the individual's interaction within and with a new group, since it is related to the psychological and social behavior of each of the other members of the group as a whole. What the leader needs is a tool to measure and characterize the individual members so that he can predict their interactions and structure his task team accordingly.

---

6. Robert D. Doering, "An Approach Toward Improving the Creative Output of Scientific Task Teams," *IEEE Transactions of Engineering Management*, February, 29-31, 1973.

5.12 DIRECTING

Directing is the implementing and carrying out (through others) of those approved plans which are necessary to achieve or exceed objectives. Directing involves such steps as

- Staffing: seeing that a qualified person is selected for each position
- Training: teaching individuals and groups how to fulfill their duties and responsibilities
- Supervising: giving others day-to-day instruction, guidance and discipline as required so that they can fulfill their duties and responsibilities
- Delegating: assigning work, responsibility, and authority so others can make maximum utilization of their abilities
- Motivating: encouraging others to perform by fulfilling or appealing to their needs
- Counseling: holding private discussions with others about how he might do better work, solve a personal problem or realize ambitions
- Coordinating: seeing that activities are carried out in relation to their importance and with a minimum of conflict

Directing subordinates is not an easy task because of both the short time duration of the project and the fact that the employees might still be assigned to a functional manager while temporarily assigned to your effort. The luxury of getting to "know" one's subordinates may not be possible in a project environment.

Project managers must be decisive and move forward rapidly whenever directives are necessary. It is better to decide an issue and be 10% wrong than it is to wait for the last 10% of a problem's input and cause a schedule delay and improper use of resources. Directives are most effective when the KISS (keep it simple, stupid) rule is applied. Directives should be written with one simple and clear objective so that subordinates can work more effectively and get things done right the first time. Orders must be issued in a manner that demands immediate compliance. The biggest reason why people will or will not obey an order depends on the amount of respect that they have for you. Therefore, never issue an order that you cannot enforce. Oral orders and directives should be disguised as suggestions or requests. The requestor should ask the receiver to repeat back the oral orders so that there is no misunderstanding.

Project managers must understand human behavior, perhaps more than functional managers. The reason for this is that project managers must continually motivate people toward successful accomplishment of project objectives. Motivation cannot be accomplished without at least a fundamental knowledge of human behavior.

Douglas McGregor advocated that most workers can be catagorized into one of two groups. The first group, often referred to as Theory X, assumes that the

Table 5-4. Planning And Requirements Policies.

PROGRAM MANAGER	FUNCTIONAL MANAGER	RELATIONSHIP
Plans and Requirements Requests the preparation of the program master schedules and provides for integration with the Division Composite Schedules. Defines work to be accomplished through preparation of the Subdivided Work Description Package.	*Plans and Requirements* Develops the details of the program plans and requirements in conjunction with the program manager. Provides proposal action in support of program manager requirements and the program master schedule.	*Plans and Requirements* Program planning and scheduling is a functional specialty; the Program Manager utilizes the services of the specialist organizations. The specialists retain their own channels to the general manager but must keep the program manager informed.
Provides program guidance and direction for the preparation of program plans which establish program cost, schedule, and technical performance; and which define the major events and tasks to ensure the orderly progress of the program.	With guidance furnished by the program manager, participates in the preparation of program plans, schedules, and work release documents which cover cost, schedule, and technical performance; and which define major events and tasks. Provides supporting detail plans and schedules.	Program planning is also a consultative operation and is provided guidelines by the program manager. Functional organizations initiate supporting plans for program manager approval, or react to modify plans to maintain currency. Functional organizations also initiate planning studies involving trade-offs and alternative courses of action for presentation to the program manager.
Establishes priorities within the program. Obtains relative program priorities between programs managed by other programs from the director, program management, manager, marketing and product development, or the general manager as specified by the policy.	Negotiates priorities with program managers for events and tasks to be performed by his organization.	The program manager and program team members are oriented to his program, whereas the functional organizations and the functional managers are "function" and multi-program oriented. The orientation of each director, manager, and team member must be mutually recognized to preclude unreasonable demands and con-

Table 5-4. (Continued) Planning And Requirements Policies.

Approves program contractual data requirements.	Conducts analysis of contractual data requirements. Develops data plans including contractor data requirements list and obtains Program Manager approval.	flicting priorities. Priority conflicts which cannot be resolved must be referred to the general manager.
Remains alert to new contract requirements, government regulations and directives which might affect the work, cost, or management of the program.	Remains alert to new contract requirements, government regulations and directives which might affect the work, cost, or management of his organization on any program.	
Provides early technical requirements definitions, and substantiates make-or-buy recommendations. Participates in the formulation of the make-or-buy plan for the program.	Provides the necessary make-or-buy data; substantiates estimates and recommendations in the area of functional specialty.	Make-or-buy concurrence and approvals are obtained in accordance with current Policies and Procedures.
Approves the program bill of material for need and compliance with program need and requirements.	Prepares the program bill of material.	
Directs data management including maintenance of current and historical files on programmed contractual data requirements.		

Table 5-5. Scheduling Policies.

PROGRAM MANAGER	FUNCTIONAL MANAGER	RELATIONSHIP
Scheduling Provides contractual data requirements and guidance for construction of program master schedules.	*Scheduling* The operations directorate shall construct the program master schedule. Data should include but not be limited to engineering plans, manufacturing plans, procurement plans, test plans, quality plans, and provides time spans for accomplishment of work elements defined in the Work Breakdown Structure to the level of definition visible in the planned Subdivided Work Description Package.	*Scheduling* The operations directorate constructs the program master schedule with data received from functional organizations and direction from the program manager, Operations shall coordinate program master schedule with functional organizations and secure program managers approval prior to release.
Concurs with Detail Schedules constructed by functional organizations Provides corrective action decisions and direction as required at any time a functional organization fails to meet program master schedule requirements or when by analysis, performance indicated by detail schedule monitoring, threatens to impact the program master schedule.	Constructs detail program schedules and working schedules in consonance with Program Manager approved Program Master Schedule. Secures program manager concurrence and forwards copies to the program manager.	Program manager monitors the functional organizations detail schedules for compliance with program master schedules and reports variance items which may impact division operations to the director, program management.

average worker is inherently lazy and requires supervision. Theory X further assumes that[7]

- The average worker dislikes work and avoids work whenever possible.
- To induce adequate effort, the supervisor must threaten punishment and exercise careful supervision.
- The average worker avoids increased responsibility and seeks to be directed.

The manager who accepts Theory X normally exercises authoritarian type control over workers and allows little participation during decision making. Theory X employees generally favor lack of responsibility, especially in decision making.

Theory Y employees advocate a willingness to get the job done without constant supervision. Theory Y further assumes that

- The average worker wants to be active and finds the physical and mental effort on the job satisfying.
- Greatest results come from willing participation which will tend to produce self-direction toward goals without coercion and control.
- The average worker seeks opportunity for personal improvement and self-respect.

The manager who accepts Theory Y normally advocates participation and a management-employee relationship. However, when working with professionals, especially engineers, special care must be exercised because these individuals often pride themselves on their ability to finding a better way to achieve the end result, regardless of the cost. The risk of this happening rises with the numbers of professional degrees that one possesses. This poses a problem in that it is the responsibility of the functional manager to determine "how" the job will be done once the project manager states "what" must be done. Project management must take a vested interest in individual, who, given free rein to accomplish an objective, must fully understand the necessity of time, cost and performance constraints. This situation holds true for several engineering disciplines where engineers consistently strive to exhibit their individuality by seeking new and revolutionary solutions to problems for which well-established solutions already exist. Under these conditions, project managers must become authoritarian leaders and change from Theory Y to Theory X. Employees must be shown how to report to two bosses at the same time. The problem occurs when the employee's line manager uses Theory Y but the project manager uses Theory X. Employees must realize that this situation will occur.

Many psychologists have established the existence of a prioritized hierarchy of needs that motivate individuals toward satisfactory performance. Maslow was

---

7. Douglas McGregor, *The Human Side of Enterprise,* New York, McGraw-Hill, 1960, p. 33-34.

- A feeling of pride or satisfaction for one's ego
- Security of opportunity
- Security of approval
- Security of advancement (if possible)
- Security of promotion (if possible)
- Security of recognition
- A means for doing a better job, instead of just keeping a job

Motivating employees so that they have feeling of security on the job is not easy, especially since the project has finite lifetime. Specific methods for producing security in a project environment include:

- Informing employees why they are where they are
- Encouraging a sense of belonging
- Placing the individuals in the positions for which they are properly trained
- Explaining to employees how their efforts fit into the big picture

Since project managers cannot motivate by promising material gains, they must appeal to each person's pride. To encourage proper motivation,

- Adopt a positive attitude
- Do not criticize management
- Do not make promises that cannot be kept
- Circulate customer reports
- Give each person the attention they require

There are several ways of motivating project personnel. Some effective ways include:

- Providing assignments that provide challenges
- Clearly defining performance expectations
- Giving proper criticism as well as credit
- Giving honest appraisals
- Providing a good working atmosphere
- Developing a team attitude
- Providing a proper direction (i.e., see Theory Y)

5.13 PROJECT AUTHORITY

Project management structures create a web of relationships which can cause chaos in the delegation of authority and the internal authority structure. Four questions must be considered in describing project authority:

- What is project authority?
- What is power and how is it achieved?

the first to identify these needs.[8] The first level is that of the basic or physio-logical needs, food, water, clothing, shelter, sleep, and sexual satisfaction. Simply, one's primal desire to satisfy these basic needs motivates one to do a good job. However, once a need becomes satisfied, the motivation ceases unless there is a higher level need. Fulfilled needs are not motivators.

Once employees fulfill physiological needs, they then turn to the next higher need of safety. Safety needs include economic security and protection from harm, disease, and violence. These needs must be considered on projects involving the handling of dangerous materials or anything which could produce bodily harm. Safety can also include security. It is important that project managers realize this because as a project nears termination, functional employees are more interested in finding a new role for themselves rather than giving their best to the current situation. The next level contains the social needs. This includes love, belonging, togetherness, approval, and group membership. It is at this level where the infor-mal organization plays a dominant role. Many people refuse promotions to proj-ect management (as project managers, project office personnel, or functional rep-resentatives) because they fear that they will lose their "membership" in the in-formal organization. This problem can occur even on short-term projects. In a project environment, project managers generally do not belong to any informal organization and therefore tend to be viewed as external to the organization. Proj-ect managers consider authority and funding to be very important in gaining proj-ect support. Functional personnel, however, prefer friendship and work assign-ments. In other words, the project manager can use the project itself as a means of helping fulfill the third level for the line employees; i.e., the team spirit.

The two highest needs are esteem and self-actualization. The esteem need in-cludes self-respect, reputation, the opinion of others, recognition, and self-confi-dence. Highly technical professionals are often not happy unless esteem needs are fulfilled. For example, many engineers strive to publish and invent as a means of satisfying these needs. These individuals often refuse promotions to project management because they believe that they cannot satisfy esteem needs in such a position. Being called a project manager does not carry as much importance as being considered an expert by one's peers. The highest need is self-actualization and includes doing what one can do best, desiring to utilize and realize one's full-est potential, constant self-development, and a desire to be truly creative. Many good project managers find this level as the most important and consider each new project as a challenge by which they can achieve this self-actualization.

Project managers must motivate these temporarily assigned individuals by ap-pealing to their desires to fullfill the highest two levels. Of course, the motivation process should not be developed by making promises which the project manager knows cannot be met. Project managers must motivate by providing:

---

8. Abraham Maslow, *Motivation and Personality,* New York, Harper and Brothers, 1954.

- How much project authority should be granted to the project manager?
- Who settles project authority interface problems?

Authority is usually defined as the legal or rightful power to command, act or direct the activities of others. Authority can be delegated from one's superiors. Power, on the other hand, is granted to an individual by subordinates and is a measure of their respect. A manager's authority is a combination of power and influence which subordinates, peers, and associates willingly accept.

Authority is the key to the project management process. The project manager must manage across functional and organizational lines by bringing together activities required to accomplish the objectives of a specific project. Project authority provides the required way of thinking to unify all organizational activities toward accomplishment of the project regardless of location. The project manager who fails to build and maintain alliances will soon find opposition or indifference to project requirements.

The amount of authority granted to the project manager varies according to project size, management philosophy and management interpretation of potential conflicts with functional managers. There does exist, however, certain fundamental elements over which the project manager must have authority in order to maintain effective control. According to Steiner and Ryan,[9]

The project manager should have broad authority over all elements of the project. His authority should be sufficient to permit him to engage all necessary managerial and technical actions required to complete the project successfully. He should have appropriate authority in design and in making technical decisions in development. He should be able to control funds, schedule and quality of product. If subcontractors are used, he should have maximum authority in their selection.

Generally speaking, project managers should have more authority than their responsibilities call for, the exact amount usually being dependent upon the amount of risk involved. The greater the risk, the greater the amount of authority. Good project managers know where their authority ends and do not hold employees responsible for duities not under their (the project manager's) jurisdiction. Some projects are directed by project managers who have only monitoring authority. These project managers are referred to as influence project managers.

Failure to establish authority relationships can result in

- Poor communication channels, often containing misleading information
- Antagonism, especially from the informal organization

---

9. Steiner and Ryan, *Industrial Project Management,* New York, Macmillan, 1968, p. 24. Copyright © 1968 by the Trustees of Columbia University in the City of New York.

- Poor working relationships with superiors, subordinates, peers, and associates
- Surprises for the customer

The project management organizational structure is an arena of continuous conflicts and negotiations. Although there are many clearly defined authority boundaries between functional and project management responsibilities, the fact that each project can be inherently different almost always creates new areas where authority negotiations are necessary. The project manager does not have unilateral authority in the project effort. There is frequent negotiation with the functional manager. The project manager has the authority to determine the "when" and "what" of the project activities, whereas the functional manager has the authority to determine "how the support will be given." The project manager accomplishes objectives by working with personnel who are largely professional. For professional personnel, project leadership must include explaining the rationale of the effort as well as the more obvious functions of planning, organizing, direction, and controlling.

Certain ground rules exist for authority control through negotiations:

- Negotiations should take place at the lowest level of interaction
- Definition of the problem in four basic terms must be the first priority
  - The issue
  - The impact
  - The alternatives
  - The recommendations
- Higher level authority should be used if, and only if, agreement cannot be reached

The critical stage of any project is planning. This includes more than just planning out the activities to be accomplished, but also the anticipation and establishment of the authority relationships that must exist for the duration of the project. Because the project management environment is constantly changing, each projet establishes its own policies and procedures, a situation which can ultimately result in a variety of authority relationships. It is therefore possible for functional personnel to have different responsibilities on different projects, even if the tasks are the same.

During the planning phase the project team develops a responsibility matrix which contain such elements as:

- General management responsibility
- Operations management responsibility
- Specialized responsibility
- Must be consulted
- May be consulted

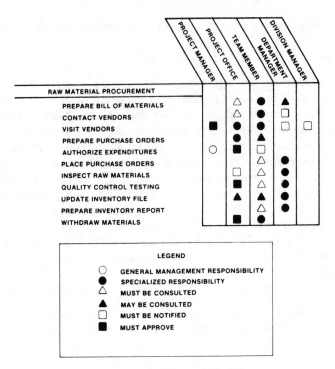

Figure 5-5. Linear Responsibility Chart.

- Must be notified
- Must approve

The responsibility matrix is often referred to as a linear responsibility chart (LRC). Linear responsibility charts identify the participants, and to what degree an activity will be performed or a decision will be made. The LRC attempts to clarify the authority relationships that can exist when functional units share common work. As described by Cleland and King:[10]

The need for a device to clarify the authority relationships is evident from the relative unity of the traditional pyramidal chart, which (1) is merely a simple portrayal of the overall functional and authority models and (2) must be combined with detailed position descriptions and organizational manuals to delineate authority relationships and work performance duties.

Figure 5-5 shows a typical linear responsibility chart. The rows indicate the activities, responsibilities, or functions required. The rows can be all of the tasks

10. From *Systems Analysis and Project Management* by David Cleland and William Richard King. Copyright © 1968, 1975 McGraw-Hill Inc. Used with permission of McGraw-Hill Book Company. p. 271.

in the work breakdown structure. The columns identify either the positions, titles, or the people themselves. If the chart will be given to an outside customer, then only the titles should appear or else the customer will call the employees directly without going through the project manager. The symbols indicate the degrees of authority or responsibility that exists between the rows and columns.

Another example of an LRC is shown in Figure 5-6. In this case, the LRC is used to describe how internal and external communications should take place. This type of chart can be used to eliminate communications conflicts. Consider a customer who is unhappy about having all of his information being filtered through the project manager, and requests that his line people be permitted to talk to your line people on a one-on-one basis. You may have no choice, but you should make sure the customer understands that:

- Functional employees cannot make commitments for additional work or resources
- Functional employees give their own opinion and not that of the company. Company policy comes through the project office.

Linear responsibility charts can be used to alleviate some of these problems.

| INITIATED FROM | REPORTED TO | | | | | | | | | | | | | |
| | INTERNAL | | | | | | | EXTERNAL (CUSTOMER)** | | | | | | |
	PROJECT MANAGER	PROJECT OFFICE	TEAM MEMBER	DEPARTMENT MANAGERS	FUNCTIONAL EMPLOYEES	DIVISION MANAGER	EXECUTIVE MANAGEMENT	PROJECT MANAGER	PROJECT OFFICE	TEAM MEMBER	DEPARTMENT MANAGER	FUNCTIONAL EMPLOYEES	DIVISION MANAGER	EXECUTIVE MANAGER
PROJECT MANAGER	///	○	◆	◁	▲	▲	◆	○	○	■	■	■	■	◁
PROJECT OFFICE	○	///	○	○	▲	▲	▲	○	○	◁	◁	■	■	◁
TEAM MEMBER	◆	○	///	◆	⬡	■	■	■	■	▲	▲	▲	■	■
DEPARTMENT MANAGER	▲	◁	○	///	○	◆	■	◁	◁	◁	◁	◁	■	■
FUNCTIONAL EMPLOYEES	▲	▲	○	○	///	■	■	▲	▲	▲	▲	▲	■	■
DIVISION MANAGERS	◁	▲	▲	▲	▲	///	◁	■	■	■	■	■	◁	◁
EXECUTIVE MANAGEMENT	◁	▲	▲	▲	▲	▲	///	◁	◁	▲	▲	■	◁	◁

*CAN VARY FROM TASK TO TASK AND CAN BE WRITTEN OR ORAL
**DOES NOT INCLUDE REGULARLY SCHEDULED INTERCHANGE MEETINGS

LEGEND	
○	DAILY
◆	WEEKLY
○	MONTHLY
▲	AS NEEDED
◁	INFORMAL
■	NEVER

Figure 5-6. Communications Responsibility Matrix.*

The responsibility matrix attempts to answer such questions as: Who has signature authority? Who must be notified? Who can make the decision? These questions can only be answered by clear definitions of authority, responsibility, and accountability:

- Authority is the right of an individual to make the necessary decisions required to achieve objectives or responsibilities.
- Responsibility is the assignment of a specific event or activity until completion.
- Accountability is the acceptance of success or failure.

The linear responsibility charts, although a valuable tool for management, does not fully describe how people interact within the program. The LRC must be combined with the organization to fully understand how interactions between individuals and organizations take place. As described by Karger and Murdick, the LRC's have merit:[11]

Obviously the chart has weaknesses, of which one of the larger ones is that it is a mechanical aid. Just because it says that something is a fact does not make it true. It is very difficult to discover, except generally, exactly what occurs in a company – and with whom. The chart tries to express in specific terms relationships that cannot always be delineated so clearly; moreover, the degree to which it can be done depends on the specific situation. This is the difference between the formal and informal organizations mentioned. Despite this, the Linear Responsibility Charts is one of the best devices for organization analysis known to the authors.

5.14 INTERPERSONAL INFLUENCES

There exists a variety of relationships (although not always clearly definable) between power and authority. This relationship is usually measured by "relative" decision power as a function of the authority structure, and is strongly dependent upon the project organizational form.

Project managers are generally known for having a lot of delegated authority but very little formal power. Project managers must therefore get the job done through the use of interpersonal influences. There are five such interpersonal influences:

- Formal Authority. The ability to gain support because project personnel perceive the project manager as being officially empowered to issue orders.
- Reward Power. The ability to gain support because project personnel perceive the project manager as capable of directly or indirectly dispensing

---

11. Karger, D.W., and Murdick, R.G., *Managing Engineering and Research*, New York, Industrial Press, 1963, p. 89.

valued organizational rewards (i.e., salary, promotion, bonus, future work assignments).

- Penalty Power. The ability to gain support because the project personnel perceive the project manager as capable of directly or indirectly dispensing penalties that they wish to avoid. Penalty power usually derives from the same source as reward power, with one being a necessary condition for the other.
- Expert Power. The ability to gain support because personnel perceive the project manager as possessing special knowledge or expertise (that functional personnel consider as important).
- Referent Power. The ability to gain support because project personnel feel personally attracted to the project manager or the project.

Consider the following two expressions made by a project manager:

- "I've had good working relations with Department A. They like me and I like them. I can usually push through anything ahead of schedule."
- (A research scientist was temporarily promoted to project management for an advanced state-of-the-art effort. He was overheard making the following remark to a team member), "I know it's contrary to department policy, but the test must be conducted according to these criteria or else the results will be meaningless."

These two statements reflect the way the project manager gets the job done.

The following six situations are examples of referent power (the first two are also reward power):

- The employee might be able to get personal favors from the project manager.
- The employee feels that the project manager is a winner and the rewards will be passed down to the employee.
- The employee and the project manager have strong ties, such as the same foursome for golf.
- The employee likes the project manager's manner of treating people.
- The employee wants identification with a specific project or product line.
- The employee has personal problems and believes that he or she can get empathy or understanding from the project manager.

Figure 5-7 shows how project managers perceive their influence style.[12]

As was the case with relative power, these interpersonal influences can also be identified with various project organizational forms as to their relative value. This is shown in Figure 5-8.

---

12. Source: *Seminar in Project Management Workbook,* © 1979 by Hans J. Thamhain, reproduced by permission.

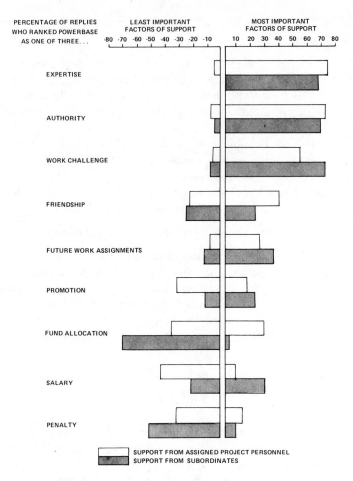

PERCENTAGE OF REPLIES
WHO RANKED POWERBASE
AS ONE OF THREE...

LEAST IMPORTANT
FACTORS OF SUPPORT

MOST IMPORTANT
FACTORS OF SUPPORT

Figure 5-7. Significance Of Factors In Support To Project Management.

For any temporary management structure to be effective, there must be a rational balance of power between functional and project management. Unfortunately, such a balance of equal power is often impossible to obtain because each project is inherently different and each project manager possesses different leadership abilities.   Organizations, nevertheless, must attempt to obtain this balance so that trade offs can be effectively accomplished according to the individual merit and not as a result of some established power structure.

Achieving this balance is a never-ending challenge facing management. If time and cost constraints on a project cannot be met, the project influence in decision-making is increased, as can be seen in Figure 5-8. If the technology or performance constraints need reappraisal, then the functional influence in decision-making will dominate.

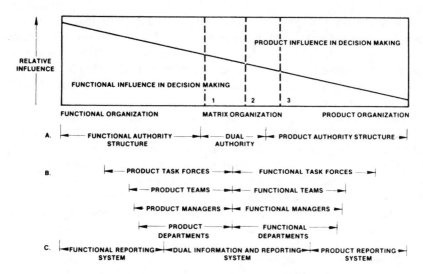

Figure 5-8. The Range Of Alternatives.

Regardless of how much authority and power a project manager develops over the course of the project, the ultimate factor in one's ability to get the job done is usually leadership style. Project managers, because of the inherent authority gaps which develop at the project-functional interface, must rely heavily upon supplementary techniques for getting the job done. These supplementary techniques include those facets which directly affect the leadership style, and include such items as developing bonds of trust, friendship, and respect with the functional workers. Of course, the relative importance to these techniques can vary depending upon the size and scope of the project.

5.15 TOTAL PROJECT PLANNING

The difference between the good project manager and poor project manager is often described in one word: planning. Unfortunately, people have a poor definition of what project planning actually involves. Project planning involves planning for

- Schedule development
- Budget development
- Project administration
- Leadership styles (interpersonal influences)
- Conflict management

The first two items involve the quantitative aspects of planning. Planning for project administration includes the development of the linear responsibility chart. Leadership styles refer to the interpersonal influence modes that a project manager can use. Project managers may have to use several different leadership styles depending upon the makeup of the project personnel. Conflict management is important because, if the project manager can predict what conflicts will occur and when they are most likely to occur, then the project manager may be able to plan for the resolution of the conflict through project administration. This will be discussed in Chapter 7.

Figure 5-9 shows the complete project planning phase for the quantitative portions. The object, of course, is to develop a project plan which shows complete distribution of resources and the corresponding costs. The figure represents an iterative process. The project manager begins with a coarse (arrow diagram) network and then decides upon the work breakdown structure. The WBS is essential to the arrow diagram and should be constructed such that reporting elements and levels are easily identifiable. Eventually, there will be an arrow diagram and detailed chart for each element in the WBS. If there exists too much detail, the project manager can refine the diagram by combining all logic into one plan and then decide upon the work assignments. There is a risk here that, by condensing the diagrams as much as possible, there may be a loss of clarity. Finally, as shown in Figure 5-9, all the charts and schedules can be integrated into one summary level figure. This can be accomplished at each WBS level until the desired plan is achieved.

Finally, both project, line, and executive management must analyze other internal and external variables before finalizing these schedules. A partial listing of these variables would include:

- Introduction or acceptance of the product in the marketplace
- Present or planned manpower availability

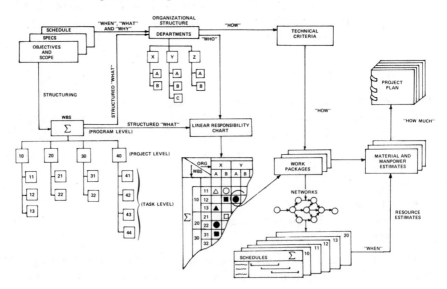

Figure 5-9. Project Planning.

- Economical constraints of the project
- Degree of technical difficulty
- Manpower availability
- Availability of personnel training
- Priority of the project

5.16 MANAGEMENT POLICIES AND PROCEDURES

Although each project manager has the authority and responsibility to establish project policies and procedures, they must fall within the general guidelines established by top management. Table 5-6 identifies sample top-management guidelines. Guidelines can also be established for planning, scheduling, controlling, and communications.

Linear responsibility charts can result from customer-imposed requirements above and beyond normal operations. For example, the customer may require as part of their quality control requirements that a specific engineer supervise and approve all testing of a certain item or that another individual approve all data released to customer over and above program office approval. Customer requirements similar to those identified above, require LRCs and can cause disruptions and conflicts within an organization.

There are several key factors which affect the delegation of authority and responsibility both from upper-level management to project management, and from project management to functional management. These key factors include:

- The maturity of the project management function
- The size, nature, and business base of the company
- The size and nature of the project
- The life cycle of the project
- The capabilities of management at all levels

Once agreement has been reached on the project manager's authority and responsibility, the results must be documented to clearly delineate that role regarding:

- Focal position
- Conflict between the project manager and functional managers
- Influence to cut across functional and organizational lines
- Participation in major management and technical decisions
- Collaboration in staffing the project
- Control over allocation and expenditure of funds
- Selection of subcontractors
- Rights in resolving conflicts
- Input in maintaining integrity of project team
- Establishment of project plans
- Provisions for a cost effective information system-for control

Table 5-6. General Management Guidelines.

PROGRAM MANAGER	FUNCTIONAL MANAGER	RELATIONSHIP
GENERAL The Program Manager is responsible for over-all program direction, control, and coordination; and is the principal contact with the program management of the customer. To achieve the program objectives, the Program Manager utilizes the services of the functional organizations in accordance with the prescribed Division Policies and Procedures affecting the functional organizations. Establishes Program and Technical policy as defined by Management Policy. The Program Manager is responsible for the progress being made as well as the effectiveness of the total program. Integrates research, development, production, procurement, quality assurance, product support, test, and financial and contractual aspects. Approves detailed performance specifications, pertinent physical characteristics and functional design criteria to meet the programs development or operational requirements.	*GENERAL* The functional organization managers are responsible for supporting the Program Manager in the performance of the contract(s) and in accordance with the terms of the contract(s) and are accountable to their cognizant managers for the total performance. The functional support organizations perform all work within their functional areas for all programs within the cost, schedule, quality, and specifications established by contract for the program so as to assist the Program Manager in achieving the program objectives. The functional support organization management seeks out or initiates innovations, methods, improvements or other means which will enable that function to better schedule commitments, reduce cost, improve quality, or otherwise render exemplary performance as approved by the Program Manager.	*GENERAL* The Program Manager determines what will be done: he obtains, through the assigned Program Team members, the assistance and concurrence of the functional support organizations in determining the definitive requirements and objectives of the program. The functional organizations determine *how* the work will be done The Program Manager operates within prescribed division policies and procedures except where requirements of a particular program necessitate deviations or modifications as approved by the General Manager. The functional support organizations provide strong, aggressive support to the Program Managers. The Program Manager relies on the functional support Program Team members for carrying out specific program assignments. Program Managers and the functional support program team members are jointly responsible for ensuring that unresolved conflicts between requirements levied on functional organizations by different Program Managers are brought to the attention of management.

Table 5-6. General Management Guidelines. (continued)

PROGRAM MANAGER	FUNCTIONAL MANAGER	RELATIONSHIP
GENERAL (Cont.)	*GENERAL (Cont.)*	*GENERAL (Cont.)*
Insures preparation of, and approves, over-all plan, budgets, and work statements essential to the integration of system elements.		Program managers do not make decisions which are the responsibility of the functional support organizations as defined in Division Policies and procedures and/or as assigned by the general manager.
Directs the preparation and maintenance of a time, cost, and performance schedule to insure the orderly progress of the program.		Functional organization managers do not request decisions of a program manager which are not within the program manager's delineated authority and responsibility and which do not affect the requirements of the program.
Coordinates and approves subcontract work statement, schedules, contract type, and price for major "Buy" items.		Functional organizations do not make program decisions which are the responsibility of the program manager.
Coordinates and approves vendor evaluation and source selections in conjunction with procurement representative to the Program Team		Joint participation in problem solution is essential to providing satisfactory decisions that fulfill over-all program and Company objectives, and is accomplished by the Program Manager and the assigned Program Team members.
Program decision authority rests with the Program Manager for all matters relating to his assigned program, consistent with Division policy and the responsibilities assigned by the general manager.		In arriving at program decisions, the Program Manager obtains the assistance and concurrence of cognizant functional support managers, through the cognizant Program Team member, since they are held accountable for their support of each program and for over-all Division functional performance.

- Provisions for leadership in preparing operational requirements
- Maintainence of prime customer liaison and contact
- Promotion of technological and managerial improvements
- Establishment of project organization for the duration
- Elimination of red tape

Documenting the project manager's authority is necessary because:

- All interfacing must be kept as simple as possible
- The project manager must have the authority to "force" functional managers to depart from existing standards and possibly incur risk
- Gaining authority over those elements of a program which are not under the project manager's control is essential. This is normally achieved by earning the respect of the individuals concerned.
- The project manager should not attempt to fully describe the exact authority and responsibilities of the project office personnel or team members. Instead, problem-solving rather than role definition should be encouraged.

CASE STUDY: THE RELUCTANT WORKERS

Tim Aston had changed employers three months ago. His new position was project manager. At first he had stars in his eyes about becoming the best project manager that his company had ever seen. Now, he wasn't sure if project management was worth the effort. He made an appointment to see Phil Davies, Director of Project Management.

Tim Aston: Phil, I'm a little unhappy about the way things are going. I just can't seem to motivate my people. Every day, at 4:30 P.M., all of my people clean off their desks and go home. I've had people walk out of late afternoon team meetings because they were afraid that they'd miss their car pool. I have to schedule morning team meetings.

Phil Davies: Look Tim. You're going to have to realize that in a project environment, people think that they come first and that the project is second. This is a way of life in our organizational form.

Tim Aston: I've continuously asked my people to come to me if they have problems. I find that the people do not think that they need help and, therefore, do not want it. I just can't get my people to communicate more.

Phil Davies: The average age of our employees is about forty-six. Most of our people have been here for twenty years. They're set in their ways. You're the first person that we've hired in the past three years. Some of our people may just resent seeing a thirty-year-old project manager.

Tim Aston: I found one guy in the accounting department who has an excellent head on his shoulders. He's very interested in project management. I asked his boss if he'd release him for a position in project management, and his boss just laughed at me saying something to the effect that as long as that guy is doing a good job for him, he'll never be released for an assignment elsewhere in the company. His boss seems more worried about his personal empire than what's best for the company.

We had a test scheduled for last week. The customer's top management was planning on flying in for first-hand observations. Two of my people said that they had programmed vacation days coming, and that they would not change, under any conditions. One guy was going fishing and the other guy was planning to spend a few days working with fatherless children in our community. Surely, these guys could change their plans for the test.

Phil Davies: Many of our people have social responsibilities and outside interests. We encourage social responsibilities and only hope that the outside interests do not interfere with their jobs.

There's one thing you should understand about our people. With an average age of forty-six, many of our people are at the top of their pay grades and have no place to go. They must look elsewhere for interests. These are the people you have to work with and motivate. Perhaps you should do some reading on human behavior.

CASE STUDY: PROJECT MANAGEMENT AT LIBERTY CONSTRUCTION[8]

Background

The stockholder's report for 1960 made it clear that Liberty Construction was a company to reckon with. The company had grown from fifty people back in 1955 to 400 people in 1960. Although Liberty had evolved primarily as an industrial facilities contractor, their business base expanded in commercial buildings, office buildings, production plants, chemical plants and even private housing. This rapid expansion was attributed mainly to Liberty's ability to work with the customer.

As Liberty began to grow, they found it more and more difficult to coordinate efforts using the traditional structure. Planning and scheduling was accomplished with great difficulty. A new organizational structure was needed.

In 1964, Liberty adopted the classical matrix structure so that individuals could be shared. The project engineering function now included project management as well as project engineering. For the most part, each project engineer was assigned full-time to one and only one project. The project engineering positions were primarily administrative and included all customer communication. In effect, the project engineer could also serve as a customer representative if the customer did not have one.

The project engineer worked closely with the functional team members, by providing direction and answering questions. When in doubt, the project engineer would coordinate with the functional manager so that conflicting direction would not be given to the functional team member.

By 1967, Liberty found themselves in a position of having their project engineers consistently arguing with the functional managers over resources and priorities. Furthermore, because key individuals were being shared on as many as four

---

8. Copyright © 1978 Harold Kerzner.

projects at one time, the project engineers felt that they did not have total accountability for a given project. In 1968, Liberty sponsored a series of in-house seminars in hopes that this would lead to better working relationships between the project engineers and the functional design groups. Below are the seven basic questions and answers that resulted from the seminars.

Questions & Answers

1. Q–Does a project engineer need more legal authority over the project group?

   A–The group consensus was that the project engineer has enough "legal" (organizational) authority.
   Amplifying remarks were:

   a. A "Partnership" of the design and project groups must be established.
   b. It is important for the project engineers to clarify goals for the purpose of minimizing conflict.
   c. If all project engineers would do a better job of using "tools" that they already have, this would be sufficient authority. Some of the tools mentioned were:
      —improved communications
      —using motivational techniques
      —creating a better team "climate"

2. Q–The project engineer has responsibility for leading a given project but does not have authority over the "who" does it and "how" it is to be done. In what ways is this a problem?

   A–Some of the problems associated with having responsibilities for a project without complete authority over the "how and who" questions are:

   a. A situation whereby the project engineer becomes demotivated as a result of his authority being diluted and as a result of organizational confusion, the group becomes demotivated.
   b. If the project engineer does not exercise what authority he already has when needed.
   c. If low quality/or performer people are assigned to a project.

3. Q–"How" and "who" decisions are made by design. Can project engineers be involved in these decisions?

   A–The group concluded that the project manager can be involved in "how" and "who" decisions by reviewing any conflicts with design group people and, in extreme cases, by reviewing problems with the manager of project engineering.

   Specifically, the group talked in detail about "who" problems. Some of the solutions to the problems offered were:

   a. Before a project is formalized, the project manager should make recommendations for lead men with design section managers.

   b. During the design stage of a project, changing key design people is a serious consideration and should be avoided whenever possible.
   c. The key to resolving "who" problems is to work with design supervision first, and if the problem has significant impact on the success of the project and cannot be resolved with design supervision, then the problem should be reviewed with the manager of project engineering.

4. Q–"What" has to be done and "when" it has to be done decisions are made by project engineers. How should these be communicated to the "who" group?

A–Not discussed in detail. However, from the research conclusions presented, it should be evident that it is critically important for project engineers to involve key design people in "what and when" decisions, assuming the project engineer does this and "stays close" to design people on "what and when" problems. The project engineer can keep such problems from creating conflicts.

5. Q–Different project engineers create different human relations "climates" on their projects. What are some of the techniques that can be used to control this?

A–Project engineers can create a positive project team climate by balancing overall goals with specific project demands and needs. (Such as evaluating people and development of people.) Group discussions centered around the need for the project engineers to emphasize mutual goals, (design, project, etc.), and to de-emphasize those areas where there may be conflict.

6. Q–What is an appropriate project communication concerning:
   —rating people (design and project)
   —feedback to people on project (successes) failures in the field

A–It was suggested that design personnel assigned to project teams should be evaluated by the project engineer. In the event design management does not request such feedback, it is suggested that project engineers routinely evaluate project people. It was also suggested that project engineers be rated by design management. (Example of an evaluation form is shown in Table 5-7)

Techniques for providing feedback for project personnel regarding success and failures of projects in the field were:
   —the need for project engineers to emphasize successes
   —evaluating new field problems, and their successful completion, the project engineer might use a variety of feedback techniques; individually, to several individuals, to the total group, or to section managers
   —letters commending individual or group efforts by project engineers were mentioned as a technique for social recognition

7. Q–How are Project Engineer decisions "validated" by project team members?

A–Not discussed in detail. However, from the research presented, "participation" of project team members in project decisions seems to be the key.

Table 5-7. Project Work Assignment Appraisal.

EMPLOYEE'S NAME _____ DATE _____
PROJECT TITLE _____ JOB NO. _____
ASSIGNMENT _____ TIME ON JOB _____

For each item below, select a number between zero and five according to the following:

        0 = not applicable
        1 = outstanding
        2 = excellent
        3 = good or average
        4 = adequate or acceptable
        5 = inadequate or unacceptable

I   TECHNICAL ABILITY

- ☐ Ability to meet quality of work standards
- ☐ Ability to meet quantity of work standards
- ☐ Ability to apply technical judgement
- ☐ Time and cost consciousness
- ☐ Safety consciousness

II   HUMAN RELATIONS

- ☐ Job attitude
- ☐ Communicative skills
- ☐ Ability to work with others
- ☐ Cooperation
- ☐ Loyalty to the company

III   PROBLEM-SOLVING ABILITY

- ☐ Originality
- ☐ Adaptability
- ☐ Judgement
- ☐ Thoroughness

IV   SELF-MOTIVATION

- ☐ Willingness to accept responsibility or accountability
- ☐ Ambitiousness
- ☐ Vigor
- ☐ Likes work challenge

V   MANAGERIAL RESPONSIBILITIES

- ☐ Planning
- ☐ Organizing
- ☐ Directing
- ☐ Motivating employees

VI   WORK HABITS

- ☐ Attendance at meetings
- ☐ Punctuality
- ☐ Housekeeping
- ☐ Stays at desk

VII   IN COMPARISON TO CONTEMPORARIES, I WOULD RATE THIS EMPLOYEE AS

- ☐ Top 10%
- ☐ Top 25%
- ☐ Average
- ☐ Bottom 25%
- ☐ Bottom 10%

VIII   ADDITIONAL COMMENTS

_____
_____
_____
_____
_____
_____

Although the group seminar did provide some relief for many of the dilemmas, there still existed many problems which created conflicts. The majority of the conflicts revolved about the fact that the project engineer did not have total responsibility for the project because of lack of control over the functional team members. For example, a buyer might be working on more than one project at a time, the project engineer would then have to compete with other projects for the services of this buyer.

Product Management

In 1972, Liberty's management decided that the only realistic means of reducing conflicts would be to reorganize. Liberty went to the product organizational form in hopes that the project engineer would be able to achieve total responsibility, accountability and control over those resources which would be needed. Liberty's management decided that all projects could be categorized as either industrial construction, home/office construction, government construction or special projects. Each of these four "product lines" would be headed up by a team manager. Each team manager had the same eight functional departments beneath him.

Each team manager was responsible for approximately sixty people. This included the project engineers. There was some concern that the best technical specialists would be assigned to the special projects team. Top level management, however, made it clear that there would be an equal division of the key people. All employees reported directly to the team managers and indirectly to the project engineers. The project engineers, however, had authority delegated to them by the team managers to utilize those people resources within their team as they see fit. In theory, the new systems looked like a matrix organizational structure within a product organizational form.

Each team manager was responsible for keeping two of the eight disciplines current with technology; the same two disciplines in all teams. In addition, the team managers would be responsible for evaluating all functional team members, regardless of their discipline.

The case writer interviewed the four team managers, the project engineers, and the functional (group) engineers as to how they foresaw the new organizational form and whether or not they felt that the problems which existed under the matrix would be carried over.

Interview With Project Engineers

Q—"What problems do you see carrying over into the new system?"

A—*Planning:* "Many times we're not even sure what our planning needs are, and this tends to create havoc. Sometimes it's our fault, but quite often the customer doesn't even know what he wants. This makes it difficult for us to work with the functional team members because we always end up replanning. The result is that the functional people may have lost confidence in us and therefore do not believe that the plan is any good. One function guy once told me, "Why should we plan at all? Nobody follows it anyway."

"If we had good planning that everyone had confidence in, then we could play "what if" games and develop contingency plans."

A—*Communications:* "We have to establish better communications with our design people. They're the people that made our system a success. Unfortunately, it's not easy working with design people and establishing a good communications network. It's difficult for a project engineer to become successful until after he has established credibility with functional people. To do this, a project engineer must make the first contact and show some interest in what they're doing. Of course, this can backfire because quite often the functional team members think that we're sticking our nose into their business and that we're going to tell them how to do their job. I guess they have a right to feel this way. This is a carry over from the matrix.

"Many times I tell our functional people everything I know about the project, but I still get the feeling that they think that I'm holding something back.

"A good project engineer is a manager, not a doer. Most of his time he is caught up in paperwork and some red tape. Sometimes I consider myself as a high-priced clerk. I wish we (project engineers) could lighten some of the load we put on our design people in the way of writing reports. If our design people think they have to do a lot of writing, perhaps they should have my job for a while.

"We need a more dedicated effort on our projects. I think the only way we can do it is by developing better communications channels, both up as well as down.

"Many of our design people have poor communicative skills. They cannot write well, read or sometimes even understand what they've read. I guess this is typical of engineers. I'm used to it now and am willing to help them out whenever I can. I just hope when I do this that they don't think that I'm trying to do their job for them."

Q–"What kind of working relationships would you like to see develop between the project engineer and the team manager?"

A–"Team managers should be managers, not doers. Their job should be administrative, for the most part. We must remember, however, that the team managers are still engineers, and damn good ones at that. I would like to see them act as consultants, not only to our team personnel, but to the other teams as well.

"The team managers have the authority to establish their own team policies, procedures and standards as they see fit (I assume as long as though they conform to Liberty's policies, procedures, and rules). The team managers could easily end up telling the design people how to structure their work. This could put the project engineer in a position of responsibility without authority. I'd like to see the team managers funnel their work through us. In the new system, team managers are like the old functional managers, but tied up more with administrative duties."

Q–"How do you feel about having new hirers attached to your project? Do you feel that you have a responsibility for on-the-job training?"

A–"Somebody's got to do it. Sure, I'd prefer having seasoned veterans. But a good project engineer assumes that whatever people are assigned to him have the technical ability."

Interview With Group Engineers

Q–What are the biggest problems that you would like to see overcome by the new system?

A–*Planning:* "I've seen several packages which are total disasters from the start. I think there is a discontinuity of effort and lack of willingness of the project engineer and the customer to do good planning. Our project engineers might need refresher courses in industrial construction, but I don't think that this is a big problem. The "biggy" is probably that the customer hasn't done any good planning and keeps coming up with different ideas. I wish our P.E.'s would keep us more informed about the total picture. I think it would give us a better understanding of their job and improve our relationships.

"Many times we do poor planning because we have to come up with too much information too quick. Because of the amount of changes we end up making, we should develop schedules as we go along.

"Someday, just someday, I'd like to have some kind of feedback or appraisal of how good our engineering package is. Contrary to popular belief, several of us group engineers are interested . . . . I should say dedicated . . . . to the total project."

A—*Communications:* "Up, down, sideways and inside out! We have severe inter-disciplinary communications problems. There are some activities that can be handled by more than one group . . . . at least this is the way it was in the old system. Overlapping efforts occurred because poor planning left several "fuzzy areas" which could not be completely resolved until half-way through the job. Hopefully, the new system will alleviate this.

"I'd like somebody to tell me how much money I'm spending in doing my job. A little feedback wouldn't hurt.

"The best P.E.'s are those that have developed good communications channels with us but keep their nose out of our business and "stop trying to help.""

A—*Loss of Flexibility:* "I'm worried that the new system is trying to isolate and define more responsibility. This may be bad if it results in less flexibility for us. We're at the mercy of the team managers in the new system. I can see them tell us; Do it my way, use this procedure, use this standard, etc. What happens if I'm tranferred or just temporarily assigned to another group? We could very easily have a loss of learning between groups and teams. The team managers have a great deal more responsibility in the new system. I can sympathize with their problem of having to control technology in all four teams, of which only one reports to them directly."

Q—How do you foresee the role of the team managers?

A—*Procedures and standards:* "Everyone has the tendency of wanting people to conform to their own standards. Sure, we here in the functional groups would like to use our own policies and procedures, but we do understand that one of the responsibilities of the team manager is to develop team procedures. This could pose a problem if each team manager has a different procedure for his team. I don't think I'd be very happy being temporarily assigned to another team and then finding a change in the way I'm supposed to do my job."

"I sure as hell hope that the team managers consult the project engineers before policies and procedures are developed. How can anyone expect the functional people to be motivated toward the successful accomplishment of a project when its obvious that there's a conflict in procedures between the team manager and the project engineer?"

A—*Character of the Team Manager:* "Sometimes I'm not sure that the right man is placed in the right position around here. Upper-level management must look at the ability of a team manager to interact with his people. We have conflicts in our group. Most of our conflicts are probably personality related. For this reason he must be able to interact. I don't care if he's the world's greatest engi-neer. If he can't interact with us (and the P.E.'s) then I question whether or not he'll be effective. This boils down to the proverbial question, Should people be assigned according to system characteristics or people characteristics? I have com-plete confidence in all four team managers. But, if one were weak, I think the new system could easily handle it by having good project engineers available. They (P.E.s) will be the guys who should make this new system go. I wonder what will happen if a team manager gets promoted? I don't think it will be easy for someone to walk in and fill his shoes. The team managers we have now have an advantage that they've worked the old system and are coming on board at the beginning of the new system so that they can have some say about how the system should be designed and operated. A new man, promoted into a team manager's slot, might not be able to readily adapt to this situation. He (the new manager) will have to work closely with the other three team managers. In the ideal situation, I'd like to see all four team managers think as one. For this reason, I feel that the team managers will probably have some say about who gets promoted to the vacant position when on exists. I'm not so sure that we'll always be able to fill this vacancy from within."

A—*Promotion and Evaluation.* "The big disadvantage I see about the new system is that we've lost our opportunity to excel. We had this chance in the old system, but it looks like it will be difficult to do in the new one."

"I can see a problem in that functional members might be worried about being evaluated by a team manager who doesn't understand their discipline. How can a team manager trained in, say electronics, effectively evaluate the performance of, say, a civil engineer or a piping engineer?"

"I expect our team manager to show favoritism during evaluation. Everyone has their favorites. I do think that, overall, everyone will get a fair shake."

Q—"Do you think that keeping in touch with technology will suffer in the new system?"

A—"No. Each team manager is responsible for keeping two functional group disciplines (i.e., civil and mechanical) up to date with technology. If he does his job, then this effort will consume a great deal of time. And even if he slacks off, I'm not worried because the company has always been good about providing in-house seminars and letting us travel to out-of-house seminars and conferences."

Interview With Team Managers

Q—Do you expect to spend a great deal of your time resolving conflicts?

A—"I want the P.E. to come to me only as a last resort."

A—"I need all information flowing up, especially problems, even if they are resolved by the P.E., so that I can understand them (the people) better and they can understand me."

A—"I expect to have disagreements with the P.E.'s. But even though we have disagreements, we must have mutual respect for each other's opinion."

Q—What do you foresee as some of your biggest problems?

A—*Personnel evaluation:* "In order for evaluation to be effective, the team managers must talk to one another in order to be consistent. This will probably be the secret to our success. I'm sure the functional people are worried about how we'll end up evaluating those whose disciplines we are not totally familiar with. We're aware of their concern."

Q—"Do you have many people that would rather be managers than engineers?"

A—"Yes, we have some. We have both a technical ladder and a management performance ladder. People can go back and forth on both, provided they commit. Some of our people place more emphasis on title than on salary."

CASE STUDY: CAPITAL INDUSTRIES

In the summer of 1976, Capital Industries undertook a material development program to see if a hard plastic bumper could be developed for medium-sized cars. By January, 1977 Project Bumper (as it was called by management) had developed a material which endured all preliminary laboratory testing.

One more step was required before full-scale laboratory testing: a three-dimensional stress analysis on bumper impact collisions. The decision to perform the stress analysis was the result of a concern on the part of the technical community that the bumper might not perform correctly under certain conditions. The cost of the analysis would require corporate funding over and above the original estimates. Since the current costs were identical to what was budgeted, the additional funding was a necessity.

Frank Allen, the project engineer in the Bumper Project Office, was assigned control of the stress analysis. Frank met with the functional manager of the engineering analysis section to discuss the assignment of personnel to the task.

Functional Manager: I'm going to assign Paul Troy to this project. He's a new man with a Ph.D. in structural analysis. I'm sure he'll do well.

Frank Allen: This is a priority project. We need seasoned veterans, not new people, regardless of whether or not they have Ph.D.s. Why not use some other project as a testing ground for your new employee?

Functional Manager: You project people must accept part of the responsibility for on-the-job training. I might agree with you if we were talking about blue collar workers on an assembly line. But this is a college graduate, coming to us with a good technical background.

Frank Allen: He may have a good background, but he has no experience. He needs supervision. This is a one-man task. The responsibility will be yours if he fouls up.

Functional Manager: I've already given him our book for cost estimates. I'm sure he'll do fine. I'll keep in close communication with him during the project.

Frank Allen met with Paul Troy to get an estimate for the job.

Paul Troy: I estimate that 800 hours will be required.

Frank Allen: Your estimate seems low. Most three-dimensional analyses require at least 1000 hours. Why is your number so low?

Paul Troy: Three-dimensional analysis? I thought that it would be a two-dimensional analysis. But no difference; the procedures are the same. I can handle it.

Frank Allen: O.K. I'll give you 1100 hours. But if you overrun it, we'll both be sorry.

Frank Allen followed the project closely. By the time the costs were 50 percent completed, performance was only 40 percent. A cost overrun seemed inevitable. The functional manager still asserted that he was tracking the job and that the difficulties were a result of the new material properties. His section had never worked with materials as these before.

Six months later, Troy announced that the work would be completed in one week, two months later than planned. The two-month delay caused major problems in facility and equipment utilization. Project Bumper was still paying for employees who were "waiting" to begin full-scale testing.

On Monday mornings, the project office would receive the weekly labor monitor report for the previous week. This week the report indicated that the publications and graphics art department had spent over 200 manhours (last week) in preparation of the final report. Frank Allen was furious. He called a meeting with Paul Troy and the functional manager.

Frank Allen: Who told you to prepare a formal report? All we wanted was a go or no-go decision as to structural failure.

Paul Troy: I don't turn in any work unless it's professional. This report will be documented as a masterpiece.

Frank Allen: Your 50 percent cost overrun will also be a masterpiece. I guess your estimating was a little off!

Paul Troy: Well, this was the first time that I had performed a three-dimensional stress analysis. And what's the big deal? I got the job done, didn't I?

CASE STUDY: WILLIAMS CONSTRUCTION

Williams Construction was a major industrial construction company based in Massachusetts. Williams maintained a full-time staff of 200 employees. The entire staff was non-union because Williams could promise their employees 50 weeks of work a year, whereas union companies could not.

Although Williams Construction was primarily concerned with industrial projects, they often accepted such small projects as homes, in order to fill the slack time between major jobs. Unfortunately, these smaller jobs often suffered because of their low priorities. However, with a reasonable amount of resources, Williams could erect and completely landscape a 3000-square-foot home in approximately two months.

On March 15, 1978, Williams contracted to build a 3000-square-foot house beginning April 15 with a guaranteed finish date of July 1, 1978. The appropriate schedules and charts were sent out to all department managers so that they could allocate their resources. (See Exhibits 1-3)

Frank Thomas was the department manager for concrete masonry and prefab walls.

"You people keep doing this to me," remarked Frank, as he stared at the project manager.

Exhibit 1. The Work Breakdown Structure.

PROJECT 1—DESIGN		
TASK		*DAYS*
A)	Topography	3
B)	Home Design	3
C)	Selections	2
D)	Working Drawings	3
E)	Order Specials	1
PROJECT 2—ROUGH STRUCTURE		
TASK		
F)	Staking	3
G)	Concrete Masonry	4
H)	Electrical Service	2
I)	Pre-Fab Walls	3
J)	Rough-in Plumbing	4
PROJECT 3—FINISH STRUCTURE		
TASK		
K)	Sheet Insulation	5
L)	Dry Wall	4
M)	Doors	3
N)	Finish Plumbing	4
O)	Blown Insulation	1
PROJECT 4—FINAL TOUCHES		
TASK		
P)	Painting	6
Q)	Inspection	2
R)	Landscaping	5

"On May 15, I have a top priority commitment for all of my people, and I do mean all. Last time we went this route, I was blamed for slowing down the work because my people were not available. I want someone to calculate the slack time in the network and tell me my limits. All of my people can do either masonry or prefab walls. Therefore, replanning should be easy. My second gripe is that I don't get the correct reports. I think that I'd rather have weekly than monthly reports. If you just look at the schedule, you'll see why. I'll come back tomorrow, if that's all right with you, and your people can tell me my limits."

Exhibit 2. GANTT Chart for the Work Breakdown Structure.

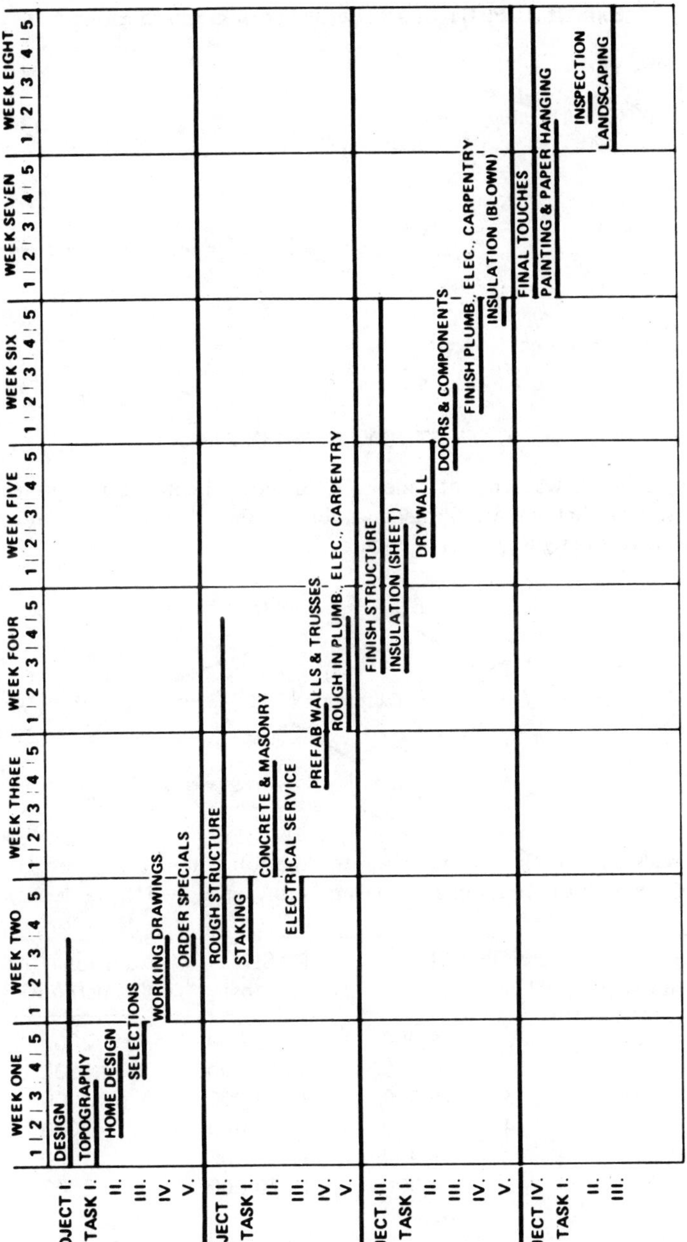

	WEEK ONE 1·2·3·4·5	WEEK TWO 1·2·3·4·5	WEEK THREE 1·2·3·4·5	WEEK FOUR 1·2·3·4·5	WEEK FIVE 1·2·3·4·5	WEEK SIX 1·2·3·4·5	WEEK SEVEN 1·2·3·4·5	WEEK EIGHT 1·2·3·4·5

PROJECT I. DESIGN
TASK I. TOPOGRAPHY
II. HOME DESIGN
III. SELECTIONS
IV. WORKING DRAWINGS
V. ORDER SPECIALS

PROJECT II. ROUGH STRUCTURE
TASK I. STAKING
II. CONCRETE & MASONRY
III. ELECTRICAL SERVICE
IV. PREFAB WALLS & TRUSSES
V. ROUGH IN PLUMB., ELEC., CARPENTRY

PROJECT III. FINISH STRUCTURE
TASK I. INSULATION (SHEET)
II. DRY WALL
III. DOORS & COMPONENTS
IV. FINISH PLUMB., ELEC., CARPENTRY
V. INSULATION (BLOWN)

PROJECT IV. FINAL TOUCHES
TASK I. PAINTING & PAPER HANGING
II. INSPECTION
III. LANDSCAPING

Exhibit 3. PERT Chart (Letters correspond to Exhibit 1).

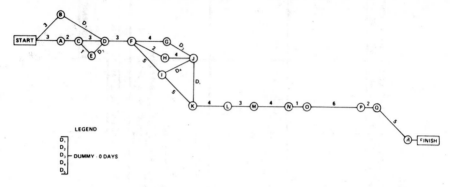

LEGEND

D₁
D₂
D₃ ⊢ DUMMY · 0 DAYS
D₄
D₅

CASE STUDY: THE MX PROJECT

On May 1, Arnie Watson sent a memo to his boss, the director of project management, stating that the MX Project would require thirteen weeks for completion according to the figure shown below.

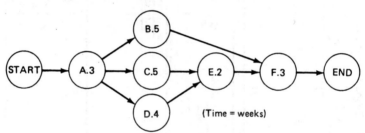

Arnie realized that the customer wanted the job completed in less time. After discussions with the functional managers, Arnie developed the table shown below:

Activity	NORMAL Time	Cost	CRASH Time	Cost	Additional (crash) Cost/Week
A	3	6,000	2	8,000	2000
B	5	12,000	4	13,500	1500
C	5	16,000	3	22,000	3000
D	4	8,000	2	10,000	1000
E	2	6,000	1	7,500	1500
F	3	14,000	1	20,000	3000
		$62,000			

a. According to the contract, there is a penalty payment of $5,000 per week for every week over six. What is the minimum amount of additional funding that Arnie should request?

b. Suppose your answer to part (a) gives you the same additional cost for both an eight-week and a nine-week project. What factors would you consider before deciding whether to do it in eight or nine weeks?

CASE STUDY: PROJECT STATUS

On March 1, the project manager received three status reports indicating resource utilization to date. Shown below are the three reports as well as the PERT diagram.

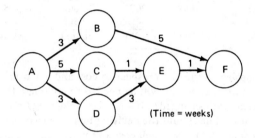

(Time = weeks)

PERCENT COMPLETION REPORT

Activity	Date Started	% Completed	Time to Complete
AB	2/1	100%	–
AC	2/1	60%	2
AD	2/1	100%	–
DE*	Not Started	–	3
BF	2/14	40%	3

Project Planning Budget. Weeks After Go-ahead.

ACTIVITY	1	2	3	4	5	6	7	8	TOTAL$
AB	2000	2000	2000						6,000
AC	4000	4000	4000	4000	4000				20,000
AD	2500	2500	2500						7,500
BF				3000	3000	3000	3000	3000	15,000
CE						2500			2,500
DE				3500	3500	3500			10,500
EF							3000		3,000
	8500	8500	8500	10500	10500	9000	6000	3000	64,500

*Note: Due to priorities, resources for activity DE will not be available until 3/14. Management estimates that this activity can be crashed from 3 weeks to 2 weeks at an additional cost of $3,000.

Cost Summary.

	WEEK ENDING 28 FEB			CUMULATIVE TO DATE		
ACTIVITY	BUDGETED COST	ACTUAL	(OVER) UNDER	BUDGETED COST	ACTUAL	(OVER) UNDER
AB	-	-	-	6000	6200	(200)
AC	4000	4500	(500)	16,000	12,500	3500
AD	-	2400	(2400)	7500	7400	100
BF	3000	2800	200	3000	5500	(2500)
DE	3500	-	-	3500	-	3500
TOTAL	10,500	9700	(2700)	36,000	31,600	4400

a. What is the project status with respect to cost and performance?
b. How much additional money will be needed to complete the project?
c. Has the critical path changed? If so, what is the new time to completion?
d. At what point in time should the decision be made to crash activities?
e. Construct a single table by which cost and performance data is more easily seen.

CASE STUDY: CONSTRUCTION OF A GAS TESTING LAB IN IRAN

With the increase in the availability of natural gas, the country of Iran had decided to embark on an extensive development program to test and evaluate the gas-utilizing appliances and accessories which might be required to satisfy future demands. The Iranian government desired to have all such items tested prior to use. The responsibility for this testing was delegated to the National Iranian Gas Company (NIGC).

Testing requires a facility. NIGC employed the American Gas Association (AGA), a non-profit organization. NIGC contracted AGA for engineering services, training, technical assistance, and special equipment fabrication work required for establishment of a testing lab. Testing for safety and performance would be in compliance with Iranian National Standards. Except for equipment installation and program startup, all work would be accomplished in the United States. The final assembly would be at the NIGC city gate station in Rey, Iran.

The project is a technical assistance contract to provide program planning, building design (but not construction), instruments purchasing, special equipment fabrication, operations personnel training, equipment installation, and program startup aid.

The contractor will furnish general design specifications and layouts including mechanical and electrical drawings. Architectural details, building construction and site preparation are furnished by the customer.

The project consists of five phases with a total time frame of twenty-one months. The five phases are:

1. Program plan and building design
2. Equipment purchase

3. Equipment construction
4. Training
5. Plant startup

Work Breakdown Structure

The analysis of the cost associated with building the project begins with the separation of the program into its basic tasks. The tasks involved with the project are defined as engineering, procurement, and training. The costs associated with each of the basic tasks are broken out and allocated to specific cost centers.

Project 1-1-00 Program Plan And Building Design

Project #1 consists of engineering and program management in the following areas:
Task 1-1-1 engineering
Engineering time required to design the testing building
Task 1-1-2 program management
Management time allocated to project planning and building design

Project 1-2-00 Equipment Purchase

Project #2 included time required to specify and purchase the equipment for the testing laboratory as follows:
Task 1-2-1 program management
Time allocated for management of the purchasing function.
Task 1-2-2 engineering
Provides the basic specifications for the equipment to be purchased
Task 1-2-3 testing and inspection
Insures that all equipment meets the established specifications
Task 1-2-4 shipping
Includes packing and storage for foreign shipment of the equipment
Task 1-2-5 procurement
Purchase all equipment and establish dates that it will be shipped

Project 1-3-00 Equipment Construction

Project #3 is required to specify, purchase and fabricate equipment that is not on the market.
Task 1-3-1 program management
Overall management of the special equipment function
Task 1-3-2 engineering
Developing the specifications for the special equipment
Task 1-3-3 procurement
The purchase and evaluation of special equipment, and the establishment of dates for shipment of the equipment
Task 1-3-4 shipping
The packing and shipment of the special equipment for foreign shipment.
Task 1-3-5 fabrication
Building and testing the equipment at selected vendors

Project 1-4-00 Training

Project #4 involves the preparation of material and equipment to train the testing
laboratory personnel

Task 1-4-1 program management
Overall management of the training function
Task 1-4-2 engineering
Developing the materials used to train the laboratory personnel
Task 1-4-3 training
The actual time required to make the testing people proficient with their new
equipment

Project 1-5-00 Plant Startup

Project #5 provides the time for field personnel to put the laboratory in operation.
Task 1-5-1 program management
Provides the overall coordination of the plant startup function
Task 1-5-2 field engineering
The time involved to provide the laboratory with startup personnel

Other Costs Associated With The Project

Purchased parts—Testing equipment
Freight—Shipping and packing
Travel—Procurement
Other—Purchased goods, freight, subcontracts, materials
Exhibit 1 contains the PERT chart for the program. Exhibit 2 shows the Bar chart
for the total program together with monthly man-hours and initial salary struc-
tures.

Exhibit 1. Critical Path Diagram

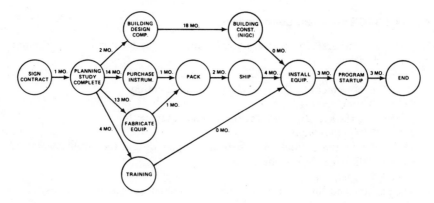

Base Case Discussion

The parameters used in the strategic planning model are listed below:

1. Salary costs will increase 6 percent per year with the increase beginning January 1 of each year.
2. Raw material costs will increase 10 percent per year with the increase beginning January 1 of each year.
3. Demanning ratio is 10 percent of following months labor and man-hour costs.
4. Termination liability on materials is 0 percent, and material commitments are based upon 6 months or less.
5. Indirect cost for each project is 14 percent of total cost of labor and materials.
6. Corporate cost for each project is 1 percent of total cost of labor and materials.
7. A profit of 12 percent is used for each project in the base case.
8. No delays or additional increased costs are assumed in the base case.
9. A separate overhead rate is included for each task. (see Exhibit 2)

The output obtained from the model using the parameters established for the program are listed below:

1. The total cost of establishing a natural gas testing laboratory is $920,322 including a 12 percent profit, overhead rates, and corporate costs.
2. Cash flow for the first year, 1978, is $642,718 and $178,999 for the second year. Profit is not included in these figures.
3. The cost for each project and total program percentage is shown below.

Project 1	$ 17,649	2%
Project 2	$250,978	31%
Project 3	$496,005	60%
Project 4	$ 25,414	3%
Project 5	$ 31,671	4%

The two projects representing 91 percent of the total program are equipment purchasing and equipment construction. (Profit is not included.)

4. Total labor expenditure for the project is 23,830 hours costing $583,410. This breaks down into 16,604 hours, costing $404,399 in 1978, and 7,226 hours, costing $179,011 in 1979.
5. Total material expenditure is $238,307 with the total commitment established in July of 1978.
6. A functional cost summary has the program divided into four major divisions, excluding material costs. The divisions and associated costs (including overhead) are as follows:

Engineering	$ 96,732	19%
Program Mgt.	$ 26,349	5%

Exhibit 2. Program Bar chart.

PROJECTS/TASKS	1977 JAN	FEB	MAR	APR	MAY	JUNE	JULY	AUG	SEPT	OCT	NOV	DEC	1978 JAN	FEB	MAR	APR	MAY	JUNE	JULY	AUG	SEPT
I. PROGRAM PLANS & BUILDING DESIGN																					
1. PROGRAM MANAGEMENT	102	50	48																		
2. ENGINEERING	20	174	283																		
II. EQUIPMENT PURCHASE																					
1. PROGRAM MANAGEMENT		52	40	40	30	30	30	30	30	30	20	20	20	20	20						
2. ENGINEERING		267	232	200	165	131	95	60	40	266	266	266	154	112							
3. TESTING & INSPECTION							154	154	154	154	154	154	154	308	308						
4. SHIPPING																					
5. PROCUREMENT				154	154	154	154	77	77												
III. EQUIPMENT CONSTRUCTION																					
1. PROGRAM MANAGEMENT			20	20	30	30	30	30	30	30	20	20	20	20	20						
2. ENGINEERING			154	154	154	154	154	154	154	154	77										
3. PROCUREMENT					154	308	308	308	308	308	308	308	308	308	308						
4. SHIPPING													47	100	308						
5. FABRICATION					308	462	616	770	924	1078	1386	1848	1848	1848	154						
IV. TRAINING																					
1. PROGRAM MANAGEMENT											20	20	20	20	5	5	5	5	5	20	
2. ENGINEERING											60	60	60	60							
3. TRAINING											154	154	154	154	154	154	308	154	154	154	
V. PLANT START-UP																					
1. PROGRAM MANAGEMENT																					
2. FIELD ENGINEERING																					

II. OTHER COSTS:

PURCHASED GOODS:	$121,981.
FREIGHT:	1,988.
OTHER:	3,049.
OVERSEAS PACKING:	6,242.
	$133,260.

III. OTHER COSTS:

PURCHASED MAT'LS:	39,527.
SUBCONTRACTS:	28,082.
OVERSEAS PACKING:	3,520.
FREIGHT:	2,598.
	$ 73,727.

IV. OTHER COSTS:

SUPPLIES:	$ 980.

	RATE	OH	
PROGRAM MANAGEMENT	11.00	120%	
ENGINEERING	10.00	120%	
TESTING	8.00	117%	} 125%
PROCUREMENT	8.00	110%	
SHIPPING	5.70	100%	
FABRICATION	10.00	125%	
TRAINING	10.50	120%	} 12%
FIELD ENGINEERING	9.00	80%	

INDIRECT COSTS	14%
CORPORATE COSTS	1%
PROFIT:	12%

RAW MATERIALS ESCALATION	10%
DEMANNING RATIO	10%
TERMINATION LIABILITY	0%
SALARY INCREASES	6%

NOTE: ONE MAN MONTH = 154 MAN HOURS

Finance	$ 14,654	3%
Operations	$368,953	73%

Problems

1. Construction of Special Equipment

   There is special test equipment required for the laboratory. Since many of the tests are unique to gas appliance testing under the American National Standards, the equipment cannot be purchased on the open market and must be constructed. The costs of construction are very difficult to estimate accurately since many of these items are unique.

2. Building Construction

   The erection of the laboratory building is the critical path in the program. The construction is being supervised and contracted for in Iran by the overburdened engineering department of NIGC. Delay of building opening shifts the entire program to the right (except for the planning stage), resulting in increased costs and scheduling problems as follows:

   a. Material costs
   b. Labor costs
   c. Scheduling problems
   d. Storage costs

3. Transportation of Equipment

   The large amount of construction in Iran will result in long delays in unloading at Persian Gulf ports. On a similar program conducted previously, just before shipment of completed equipment and instruments, the contractor was made aware by the customer that there would be a delay of up to eighteen months. Alternate shipping plans were worked out by the customer (who was responsible for shipment from New York to the site in Tehran) involving shipment to Hamburg, Germany, and overland shipment by truck from Hamburg to Tehran. This shipping route took about four months.

4. Language Difficulties

   There was great uncertainty at the outset of the contract about accurate communication because of the language problem. All parties at the customer could speak English, but not well. This resulted in occasional misunderstandings.

5. Building Subcontractor

   The building work was contracted out by NIGC to a local construction firm.

Results

The company's strategy for shipping the building materials was to fabricate components prior to shipping. The shipping schedule was of prime importance because a delay in shipping, for whatever cause, would immediately put the project behind.

It was projected that any sizable delay would increase costs in the area of materials and labor.

Plans were initiated to commence with a screening of Iranian labor and for training of selected personnel in the event of a shipping delay. An analysis of costs was made based on an extension of the construction period over an additional twenty months, otherwise the training would take place at the completion of the construction. Iran had a shortage of labor and might be hard pressed in finding an ample work force for this project.

Alternative plans were set up in the event of a delay in the construction schedule, problems involving scheduling personnel for transportation to the project, and storage of materials and supplies.

The following schedule is a comparative analysis of the two periods:

	18 mo.	38 mo.	Unfavorable Variance
Engineering	$ 96,731	$105,382	$ 8,651
Program Management	26,349	28,424	2,075
Finance	14,654	15,980	1,326
Operations	368,953	406,567	37,614
Materials	206,987	216,749	9,762
Indirect Costs	99,916	108,234	8,318
Corporate Costs	8,127	8,806	679
Total Costs	$821,717	$890,142	$68,425

Plans were made to construct energy supply generators to combat the possibility of a power shortage since there is a utility shortage in Iran.

A comparison of the base cost is estimated on an 18-month construction period extended to the 38 months. The above analysis for the two periods does not reflect a profit factor, which, however, is a ten percent escalation factor for raw materials and a demanning ratio of 10 percent. The termination liability ratio is 0 percent and salary increases are equal to 6 percent per year. Corporate costs and indirect costs are 1 percent and 14 percent, respectively.

CASE STUDY: POLYPRODUCTS INCORPORATED

Polyproducts Incorporated, a major producer of rubber components employs 800 people and is organized with a matrix structure. Exhibit 1 shows the salary structure for the company and Exhibit 2 identifies the overhead rate projections for the next two years.

Polyproducts has been very successful at maintaining its current business base with approximately 10 percent overtime. Both exempt and non-exempt employees are paid overtime at the rate of time and half. All overtime hours are burdened at an overhead rate of 30 percent.

On April 16, Polyproducts received a request for proposal from Capital Corporation (see Exhibit 3). Polyproducts had an established policy for competitive

Exhibit 1. Salary Structure.

	PAY SCALE	
GRADE		HOURLY RATE
1		3.00
2		4.00
3		5.00
4		7.00
5		9.00
6		11.00
7		13.00
8		14.00
9		15.00

Number of Employees per grade

Department	1	2	3	4	5	6	7	8	9	Total
R&D			5	40	20	10	12	8	5	100
Design		3	5	40	30	10	10	2		100
Project Engineering						30	15	10	5	60
Project Management							10	10	10	30
Cost Accounting				20	10	10	10	10		60
Contracts						3	4	2	1	10
Publication		3	5	3	3	3	3			20
Computers				2	3	3	1	1		10
Manufacturing Engineering				2	7	7	3	1		20
Industrial Engineering					4	3	2	1		10
Facilities					8	9	10	7	1	35
Quality Control				3	4	5	5	2	1	20
Production Line				55	50	50	30	10	5	200
Traffic				2	2	1				5
Procurement				2	2	2	2	1	1	10
Safety						2	2	1		5
Inventory Control		2	2	2	2	1	1			10

bidding. First, they would analyze the marketplace to see whether or not it would be advantageous for them to compete. This task was normally assigned to the marketing group (which operated on overhead). If the marketing group responded favorably, then Polyproducts would go through the necessary pricing procedures to determine a bid price.

On April 24, the marketing group displayed a prospectus on the four companies which would most likely be competing with Polyproducts for the Capital contract. This is shown in Exhibit 4.

At the same time, top management of Polyproducts made the following projections concerning the future business over the next 18 months:

1. Salary increases would be given to all employees at the beginning of the 13th month.

Exhibit 2. Overhead Structure.

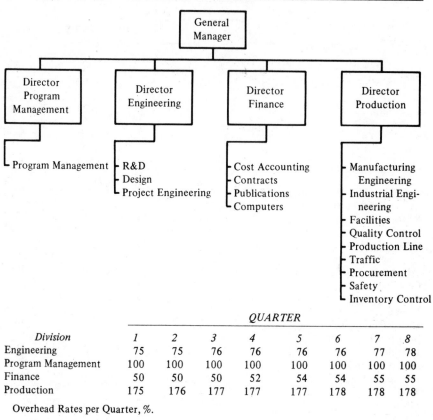

	QUARTER							
Division	*1*	*2*	*3*	*4*	*5*	*6*	*7*	*8*
Engineering	75	75	76	76	76	76	77	78
Program Management	100	100	100	100	100	100	100	100
Finance	50	50	50	52	54	54	55	55
Production	175	176	177	177	177	178	178	178

Overhead Rates per Quarter, %.

2. If the Capital contract was won, then the overhead rates would go down 0.5 percent each quarter (assuming no strike by employees).
3. There was a possibility that the union would go out on strike if the salary increases were not satisfactory. Based upon previous experience, the strike would last between one and two months. It was possible that, due to union demands, the overhead rates would increase by 1 percent per quarter for each quarter after the strike (due to increased fringe benefit packages).
4. With the current work force, the new project would probably have to be done on overtime. (At least 75 percent of all namhours were estimated to be performed on overtime). The alternative would be to hire additional employees.
5. All materials could be obtained from one vendor. It can be assumed that raw materials cost $200/unit (without scrap factors) and that these raw materials are new to Polyproducts.

On May 1, Roger Henning was selected by Jim Grimm, the Director of Project Management, to head up the project.

Grimm: Roger, we've got a problem on this one. When you determine your final bid, see if you can account for the fact that we may lose our union. I'm not sure exactly how that will impact our bid. I'll leave that up to you. All I know is that a lot of our people are getting unhappy with the union. See what numbers you can generate.

Henning: I've read the RFP and have a question about inventory control. Should I look at quantity discount buying for raw materials?

Grimm: Yes. But be careful about your assumptions. I want to know all of the assumptions you make.

Henning: How stable is our business base over the next eighteen months?

Grimm: You had better consider both an increase and a decrease of 10 percent. Get me the costs for all cases. Incidentally, the grapevine says that there might be follow-on contracts if we perform well. You know what that means.

Henning: Okay. I get the costs for each case and then we'll determine what our best bid will be.

Exhibit 3. Request for Proposal

Capital Corporation is seeking bids for 10,000 rubber components which must be manufactured according to specifications supplied by the customer. The contractor will be given sufficient flexibility for material selection and testing provided that all testing include latest developments in technology. All material selection and testing must be within specifications. All vendors selected by the contractor must be (1) certified as a vendor for continuous procurement (follow-on contracts will not be considered until program completion), and (2) operating with a quality control program that is acceptable to both the customer and contractor.

The following timetable must be adhered to:

Month after Go-ahead	Description
2	R & D completed and preliminary design meeting held
4	Qualification completed and final design review meeting held
5	Production set-up completed
9	Delivery of 3000 units
13	Delivery of 3500 units
17	Delivery of 3500 units
18	Final report and cost summary

The contract will be firm-fixed-price and the contractor can develop his own work breakdown structure upon final approval by the customer.

Exhibit 4. Prospectus.

COMPANY	BUSINESS BASE $ MILLION	GROWTH RATE LAST YEAR (%)	PROFIT %	R&D PERSONNEL	CONTRACTS IN HOUSE	NUMBER OF EMPLOYEES	OVERTIME (%)	PERSONNEL TURNOVER (%)
Alpha	10	10	5	Below Avg.	6	30	5	1.0
Beta	20	10	7	Above Avg.	15	250	30	0.25
Gamma	50	10	15	Avg.	4	550	20	0.50
Poly-products	100	15	10	Avg.	30	800	10	1.0

On May 15, Roger Henning received a memo from the pricing department summing up the base case man-hour estimates. (This is shown in Exhibit 5 and 6) Now Roger Henning wondered what people he could obtain from the functional departments and what would be a reasonable bid to make.

EXHIBIT 5

To: Roger Henning
From: Pricing Department
Subject: Rubber Components Production

1. All manhours in the Exhibit 6 are based upon performance standards for a Grade 7 employee. For each grade below 7, add 10% of the Grade 7 standard and subtract 10% of the Grade standard for each employee above Grade 7. This applies to all departments as long as they are direct labor hours (i.e., not administrative support as in Project 1).
2. Time duration is fixed at 18 months.
3. Each production run normally requires four months. The company has enough raw materials on hand for R & D, but must allow 2 months lead time for purchases that would be needed for a production run. Unfortunately, the vendors cannot commit large purchases, but will commit to monthly deliveries up to a maximum of 1000 units of raw materials per month. Furthermore, the vendors will guarantee a fixed cost of $200 per raw material unit during the first 12 months of the project only. Material escalation factors are expected at month 13 due to renegotiation of the United Rubber Workers contracts.
4. Use the following Work Breakdown Structure:

> Program: Rubber Component Production
>   Project 1: Support
>   TASK 1: Project Office
>   TASK 2: Functional Support
>   Project 2: Preproduction
>   TASK 1: R & D
>   TASK 2: Qualification
>   Project 3: Production
>   TASK 1: Set-up
>   TASK 2: Production

CASE STUDY: SMALL PROJECT COST ESTIMATING AT PERCY COMPANY

Paul graduated from college in June, 1970, with a degree in industrial engineering. He accepted a job as a manufacturing engineer in the Manufacturing Division of Percy Company. His prime responsibility was performing estimates for the Manufacturing Division. Each estimate was then given to the appropriate project office for consideration. The estimation procedure history had shown the estimates to be valid.

In 1975, Paul was promoted to project engineer. His prime responsibility was the coordination of all estimates for work to be completed by all of the divisions. For one full year Paul went by the book and did not do any estimating except for project office personnel manpower. After all, he was now in the project management division which contained job descriptions including such words as "coordinating and integrating."

In 1976 Paul was transferred to small program project management. This was a new organization designed to perform low-cost projects. The problem was that these projects could not withstand the expenses needed for formal divisional cost estimates. For five projects, Paul's estimates were "right on the money." But the sixth project incurred a cost overrun of $20,000 in the Manufacturing Division.

In November, 1977, a meeting was called to resolve the question of "Why did the overrun occur?" The attendees included the general manager, all division managers and directors, the project manager and Paul. Paul now began to worry about what he should say in his defense.

CASE STUDY: THE BATHTUB PERIOD

The award of the Scott contract on January 3, 1977, left Park Industries elated. The Scott Project, if managed correctly, offered tremendous opportunities for follow-on work over the next several years. Park's management considered the Scott Project as strategic in nature.

The Scott Project was a ten month endeavor to develop a new product for Scott Corporation. Scott informed Park Industries that sole-source production contracts would follow, for at least five years, assuming that the initial R & D effort proved satisfactory. All follow-on contracts were to be negotiated on a year-to-year basis.

Jerry Dunlap was selected as project manager. Although he was young and eager, he understood the importance of the effort for future growth of the company. Dunlap was given some of the best employees to fill out his project office as part of Park's matrix organization. The Scott Project maintained a project office of seven full-time people, including Dunlap, throughout the duration of the project In addition, eight people from the functional department were selected for representation as functional project team members; four full-time and four half-time.

Although the work load fluctuated, the man-power level for the project office and team members was constant for the duration of the project at 2080 hours per month. The company assumed that each hour worked incurred a cost of $20.00 per person, fully burdened.

At the end of June, with four months remaining on the project, Scott Corporation informed Park Industries that, due to a projected cash flow problem, follow-on work would not be awarded until the first week in March (1978). This posed a tremendous problem for Jerry Dunlap because he did not wish to break up the project office. If he permitted his key people to be assigned to other projects, there would be no guarantee that he could get them back at the beginning of the follow-on work. Good project office personnel are always in demand.

Exhibit 6. Program: Rubber Component Production.

PROJECT	TASK	DEPARTMENT	1	2	3	4	5	6	7	8	9	10	11	12	13	14	15	16	17	18
											MONTH									
1	1	Prog. Mgt.	480	480	480	480	480	480	480	480	480	480	480	480	480	480	480	480	480	480
1	2	R & D	16	16	16	16	16	16	16	16	16	16	16	16	16	16	16	16	16	16
		Proj. Eng.	320	320	320	320	320	320	320	320	320	320	320	320	320	320	320	320	320	320
		Cost Acct.	80	80	80	320	320	320	320	320	320	320	320	320	320	320	320	320	320	320
		Contracts	320	320	320	320	320	320	320	320	320	320	320	320	320	320	320	320	320	320
		Manu. Eng.	320	320	320	320	320	320	320	320	320	320	320	320	320	320	320	320	320	320
		Quality Cont.	160	160	160	160	160	160	160	160	160	160	160	160	160	160	160	160	160	160
		Production	160	160	160	160	160	160	160	160	160	160	160	160	160	160	160	160	160	160
		Procurement	80	80	80	80	80	80	80	80	80	80	80	80	80	80	80	80	40	40
		Publications	80	80	80	80	80	80	80	80	80	80	80	80	80	80	80	80	80	600
		Invent. Cont.	80	80	80	80	80	80	80	80	80	80	80	80	80	80	80	80	40	40
2	1	R & D	480	480																
		Proj. Eng.	160	160																
		Manu. Eng.	160	160																
2	2	R & D			80	80														
		Proj. Eng.			160	160														
		Manu. Eng.			160	160														
		Ind. Eng.			40	40														
		Facilities			20	20														
		Quality Cont.			160	160														
		Production			600	600														
		Safety			20	20														
3	1	Proj. Eng.					160													
		Manu. Eng.					160													
		Facilities					80													
		Quality Cont.					160													
		Production					320													
3	2	Proj. Eng.						160	160	160	160	160	160	160	160	160	160	160	160	160
		Manu. Eng.						320	320	320	320	320	320	320	320	320	320	320	320	320
		Quality Cont.						320	320	320	320	320	320	320	320	320	320	320	320	320
		Production						1600	1600	1600	1600	1600	1600	1600	1600	1600	1600	1600	1600	1600
		Safety						20	20	20	20	20	20	20	20	20	20	20	20	20

Jerry estimated that he needed $40,000 per month during the "bathtub" period to support and maintain his key people. Fortunately, the bathtub period fell over Christmas and New Years, a time when the plant would be shut down for seventeen days. Between the vacation days that his key employees would be taking, and the small special projects that his people could be temporarily assigned to on other programs, Jerry revised his estimate to $125,000 for the entire bathtub period.

At the weekly team meeting, Jerry told the program team members that they would have to "tighten their belts" in order to establish a management reserve of $125,000. The project team understood the necessity for this action and began rescheduling and replanning until a management reserve of this size could be realized. Because the contract was firm-fixed-price, all schedules for administrative support (i.e., project office and project team members) were extended through February 28 on the supposition that this additional time was needed for final cost data accountability and program report documentation.

Jerry informed his boss, Frank Howard, the division head for project management, as to the problems with the bathtub period, Frank was the intermediary between Jerry and the general manager. Frank agreed with Jerry's approach to the problem and requested to be kept informed.

On September 15, Frank told Jerry that he wanted to "book" the management reserve of $125,000 as excess profit since it would influence his (Frank's) Christmas bonus. Frank and Jerry argued for a while, with Frank constantly saying, "Don't worry! You'll get your key people back. I'll see to that. But I want those uncommitted funds recorded as profit and the program closed out by November 1."

Jerry was furious with Frank's lack of interest in maintaining the current organizational membership.

a. Should Jerry go to the general manager?
b. Should the key people be supported on overhead?
c. If this were a cost-plus program, would you consider approaching the customer with your problem in hopes of relief?
d. If you were the customer of this cost-plus program, what would your response be for additional funds for the bathtub period, assuming cost overrun?
e. Would your previous answer change if the program had the money available as a result of an underrun?
f. How do you prevent this situation from reoccurring on all yearly follow-on contracts?

CASE STUDY: MARGO COMPANY

"I've called this meeting, gentlemen, because that paper factory we call a computer organization is driving up our overhead rates," snorted Richard Margo, president, as he looked around the table at the vice-presidents of Project Management, Engineering, Manufacturing, Marketing, Administration, and Information Systems. We seem to be developing reports faster than we can update our computer facility. Just one year ago, we updated our computer and now we're operating three shifts a day, seven days a week. Where do we go from here?"

V.P. Information: As you all know, Richard asked me about two months ago to investigate this gigantic increase in the flow of paperwork. There's no question that we're getting too many reports. The question is, are we paying too much money for the information that we get? I've surveyed all of our departments and their key personnel. Most of the survey questionnaires indicate that we're getting too much information. Only a small percentage of each report appears to be necessary. In addition, many of the reports arrive too late. I'm talking about scheduled reports, not planning, demand or exception reports.

V.P. Project Management: Every report my people receive is necessary for us to effectively make decisions with regard to planning, organizing and controlling each project. My people are the biggest users and we can't live with less reports.

V.P. Information: Can your people live with less information in each report? Can some of the reports be received less frequently?

V.P. Project Management: Some of our reports have too much information in them. But we need them at the frequency we have now.

V.P. Engineering: My people utilize about 20 percent of the information in most of our reports. Once our people find the information they want, the report is discarded. That's because we know that each project manager will retain a copy. Also, only the department managers and section supervisors read the reports.

V.P. Information: Can engineering and manufacturing get the information they need from other sources, as the project office?

V.P. Project Management: Wait a minute! My people don't have time to act as paper pushers for each department manager. We all know that the departments can't function without these reports. Why should we assume the burden?

V.P. Information: All I'm trying to say is that many of our reports can be combined into smaller ones and possibly made more concise. Most of our reports are flexible enough to meet changes in our operating business. We have two sets of reports; one for the customer and one for us. If the customer wants the report in a specific fashion, he pays for it. Why can't we act as our own customer and try to make a reporting system which we can all use?

V.P. Engineering: Many of the reports obviously don't justify the cost. Can we generate the minimum number of reports and pass it on to someone higher or lower in the organization?

V.P. Project Management: We need weekly reports, and we need them on Monday mornings. I know our computer people don't like to work on Sunday evenings, but we have no choice. If we don't have those reports on Monday mornings, we can't control time, cost, and performance.

V.P. Information: There are no reports generated from the pertinent data in our original computer runs. This looks to me like every report is a one-shot deal. There has to be room for improvement. I have prepared a checklist for each of you with four major questions. Do you want summary or detailed information? How do you want the output to look? How many copies do you need? How often do you need these reports?

Richard Margo: In project organizational forms, the project exists as a separate entity except for administrative purposes. These reports are part of that administrative purpose. Combining this with the high cost of administration in our project structure, we'll never remain competitive unless we lower our overhead. I'm gonna leave it up to you guys. Try to reduce the number of reports, but don't sacrifice the necessary information you need to control the projects and your resources.

CASE STUDY: PAYTON CORPORATION

Payton Corporation had decided to respond to a government RFP for the R & D phase on a new project. The statement of work specified that the project must be completed within 90 days after go-ahead and that the contract would be at a fixed cost and fee.

The majority of the work would be accomplished by the development lab. According to government regulations, the estimated cost must be based upon the *average* cost of the entire department, which was $9.50 per hour (unburdened).

Payton won the contract for a total package (cost plus fee) of $102,000. After the first weekly labor report was analyzed, it became evident that the development lab was spending $13.75 per hour. The project manager decided to discuss the problem with the manager of the development lab.

Project Manager: Obviously you know why I'm here. At the rate that you're spending money, we'll overrun our budget by 50 percent.

Lab Manager: That's your problem, not mine. When I estimate the cost to do a job, I submit only the hours necessary based upon historical standards. The pricing department converts the hours to dollars based upon department averages.

Project Manager: Well, why are we using the most expensive people? Obviously there must be lower-salaried people capable of performing the work.

Lab Manager: Yes, I do have lower salaried people, but none who can complete the job within the two months required by the contract. I have to use people high on the learning curve, and they're not cheap. You should have told the pricing department to increase the average cost for the department.

Project Manager: I wish I could, but government regulations forbid this. If we were ever audited, or if this proposal were compared to other salary structures in other proposals, we would be in deep trouble. The only legal way to accomplish this would be to set up a new department for those higher-paid employees working on this project. Then the average department salary would be correct. Unfortunately, the administrative costs of setting up a temporary unit for only two months is prohibitive. For long duration projects, this technique is often employed. Why couldn't you have increased the hours to compensate for the increased dollars required?

Lab Manager: I have to submit labor justifications for all hours I estimate. If I were to get audited, my job would be on the line. Remember, we had to submit labor justification for all work as part of the proposal. Perhaps next time management might think twice before bidding on a short-duration project. You might try talking to the customer to get his opinion.

Project Manager: His response would probably be the same regardless of whether I explained the situation to him before we submitted the proposal or now, after we have negotiated it. There's a good chance that I've just lost my Christmas bonus.

    a. What is the basis for the problem?
    b. Who is at fault?
    c. How can the present situation be corrected?
    d. Is there any way that this situation can be prevented from reoccurring?
    e. How would you handle this situation on a longer duration project, say one year, assuming that multiple departments are involved and that no new departments were established other than possibly the project office?
    f. Should a customer be willing to accept monetary responsibility for this type of situation, possibly by permitting established standards to be deviated from? If so, then how many months should be considered as a short duration project?

CASE STUDY: CROSBY MANUFACTURING CORPORATION

"I've called this meeting to resolve a major problem with our Management Cost and Control System (MCCS)," remarked Wilfred Livingston, president. "We're having one hell of a time trying to meet competition with our antiquated MCCS reporting procedures. Last year we were considered non-responsive to three large government contracts because we could not adhere to the customer's financial reporting requirements. The government has recently shown a renewed interest in Crosby Manufacturing Corporation. If we can computerize our project financial reporting procedure, we'll be in great shape to meet the competition head-on. The customer might even waive the financial reporting requirements if we show our immediate intent to convert."

    Crosby Manufacture was $5 million a year electronics component manufacturing firm in 1975, at which time Wilfred "Willy" Livingston became president. His first major act was to reorganize the 700 employees into a modified matrix structure. This reorganization was the first step in Livingston's long-range plan to obtain large government contracts. The matrix provided the customer focal point policy that government agencies prefer. After three years, the matrix seemed to be working. Now we can begin the second phase; an improved MCCS policy.
    On October 20, 1978 Livingston called a meeting with department managers from project management, cost accounting, MIS, data processing and planning.

Livingston: We have to replace our present computer with a more advanced model so as to update our MCCS reporting procedures. In order for us to grow, we'll have to develop capabilities for keeping two or even three different sets of books for our customers. Our present computer does not have this capability. We're talking about a sizable cash outlay, not necessarily to impress our customers, but to increase our business base and grow. We need weekly, or even daily, cost data so as to better control our projects.

MIS Manager: I guess the first step in the design, development and implementation process would be the feasibility study. I have prepared a list of the major topics which are normally included in a feasibility study of this sort. (See Exhibit 1).

Livingston: What kind of costs are you considering in the feasibility study?

MIS Manager: The major cost items include input/output demands; processing; storage capacity; rental, purchase or lease of a system; non-recurring expenditures; recurring expenditures; cost of supplies; facility requirements; and training requirements. We'll have to get a lot of this information from the EDP department.

EDP Manager: You must remember that, for a short period of time, we'll end up with two computer systems in operation at the same time. This cannot be helped. However, I have prepared a typical (abbreviated) schedule of my own. (See Exhibit 2). You'll notice from the right-hand column that I'm somewhat optimistic as to how long it should take us."

Livingston: Have we prepared a checklist on how to evaluate a vendor?

EDP Manager: Besides the 'benchmark' test, I have prepared a list of topics which we must include in evaluation of any vendor. (See Exhibit 3). We should plan to either call on or visit other installations that have purchased the same equipment and see the system in action. Unfortunately, we may have to commit real early and begin developing software packages. As a matter of fact, using the principle of concurrency, we should begin developing our software package right now.

Livingston: Because of the importance of this project, I'm going to violate our normal structure and appoint Tim Emary from our planning group as project leader. He's not as knowledgeable as you people are in regard to computers, but he does know how to lay out a schedule and get the job done. I'm sure your

Exhibit 1. Feasibility Study

- Objectives of the study
- Costs
- Benefits
- Manual or computer-based solution?
- Objectives of the system
- Input requirements
- Output requirements
- Processing requirements
- Preliminary system description
- Evaluation of bids from the vendors
- Financial analysis
- Conclusions

Exhibit 2. Typical Schedule (in months).

ACTIVITY	NORMAL TIME TO COMPLETE	CRASH TIME TO COMPLETE
Management Go-ahead	0	0
Release of preliminary system specs.	6	2
Receipt of bids on specs	2	1
Order hardware and systems software	2	1
Flowcharts completed	2	2
Applications programs completed	3	6
Receipt of hardware and systems software	3	3
Testing and debugging done	2	2
Documentation, if required	2	2
Changeover completed	22	15*

*This assumes that some of the activities can be run in parallel, instead of series.

people will give him all the necessary support he needs. Remember, I'll be behind this project all the way. We're going to convene again one week from today, at which time I expect to see a detailed schedule with all major milestones, team meetings, design review meetings, etc. . . . shown and identified. I'd like the project to be complete in 18 months, if possible. If there are risks in the schedule, identify them. Any questions?

CASE STUDY: NUCLEONIX INCORPORATED

"Fabrication of so little as one component of a nuclear-fueled, steam generation system may include hundreds of complex operations involving scores of outside vendors," remarked Paul Gibby, President. "The unit can weigh as much as two hundred and fifty tons upon completion. Most contracts are fixed-price, fixed incentive types, where there is an automatic ceiling on the amount of money available. We must do good and accurate planning such that the negative effects of

Exhibit 3. Vendor Support Evaluation Factors.

- Availability of hardware and software packages
- Hardware performance, delivery and past track record
- Vendor proximity and service and support record
- Emergency backup procedure
- Availability of applications programs and their compatability with our other systems
- Capacity for expansion
- Documentation
- Availability of consultants for systems programming and general training
- Who burdens training cost?
- Risk of obsolescence.
- Ease of use

changes in operating variables can be adequately assessed. Any increase in costs due to changes in the operation can only come out of profits. Emphasis is placed on minimizing costs and maintaining or increasing our target profit of 13 percent."

PROJECTS	INDUSTRIAL	NUCLEAR
short term	1 year	5 years
tactical	2-3 years	10 years
long term	5 years	20 years

Background

The strategy of Nucleonix is first of all to continue to be a viable concern and to remain a major competitor in the power generation industry. This had been accomplished by keeping operations as efficient as possible and by achieving respectable returns on investments so that the company can continue to grow and remain a technological leader. The company also believes that it has a social commitment to the communities in which it resides and to the employees. Since the employees are considered to be the company's most valuable asset, it would be a fatal mistake to neglect them in the setting of the company's strategies.

To achieve company goals, management must deal with the operating variables which, in the long run, may not be controllable or predictable. Operating variables for the nuclear power generation industry can be classified as external and internal. External variables are normally completely out of the hands of the company. These include demand for new power plants, government regulations, costs of fuels, government policies, and research expenditures.

Of particular interest are the internal variables. These variables affect the day-to-day operations, particularly for contracts that have already been signed. The variables include overhead rates, labor costs, material costs, energy costs, the availability of skilled labor, and the availability of raw materials. These variables are often estimated for future periods for purposes of deriving costs for contracts being negotiated or to be negotiated at a later date. Estimates cannot include unforeseen circumstances such as an unusually severe winter, increased inflation, or a prolonged labor strike. Management's job is to adjust the operation so that such occurrences have a minimal effect, if possible.

Management can effectively counter increased costs of one variable by decreasing the costs of another variable. The availability of skilled labor can be met by company-sponsored training programs and the availability of raw materials can be met by stockpiles or company supplied materials. If proper management controls are used, the effects of changing internal variables can be determined and proper steps can be taken to assure that the corporate strategies are adhered to.

Planning The Grove Electric Project

On March 15, 1976 Paul Gibby decided that Nucleonix had the necessary resources to bid and win the Grove Electric Project for development and construction of nuclear power generation equipment. Paul selected John Wight as project manager, and Henry Ash as the chief pricing specialist. Both men had over ten years experience with Nucleonix and were highly capable individuals.

Gibby: We've gotten burned the last several times on some of our proposals. We haven't done a good job on predicting what can go wrong and trying to anticipate increased costs. Let's see if we can do better on this one. We're also under a tight budget of $50,000 for bid and proposal activities on the Grove Electric Project, so try to minimize the amount of pricing that's necessary, especially the size of the Work Breakdown Structure.

Wight: Henry and I have already developed a tenative Work Breakdown Structure. The RFP requires that four units be produced over a sixty month period. Because of the similarity between units, we can reduce the size of the WBS. We could have just as easily broken down such operations as fabrication of components into hundreds of subtasks. We're just considering these as a single task (i.e., level three of the WBS), and we'll let the department managers worry about the subtask breakdown during internal control activities. We, therefore, found it possible to have just three projects, with a total of nine tasks. This should be adequate for us to do some perturbation analysis. Later, if the customer wants additional cost breakdowns, we'll either give it to him or bill him for it.

The work breakdown structure for the program being considered is presented below. Due to the magnitude of the problem, it is impractical to consider the program in its entirety. For this reason, such operations as fabrication, which may be broken down into hundreds of sub-tasks, are considered as single tasks. The work breakdown structure that is presented, although relatively gross in detail, includes all the major operations necessary for program completion.

Work Breakdown Structure

Program: Nuclear Component Fabrication

Project I. Engineering
Task 1. Design and Analysis — To do all functional and structural design work

Task 2. Engineering Graphics Design — To provide all sketches, forgoing drawings for the components being fabricated

Task 3. Materials Engineering — To procure needed materials and to assure all materials meet contract requirements and schedules

Project II. Manufacturing
Task 1. Shop Fabrication — To perform all machinery, welding, grinding, and assembly operations

Task 2. Quality Control — To check contract compliance with drawings and quality standards set forth through contract specifications

Task 3. Component Testing — To pressure test the component to assure operational acceptability

Task 4. Component Shipment — To prepare the component for shipment and proper shipping equipment

Project III. General Support

Task 1. Production Control — To set up production schedules and to coordinate manufacturing with material procurements and with engineering

Task 2. Inventory Control — To store and supply all manufacturing related materials to assure their availability when they are needed

"All work associated with the program being analyzed is done through the use of four divisions and thirteen departments. The divisions and departments involved and their respective responsibilities are as follows:"

Division I. Engineering

Dept. 1. Technology — To keep the company current on all technologies related to the power generation industry

Dept 2. Contract Engineering — To do all design and analysis work as well as to provide engineering support for manufacturing

Dept 3. Engineering Graphics — To provide all drawings for the various departments

Division II. Program Management

— To coordinate the efforts of all disciplines for the various programs

Division III. Finance

Dept. 1. Proposition Dept. — To prepare estimates and to negotiate new contracts and changes to present contracts

Dept. 2. Material Procurement — To procure all materials needed for the completion of a contract

Dept. 3. Cost Accounting — To keep accurate records of costs in all departments for future and present reference

Division IV. Manufacturing

Dept. 1. Fabrication — To perform all assembly operations

Dept. 2. Manufacturing Engineering — To supervise the manufacturing processes

Dept. 3. Quality Control — To perform all quality control activities

Dept. 4. Inventory Control — To supervise and perform inventory controls for manufacturing

Dept. 5. Production Control — To schedule and coordinate the manufacturing efforts

Dept. 6. Shipping Dept. — To prepare the units for shipment and to provide a means of transportation

Henry Ash: I have a brief meeting with our key function people to develop the PERT and Bar Charts that we'll need for pricing out the proposal. (See Figures 1 and 2). The sixty-month activity has three critical paths; engineering, engineering graphics and cost accounting, all of which are support-type activities. This is the reason for man-hours extending beyond shipment of the fourth unit. Even though fabrication is complete at this point, these three support activities are necessary for program administration, final cost analysis, final document preparation, and customer coordination and follow-up.

Paul Gibby: O.K. Looks like you're on the right track. Since we're under a time constraint to get all of our costs together, let's meet a week from today. I'm sure you can have the base case figures by then.

Developing The Base Case

For the next seven days, Henry and John worked furiously to develop the base case cost estimates. The functional managers understood the necessity of rapid cost estimate responses, and were eager to do their part. Finally, Henry and John were ready to meet with Paul Gibby on base case cost estimates.

Ash: Well, we've developed our base case. I'm not sure that, in the little amount of time we've had, the base case is truly optimized as to activity starting points. However, it should be close enough for all practical purposes.

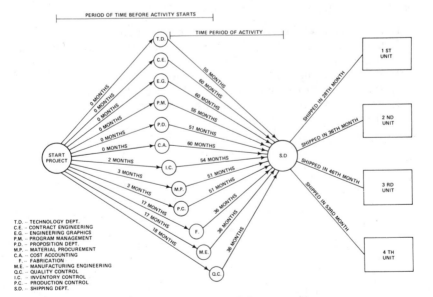

Figure 1. PERT Chart (In months).

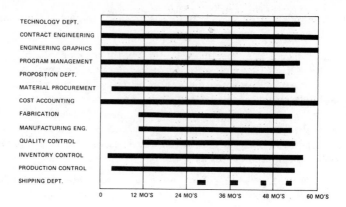

Figure 2. Bar Chart (In months).

I have graphically represented the manloading curves for each of the departments necessary to support the project. These are shown in Figures 3 through 15. The histograms indicate that for some of the department, manpower loadings are somewhat erratic while others follow predicable trends. We're going to have to smooth out our manloading. I'm sure most of our department managers can do it within cost.

Gibby: What assumptions did you put into the model? I hope they're based upon substantial data. You know, this is where we've gotten burned in the past.

Ash: I've made the following assumptions:

1. Escalation factor on raw materials = 8 percent/year
2. Demanning ratio = 70.0 percent of the following months labor and man-hour costs
3. Material commitments are 6 months or less
4. Termination liability on materials is 45 percent of commitments
5. Anticipated yearly salary increases are 7 percent
6. Profit Margin = 13 percent

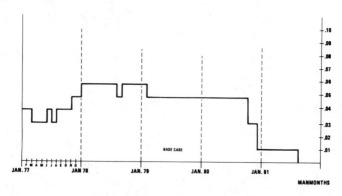

Figure 3. Technology Department.

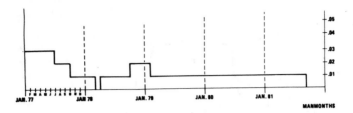

Figure 4. Program Management.

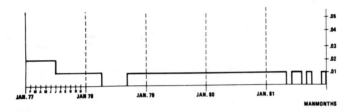

Figure 5. Proposition Department.

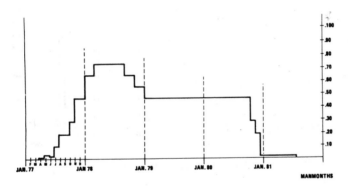

Figure 6. Material Procurement.

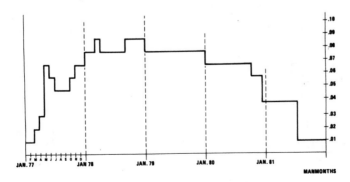

Figure 7. Cost Accounting.

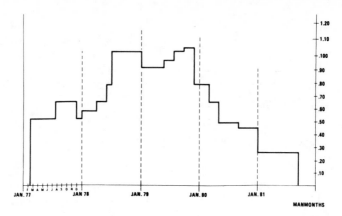

Figure 8. Inventory Control.

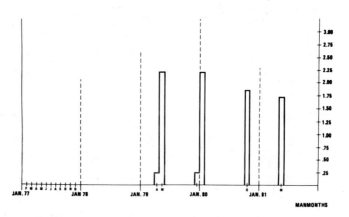

Figure 9. Shipping Department.

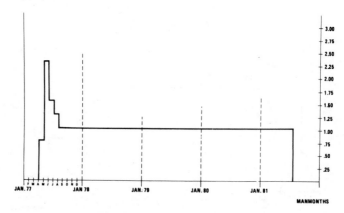

Figure 10. Production Control.

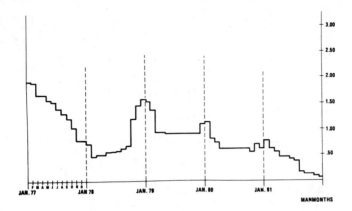

Figure 11. Contract Engineering.

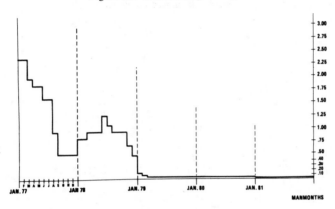

Figure 12. Engineering Graphics.

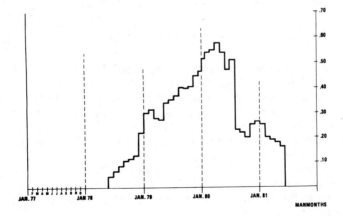

Figure 13. Fabrication.

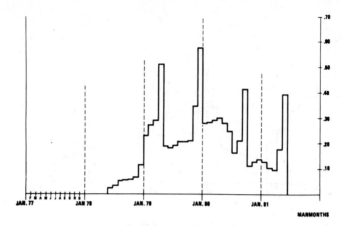

Figure 14. Manufacturing Engineering.

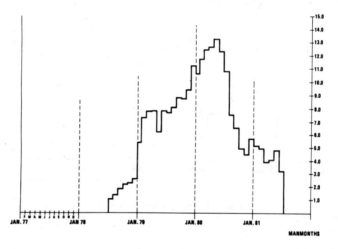

Figure 15. Quality Control.

The results of the base case analysis are graphically represented in Figures 16 through 27. These figures illustrate the total costs for each project and a breakdown of the costs for each task. It is clear from these curves that Shop Fabrication (Task 1. Project 2) is the most costly task. If significant savings are desired or required, then careful analysis of this task must be made. The perturbation which deals with the possibility of a strike illustrates the effects that the shifting of costs of this task will have on the overall program.

Since the program is considered to be a fixed-price, fixed-fee program, the company is locked into the profit, $1,903,906, which is determined by the operating variables set in the base case. Any changes in costs will either add to or subtract from the profit of the base case.

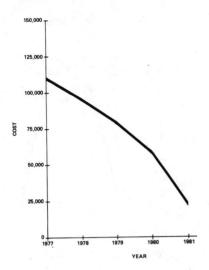

Figure 16. Yearly Cost Distribution
Project 1 (Total) Base Case.

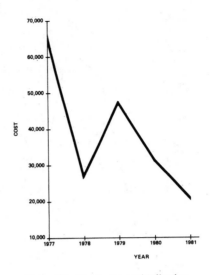

Figure 17. Yearly Cost Distribution
Task 1 Project 1 Base Case.

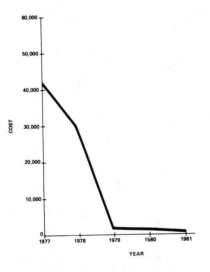

Figure 18. Yearly Cost Distribution
Task 2 Project 1 Base Case.

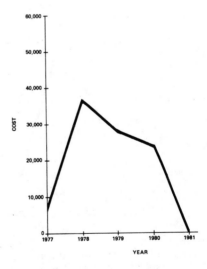

Figure 19. Yearly Cost Distribution Task
Task 3 Project 1 Base Case.

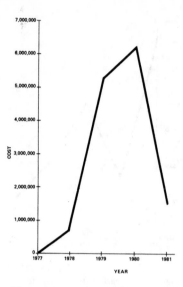

Figure 20. Yearly Cost Distribution
Project 2 (Total Base Case.

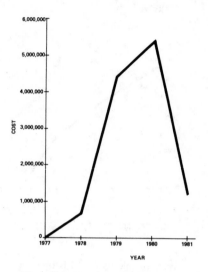

Figure 21. Yearly Cost Distribution
Task 1 Project 2 Base Case.

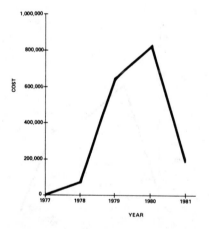

Figure 22. Yearly Cost Distribution
Task 2 Project 2 Base Case.

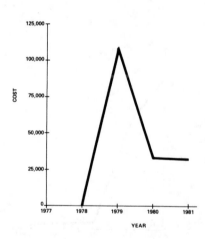

Figure 23. Yearly Cost Distribution
Task 3 Project 2 Base Case.

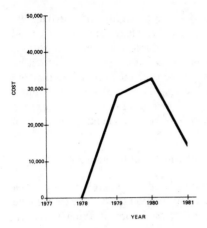

Figure 24. Yearly Cost Distribution
Task 4 Project 2 Base Case.

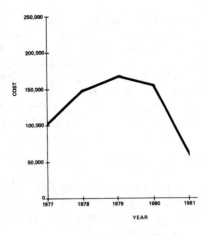

Figure 25. Yearly Cost Distribution
Project 3 (Total) Base Case.

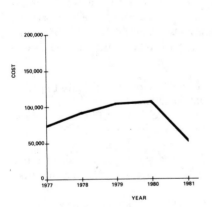

Figure 26. Yearly Cost Distribution
Task 1 Project 3 Base Case.

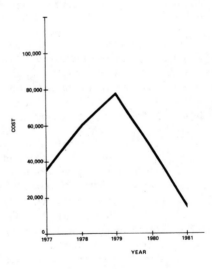

Figure 27. Yearly Cost Distribution
Task 2 Project 3 Base Case.

Gibby: I'm glad to see that you're considering the possibility of a strike. We fouled up on that one last time, and it cost us plenty. Make sure you do a good analysis on the effect of changes in the operating variables. The most important aspect for non-predictable changes in the operating variables is that the effect be noted at the time of occurrence and that proper steps be taken to assure that the changing variables do not upset corporate strategies. There is no limit to the number of changes (and combination of changes) that can occur in the operating variables. Have you made a list of what perturbations you'll be making on the base case?

Ash: Yes, we have. The following three pertubations will be made:

Two variations in salary increases will be considered. The base case assumed a normal 7 percent annual increase in salaries. Modification to the base case will be performed by changing the rate of salary increase to 5 percent and 10 percent.

Three variations in material escalation rates will be considered. The base case allowed for an 8 percent material escalation rate. A change in this rate to 10 percent and 12 percent will be analyzed and compared to the base case as well as a combination of a 10 percent materials increase and a 5 percent anticipated salary increase.

A major problem that may develop is the possibility of a labor strike. A strike may not only delay shipment dates but may push work schedules into more expensive periods which may have an adverse effect on profits. The effects that a strike would have on the base case will be considered. Several variations of a strike will also be considered to determine the best way to make up lost time. The variations of a strike that will be considered are as follows:

1. One month strike with lost time being made up over a three month period following the strike utilizing additional manpower.
2. One month strike with the lost time being made up over a five month period prior to the strike through the use of additional manpower. This assumes that the strike was anticipated.
3. One month strike which results in a general delay of the contract of a time period equal to the duration of the strike. Thus, shipments after the strike are delayed one month.
4. One month strike with the lost time being made up during a two month period following the strike through the use of overtime.

In each case, the appropriate operating variable will be changed in the base case and an analysis will be done to determine what effect the changed variable has on the total program. Special attention will be paid to the effects each perturbation has on the profit of the program.

Two weeks later, John Wight and Henry Ash presented a formal report to Paul Gibby on the results of the perturbation analysis. The report included the following information:

A. Perturbation On Anticipated Yearly Salary Increases

Background

In a bid situation, all variables must be considered when determining bottom line costs. Figure 28 shows how the overall program costs can vary with yearly salary increases. The curve is a straight line due to the fact that the overall program is labor intensive.

The base case was run assuming the average salary increase throughout the life of the program would be 7.0 percent. The next question is, "What could go wrong?" The answer is obvious that the salary increases would not be 7.0 percent, but rather 5.0 percent or 10.0 percent.

The profit for the program is figured at 13 percent of total costs and is based on an anticipated salary increase of 7.0 percent. Because the amount of profit is fixed, all salary increases above 7.0 percent must decrease overall profits.

Analysis

The overall cost of the program and projects 1, 2, and 3 increased lineary as the salary increased. It, therefore, followed that profits varied inversely with percent salary increases. This effect can be seen in Figures 29 through 32. Taking the analysis one step further, the percentage increase or decrease in profits as related to salary increases can be seen in Figures 33 through 36. Project 1 will suffer the least if in fact salaries increased at a rate of 10.0 percent rather than 7.0 percent. Project 3 will suffer the most by having salaries increased 10.0 percent annually rather than 7.0 percent. The profits for the overall program will be 8.9 percent if salaries increased 10.0 percent annually, 13.0 percent if salaries increase 7.0 percent annually, and 15.62 percent if salaries increased 5.0 percent annually.

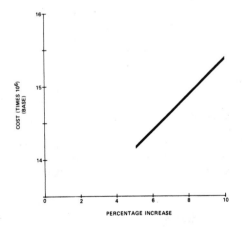

Figure 28. Overall Total Program Cost With Varying Salary Increases.

Figure 29. Profits As A Result Of
Varying Salary Increases Ref - Base
Case Project 1.

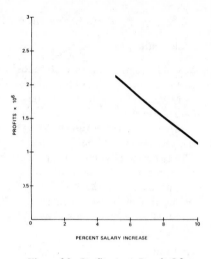

Figure 30. Profits As A Result Of
Varying Salary Increases Ref - Base
Case Project 2.

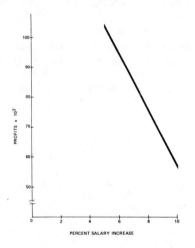

Figure 31. Profits As A Result Of
Varying Salary Increases Ref - Base
Case Project 3.

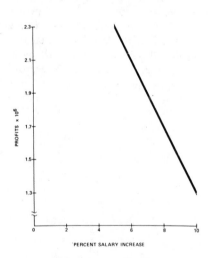

Figure 32. Profits As A Result Of
Varying Salary Increases Ref - Base
Case Overall Program

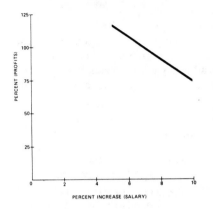

Figure 33. Percent Profit Increase/Decrease
Vs Percent Salary Increase
(Base = 7.0%) Project 1.

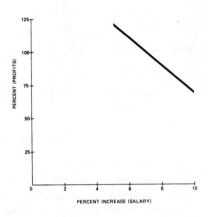

Figure 34. Percent Profit Increase/Decrease
Vs Percent Salary Increase
(Base = 7.0%) Project 2.

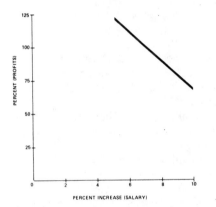

Figure 35. Percent Profit Increase/Decrease
Vs Percent Salary Increase
(Base = 7.0%) Project 3.

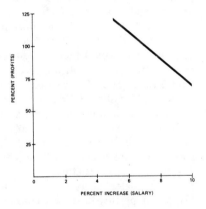

Figure 36. Percent Profit Increase/Decrease
Vs Percent Salary Increase
(Base = 7.0%) Overall Program.

Conclusion

Salary increases are real. If anticipated annual salary increases are less than the actual increases, the profit will decrease resulting in program or any project in the program being cut short. Therefore, past history of salary trends, plus sound management decisions, should be used when speculating salary trends for the life of the program.

B. Material Escalation Rate

The base case assumed an 8 percent escalation factor on raw materials. Two perturbations were considered to determine the effect that a 10 percent and 12 percent escalation factor would have on the base case. A third perturbation using a 10 percent escalation factor in combination with a 5 percent salary increase was also performed. The latter perturbation was analyzed to determine whether or not salary decreases could offset a material increase in order to keep the profit at 13 percent of costs.

For a 10 and 12 percent materials escalation factor, the output of the computer program was examined and compared to the base case in order to determine what projects and tasks are affected and how much they are affected. Once this was determined the effect on the entire program could be established.

Examination of the base case indicates that the only project which involves materials, and would therefore suffer increased costs as well as contribute to increased costs of the entire project, is Project 2, Operations. Within that project, only Task 1 (Shop Fabrication) involves materials cost. Exhibit I indicates summary costs for Shop Fabrication, Task Package 1-2-1.

Increased materials costs will affect the total program. Since this is a fixed-price, fixed-fee contract, any increased costs will have to come out of the expected profit, which in this program is 13 percent of total costs. Exhibit I shows the amount by which profit will be reduced assuming a 10 percent and a 12 percent cost of materials escalation.

If anticipated salary increases can be reduced, increased materials cost can be offset. A perturbation was considered using a 10 percent materials escalation factor and a 5 percent anticipated salary increase. The base case assumed a 7 percent anticipated salary increase. Exhibit II indicates the differences in the two perturbations compared to the base case. Loss of profit by increased materials cost can be offset by reduced salary increases. Actually, profits are increased by $16,825 in a combination salary decrease/materials cost increase, indicating that salary increases would not have to be reduced to as much as 5 percent in order to realize the expected profit.

Exhibit III shows total program costs by year and indicates overall increases in the total five year program for a 10 percent and a 12 percent escalation factor. It is also apparent from Exhibit III that increased materials costs do not affect the project until the second year and then only slightly. The fourth year of the project shows the greatest material expenditures.

Exhibit I. Shop Fabrication, Task Package: 1-2-1.

COST	ESCALATION FACTOR		
	8%*	10%	12%
Materials	3,495,099	3,671,167	3,853,409
Total (Incl. Labor)	9,400,000	9,576,076	9,758,318
Indirect Costs	1,506,133	1,533,622	1,562,044
Total	10,906,141	11,109,698	11,320,362
Corporate Costs	757,384	771,244	785,575
Total	11,663,525	11,880,942	12,105,937
Profit (13%)	1,516,258	1,544,522	1,573,771
Total	13,179,783	13,425,464	13,679,708
Amt. Profit Reduced:		28,264	57,513
Percent Profit:	13	12.8	12.6

*Base Case.

Increased materials costs will also increase the amount of commitments, amount of termination liability, and amount of expenditures needed to run the program. To illustrate these types of increased material costs effects, consider Exhibit IV which shows the materials expenditures for the program assuming 8 percent, 10 percent, and 12 percent materials escalation factors.

Exhibit II. Shop Fabrication, Task Package: 1-2-1.
Combination Materials Labor Perturbation.

COST	ESCALATION FACTOR		
	8%/7%*	10%/7%	10%/5%
Materials	3,495,099	3,671,167	3,671,167
Total (Incl. Labor)	9,400,000	9,576,076	9,295,703
Indirect Costs	1,506,133	1,533,622	1,489,445
Total	10,906,141	11,109,698	10,785,148
Corporate Costs	757,384	771,244	748,958
Total	11,663,525	11,880,942	11,534,106
Profit	1,516,258	1,544,522	1,499,433
Total	13,179,783	13,425,464	13,033,539
Amt. Profit Reduced:		28,264	
Amt. Profit Increased:			16,825
Percent Profit:	13	12.8	13.11

*Base Case, Materials Escalation/Salary Increase.

Exhibit III. Total Program Costs.

	YEAR					
	1977	1978	1979	1980	1981	Total
MATERIAL ESCALATION						
8%	212,857	966,442	5,524,810	6,408,881	1,532,446	14,645,436
10%	212,857	970,099	5,584,806	6,521,622	1,573,469	14,862,853
12%	212,857	973,754	5,645,910	6,638,539	1,616,788	15,087,848

Exhibit IV. Expenditure Forecast.

	8%	10%	12%
1978 July	17,755	18,084	18,412
Aug.	23,837	24,279	24,720
Sept.	31,738	32,326	32,913
Oct.	38,485	39,198	39,910
Nov.	40,394	41,141	41,890
Dec.	45,233	46,071	46,909
1979 Jan.	85,406	88,598	91,849
Feb.	117,186	121,566	126,027
Mar.	122,398	126,974	131,633
Apr.	108,743	112,808	116,947
May	106,583	110,567	114,625
June	133,273	138,254	143,328
July	137,594	142,736	147,975
Aug.	144,494	149,895	155,396
Sept.	156,909	162,775	168,748
Oct.	156,163	162,001	167,946
Nov.	159,639	165,606	171,683
Dec.	176,696	183,300	190,027
1980 Jan.	190,209	200,972	212,137
Feb.	210,710	222,634	235,001
Mar.	222,699	235,301	248,371
Apr.	226,540	239,360	252,655
May	236,720	250,114	264,001
June	220,313	232,780	245,710
July	192,546	203,442	214,742
Aug.	127,930	135,171	142,678
Sept.	93,936	99,253	104,765
Oct.	89,006	94,043	99,266
Nov.	80,443	84,996	89,717
Dec.	101,201	106,929	112,868
1981 Jan.	113,655	122,311	131,453
Feb.	109,241	117,561	126,347
Mar.	85,297	91,793	98,653
Apr.	81,102	87,280	93,803
May	78,068	84,013	90,292
June	71,255	76,682	82,412

C. Labor Strike

1. One Month Strike Made Up In Three Month Period Afterwards (No Overtime, Use Of Additional Manpower)

While the discussion thus far has dealt with the financial aspects of the strike as a bottom-line decision making tool, some analysis must be directed where the strike can be most graphically seen, man-month loading. This will be accomplished by first examining the man-month loading effect of the strike followed by a three-month makeup period.

I. Perturbation analysis of a strike and a three-month makeup

A. *Engineering Division.* The impact was not felt too severely here. No changes were noted in the Technology Department, or in Engineering Graphics. Contract Engineering experienced about a one half man-month reduction requirement in September, (the month of the strike) with moderate peaking in the three-month follow-on period. This represented a displacement of work and cost and did not result in any increased cost.

B. *Program Management.* The strike did not affect this division.

C. *Finance Division.* This major division, which included the Proposition Department, Material Procurement, and Cost Accounting, experienced no impact from the strike. Neither was there placement, increased labor, or cost.

D. *Operation.* As might be expected, this division was heavily impacted by the strike.

1. *Fabrication.* A total drop in activity is noted in the strike month, with an immediate severe peaking of manpower requirements immediately after. This peaking aggravates the already appreciable peaking which is experienced in the base case from roughly August, 1979 through July, 1980. Management will have to deal with both the hiring and learning curve problems which the strike accentuates by adding a 25% increase in manning requirements from October, through December of 1979. Financially, the impact is not as great, as September savings free up dollars to be spread over the rest of the year for additional manpower.

2. *Manufacturing Engineering.* This department is troubled by the strike. Additional man-hour recruitment and employment is necessary for catch up. There is some displacement by several months of an already severe peak requirement, but the main significance is the 315 hour increase required, producing additional costs of $2,943.

3. *Quality Control.* Quality control requirements drop to zero during the strike with a displacement of the activity to the period immediately following. Cost remains the same.

4. *Inventory Control.* This department is impacted by the strike. A very damaging peaking occurs in manpower requirements immediately following the strike. The full impact continues through April, 1980. Costs of the strike are increased $1,743.

5. *Production Control.* This department is also impacted by the strike. A peaking trend, though mild, is generated by the strike (about 0.4 man-months for three months). Additional costs of $1,563 are accrued.
6. *Shipping.* In this perturbation, the catch up nature of the strike follow-on activity and associated delays results in a one-month displacement of shipping activity as 1979 moves into 1980. The costs, however, are roughly the same. Management must evaluate the down-the-line impact of delayed shipment.

The direct manpower and cost analysis of the perturbation shows some changes in overall cost. The real effect cannot be appreciated until the impact of direct hours and overhead dollars are combined. Operations, with a 296% overhead figure, was directly affected by the strike. As a result, the total cost of the strike was $25,525 (labor). There was no difference in materials. The $25,000 additional costs is not the most damaging aspect of this pertubation. What is damaging is the increased stress brought on management in the area of manning, demanning, and training.

2. One Month Strike With A Five Month Anticipation Of The Strike

II. Perturbation analysis of a strike and a five month anticipation

A. *Engineering Division.* Again, neither the Technology Department nor the Engineering Graphics are changed as a result of the strike. In Contract Engineering, however, total hours and costs changed slightly (upward). The five month preparation for the strike made it possible to spread out the anticipated increases in lower cost periods. Only about a $200 direct cost increase was noted.
B. *Program Management.* Here also the strike had no effect on manpower or cost. It should be noted, however, that management activities internal to the department would reflect the strike.
C. *Finance Division.* No direct impact is noted as a result of the strike.
D. *Operations.* This division was again affected by the strike.

1. *Fabrication.* An increase in manning over the five month period preceding the strike offsets the drop to zero manmonth requirements in September, 1979. This contrasts significantly with the sharp peaking experienced with the work done in a "make up" mode. The overall effect is made much smoother by anticipating the strike. The earlier spending of five months extra manning is offset by the zero requirement in September so that costs are almost identical.
2. *Manufacturing Engineering.* Additional manpower has to be employed in the five month period preceding the strike. An additional direct cost of $2,560 is reflected.
3. *Quality Control.* Requirements in this area drop to zero during the strike. The work is almost smoothly displaced to the preceding five months with no direct cost increase noted.
4. *Inventory Control.* An earlier peaking of manpower requirements occurs, with an added direct cost of $1,285.

5. *Production Control.* Additional costs of $1,670 in direct hours are accrued. The effect is spread smoothly over the five months preceding the strike.

6. *Shipping.* No change required.

The direct manpower cost analysis of this perturbation shows changes. A burdened labor cost of an additional $22,500 can be seen as a result of the strike, mostly in the operations division.

3. One Month Strike Made Up In Delay In Contract

Background

In this perturbation, assume that management has decided that the entire project will be delayed one month and the work will be made up at the end of each activity.

The strike is again anticipated for September, 1979. The major departments burdening the increased costs (the fabrication and quality control activities) are materials procurement, manufacturing engineering, inventory control, production control and shipping. Some of the other activities are indirectly affected because the personnel in these departments are on salary. These people, therefore, may be required to track the program during the strike.

Analysis

The overall cost of the project took into account the anticipated salary increases, material increases, and overhead rate increases and decreases. Analysis did not take into consideration the effect of a strike where the work is made up at a period approximately one and one-half years later. The reason for this is that the overhead rates are expected to decrease because of an increased business base and, therefore, any work delayed until the end of the project may benefit by being in a period of lower burden. Likewise, indirect costs and corporate costs may be influenced.

Conclusion

The profit percentage as a result of making up the strike at the end of the activities increased to 13.58 percent since the overhead rates were lower. This conclusion can be beneficial if in fact management can succeed in obtaining additional contracts that would maintain lower overhead rates.

4. One Month Strike Made Up By Working Overtime In Next Two Months

Background

In this case, the strike is again anticipated to occur in September, 1979. Management has decided to make up lost time over a two month period using overtime. The hours lost, both direct and indirect, would be made up in October and November of 1979. The overhead rates were adjusted to reflect the overtime being worked and likewise were the indirect costs and corporate costs.

Analysis

The strike occurred in September, 1979, and the hours lost were made up in the next two succeeding months. What were the benefits of this timing? The main advantage was that the salary increases were not a factor. The main disadvantage was the high overhead rates. As indicated in the base case, the overhead rates were the highest in the third year of the project. Another disadvantage is the indirect costs and corporate costs. The resulting profit percentage was reduced to 11.94 percent.

Conclusion

Based on the overhead rates and other alternatives, management should also consider the possibility of overtime in other periods as to the effect on the profit percentage. In comparing the delay to the overtime situation it would be in management's favor to go with the delay because of the increased profit percentage possibility.

Because the fabrication project is part of a fixed price contract, the effect of the strike upon the bottom line profit is critical.

The percentage of profit in each perturbation is calculated using the following formula:

$$\text{Profit} = 1 - \frac{\text{Total Perturbation Cost}}{\text{Base Case Total Price}}$$

The four strike perturbations can be listed as follows:

Variation	Price ($)	Cost ($)	Profit (%)
Base Case	16,549,342	14,645,436	13.00
Delay Contract 1 Month	"	14,559,656	13.58
Overtime in Following 2 Months	"	14,799,374	11.94
Work 5 Months Prior, No Overtime (Additional Manpower)	"	14,673,980	11.33
Work 3 Months After, No Overtime (Additional Manpower)	"	14,676,300	11.31

Management now has a tool for evaluating which alternative is the more desirable if, in fact, a strike of one month duration proved to be inevitable. It should be noted that an almost infinite variety of perturbations on a strike is possible. These figures hold true only for a one month (September, 1979) strike. A strike of longer or shorter duration or at a different time would undoubtedly impact the base case differently.

Paul Gibby read the report and was delighted over the amount of detail that went into the perturbation analysis. Only one question remained to be answered; "What bid should we go in with such that we still remain competitive?"

CASE STUDY: REPUBLIC OIL OF CANADA (TORONTO DIVISION)

Republic Oil of Canada decided to embark on a $100 million construction project for a new chemical refining plant. Republic felt that the number of companies competing for this contract would be small, and that many of those submitting bids would be the result of joint ventures in as much there are very few construction management companies with sufficient resources to manage a project of this magnitude.

The front runner in the proposal evaluation process was the joint venture bid submitted by Casper Construction Corporation of Toronto, Canada. "My work is just beginning," remarked Paul Worthington, Head of the proposal evaluation team. "Once we narrow the field down to the leading candidate, we must go over their proposal with a fine-toothed comb. With a joint venture, especially if the contractors are located geographically apart, our job becomes even more difficult because we must not only guard against duplication of effort, but we must make sure that nothing has fallen through the crack and that everything will be accounted for. Unfortunately, our team meets perhaps once every three or four years to evaluate some proposal for a construction project. You know that we just don't go around throwing up $100 million buildings each year. Therefore, to help us evaluate the contractors' proposals, we quite often bring in outside consultants. Many times they're more familiar with current construction technology than we are. Below are excerpts from the project management, work plan and construction sections of the Casper-Lane proposal. Perhaps now you'll see why my job isn't an easy one."

Project Management

Organization: Phase I

The joint venture of Casper-Lane will form a coherent project organization centered in Toronto, which will operate independently from any other projects which may concurrently be undertaken by the individual partners. This organization will be headed by the **PROJECT DIRECTOR**. All project control functions will be directed from this center, as well as all liaison with Republic of Canada.

Some specialized functions or technical packages which can be more economically performed in the partner's home offices will be subcontracted to these offices under the control of the project director. The terms of such contracts will define costs and schedules for this work, and these will be shown as individual items in the overall schedule and cost reports.

Regulatory Approval Requirements

We have developed a consistent approach to obtaining regulatory and environmental approvals in Canada which is based on early contracts with all involved governmental agencies. We have found that putting the agencies in the picture early assures a good dialog on basic regulatory concerns and thus avoids potential problem areas and minimizes hold-ups on approvals.

This project will require essentially two approvals of the Environmental Impact Assessment (EIA) and the formal permit applications. This approach normally meets with favorable response in that third party consultants can retain their objectivity and avoid charges of bias, while the staff environmental coordinator provides the continuing environmental liaison throughout the project. The staff environmental coordinator's duties during detailed design and construction are primarily to ensure that environmental guidelines and restrictions are met and fulfilled. At the completion of the project he prepares a final environmental report summarizing all EI activities, attempts to mitigate impacts, and evaluates the overall success of the program.

Site Selection

Site selection will depend upon three main areas of concern: political, environmental, and economic considerations.

The governments of Toronto and Canada will be keenly interested in the selection of a potential location both from an inter-provincial rivalry aspect and also as a move to establish industry in depressed areas. Early contact will be required to pursue these matters as an extension of the efforts already undertaken by Republic.

Environmental screening of all potential sites to clearly define the positive and negative potentials of each will be the first phase of the environmental study. The screening will include analysis of ecological and socio-economic impact potential at each site, as well as an analysis of the available supporting infra-structure (availability of manpower, services, housing, utilities, etc.)

The economic analysis will consider the financial impact upon the project of locating at various sites as determined by the proximity to feedstocks, fuel supplies, distribution facilities, costs associated with establishing adequate labor, equipment and support facilities, an analysis of potential tax incentives, and government financing associated with each location.

The Economic Reports will evaluate the effect on investment and operating costs of project variables such as but not limited to:

- Soil Conditions
- Meteorological effects
- Potable and cooling water supply
- Disposal facilities for atmospheric, liquid and soil wastes
- Construction camp and permanent housing facilities, utilities, etc., for temporary construction and permanent operating personnel
- Crude feed and product transportation facilities (pipelines and pumping stations)
- Company financed roads and railroads to outside public transportation facilities
- Educational facilities for construction and operating personnel families
- Power supply
- Telephone systems

- Available firefighting facilities
- Provincial and local codes, standards, design factors, anti-pollution requirements, etc.
- Availability of part-time maintenance, labor and supplies versus cost of permanent maintenance labor and material inventories
- Taxes, duties, licenses, and government subsidies (if any)
- Availability of road and concrete aggregates

Upon completion of the screening studies, all sites will be graded to establish the overall desirability of each location, and to recommend the site selected.

After choice of a site based on economical, political, and environmental considerations, the environmental screening report will be finalized. Sufficient data and planned environmental protection provisions will be furnished in an Environmental Impact Assessment report for approval of local and provincial governing bodies.

The report will include details and solutions to the following problem areas:

- Air pollution control
- Solid waste disposal
- Water pollution control
- Surface drainage and erosion control
- Surface rehabilitation and revegetation
- Protection of fish and wildlife
- Aesthetic value considerations in refinery design
- Fire protection and control
- Plans for prevention and cleanup of oil and hazardous material
- Spills
- Prevention of hazards to public health and safety for employees and neighboring populated areas

The report will also include a comprehensive program for monitoring the above environmental protection procedures during project construction and during plant operation. This will establish the objective provided on parameters and monitoring methodology, data handling, etc.

The monitoring program will include air and water pollution, refinery effluent receiving bodies, solid waste, noise pollution, and biota monitoring.

Management Of Multi-office Organization

As discussed under "Organization" above, the core of the Project Organization will be situated in Toronto. Any work performed in the home office of a Joint Venture Partner will be on a subcontract basis; the term of the section subcontract defining exactly the terms and boundries of most work. The Project Staff in Toronto will ensure that these terms are met and will coordinate the interfaces of such work packages so that overlaps and omissions are avoided.

The individual offices are linked with each other and with the Project office by the normal telecommunication facilities such as Telex and Telecopier as well as by common Computer Terminals and software for data transmittal. Cost and schedule information of individual work may then be fed into the overall system directly from the participating offices.

Each office will be responsible to the Project Office in Toronto in essentially the same way as they would be if the Project Office were their client.

Determining Depth Of Process Studies

We expect that we will be able to assess the error that may be involved in the approximations we will use for each process study. The simplest approximations will be used that cause errors that are small compared to the differences between process alternatives.

Potential Problems

Site selection and environmental approvals will of necessity be heavily dependent upon governmental input. We see this potentially as a two-fold problem:

- Delays in the processing and approval of permits required for the project.
- The possibility that political considerations may over-ride technical and environmental recommendations.

A third concern is that changing availabilities of certain crude oils may delay the "freezing" of the final design basis and thus detrimentally influence the cost of the project.

We expect to find the most difficult problems in process design to be concerned with reconciling licensors' estimates of costs with our own. Such problems could easily delay further process design work and, of course, the choice of processes. Changes in licensor data after pilot work is done also could require repetition of process design work that will have been done before the reports on pilot work.

We know that many of our clients have different preferences in the solutions of many process problems. If Republic's representatives do not include a man experienced in operation of refinery plants to make his company's preferences known, the process design may be less satisfactory than it otherwise would be.

Client Involvement

A close hand-in-hand working arrangement between the client and the contractor will contribute significantly to the success of any project. We would, therefore, encourage this cooperation right from the start of the project and would expect Republic's staff to be involved in the decision-making process on a day-to-day basis.

We anticipate that a tight client-contractor team will thus evolve soon after project award which will solve difficulties on an "our problem basis" rather than a "client's problem" or "contractor's problem." This will, of course, require the full confidence of Republic not only in our ability but in our willingness to disclose problems, difficulties, and errors, as they occur, and we emphasize that this is our usual approach to our clients.

It should be emphasized that this close client involvement does not in any way reduce our responsibility for the design and construction of the facilities on schedule and within budget.

Main Priorities For The First Two Months

Considering the very tight schedule of the Phase II work, we consider the following items having top priority immediately after contract award:

- The availability for review and discussion of Republic's work to date.
- Establishment of close communication links with Republic's personnel.
- Identifying all influences outside the process battery limits which may affect the site selection, i.e., transport systems, labor availability, fuel supplies, others.
- Choice of process alternatives for evaluation
- Preparation of specifications for all chosen process alternatives
- Preparation of expected or hoped-for properties of products from all processes
- Preparation and transmittal of requests for licensors' information for evaluation of their processes
- Negotiation of necessary secrecy agreements
- Initiating contacts with regulatory agencies

Financial Ability

Our financial ability to handle this size of a project is demonstrated by the latest annual reports of our parent companies in the section tabbed "Company Data."

Modularization

The design and engineering of individual process unit modules will be identified during the Phase II stage and some of these may be handled on a subcontract basis as explained in "Organization" above.

For the construction, it is not necessary to modularize the entire refinery but several physical equipment modules will be used, such as assembled and housed analyzer shelters control boards, and small auxiliary units. This will take advantage of specialty jobs and make maximum use of the available winter labor pool.

Some of the objectives of modularization are:

- Schedule improvement by more efficient use of time and labor
- Permit use of local specialty shops and contractors, thus saving cost of importing and housing equivalent labor at jobsite
- Permit winter work in an enclosed or sheltered work area, thus improving labor productivity
- Provide cost benefits of shop work over field construction

- Participation of local shops and contractors contributes greatly to improved public relations

Planning And Scheduling

Organizing and Staffing

Immediately upon project award, we will put into action a comprehensive system of planning, scheduling and time control. This program is designed to meet project requirements through the internal control of our operations. Planning, scheduling and time control will initially be performed in the engineering office concurrent with engineering and procurement operations. When project time control needs shift to construction, the Planner/Scheduler assigned to the Project will be resident at the jobsite.

Methods and Systems

We will use the Critical Path Method as a basic tool in planning and scheduling the project. In support of the CPM schedules and to further verify and develop the schedule logic, the following studies and programs will be initiated as required:

- Craft Manpower Loading Study
- Priority Work Area Program
- Craft Work Availability Study
- Pipe Spool Engineering, Fabrication and Erection Curves
- Pipefitter Allocation Program
- Subcontract Plan

The Craft Manpower Loading Study assigns budget construction man-hours to CPM schedule durations to obtain craft manpower requirements. Once an initial pass has been completed, necessary adjustments are made to the planned start and finish of key leveling activities in order that manpower will be scheduled as effectively as possible. Our experience shows there is significant benefit to be gained from this approach, particularly on multi-area projects.

The Priority Work Area Program provides a method for coordinating production and spool fabrication with equipment deliveries in order to ensure a coordinated, early-start construction program. As a spin-off from this program, a Work Availability Study can be done which plots percent work availability against time for overhead piping. The Pipefitter Allocation Program can be developed for the purpose of planning the utilization of available pipefitters to the best advantage.

The Subcontract Plan is a document used to coordinate the preparation of bid packages, procurement of subcontracts, and subcontract field start and completion dates with the remainder of the Project Information are input into this document from the CPM schedules.

Project Plans and Schedules

The planning begins with determining the construction approach to the project based on currently available major equipment delivery information and anticipated manpower requirements. Engineering and Procurement activities are directed to meeting the established Construction approach, with all inter-related restraints clearly identified.

Engineering activities identified in the CPM schedule include equipment specifications and bills of material for major equipment and materials, layout and modeling activities, design and drawing activities by discipline and vendor print requirements. Clearly defined start and finish dates and 95 percent completion dates are shown for each engineering discipline.

Procurement activities reflect the placement of orders with suppliers of major equipment and materials, the procurement of vendor prints, the placement of all subcontracts and the fabrication and delivery of major equipment and materials. Sequential delivery requirements for equipment established during the planning phase are also reflected in the procurement schedule.

Construction activities include each major element involved in the construction of the project including set up time, site clearance, demolition, underground work, foundations, structures, equipment erections, piping, electrical, instrumentation, insulation, painting, all major subcontracts, etc. Also shown are testing, check out, run-in, and other special requirements. Mechanical completion is shown as a key date with a limited duration work clean-up activity following. A supplemental breakdown on the Critical Path Diagram supplies information on the type of work involved within the overall work activity.

Project Time Control

Engineering and procurement time control begins with monitoring of the Project Plans and Schedules based on internal documentation. Comparison of actual, expected and scheduled times supplies time control information which is communicated directly by the Planner/Scheduler to key members of the Project Team.

Construction time control begins with computer generated "STATUS" reports (Scheduled Time And Time Updating System) based on times extracted directly from the Project Schedule. These "STATUS" reports are issued to responsible construction people at the project site for control and feedback purposes. It is the continuing responsibility of construction personnel to mark-up the "STATUS" reports showing a detailed breakdown of the work included in the work package; to show expected accomplishment dates and to give causes for delays beyond the scheduled dates. The original copy of the marked-up "STATUS" reports are forwarded to the Project Manager to review any indicated major delays to the project.

Project Management, the Project Control Manager, and the Planner/Scheduler will meet on a regular basis to review the updated plans and schedules, analyze the effects on the overall project and determine and implement any necessary corrective or recouping actions.

Cost Reporting

Effective cost control is exercised through systems which emphasize cost control participation by all members of the project team. Our Project Director is responsible for control of the project. Our Cost Engineer is responsible for cost forecasting, reporting, and cost control recommendations to the Project Director.

Data flowing to the cost engineer originates in the functional areas of the project. Estimating prepares the project control budget and estimates of all changes. Drawings, engineering requisitions, and quantity sampling reports are transmitted from Engineering. Purchasing provides inquiries, quotations, bid tabulations, purchase orders, and input of commitments to the cost reporting system. Accounts payable, cost records and input to the cost reporting system of costs incurred to date are the responsibility of Accounting.

Our methods recognize two (2) principles:

- The Budget, including its specified basis, is the document against which the project is controlled.
- The measurement of cost vs. progress is the primary function of the project cost engineer and is the basis for cost forecasting and control recommendations.

These principles are applied in a continuous trending/reporting/controlling cycle based on monitoring cost versus progress for all elements of the work.

The results of, and recommendations for, this control activity are summarized in regular cost reports.

- Engineering progress, man-hour and salary expenditures and other cost expenditures are continuously monitored and reported on the Home Office Cost Report.
- Any significant changes in projected final costs are identified and advised to the Project Director at the earliest realistic point in time on the Interim Variance Report. In addition, this report provides review of significant cost changes by the project team prior to entry in the Monthly cost Progress Report.
- The cost engineer in the field monitors all phases of construction costs and prepares a monthly Construction Cost Report, including labor progress, productivity, unit man-hours, and construction indirect costs and trends.
- The Cost Progress Report provides a comprehensive status report of the Current Budget, Commitments, Costs to Date, Final Cost Forecast, and Variances in a standard cost code format. The Report also includes a written analysis of significant cost trends and changes, charts illustrating cost versus progress for major cost elements and cash flow curves.

The levels of reporting detail available allow the identification of critical cost areas and permits effective and timely corrective action.

Work Plan

Phase II

Immediately following contract award, we shall begin to develop the two major processing routes, i.e., coking or resid hydro-processing. Each scheme will have several alternates that must be evaluated in detail in parallel.

These evaluations will include, in addition to normal process work, definition of maximum resid processing unit size to determine the number of trains vs. total plant size. For each total process scheme under consideration, heat integration, utility requirements, tankage and environmental needs will be developed.

At the end of six months the following process information will be provided:

- Complete material balances
- Hydrogen requirements and balances
- Heat balances around critical process units
- Utility requirements for non-critical units and offsites
- Process flow diagrams for the major units
- Major equipment size for the process units
- Tankage, offsite, and utility requirements
- Identification of time-critical items

Our attached milestone schedule indicates the sequence in which we expect to develop the key activities of our work plan. It is our intention to keep Republic continuously informed on the status of our work. At the end of four months, we plan to have developed sufficient information to permit a directional decision on process selection.

With Republic's concurrence, one scheme will be selected for more detailed process engineering from which the capital cost estimate will be prepared by the eight-month milestone. This estimate will serve as the basis for trending the project costs prior to the preparation of a definitive estimate. We feel that the capital cost estimate prepared for the selected processing scheme will provide a better trending tool than the investment estimate prepared for several processing schemes.

During the initial six months we will be making contact with the governmental regulatory agencies to develop the basis for your submittals. We will also be investigating potential plant sites and compiling the data necessary to make a recommendation considering all the economic factors. We will begin early to develop a dialog with the environmental regulatory agencies. The sequence of these activities is indicated on the attached milestone schedule. All Phase II work will be directed out of Toronto.

Phase III

Phase III is defined as the engineering and procurement phase. There is an initial period of about six months duration where we would continue with process design and estimating and complete certain other milestone targets. During this initial period of Phase III, we would maintain project control in Toronto but utilize two principal work centers; Cleveland and Toronto. The primary milestones during this early period are as follows:

- Confirm process design
- Pilot plant monitoring
- Schedule "A" packages
- Capital cost estimate
- Utility and operating cost estimates
- Critical equipment inquires
- General specifications

- Evaluation of selected site
- Regulatory approvals
- Environmental approvals
- Detailed project execution plan

We will consider an engineering work split which provides for front-end design work for major conversion units in Cleveland and all other design engineering in Canada. Worldwide procurement activities will be centered in Toronto. Overall project controls will be developed and maintained in Toronto.

We estimate that 80 percent of the man-hours expended in the total Phase III effort will be expended in Canada, primarily Toronto.

Process support will be provided by Casper. The joint venture headquarters in Toronto will provide project management, purchasing, construction coordination, controls, and subcontract administration. Lane Construction will be responsible for pipeline systems. Detailed engineering design, therefore, will be done in Toronto except for some front-end design work on the conversion units as noted. During the development of the project execution plan, we will review with you two options. First, we will review the availability of Toronto subcontractors to engineer selected general facilities. Second, we will review the utilization of Toronto to handle offsites, such as the tank farm, and utilities, such as the boiler system.

Construction

Approach

Our approach to construction is to assign a full time construction manager to the project very early in the planning stage to establish guidelines and philosophy and to participate in the planning and scheduling activities. He then establishes the requirements for the construction team and assumes full responsibility for the construction and field control of the project.

One of the first tasks of the construction manager is to investigate and analyze the working conditions at the project site, and the availability of labor craftsmen. He must develop solutions to logistic problems involved in transporting workers, materials, and equipment to the site.

It is possible that local housing facilities will not be adequate to provide accommodations for the anticipated construction work force at any of the prospective plant sites. It is the responsibility of the construction manager and his construction team to arrange adequate accommodations for the on-site work force during the construction phase of the project.

Since construction site activities will take place over one or more winter work periods, the entire project strategy must be developed to minimize weather effects. A careful study will be made of the specific requirements of a cold weather construction program at the selected project location.

Two considerations are of paramount importance. First, project planning must take into account overall craft labor requirements, including seasonal anticipated adjustments. Major outside work should be scheduled during mild weather periods, but work which can be done indoors should be scheduled during cold weather periods when craft surplus frequently exists. Second, for any work scheduled or forced into the winter period, the capabilities and judgement of construction personnel experienced in cold weather operations must be fully utilized.

The building block for winter planning is the thorough understanding of the difficulty and cost of performing each work activity. An organized approach is required for any group of activities comprising a segment of system. Two principal factors control the analysis of most activities. First, the feasibility and cost of enclosing and heating work spaces; and second, the loss of productivity which will occur for different field craft activities under such conditions when compared to the norm.

Good productivity analysis capabilities are essential in such a planning effort.

For example, if summer productivity is required, then an anticipated productivity rating for various construction activities in a refinery in the specified regions would be about as follows:

CONDITION	DEFINITION	PRODUCTIVITY
1	Inside building, heat and light.	1.0
2	Major temporary enclosure, heat and light.	0.9
3	Temporary enclosure, such as sheeting draped from pipe supports or structures, minimum heat and light.	0.8
4	Windbreaks only, no heating light.	0.7
5	Outdoor work, principally support for above, isolated work, bare hand work such as wiring.	0.5

Condition 5 work is costly and is limited to support work only. Discounting condition 5 work, except for absolute minimum support, a typical winter mix productivity is about 0.8. Weighting summer and winter work periods and craft loading and including an allowance for unplanned condition 5 work as a contingency, a year-round weighted average of 1.0 is obtained, which is considered norm.

"Climatology Guidelines" are used as a planning tool. These provide a basis for design, and are a source of extreme weather data for any area. These are a major source of data for developing project strategy where the considerations applicable to every phase of the work including the guidelines for engineering, procurement, construction, time control and cost control are defined.

In addition to scheduling work out of the winter and having the capability to do required work during the winter, the availability of the winter labor pool and the year-round gain from shop labor efficiency is utilized by planning and operating off-site a large multi-craft shop producing modularized components.

A multi-craft shop would be established in a location in Toronto where surplus skilled labor and accommodations would be available during the winter months.

Careful evaluation of all factors during the early project planning stages will provide the least costly solution within the available time frame, and our first-hand experience obtained through many projects under similar conditions assures that this will be accomplished.

Labor Relations In Toronto

Organized labor in Toronto engaged in refinery construction is represented by the major International Unions such as the Teamsters, Plumbers and Pipefitters, Electricians, Ironworkers, Carpenters and General Labourers. Negotiations with the unions are generally carried out by contractor associations such as the Toronto Construction Labour Relations Association. Agreements reached by these Associations and the labor unions are later incorporated into the union agreements between the individual contractors and the unions.

Over the past few years, it has been the practice of contractors engaged in major petrochemical construction projects in Toronto to meet with the business agents of the unions involved in the work in a pre-job conference. The purpose of this conference is to come to an agreement concerning wage rates in the work area, travel and subsistance allowances, camp conditions if applicable, and other matters that may be controversial or outside the existing agreements, and if possible, to include a "no strike, no lockout" clause.

This "no strike, no lockout" clause does not necessarily forestall all wildcat walkouts and work stoppages by individual unions during the life of the project, but it has, in some instances, proven highly successful in preventing serious delays in the progress of the work due to prolonged strikes.

We feel that a "no strike, no lockout" clause would be highly advantageous for this project, and we are confident that we can negotiate such an agreement.

Productivity

One of the keys to maintaining a high level of productivity during the construction phase of a large project is the involvement of the construction manager and the project staff in the work planning and material scheduling from the earliest planning phase of the program.

The construction manager's continuous involvement and input into the preliminary planning and later into the CPM program insures that a reasonable labor density is maintained in all work areas and that highly labor intensive programs involving particular trades are not scheduled simultaneously. The construction manager is particularly aware of the need to avoid large short-term changes in the composition of the work force.

The construction manager and project staff, by careful planning, the avoidance of over optimistic delivery schedules and through the use of on-the-spot expediting and quality control, insure that major slowdowns and work stoppages do not occur as a result of delays in delivery of material and major equipment packages.

The efficient use of models by the construction manager and his construction team is a valuable aid in planning and scheduling work assignments. The full construction model gives an overview of the project. Areas of potential overcrowding becomes immediately apparent. A further study of individual process model tables provides solutions to the problem of overcrowding by distributing the workload to areas which might otherwise be overlooked. Design models provide a great assist to modularized construction planning and winter work enclosure planning.

In addition, the use of models in planning can assist the construction manager to maintain a reasonable work force mix by suggesting areas where particular crafts can work simultaneously without interfering with the work of other crafts.

The project director and construction manager chosen for this project will be completely conversant with productivity problems inherent in large scale construction projects and will have the means at their disposal to overcome these problems and maintain a high level of productivity through the construction period.

Recruiting Techniques

Our recruiting techniques are governed largely by the availability of both skilled tradesmen and unskilled laborers in the work area in which we operate. The availability of workmen, in turn, is dependent on the general level of construction activity in the area.

Well before the start of construction we will conduct labor surveys as a check on the surveys prepared by major oil companies in which we participate in continuously monitoring labor conditions. Our second source of labor data will be discussions with area business and labor leaders which will provide us with current productivity information. Our third source of information will be subcontractor surveys. A fourth source will be a subjective analysis of the effect of conditions in the specific area of the project on productivity, taking into consideration such factors as the weather, distance from storage area to work area, distance from accommodations to work area, need for work camps and other factors.

Using information from these surveys and studies and from other sources, we will plot our anticipated manpower requirements over the life of the project. With this information and with information from previously compiled local manpower surveys, we will obtain a good indication of the types and numbers of tradesmen and laborers that we must recruit from other areas of the prairies and from Eastern Canada and the West Coast. Should employment levels remain unchanged, and assuming that certain large projects presently underway are completed, it is anticipated that the main work force will be available in Western Canada and that a vigorous recruiting program in Eastern Canada and the West Coast will provide all the remaining skilled and unskilled labor required.

We are familiar with the program of Canada Manpower and have worked with them in the past. We have also conducted on the job training programs to upgrade the skills of local labor.

Construction Progress

Definition and Application

Productivity is one measure of job performance. It is calculated as:

$$\frac{\text{Quantity produced X man-hour units at norm}}{\text{Actual man-hours spent}} = \text{productivity}$$

Productivity is affected by:

- Local labor rules
- Quality and quantity of supervision
- Worker attitude
- Weather
- Site conditions
- Rate of manpower buildup
- Labor availability
- Quality of engineering
- Delivery of material
- Overtime

In addition, the accuracy of reported productivity is dependent on:

- Proper identification of work activities
- Assignment of standard work units
- Accurate survey of work quantities performed
- Accurate coding of actual man-hours spent

The measurement of productivity, and associated physical progress is an essential tool for construction management. For direct hire and cost reimbursable subcontracts, the information is a basis for control decisions affecting:

- Manpower requirements
- Construction schedule
- Deployment of supervision
- Material handling
- On-site vs. off-site fabrication of piping and structures

The information is also essential for fixed price subcontracts to determine:

- Subcontractor progress
- Adequacy of subcontractor manpower levels
- Validity of subcontractor claims

CASE STUDY: ESTABLISHING PLANNING PRIORITIES

The Director of Project Management has just called you into his office and informed you that you are the project manager on a top priority project requested by corporate headquarters. The Director hands you two sheets of paper. On the first sheet, there is a brief description of the corporate request, together with a not-to-exceed funding limitation. On the second page, you find a list containing the names of four project office individuals which the Director has personally picked to make up your project office. You may negotiate for the functional employees of your choice with the functional managers in order to complete the project team.

The Director informs you that he knows very little about the project except that it is a top priority effort for corporate and that the other four project office members will be here in about twenty minutes to meet with you and hear your first briefing on the project.

Despite the lack of information you have regarding the project, you must design a preliminary package of logical steps in order to manage the project. In Figure 1 you will find a list of 26 activities for managing the project. Without discussing it with anyone, prioritize the list according to what you feel the proper sequence should be. Then, meet with your team and determine the team's order.

Remember: This is an exercise designed to show you some of the procedures needed to successfully plan and manage a project. Appendix B will give you the "expert's order" so that you may complete the table. Some of the activities can overlap and others may be controlled through company policy. This exercise can be done either individually, as a group, or both.

CASE STUDY: THE MARKETING GROUP

Joe Walton wasn't sure if he would really like his new position of product manager. His job description stated that he would work with R & D in the development stages of the product and then he would have to "pick up the ball and run with it" through marketing, sales, advertising, finance, and manufacturing. The most difficult part of the job appeared to be the necessity for working with the diverse functional groups, none of which understood the total picture.

Joe would have to develop the "big picture" by obtaining reasonable estimates from the line groups and then integrating all of the information into one viable plan. The functional group had the reputation of giving poor estimates and over-inflating the time and manpower requirements so that there would be a sufficient cushion in case something went wrong. Joe was a little nervous as to how the line managers would react if he had to take the "fat" out of their estimates.

Joe was informed that engineering next month would be completing the R & D phase of a new product, and that the product would be ready for market introduction within the next 60 days. The vice-president for marketing then gave Joe the following instructions:

Joe, I'm going to give you a little bit of help on this project. Here is a check list which includes the major items needed for new product introduction (see Exhibit I). I want you to determine, by yourself, the time needed for each element. Then, develop the work breakdown structure, the logic or arrow diagram, and the PERT/CPM. After you have identified the critical path, come on in and see me and we'll discuss your major milestones, the end date, and how to convince line managers that your estimates are correct. Try to 'marry' the work breakdown structure to the arrow diagram.

ACTIVITY	DESCRIPTION	COLUMN 1: YOUR SEQUENCE	COLUMN 2: GROUP SEQUENCE	COLUMN 3: EXPERT's SEQUENCE	COLUMN 4: DIFFERENCE BETWEEN 1 & 3	COLUMN 5: DIFFERENCE BETWEEN 2 & 3
1.	Develop Linear Responsibility Chart					
2.	Negotiate for qualified functional personnel					
3.	Develop specifications					
4.	Determine means for measuring progress					
5.	Prepare final report					
6.	Authorize departments to begin work					
7.	Develop work breakdown structure					
8.	Close out functional work orders					
9.	Develop scope statement and set objectives					
10.	Develop gross schedule					
11.	Develop priorities for each project element					
12.	Develop alternative courses of action					
13.	Develop PERT network					
14.	Develop detailed schedules					
15.	Establish functional personnel qualifications					
16.	Coordinate on-going activities					
17.	Determine resource requirements					
18.	Measure progress					
19.	Decide upon basic course of action					
20.	Establish costs for each WBS element					
21.	Review WBS costs with each functional manager					
22.	Establish project plan					
23.	Establish cost variances for base case elements					
24.	Price out WBS					
25.	Establish logic network with check points					
26.	Review "base case" costs with Director					
	TOTAL					

Figure 1. Project Management Priority List.

CASE STUDY: CORY ELECTRICAL

"Frankly speaking, Jeff, I didn't think that we would stand a chance in winning this $20 million program. I was really surprised when they said that they'd like to accept our bid and begin contract negotiations. As chief contract administrator, you'll head up the negotiation team," remarked Gus Bell, Vice-President and General Manager of Cory Electric. "You have two weeks to prepare your data and line up your team. I want to see you when you're ready to go."

Exhibit I.

- Production layout
- Market testing
- Analyze selling cost
- Analyze customer reaction
- Storage and shipping costs
- Select salesmen
- Train salesmen
- Train distributors
- Literature to salesmen
- Literature to distributors
- Print literature
- Sales promotion
- Sales manual
- Trade advertising

- Review plant costs
- Select distributors
- Layout artwork
- Approve artwork
- Introduce at trade show
- Distribute to salesmen
- Establish billing procedure
- Establish credit procedure
- Revise cost of production
- Revise selling cost
- Approvals*
- Review meetings*
- Final specifications
- Material requisitions

*Approvals and review meetings can appear several times.

Jeff Stokes was chief contract negotiator for Cory Electric, a $250 million-a-year electrical components manufacturer serving virtually every major U.S. industry. Cory Electric had a well-established matrix structure which had withstood fifteen years of testing. Job casting standards were well established, but did include some "fat" upon the discretion of the functional manager.

Two weeks later, Jeff meet with Gus Bell to discuss the negotiation process:

Gus: Have you selected an appropriate team? You had better make sure that you're covered on all sides.

Jeff: There will be four, plus myself at the negotiating table; the program manager, the chief project engineer who developed the engineering labor package; the chief manufacturing engineer who developed the production labor package; and a pricing specialist who has been on the proposal since the kick-off meeting. We have a strong team and should be able to handle any questions.

Gus: Okay, I'll take your word for it. I have my own checklist for contract negotiations. I want you to come back with a guaranteed fee of $1.6 million for our stockholders. Have you worked out the possible situations based upon the negotiated costs?

Jeff: Yes! Our minimum position if $20 million plus an 8 percent profit. Of course, this profit percentage will vary depending upon the negotiated cost. We can bid the program at a $15 million cost; that's $5 million below our target, and still book a $1.6 million profit by overrunning the cost-plus-incentive-fee contract. Here is a list of the possible cases. (See Exhibit 1)

Gus: If we negotiate a cost overrun fee, make sure that cost accounting knows about it. I don't want the total fee to be booked as profit if we're going to need it later to cover the overrun. Can we justify our overhead rates, general and administrative costs and our salary structure?

Exhibit 1. Cost Positions.

NEGOTIATED COST	%	NEGOTIATED FEE			
		TARGET FEE	OVERRUN FEE	TOTAL FEE	TOTAL PACKAGE
15,000,000	14.00	1,600,000	500,000	2,100,000	17,100,000
16,000,000	12.50	1,600,000	400,000	2,000,000	18,000,000
17,000,000	11.18	1,600,000	300,000	1,900,000	18,900,000
18,000,000	10.00	1,600,000	200,000	1,800,000	19,800,000
19,000,000	8.95	1,600,000	100,000	1,700,000	20,700,000
20,000,000	8.00	1,600,000	0	1,600,000	21,600,000
21,000,000	7.14	1,600,000	-100,000	1,500,000	22,500,000
22,000,000	6.36	1,600,000	-200,000	1,400,000	23,400,000
23,000,000	5.65	1,600,000	-300,000	1,300,000	24,300,000
24,000,000	5.00	1,600,000	-400,000	1,200,000	25,200,000

Assume total cost will be spent:

NEGOTIATED COST	% FEE		
21,000,000	7.61		
22,000,000	7.27	Minimum Position	= $20,000,000
23,000,000	6.96	Minimum Fee	= 1,600,000 = 8% of Minimum Position
24,000,000	6.67	Sharing Ratio	= 90/10 %

Jeff: That's a problem. You know that 20 percent of our business comes from Mitre Corporation. If they fail to renew our contract for another two-year follow-on effort, then our overhead rates will jump drastically. Which overhead rates should I use?

Gus: Let's put in a renegotiation clause to protect us against a drastic change in our business base. Make sure that the customer understands that as part of the terms and conditions. Are there any unusual terms and conditions?

Jeff: I've read over all terms and conditions, and so have all of the project office personnel as well as the key functional managers. The only major item is that the customer wants us to qualify some new vendors as sources for raw material procurement. We have included in the package the cost of qualifying two new raw material suppliers.

Gus: Where are the weak points in our proposal? I'm sure we have some.

Jeff: Last month, the customer sent in a fact-finding team to go over all of our labor justifications. The impression that I get from our people is that we're covered all the way around. The only major problem might be where we'll be performing on our learning curve. We put into the proposal a 45 percent learning curve efficiency. The customer has indicated that we should be up around 50 to 55 percent efficiency, based upon our previous contracts with him. Unfortunately, those contracts which the customer referred to, were four years ago. Several of the employees who worked on those programs have left the company. Others are assigned to on going projects here at Cory. I estimate that we could put together about 10 percent of the people we used previously. That learning curve percentage will be a big point for disagreements. We finished off the previous programs with the customer at a 35 percent learning curve position. I don't see how they can expect us to be smarter, given these circumstances.

Gus: If that's the only weakness, then we're in good shape. It sounds like we have a fool-proof audit trail. That's good! What's your negotiation sequence going to be?

Jeff: I'd like to negotiate the bottom line only, but that's a dream. We'll probably negotiate the raw materials, the manhours, the learning curve, the overhead rate, and the profit percentage. Hopefully, we can do it in that order.

Gus: Do you think that we'll be able to negotiate a cost above our minimum position?

Jeff: Our proposal was for $22.2 million. I don't foresee any problem which will prevent us from coming out ahead of the minimum position. The five percent change in learning curve efficiency amounts to approximately $1 million. We should be well covered. The first move will be up to them. I expect that they'll come in with an offer of $18 to $19 million. Using the binary chop procedure, that'll give us our guaranteed minimum position.

Gus: Do you know the guys who you'll be negotiating with?

Jeff: Yes. I've dealt with them before. The last time, the negotiations took three days. I think we both got what we wanted. I expect this one to go just as smoothly.

Gus: Okay Jeff. I'm convinced we're prepared for negotiations. Have a good trip.

The negotiations began at 9:00 A.M. on Monday morning. The customer countered the original proposal of $22.2 million with an offer of $15 million. After six solid hours of arguments, Jeff and his team adjourned. Jeff immediately called Gus Bell at Cory Electronics.

Jeff: Their counter-offer to our bid is absurd. They've asked us to make a counter-offer to their offer. We can't do that. The instant we give them a counter-offer, we are in fact giving credibility to their absurd bid. Now, they're claiming that, if we don't give them a counter-offer, then we're not bargaining in good faith. I think we're in trouble.

Gus: Has the customer done their homework to justify their bid?

Jeff: Yes. Very well. Tomorrow we're going to discuss every element of the proposal, task by task. Unless something drastically changes in their position within the next day or two, contract negotiations will probably take up to a month.

Gus: Perhaps this is one program that should be negotiated at the top levels of management. Find out if the person that you're negotiating with reports to a vice-president and general manager, as you do. If not, break off contract negotiations until the customer gives us someone at your level. We'll negotiate this at my level, if necessary.

6

The Project Environment: Problems and Pitfalls

6.0 INTRODUCTION

The two major problem areas in the project environment are the determination of the "who has what authority and responsibility" question, and the resulting conflicts associated with the individual at the project/functional interface. Almost all project problems in some way or another involve these two major areas. Other problem areas found in the project environment include:

- The pyramidal structure
- Superior-subordinate relationships
- Departmentation
- Scalar chain of command
- Organizational chain of command
- Power and authority
- Planning goals and objectives
- Decision making
- Reward and punishment
- Span of control

6.1 EMPLOYEE PROBLEMS

The two most common employee problems involve the assignment and resulting evaluation processes. Personnel assignments have already been discussed in chapter four. In summary:

- People should be assigned to tasks which are commensurate with their skills.
- Whenever possible, the same person should be assigned to related tasks.
- The most critical tasks should be assigned to the more responsible people.

The evaluation process in a project environment is difficult for an employee at the functional/project interface, especially if hostilities develop between the functional and project managers. In this situation, the interfacing employee almost always suffers due to a poor rating by either the project manager or his supervisor. Unless the employee continually keeps his superior abreast of his performance and achievements, the supervisor must rely solely upon the input received from project office personnel. This can result in a performance evaluation process which is subject to error.

Three additional questions must be answered with regard to employee evaluation:

- Of what value are job descriptions?
- How do we maintain wage and salary grades?
- Who provides training and development, especially under conditions where variable manloading can exist?

If each project is, in fact, different then it becomes almost an impossible task to develop accurate job descriptions. In many cases, wage and salary grades are functions of a unit manning document which specifies the number, type and grade of all employees required on a given project. Although this might be a necessity in order to control costs, it also is difficult to achieve because variable manloading changes project priorities. Variable manloading creates several difficulties for project managers, especially if new employees are included. Project managers like seasoned veterans assigned to their activities because there generally does not exist sufficient time for proper and close supervision of the training and development of new employees. Functional managers, however, contend that the training has to be accomplished on someone's project, and sooner or later all project managers must come to this realization.

6.2 MANAGER PROBLEMS

On the manager level, the two most common problems involve personal values and conflicts. Personal values are often attributed to the "changing of the guard." New managers have a different sense of values than do the older more experienced managers. Miner identifies some of these personal values attributed to new managers:[1]

- Less trusting, especially of people in positions of authority.
- Increased feelings of being controlled by external forces and events, and thus believing that they cannot control their own destinies. This is a kind of change that makes for less initiation of one's own activities and a greater likelihood of responding in terms of external pressures. There is a sense of powerlessness, although not necessarily a decreased desire for power.

---

1. John B. Miner, "The OD-Management Development Conflict," *Business Horizons,* December 1973, p. 32.

- Less authoritarian and more negative attitudes toward persons holding positions of power.
- More independent, often to the point of rebelliousness and defiance.
- More free and uncontrolled in expressing feelings, impulses, and emotions.
- More inclined to live in the present and to let the future take care of itself.
- More self-indulgent.
- Moral values that are relative to the situation, less absolute and less tied to formal religion.
- A strong and increasing identification with their peer and age groups, with the youth culture.
- Greater social concern and greater desire to help the less fortunate.
- More negative toward business, the management role in particular. A professional position is clearly preferred to managing.
- A desire to contribute less to an employing organization and to receive more from the organization.

Previously we defined one of the attributes of a project manager as liking risks. Unfortunately, the amount of risk which today's managers are willing to accept varies not only with their personal values but also with the impact of current economic conditions and top management philosophies. If top management views a specific project as vital for the growth of the company, then the project manager may be so directed to assume virtually no risks during the execution of the project. In this case the project manager may attempt to pass all responsibility to higher or lower management claiming that "his hands are tied." Wilemon and Cicero identify problems with risk identification:[2]

- The project manager's anxiety over project risk varies in relation with his willingness to accept final responsibility for the technical success of his project. Some project managers may be willing to accept full responsibility for the success or failure of their projects. Others, by contrast, may be more willing to share responsibility and risk with their superiors.
- The greater the length of stay in project management, the greater the tendency for project managers to remain in administrative positions within an organization.
- The degree of anxiety over professional obsolescence varies with the length of time the project manager spends in project management positions.

The amount of risk that a manager will accept also varies with age and experience. Older, more experienced managers tend to take little risks whereas the younger, more aggressive managers may adopt a risk-lover policy in hopes of achieving a name for themselves.

2. D.L. Wilemon, and John P. Cicero, "The Project Manager: Anomolies and Ambiguities," *Academy of Management Journal,* 13, 269-282, 1970.

Conflicts exist at the project/functional interface regardless of how hard we attempt to structure the work. Authority and responsibility relationships can vary from project to project. In general, however, there does exist a relatively definable boundary between the project and functional manager. According to Cleland and King, this interface can be defined by the following relationships:[3]

- Project Manager
  - *What* is to be done?
  - *When* will the task be done?
  - *Why* will the task be done?
  - *How much* money is available to do the task?
  - *How well* has the total project been done?
- Functional Manager
  - *Who* will do the task?
  - *Where* will the task be done?
  - *How* will the task be done?
  - *How well* has the functional input been integrated into the project?

Another difficulty arises from the way the functional manager views the project. Many functional managers consider the project as simply a means toward an end and therefore identify problems and seek solutions in terms of their immediate duties and responsibilities rather than looking beyond them. This problem also exists at the horizontal hierarchy level. The problem comes about as a result of authority and responsibility relationships, and may not have anything at all to do with the competence of the individuals concerned. This situation breeds conflicts which can also have an impact on the amount of risk that a manager wishes to accept. William Killain defined this inevitable conflict between the functional and project manager:[4]

The conflicts revolve about items such as project priority, manpower costs, and the assignment of functional personnel to the project manager. Each project manager will, of course, want the best functional operators assigned to his project. In addition to these problems, the accountability for profit and loss is much more difficult in a matrix organization than in a project organization. Project managers have a tendency to blame overruns on functional managers, stating that the cost of the function was excessive. Whereas functional managers have a tendency to blame excessive costs on project managers with the argument that there were too many changes, more work required than defined initially, and other such arguments.

---

3. From *Systems Analysis and Project Management* by David I. Cleland and William Richard King. Copyright © 1968, 1975 by McGraw-Hill, Inc. Used with permission of McGraw-Hill Book Company. p. 237.
4. William P. Killian, "Project Management—Future Organizational Concepts," *Marquette Business Review,* 2: 90-107, 1971.

Another major trouble area is in problem reporting and resolution. Major conflicts can arise during problem resolution sessions, not only because of the above-mentioned reasons, but also because the time constraints imposed on the project often prevent both parties from taking a logical approach. Project managers have the tendency of wanting to make immediate decisions, after which the functional manager asserts that his way is "the only way" the problem can be resolved. One of the major causes for prolonged problem-solving is the lack of pertinent information. In order to ease potential conflicts, all pertinent information should be made available to all parties concerned as early as possible. The following information should be reported by the project manager:[5]

- The problem
- The cause
- The expected impact on schedule, budget, profit or other pertinent area
- The action taken or recommended and the results expected of that action
- What top management can do to help

6.3 LEADERSHIP IN A PROJECT ENVIRONMENT

Leadership can be defined as a style of behavior designed to integrate both the organizational requirements and one's personal interests into the pursuit of some objective. All managers have some sort of leadership responsibility. If time permits, successful leadership techniques and practices can be developed.

Leadership is the composition of several complex elements, the three most common being:

- The person leading
- The people being led
- The situation (i.e., the project environment)

Project managers are often selected or not selected because of their leadership styles. The most common reason for not selecting an individual is his inability to balance the technical and managerial project functions. Wilemon and Cicero have defined four characteristics of this type of situation:[6]

- The greater the project manager's technical expertise, the higher the propensity that he will overly involve himself in the technical details of the project.
- The greater the project manager's difficulty in delegating technical task responsibilities, the more likely it is that he will over involve himself in the technical details of the project (depending upon his expertise to do so).

---

5. Russell D. Archibald, *Managing High-Technology Programs and Projects,* New York, Wiley, 1976, p. 230.
6. D.L. Wilemon, and John P. Cicero, "The Project Manager: Anomalies and Ambiguities," *Academy of Management Journal,* 13, 269-282, 1970.

- The greater the project manager's interest in the technical details of the project, the more likely it is that he will defend the project manager's role as one of a technical specialist.
- The lower the project manager's technical expertise, the more likely it is that he will overstress the non-technical project functions (administrative functions).

There have been several surveys to determine what leadership techniques are best. The following are the results of a survey by Richard Hodgetts:[7]

- Human Relations-Oriented Leadership Techniques
  - "The Project manager must make all the team members feel that their efforts are important and have a direct effect on the outcome of the program."
  - "The project manager must educate the team concerning what is to be done and how important its role is."
  - "Provide credit to project participants."
  - "Project members must be given recognition and prestige of appointment."
  - "Make the team members feel and believe that they play a vital part in the success (or failure) of the team."
  - "By working extremely close with my team I believe that one can win a project loyalty while to a large extent minimizing the frequency of authority-gap problems."
  - "I believe that a great motivation can be created just by knowing the people in a personal sense. I know many of the line people better than their own supervisor does. In addition. I try to make them understand that they are an indispensable part of the team."
  - "I would consider the most important technique in overcoming the authority-gap to be understanding as much as possible the needs of the individuals with whom you are dealing and over whom you have no direct authority."
- Formal Authority Oriented Leadership Techniques
  - "Point out how great the loss will be if cooperation is not forthcoming."
  - "Put all authority in functional statements."
  - "Apply pressure beginning with a tactful approach and minimum application warranted by the situation and then increasing it."
  - "Threaten to precipitate high-level intervention and do it if necessary."
  - "Convince the members that what is good for the company is good for them."

---

7. Richard M. Hodgetts, "Leadership Techniques in Project Organizations," *Academy of Management Journal* , 11, 211-219, 1968.

- "Place authority on full-time assigned people in the operating division to get the necessary work done."
- "Maintain control over expenditures."
- "Utilize implicit threat of going to general management for resolution."
- "It is most important that the team members recognize that the project manager has the charter to direct the project."

6.4 ORGANIZATIONAL IMPACT

In most companies, whether or not project oriented, the impact of management emphasis upon the organization is well known. In the project environment there also exists a definite impact due to leadership emphasis. The leadership emphasis is best seen by employee contributions, organizational order, employee performance, and the project manager's performance.

- Contributions from people:
  - A good project manager encourages active cooperation and responsible participation. The result is that both good and bad information is contributed freely.
  - A poor project manager maintains an atmosphere of passive resistance with only responsive participation. This results in information being withheld.
- Organizational Order:
  - A good project manager develops policy and encourages acceptance. A low price is paid for contributions.
  - A poor project manager goes beyond policies and attempts to develop procedures and measurements. A high price is normally paid for contributions.
- Employee Performance:
  - A good project manager keeps people informed and satisfied (if possible) by aligning motives with objectives. Positive thinking and cooperation is encouraged. A good project manager is willing to give more responsibility to those willing to accept it.
  - A poor project manager keeps people uninformed, frustrated, defensive, and negative. Motives are aligned with incentives rather than objectives. The poor project manager develops a "stay out of trouble" atmosphere.
- Performance of the Project Manager:
  - A good project manager assumes that employee misunderstandings can and will occur, and therefore blames himself. A good project manager contantly attempts to improve and be more communicative. He relies heavily on moral persuasion.

- A poor project manager assumes that employees are unwilling to cooperate and therefore blames subordinates. The poor project manager demands more through authoritarian attitudes and relies heavily on material incentives.

Management emphasis also impacts the organization. The following four categories show this management emphasis resulting for both good and poor project management:

- Management Problem Solving:
  - A good project manager performs his own problem solving at the level for which he is responsible through delegation of problem solving responsibilities.
  - A poor project manager will do subordinate problem solving in known areas. For areas which he does not know, he requires that his approval be given prior to idea implementation.
- Organizational Order:
  - A good project manager develops, maintains, and uses a single integrated management system in which authority and responsibility are delegated to the subordinates. In addition, he knows that occasional slippages and overruns will occur, and simply tries to minimize their effect.
  - A poor project manager delegates as little authority and responsibility as possible, and runs the risk of continual slippages and overruns. A poor project manager maintains two management information systems; one informal system for himself and one formal (eyewash) system simply to impress his superiors.
- Performance of People:
  - A good project manager finds that subordinates willingly accept responsibility, are decisive in attitude toward the project, and are satisfied.
  - A poor project manager finds that his subordinates are reluctant to accept responsibility, are indecisive in their actions, and seem frustrated.
- Performance of the Project Manager:
  - A good project manager assumes that his key people can "run the show." He exhibits confidence in those individuals working in areas in which he has no expertise, and exhibits patience with people working in areas where he has a familiarity. A good project manager is never too busy to help his people solve personal or professional problems.
  - A poor project manager considers himself indispensable, is over-cautious with work performed in unfamiliar areas, and becomes overly interested in work he knows. A poor project manager is always tied up in meetings.

6.5 PREDICTING PROJECT SUCCESS

One of the most difficult tasks is predicting of whether the project will be successful. Most goal-oriented managers look only at the time, cost, and performance parameters. If an out-of-tolerance condition exists, then additional analysis is required to identify the cause of the problem. Looking only at time, cost, and performance might identify immediate contributions to profits, but will not identify whether or not the project itself was managed correctly. This takes on paramount importance if the survival of the organization is based upon a steady stream of successfully managed projects. Once or twice a program manager might be able to force a project to success by continually swinging a large baseball bat. After a while, however, the effect of the big bat will either become tolerable or people will avoid working on his projects.

Project success is often measured by the "actions" of three groups: the project manager and team; the parent organization; and finally the customer organization. There are certain actions that the project manager and team can take in order to stimulate project success. These actions include:

- Insist upon the right to select key project team members.
- Select key team members with proven track records in their fields.
- Develop commitment and sense of mission from the outset.
- Seek sufficient authority and a projectized organizational form.
- Coordinate and maintain good relationship with client, parent, and team.
- Seek to enhance public's image of the project.
- Have key team members assist in decision making and problem solving.
- Develop realistic cost, schedule, and performance estimates and goals.
- Have back-up strategies in anticipation of potential problems.
- Team structure should be appropriate, yet flexible and flat.
- Go beyond formal authority to maximize influence over people and key decisions.
- Employ a workable set of project planning and control tools.
- Avoid over-reliance on one type of control tool.
- Stress importance of meeting cost, schedule, and performance goals.
- Give priority to achieving the mission or function of the end item.
- Keep changes under control.
- Seek to find ways of assuring job security for effective project team members.

In Chapter Four we stated that a project cannot be successful unless it is recognized as a project and has the support of top-level management. Top-level management must be willing to commit company resources and provide the necessary administrative support so that the project easily adapts to the company's day-to-day routine of doing business. Furthermore, the parent organization must develop an atmosphere conducive to good working relationships between the project manager, parent organization, and client organization.

With regard to the parent organization, there exists several variables which can be used to evaluate parent organization support. These variables include:

- A willingness to coordinate efforts
- A willingness to maintain structural flexibility
- A willingness to adapt to change
- Effective strategic planning
- Rapport maintenance
- Proper emphasis on past experience
- External buffering
- Prompt and accurate communications
- Enthusiastic support
- Identification to all concerned parties that the project does in fact, contribute to parent capabilities

The mere identification and existence of these variables does not guarantee project success in dealing with the parent organization. Instead, it implies that there exists a good foundation to work with such that if the project manager and team, and the parent organization take the appropriate actions then project success is likely. The following actions must be taken:

- Select at an early point, a project manager with a proven track record of technical skills, human skills, and administrative skills (in that order) to lead the project team.
- Develop clear and workable guidelines for the project manager.
- Delegate sufficient authority to the project manager and let him make important decisions in conjunction with key team members.
- Demonstrate enthusiasm for and commitment to the project and team.
- Develop and maintain short and informal lines of communication.
- Avoid excessive pressure on the project manager to win contracts.
- Avoid arbitrarily slashing or ballooning project team's cost estimate.
- Avoid "buy-ins."
- Develop close, not meddling, working relationships with the principal client contact and project manager.

Both the parent organization and the project team must employ proper managerial techniques to insure that judicious and adequate, but not excessive use of the planning, controlling, and communications systems can be made. These proper management techniques must also include pre-conditioning, such as:

- Clearly established specifications and designs
- Realistic schedules
- Realistic cost estimates
- Avoidance of "buy-ins"
- Avoidance of over-optimism

The client organization can have a great deal of influence toward project success by minimizing team meetings, making rapid responses to requests for information, and simply by letting the contractor "do his thing" without any interference. The variables which exist for the client organization include:

- A willingness to coordinate efforts
- Rapport maintenance
- Establishment of reasonable and specific goals and criteria
- Well-established procedures for changes
- Prompt and accurate communications
- Commitment of client resources
- Minimization of red tape
- Providing sufficient authority to the client contact (especially for decision making)

With these variables as the basic foundation, the following actions should result:

- Encourage openness and honesty from the start from all participants.
- Create an atmosphere that encourages healthy, but not cut-throat, competition, or "liars" contests.
- Plan for adequate funding to complete the entire project.
- Develop clear understandings of the relative importance of cost, schedule, and technical performance goals.
- Develop short and informal lines of communication and flat organizational structures.
- Delegate sufficient authority to the principal client contact and allow prompt approval or rejection important project decisions.
- Reject "buy-ins."
- Make prompt decisions regarding contract award or go ahead.
- Develop close, not meddling, working relationships with project participants.
- Avoid arms-length relationships.
- Avoid excessive reporting schemes.
- Make prompt decisions regarding changes.

By combining the relevant actions of the project team, parent organization, and client organization, we can identify the fundamental lessons for management. These include:

- When starting off in project management, plan to go all the way
  - Recognize authority conflicts: resolve
  - Recognize change impact: be a change agent
- Match the right people for the right jobs
  - No system is better than the people that implement it

- Allow adequate time and effort for laying out the project groundwork and defining work
  - Work breakdown structure
  - Network planning
- Insure that work packages are the proper size
  - Manageable and have organizational accountability
  - Realistic in terms of effort and time
- Establish and use planning and control systems as the focal point of project implementation
  - know where you're going
  - Know when you've gotten there
- Be sure information flow is realistic
  - Information is the basis for problem solving and decision making
  - Communication "pitfalls" greatest contributor to project difficulties
- Be willing to replan—do so
  - The best laid plans can often go astray
  - Change is inevitable
- Tie together responsibility, performance, and rewards
  - Management by objectives
  - Key to motivation and productivity
- Long before project ends—plan for its end
  - Disposition of personnel
  - Disposal of material and other resources
  - Transfer of knowledge
  - Closing out work orders
  - Customer/contractor financial payments and reporting

The last lesson, project termination, has been the downfall for many a good project manager. As projects get near completion, there is the natural tendency to want to minimize costs by transferring people as soon as possible and by closing out work orders. This often leaves the project manager with the responsibility for writing the final report and transferring raw materials to other programs. Many projects require one or two months after work completion simply for administrative reporting and final cost summary.

Having defined project success, we can now identify some of the major causes for the failure of project management. These causes include:

- Selecting a concept which was not applicable. Since each application is unique, selecting a project that does not have a sound basis, or forcing a change when the time is not appropriate, can lead to immediate failure.
- The wrong person selected as project manager. The individual selected must be a manager, not a doer. He must place emphasis on all aspects of the work, not merely technical.

- Upper management not supportive. Upper management must concur in the concept and must behave accordingly.
- Inadequately defined tasks. There must exist an adequate system for planning and control such that a proper balance between cost, schedule, and technical performance can be maintained.
- Management techniques misused. There exists the inevitable tendency in technical communities to attempt to do more than is initially required by contract. Technology must be watched and individuals must buy only what is needed.
- Project termination not planned. By definition, each project must stop. Termination must be planned so that the impact can be identified.

It is often said that more can be learned from failure than from success. The lessons that can be learned from project failure include:[8]

- When starting off in project management, plan to go all the way
- Don't skimp on the project manager's qualifications
- Do not spare time and effort in laying out the project groundwork and defining work
- Insure that the work packages in the project are of proper size
- Establish and use network planning techniques, having the network as the focal point of project implementation
- Be sure that the information flow related to the project management system is realistic
- Be prepared to continually replan jobs to accommodate frequent changes on dynamic programs
- Whenever possible, tie together responsibility, performance, and rewards
- Long before a project ends, provide some means for accommodating the employees' personal goals
- If mistakes in project implementation have been made, make a fresh try

6.6 MANAGEMENT PITFALLS

The project environment offers numerous opportunities for project managers and team members to get into trouble. These activities which readily create problems are referred to as management pitfalls. The lack of planning, for example, can be considered as a management pitfall. Other common types of management pitfalls are:

- Lack of self-control ("knowing oneself")
- Activity traps

---

8. Ivars Avots, "Why Does Project Management Fail?" *California Management Review,* Vol. 12, 1969, pp. 77-82.

- Managing versus doing
- People versus task skills
- Ineffective communications
- Time management
- Management bottlenecks

Knowing oneself, especially one's capabilities, strengths, and weaknesses, is the first step toward successful project management. Too often, managers will assume that they are jacks-of-all-trades and indispensable to the organization. The ultimate result is that such managers tend to "bite off more than they can chew." and then find that insufficient time exists for training additional personnel. This, of course, assumes that the project budget provided sufficient funding for additional positions which were never utilized.

The following two poems illustrate this self-concept:

The "me" I think I am
The "me" I wish I were
The "me" I really am
The "me" I try to project
The "me" others perceive
The "me" I used to be
The "me" others try to make me.

Author Unknown

Four Men
It chanced upon a winters night
Safe sheltered from the weather.
The board was spread for only one,
Yet four men dined together.
There sat the man I meant to be
In glory, spurred and booted.
And close beside him, to the right
The man I am reputed.
The man I think myself to be
His seat was occupying
Hard by the man I really am
To hold his own was trying.
And all beneath one roof we met
Yet none called his fellow brother
No sign of recognition passed.
They knew not one another.

Author Unknown

Activity traps result when the means becomes the end, rather than the means to achieve the end. The most common activity traps are team meetings and customer technical interchange meetings. Another common activity trap is the development of special schedules and charts which cannot be used for customer reporting, but are used to inform upper-level management of project status. Managers must always evaluate whether or not the time spent to develop these charts is worth the effort. Sign-off documents, such as manufacturing plans, provide yet another activity trap by requiring that the project manager and/or several key project team members sign off all documentation. Proper project planning and the delegation of authority and responsibility can reduce this activity trap.

We previously defined one of the characteristics of poor leadership as being the inability to obtain a balance between the management functions and the technical functions. This can easily develop into an activity trap where the individual becomes a doer rather than a manager. Unfortunately, there often exists a very fine line between manageing and doing. As an example, consider a project manager who was asked by one of his technical people to make a telephone call to assist him in solving a problem. Simply making the phone call is doing work which should be done by the project team members or even the functional manager. However, if the person being called requires that someone in absolute authority be included in the conversation, then this can be considered managing instead of doing.

There are several other cases where one must become a doer in order to be an effective manager and command the loyalty and respect of your subordinates. Assume a special situation where you must schedule subordinates to work overtime, say on special holidays or even weekends. By showing up at the plant during these times, just to make a brief appearance before the people in question, you can create a better working atmosphere and understanding with the subordinates.

Another major pitfall is the decision to utilize either people skills or task skills. Is it better to utilize subordinates with whom you can obtain a good working relationship, or to employ highly skilled people simply to get the job done? Obviously, the project manager would like nothing better than to have the best of both worlds. Unfortunately, this is not always possible. Consider the following situations:

- There exists a task which will take three weeks to complete. John has worked for you before, but not on such a task as this. John, however, understands how to work with you. Paul is very competent but likes to work alone. He can get the job done within constraints. Should you employ people or task skills? (Would your answer change if the task were three months instead of three weeks?)

- There exist three tasks, each one requiring two months of work. Richard has the necessary people skills to handle all three tasks, but he will not be able to do so as efficiently as a technical specialist. The alternate choice is to utilize three technical specialists.

In both situations there should be more information made available to assist in the final decision. However, based upon the amount of information given, the author prefers task skills so as not to hinder the time or performance constraints on the project. Generally speaking, for long-duration projects which require constant communications with the customer, it might be better to have permanently assigned employees who can perform a variety of tasks. Customers dislike seeing a steady stream of new faces.

Highly technical industries are modifying the marketing function because of this distinction between people and task skills. In the past, people skills were considered to be of extreme importance in marketing technology. Today the trend is toward giving more importance to the task skill. The result has been that the project manager and project engineer must undertake marketing efforts in addition to their everyday duties. The marketing function has therefore moved down to middle management.

It is often said that a good project manager must be willing to work sixty to eightly hours a week to get the job done. This might be true if continually fighting fires or if budgeting constraints pervent employing additional staff. The major reason, however, is the result of ineffective time management. Prime examples might include the continuous flow of paperwork, unnecessary meetings, unnecessary phone calls, and acting as a tour guide for visitors. Improper time management becomes an activity trap where the project manager becomes controlled by the job rather than controlling the job himself. The final result is that the project manager must work long and arduous hours in order to find time for creative thinking.

To be effective, the project manager must establish time management rules and then ask himself four questions:

- Rules for Time Management
  - Conduct a time analysis (time log)
  - Plan solid blocks for important things
  - Classify your activities
  - Establish priorities
  - Establish opportunity cost on activities
  - Train your system (boss, subordinate, peers)
  - Practice delegation
  - Practice calculated neglect
  - Practice management by exception
  - Focus on opportunities—not on problems
- Questions
  - What am I doing that I don't have to be doing at all?
  - What am I doing that can be done better by someone else?
  - What am I doing that could be done sufficiently well by someone else?
  - Am I establishing the right priorities for my activities?

This type of time management analysis can greatly reduce such proverbial "time robbers," as:

- Incomplete work
- A job poorly done—must be done over
- Delayed decisions
- Poor communications channels
- Uncontrolled telephone calls
- Casual visitors
- Waiting for people
- Failure to delegate
- Poor retrieval system

Proper communications is vital to the success of the project. Communications is the process by which information is exchanged. Communications can be

- Written formal
- Written informal
- Oral formal
- Oral informal

Noise tends to distort or destroy the information within the message. Noise results from our own personality screens which dictate the way we present the message, and perception screens which may cause us to "perceive" what we thought was said. Noise can therefore cause ambiguity.

- Ambiguity causes us to hear what we want to hear
- Ambiguity causes us to hear what the group wants
- Ambiguity causes us to relate to past experiences without being discriminatory

Communications is more than simply conveying a message; it is also a source for control. Proper communications let the employees in on the act since employees need to know and understand. Communication must convey both information and motivation. The problem, therefore, is how to communicate. Below are six simple steps:

- Think through what you wish to accomplish.
- Determine the way you will communicate.
- Appeal to the interest of those affected.
- Give playback on ways others communicate to you.
- Get playback on what you communicate.
- Test effectiveness through reliance on others to carry out your instructions.

Knowing how to communicate does not guarantee that a clear message will be generated. There are techniques that can be used to improve communications. These techniques include:

- Obtaining feedback, possibly in more than one form
- Establishing multiple communications channels
- Using face-to-face communications if possible
- Determining how sensitive the receiver is to your communications
- Being aware of symbolic meanings as expressions on people's faces
- Communicating at the proper time
- Reinforcing words with actions
- Using a simple language
- Using redundancy (i.e., saying it two different ways) whenever possible

Techniques can vary from project to project. For example, on one project the customer may require that all test data be made available, in writing, as soon as testing occurs and possibly before your own people have had a chance to examine the results. This type of clear and open communication cannot exist indefinitely because the customer might form his own opinion of the data before hearing the project office position. Similarly, project managers should not expect functional managers to provide them with immediate raw test data until functional analysis is conducted.

With every effort to communicate there are always barriers. These barriers include:

- Receiver hearing what he wants to hear. This results from people doing the same job so long that they no longer listen.
- Sender and receiver having different perceptions. This is vitally important in interpreting contractual requirements, statements of work and proposal information requests.
- Receiver evaluating the source before accepting the communications.
- Receiver ignoring conflicting information and doing as he pleases.
- Words meaning different things to different people.
- Ignoring non-verbal cues.
- Receiver being emotionally upset.

The scalar chain of command can also become a barrier with regard to inhouse communications. The project manager must have the authority to go to the general manager or counterpart to communicate effectively. Without direct upward communication it is possible that filters can develop such that the final message gets distorted.

Three important conclusions can be drawn from communications techniques and barriers:

- Don't assume that the message you sent will be received in the form you sent it.
- The swiftest and most effective communications take place among people with common points of view. The manager who fosters a good relationship with his associates will have less difficulty in communicating with them.
- Communications must be established early in the project.

Communications is also listening. Good project managers must be willing to listen to their employees, both professionally and personally. The advantages of listening properly are that

- Subordinates know you are sincerely interested
- You obtain feedback
- Employee acceptance is fostered.

The successful manager must be willing to listen to a man's story from beginning to end, without interruptions. The manager must be willing to see the problem through the eyes of the subordinate. Finally, before making a decision, the manager should ask the subordinate for his solutions to the problem.

Project managers should ask themselves four questions:

- Do I make it easy for employees to talk to me?
- Am I sympathetic to their problems?
- Do I attempt to improve human relations?
- Do I make an extra effort to remember names and faces?

Team meetings are supposedly meetings of the mind where information giving, receiving and listening take place. Team meetings must be effective or else they become time management pitfalls. It is the responsibility of the project manager to insure that meetings are valuable and necessary for the exchange of information. The following are general guides for conducting a more effective meeting:

- Start on time. If you wait for people, you reward tardy behavior.
- Develop agenda "objectives". Generate a list and proceed: avoid getting hung up on the order of topics.
- Conduct one piece of business at a time.
- Allow each member to contribute in their way. Support, challenge, and counter . . . view differences as helpful, dig for reasons or views.
- Silence does not always mean agreement. Seek opinions: "What's your opinion on this, Peggy?"
- Be ready to confront the verbal member: "Okay, we've heard from Mike on this matter, now how about some other views?"
- Test for readiness to make a decision.
- Make the decision.
- Test for commitment to the decision.

- Assign roles and responsibilities (only after decision-making).
- Agree on follow-up or accountability dates.
- Indicate the next step for this group.
- Set the time and place for the next meeting.
- End on time.
- Was the meeting necessary?

Team meetings quite often provide individuals with means of exhibiting suppressed ideas. The following three humorous quotations identify these:

- In any given meeting, when all is said and done, 90 percent will be said—10 percent will be done.-Orben's *Current Comedy*
- A committee meeting provides a great chance for some people who like to hear their own voices talk and talk, while others draw crocodiles or a lady's legs. It also prevents the men who can think and make quick decisions from doing so.-Lin Yutang, *The Pleasures of a Nonconformist (World)*
- Having served on various committees, I have drawn up a list of rules: Never arrive on time or you will be stamped a beginner. Don't say anything until the meeting is half over; this stamps you as being wise. Be as vague as possible; this prevents irritating the others. When in doubt, suggest that a subcommittee be appointed. Be the first to move for adjournment; this will make you popular—it's what everyone is waiting for.-Harry Chapman, quoted in *Think*

Many times, company policies and procedures can be established for the development of communications channels for project personnel. Table 6-1 illustrates such communications guidelines.

6.7 PROJECT MANAGEMENT BOTTLENECKS

Poor communications can easily produce communications bottlenecks. These bottlenecks can occur in both the parent and client organizations. The most common bottleneck occurs when all communications between the customer and the parent organization must flow through the project office. There are two major disadvantages to this type of arrangement. First, requiring that all information pass through the project office may be a necessity but develops slow reaction times. Second, regardless of the qualifications of the project office members, the client always fears that the information which he receives will be "filtered" prior to disclosure.

Customers not only like first-hand information, but also prefer that their technical specialists be able to communicate directly with the parent's technical specialists. Many project managers dislike this arrangement, for they fear that the technical specialists may say or do something which may be contrary to project strategy or thinking. These fears can be allayed by telling the customer that this situation

Table 6-1. Communications Policy.

PROGRAM MANAGER	FUNCTIONAL MANAGER	RELATIONSHIP
Communications The program manager utilizes existing authorized communications media to the maximum extent rather than create new ones.	*Communications*	*Communications* Communications up, down, and laterally are essential elements to the success of programs in a multi-program organization, and to the morale and motivation of supporting functional organizations. In principle, communication from the program manager should be channeled through the program team member to functional managers.
Approves program plans, Subdivided Work Description and/or work authorizations, and schedules defining specific program requirements.	Assures his organization's compliance with all such program direction received.	Program definition must be within the scope of the contract as expressed in the program plan and Work Breakdown Structure.
Signs correspondence which provides program direction to functional organizations. Signs correspondence addressed to the customer that pertains to the program except that which has been expressly assigned by the general manager the function organizations or higher management in accordance with division policy.	Assures his organization's compliance with all such program direction received. Functional manager provides the program manager with copies of all "Program" correspondence released by his organization which may affect program performance. Ensures that the program manager is aware of correspondence with unusual content, on an exception basis, through the cognizant Program Team member or directly is such action is warranted by the gravity of the situation.	In the program manager's absence, the signature authority is transferred upward to his reporting superior unless an acting Program Manager has been designated. Signature authority for correspondence will be consistent with established Division Policy.

Table 6-1 Communications Policy. Continued

PROGRAM MANAGER	FUNCTIONAL MANAGER	RELATIONSHIP
Reports program results and accomplishments to the customer and to the general manager, keeping them informed of significant problems and events.	Participates in program reviews, being aware of and prepared in matters related to his functional specialty. Keeps his line or staff management and cognizant program team member informed of significant problems and events relating to any program in which his personnel are involved.	Statusing and reporting is the responsibility of functional specialists. The program manager utilizes the specialist organizations. The specialists retain their own channels to the general manager but must keep the program manager informed.

will be permitted if, and only if, the customer realizes that the remarks made by the technical specialists do not, in any way, shape or form, reflect the position of the project office or company. Furthermore, only the project office can authorize commitment of resources or the providing of information for a customer request. This will alleviate the necessity for having a project representative present during all discussions, but will require that records be provided to the project office of all communications with the customer.

For long-duration projects the customer may require that the contractor have an established customer representative office in the contractor's facilities. The idea behind this is sound in that all information to the customer must flow through the customer's project office at the contractor's facility. This creates a problem in that it attempts to sever direct communications channels between the customer and contractor project managers. The result is that in many situations, the establishment of a local project office is merely an "eyewash" situation to satisfy contractual requirements, whereas actual communications go from customer to contractor as though the local project office did not exist. This creates an antagonistic local customer project office.

The last bottleneck to be discussed occurs when the customer's project manager considers himself to be in a higher position than the contractor's project manager and therefore seeks some higher authority to which to communicate. As an example, the customer has a $130 million program and subcontracts $5 million out to you. Even though you are the project manager and report to either the vice-president and general manager or the director of program management, the customer's project manager may wish to communicate directly with the vice-president or one of the directors. Project managers who seek status can often jeopardize the success of the project by creating rigid communications channels.

Figure 6-1 identifies why communications bottlenecks such as these occur. These almost always exist a minimum of two paths for communications flow to

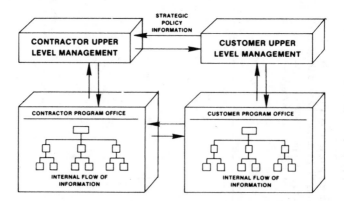

Figure 6-1. Information Flow Pattern From Contractor Program Office.

and from the customer. Many times, strategic project planning is accomplished between the customer and contractor at a level above the respective project managers. This type of situation can have a strongly demoralizing effect.

6.8 COMMUNICATION TRAPS

Projects are run by communications. The work is defined by the communications tool known as the work breakdown structure. Actually, this is the easy part of communications, where everything is well defined. Unfortunately, project managers cannot document everything they wish to say or relate to other people, regardless of the level in the company. The worst possible situation is when an outside customer loses faith in the contractor. When a situation of mistrust prevails, the logical sequence of events would be:

- More documentation
- More interchange meetings
- Customer representation on your site

In each of these situations, the project manager becomes severely overloaded with work. This situation can also occur in-house when a line manager begins to mistrust a project manager, or vice versa. There may suddenly appear an exponential increase in the flow of paperwork and everyone is writing "protection" memos. Previously, everything was verbal.

Communication traps occur more frequently with customer-contractor relationships. The following are examples of this:

- Phase I of the program has just been completed successfully. The customer, however, was displeased because he had to wait three weeks to a month after all tests were completed before the data was presented. For Phase II, the customer is insisting that his people be given the raw data the same time your people receive it.
- The customer is unhappy with the technical information that is being given by the project manager. As a result, he wants his technical people to be able to communicate with your technical people on an individual basis without having to go through the project office.
- You are a subcontractor to a prime contractor. The prime contractor is a little nervous about what information you might present during a technical interchange meeting where the customer will be represented and therefore wants to review all material before the meeting.
- You are a subcontractor to a prime contractor. During negotiations between the customer and the prime contractor, your phone rings. You find out that it is the customer asking for certain information.

- The customer has asked to have a customer representative office set up in the same building as the project office. Furthermore, the customer's project manager wants his office next to yours.
- During an interchange meeting with the customer, one of your company's functional employees presents data to the customer and concludes with the remarks, "I personally disagree with our company's solution to this problem and I think that the company is all wet in their approach. Let me show you my solution to this problem."
- Functional employees are supposed to be experts. In front of the customer (or even your top management) an employee makes a statement that you the project manager do not believe is completely true or accurate.
- On Tuesday morning, the customer's project manager calls your project manager and asks him a question. On Tuesday afternoon, the customer's Project engineer calls your project engineer and asks him the same question.

Communication traps can also occur between the project office and line managers. Below are several examples:

- The project manager can hold too many "useless" team meetings
- The project manager can hold too few team meetings
- People refuse to make decisions and ultimately the team meetings are flooded with agenda items which are irrelevant
- Last month Larry completed an assignment as an assistant project manager on an activity where the project manager kept him continuously informed as to project status. Now, Larry is working for a project manager that tells him only what he needs to know to get the job done.

In a project environment, the line manager is not part of any project team, otherwise he would spend 40 hours per week simply attending team meetings. Therefore, how does the line manager learn of the true project status? Written memos will not do it. The information must come first hand from either the project manager or the assigned functional employee. Line managers would rather hear it from the project manager because line employees have the tendency to censor bad news from the respective line manager. Line managers must be provided true status by the project office. Consider the following example:

John is a functional support manager with fourteen highly competent individuals beneath him. John's main concern is performance. He has a tendency to leave scheduling and cost problems up the the project managers. During the past two months John has intermittently received phone calls and casual visits from upper-level management and senior executives asking him about his department's costs and schedules on a variety of projects. Although he can answer almost all of the performance questions, he has found great difficulty in responding to time and cost questions. John is a little nervous that if this situation continues it may affect his evaluation and merit increase.

Sometimes, project managers expect too much out of their employees during problem-solving or brainstorming sessions, and communications become inhibited. There are several possible causes for having unproductive team meetings.

- Because of superior, subordinate relationships (i.e., pecking orders), creativity is inhibited.
- Criticism and ridicule have a tendency to inhibit spontaneity.
- Pecking orders, unless adequately controlled, can inhibit teamwork and problem-solving.
- All seemingly crazy or unconventional ideas were ridiculed and eventually discarded. Contributors do not wish to contribute anything further.
- Many lower-level people, who could have good ideas to contribute felt inferior and therefore refused to contribute.
- Meetings were dominated by upper-level management personnel.
- The meetings were held at an inappropriate place and time.
- Many people were not given adequate notification of meeting time and subject matter.

As a brief exercise, below are eight often found methods that project and functional employees can use to provide communications:

a. Counseling sessions
b. Telephone conversation
c. Individual conversation
d. Formal letter
e. Project office memo
f. Project office directive
g. Project team meeting
h. Formal report

For each of the items below, select one and only one communications media from the list above which you would utilize.

1. Defining the project organizational structure to functional managers
2. Defining the project organizational structure to team members
3. Defining the project organizational structure to executives
4. Explaining to a functional manager the reasons for the conflict between his employee and your assistant project managers
5. Requesting overtime because of schedule slippages
6. Reporting an employee's violation of company policy
7. Reporting an employee's violation of project policy
8. Trying to solve a functional employee's grievance
9. Trying to solve a project office team member's grievance
10. Directing employees to increase production

11. Directing employees to perform work in a manner which violates company policy
12. Explaining the new indirect project evaluation system to project team members
13. Asking for downstream functional commitment of resources
14. Reporting daily status to executives or the customer
15. Reporting weekly status to executives or the customer
16. Reporting monthly or quarterly status to executives or the customer
17. Explaining the reason for the overrun
18. Establishing project planning guidelines
19. Requesting a vice-president to attend your team meeting
20. Informing functional managers of project status
21. Informing functional team members of project status
22. Asking a functional manager to perform work not originally budgeted for
23. Explaining customer grievances to your people
24. Informing employees of the results of customer interchange meetings
25. Requesting that a functional employee be removed from your project because of incompetence.

6.9 WHAT CAN GO WRONG?

Many people feel that best project managers are those who can anticipate what can go wrong and then take preventive actions well in advance. As a brief exercise on this, consider the following example:

Good project managers know what type of trouble can occur at the various stages in the development of a project. The activities on the left indicate the various stages of a project. The list on the right identifies major problems. For each item on the left, select all of those items on the right which are applicable.

1. Request for proposal

2. Submittal to customer

3. Contract award

4. Design review meetings

5. Testing the product

6. Customer acceptance

a. Engineering does not request manufacturing input for end-item productibility

b. Poorly defined work breakdown structure

c. Customer does not fully realize the impact that a technical change will have upon cost and schedule

d. Time and cost constraints are not compatible with the state of the art

e. Poor project/functional interface definition

f. Improper systems integration has created conflicts and a communications breakdown

g. Several functional managers did not realize that they were responsible for certain tasks

h. The impact of design changes are not systematically evaluated

Not all problems can be anticipated. Consider each of the situations below and decide what you would do:

- One of your employees appears to have more loyalty to his profession, discipline, or expertise, than to the project.
- You are the project manager of a nine month effort. You are now in the fifth month of the project and are more than two weeks behind schedule, with very little hope of catching up. The dam breaks in a town nearby and massive flooding and mudslides take place. Fifteen of your key functional people request to take off three days from the following week to help fellow church members dig out. Their functional managers have left the entire decision up to you.
- You decide to wait for long-term changes to a problem instead of seeking immediate response. The long-term change does not happen.
- Your functional team members are performing a repetitive task and have done it so often, they no longer listen to your instructions.
- You have read an article called "Know the Energy Cycles of Your People." You decide to implement the results of the article and let your people work occasional overtime. They produce eight units in eight hours and ten units in twelve hours (which includes four hours of overtime).
- Alpha Company, a project-driven organization, pays its department managers a quarterly bonus dependent upon two factors: The departmental overhead rate and direct labor dollars. The exact value of the bonus is proportional to how much these two factors are underrun.

  Department man-hours are priced out against the department average, which does not include the department manager's salary which is included under the departmental overhead rate, but without the option of charging overtime as direct labor to the projects that he must supply resources for. Last week's report indicated that a functional manager was charging 40 hours to your project.
- Your company has a policy that employees can participate in the educational tuition reembursement program provided that the degree will benefit the company and that the employee's immediate superior gives his permission. As a project manager, you authorize George, your assistant project manager who reports directly to you, to take courses leading to an M.B.A. degree.

  Midway through your project, you find that overtime is required on Monday and Wednesday evenings, the same two evenings that George has classes. George cannot change the evenings that his classes are offered. You try without success to reschedule the overtime to early mornings or other evenings. According to company policy the project office must supervise all overtime. Since the project office consists of only you and George, you must perform the overtime if George does not.

Below are 20 project management proverbs that show you what can go wrong:[9]

- You cannot produce a baby in one month by impregnating nine women.
- The same work under the same conditions will be estimated differently by ten different estimators or by one estimator at ten different times.
- The most valuable and least used word in a project manager's vocabulary is "NO."
- You can con a sucker into committing an unreasonable deadline, but you can't bully him into meeting it.
- The more ridiculous the deadline, the more it costs to try to meet it.
- The more desperate the situation, the more optimistic the situatee.
- Too few people on a project can't solve the problems — too many create more problems than they solve.
- You can freeze the user's specs but he won't stop expecting.
- Frozen specs and the abominable snowman are alike: They are both myths and they both melt when sufficient heat is applied.
- The conditions attached to a promise are forgotten and the promise is remembered.
- What you don't know hurts you.
- A user will tell you anything you ask about — nothing more.
- Of several possible interpretations of a communication, the least convenient one is the only correct one.
- What is not on paper has not been said.
- No major project is ever installed on time, within budget, with the same staff that started it.
- Projects progress quickly until they become 90 percent complete; then they remain at 90 percent complete forever.
- If project content is allowed to change freely, the rate of change will exceed the rate of progress.
- No major system is ever completely debugged; attempts to debug a system inevitably introduce new bugs that are even harder to find.
- Project teams detest progress reporting because it vividly demonstrates their lack of progress.
- Parkinson and Murphy are alive and well — in your project.

6.10 TIME MANAGEMENT TRAPS

Working with a variety of new people on short term projects plays havoc with the project manager's ability to make effective utilization of his time. The fol-

---

9. Source unknown.

lowing people characteristics can require continuous redirecting of a project manager's self-planning:

- People tend to resist explorations of new ideas
- People tend to mistrust each other in temporary management situations
- People tend to protect themselves
- Functional people tend to look at day-to-day activities rather than long-range efforts
- Both functional and project personnel often look for individual rather than group recognition
- People tend to create win or lose positions

On the following pages the reader will find a time management exercise to illustrate the problems that can occur. The reader should pay particular attention to the daily activities because they indicate the most common problems that can occur.

Time Management For Project Managers

Effective time management is one of the most difficult chores facing even the most experienced managers. For a manager who manages well-planned repetitive tasks, effective time management can be accomplished without very much pain. But for a project manager who must plan, schedule, and control resources and activities on unique, one-of-a-kind projects or tasks, effective time management may not be possible because of the continuous stream of unexpected problems that develop.

This exercise is designed to make you aware of the difficulties of time management both in a traditional organization as well as a project environment. Before beginning the exercise you must make the following assumptions concerning the nature of the project:

- You are the project manager on a project for an outside customer.
- The project is estimated at $3.5 million with a time span of two years.
- The two year time span is broken down into three phases: Phase I – one year, beginning February 1. Phase II – six months; Phase III – six months. You are now at the end of Phase I. (Phase I and II overlap by approximately two weeks. You are now in the Monday of the next to the last week of Phase I.) Almost all of the work has been completed.
- Your project employs between 35 to 60 people, depending upon the phase that you are in.
- You, as the project manager, have three full-time assistant project managers that report directly to you in the project office; an assistant project manager for engineering, cost control, and manufacturing. (Material procure-

ment is included as part of the responsibilities of the manufacturing assistant project manager.)

- Phase I appears to be proceeding within the time, cost, and performance constraints.
- You have a scheduled team meeting each Wednesday from 10-12 a.m. The meeting will be attended by all project office team members and the functional team members from all participating line organizations. Line managers are not team members and therefore do not show up at team meetings. It would be impossible for them to show up at the team meetings for all projects and still be able to function as a line manager. Even when requested, they may not show up at the team meeting because it is not effective time management for them to show for a two hour meeting simply to discuss ten minutes of business. (Disregard the possibility that a team meeting agenda could resolve this problem.)

It is now Monday morning. As soon as you enter your office, you will be informed about problems, situations, tasks, and activities which have to be investigated. Your problem will be to accomplish effective time management for this entire week based upon the problems and situations that occur.

You will take each day one at a time. You will be given ten problems and/or situations that will occur for each day, and the time necessary for resolution. You must try to optimize your time for each of the next five days and get the maximum amount of productive work accomplished. Obviously, the word "productive" can take on several meanings. You must determine what is meant by productive work. For simplicity sake, let us assume that your energy cycle is such that you can do eight hours of productive work in an eight hour day. You do not have to schedule idle time, except for lunch. However, you must be aware that in a project environment, the project manager occasionally becomes the catch-all for all work that line managers, line personnel and even executives do not feel like accomplishing.

Following the ten tasks for each day, you will find a worksheet which breaks down each day into half hour blocks between 9:00 a.m. and 5:00 p.m. Your job will be to determine which of the tasks you wish to accomplish during each half-hour block. The following assumptions are made in scheduling work:

- Because of car pool requirements, overtime is not permitted.
- Your wife has threatened you with large child support and alimony payments if you persist in taking work home from the office. Therefore, you will not schedule any work after 5:00 p.m.
- The project manager is advised of the 10 tasks as soon as he arrives at work.
- You start work at 8:30 each morning, but the first half hour is devoted to planning your day.

The first step in the solution to the exercise is to establish the priorities for each activity based upon:

- *Priority A:* This activity is urgent and must be completed today. (However, some A priorities can be withheld until the team meeting.)
- *Priority B:* This activity is important but not necessarily urgent.
- *Priority C:* This activity can be delayed, perhaps indefinitely.

Fill in the space after each activity as to the appropriate priority. Next you must determine which of the activities you have time to accomplish for this day. You have either seven or seven and one half hours to use for effective time management, depending whether you want a half hour or a full hour for lunch.

You have choices as to how to accomplish each of the activities. These choices are shown below:

- You can do the activity yourself. (Symbol = Y)
- You can delegate the responsibility to one of your assistant project managers (Symbol = D). If you use this technique, you can delegate only one hour's work of *your* work to each of your assistants without incurring a penalty. The key word here is that you are delegating *your work.* If the task that you wish to delegate is one which the assistant project manager would normally perform, then it does *not* count toward the one hour's worth of your work. This type of work is transmittal work and will be discussed below. For example, if you wish to delegate five hours of work to one of your assistant project managers and four of those hours are activities which would normally be his responsibility, then no penalty will be assessed. You are actually transmitting four hours and delegating one. You may assume that whatever work you assign to an assistant project manager will be completed on the day it is assigned, regardless of the priority.
- Many times the project manager and his team are asked to perform work which is normally the responsibility of someone else, say an executive or a line manager. As an example, a line employee states that he doesn't have sufficient time to write a report and he wants you to do it since you are the project manager. These types of requests can be returned to the requestor since they normally do not fall within the project manager's responsibilities. You may therefore, select one of the following four choices:
  - You can return the activity request back to the originator, whether line manager, executive or employee, since it is not your responsibility (Symbol = R). Of course, you might want to do this activity, if you have time, in order to build up good will with the requestor.
  - Many times, work that should be requested of an assistant project manager is automatically sent to the project manager. In this case, the project manager will automatically transmit this work to the appropriate assistant project manager (Symbol = T). As before, if the project manager feels that he has sufficient time available or if his assistants are burdened, he may wish to do the work himself. Work which is normally the responsibility of an assistant project manager is transmitted, not delegated.

Thus, the project manager can transmit four hours of work (T) and still delegate one hour of work (D) to the same assistant project manager without incurring any penalty.

- You can postpone work from one day to the next (Symbol = P). As an example, you decide that you want to accomplish a given Monday activity but do not have sufficient time. You can postpone the activity until Tuesday. If you do not have sufficient time on Tuesday, you may then decide to transmit (T) the activity to one of your assistants, delegate (D) the activity to one of your assistants, return (R) the activity to the requestor or postpone (P) the activity another day. Postponing activities can be a trap. On Monday you decide to postpone a Category B priority. On Tuesday, the activity may become a Category A priority and you have no time to accomplish it. If you make a decision to postpone an activity from Monday to Tuesday and find that you have made a mistake by not performing this activity on Monday, you *cannot* go back in time and correct the situation.

- You can simply consider the activity as unnecessary and avoid doing it (Symbol = A).

After you have decided which activities you will perform each day, place them in the appropriate time slot based upon *your own* energy cycle. Later we will discuss energy cycles and the order of the activities accomplished each day. You will find one worksheet for each day. The worksheets follow the 10 daily situations and/or problems.

Repeat the procedure for each of the five days. Remember to keep track of the activities that are carried over from the previous days. Several of the problems can be resolved with more than one method. If you are thoroughly trapped between two or more choices on setting priorities or modes of resolution, then write a note or two to justify your answer in space beneath each activity.

Scoring System

Briefly look at the sample work plan on the next page (Figure 1). Under the column labeled "priority," the 10 activities for each day will be listed. You must first identify the priorities for each activity. Next, under the column labeled "method," you must select the method of accomplishment according to the legend at the bottom of the page. At the same time, you must fill in the activities you wish to perform yourself under the "accomplishment" column in the appropriate time slot because your method for accomplishment may be dependent upon whether or not you have sufficient time to accomplish the activity.

Notice that there is a space provided for you to keep track of activities that have been carried over. This means that if you have three activities on Monday's list that you wish to carry over until Tudesday, then you must turn to Tuesday's work plan and record these activities so that you will not forget.

Priority			Method		Accomplishment		
Activity	Priority	Points	Method of Accomplishment	Points	Time	Activity	Points
					9:00-9:30		
					9:30-10:00		
					10:00-10:30		
					10:30-11:00		
					11:00-11:30		
					11:30-12:00		
					12:00-12:30		
					12:30-1:00		
					1:00-1:30		
					1:30-2:00		
	Total		Total		2:00-2:30		
					2:30-3:00		

Activities Postponed Until today	Today's Priority

3:00-3:30	
3:30-4:00	
4:00-4:30	
4:30-5:00	
Total	

Points	
Priority Points	
Method Points	
Accomplishment Points	
Today's Points	

Legend
Method of Accomplishment:
Y= you
D= delegate
T= transmit
R= return
A= avoid
P= postpone

Figure 1. Work Plan.

You will not score any points until you complete Friday's work plan. Using the scoring sheets which follow Friday's work plan, you can return to the daily work plans and fill in the appropriate points. You will receive either positive points or negative points for each decision that you make. Negative points should be subtracted when calculating totals.

After completing the work plans for all five days, fill in the summary work plan which follows and be prepared to answer the summary questions.

You will not be told at this time how the scoring points will be awarded because it may impact your answers.

Turn the page and begin when ready.

MONDAY'S ACTIVITIES

ACTIVITY   DESCRIPTION   PRIORITY

1.   The detailed schedules for Phase II must be up-
        dated prior to Thursday's meeting with the cus-
        tomer. (Time = 1 hr.)

2.   The Manufacturing Manager calls you and states
        that he cannot find a certain piece of equipment
        for tomorrow's production run test. (Time =
        1/2 hr.)

3.   The local university has a monthly distinguished
        lecturer series scheduled for 3-5 p.m. today. You
        have been directed by the vice-president to attend
        and hear the lecture. The company will give you
        a car. Driving time to the university is one hour.
        (Time = 3 hrs.)

4.   A manufacturer's representative wants to call on
        you today to show you why his product is supe-
        rior to the one that you are now using. (Time =
        1/2 hr.)

5.   You must write a two page weekly status report
        for the vice-president. Report is due on his desk
        by 1:00 p.m. Wednesday. (Time = 1 hr.)

6.   A vice-president calls you and suggests that you
        contact one of the other project managers about
        obtaining a uniform structure for the weekly prog-
        ress reports. (Time = 1/2 hr.)

7.   A functional manager calls to inform you that,
        due to a schedule slippage on another project,
        your beginning milestones on Phase II may slip
        to the right because his people will not be avail-
        able. He wants to know if you can look at the
        detailed schedules and modify them. (Time =
        2 hrs.)

8.   The Director of Personnel wants to know if you
        have reviewed the three resumes that he sent you
        last week. He would like your written comments
        by quitting time today. (Time = 1 hr.)

ACTIVITY	DESCRIPTION	PRIORITY
9.	One of your assistant project managers asks you to review a detailed Phase III schedule which appears to have errors. (Time = 1 hr.)	
10.	The Procurement Department calls with a request that you tell them approximately how much money you plan to spend on raw materials for Phase III. (Time = 1/2 hr.)	

Priority			Method	
Activity	Priority	Points	Method of Accomplishment	Points
1				
2				
3				
4				
5				
6				
7				
8				
9				
10				
	Total		Total	

Accomplishment		
Time	Activity	Points
9:00-9:30		
9:30-10:00		
10:00-10:30		
10:30-11:00		
11:00-11:30		
11:30-12:00		
12:00-12:30		
12:30-1:00		
1:00-1:30		
1:30-2:00		
2:00-2:30		
2:30-3:00		
3:00-3:30		
3:30-4:00		
4:00-4:30		
4:30-5:00		
Total		

Activities Postponed Until today	Today's Priority

Points	
Priority Points	
Method Points	
Accomplishment Points	
Today's Points	

Legend
Method of Accomplishment:
Y= you
D= delegate
T= transmit
R= return
A= avoid
P= postpone

Work Plan: Monday

TUESDAY'S ACTIVITIES

ACTIVITY	DESCRIPTION	PRIORITY
11.	A functional manager calls you wanting to know if his people should be scheduled for overtime next week. (Time = 1/2 hr.)	
12.	You have a Safety Board Meeting today from 1-3 p.m. and must review the agenda. (Time = 2.1/2 hrs.)	
13.	Because of an impending company cash flow problem, your boss has asked you for the detailed monthly labor expenses for the next three months. (Time = 2 hrs.)	
14.	The vice-president has just called to inform you that two Congressmen will be visiting the plant today and are requested to conduct the tour of the facility from 3-5 p.m. (Time = 2 hrs.)	
15.	You have developed a new policy for controlling overtime costs on Phase II. You must inform your people either by memo, phone, or team meeting. (Time = 1/2 hr.)	
16.	You must sign and review 25 purchase order requisitions for Phase III raw materials. It is company policy that the project manager sign all forms. Almost all of the items require a three month lead time. (Time = 1 hr.)	
17.	The Engineering Divison Manager has asked you to assist one of his people this afternoon in the solution of a technical problem. You are not required to do this. It would be as a personal favor for the Engineering Manager, a man whom you reported to for the six years that you were an engineering functional manager. (Time = 2 hrs.)	
18.	The Data Processing Department Manager informs you that the company is trying to eliminate unnecessary reports. He would like you to tell him which reports you can do without. (Time = 1/2 hr.)	
19.	The Assistant Project Manager for Cost informs you that he does not know how to fill out the revised corporate project review form. (Time = 1/2 hr.)	

ACTIVITY	DESCRIPTION	PRIORITY

20. One of the functional managers wants an immediate explanation of why the scope of effort for Phase II was changed this late into the project and why he wasn't informed. (Time = 1 hr.)

Priority			Method	
Activity	Priority	Points	Method of Accomplishment	Points
11				
12				
13				
14				
15				
16				
17				
18				
19				
20				
	Total		Total	

Accomplishment		
Time	Activity	Points
9:00-9:30		
9:30-10:00		
10:00-10:30		
10:30-11:00		
11:00-11:30		
11:30-12:00		
12:00-12:30		
12:30-1:00		
1:00-1:30		
1:30-2:00		
2:00-2:30		
2:30-3:00		
3:00-3:30		
3:30-4:00		
4:00-4:30		
4:30-5:00		
Total		

Activities Postponed Until today	Today's Priority

Points	
Priority Points	
Method Points	
Accomplishment Points	
Today's Points	

Legend
Method of Accomplishment:
Y= you
D= delegate
T= transmit
R= return
A= avoid
P= postpone

Work Plan: Tuesday

WEDNESDAY'S ACTIVITIES

ACTIVITY	DESCRIPTION	PRIORITY

21.   A vice-president calls you stating that he has just read the rough draft of your Phase I report and wants to discuss some of the conclusions with you before the report is submitted to the customer on Thursday. (Time = 2 hrs.)

22.   The Reproduction Department informs you that they are expecting the final version of the in-house quarterly report for your project by noon today. The report is on your desk waiting for final review. (Time = 1 hr.)

23.   The Manufacturing Department Manager calls to say that they may have to do more work than initially defined for in Phase II. A meeting is requested. (Time = 1 hr.)

24.   Quality Control sends you a memo stating that, unless changes are made, they will not be able to work with the engineering specifications developed for Phase III. A meeting will be required with all assistant project managers in attendance. (Time = 1 hr.)

25.   A functional manager calls to tell you that the raw data from yesterday's tests are terrific and invites you to come up to the laboratory and see the results yourself. (Time = 1 hr.)

26.   Your assistant project manager is having trouble resolving a technical problem. The functional manager wants to deal with you directly. This problem must be resolved by Friday or else a major Phase II milestone might slip. (Time = 1 hr.)

27.   You have a technical interchange meeting with the customer scheduled for 1-3 p.m. on Thursday, and must review the handout before it goes to publication. The Reproduction Department has requested at least 12 hours notice. (Time = 1 hr.)

28.   You have a weekly team meeting from 10-12 a.m. (Time = 2 hrs.)

ACTIVITY	DESCRIPTION	PRIORITY
29.	You must dictate minutes to your secretary concerning your weekly team meeting. (Time = 1/2 hr.)	
30.	A new project problem has occurred in the manufacturing area and your manufacturing functional team members are reluctant to make a decision. (Time = 1 hr.)	

Priority			Method		Accomplishment		
Activity	Priority	Points	Method of Accomplishment	Points	Time	Activity	Points
21					9:00-9:30		
22					9:30-10:00		
23					10:00-10:30		
24					10:30-11:00		
25					11:00-11:30		
26					11:30-12:00		
27					12:00-12:30		
28					12:30-1:00		
29					1:00-1:30		
30					1:30-2:00		
Total			Total		2:00-2:30		
					2:30-3:00		
					3:00-3:30		
					3:30-4:00		
					4:00-4:30		
					4:30-5:00		
					Total		

Activities Postponed Until today	Today's Priority

Points	
Priority Points	
Method Points	
Accomplishment Points	
Today's Points	

Legend
Method of Accomplishment;
Y= you
D= delegate
T= transmit
R= return
A= avoid
P= postpone

Work Plan: Wednesday

THURSDAY'S ACTIVITIES

ACTIVITY   DESCRIPTION   PRIORITY

31.   The Electrical Engineering Department informs
        you that they have completed some Phase II
        activities ahead of schedule and want to know
        if you wish to push any other activities to the
        left. (Time = 1 hr.)

32.   The Assistant Project Manager for Cost informs
        you that the corporate overhead rate is increasing
        faster than anticipated. If this continues, severe
        costs overruns will occur in Phases II and III. A
        schedule and cost review is necessary. (Time =
        2 hrs.)

33.   Your insurance man is calling to see if you wish
        to increase your life insurance. (Time = 1/2 hr.)

34.   You cannot find one of last week's manufacturing
        line manager's technical reports as to departmental
        project status. You'll need it for the customer tech-
        nical interchange meeting. (Time = 1/2 hr.)

35.   One of your carpool members wants to talk to you
        concerning next Saturday's golf tournament. (Time
        = 1/2 hr.)

36.   A functional manager call to inform you that, due
        to a change in his division's workload priorities,
        people with the necessary technical expertise may
        not be available for next week's Phase II tasks.
        (Time = 2 hrs.)

37.   An employee calls you stating that he is receiving
        conflicting instructions from one of your assistant
        project managers and his line manager. (Time =
        1 hr.)

38.   The customer has requested bi-monthly instead of
        monthly team meetings for Phase II. You must de-
        cide whether or not to add an additional project
        office team member to support the added workload.
        (Time = 1/2 hr.)

39.   Your secretary reminds you that you must make a
        presentation to the Rotary Club tonight on how

ACTIVITY	DESCRIPTION	PRIORITY

your project will affect the local economy. You must prepare your speech. (Time = 2 hrs.)

40. The bank has just called you concerning your overdrawn checking account. (Time = 1/2 hr.)

Priority			Method		Accomplishment		
Activity	Priority	Points	Method of Accomplishment	Points	Time	Activity	Points
31					9:00-9:30		
32					9:30-10:00		
33					10:00-10:30		
34					10:30-11:00		
35					11:00-11:30		
36					11:30-12:00		
37					12:00-12:30		
38					12:30-1:00		
39					1:00-1:30		
40					1:30-2:00		
	Total		Total		2:00-2:30		
					2:30-3:00		
					3:00-3:30		
					3:30-4:00		
					4:00-4:30		
					4:30-5:00		
					Total		

Activities Postponed Until today	Today's Priority

Points	
Priority Points	
Method Points	
Accomplishment Points	
Today's Points	

Legend
Method of Accomplishment:
Y= you
D= delegate
T= transmit
R= return
A= avoid
P= postpone

Work Plan: Thursday

FRIDAY'S ACTIVITIES

ACTIVITY	DESCRIPTION	PRIORITY

41.   An assistant project manager has asked for your
        solution to a recurring problem. (Time = 1/2 hr.)

42.   A functional employee is up for a merit review.
        You must fill out a brief checklist form and dis-
        cuss it with the employee. The form must be on
        the functional manager's desk by next Tuesday.
        (Time = 1/2 hr.)

43.   The Personnel Department wants you to review the
        summer vacation schedule for your project office
        personnel. (Time = 1/2 hr.)

44.   The vice-president calls you into his office stating
        that he has seen the excellent test results from
        this week's work, and feels that a follow-on con-
        tract should be considered. He wants to know if
        you can develop reasonable justification for re-
        questing a follow-on contract at this early date.
        (Time = 1 hr.)

45.   The travel department says that you'll have to make
        your own travel arrangements for next month's
        trip to one of the customers since you are taking
        a planned vacation trip in conjunction with the
        customer visit. (Time = 1/2 hr.)

46.   The Personnel Manager has asked if you would be
        willing to conduct a screening interview for an ap-
        plicant who wants to be an assistant project man-
        ager. The applicant will be available this afternoon
        from 1-2 p.m. (Time = 1 hr.)

47.   Your assistant project manager wants to know why
        you haven't approved his request to take MBA
        courses this quarter. (Time = 1/2 hr.)

48.   Your assistant project manager wants to know if
        he has the authority to visit vendors without in-
        forming procurement. (Time = 1/2 hr.)

49.   You have just received your copy of *Engineering
        Review Quarterly* and would like to look it over.
        (Time = 1/2 hr.)

ACTIVITY	DESCRIPTION	PRIORITY

50. You have been asked to make a statement before the Grievance Committee (this Friday, 10-12 a.m.) because one of the functional employees has complained about working overtime on Sunday mornings. You'll have to be in attendance for the entire meeting. (Time = 2 hrs.)

Priority			Method		Accomplishment		
Activity	Priority	Points	Method of Accomplishment	Points	Time	Activity	Points
41					9:00-9:30		
42					9:30-10:00		
43					10:00-10:30		
44					10:30-11:00		
45					11:00-11:30		
46					11:30-12:00		
47					12:00-12:30		
48					12:30-1:00		
49					1:00-1:30		
50					1:30-2:00		
	Total		Total		2:00-2:30		
					2:30-3:00		
					3:00-3:30		
					3:30-4:00		
					4:00-4:30		
					4:30-5:00		
					Total		

Activities Postponed Until today	Today's Priority

Points	
Priority Points	
Method Points	
Accomplishment Points	
Today's Points	

```
            Legend
Method of Accomplishment:
       Y= you
       D= delegate
       T= transmit
       R= return
       A= avoid
       P= postpone
```

Work Plan: Friday

Rationale And Point Awards

In the answers which follow, your recommendations may differ from those of the author because of the type of industry or the nature of the project. You will be given the opportunity to defend your answers at a later time.

(a) If you selected the correct priority according to the table on the following page, then the following system should be employed for awarding points:

PRIORITY	POINTS
A	10
B	5
C	3

(b) If you selected the correct accomplishment mode according to the table on the following page, then the following system should be employed for assigning points:

METHOD OF ACCOMPLISHMENT	POINTS
Y	10
T	10
P	8
D	8
A	6

(c) You will receive 10 bonus points for each correctly postponed or delayed activity accomplished during the team meeting.

(d) You will receive 5 points for each half hour time slot in which you perform a Priority A activity (one which is correctly identified as priority A).

(e) You will receive a 10 point penalty for any activity which is split.

(f) You will receive a 20 point penalty for each Priority A or B activity not accomplished by you or your team by Friday at 5:00 p.m.

Activity	Rationale

1.   The updating of schedules, especially for Phase II, should be of prime importance because of the impact on functional resources. These schedules can be delegated to assistant project managers. However, with a team meeting scheduled for Wednesday, it should be an easy task to update the schedules when all of the players are present. The updating of the schedules should *not* be delayed until Thursday. Sufficient time must be allocated for close analysis and reproduction services.

2.   This must be done immediately. Your assistant project manager for manufacturing should be able to handle this activity.

3.   You must handle this yourself.

4.   Here, we assume that the representative is available only today. The assistant project managers can handle this activity. This activity may be important if you were unaware of this vendor's product.

5.   This could be delegated to your assistants provided that you allow sufficient time for personal review on Wednesday.

6.   Delaying this activity for one more week should not cause any problems. This activity can be delegated.

7.   You must take charge at once.

8.   Even though your main concern is the project, you still must fulfill your company's administrative requirements.

9.   This can be delayed until Wednesday's team meeting, especially since these are Phase III schedules. However, there is no guarantee that line people will be ready or knowledgeable to discuss phase III this early. You will probably have to do this yourself.

10.   The procurement request must be answered. Your assistant project manager for manufacturing should have this information available.

11.   This is urgent and should *not* be postponed until the team meeting. Good project managers will give functional managers as much information as possible and as early as possible for resource control. This task can be delegated to the assistant project managers, but it is not recommended.

12.   This belongs to the project manager. The agenda review and the meeting can be split, but it is not recommended.

13.   This must be done immediately. The results could severely limit your resources (especially if overtime would normally be required). Although your assistant project managers will probably be involved, the majority of the work is yours.

14.   Most project managers hate a request as this but know that situations as this are inevitable.

Activity	Rationale
15.	Project policies should be told by the project manager himself. Policy changes should be announced as early as possible. Team meetings are appropriate for such actions.
16.	Obviously, the project manager must do this task himself. Fortunately, there is sufficient time if the lead times are accurate.
17.	The priority of this activity is actually your choice, but an A priority is preferred if you have time. This activity cannot be delegated.
18.	This activity must be done, but the question is when. Parts of this task can be delegated, but the final decision must be made by the project manager.
19.	Obviously you must do this yourself. Your priority, of course, depends upon the deadline on the corporate project review form.
20.	The project manager must perform this activity immediately.
21.	Top level executives from both the customer and contractor often communicate project status among themselves. Therefore, since the conclusions in the report reflect corporate policy, this activity should be accomplished immediately.
22.	The reproduction department considers each job as a project and therefore you should not try to violate their milestones. This activity can be delegated depending upon the nature of the report.
23.	This could have a severe impact on your program. Although you could delegate this to one of your assistants, you should do this yourself because of the ramifications.
24.	This must be done and the team meeting is the ideal place.
25.	You personally should give the functional manager the courtesy of showing you his outstanding results. However, it is not a high priority and could even be delegated or postponed since you'll see the data eventually.
26.	The question here is the importance of the problem. The problem must be resolved by Thursday in case an executive meeting needs to be scheduled to establish company direction. Waiting until the last minute can be catastrophic here.
27.	The project manager should personally review all data presented to the customer. Check Thursday's schedule. Did you forget the interchange meeting?
28.	This is your show.
29.	This should be done immediately. Non-participants need to know project status. The longer you wait, the greater the risk that you will neglect something important. This activity can be delegated but it is not recommended.

Activity	Rationale
30.	You may have to solve this yourself even though you have an assistant project manager for manufacturing. The decision may impact the schedule and milestones.
31.	Activities as this do not happen very often. But when they do, the project manager should make the most of them, as fast as he can. These are gold mine activities. They can be delegated, but not postponed.
32.	If this activity is not accomplished immediately, the results can be catastrophic. Regardless of the project manager's first inclination to delegate, this activity should be done by the project manager himself.
33.	This activity can be postponed or even avoided, if necessary.
34.	Obviously, if the report is that important, then your assistant project managers should have copies of the report and the activity can be delegated.
35.	This activity should be discussed in the carpool, not on company time.
36.	This is extremely serious. The line manager would probably prefer to work directly with the project manager on this problem.
37.	This is an activity which you should handle. Transmitting this to one of your assistants may aggravate the situation further. Although it is possible that this activity could be postponed, it is highly unlikely that time would smooth out the conflict.
38.	This is a decision for the project manager. Extreme urgency may not be necessary.
39.	Project managers also have a social responsibility.
40.	The solution to this activity is up for grabs. The inability of an employee to pay his bills reflects not only upon the employee, but can provide embarrassment to the company. Therefore, the company must realize that employees occasionally need company time to complete personal business.
41.	Why is he asking you about a recurring problem? How did he solve it last time? Let him do it again.
42.	You must do this personally, but it can wait until Monday.
43.	This activity is not urgent and can be accomplished by your assistant project managers.
44.	This could be your lucky day.
45.	Although most managers would prefer to delegate this activity to their secretary, it is really the responsibility of the project manager since it involves personal business.
46.	This is an example of an administrative responsibility which is required of all personnel regardless of the job title or management level. This activity must be accomplished today, if time permits.

Activity	Rationale
47.	Although you might consider this as a B priority or one which can be postponed, you must remember that your assistant project manager considers this as an A priority and would like an answer today. You are morally obligated to give him the answer today.
48.	Why can't he get the answer himself? Whether or not you handle this activity might depend on the priority and how much time you have available.
49.	How important is it for you to review the publication?
50.	This is mandatory attendance on your behalf. You have total responsibility for all overtime scheduled on your project. You may wish to bring one of your assistant project managers with you for moral support.

ACTIVITY	Monday PRIOR.	Monday ACCOM.	Tuesday PRIOR.	Tuesday ACCOM.	Wednesday PRIOR.	Wednesday ACCOM.	Thursday PRIOR.	Thursday ACCOM.	Friday PRIOR.	Friday ACCOM.
1	B	D,Y,T,P	B	D,Y,T,P	A	D,Y,T				
2	A	D,Y,T								
3	A	Y								
4	A/B	D,Y,T								
5	B	D,Y,P	B	D,Y,P	A	D,Y				
6	B	D,Y,P	B	D,Y,P	B	D,Y,P	B	D,Y,P	B	D,Y,P
7	A	Y								
8	A	Y								
9	B	Y,P	B	Y,P	A	Y				
10	B	Y,T,P	B	Y,T,P	B	Y,T,P	B	Y,T,P	B	Y,T,P
11			A	D,Y,T						
12			A	Y						
13			A	Y,P						
14			A	Y						
15			B	P,Y	A	Y				
16			B	Y,P	B	Y,P	B	Y,P	B	Y,P
17			C	A,Y						
18			B/C	D,Y,P	B	D,Y,P	B	D,Y,P	B	D,Y,P
19			A/B	Y,P	A/B	Y,P	A/B	Y,P	A/B	Y,P
20			A	Y						
21					A	Y				
22					A	D,Y				
23					A	D,Y,T				
24					A	Y				
25					B	Y,T,P,D	B	Y,T,P,D	B	Y,T,P
26					B	Y	A	Y		
27					A	Y				
28					A	Y				
29					A	Y,D				
30					A	Y,T				
31							A	Y,D		
32							A	Y		
33							C	Y,P	C	Y,P
34							A	Y,T		
35							C	A,P	C	A,P
36							A	Y,T		
37							A	Y		
38							B	Y,P	B	Y,P
39							A	Y		
40							A	Y		
41									A/B	R
42									B	Y,P
43									B	Y,P,D
44									A	Y
45									B	Y,P
46									A	Y,T,D
47									A	Y
48									B	Y,T,P,D
49									C	Y,P,A
50									A	Y

Priority/Accomplishment Mode.

Now take the total points for each day and comple the following table:

SUMMARY WORK PLAN	
DAY	POINTS
Monday	
Tuesday	
Wednesday	
Thursday	
Friday	
TOTAL	

Conclusions And Summary Questions:

1. Project managers have a tendency of wanting to carry the load themselves, even if it means working 60 hours a week. You were told to do everything within your normal working day. But, as a potentially good project manager, you probably have the natural tendency of wanting to postpone some work until a later date so that you can do it yourself. Doing the activities, when they occur, even through transmittal or delegation, is probably the best policy. You might wish to do the game again at a later time and see if you can beat your present score. Only this time, try to do as many tasks as possible on each day, even if it means delegation.

2. Several of the activities were company, not project requests. Project managers have a tendency to avoid administrative responsibilities unless it deals directly with their project. This process of project management "tunnel vision" can lead to antagonism and conflicts if the proper attitude is not developed on the part of the project manager. This can easily carry down to his assistants as well.

3. Several of the activities could have been returned to the requestor. However, in a project environment where the project manager cannot be successful without the functional manager's support, most project managers would never turn away a line employee's request for assistance.

4. Make a list of the activities where your answers differ from those of the answer key and where you feel that there exists sufficient justification for your interpretation.

5. Quite often self-productivity can be increased by knowing one's own energy cycle. Are your more important meetings in the mornings or afternoons? What time of day do you perform your most productive work?

When do you do your best writing? Does your energy cycle vary according to the day of the week?

In the space provided below, set up your criteria for your own energy cycle based upon the above questions. Try to be specific as to the hours of the day.

Criteria 1: _____

Criteria 2: _____

Criteria 3: _____

Criteria 4: _____

Criteria 5: _____

Criteria 6: _____

6. Now let's see if you can truly optimize your time once you know the energy cycle. On the following pages you will find an energy cycle and two tables. Assume that the energy cycle in the figure is yours. Fill in the tables based upon this energy cycle and assuming that:

  A. You can reschedule the following meetings to any day of the week, or any time of day:
  a. Customer interchange meeting
  b. Weekly team meeting
  c. Safety Board meeting
  d. Grievance Committee meeting
  B. You *cannot* change the following:
  a. Tour for the two congressmen
  b. Rotary Club presentation
  C. You can schedule or reschedule any of the other activities for mornings or afternoons, and any day of the week.
  D. You can delegate or transmit only those activities that are so specified according to the answer key for the first part of the exercise.
  E. You can work a maximum of one hour of overtime per day provided that the work can be accomplished at home. (Remember, you are part of a carpool.)

Fill in the tables using the given energy cycle. Try to include the fact that the energy cycle can also vary according to days of the week.

Table 1.

ACTIVITY	PRIORITY	TO BE DONE IN THE			
		EARLY A.M.	LATE A.M.	EARLY P.M.	LATE P.M.
1					
2					
3					
4					
5					
6					
7					
8					
9					
10					
11					
12					
13					
14					
15					
16					
17					
18					
19					
20					
21					
22					
23					
24					
25					
26					
27					
28					
29					
30					
31					
32					
33					
34					
35					
36					
37					
38					
39					
40					
41					
42					
43					
44					
45					
46					
47					
48					
49					
50					

CASE STUDY: THE BLUE SPIDER PROJECT*

"This is impossible! Just totally impossible! Ten months ago I was sitting on top of the world. Upper-level management considered me one of the best, if not the best, engineer in the plant. Now look at me! I have bags under my eyes, I haven't slept soundly in the last six months, and here I am, cleaning out my desk. I'm sure glad they gave me back my old job in engineering. I guess I could have saved myself a lot of grief and aggravation had I not accepted the promotion to project manager."

History

Gary Anderson had accepted a position with Parks Corporation right out of college. With a Ph.D. in mechanical engineering, Gary was ready to solve the world's

---

*Copyright © 1978 by Harold Kerzner

Table 2.

TIME	MONDAY	TUESDAY	ACTIVITIES WEDNESDAY	THURSDAY	FRIDAY
9:00-9:30					
9:30-10:00					
10:00-10:30					
10:30-11:00					
11:00-11:30					
11:30-12:00					
12:00-12:30					
12:30-1:00					
1:00-1:30					
1:30-2:00					
2:00-2:30					
2:30-3:00					
3:00-3:30					
3:30-4:00					
4:00-4:30					
4:30-5:00					
5:00-5:30					
5:30-6:00					
6:00-6:30					
6:30-7:00					

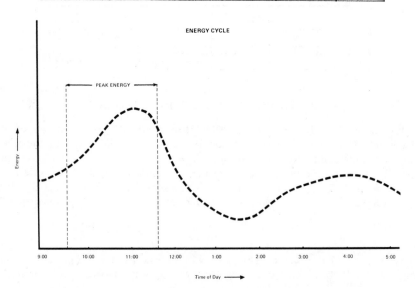

Figure 1. Energy Cycle Per Day.

most traumatic problems. At first, Parks Corporation offered Gary little opportunity to do the pure research which he eagerly wanted to undertake. However, things soon changed. Parks grew into a major electronics and structural design corporation during the big boom of the late fifties and early sixties when the Department of Defense (DoD) contracts were plentiful.

Parks Corporation grew from a handful of engineers to a major DoD contractor, employing some 6500 people. During the recession of the late sixties, money became scarce and major layoffs resulted in lowering the employment level to 2200 employees. At that time, Parks decided to get out of the R & D business and compete as a low-cost production facility while maintaining an engineering organization solely to support production requirements.

After attempts at virtually every project management organizational structure, Parks Corporation selected the matrix form. Each project had a program manager who reported to the director of program management. Each project also maintained an assistant project manager, normally a project engineer, who reported directly to the project manager and indirectly to the director of engineering. The program manager spent most of his time worrying about cost and time whereas the assistant program manager worried more about technical performance.

With the poor job market for engineers, Gary and his colleagues began taking coursework toward an MBA degree should the job market deteriorate further.

In 1975, with the upturn in DoD spending, Parks had to change its corporate strategy. Parks had spent the last seven years bidding on the production phase of large programs. But now, with the new evaluation criteria set forth for contract awards, those companies winning the R & D and qualification phases had a definite edge on being awarded the production contract. The production contract was where the big profits could be found. In keeping with this new strategy, Parks began to beef up its R & D engineering staff. By 1978, Parks had increased in size to 2700 employees. The increase was mostly in engineering. Experienced R & D personnel were difficult to find for the salaries that Parks was offering. Parks was, however, able to lure some employees away from the competitors, but relied mostly upon the younger, inexperienced engineers fresh out of college.

With the adoption of this corporate strategy, Parks Corporation administered a new wage and salary program which included job upgrading. Gary was promoted to senior scientist, responsible for all R & D activities performed in the mechanical engineering department. Gary had distinguished himself as an outstanding production engineer during the past several years, and management felt that his contribution could be extended to R & D as well.

In January, 1978 Parks Corporation decided to compete for Phase I of the Blue Spider Project, an R & D effort which, if successful, could lead into a $500 million program spread out over twenty years. The Blue Spider Project was an attempt to improve the structural capabilities of the Spartan Missile, a short-range tactical missile used by the Army. The Spartan Missile was exhibiting fatigue failure after six years in the field. This was three years less than what the original design specifications called for. The Army wanted new materials which could result in a longer age life for the Spartan Missile.

Lord Industries was the prime contractor for the Army's Spartan Program. Parks Corporation would be a subcontractor to Lord if they could successfully bid and win the project. The criteria for subcontractor selection was based not only on low bid, but also on technical expertise as well as management performance on other projects. Parks' management felt that they had a distinct advantage over most of the other competitors because they had successfully worked on other projects for Lord Industries.

The Blue Spider Project Kickoff

On November 3, 1977 Henry Gable, the Director of Engineering, called Gary Anderson into his office.

Henry: Gary, I've just been notified through the grapevine that Lord will be issuing the RFP for the Blue Spider Project by the end of this month, with a thirty-day response period. I've been waiting a long time for a project like this to come along so that I can experiment with some new ideas that I have. This project is going to be my baby all the way! I want you to head up the proposal team. I think it must be an engineer. I'll make sure that you get a good proposal manager to help you. If we start working now, we can get close to two months of research in before proposal submittal. That will give us a one month edge on our competitors.

Gary was pleased to be involved in such an effort. He had absolutely no trouble in getting functional support for the R & D effort necessary to put together a technical proposal. All of the functional managers continually remarked to Gary that, "This must be a biggy. The director of engineering has thrown all of his support behind you."

On December 2, the RFP was received. The only trouble area that Gary could see was that the technical specifications stated that all components must be able to operate normally and successfully through a temperature range of -65°F to 145°F. Current testing indicated the Parks Corporation's design would not function above 130°F. An intensive R & D effort was conducted over the next three weeks. Everywhere Gary looked, it appeared that the entire organization was working on his technical proposal.

A week before the final proposal was to be submitted, Gary and Henry Gable met to develop a company position concerning the inability of the preliminary design material to be operated above 130°F.

Gary: Henry, I don't think it is going to be possible to meet specification requirements unless we change our design material or incorporate new materials. Everything I've tried indicates we're in trouble.

Henry: We're in trouble only if the customer knows about it. Let the proposal state that we expect our design to be operative up to 155°F. That'll please the customer.

Gary: That seems unethical to me. Why don't we just tell them the truth?

Henry: The truth doesn't always win proposals. I picked you to head up this effort because I thought that you'd understand. I could have just as easily selected one of our many moral project managers. I'm considering you for program manager after we win the program. If you're going to pull this conscientious crap on me like the other project managers do, I'll find someone else. Look at it this way; later we can convince the customer to change the specifications. After all, we'll be so far down stream that he'll have no choice.

After two solid months of sixteen-hour days, the proposal was submitted. On February 10, 1978 Lord Industries announced that Parks Corporation would be awarded the Blue Spider Project. The contract called for a ten-month effort, negotiated at $2.2 million at a firm-fixed price.

Selecting the Project Manager

Following contract award, Henry Gable called Gary in for a conference.

Henry: Congratulations Gary! You did a fine job. The Blue Spider Project has great potential for on-going business over the next ten years, provided that we perform well during the R & D phase. Obviously you're the most qualified person in the plant to head up the project. How would you feel about a transfer to program management?

Gary: I think it would be a real challenge. I could make maximum use of the MBA degree I earned last year. I've always wanted to be in program management.

Henry: Having several masters degrees, or even doctorates for that matter, does not guarantee that you'll be a successful project manager. There are three requirements for effective program management; you must be able to communicate both in writing and orally; you must know how to motivate people; and you must be willing to give up your car pool. The last one is extremely important in that program managers must be totally committed and dedicated to the program, regardless of how much time is involved.

But this is not the reason why I asked you to come here. Going from project engineering to program management is a big step. There are only two places you can go from program management; up the organization or out the door. I know of very, very few engineers that failed in program management and were permitted to return.

Gary: Why is that? If I'm considered to be the best engineer in the plant, why can't I return to engineering?

Henry: "Program management is a world of its own. It has its own formal and informal organizational ties. Program managers are outsiders. You'll find out. You might not be able to keep the strong personal ties you now have with your fellow employees. You'll have to force even your best friends to comply with your standards. Program managers can go from program to program but functional departments remain intact.

I'm telling you all this for a reason. We've worked well together the past several years. But if I sign the release so that you can work for Grey in Program Management, you'll be on your own, like hiring into a new company. I've already signed the release but you still have some time to think about it.

Gary: One thing I don't understand. With all of the good program managers we have here, why am I given this opportunity?

Henry: Almost all of our program managers are over 45 years old. This resulted from our massive layoffs several years ago when we were forced to let go of the younger, inexperienced program managers. You were selected because of your age and because all of our other program managers have worked on only production-type programs. We need someone at the reins who knows R & D. Your counterpart at Lord Industries will be an R & D type. You have to fight fire with fire.

I have an ulterior motive for wanting you to accept this position. Because of the division of authority between program management and project engineering, I need someone in program management who I can communicate with concerning R & D work. The program managers we have now are interested only in time and cost. We need a manager who will bend over backwards to get performance also. I think you're that man. You know the commitment we made to Lord when we submitted that proposal. You have to try to achieve that. Remember, this program is my baby. You'll get all the support you need. I'm tied up on another project now. But when it's over, I'll be following your work like a hawk. We'll have to get together occasionally and discuss new techniques.

"Take a day or two to think it over. If you want the position, make an appointment to see Elliot Grey, the Director of Program Management. He'll give you the same speech I did. I'll assign Paul Evans to you as chief project engineer. He's a seasoned veteran and you should have no trouble working with him. He'll give you good advice. He's a good man.

The Work Begins

Gary accepted the new challenge. His first major hurdle occurred in staffing the project. The top priority given to him to bid the program did not follow through for staffing. The survival of Parks Corporation depended upon the profits received from the production programs. In keeping with this philosophy Gary found that engineering managers (even his former boss) were reluctant to give up their key people to the Blue Spider Program. However, with a little support from Henry Gable, Gary formed an adequate staff for the program.

Right from the start Gary was worried that the test matrix called out in the technical volume of the proposal would not produce results which could satisfy specifications. Gary had a milestone, 90 days after go-ahead, to identify the raw materials which could satisfy specification requirements. Gary and Paul Evans held a meeting to map out their strategy for the first few months.

Gary: Well Paul, we're starting out with our backs against the wall on this one. Any recommendations?

Paul: I also have my doubts in the validity of this test matrix. Fortunately, I've been through this before. Gable thinks this is his project and he'll sure as hell try to manipulate us. I have to report to him every morning at 7:30 A.M. with the raw data results of the previous day's testing. He wants to see it before you do. He also stated that he wants to meet with me alone. Lord will be the big problem. If the test matrix proves to be a failure, we're going to have to change the scope of effort. Remember, this is an FFP contract. If we change the scope of work and do additional work in the earlier phases of the program, then we should prepare a tradeoff analysis to see what we can delete downstream so as to not overrun the budget.

Gary: I'm going to let the other project office personnel handle the administrating work. You and I are going to live in the research labs until we get some results. We'll let the other project office personnel run the weekly team meetings.

For the next three weeks Gary and Paul spent virtually twelve hours per day, seven days a week, in the research and development lab. None of the results showed any promise. Gary kept trying to set up a meeting with Henry Gable but always found him unavailable.

During the fourth week, Gary, Paul, and the key functional department managers met to develop an alternate test matrix. The new test matrix looked good. Gary and his team worked frantically to develop a new workable schedule that would not have impact on the second milestone which was to occur at the end of 180 days. The second milestone was the final acceptance of the raw materials and preparation of production runs of the raw materials to verify that there would be no scale-up differences between lab development and full scale production.

Gary personally prepared all of the technical handouts for the interchange meeting. After all, he would be the one presenting all of the data. The technical interchange meeting was scheduled for two days. On the first day, Gary presented all of the data, including test results, and the new test matrix. The customer appeared displeased with the progress to date and decided to have their own in-house caucus that evening to go over the material which was presented. The following morning the customer stated their position:

First of all, Gary, we're quite pleased to have a project manager who has such a command of technology. That's good. But every time we've tried to contact you last month, you were unavailable or had to be paged in the research laboratories. You did an acceptable job presenting the technical data, but the administrative data was presented by your project office personnel. We, at Lord, do not think that you're maintaining the proper balance between your technical and administrative responsibilities. We prefer that you personally give the administrative data and your chief project engineer present the technical data.

We did not receive any agenda. Our people like to know what will be discussed, and when. We also want a copy of all handouts to be presented at least three days in advance. We need time to scrutinize the data. You can't expect us to walk in here blind and make decisions after seeing the data for ten minutes.

To be frank, we feel that the data to date is totally unacceptable. If the data does not improve, we will have no choice but to issue a stop workage order and look for a new contractor. The new test matrix looks good, especially since this is a firm-fixed-price contract. Your company will burden all costs for the additional work. A tradeoff with later work may be possible, but this will depend upon the results presented at the second design review meeting, ninety days from now.

We have decided to establish a customer office at Parks to follow your work more closely. Our people feel that monthly meetings are insufficient during R & D activities. We would like our customer representative to have daily verbal meetings with you or your staff. He will then keep us posted. Obviously, we had expected to review much more experimental data than you have given us.

Many of our top quality engineers would like to talk directly to your engineering community, without having to continually waste time by having to go through the project office. We must insist upon this last point. Remember, your effort may be only $2.2 million but our total package is $100 million. We have a lot more at stake than you people do. Our engineers do not like to get information that has been filtered by the project office. They want to help you.

And last, don't forget that you people have a contractual requirement to prepare complete minutes for all interchange meetings. Send us the original for signature before going to publication.

Although Gary was unhappy with the first team meeting, especially with the requests made by Lord Industries, he felt that they had sufficient justification for their comments. Following the team meeting, Gary personally prepared the complete minutes. "This is absured," thought Gary. "I've wasted almost one entire week doing nothing more than administrative paperwork. Why do we need such detailed minutes? Can't a rough summary just as well suffice? Why is it that customers want everything documented? That's like an indication of fear. We've been completely cooperative with them. There has been no hostility between us. If we've gotten this much paperwork to do now, I hate to imagine what it will be like if we get into trouble."

A New Role

Gary completed and distributed the minutes to the customer as well as to all key team members.

For the next five weeks testing went according to plan, or at least Gary thought that it had. The results were still poor. Gary was so caught up in administrative paperwork that he hadn't found time to visit the research labs in over a month. On a Wednesday morning, Gary entered the lab to observe the morning testing. Upon arriving in the lab, Gary found Paul Evans, Henry Gable and two technicians testing a new material, JXB-3.

Henry: "Gary, your problems will soon be over. This new material, JXB-3, will permit you to satisfy specification requirements. Paul and I have been testing it for two weeks. We wanted to let you know, but were afraid that if the word leaked out to the customer that we were spending his money for testing materials that were not called out in the program plan, then he would probably go crazy and might cancel the contract. Look at these results. They're super!"

Gary: Am I supposed to be the one to tell the customer now? This could cause a big wave.

Henry: There won't be any wave. Just tell them that we did it with our own IR & D funds. That'll please them because they'll think we're spending our own money to support their program.

Before presenting the information to Lord, Gary called a team meeting to present the new data to the project personnel. At the team meeting, one functional manager spoke out:

This is a hell of a way to run a program. I like to be kept informed about everything that's happening here at Parks. How can the project office expect to get support out of the functional departments if we're kept in the dark until the very last minute? My people have been working with the existing materials for the last two months and you're telling us that it was all for nothing. Now you're giving us a material that's so new that we have no information on it whatsoever. We're now going to have to play catch-up, and that's going to cost you plenty.

One week before the 180-day milestone meeting, Gary submitted the handout package to Lord Industries for preliminary review. An hour later the phone rang.

Customer: "We've just read your handout. Where did this new material come from? How come we were not informed that this work was going on? You know, of course, that our customer, the Army, will be at this meeting. How can we explain this to them? We're postponing the review meeting until all of our people have analyzed the data and are prepared to make a decision. The purpose of a review or interchange meeting is to exchange information when *both* parties have familiarity with the topic. Normally, we (Lord Industries) require almost weekly interchange meetings with our other customers because we don't trust them. We disregarded this policy with Parks Corporation based upon past working relationships. But with the new state of developments, you have forced us to revert to our previous position since we now question Parks Corporation's integrity in communicating with us. At first we believed this was due to an inexperienced program manager, Now, we're not sure.

Gary: I wonder if the real reason we have these interchange meetings isn't to show our people that Lord Industries doesn't trust us. You're creating a hell of a lot of work for us, you know.

Customer: You people put yourself in this position. Now you have to live with it.

Two weeks later Lord reluctantly agreed that the new material offered the greatest promise. Three weeks later the design review meeting was held. The Army was definitely not pleased with the prime contractor's recommendation to put a new untested material into a multimillion dollar effort.

The Communications Breakdown

During the week following the design review meeting Gary planned to make the first verification mix in order to establish final specifications for selection of the raw materials. Unfortunately, the manufacturing plans were a week behind schedule, primarily due to Gary, since he had decided to reduce costs by accepting the responsibility for developing the bill of materials himself.

A meeting was called by Gary to consider rescheduling of the mix.

Gary: As you know we're about a week to ten days behind schedule. We'll have to reschedule the verification mix for late next week.

Production Manager: Our resources are committed until a month from now. You can't expect to simply call a meeting and have everything reshuffled for the Blue Spider Program. We should have been notified earlier. Engineering has the responsibility for preparing the bill of materials. Why aren't they ready?

Engineering Integration: We were never asked to prepare the bill of materials. But I'm sure that we could get it out if we work our people overtime for the next two days.

Gary: When can we remake the mix?

Production Manager: We have to redo at least 500 sheets of paper every time we reschedule mixes. Not only that, we have to reschedule people on all three shifts. If we are to reschedule your mix, it will have to be performed on overtime. That's going to increase your costs. If that's agreeable with you, we'll try it. But this will be the first and last time that production will bail you out. There are procedures that have to be followed.

Testing Engineer: I've been coming to these meetings since we kicked off this program. I think I speak for the entire engineering division when I say that the role that the Director of Engineering is playing in this program is suppressing individuality among our highly competent personnel. In new projects, especially those involving R & D, our people are not apt to stick their necks out. Now our people are becoming ostriches. If they're impeded from contributing, even in their own slight way, then you'll probably lose them before the project gets completed. Right now I feel that I'm wasting my time here. All I need are minutes of the team meetings and I'll be happy. Then I won't have to come to these pretend meetings anymore.

The purpose of the verification mix was to make a full-scale production run of the material to verify that there would be no material property changes in scale-up from the small mixes made in the R & D laboratories. After testing, it became obvious that the wrong lots of raw materials were used in the production verification mix.

A meeting was called by Lord Industries for an explanation of why the mistake had occurred and what the alternatives were.

Lord: Why did the problem occur?

Gary: Well, we had a problem with the bill of materials. The result was that the mix had to be made on overtime. And when you work people on overtime, you have to be willing to accept mistakes as being a way of life. The energy cycles of our people are slow during the overtime hours.

Lord: The ultimate responsibility has to be with you, the program manager. We, at Lord, think that you're spending too much time doing and not enough time managing. As the prime contractor, we have a hell-of-a-lot more at stake than you do. From now on we want documented weekly technical interchange meetings and closer interaction by our quality control section with yours.

Gary: These additional team meetings are going to tie up our key people. I can't spare people to prepare handouts for weekly meetings with your people.

Lord: Team meetings are a management responsibility. If Parks does not want the Blue Spider Program, I'm sure we can find another subcontractor. All you (Gary) have to do is give up taking the material vendors to lunch and you'll have plenty of time for handout preparation.

Gary left the meeting feeling as though he had just gotten raked over the coals. For the next two months, Gary worked sixteen hours a day, almost every day. Gary did not want to burden his staff with the responsibility of the handouts, so he began preparing them himself. He could have hired additional staff, but with such a tight budget, and having to remake the verification mix, cost overruns appeared inevitable.

As the end of the seventh month approached, Gary was feeling pressure from within Parks Corporation. The decision-making process appeared to be slowing down and Gary found it more and more difficult to motivate his people. In fact, the grapevine was referring to the Blue Spider Project as a loser, and some of his key people acted as though they were on a sinking ship.

By the time the eighth month rolled around, the budget had nearly been expended. Gary was tired of doing everything himself. "Perhaps I should have stayed an engineer," thought Gary. Elliot Grey and Gary Anderson had a meeting to see what could be salvaged. Grey agreed to get Gary additional corporate funding to complete the project. But performance must be met since there is a lot riding on the Blue Spider Project," asserted Grey. He called a team meeting to identify the program status.

Gary: It's time to map out our strategy for the remainder of the program. Can engineering and production adhere to the schedule that I have laid out before you?

Team Member (Engineering): This is the first time that I've seen this schedule. You can't expect me to make a decision in the next ten minutes and commit the resources of my department. We're getting a little unhappy being kept in the dark until the last minute. What happened to effective planning?

Gary: We still have effective planning. We must adhere to the original schedule, or at least try to adhere to it. This revised schedule will do that.

Team Member (Engineering): Look Gary! When a project gets in trouble it is usually the functional departments that come to the rescue. But if we're kept in the dark, then how can you expect us to come to your rescue? My boss wants to know, well in advance, every decision that you're contemplating with regard to our departmental resources. Right now, we . . .

Gary: Granted, we may have had a communications problem. But now we're in trouble and have to unite forces. What is your impression as to whether your department can meet the new schedule?

Team Member (Engineering): When the Blue Spider Program first got in trouble, my boss exercised his authority to make all departmental decisions regarding the program himself. I'm just a puppet. I have to check with him on everything.

Team Member (Production): I'm in the same boat, Gary. You know we're not happy having to reschedule our facilities and people. We went through this once before. I also have to check with my boss before giving you an answer about the new schedule.

The following week the verification mix was made. Testing proceded according to the revised schedule, and it looked as though the total schedule milestones could be met, provided that specifications could be adhered to.

Because of the revised schedule, some of the testing had to be performed on holidays. Gary wasn't pleased with asking people to work on Sundays and holidays, but had no choice since the test matrix called for testing to be accomplished at specific times after end-of-mix.

A team meeting was called on Wednesday to resolve the problem of who would work on the holiday which would occur on Friday, as well as staffing Saturday and Sunday. During the team meeting Gary became quite disappointed. Phil Rodgers, who had been Gary's test engineer since the project started, was assigned to a new project which the grapevine called Gable's new adventure. His replacement was a relatively new man, only eight months with the company. For an hour and a half, the team members argued about the little problems and continually avoided the major question, stating that they would have to first coordinate commitments with their boss. It was obvious to Gary that his team members were afraid to make major decisions and therefore "ate up" a lot of time on trivial problems.

On the following day, Thursday, Gary went to see the department manager responsible for testing, in hopes that he could use Phil Rodgers this weekend.

Department Manager: I have specific instructions from the boss (director of engineering) to use Phil Rodgers on the new project. You'll have to see the boss if you want him back.

Gary: But we have testing that must be accomplished this weekend. Where's the new man you assigned yesterday?

Department Manager: Nobody told me you had testing scheduled for this weekend. Half of my department is already on an extended weekend vacation, including Phil Rodgers and the new man. How come I'm always the last to know when we have a problem?

Gary: The customer is flying down his best people to observe this weekend's tests. It's too late to change anything. You and I can do the testing.

Department Manager: Not on your life. I'm staying as far away as possible from the Blue Spider Project. I'll get you someone, but it won't be me. That's for sure!

The weekend's testing went according to schedule. The raw data was made available to the customer under the stipulation that the final company position would be announced at the end of next month, after the functional departments had a chance to analyze it.

Final testing was completed during the second week of the ninth month. The initial results looked excellent. The materials were within contract specifications, and although they were new, both Gary and Lord's management felt that there would be little difficulty in convincing the Army that this was the way to go. Henry Gable visited Gary and congratulated him on a job well done.

All that now remained was the making of four additional full-scale verification mixes in order to determine how much deviation there would be in material properties between full-sized production-run mixes. Gary tried to get the customer to concur (as part of the original trade-off analysis) that two of the four production runs could be deleted. Lord's management refused, insisting that contractual requirements must be met at the expense of the contractor.

The following week, Elliot Grey called Gary in for an emergency meeting concerning expenditures to date.

Elliot: Gary, I just received a copy of the financial planning report for last quarter in which you stated that both the cost and performance of the Blue Spider Project were 75 percent complete. I don't think you realize what you've done. The target profit on the program was $200,000. Your memo authorized the vice-president and general manager to book 75 percent of that, or $150,000, for corporate profit spending for stockholders. I was planning on using all $200,000 together with the additional $300,000 I personally requested from corporate headquarters to bail you out. Now I have to go back to the vice-president and general manager and tell them that we've made a mistake and that we'll need an additional $150,000.

Gary: Perhaps I should go with you and explain my error. Obviously, I take all responsibility.

Elliot: No, Gary. It's our error, not yours. I really don't think you want to be around the general manager when he sees red at the bottom of the page. It takes an act of God to get money back once corporate books it as profit. Perhaps you should reconsider project engineering as a career instead of program management. Your performance hasn't exactly been sparkling, you know.

Gary returned to his office quite disappointed. No matter how hard he worked, the bureaucratic red tape of project management seemed to always do him in. But late that afternoon, Gary's disposition improved. Lord Industries called to say that, after consultation with the Army, Parks Corporation would be awarded a sole-source contract for qualification and production of Spartan Missile components using the new longer-life raw materials. Both Lord and the Army felt that the sole-source contract was justified, provided that continued testing showed the same results, since Parks Corporation had all of the technical experience with the new materials.

Gary received a letter of congratulations from corporate headquarters, but no additional pay increase. The grapevine said that a substantial bonus was given to the Director of Engineering.

During the tenth month, results were coming back from the accelerated aging tests performed on the new materials. The results indicated that although the new materials would meet specifications, the age life would probably be less than five years. These numbers came as a shock to Gary. Gary and Paul Evans had a conference to determine the best strategy to follow.

Gary: Well, I guess we're now in the fire instead of the frying pan. Obviously, we can't tell Lord Industries about these tests. We ran them on our own. Could the results be wrong?

Paul: Sure, but I doubt it. There's always margin for error when you perform accelerated aging tests on new materials. There can be reactions taking place which we know nothing about. Furthermore, the accelerated aging tests may not even correlate well with actual aging. We must form a company position on this as soon as possible.

Gary: I'm not going to tell anyone about this, especially Henry Gable. You and I will handle this. It will be my throat if word of this leaks out. Let's wait until we have the production contract in hand.

Paul: That's dangerous. This has to be a company position, not a project office position. We had better let them know upstairs.

Gary: I can't do that. I'll take all responsibility. Are you with me on this?

Paul: I'll go along. I'm sure I can find employment elsewhere when we open Pandora's Box. You had better tell the department managers to be quiet also.

Two weeks later, as the program was winding down into the testing for the final verification mix and final report development, Gary received an urgent phone call asking him to report immediately to Henry Gable's office.

Henry: When this project is over, you're through. You'll never hack it as a program manager, or possibly a good project engineer. We can't run projects around here without honesty and open communications. How the hell do you expect top management to support you when you start censoring bad news to the top? I don't like surprises. I like to get the bad news from the program managers and project engineers, not second hand from the customer. And of course, we cannot forget the cost overrun. Why didn't you take some precautionary measures?

Gary: How could I when you were asking our people to do work such as accelerated aging tests which would be charged to my project and was not part of program plan? I don't think that I'm totally the blame for what's happened.

Henry: Gary, I don't think its necessary to argue the point any further. I'm willing to give you back your old job, in engineering. I hope you didn't lose too many friends while working in program management. Finish up final testing and the program report. Then I'll reassign you.

Gary returned to his office and put his feet up on the desk. "Well," thought Gary, "perhaps I'm better off in engineering. At least I can see my wife and kids once in a while." As Gary began writing the final report, the phone rang:

Functional Manager: Hello Gary. I just thought I'd call to find out what charge number you want us to use for experimenting with this new procedure to determine accelerated age life."

Gary: Don't call me! Call Gable. After all, the Blue Spider Project is his baby.

CASE STUDY: NORTHEAST RESEARCH LABORATORY (B)*

On a Friday morning in late December, 1973, Sam Lacy, Head of the Physical Sciences Division of Northeast Research Laboratory (NRL) thought about two letters which lay on his desk. One, which he had received a few weeks before, was a progress report from Robert Kirk, recently assigned project leader of the Exco Project, who reported that earlier frictions between the NRL team and the client had lessened considerably, that quality research was under way, and that the prospects for retaining the Exco project on a long-term basis appeared fairly good. The other letter, which had just arrived in the morning's mail, came from Gray Kenney, a Vice President of Exco, and stated that the company wished to terminate the Exco contract effective immediately.

Lacy was puzzled. He remembered how pleased Gray Kenney had been only a few months before when the Exco project produced its second patentable process. On the other hand, he also recalled some of the difficulties the project had encountered within NRL which had ultimately led to the replacement of project leader Alan North in order to avoid losing the contract. Lacy decided to call in the participants in an effort to piece together an understanding of what had happened. Some of what he learned is described below. But the problem remained for him to decide what he should report to top management. What should he recommend to avoid the recurrence of such a situation in the future?

Company Background

Northeast Research Laboratory was a multidisciplinary research and development organization employing approximately 1,000 professionals. It was organized into two main sectors, one for economics and business administration and the other for the physical and natural sciences. Within the physical and natural sciences sector, the organization was essentially by branches of science. The main units were called divisions and the subunits were called laboratories. A partial organization chart is shown in Exhibit 1.

---

*Copyright © 1975 by the President and Fellows of Harvard College. Reproduced by permission. This case was prepared by Richard Johnson under the supervision of Robert N. Anthony.

Exhibit 1. Northeast Research Laboratory (B) Organization Chart (Simplified).

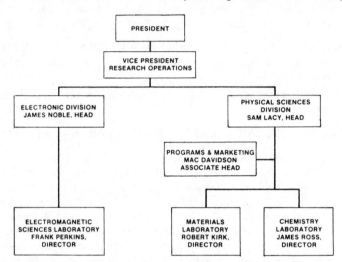

Most of the company's work was done on the basis of contracts with clients. Each contract was a project. Responsibility for the project was vested in a project leader, and through him up the organizational structure in which his laboratory was located. Typically, some members of the project team were drawn from laboratories other than that in which the project leader worked; it was the ability to put together a team with a variety of technical talents that was one of the principal strengths of a multidisciplinary laboratory. Team members worked under the direction of the project leader during the period in which they were assigned to the project. An individual might be working on more than one project concurrently. The project leader could also draw on the resources of central service organizations, such as model shops, computer services, editorial, and drafting. The project was billed for the services of these units at rates which were intended to cover their full costs.

Inception of the Exco Project

In October, 1972, Gray Kenney, Vice President of Exco, had telephoned Mac Davidson of NRL to outline a research project which would examine the effect of microwaves on various ores and minerals. Davidson was Associate Head of the Physical Sciences Divisions and had known Kenney for several years. During the conversation Kenney asserted that NRL ought to be particularly intrigued by the research aspects of the project, and Davidson readily agreed. Davidson was also pleased because the Physical Sciences Division was under pressure to generate more revenue, and this potentially long-term project from Exco would make good use of available manpower. In addition, top management of NRL had recently circulated several memos indicating that more emphasis should be put on commercial rather than government work. Davidson was, however, a little concerned that the project did not fall neatly into one laboratory or even one division, but in fact required assistance from the Electronics Division to complement work that would be done in two different Physical Sciences Laboratories (the Chemistry Laboratory and the Materials Laboratory).

A few days later Davidson organized a joint client-NRL conference to determine what Exco wanted and to plan the proposal. Kenney sent his assistant, Tod Denby, who was to serve as the Exco liaison officer for the project. Representing NRL were Davidson; Sam Lacy; Dr. Robert Kirk, director of the Materials Laboratory (one of the two Physical Sciences laboratories involved in the project); Dr. Alan North, manager of Chemical Development & Engineering (and associate director of the Chemistry Laboratory); Dr. James Noble, Executive of the Electronics Division; and a few researchers chosen by Kirk and North. Davidson also would like to have invited Dr. James Ross, director of the Chemistry Laboratory, but Ross was out of town and couldn't attend the preproposal meeting.

Denby described the project as a study of the use of microwaves for the conversion of basic ores and minerals to more valuable commercial products. The study was to consist of two parts:

Task A—An experimental program to examine the effect of microwaves on some 50 ores and minerals, and to select those processes appearing to have the most promise.

Task B—A basic study to obtain an understanding of how and why microwaves interact with certain minerals.

It was agreed that the project would be a joint effort of three laboratories: (1) Materials, (2) Chemistry, and (3) Electromagnetic. The first two laboratories were in the Physical Sciences Division, and the last was in the Electronics Division.

Denby proposed that the contract be open-ended, with a level of effort of around $10,000–$12,000 per month. Agreement was quickly reached on the content of the proposal. Denby emphasized to the group that an early start was essential if Exco were to remain ahead of its competition.

After the meeting, Lacy, who was to have overall responsibility for the project, discussed the choice of project leader with Davidson. Davidson proposed Alan North, a 37-year-old chemist who had had experience as a project leader on several projects. North had impressed Davidson at the pre-proposal meetings and seemed well suited to head the interdisciplinary team. Lacy agreed. Lacy regretted that Dr. Ross (head of the Laboratory in which North worked) was unable to participate in the decision of who should head the joint project. In fact, because he was out of town, Ross was neither aware of the Exco project nor of his laboratory's involvement in it.

The following day, Alan North was told of his appointment as project leader. During the next few days, he conferred with Robert Kirk, head of the other Physical Sciences laboratory involved in the project. Toward the end of October, Denby began to exert pressure on North to finalize the proposal, stating that the substance had been agreed upon at the pre-proposal conference. North thereupon drafted a five-page letter as a substitute for a formal proposal, describing the nature of the project and outlining the procedures and equipment necessary. At Denby's request, North included a paragraph which authorized members of the client's staff to visit NRL frequently and observe portions of the research program. The proposal's cover sheet contained approval signatures from the laboratories and divisions involved. North signed for his own area and for laboratory director Ross. He telephoned Dr. Noble of the Electronics Division, relayed the client's sense of urgency, and Noble authorized North to sign for him. Davidson signed for the Physical Sciences Division as a whole.

At this stage, North relied principally on the advice of colleagues within his own division. As he did not know personally the individuals in the Electronics Division, they were not called upon at this point. Since North understood informally that the director of the Electromagnetic Sciences Laboratory, Dr. Perkins, was quite busy and often out of town, North did not attempt to discuss the project with Perkins.

After the proposal had been signed and mailed, Dr. Perkins was sent a copy. It listed the engineering equipment which the client wanted purchased for the project and prescribed how it was to be used. Perkins worried that performance characteristics of the power supply (necessary for quantitative measurement) specified in the proposal were inadequate for the task. He asked North about it and North said that the client had made up his mind as to the microwave equipment he wanted and how it was to be used. Denby had said he was paying for that equipment and intended to move it to Exco's laboratories after the completion of the NRL contract.

All these events had transpired rather quickly. By the time Dr. Ross, director of the Chemistry Laboratory, returned to the Institute, the proposal for the Exco project had been signed and accepted. Ross went to see Lacy and said that he had dealt with Denby on a previous project and had serious misgivings about working with him. Lacy assuaged some of Ross's fears by observing that if anyone could succeed in working with Denby it would be North—a flexible man, professionally competent, who could move with the tide and get along with clients of all types.

Conduct of the Project

Thus the project began. Periodically, when decisions arose, North would seek opinions from division management. However, he was somewhat unclear about whom he should talk to. Davidson had been the person who had actually appointed him project leader. Normally, however, North worked for Ross. Although Kirk's laboratory was heavily involved in the project, Kirk was very busy with other Materials Laboratory work. Adding to his uncertainty, North periodically received telephone calls from Perkins of the Electronics Division, whom he didn't know well. Perkins expected to be heavily involved in the project.

Difficulties and delays began to plague the project. The microwave equipment specified by the client was not delivered by the manufacturer on schedule, and there were problems in filtering the power supply of the radio-frequency source. Over the objection of NRL Electromagnetic Sciences engineers, but at the insistence of the client, one of the chemical engineers tried to improve the power supply filter. Eventually the equipment had to be sent back to the manufacturer for modification. This required several months.

In the spring of 1973, Denby, who had made his presence felt from the outset, began to apply strong pressure. "Listen," he said to North, "top management of Exco is starting to get on my back and we need results. Besides, I'm up for review in four months and I can't afford to let this project affect my promotion." Denby was constantly at NRL during the next few months. He was often in the labs conferring individually with members of the NRL teams. Denby also visited North's office frequently.

A number of related problems began to surface. North had agreed to do both experimental and theoretical work for this project, but Denby's constant pushing for experimental results began to tilt the emphasis. Theoretical studies began to lapse, and experimental work became the focus of the Exco project. From time to time North argued that the theoretical work should precede or at least accompany the experimental program, but Denby's insistence on concrete results led North to temporarily deemphasize the theoretical work. Symptoms of this shifting emphasis were evident. One day a senior researcher from Kirk's laboratory came to North to complain that people were being "stolen" from his team. "How can we do a balanced project if the theoretical studies are not given enough manpower?" he asked. North explained the client's position and asked the researcher to bear with this temporary realignment of the project's resources.

As the six-month milestone approached, Denby expressed increasing dissatisfaction with the project's progress. In order to have concrete results to report to Exco management, he directed North a number of times to change the direction of the research. On several occasions various members of the project team had vigorous discussions with Denby about the risks of chasing results without laying a careful foundation. North himself spent a good deal of time talking with Denby on this subject, but Denby seemed to discount its importance. Denby began to avoid North and to spend most of his time with the other team members. Eventually the experimental program, initially dedicated to a careful screening of some 50 materials, deteriorated to a somewhat frantic and erratic pursuit of what appeared to be "promising leads." Lacy and Noble played little or no role in this shift of emphasis.

On June 21, 1973, Denby visited North in his office and severely criticized him for proposing a process (hydrochloric acid pickling) that was economically infeasible. In defense, North asked an NRL economist to check his figures. The economist reported back that North's numbers were sound and that, in fact, a source at U.S. Steel indicated that hydrochloric acid pickling was "generally more economic than the traditional process and was increasingly being adopted." Through this and subsequent encounters, the relationship between Denby and North became increasingly strained.

Denby continued to express concern about the Exco project's payoff. In an effort to save time, he discouraged the NRL team from repeating experiments, a practice that was designed to insure accuracy. Data received from initial experiments were frequently taken as sufficiently accurate, and after hasty analysis

were adopted for the purposes of the moment. Not surprisingly Denby periodically discovered errors in these data. He informed NRL of them.

Denby's visits to NRL became more frequent as the summer progressed. Some
days he would visit all three laboratories, talking to the researchers involved and
asking them about encouraging leads. North occasionally cautioned Denby against
too much optimism. Nonetheless, North continued to oblige the client by restructuring the Exco project to allow for more "production line" scheduling of experiments and for less systematic research.

In August, North discovered that vertile could be obtained from iron ore. This
discovery was a significant one, and the client applied for a patent. If the reaction
could be proved commercially, its potential would be measured in millions of
dollars. Soon thereafter, the NRL team discovered that the operation could, in
fact, be handled commercially in a rotary kiln. The client was notified and soon
began planning a pilot plant that would use the rotary kiln process.

Exco's engineering department, after reviewing the plans for the pilot plant,
rejected them. It was argued that the rotary process was infeasible and that a
fluid bed process would have to be used instead. Denby returned to NRL and
insisted on an experiment to test the fluid bed process. North warned Denby
that agglomeration (a sticking together of the material) would probably take place.
It did. Denby was highly upset, reported to Gray Kenney that he had not received
"timely" warning of the probability of agglomeration taking place, and indicated
that he had been misled as to the feasibility of the rotary kiln process.*

Work continued, and two other "disclosures of invention" were turned over
to the client by the end of September.

Personnel Changes

On September 30, Denby came to North's office to request that Charles Fenton be
removed from the Exco project. Denby reported he had been watching Fenton in
the Electromagnetic Laboratory, which he visited often, and had observed that
Fenton spent relatively little time on the Exco project. North, who did not know
Fenton well, agreed to look into it. But Denby insisted that Fenton be removed immediately and threatened to terminate the contract if he were allowed to remain.

North was unable to talk to Fenton before taking action because Fenton was
on vacation. He did talk to Fenton as soon as he returned, and the researcher
admitted that due to the pressure of other work he had not devoted as much time
or effort to the Exco work as perhaps he should have.

Three weeks later, Denby called a meeting with Mac Davidson and Sam Lacy.
It was their first meeting since the pre-proposal conference for the Exco project.
Denby was brief and to the point:

Denby: I'm here because we have to replace North. He's become increasingly
difficult to work with and is obstructing the progress of the project.

---

*Ten months later the client was experimenting with the rotary kiln process for producing
vertile from iron ore in his own laboratory.

Lacy: But North is an awfully good man . . .

Davidson: Look, he's come up with some good solid work thus far. What about the process of extracting vertile from iron ore he came up with. And . . .

Denby: I'm sorry, but we have to have a new project leader. I don't mean to be abrupt, but it's either replace North or forget the contract.

Davidson reluctantly appointed Robert Kirk project leader and informed North of the decision. North went to see Davidson a few days later. Davidson told him that although management did not agree with the client, North had been replaced in order to save the contract. Later Dr. Lacy told North the same thing. Neither Lacy nor Davidson made an effort to contact Exco senior management on the matter.

Following the change of project leadership, the record became more difficult to reconstruct. It appeared that Kirk made many efforts to get the team together, but morale remained low. Denby continued to make periodic visits to the Institute but found that the NRL researchers were not talking as freely with him as they had in the past. Denby became skeptical about the project's value. Weeks slipped by. No further breakthroughs emerged.

Lacy's Problem

Dr. Lacy had received weekly status reports on the project, the latest of which is shown in Exhibit 2. He had had a few informal conversations about the project, principally with North and Kirk. He had not read the reports submitted to Exco. If the project had been placed on NRL's "problem list," which comprised about 10 percent of the projects which seemed to be experiencing the most difficulty, Lacy would have received a written report on its status weekly, but the Exco project was not on that list.

With the background given above, Lacy reread Kenney's letter terminating the Exco contract. It seemed likely that Kenney, too, had not had full knowledge of what went on during the project's existence. In his letter, Kenney mentioned the "glowing reports" which reached his ears in the early stages of the work. These reports, which came to him only from Denby, were later significantly modified, and Denby apparently implied that NRL had been "leading him on." Kenney pointed to the complete lack of economic evaluation of alternative processes in the experimentation. He seemed unaware of the fact that at Denby's insistence all economic analysis was supposed to be done by the client. Kenney was most dissatisfied that NRL had not complied with all the provisions of the proposal, particularly those that required full screening of all materials and the completion of the theoretical work.

Lacy wondered why Denby's changes of the proposal had not been documented by the NRL team. Why hadn't he heard more of the problems of the Exco project before? Lacy requested a technical evaluation of the project from the economics process director and asked Davidson for *his* evaluation of the project. These reports are given in Exhibits 3 and 4. When he reviewed these reports, Lacy wondered what, if any, additional information he should submit to NRL top management.

Exhibit 2. Northeast Research Laboratory (B) Weekly Project Status Report.

MICROWAVES IN CONVERSION OF BASIC ORES AND MINERALS

TRANSACTIONS RECORDED 12-15-73 - 12-22-73

LABOR

ORG	ID	W/E DATE	T/S NO	OBJ	NAME	WEEK	TO DATE
						HOURS	
322	02345	12-22-73	363073	13	KIRK	6.0	150
322	02345	12-22-73	363073	22	KIRK	6.0	
322	03212	12-22-73	363082	13	DENSMORE	8.0	25
322	03260	12-22-73	236544	14	COOK	15.0	30
325	12110	12-08-73	C30093	15	HOWARD	15.0	82
325	12110	12-15-73	236548	15	HOWARD	36.0	
325	12110	12-22-73	376147	15	HOWARD	8.0	
325	12357	12-22-73	376149	15	SPELTZ	15.0	68
325	12369	12-22-73	376150	15	GYUIRE	15.0	17
325	12384	12-22-73	R08416	15	DILLON	40.0-	44
325	12397	12-22-73	336527	15	NAGY	31.0	31
325	12397	12-22-73	336527	21	NAGY	15.0	
652	12475	12-22-73	236548	15	KAIN	8.0	20
652	12475	12-22-73	236548	21	KAIN	15.0	

	HOURS	DOLLARS
LABOR (STRAIGHT TIME)	117.0	943
PAYROLL BURDEN		248
OVERHEAD RECOVERY		1227
OVERTIME PREMIUM LABOR	30.0	160
OTHER PREMIUM LABOR	6.0	242
TOTAL PERSONNEL COSTS		2820 S

MATERIALS & SERVICES

PO NO	REF NO	OBJ	DESCRIPTION	REQUESTOR	
61289	54065	48	438 REA EXPRESS	KIRK	42
	87413	48	456 GED SUPPLY CO	COOK	10
17234	04461	71	448 P.T.& T. 326-6200	NAGY	2
			TOTAL M&S COSTS		56 S
			FEE		158
			TRANSACTION TOTAL		8034 T

PROJECT/ACCOUNT STATUS REPORT

PHYSICAL SCI	CHEMISTRY LAB	ROBERT KIRK	ROBERT KIRK

ORG	FIRM/ACCT SUB	W/O	FIRM/CLOSING DATE	WEEK ENDING DATE	TYPE	REV TYPE	PROJ	FEE %
325	3273	0000 000	12-22-73	PROJ	INDUS	SCA YD 3 ON DOMESTIC		15.00

EXCO — START DATE 11-06-72 · PROF WORK DATE 11-06-74 · TERM DATE 11-06-74 · BURDEN % 28.00 · OVERHEAD % 105.00

COST CATEGORIES	OBJECT CODE	DOLLARS YTD	13 WK	TO DATE	LABOR HOURS ESTIMATE	TO DATE	BALANCE
SUPERVISOR	(11, 12)			560		36	
SENIOR	(13)	192		17986		1348	
PROFESSIONAL	(14)	150		16787		1678	
TECHNICAL	(15)	629		5299		1037	
CLER/SUPP	(16, 17, 18)			301		84	
OTHER	(19)	72		72		12	
LABOR (S.T.)		943		41005		1644	
BURDEN		248		11481			
OVERHEAD		1227		55110	LAST BILLING:		
OVERTIME PREM	(21)	160		1540	DATE	11-30-73	
OVS./OTIL. PREM	(23-29)	242		476	AMOUNT	11350	
TOTAL PERSONNEL COSTS		2820		109612	ACCOUNT STATUS TO DATE:	154583	
TRAVEL	(55-59)	766			BILLED	154583	
SUBCONTRACT				3726	PAID	154583	
MATERIAL	(41, 42)						
EQUIPMENT	(43)						
COMPUTER	(37, 45)	2		507	TIME BALANCE %	39.4	
COMMUN	(62, 63, 70, 71)				COST BALANCE %	43.5	
CONSULTANT	(74, 75)	54		99	TIME BALANCE WKS.	41	
REPORT COST	(44, 47)	56		5098		ESTIMATED	BALANCE
OTHER M&S							
TOTAL M&S COST		56		26847		250435	108878
COMMITMENTS		2876		141557		37565	13189
TOTAL LESS FEE		158		24376		288000	122067
FEE (15.00)		3031		165933			
TOTAL							

COMMITMENT STATUS TO DATE

PO NO	DATE	OBJ	VENDOR/DESCRIPTION	TOTAL	CHARGES	BALANCE
A61289	11-21-73	41	MINNESOTA MINING	111	61	50
A61313	11-23-73	41	ALDRICH CHEMICAL	348		348
A95209	11-28-73	43	TENNECO CHEMICAL CO	5		5
A95093	11-15-73	41	UNION CARBIDE CORP	23194		23194
B95104	11-19-73	37	SCIENTIFIC PRODUCTS	600		600
B95232	11-25-73	41	VAN WATERS & ROGERS	2500		2500
018046	12-15-73	57	ROGER MD	300	150	150
			TOTAL			26847 T

EXHIBIT 3 NORTHEAST RESEARCH LABORATORY (B):
TECHNICAL EVALUATION
by Ronald M. Benton,
Director, Process Economics Program

Principal Conclusions

1. The original approach to the investigation as presented in the proposal is technically sound. The accomplishments could have been greater had this been followed throughout the course of the project, but the altered character of the investigation did not prevent accomplishment of fruitful research.
2. The technical conduct of this project on NRL's part was good, despite the handicaps under which the work was carried out. Fundamental and theoretical considerations were employed in suggesting the course of research and in interpreting the data. There is no evidence to indicate that the experimental work itself was badly executed.
3. Significant accomplishments of this program were as follows:
   a. *Extraction of vertile from iron ore by several alternative processes.* Conception of these processes was based on fundamental considerations and demonstrated considerable imagination. As far as the work was carried out at NRL, one or more of these processes offers promise of commercial feasibility.
   b. *Nitrogen fixation.* This development resulted from a laboratory observation. The work was not carried far enough to ascertain whether or not the process offers any commercial significance. It was, however, shown that the yield of nitrogen oxides was substantially greater than has previously been achieved by either thermal or plasma processes.
   c. *Reduction of nickel oxide and probably also garnerite to nickel.* These findings were never carried beyond very preliminary stages and the ultimate commercial significance cannot be assessed at this time.
   d. *Discovery that microwave plasmas can be generated at atmospheric pressure.* Again the commercial significance of this finding cannot be appraised at present. However, it opens the possibility that many processes can be conducted economically that would be too costly at the reduced pressures previously thought to be necessary.
4. The proposal specifically stated that the selection of processes for scale-up and economic studies would be the responsibility of the client. I interpret this to mean that NRL was not excluded from making recommendations based on economic considerations. Throughout the course of the investigation, NRL did take economic factors into account in its recommendations.
5. Actual and effective decisions of significance were not documented by NRL and only to a limited extent by the client. There was no attempt on NRL's part to convey the nature or consequences of such decisions to the client's management.

6. The NRL reports were not well prepared even considering the circumstances under which they were written.

7. It is possible that maximum advantage was not taken off the technical capabilities of personnel in the Electromagnetic Sciences Laboratory. Furthermore, they appeared to have been incompletely informed as to the overall approach to the investigation.

8. There was excessive involvement of the client in the details of experimental work. Moreover, there were frequent changes of direction dictated by the client. Undoubtedly these conditions hampered progress and adequate consideration of major objectives and accomplishments.

9. In the later stages of the project, the client rejected a number of processes equipment types proposed by the NRL for investigation of their commercial feasibility. From the information available to me, I believe that these judgments were based on arbitrary opinions as to technical feasibility and superficial extrapolations from other experience as to economic feasibility that are probably not valid.

Evaluation of Client's Complaints

Following are the comments responding to the points raised by the client management during your conversation:

1. *Client anticipated a "full research capability." He had hoped for participation by engineers, chemists, economists and particularly counted on the provision of an "analytical capability." It was this combination of talents that brought him to NRL [rather than a competitor]. He feels that the project was dominated almost exclusively by chemists.*

   This complaint is completely unfounded. All the disciplines appropriate to the investigation (as called for in the proposal) were engaged on the project to some degree. In addition, men of exceptional capabilities devoted an unusually large amount of time to the project. The client never officially altered the conditions of the proposal stating that no economic studies should be performed by NRL and there was no explicit expression of this desire on the part of the client until near the project termination.

2. *The analytical services were poor. They were sometimes erroneous and there were frequent "deviations." Data was given to the client too hastily, without further experiment and careful analysis, and as a result a significant amount of the data was not reproducible. NRL was inclined to be overly optimistic. "Glowing reports" would be made only to be cancelled or seriously modified later.*

   There is no way of determining whether the analytical services were good or bad, but one can never expect all analytical work to be correct or accurate. Because the client insisted on obtaining raw data they would certainly receive some analyses that were erroneous. With respect to the allegation that NRL was overly optimistic, there were no recommendations or opinions expressed in the NRL reports or included in the client's notes that can be placed in this category. Whether or not there were verbal statements of this kind cannot of course be ascertained.

3. *There were "errors in the equations and the client was not informed of the changes." This refers to the case of a computer program that had not been "de-bugged." It was the client who discovered the errors and informed NRL of the discrepancies. (The program was eventually straightened out by the Math Sciences Department.)*

The client's complaint that they were given a computer program which had not been "de-bugged" is valid, but it is not certain that the project leadership gave them the program without exercising normal precautions for its accuracy. The program was developed by a person not presently with NRL and for another project. He transmitted it without any warning that "de-bugging" had not been conducted. It is even possible that the existence and source of error could not have been determined in his usage and would only appear in a different application.

4. *NRL told the client that the "vertile from iron ore" process could be handled commercially in a rotary kiln. Client prepared elaborate plans for this rotary kiln process and then was informed by his Engineering Division that this was completely infeasible. Plans were then shifted to a fluid bed process and much time and money had been wasted. Client claims that he was not warned that in the fluid bed agglomeration would probably take place. Agglomeration did take place the first time this process was tried ("open boats") and the client was greatly upset.*

It is unclear whether the original suggestion that a rotary kiln be used in the vertile process came from the client or NRL. In any event, it is a logical choice of equipment and is used for the production of such low cost items as cement. Without the benefit of at least pilot plant experience that revealed highly abnormal and unfavorable conditions leading to excessive costs, no one would be in a position to state that such equipment would be uneconomic. It is true that a completely standard rotary kiln probably could not be employed, if for no other reasons than to prevent the escape of toxic hydrogen sulfide gas from the equipment. At least special design would be needed and probably some mechanical development. However, it is rare that any new process can be installed without special design and development and it is naive to expect otherwise.

I do not know, of course, how much time was actually spent on the "elaborate plans" for the vertile process using a rotary kiln. I can, however, compare it with generally similar types of studies that we carry out in the Process Economics Program. For this kind of process we would expend about 45 engineering man-hours, and the design calculations would be more detailed than the client's engineer made (his cost estimates incidentally reflected inexperience in this field). I doubt, therefore, that this effort represented a serious expenditure of money and would not have been a complete waste even if the process had been based on a partially false premise.

The contention that the client was not informed of the agglomerating properties of the vertile while the reaction was taking place seems unlikely. The client's representatives were so intimately concerned with the experimental work that it would be unusual if the subject had not been raised. Moreover, it is doubtful that the client would have been deterred by NRL's warning, in view of their subsequent insistence that considerable effort be devoted to finding means by which a fluid bed could be operated.

5. *The meetings were poorly planned by NRL.*

There is no way of evaluating this complaint, but certainly the extreme frequency of the meetings would not be conducive to a well organized meeting.

6. *Experimental procedures were not well planned.*

Apparently this refers to the client's desire that experiments be planned in detail as much as three months in advance. Such an approach might conceivably be useful merely for purposes of gathering routine data. It is naive to think that research can or should be planned to this degree and certainly if NRL had acceded to the request it would have been a fruitless time-consuming exercise.

7. *Economic support was not given by NRL.*

As mentioned above, the proposal specifically excluded NRL from economic evaluations, but NRL did make use of economic consideration in its suggestions and recommendations.

8. *NRL promised to obtain some manganese nodules but never produced them.*

Manganese nodules were obtained by NRL but no experiments were ever run with them. Many other screening experiments originally planned were never carried out because of the changed direction of the project. It seems likely, therefore, that the failure to conduct an experiment with manganese nodules was not NRL's responsibility.

9. *The client claims that he does not criticize NRL for failing "to produce a process." He says that he never expected one, that he wanted a good screening of ores and reactions as called for in the proposal, and that he had hoped for results from the theoretical studies—Task B. This he feels he did not get. We did not do what the proposal called for.*

The statement that a process was not expected seems entirely contrary to the course of the project. There was universal agreement among NRL personnel involved that almost immediately after the project was initiated it was converted into a crash program to find a commercial process. In fact, the whole tenor of the project suggests a degree of urgency incompatible with a systematic research program. It is quite true that the theoretical studies as a part of Task B were never carried out. According to the project leader this part of the proposal was never formally abandoned, it was merely postponed. Unfortunately, this situation was never documented by the NRL, as was the case with other significant effective decisions.

Additional Comments

1. It appears that the first indication that the client expected economic studies or evaluations of commercial feasibility occurred during the summer of 1973. At this time the project leader was severely criticized by the client's representatives for having proposed a process (hydrochloric acid pickling) that was economically infeasible. The basis for this criticism was that hydrochloric acid pickling of steel had not proved to be economically feasible. It is totally unreasonable to expect that NRL would have access to information of this kind, and such a reaction would certainly have the effect of discouraging any further contributions of an economic or commercial nature by NRL rather than encouraging them.

   Actually it is patently ridiculous to directly translate economic experience of the steel industry with steel pickling to leaching a sulfided titanium ore. Nevertheless, I directed an inquiry to a responsible person in U.S. Steel as to the status of hydrochloric acid pickling. His response (based on the consensus of their experts) was diametrically opposite to the client's information. While there are situations that are more favorable to sulfuric acid pickling, hydrochloric acid pickling is generally more economic and is becoming increasingly adopted.

2. The reports written by NRL were requested by the client, but on an urgent and "not fancy" basis. If such were the case, it is understandable that the project leader would be reluctant to expend enough time and money on the report to make it representative of NRL's normal reports. However, the nature of the reports seems to indicate that they are directed toward the same individuals with whom NRL was in frequent contact, or persons with a strong interest in the purely scientific aspects. The actual accomplishments of the project were not brought out in a manner that would have been readily understandable to client's management.

Recommendations

It is recommended that consideration be given to the establishment of a simple formal procedure by which high risk projects could be identified at the proposal stage and brought to the attention of the Division Vice President. There should also be a formal procedure, operative after project acceptance, in which specific responsibilities are assigned for averting or correcting subsequent developments that would be adverse to NRL's and the client's interests.

Some of the factors that would contribute to a high risk condition are insufficient funding, insufficient time, low chance of successfully attaining the objectives, an unsophisticated client, public or private political conditions, etc. The characteristics that made this a high risk project were certainly apparent at the time the proposal was prepared.

EXHIBIT 4
NORTHEAST RESEARCH LABORATORY (B)
MEMORANDUM.

To: Sam Lacy   Date: January 8, 1974
From: Mac Davidson
Re: The Exco Project—Conclusions

- The decision to undertake this project was made without sufficient consideration of the fact that this was a "high risk" project.
- The proposal was technically sound and within the capabilities of the groups assigned to work on the project.
- There was virtually no coordination between the working elements of Physical Sciences and Electronics in the preparation of the proposal.
- The technical conduct of this project, with few exceptions, was, considering the handicaps under which the work was carried out, good and at times outstanding. The exceptions were primarily due to lack of attention to detail.
- The NRL reports were not well prepared, even considering the circumstances under which they were written.
- The client, acting under pressure from his own management, involved himself excessively in the details of experimental work and dictated frequent changes of direction and emphasis. The proposal opened the door to this kind of interference.
- There was no documentation by NRL of the decisions made by the client which altered the character, direction and emphasis of the work.
- There was no serious attempt on the part of NRL to convey the nature or performance are valid.
- The project team acquiesced too readily in the client's interference and management too easily to the client's demands.
- Management exercised insufficient supervision and gave inadequate support to the project leader in his relations with the client.
- There were no "overruns" either in time or funds.

CASE STUDY: TELESTAR INTERNATIONAL

On November 15, 1978 The Department of Energy Resources awarded Telestar a $475,000 contract for the developing and testing of two waste treatment plants. Telestar had spent the better part of the last two years developing waste treatment technology under their own R & D activities. This new contract would give Telestar the opportunity to "break into a new field," of waste treatment.

The contract was negotiated at a firm-fixed price. Any cost overruns would have to be incurred by Telestar. The original bid was priced out at $847,000. Telestar's management, however, wanted to win this one. The decision was made that Telestar would "buy in" at $475,000 so that they could at least get their foot into the new marketplace.

The original estimate of $847,000 was very "rough" because Telestar did not have any good man-hour standards, in the area of waste treatment, upon which to base their man-hour projections. Corporate management was willing to spend up to $400,000 of their own funds in order to compensate the bid of $475,000.

By February 15, 1979, costs were increasing to such a point where overrun would be occurring well ahead of schedule. Anticipated costs to completion were now $943,000. The project manager decided to stop all activities to certain functional departments, one of which was structural analysis. The manager of the structural analysis department strongly opposed the closing out of the work order prior to the testing of the first plant's high-pressure pneumatic and electrical systems.

Structures Manager: You're running a risk if you close out this work order. How will you know if the hardware can withstand the stresses that will be imposed during the test? After all, the test is scheduled for next month and I can probably finish the analysis by then.

Project Manager: I understand your concern, but I cannot risk a cost overrun. My boss expects me to do the work within cost. The plant design is similar to one which we have tested before, without any structural problems being detected. On this basis I consider your analysis as unnecessary.

Structures Manager: Just because two plants are similar does not mean that they will be identical in performance. There can be major structural deficiencies.

Project Manager: I guess the risk is mine.

Structures Manager: Yes, but I get concerned when a failure can reflect upon the integrity of my department. You know, we are performing on schedule and within the time and money budgeted. You're setting a bad example by cutting off our budget without any real justification.

Project Manager: I understand your concern, but we must pull out all stops when overrun costs are inevitable.

Structures Manager: There's no question in my mind that this analysis should be completed. However, I'm not going to complete it on my overhead budget. I'll reassign my people tomorrow. Incidentally, you had better be careful; my people are not very happy to work for a project that can be cancelled immediately. I may have trouble getting volunteers next time.

Project Manager: Well, I'm sure you'll be able to adequately handle any future work. I'll report to my boss that I have issued a work stoppage order to your department.

During the next month's test, the plant exploded. Post analysis indicated that the failure was due to a structural deficiency.

    a. Who is at fault?
    b. Should the structures manager have been dedicated enough to continue the work on his own?
    c. Can a functional manager, who considers his organization as strictly support, still be dedicated to total project success?

CASE STUDY: THE TWO-BOSS PROBLEM

On May 15, 1977 Brian Richards was assigned full-time to Project Turnbolt by Fred Taylor, manager of the thermodynamics department. All work went smoothly for four-and-one-half of the five months necessary to complete this effort. During this period of successful performance Brian Richards had good working relations with Edward Compton (the Turnbolt Project Engineer) and Fred Taylor.

Fred treated Brian as a Theory Y employee. Once a week Fred and Brian would chat about the status of Brian's work. Fred would always conclude their brief meeting with, "You're doing a fine job, Brian. Keep it up. Do anything you have to do to finish the project."

During the last month of the project Brian began receiving conflicting requests from the project office and the department manager as to the preparation of the final report. Compton told Brian Richards that the final report was to be assembled in viewgraph format (i.e., "bullet" charts) for presentation to the customer at the next technical interchange meeting. The project did not have the funding necessary for a comprehensive engineering report.

The theromodynamics department, on the other hand, had a policy that all engineering work done on new projects would be documented in a full and comprehensive report. This new policy was implemented about one year ago when Fred Taylor became department manager. Rumor had it that Fred wanted formal reports so that he could put his name on them and either publish or present them at technical meetings. All work performed in the thermodynamics department required Taylor's signature before it could be released to the project office as an official company position. Upper-level management did not want their people to publish and therefore did not maintain a large editorial or graphic arts department. Personnel desiring to publish had to get the department manager's approval and, upon approval, had to prepare the entire report themselves, without any "overhead" help. Since Taylor had taken over the reins as department head, he had presented three papers at technical meetings.

A meeting was held between Brian Richards, Fred Taylor, and Edward Compton.

Edward: I don't understand why we have a problem? All the project office wants is a simple summary of the results. Why should we have to pay for a report which we don't want or need?

Fred: We have professional standards in this department. All work that goes out must be fully documented for future use. I purposely require that my signature be attached to all communications leaving this department. This way we obtain uniformity and standardization. You project people must understand that, although you can institute your own project policies and procedures (within the constraints and limitations of company policies and procedures), we department personnel also have standards. Your work must be prepared within our standards and specifications.

Edward: The project office controls the purse strings. We (the project office) specified that only a survey report was necessary. Furthermore, if you want a more comprehensive report, then you had best do it on your own overhead account. The project office isn't going to foot the bill for your publications.

Fred: The customary procedure is to specify in the program plan the type of report requested from the departments. Inasmuch as your program plan does not specify this, I used my own discretion as to what I thought you meant.

Edward: But I told Brian Richards what type of report I wanted. Didn't he tell you?

Fred: I guess I interpreted the request a little differently from what you had intended. Perhaps we should establish a new policy that all program plans must specify reporting requirements. This would alleviate some of the misunderstandings, especially since my department has several projects going on at one time. In addition, I am going to establish a policy for my department that all requests for interim, status or final reports be given to me directly. I'll take personal charge of all reports.

Edward: That's fine with me! And for your first request I'm giving you an order that I want a survey report, not a detailed effort.

Brian: Well, since the meeting is over, I guess I'll return to my office (and begin updating my resume just in case).

CASE STUDY: CAMDEN CONSTRUCTION CORPORATION

"For five years I've heard nothing but flimsy excuses from you people as to why the competition was beating us out in the downtown industrial building construction business," remarked Joseph Camden, President. "Excuses, excuses, excuses; that's all I ever hear! Only 15 percent of our business over the past five years has been in this area, and virtually all of that was with our established customers. Our growth rate is terrible. Everyone seems to just barely outbid us. Maybe our bidding process leaves something to be desired. If you three vice-presidents don't come up with the answers then we'll have three positions to fill by mid-year. We have a proposal request coming in next week, and I want to win it. Do you guys understand that?

Background

Camden Construction Corporation matured from a $1 million to a $26 million construction company between 1969 and 1979. Camden's strength was in their ability to work well with the customer. Their reputation for quality work far exceeded the local competitors.

Most of Camden's contracts in the early seventies were with long-time customers who were willing to go sole-source procurement and pay the extra price for quality and service. With the recession of 1975, Camden found that, unless they penetrated the competitive bidding market, their business base would decline.

In 1976, Camden was "forced" to go union in order to bid government projects. Unionization drastically reduced Camden's profit margin, but offered a greater promise for increased business. Camden had avoided the major downtown industrial construction market. But with the availability of multimillion dollar skyscraper projects, Camden wanted their share of the pot of gold that follows the rainbow.

Meeting of The Minds

On January 17, 1979 the three vice-presidents met to consider ways of improving Camden's bidding technique.

V.P. Finance: You know fellas, I hate to say it, but we haven't done a good job in developing a bid. I don't think that we've been paying enough attention to the competition. Now's the time to begin.

V.P. Operations: What we really need is a list of who our competitors have been on each project over the last five years. Perhaps we can find some bidding trends.

V.P. Engineering: I think the big number we need is to find out the overhead rates of each of these companies. After all, union contracts specify the rate at which the employees will work. Therefore, except for the engineering design packages, all of the companies should be almost identical in direct labor man-hours and union labor wages for similar jobs.

V.P. Finance: I think I can hunt down past bids by our competitors. Many of them are in public records. That'll get us started.

V.P. Operations: What good will it do? The past is past. Why not just look toward the future?

V.P. Finance: What we want to do is to maximize our chances for success and maximize profits at the same time. Unfortunately, these two cannot be met at the same time. We must find a compromise.

V.P. Engineering: Do you think that the competition looks at our past bids?

V.P. Finance: They're stupid if they don't. What we have to do is to determine their target profit and target cost. I know many of the competitors personally and have a good feel for what their target profits are. We'll have to assume that their target direct cost equals ours, otherwise we will have a difficult time making a comparison.

V.P. Engineering: What can we do to help you?

V.P. Finance: You'll have to tell me how long it takes to develop the engineering design packages and how our personnel in engineering design stack up against the competition's salary structure. See if you can make some contacts and find out how much money the competition put into some of their proposals for engineering design activities. That'll be a big help. We'll also need good estimates from engineering and operations for this new project we're suppose to bid. Let me pull my data together and we'll meet again in two days, if that's all right with you two.

Reviewing The Data

The executives met two days later to review the data. The vice-President for Finance presented the data on the three most likely competitors. (See Exhibit 1) These companies were Ajax, Acme, and Pioneer. The vice-President for Finance made the following comments:

1. In 1970, Pioneer was in danger of bankruptcy. It was estimated that they needed to win one or two in order to hold their organization together.
2. The 1972 contract was probably a buy-in based upon the potential for follow-on work.
3. In 1973, Acme was contract rich and had a difficult time staffing all of their projects.
4. The 1974 contract was for an advanced state-of-the art project. It is estimated that Ajax bought in so that they could break into a new field.

The vice-President for Engineering and Operations presented data indicating that the total project cost (fully burdened) was approximately $5 million. "Well," thought the vice-President of Finance, "I wonder what we should bid so that we will have at least a reasonable chance of winning the contract?"

Exhibit 1. Proposal Data Summary (Cost in Ten Thousands).

YEAR	ACME	AJAX	PIONEER	CAMDEN BID	CAMDEN COST
1970	270	244	260	283	260
1970	260	250	233	243	220
1970	355	340	280	355	300
1971	836	830	838	866	800
1971	300	288	286	281	240
1971	570	560	540	547	500
1972	240*	375	378	362	322
1972	100*	190	180	188	160
1972	880	874	883	866	800
1973	410	318	320	312	280
1973	220	170	182	175	151
1973	400	300	307	316	283
1974	408	300*	433	449	400
1975	338	330	342	333	300
1975	817	808	800	811	700
1975	886	884	880	904	800
1976	384	385	380	376	325
1976	140	148	158	153	130
1977	197	193	188	200	165
1977	750	763	760	744	640

*Buy-in contracts

CASE STUDY: PROJECT OVERRUN

The Green Company production project was completed three months behind schedule and at a cost overrun of approximately 60 percent. Following submittal of the final report, Phil Graham, the Director of Project Management, called a meeting to discuss the problems encountered on the Green Project.

Phil: We're not here to point the finger at anyone. We're here to analyze what went wrong and to see if we can develop any policies and/or procedures which will prevent this from happening in the future. What went wrong?

Project Manager: When we accepted the contract, Green did not have a fixed delivery schedule for us to go by because they weren't sure when their new production plant would be ready to begin production activities. So, we estimated 3000 units per month for months five through twelve of the project. When they found that the production plant would be available two months ahead of schedule, they asked us to accelerate our production activities. So, we put all of our production people on overtime in order to satisfy their schedule. This was our mistake, because we accepted a fixed delivery data and budget before we understood everything.

Functional Manager: Our problem was that the customer could not provide us with a fixed set of specifications, because the final set of specifications depended upon the OSHA and EPA requirements which could not be confirmed until initial testing of the new plant. Our people, therefore, were asked to commit to man-hours before specifications could be reviewed. Six months after project go-ahead, Green Company issued the final specifications. We had to remake 6000 productions units because they did not live up to the new specifications.

Project Manager: The customer was willing to pay for the remake units. This was established in the contract. Unfortunately, our contract people didn't tell me that we were still liable for the penalty payments if we didn't adhere to the original schedule.

Phil: Don't you feel that misinterpretation of the terms and conditions is your responsibility?

Project Manager: I guess I'll have to take some of the blame.

Functional Manager: We need specific documentation on what to do in case of specification changes. I don't think that our people realize that user approval of specifications is not a contract agreed to in blood. Specifications can change, even in the middle of a project. Our people must understand that, as well as the necessary procedures for implementing change.

Phil: I've heard that the functional employees on the assembly line are grumbling about the Green Project. What's their gripe?

Functional Manager: We were directed to cut out all overtime on all projects. But when the Green Project got into trouble, overtime became a way of life. For nine months, the functional employees on the Green Project had as much overtime as they wanted. This made the functional employees on other projects very unhappy. To make matters worse, the functional employees got used to a big take-home paycheck and started living beyond their means. When the project ended, so did their overtime. Now, they claim that we should give them the opportunity for more overtime. Everybody hates us.

Phil: Well, now we know the causes of the problem. Any recommendations for cures and future prevention activities?

CASE STUDY: COPPER INTERNATIONAL INC.*

Copper International Incorporated (CII) is a $100 million corporation located in Pittsburgh. The company has one large plant located on 88 acres. CII is strictly a manufacturing company operating in a relatively static technological environment. CII is a traditional company with a traditional organizational structure.

With increasing costs for gas, oil, electricity, and labor, top management embarked on a three year severe cost reduction program. As part of this program, management decreed that there would be a freeze on all hiring and employees leaving the company due to retirement, layoffs, etc. would not be replaced. Emphasis was being placed upon purchasing new equipment which would increase production without having to increase labor costs.

In January, 1980 CII held an in-house seminar for 50 lower and middle managers. The subject of the seminar was engineering project management on the supposition that project management would permit CII to perform the same amount of work with less human resources. During the two days of the seminar, several topics and/or conclusions were reached:

- The organizational hierarchy, in terms of authority, is the vice-president and general manager, department managers, section managers, subsection managers, and unit managers. The need for project management was first identified at the unit and subsection management level. Upper-level management were then "sold" on the idea that project management would make resource control easier and decided to sponsor in-house seminars. Top management appeared to be totally supportive.
- A major problem area which was adressed in the seminar was, "which activities at CII should be defined as a project?" CII handles about 100 projects a year. Sixty of these projects are rather informal and generally remain within one unit or subsection. There is virtually no paperwork required for these informal projects. The other 40 projects are capital expenditure and equipment projects involving the purchasing and installation of new equipment and the updating of old facilities and processes. These projects require a great deal of paperwork and can cut across all line organizations within a given department. The majority of these projects are inter- rather than intradepartmental.
- Because the majority of the projects are capital equipment projects, the seminar participants wanted project management to be expanded on an informal basis rather than on the usual formal basis which could easily create more paperwork and conflicts. To keep project management informal, it

---

*This is an actual situation which has been disguised. The forms at the end of the case study are the actual forms with some slight modifications. Several of the comments and conclusions are those of the consultant, not necessarily the company.

was decided that the project manager should report low in the organizational structure. The group felt that informal project management could be established with the project managers reporting to the subsection or section level. Placing the project managers at the departmental level appears to be an open invitation for formal project management to be incorporated.

- Although the majority of project managers in industry today are between the ages of 32 and 38, almost all managers felt that the perspective project managers at CII would be much older, say 50 to 55. Experience with existing equipment and an understanding of manufacturing processes was considered to be of prime importance. This is quite common in manufacturing organizations.

Exhibit 1. Program/Project/Task Breakdown Chart.

PROGRAM/PROJECT/TASK _____

RESPONSIBILITY _____

TASK	RESPONSIBILITY	J	F	M	A	M	J	J	A	S	O	N	D	TOTAL
MANHOURS	BUDGET / ACTUAL													
TOTAL DOLLARS	BUDGET / ACTUAL													

SIGN OFF _____ DATE _____

- The major problem addressed by the seminar participants was the paper-work necessary to control a project. With the informal projects, there is no paperwork requirements. But the formal or capital equipment projects are another story. These projects begin with an appropriation request (A/R) form. This form is prepared by the requestor and includes such items as cash flow, total costs, milestones, scope and feasibility. The requestor can fill out this entire form without any interfacing with other line organizations, even though several other line organizations would eventually be involved. The A/R then gets submitted to all levels of management for approval, in-cluding the vice-president and general manager. Even though line managers sign off on the A/R and their signature implies concurrence with the idea and scope of the A/R, this does *not* constitute a commitment of resources

Exhibit 2. Unit Manager Resources.

PROJECT ACTIVITY	J	F	M	A	M	J	J	A	S	O	N	D	
OTHER													
PRODUCTION SUPPORT													
MAINTENANCE													
TOTAL													

according to the milestone schedule in the A/R. Therefore, the project manager has to commit to upper-level management to perform the required work called out within the A/R within time, cost and performance when, in fact, no functional commitments were made. This problem is further complicated when top management arbitrarily moves the A/R milestones to the left without discussing the ramifications with anyone.

- The A/R is only one of the major problem areas facing the project manager. Recently, the project managers have come under severe criticism for not controlling projects within the original estimates. Project managers are required to spend *all* money allocated to them for capital equipment projects, even if large savings are possible. This philosophy by management appears to be in conflict with management's policy of cost reduction where possible.

Exhibit 3. Program Priorities Staff Monthly Review.

PRIORITY	PROGRAM	J	F	M	A	M	J	J	A	S	O	N	D	
1														
2														
3														
4														
5														
6														
7														
8														
9														
10	THESE 20 PROGRAMS ARE PRIORITIZED BY THE DEPARTMENT MANAGERS. OTHER PROGRAMS ARE PRIORITIZED BY THE SECTION AND UNIT STAFF.													
11														
12														
13														
14														
15														
16														
17														
18														
19														
20														
(21)–X	SECTION STAFF UNIT STAFF													

- The major conclusions reached from the two-day seminar were the inappropriateness of the A/R, the inability to obtain functional commitment, and poor project planning. Although there is no guarantee that management will approve an A/R request for capital expenditure projects, the managers still felt that functional personnel should be involved as much as possible in developing detailed schedules and *total* project milestones. With this in mind, a one-day workshop was conducted to develop the necessary forms and paperwork to plan, schedule, and control all capital equipment projects.

Exhibit 4. Notification Of Intent (NOI).

A. SCOPE: _____

B. BENEFITS (DISCOUNTED RATE OF RETURN AND PAYBACK): _____

C. ESTIMATE COST/MANPOWER: _____

D. ESTIMATED TIMING: _____

E. CONFORMANCE TO STRATEGIC PLAN: _____

F. LINE FUNCTIONS INVOLVED: _____

G. POTENTIAL ADVERSE EFFECTS: _____

H. PROBABILITY OF SUCCESS/SEVERITY: _____

I. INITIATOR/ORIGINATOR: _____

J. DEPARTMENT PRIORITY: ☐ A   ☐ B   ☐ C

K. BUDGET CATEGORY: ☐ A   ☐ B   ☐ C   ☐ D

L. APPROVALS: _____ UNIT MGRS _____ SUBSECTION _____ SECTION   DEPT. __

M. FINAL APPROVAL/AUTHORIZATION: _____

GENERAL MANAGER: _____

DATE: _____

Exhibit 5. Task/Project/Program Form.

PROGRAM TITLE: _____ TIMING

PROJECT TITLE: _____ ORIG. EST. REV. EST. ACTUAL CHARGE NUMBER: _____

PROJECT MGR.: _____ START: _____ _____ _____ UNIT: _____

PRIORITY: _____ COMPLETE: _____ _____ _____ UNIT APPROVAL _____

_____ DATE: _____ DATE: _____

DEFINITION OF WORK: _____

PEOPLE	ORIG. EST.	REV. EST.	ACTUAL	COST:	ORIG. EST.	REV. EST.	ACTUAL
EXEMPT HOURS:	_____	_____	_____	EXPENSES:	_____	_____	_____
N/E HOURS:	_____	_____	_____	INVESTMENT:	_____	_____	_____
HOURLY:	_____	_____	_____	DATE:	_____	_____	_____

ELEMENTS	RESPONSIBILITY	CATEGORY		MONTHS													TOTAL
				J	F	M	A	M	J	J	A	S	O	N	D		
ELEMENTS OR PROJECTS OR TASKS	THESE ARE REPEATED FOR EACH ELEMENT	MAN HOURS	EST.														
			ACT.														
		DOLLARS EXPENSE	EST.														
			ACT.														
		DOLLARS INVEST.	EST.														
			ACT.														

COMMENTS: _____

Exhibit 6. Detail Plan.

DATE: _____

REVISION: _____

PROJECT TITLE _____

BRIEF DESCRIPTION _____

BENEFITS _____

RISK _____

COST _____

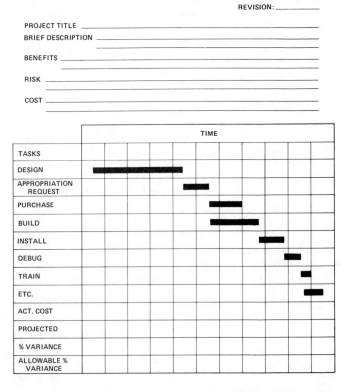

	TIME										
TASKS											
DESIGN											
APPROPRIATION REQUEST											
PURCHASE											
BUILD											
INSTALL											
DEBUG											
TRAIN											
ETC.											
ACT. COST											
PROJECTED											
% VARIANCE											
ALLOWABLE % VARIANCE											

- Thirty members of the original seminar were invited to attend a one-day workshop held two weeks later in order to develop project control documents. The participants were broken down into six groups. Each group was to develop their own forms and present their results to the other groups. Exhibits 1 through 9 show the results.* Several of the forms contain duplication of effort.

The workshop group, as a whole, appeared to define all of the information that would be necessary to identify, approve, plan, schedule, and control a capital equipment project. But now there appeared to be four major questions which had to be answered:

- Which information is actually pertinent?
- How can these forms be combined so as to maintain the minimum amount of paperwork?
- What is the proper chronological order for these forms to be filled out?
- Who should have final signature authority for the approval of each form?

Exhibit 7. Preplanning.

PROJECT TITLE _____

BRIEF DESCRIPTION _____

BENEFITS _____

RISK _____   PRIORITY: _____

COST _____   (ASSIGNED BY THE DEPT. MGR.)

GROSS SCHEDULE (TIME)

TASK

SUB—SEC. MGR.

UNIT MGR.

ORIGINATOR

---

*Only those forms pertinent to the case study are included. Several of these forms have been modified for easier understanding and use.

Exhibit 8. Project Analysis.

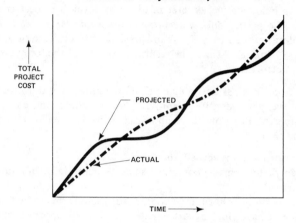

COST BREAKDOWN (HOURS OR DOLLARS)

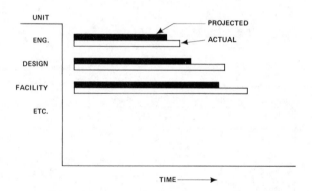

CASE STUDY: ROYAL TOOL COMPANY

"I've called you here, Tom, because I think Royal Tool is heading for big trouble unless we do something right away," remarked Keith Royal, President. "I want you to head up our inventory computerization projects. This is our first priority right now. We have some 1000 projects going on at almost the same time and we have no idea as to where our inventory is, what goods are finished, and where the finished goods are located. This is a three year project," added Keith, as he took a deep breath. "We need an integrated material handling system at Royal Tool."

"I would like to solve these problems and computerize our inventory with as little disturbance as possible to the flow of work," stated Keith. "Make sure you consider the human element in all of your planning. Also, try to develop a cost/benefit analysis as you go along. I'd like a little help from you so that I can convince our stockholders that we're spending their money wisely."

Exhibit 9. Project Diary.

PROBLEM	DATE	ACTION TAKEN	DATE	DATE CORRECTED
1.				
2.				
3.				
4.				
5.				
6.				
7.				
8.				
9.				
10.				
''				
''				
''				
''				
''				
''				
''				
''				

Background

The Royal Tool Company produces tools and machines for the construction industry, primarily for plumbing. This includes wrenches, pipe threading machines,
vises, pipe benders, and pipe and tubing cutters. The company also makes drain
cleaning equipment, band saws and portable heaters. The Royal Tool Company
does an annual business of approximately $100 million, employing over 1,000
people.

The specific subsystem to be dealt with is production control. This subsystem
has the responsibility to order material from outside sources through purchasing,
write orders for the production facilities, write orders for assembling the finished
products, monitor the amounts of material in raw and finished stocks, and expedite
the orders to the production and assembly floors.

The production control subsystem receives the larger system's needs through
forecasts produced by the marketing department. These forecasts are interpreted
into needs for specific parts. A determination is made whether these are needed
from outside sources or presently in stock. If parts are needed that are in the
finished parts inventory, orders are written to move them to assembly.

Production orders are written when raw parts are either received or in inventory. The determination of when orders need to be written has recently been computerized. The system is the Material Requirements Planning System (MRP). The
system tells the production planner when to write a purchase, production, or assembly order. It also tells him the quantity that should be ordered.

The MRP system has been installed since late 1974. It has been altered several times since then, as problems arose. The system has met most of its original goals of inventory reduction and customer service, but there still exists much room for improvement.

Monitoring of the finished and raw inventories is accomplished by a perpetual computerized inventory listing that is updated on a daily basis. Daily reports are produced for all items for which there is a transaction and weekly and monthly reports give a listing of all parts.

The inventory monitoring is a very weak link in the system's chain. Royal presently stores finished stock in 13 different locations within the plant. These are, in some cases, merely corners to shove things into. Royal does not assign specific parts to specific areas. This situation causes havoc with the MRP system and for the production facility who then must rush "hot" material through.

The third link in Royal Tool's production and inventory control system is the shop floor control system. This link is not really operative to an effective extent. It exists as a black box situation. Material goes in one end and finished product comes out the other end. Controlling what goes on in between is beyond the ineffectual approach now taken. Production control does not know where material is in the production sequence or how many there are remaining.

Problem Areas

1. *Poor Customer Service.*
   Royal Tool presently finds itself in a situation of stagnated customer service. They have reached a point of customer order fill rate which is approximately 80%. This is not poor, but there is much room for improvement.

   The inability to improve this percentage is a direct result of the MRP system, inventory control system, and the lack of a shop floor control system. The system causes stockouts because MRP does not react to special conditions such as sales promotions and sharply increased demand. It is driven by a forecast which fluctuates from week to week because it is generated by a weighted average. This fluctuation causes orders for material to fluctuate in terms of due dates. Because of this, material orders are constantly expedited and deexpedited causing mix-ups and occasional stockouts. The solution for these problems is the development of a master production schedule which will take into consideration sales promotions and increased demand. (It must also restrict the fluctuation in gross requirements or forecast level.)

   Stockouts are also caused by surprise "losses" of material which was supposedly finished. The lack of satisfactory controls on the inventory causes this problem. The automated inventory stacker will solve this problem as it will be a secure inventory storage facility. After implementation the inventory accuracy should be nearly perfect.

   The present shop floor control situation causes many parts to get delayed on the production floor. The parts do not make it to assembly on the required date, thus causing stockouts in shipping. The proposed shop floor control system must allow production control to set priorities on the production floor. Also, a means of tracking the progress of parts on the floor must be provided.

With these three new systems implemented, the customer service level should improve dramatically.

2. *Continued Generation of Excess Inventory and Lost Inventory.*

Excess inventory is a problem because of two reasons. The first is the lack of a shop floor control system. As material is delayed in the plant past its due date, a product that should have been assembled and shipped is not assembled. This means that all the other component parts are still sitting in inventory when they should be on their way to the customers. Excess inventory is the result of components not matching up when needed. The new shop floor control system should alleviate this problem by providing a tool which can control the progress of material towards meeting the due dates.

The present inventory control system also produces, at much too regular of a pace, surprises. When material that thought to be on hand turns up missing, many operations are affected; shipments are not met; material is rushed through the plant, disrupting other parts; and vendors are pressured to get material in as soon as possible.

The stacker (automated inventory storage facility) will elimate this nearly weekly occurrence.

3. *Poor Production Schedule Realization.*

This is a definite problem because of the effects on customer service and, therefore, possible sales. The real problem is that there is no formalized or stable production schedule. The MRP is fluctuating the demands constantly. What is "hot" this week may not even be needed next week. This will be alleviated by the Master Production Schedule (MPS) which is really a formalized and stable production schedule for a set period of time.

Even when there exists a master production schedule, there must also be a means of controlling the shop floor. The computerized shop floor control system will fill this need.

4. *Inability to Respond to Special Conditions.*

At present, there exists no way of responding to unforecasted demands. The MPS will not allow quick reaction to unplanned demand. MPS does provide a forum at which sales and marketing will be required to tell production control of pending promotions, large single orders, or other special conditions that exist. This information will then be incorporated into the master production schedule.

5. *Inability to Plan Facility and Manpower Requirements.*

At the present, Royal Tool does not have any means of matching capacity to the demands being made on the facilities. When a material requirements plan is run on the computer and given to the production planners, it is not known how much capacity and manpower is needed. Therefore, the manufacturing facilities cannot react sufficiently to the plan. The Master Production Schedule is the means by which production control can plan the use of the given capacity and manpower. A firm plan will allow the movement of workers from department to department, as needed. It will also pinpoint machine capacity bottlenecks which will allow action to be taken on the part of plant management. If it is an insurmountable problem, then products can be rescheduled to match that capacity.

6. *Excess Overtime Costs.*

The historical performance at Royal Tool has been to work almost the entire plant on a six-day basis. This causes very high operating and production costs. This is an area in which all three projects will be helpful in maintaining some control.

The Master Production Schedule will be furnishing the firm plan which will be the basis for a shop floor control system. The shop floor control system will supply production control with precise information as to where each piece of material is in the production phase. It will also supply to production management a daily priority list of what should be running and where. This will insure that the manufacturing facility is getting out the material as needed and in an orderly fashion. This will relieve the congestion of the floor and will therefore decrease the lead time needed to get the material through the shop. Whenever lead times are reduced, so is inventory and the need for overtime.

The stacker will assist the process by providing accurate inventory records which will reduce the need to rush lost material through the shop. This will reduce the amount of overtime being used to produce the lost material. Accurate inventory will also help keep the Master Production Schedule stable.

7. *Date for Decision Making Is Always Out of Date and Inaccurate.*

At present, the information flow from the shop floor to production control is old information. In a dynamic production control environment, information is needed on a timely basis and must be accurate. Information from the shop floor concerning material whereabouts is nonexistent. Information about material received, completed, and shipped is inaccurate and several days old. Information concerning priorities gets to the shop floor several days late or not at all.

In order for management to make sound decisions they must have at their disposal all required information. The shop floor control system will supply up-to-the-minute information on plant activities. The stacker will ensure accurate and daily information on inventory levels. These two systems will provide management the information necessary for decision making.

Cost Review

The basis for the project at Royal Tool is to determine the costs and cost effectiveness of incorporating the following three subsystems into the overall production and control system now in operation:

1. A Master Production Schedule
2. An Automated Stacker System
3. A Shop Floor Control System

The program being proposed also attempts to bring together all functional areas of the business. It is an effort at making the material ordering, production floor control, and inventory control systems at Royal Tool an integrated system to be used by production control. The goal is to improve material ordering, gain control of the shop floor, obtain accurate and timely information and react to changing business conditions.

Tom developed the Work Breakdown Structure and Bar Chart (see Exhibit 1) for a rather optimistic 16 month program. The Pricing and Forecasting Departments then analyzed the activities to determine the total cost package. Tom then met with Keith Royal to discuss the project.

Keith: I've looked over your cost data and cost/benefit analysis sheets (Exhibit 2) and find the figures compatible with my original estimates. The Bar Chart that you have laid out poses some questions. As you know, I'm rather pessimistic about the timetable you've laid out. I've estimated this project at three years to implementation and 16 months seems impossible. I don't think you've considered the people problems. Do we have enough manpower to push the project through at this rate? You also gave me a memo listing several problem areas we now have. What impact will this schedule have on these problems? I don't want to worsen our present situation just to complete this project early. I'd also like you to develop an organizational structure that would make it easier for you to direct and control the project. See what you can come up with.

Tom: O.K. Let me do some more figuring and I'll get back to you in a couple of days.

Exhibit 1. Work Breakdown Structure.

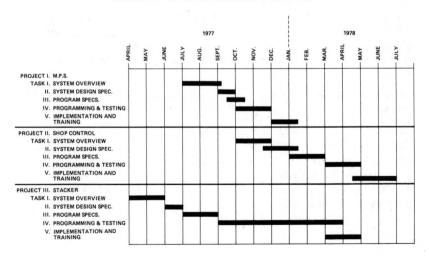

Exhibit 2. Cost Data.

Inventory Level Reduction of $2,500,000 at 7% interest	$ 175,000
Overtime Reduction — 25 people at $16,500 apiece	$ 412,500
Increased sales due to better product availability	
$1,400,000 Net Income after taxes	$ 185,000
Personnel released	
Production Control: 1 typist	
1 expediter	$ 20,000
Time booth personnel: 10 at $9,600	$ 96,000
Indirect labor (Stockroom)	$ 190,000
Eliminate physical inventory	$ 25,000
Reduction of direct labor	
Idle time	$ 17,000
Elimination of fork truck rental	
(Physical inventory)	$ 9,000
	$1,129,500

COST

Master Production Schedule	$ 53,056
Shop Floor Control	$ 335,404
Inventory Stacker	$2,005,826
	$2,394,286

COST vs. BENEFIT

There will be no new recurring cost because all three systems will be operated by existing personnel.

The development and purchase cost of the projects together will be considered a one time expense. The total cost for the program is $2,394,286. The total recurring savings is equal to $1,129,500. This is a return of 47%.

There will also be an avoided cost due to the stacker freeing up floor space in the plant.

High density vertical storage uses only 25% of floor space required by conventional methods:

— The proposed stacker will require 10,000 ft.^{2} building
— Floor space freed up 38,000 ft.^{2}
— An additional 25,000 ft.^{2} can be freed up by relayout of certain sections of the plant after stacker is installed
— The stacker will permit Royal to operate in existing facilities; therefore no new building will be needed
— The cost avoidance will equal $500,000

CASE STUDY: FARGO FOODS*

Fargo foods is a $2 billion a year international food manufacturer with canning facilities in 22 countries. Fargo products include meats, poultry, fish, vegetables, vitamins, and cat and dog foods. Fargo Foods has enjoyed a 12.5% growth rate each of the past eight years primarily due to the low overhead rates in the foreign companies.

During the past five years, Fargo had spent a large portion of retained earnings on capital equipment projects in order to increase productivity without increasing labor. An average of three new production plants have been constructed in each of the last five years. In addition, almost every plant has undergone major modifications each year in order to increase productivity.

In 1975, the president of Fargo Foods implemented formal project management for all construction projects using a matrix. By 1979, it became obvious that the matrix was not operating effectively or efficiently. In December, 1979, the author consulted for Fargo Foods by interviewing several of the key managers and a multitude of functional personnel. Below are the several key questions and responses addressed to Fargo Foods:

Q. Give me an example of one of your projects.
A. The project begins with an idea. The idea can originate anywhere in the company. The planning group picks up the idea and determines the feasibility. The planning group then works "informally" with the various line organizations to determine rough estimates for time and cost. The results are then fed back to the planning group and to the top management planning and steering committees. If top management decides to undertake the project, then top management selects the project manager and we're off and running.

Q. Do you have any problems with this arrangement?
A. You bet! Our executives have the tendency of equating rough estimates as detailed budgets and rough schedules as detailed schedules. Then, they want to know why the line managers won't commit their best resources. We almost always end up with cost overruns and schedule slippages. To make matters even worse, the project managers do not appear to be dedicated to the projects. I really can't blame them. After all, they're not involved in planning the project, laying out the schedule and establishing the budget. I don't see how any project manager can become dedicated to a plan in which the project manager has no input and may not even know the assumptions or considerations that were included. Recently, some of our more experienced project managers have taken a stand on this and are virtually refusing to accept a project assignment unless they can do their own detailed planning at the beginning of the project in order to verify

---

*Disguised case

the constraints established by the planning group. If the project managers come up with different costs and schedules (and you know that they will), the planning group feels that they have just gotten slapped in the face. If the costs and schedules are the same, then the planning group runs upstairs to top management asserting that the project managers are wasting money by continuously wanting to replan.

Q. Do you feel that replanning is necessary?

A. Definitely! The planning group begins their planning with a very crude statement of work, expecting our line managers (the true experts) to read in between the lines and fill in the details. The project managers develop a detailed statement of work and a work breakdown structure, thus minimizing the chance that anything would fall through the crack. Another reason for replanning is because the ground rules may have changed between the time that the project was originally adopted by the planning group and the time that the project begins implementation. Another possibility, of course is that technology may have changed or people can be smarter now and can perform at a higher position on the learning curve.

Q. Do you have any problems with executive meddling?

A. Not during the project, but initially. Sometimes executives want to keep the end date fixed but take their time in approving the project. As a result, the project manager may find himself a month or two behind scheduling before he even begins the project. The second problem is when the executive decides to arbitrarily change the end date milestone but keep the front end milestone fixed. On one of our projects it was necessary to complete the project in half the time. Our line managers worked like dogs to get the job done. On the next project, the same thing happened and once again, the line managers came to the rescue. Now, management feels that line managers cannot make good estimates and that they (the executives) can arbitrarily change the milestones on any project. I wish that they would realize what they're doing to us. When we put forth all of our efforts on one project, then all of the other projects suffer. I don't think our executives realize this.

Q. Do you have any problems selecting good project managers and project engineers?

A. We made a terrible mistake several years by selecting our best technical experts as the project managers. Today, our project managers are doers, not managers. The project managers do not appear to have any confidence in our line people and often try to do all of the work themselves. Functional employees are taking technical direction from the project managers and project engineers instead of the line managers. I've heard one functional employee say, 'Here come those project managers again to beat me up. Why can't they leave me alone and let me do my job?' Our line employees now feel that this is the way that project management is supposed to work. Somehow, I don't think so.

Q. Do you have any problems with the line manager/project manager interface?

A. Our project managers are technical experts and therefore feel qualified to do all of the engineering estimates without consulting with the line managers. Sometimes this occurs because not enough time or money is allocated for proper estimating. This is understandable. But when the project managers have enough time and money and refuse to get off their ivory towers and talk to the line managers, then the line managers will always find fault with the project manager's estimate even if it is correct. Sometimes I just can't feel any sympathy for the project managers. There is one special case that I should mention. Many of our project managers do the estimating themselves but have courtesy enough to ask the line manager for his blessing. I've seen line managers who were so loaded with work that they look the estimate over for two seconds and say, 'It looks fine to me. Let's do it.' Then when the cost overrun appears, the project manager gets blamed.

Q. Where are your project engineers located in the organization?

A. We're having trouble deciding that. Our project engineers are primarily responsible for coordinating the design efforts (i.e., electrical, civil, NVAC, etc. . .). The design manager wants these people reporting to him if they are responsible for coordinating efforts in his shop. The design manager wants control of these people even if they have their name changed to assistant project managers. The project managers, on the other hand, want the project engineers to report to them with the argument that they must be dedicated to the project and must be willing to complete the effort within time, cost, and performance. Furthermore, the project managers argue that project engineers will be more likely to get the job done within the constraints if they are not under the pressure of being evaluated by the design manager. If I were the design manager, I would be a little reluctant to let someone from outside of my shop integrate activities which utilize the resources under my control. But I guess this gets back to interpersonal skills and the attitudes of the people. I do not want to see a "brick wall" set up between project management and design.

Q. I understand that you've created a new estimating group. Why was that done?

A. In the past we have had several different type of estimates such as first guess, detailed, 10% complete, etc. . . . . Our project managers are usually the first people at the job site and give a shoot-from-the-hip estimate. Our line managers do estimating as do some of our executives and functional employees. Because we're in a relatively slow changing environment, we should have well established standards and the estimating department can maintain uniformity in our estimating policies. Since most of our work is approved based upon first guess estimates, the question is, "Who should give the first guess estimate?" Should it be the estimator who does not understand the processes but knows the estimating criteria, or the project engineer who understands the processes but does not know the estimates, or the project manager who is an expert in project management? Right now, we are not sure where to place the estimating group. The vice-President of Engineering has three operating groups beneath him; project management, design and procurement. We're contemplating putting estimating under procurement, but I'm not sure how this will work.

Q. How can we resolve these problems that you've mentioned?
A. I wish I knew!

CASE STUDY: QUASAR COMMUNICATIONS, INC.

Quasar Communications, Inc. (QCI) is a 30 year old, $50 million division of Communication Systems International, the world's largest communications company. QCI employs about 340 people of which more than 200 are engineers. Ever since the company was founded 30 years ago, engineers have held every major position within the company, including president and vice-president. The vice-president for accounting and finance, for example, has an electrical engineering degree from Purdue and a Masters Degree in Business Administration from Harvard.

QCI, up until 1976, was a traditional organization where everything flowed up and down. In 1976, QCI hired a major consulting company to come in and train *all* of their personnel in project management. Because of the reluctance of the line managers to accept formalized project management, QCI adopted an informal, fragmented project management structure where the project managers had lots of responsibility but very little authority. The line managers were still running the show.

In 1979, QCI had grown to a point where the majority of their business based revolved around 12 large customers and 30 to 40 small customers. The time had come to create a separate line organization for project managers, where each individual could be shown a career path in the company and the company could benefit by creating a body of planners and managers which were dedicated to the completion of a project. The project management group was headed up by a vice-president and included the following full-time personnel:

- 4 individuals to handle the 12 large customers
- 5 individuals for the 30-40 small customers
- 3 individuals for R & D projects
- 1 individual for capital equipment projects.

The nine customer project managers were expected to be able to handle two to three projects at one time if necessary. Because the customer requests did not usually come in at the same time, it was anticipated that each project manager would handle only one project at a time. The R & D and capital equipment project managers were expected to handle several projects at once.

In addition to the above personnel, the company also maintained a staff of four product managers who controlled the profitable off-the-shelf product lines. The product managers reported to the vice-president of marketing and sales.

In October, 1979 the vice-president for project management decided to take a more active role in the problems that his project managers were having and held counseling sessions for each project manager. The following major problem areas were discovered:

R & D Project Management

P.M.: My biggest problem is working with these diverse groups that aren't sure what they want. My job is to develop new products that can be introduced into the market place. I have to work with engineering, marketing, product management, manufacturing, quality assurance, finance, and accounting. Everyone wants a detailed schedule and product cost breakdown. How can I do that when we aren't even sure what the end item will look like or what materials are needed? Last month I prepared a detailed schedule for the development of a new product, assuming that everything would go according to the plan. I work with the R & D engineering group to establish what we considered to be a realistic milestone. Marketing pushed the milestone to the left because they wanted the product to be introduced into the market place earlier. Manufacturing then pushed the mile- stone to the right, claiming that they would need more time to verify the engineering specifications. Finance and accounting then pushed the milestone to the left asserting that management wanted a quicker return on investment. Now, how can I make all of the groups happy?

V.P.: Who do you have the biggest problems with?

P.M.: That's easy; marketing! Every week marketing gets a copy of the project status report and decides whether or not to cancel the project. Several times marketing has cancelled projects without even discussing it with me, and I'm supposed to be the project leader.

V.P.: Marketing is in the best position to cancel the project because they have the inside information on the profitability, risk, return on investment, and competitive environment.

P.M.: The situation that we're in now makes it impossible for the project manager to be dedicated to a project where he does not have all of the information at hand. Perhaps we should either have the R & D project managers report to someone in marketing or have the marketing group provide additional information to the project managers.

Small Customer Project Management

P.M.: I find it virtually impossible to be dedicated to and effectively manage three projects which have priorities that are not reasonably close. My low priority customer always suffers. And even if I try to give all of my customers equal status, I do not know how to organize myself and have effective time management on several projects.

P.M.: Why is it that the big projects carry all of the weight and the smaller ones suffer?

P.M.: Several of my projects are so small that they stay in one functional department. When that happens, the line manager feels that he is the true project manager operating in a vertical environment. On one of my projects I found that a line manager had promised the customer that additional tests would be run. This additional testing was not priced out as part of the original statement of work. On another project the line manager made certain remarks about the technical requirements of the project. The customer assumed that the line manager's remarks reflected company policy. Our line managers don't realize that only the project manager can make commitments (on resources) to the customer as well as company policy. I know this can happen on large projects as well, but it is more pronounced on small projects.

Large Customer Project Management

P.M.: Those of us who manage the large projects are also marketing personnel and occasionally we are the ones who bring in the work. Yet, everyone appears to be our superior. Marketing always looks down upon us and when we bring in a large contract, marketing just looks down upon us as if we're riding their coat tails or as if we were just lucky. The engineering group outranks us because all managers and executives are promoted from there. Those guys never live up to commitments. Last month I sent an inflammatory memo to a line manager because of his poor response to my requests. Now, I get no support at all from him. This doesn't happen all of the time, but when it does, it's frustrating.

P.M.: On large projects, how do we, the project managers, know when the project is in trouble? How do we decide when the project will fail? Some of our large projects are total disasters and should fail, but management comes to the rescue and pulls the best resources off of the good projects to cure the ailing projects. We then end up with six marginal projects and one partial catastrophe as opposed to six excellent projects and one failure. Why don't we just let the bad projects fail?

V.P.: We have to keep up our image for our customers. In most other companies, performance is sacrificed in order to meet time and cost. Here at QCI, with our professional integrity at stake, our engineers are willing to sacrifice time and cost in order to meet specifications. Several of our customers come to us because of this. Last year we had a project where, at the scheduled project termination date, engineering was able to satisfy only 75% of the customer's performance specifications. The project manager showed the results to the customer, and the customer decided to change his specification requirements to agree with the product that we designed. Our engineering people thought that this was a 'slap in the face' and refused to sign off the engineering drawings. The problem went all the way up to the president for resolution. The final result was that the customer would give us an additional few months if we would spend our own money to try to meet the original specification. It cost us a bundle, but we did it because our integrity and professional reputation was at stake.

Capital Equipment Project Management

P.M.: My biggest complaint is with this new priority scheduling computer package we're supposedly considering to install. The way I understand it, the computer program will establish priorities for *all* of the projects in house, based upon the feasibility study, cost benefit analysis, and return on investment. Somehow I feel as though my projects will always be the lowest priority and I'll never be able to get sufficient functional resources.

P.M.: Everytime I lay out a reasonable schedule for one of our capital equipment projects, a problem occurs in the manufacturing area and the functional employees are always pulled off of my project to assist manufacturing. And now I have to explain to everyone why I'm behind schedule. Why am I always the one to suffer? The vice-president carefully weighed the remarks of his project managers. Now came the difficult part. What, if anything, could the vice-president do to amend the situation given the current organizational environment?

7
Conflicts

7.0 INTRODUCTION

In Chapter six, *The Project Environment,* we purposely avoided the discussion of what may be the single, most important characteristic of the project environment: conflicts. Opponents of project management assert that the major reason why many companies avoid changeover to a project management organizational structure is either because of fear, or because of an inability to handle the resulting conflicts. Conflicts are a way of life in a project structure and can generally occur at any level in the organization, usually the result of conflicting objectives.

The project manager has often been described as a conflict manager. In many organizations the project manager continually fights fires and crises evolving from conflicts, and delegates the day-to-day responsibility of running the project to the project team members. Although this is not the best situation, it cannot always be prevented from occurring, especially after organizational restructuring or the initiation of projects requiring new resources.

The ability to handle conflicts requires an understanding of why conflicts occur. Four questions can be asked, the answers to which should be beneficial in handling, and possibly preventing, conflicts.

- What are the project objectives and can they be in conflict with other projects?
- Why do conflicts occur?
- How do we resolve conflicts?
- Is there any type of preliminary analysis which could identify possible conflicts before they occur?

7.1 OBJECTIVES

Each project identified as such by management must have at least one objective. The objectives of the project must be made known to all project personnel and all managers, at every level of the organization. If this information is not communicated accurately, then it is entirely possible that upper-level managers, project managers, and functional managers may all have a different interpretation of the ultimate objective, a situation which invites conflicts to occur. As an example, Company X has been awarded a $100,000 government contract for surveillance of a component which appears to be fatiguing. Top management might view the objective of this project to be the discovery of the cause of the fatigue and elimination of it in future component production. This might give Company X a "jump" on the competition. The division manager might just view it as a means of keeping people employed, with no follow-on possibilities. The department manager can consider the objective as either another job that has to be filled, or as a means of establishing new surveillance technology. The department manager, therefore, can staff the necessary positions with any given degree of expertise, depending upon the importance and definition of the objective.

Projects are established with objectives in mind. Project objectives must be:

- Specific, not general
- Not overly complex
- Measurable, tangible, and verifiable
- Realistic and attainable
- Established within resource bounds
- Consistent with resources available or anticipated
- Consistent with organizational plans, policies, and procedures

Unfortunately, the above characteristics are not always evident, especially if we consider that the project might be unique to the organization in question. As an example, research and development projects sometimes start out general, rather than specific. Research and development objectives are re-established as time goes on because the initial objective may not be attainable. As an example, Company Y believes that they can develop a high-energy rocket-motor propellant. A proposal is submitted to the government and, after a review period, the contract is awarded. However, as is the case with all R & D projects, there always exists the question as to whether the objective is attainable within time, cost, and performance constraints. It might be possible to achieve the initial objective, but at an incredibly high production cost. In this case, the specifications of the propellant (i.e., initial objectives) may be modified so as to align them closer to the available production funds.

Re-establishment of objectives occurs most frequently during the definition phase of system/project development. If resources are not available, then alternatives must be considered. This type of analysis exists during the initial stages of feasibility studies, construction, design, and estimates, and new faculty and equipment purchases.

Once the total project objective is set, subobjectives are defined in order that cost and performance may be tracked. (This procedure will be described in later chapters.) Subobjectives are a vital link in establishing proper communications between the project and functional managers. In a project environment employees are evaluated according to accomplishment, rather than to how they spend their time. Since the project manager has temporarily assigned personnel, many of whom may have never worked for him either part-time or full-time, it is vital that employees have clearly defined objectives and subobjectives. In order to accomplish this effectively, without wasting valuable time, employees should have a part in setting their own objectives and subobjectives.

Many projects are directed and controlled using a management-by-objective approach based upon effective project/functional communications and working relations as stated above. The philosophy of management by objectives

- Is proactive rather than reactive management
- Is results-oriented emphasizing accomplishment
- Focuses on change to improve individual and organizational effectiveness

Management by objectives is a systems approach for aligning project goals with organizational goals, project goals with the goals of other subunits of the organization, and project goals with individual goals. Furthermore, management by objectives (MBO) can be regarded as a

- Systems approach to planning and obtaining project results for an organization
- Strategy of meeting individual needs at the same time that project needs are met
- Method of clarifying what each individual and organizational unit's contribution to the project should be.

MBO professes to have a framework which can promote the effective utilization of time and other project resources. Many organizations, however, do not utilize the MBO philosophy. Whether or not MBO is utilized, project objectives must be set.

- If you do not have the right objectives, you may not have any idea of whether or not you are on the right road.
- Without objectives it is difficult to measure results against prior expectations.
- Objectives are utilized to determine individual goals which will provide maximum effectiveness of the whole.

7.2 THE CONFLICT ENVIRONMENT

In the project environment, conflicts are inevitable. However, as described in Chapter 5, conflicts and their resolution can be planned for. For example, conflicts can easily develop out of a situation where members of a group have a misunderstanding of each other's roles and responsibilities. Through documentation, such as the Linear Responsibility Charts, it is possible to establish formal organizational procedures (either at the project level or company-wide) for resolution means collaboration in which people must rely upon one another. Without this, mistrust will prevail and activity documentation can be expected to increase.

The most common types of conflicts involve:

- Manpower resources
- Equipment and facilities
- Capital expenditures
- Costs
- Technical opinions and trade offs
- Priorities
- Administrative procedures
- Scheduling
- Responsibilities
- Personality clashes

Each of these conflicts can vary in relative intensity over the life cycle of a project. The relative intensity can vary as a function of:

- Getting closer to project constraints
- Having only two constraints instead of three (i.e., time and performance, but not cost)
- The project life cycle itself
- The person with whom the conflict is with

Sometimes conflict is "meaningful" and produces benefical results. These meaningful conflicts should be permitted to continue as long as project constraints are not violated and benefical results are being received. An example of this would be two technical specialists arguing that each has a better way of solving a problem, and each tries to find additional supporting data for his hypothesis.

Some conflicts are inevitable and continuously reccur. As an example, let us consider the raw material and finished goods inventory. Manufacturing wants the largest possible inventory of raw materials on hand so as not to shut down production; sales and marketing want the largest finished goods inventory so that customer demands will be met; and finally, finance and accounting want the smallest raw material and finished goods inventory so the books will look better and no cash flow problems will occur.

Conflicts appear differently depending on the organizational structure. In the traditional structure, conflict should be avoided; in the project structure, conflict is part of change and therefore inevitable. In the traditional structure, conflict is the result of troublemakers and egoists; in the project structure, conflict is determined by the structure of the system and relationship among components. In the traditional structure, conflict is bad; in the project structure, conflict may be beneficial.

Conflicts can occur with anyone and over anything. Some people contend that personality conflicts are the most difficult to resolve. Below are several situations. The reader might consider what he or she would do if placed in this situation.

- Two of your functional team members appear to have personality clashes and almost always assume opposite points of view during decision-making. They are both from the same line organization. Conflicts are inevitable.
- Two of your line managers continuously argue as to who should perform a certain test. You know that this situation exists, and that the department managers are trying to work it out themselves, often with great pain. However, you are not sure for how long they will be able to resolve the problem themselves.
- Manufacturing says that they cannot produce the end item according to engineering specifications.
- R & D quality control and manufacturing operations quality control argue as to who should perform a certain test on an R & D project. R & D postulates that it is their project and manufacturing argues that it will eventually go into production and that they wish to be involved as early as possible.
- During contract negotiations, a disagreement occurs. The vice-president of Company A orders his Director of Finance, the contract negotiator, to break off negotiations with Company B because the contract negotiator for Company B does not report directly to a vice-president.
- Mr. X is the project manager of a $65 million project of which $1 million is subcontracted out to another company in which Mr. Y is the project manager. Mr. X does not consider Mr. Y as his counterpart and continuously communicates with the Director of Engineering in Mr. Y's company.

Ideally, the project manager should report high enough so that he can get timely assistance in resolving conflicts. Unfortunately, this is easier said than done. Therefore, project managers must plan for conflict resolution. As examples of this,

- The project manager might wish to concede on a low intensity conflict if he knows that a high intensity conflict is expected to occur at a later point in the project.
- Jones Construction Company has recently won a $120 million effort for a local company. The effort includes three separate construction projects, each one beginning at the same time. Two of the projects are 24 months in duration and the third one is 36 months. Each project has its own project manager. When resource conflicts occur between the projects, the customer is usually called in.

- Richard is a department manager who must supply resources to four different projects. Although each project has an established priority, the project managers continuously argue that departmental resources are not being allocated effectively. Richard now holds a monthly meeting with all four of the project managers and lets them determine how the resources should be allocated.

Many executives feel that the best way of resolving conflicts is by establishing priorities. This may be true as long as priorities are not continuously shifted around. As an example, Minnesota Power and Light establishes priorities as:

- Level 0: no completion date
- Level 1: to be completed on or before a specific date
- Level 2: to be completed on or before a given fiscal quarter
- Level 3: to be completed within a given year.

This type of technique will work as long as we do not have a large number of projects in any one group, say Level 1. How would we then distinguish between projects?

Executives are responsible for establishing priorities and often make the mistake of *not* telling the project managers the reasons for the priority level. There may be sound reasons for concealing this information, but this practice should be avoided whenever possible.

The most common factors influencing the establishment of project priorities include:

- The technical risks in development
- The risks that the company will incur, financially of competitively
- The nearness of the delivery date and the urgency
- The penalties which can accompany late delivery dates
- The expected savings, profit increase, and return on investment
- The amount of influence that the customer possesses, possibly due to the size of the project
- The impact on other projects
- The impact on affiliated organizations
- The impact on a particular product line

The ultimate responsibility for establishing priorities rests with top level management. Yet even with priority establishment, conflicts still develop. David Wilemon has identified several reasons why conflicts still occur:[1]

---

1. David L. Wilemon, "Managing Conflict in Temporary Management Situations," *The Journal of Management Studies,* 282-296, 1973.

- The greater the diversity of disciplinary expertise among the participants of a project team the greater the potential for conflict to develop among members of the team.
- The lower the project manager's degree of authority, reward and punishment power over those individuals and organizational units supporting his project the greater the potential for conflict to develop.
- The less the specific objectives of a project (cost, schedule, and technical performance) are understood by the project team members the more likely that conflict will develop.
- The greater the role ambiguity among the participants of a project team the more likely that conflict will develop.
- The greater the agreement on superordinate goals by project team participants, the lower the potential for detrimental conflict.
- The more the members of functional areas perceive that the implementation of a project management system will adversely ursurp their traditional roles, the greater the potential for conflict.
- The lower the percent need for interdependence among organizational units supporting a project, the greater the potential for dysfunctional conflict.
- The higher the managerial level within a project or functional area, the more likely that conflicts will be based upon deep seated parochial resentments. By contrast, at the project or task level, the more likely cooperation will be facilitated by task orientation and professionalism that a project requires for completion.

7.3 MANAGING CONFLICT

Temporary management situations produce conflicts. This is a natural occurrence resulting from the differences in the organizational behavior of individuals, the differences in the way that functional and project managers view the work required, and the lack of time necessary for project managers and functional personnel to establish ideal working relationships.

Regardless of how well planning is developed, project managers must be willing to operate in an environment that is characterized by constant and rapid change. This turbulent environment can be the result of changes in the scope of work, a shifting of key project and functional personnel due to new priorities and other unforeseen developments. The success or failure of a project manager is quite often measured by the ability to deal with change.

In contrast to the functional manager who works in a more standardized and predictable environment, the project manager must live with constant change. In his effort to integrate various disciplines across functional lines, he must learn to cope with the pressures of the changing work environment. He has to foster a climate that promotes the ability of his personnel to adapt to this continuously changing work environment. Demanding compliance to rigid rules, principles, and techniques is often counter-productive. In such situations, an environment conducive to effective project management is missing and the project leader too often suffers the same fate as heart-transplant patients—rejection![2]

There is no one single method which will suffice for managing all conflicts in temporary management situations because:

- There exist several types of conflicts.
- Each conflict can assume a different relative intensity over the life cycle of the project.

The detrimental aspects of these conflicts can be minimized if the project manager can anticipate their occurrence and understand their composition. The prepared manager can then resort to one of several conflict resolution modes in order to more effectively manage the disagreements which can occur.[3]

Thamhain and Wilemon surveyed 150 project managers on conflict management. Their research tried to determine the type and magnitude of the particular type of conflict which is most common at specific life cycle stages, regardless of the particular nature of the project. For the purpose of their paper the authors stated the following definitions:

Conflict is defined as the behavior of an individual, a group, or an organization which impedes or restricts (at least temporarily) another party from attaining its desired goals. Although conflict may impede the attainment of one's goals, the consequences may be beneficial if they produce new information which, in turn, enhances the decision-making process. By contrast, conflict becomes dysfunctional if it results in poor project decision-making, lengthy delays over issues which do not importantly affect the outcome of the project, or a disintegration of the team's efforts.[4]

The study presented in their paper was part of an ongoing and integrated research effort on conflict in the project-oriented work environment.[4-8]

2. H.S. Dugan, H.J. Thamhain, and D.W. Wilemon, "Managing Change in Project Management," *Proceedings of The Ninth Annual International Seminar/Symposium on Project Management,* Chicago, October 22-26, 1977, pp. 178-188.
3. The remainder of Section 7.3 is devoted to Hans J. Thamhain and David L. Wilemon, "Conflict Management in Project Life Cycles," *Sloan Management Review,* Summer, 1975, pp. 31-50. Reprinted by permission.
4. Thamhain, H.J., and Wilemon, D.L., "Conflict Management in Project-Oriented Work Environments," *Proceedings of the Sixth International Meeting of the Project Management Institute,* Washington, D.C., September 18-21, 1974.
5. "Diagnosing Conflict Determinants in Project Management," *IEEE Transactions on Engineering Management,* Vol. 22, 35-44, 1975.
6. Wilemon, D.L., and Cicero, J.P., "The Project Manager—Anomalies and Ambiguities," *Academy of Management Journal,* pp. 269-282, Fall, 1970.
7. Wilemon, D.L. "Project Management Conflict: A View From Apollo," *Proceedings of the Third Annual Symposium of the Project Management Institute,* Houston, Texas, October, 1971.
8. Wilemon, D.L. "Project Management and its Conflicts: A View from Apollo," *Chemical Technology,* Vol. 2, no. 9: 527-534, 1972.

Project managers frequently indicate that one of the requirements for effective performance is the ability to effectively manage various conflicts and disagreements which invariably arise in task accomplishment. While several research studies have reported on the general nature of conflict in project management, few studies have been devoted to the cause and management of conflict in specific project life-cycle stages. If project managers are aware of some of the major causes of disagreements in the various project life-cycle phases, there is a greater likelihood that the detrimental aspects of these potential conflict situations can be avoided or minimized.

This study first investigates the mean intensity of seven potential conflict determinants frequently thought to be prime causes of conflict in project management. Next, the intensity of each conflict determinant is viewed from the perspective of individual project life-cycle stages. An examination is then made of various conflict-handling modes used by project managers which leads to a number of suggestions for minimizing the detrimental effects of conflict over the project life cycle.

Research Design

Approximately 150 managers from a variety of technology-oriented companies were asked to participate in this comprehensive research project. A usable sample of 100 project managers was eventually selected for this study.

A questionnaire was used as the principal data collection instrument. In addition, discussions were held with a number of project managers on the subject under investigation to supplement the questionnaire data and the resulting conclusions. This process proved helpful in formulating a number of recommendations for minimizing detrimental conflicts.

The development of the questionnaire relied on several pilot studies. It was designed to measure values on three variables: (1) the average intensity of seven potential conflict determinants over the entire project life cycle; (2) the intensity of each of the seven conflict sources in the four project life-cycle phases; and (3) the conflict resolution modes used by project managers.

Mean Conflict Intensity

The average conflict intensity perceived by the project managers was measured for various conflict sources and for various phases of the project life cycle. Project managers were asked to rank the intensity of conflict they experienced for each of seven potential conflict sources on a standard four-point scale. The seven potential sources are:

- CONFLICT OVER PROJECT PRIORITIES. The views of project participants often differ over the sequence of activities and tasks which should be undertaken to achieve successful project completion. Conflict over priorities may occur not only between the project team and other support groups but also within the project team.
- CONFLICT OVER ADMINISTRATIVE PROCEDURES. A number of managerial and administrative-oriented conflicts may develop over how the project will be managed; i.e., the definition of the project manager's reporting relationships, definition of responsibilities, interface relationships, project scope, operational requirements, plan of execution, negotiated work agreements with other groups, and procedures for administrative support.
- CONFLICT OVER TECHNICAL OPINIONS AND PERFORMANCE TRADE-OFFS. In technology-oriented projects, disagreements may arise over technical issues, performance specifications, technical trade-offs, and the means to achieve performance.
- CONFLICT OVER MANPOWER RESOURCES. Conflicts may arise around the staffing of the project team with personnel from other functional and staff support areas or from the desire to use another department's personnel for project support even though the personnel remain under the authority of their functional or staff superiors.
- CONFLICT OVER COST. Frequently, conflict may develop over cost estimates from support areas regarding various project work breakdown packages. For example, the funds allocated by a project manager to a functional support group might be perceived as insufficient for the support requested.
- CONFICT OVER SCHEDULES. Disagreements may develop around the timing, sequencing, and scheduling of project-related tasks.
- PERSONALITY CONFLICT. Disagreements may tend to center on interpersonal differences rather than on "technical" issues. Conflicts often are "ego-centered."

Intensity of Specific Conflict Sources by Project Life-cycle Stage

The conflict intensity experienced by project managers for each source over the four life-cycle stages was measured on a special grid. The x-axis of the grid identifies four standard life-cycle phases: project formation, project build-up, main program phase, and phaseout. The y-axis delineates the seven potential sources of conflict. The respondents were asked to indicate on a standard four-point scale the intensity of the conflict they experienced for each of the seven potential sources of conflict within each of the four project life-cycle stages.

Conflict-handling Modes

A number of research studies indicate that managers approach and resolve conflicts by utilizing various conflict resolution modes. Blake and Mouton,[9] for example, have delineated five modes for handling conflicts:

- WITHDRAWAL. Retreating or withdrawing from an actual or potential disagreement.
- SMOOTHING. Deemphasizing or avoiding areas of difference and emphasizing areas of agreement.
- COMPROMISING. Bargaining and searching for solutions which bring some degree of satisfaction to the parties in a dispute. Characterized by a "give-and-take" attitude.
- FORCING. Exerting one's viewpoint at the potential expense of another. Often characterized by competitiveness and a win/lose situation.
- CONFRONTATION. Facing the conflict directly which involves a problem-solving approach whereby affected parties work through their disagreements.[10]

Aphorisms or statements of folk wisdom were used as surrogates for each conflict resolution mode.[11] The project managers were asked to rank the accuracy of each proverb in terms of how accurately it reflected the actual way in which they handled disagreements in the project environment. Fifteen proverbs were selected to match the five conflict-handling modes identified by Blake and Mouton.[12,13] This analysis provides an insight into the perceived conflict-handling mode of the project managers.

Analysis of Results

The results of the study are presented in three parts.

9. Blake, R.R. and Mouton, J.S. *The Managerial Grid*. Houston, Gulf Publishing, 1964.
10. For a fuller description of these definitions, see Burke, R.J. "Methods of Resolving Interpersonal Conflict," *Personnel Administration,* July-August 1969, pp. 48-55. Also see Thamhain, H.J., and Wilemon, D.L. "Conflict Management in Project-Oriented Work Environments," *Proceedings of the Sixth International Meeting of the Project Management Institute,* Washington, D.C., September 18-21, 1974.
11. Specifically, the measurements rely on the research of Lawrence, P.R., and Lorsch, J.W. "New Management Job: The Integrator," *Harvard Business Review,* November-December, 142-152, 1967.
12. See Ref. 9.
13. These proverbs have been used in other research of a similar nature to avoid the potential bias that might be introduced otherwise by the use of social science jargon. For further details, see Burke, R.J. "Methods of Managing Superior-Subordinate Conflict," *Canadian Journal of Behavioral Science,* 2,2, 124-135, 1970.

Mean Conflict Intensity over the Project Life Cycle

The mean intensity experienced for each of the potential conflict sources over the entire life of projects is presented in Figure 7-1. As indicated, relative to other situations, disagreements over schedules result in the most intense conflict over the total project. Scheduling conflicts often occur with other support departments over whom the project manager may have limited authority and control. Scheduling problems and conflicts also often involve disagreements and differing perceptions of organizational departmental priorities. For example, an issue urgent to the project manager may receive a low priority treatment from support groups and/or staff personnel because of a different priority structure in the support organization. Conflicts over schedules frequently result from the technical problems and manpower resources.

Conflict over project priorities ranked second highest over the project life cycle. In our discussions with project managers, many indicated that this type of conflict frequently develops because the organization did not have prior experience with a current project undertaking. Consequently, the pattern of project priorities may change from the original forecast, necessitating the reallocation of crucial resources and schedules, a process which is often susceptible to intense disagreements and conflicts. Similarly, priority issues often develop into conflict

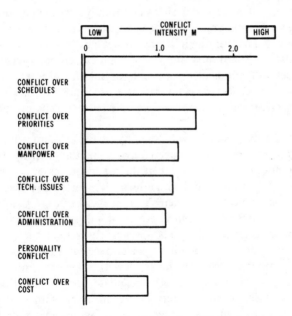

Figure 7-1. Mean Conflict Intensity Profile Over Project Life Cycle. Source: Hans J. Thamhain, and David L. Wilemon, "Conflict Management in Project Life Cycles," Sloan Management Review, Summer 1975. pp. 31-50 Reprinted by permission.

with other support departments whose established schedules and work patterns are disturbed by the changed requirements.

Conflict over manpower resources was the third most important source of conflict. Project managers frequently lament when there is little "organizational slack" in terms of manpower resources, a situation in which they often experience intense conflicts. Project managers note that most of the conflicts over personnel resources occur with those departments who either assign personnel to the project or support the project internally.

The fourth strongest source of conflict involved disagreements over technical opinions and trade-offs. Often the groups who support the project are primarily responsible for technical inputs and performance standards. The project manager, on the other hand, is accountable for the cost, schedule, and performance objectives. Since support areas are usually responsible for only parts of the project, they may not have the broad management overview of the total project. The project manager, for example, may be presented with a technical problem. Often he must reject the technical alternative due to cost or schedule restraints. In other cases, he may find that he disagrees with the opinions of others on strictly technical grounds.

Conflict over administrative procedures ranked fifth in the profile of seven conflict sources. It is interesting to note that most of the conflict over administrative procedures that occurs is almost uniformly distributed with functional departments, project personnel, and the project manager's superior.[14] Examples of conflict originating over administrative issues may involve disagreements over the project manager's authority and responsibilities, reporting relationships, administrative support, status reviews, or interorganizational interfacing. For the most part, disagreements over administrative procedures involve issues of how the project manager will function and how he relates to the organization's top management.

Personality conflict ranked low in intensity by the project managers. Our discussions with project managers indicated that while the intensity of personality conflicts may not be as high as some of the other sources of conflict, they are some of the most difficult to deal with effectively. Personality issues also may be obscured by communication problems and technical issues. A support person, for example, may stress the technical aspect of a disagreement with the project manager when, in fact, the real issue is a personality conflict.

Cost, like schedules, is often a basic performance measure in project management. As a conflict source, cost ranked lowest. Disagreements over cost frequently develop when project managers negotiate with other departments who will perform subtasks on the project. Project managers with tight budget constraints often want to minimize cost while support groups may want to maximize

---

14. See Thamhain and Wilemon in Ref. 10.

their part of the project budget. In addition, conflicts may occur as a result of technical problems or schedule slippages which may increase costs.

Conflict Sources and Intensity in the Project Life Cycle

While it is important to examine some of the principal determinants of conflict from an aggregate perspective, more specific and useful insights can be gained by exploring the intensity of various conflict sources in each life-cycle stage, namely, project formation, project build-up, main program phase, and phase-out. See Figure 7-2.

1. PROJECT FORMATION: As Figure 7-2 illustrates, during the project formation stage, the following conflict sources listed in order of rank were found:[15]

1. Project priorities
2. Administrative procedures
3. Schedules
4. Manpower

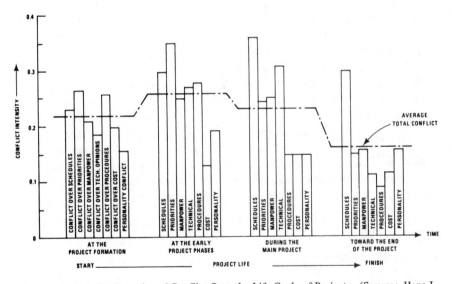

Figure 7-2. Relative Intensity of Conflict Over the Life Cycle of Projects. (Source: Hans J. Thamhain and David L. Wilemon, "Conflict Management in Project Life Cycles," *Sloan Management Review,* Summer, 1975.) pp. 31-50 Reprinted by permission.

15. The Conflict Intensity is computed as the total frequency (F) X magnitude (M) product of conflict experienced within the sample of project managers. When $0 \leqslant M \leqslant 3$. For example, if the average conflict intensity experienced by project managers on schedules with all interfaces was $M = 1.65$ (considerable) and $F = 14\%$ of all project managers indicated that "most" of this conflict occurred during the Project Formation Phase, then "Conflict over Schedules" would be $M \times F = 1.65 \times 0.14 = 0.23$ during project formation.

5. Cost
6. Technical
7. Personality

Unique to the project formation phase are some characteristics not typical of the other life-cycle stages. The project manager, for example, must launch his project within the larger "host" organization. Frequently, conflict develops between the priorities established for the project and the priorities which other line and staff groups believe important. To eliminate or minimize the detrimental consequences which could result, project managers need to carefully evaluate and plan for the impact of their projects on the groups that support them. This should be accomplished as early as possible in the program life cycle. The source of conflict ranked second was administrative procedures which are concerned with several critically important management issues. For example—How will the project organization be designed? Who will the project manager report to? What is the authority of the project manager? Does the project manager have control over manpower and material resources? What reporting and communication channels will be uses? Who establishes schedules and performance specifications? Most of these areas are negotiated by the project manager and conflict frequently occurs during the process. To avoid prolonged problems over these issues, it is important to clearly establish these procedures as early as possible.

Schedules typify another area where established groups may have to accommodate the newly formed project organization by adjusting their own operations. Most project managers attest that this adjustment is highly susceptible to conflict, even under ideal conditions, since it may involve a reorientation of present operating patterns and "local" priorities in support departments. These same departments might be fully committed to other projects. For similar reasons, negotiations over support personnel and other resources can be an important source of conflict in the project formation stage. Thus, effective planning and negotiation over these issues at the beginning of a project appear important.

2. PROJECT BUILD-UP: The conflict sources for the project build-up are listed below in order of rank.

1. Project priorities
2. Schedules
3. Administrative procedures
4. Technical
5. Manpower
6. Personality
7. Cost

Disagreements over project priorities, schedules, and administrative procedures continue as important determinants of conflict. Some of these sources of conflict appear as an extension from the previous program phase. Additional conflicts surface during negotiations with other groups in the build-up phase. It is interesting to note that while schedules ranked third in conflict intensity in the project formation phase, they are the second major conflict determinant in the build-up phase. Many of the conflicts over schedules arise in the first phase because of the disagreements that develop over the establishment of schedules. By contrast, in the build-up phase, conflict may develop over the enforcement of schedules according to objectives of the overall project plan.

An important point is that conflict over administrative procedures becomes less intense in the build-up phase, indicating the diminishing magnitude and frequency of administrative problems. It also appears that it is important to resolve potential conflicts, such as administrative disagreements, in the earlier phase of a project to avoid a replication of the same problems in the more advanced project life-cycle phases.

Conflict over technical issues also becomes more pronounced in the build-up phase, rising from the sixth ranked conflict source in the project formation phase to fourth in the build-up phase. Often this results from disagreements with a support group not being able to meet technical requirements, or their wanting to enhance the technological input for which they are responsible. Such action can adversely affect the project manager's cost and schedule objectives.

Project managers emphasized that personality conflicts are particularly difficult to handle. Even apparently small and infrequent personality conflicts might be more disruptive and detrimental to overall program effectiveness than intense conflicts over nonpersonal issues, which can often be handled on a more rational basis. Many project managers also indicated that conflict over cost in the build-up phase generally tends to be low for two primary reasons. First, conflict over the establishment of cost targets does not appear to create intense conflicts for most project managers. Second, some projects are not yet mature enough in the build-up phase to cause disagreements over cost between the project manager and those who support him.

3. MAIN PROGRAM: The main program phase reveals a different conflict pattern. The seven potential causes of conflict are listed in rank order below.

1. Schedules
2. Technical
3. Manpower
4. Priorities
5. Procedures
6. Cost
7. Personality

In the main program phase, the meeting of schedule commitments by various support groups becomes critical to effective project performance. In complex task management, the interdependency of various support groups dealing with complex technology frequently gives rise to slippages in schedules. When several groups or organizations are involved, this in turn can cause a "whiplash" effect throughout the project. In other words, a slippage in schedule by one group may affect other groups if they are on the critical path of the project.

As noted, while conflicts over schedules often develop in the earlier project phases, they are frequently related to the establishment of schedules. In the main program phase, our discussions with project managers indicated that conflicts frequently develop over the "management and maintenance" of schedules. The latter, as indicated in Figure 7-2, produce more intense conflicts.

Technical conflicts are also one of the most important sources of conflict in the main program phase. There appear to be two principal reasons for the rather high level of conflict in this phase. First, the main program phase is often characterized by the integration of various project subsystems for the first time, such as configuration management. Due to the complexities involved in this integration process, conflicts frequently develop over lack of subsystem integration and poor technical performance of one subsystem which may, in turn, affect other components and subsystems. Second, simply because a component can be designed in prototype, it does not always assure that all the technical anomalies will be eliminated. In extreme cases, the subsystem may not even be producible in the main program phase. Such problems can severely impact the project and generate intense conflicts. Disagreements also may arise in the main program phase over reliability and quality control standards, various design problems, and testing procedures. All these problems can severely impact the project and cause intense conflicts for the project manager.

Manpower resources ranked third as a determinant of conflict. The need for manpower reaches the highest levels in the main program phase. If support groups also are providing personnel to other projects, severe strains over manpower availability and project requirements frequently develop.

Conflict over priorities continues its decline in importance as a principal cause of conflict. Again, project priorities tend to be a form of conflict most likely to occur in the earlier project phases. Finally, administrative procedures, cost, and personality were about equal as the lowest ranked conflict sources.

4. PHASEOUT: The final stage, project phaseout, illustrates an interesting shift in the principal cause of conflict. The ranking of the conflict sources in this final project phase are:

1. Schedules
2. Personality
3. Manpower
4. Priorities
5. Cost
6. Technical
7. Procedures

Schedules are again the most likely form of conflict to develop in project phaseout. Project managers frequently indicated that many of the schedule slippages that developed in the main program phase tended to carry over to project phaseout. Schedule slippages often become cumulative and impact the project most severely in the final stage of a project.

Somewhat surprisingly, personality conflict was the second ranked source of conflict. It appears that much of the personality-oriented conflict can be explained in two ways. First, it is not uncommon for project participants to be tense and concerned with future assignments. Second, project managers frequently note that interpersonal relationships may be quite strained during this period due to the pressure on project participants to meet stringent schedules, budgets, and performance specifications and objectives.

Somewhat related to the personality issue are the conflicts which arise over manpower resources, the third ranked conflict source. Disagreements over manpower resources may develop due to new projects phasing in, hence creating competition for personnel during the critical phaseout stage. Project managers, by contrast, also may experience conflicts over the absorption of surplus manpower back into the functional areas where they impact the budgets and organizational variables.

Conflict over priorities in the phaseout stage often appears to be directly or indirectly related to competition with other project start-ups in the organization. Typically, newly organized projects or marketing support activities might require urgent, short-notice attention and commitments which have to be squeezed into tight schedules. At the same time, personnel might leave the project organization prematurely because of prior commitments which conflict with a slipped schedule on the current project or because of a sudden opportunity for a new assignment elsewhere. In either case, the combined pressure on schedules, manpower, and personality creates a climate which is highly vulnerable to conflicts over priorities.

As noted in Figure 7-2, cost, technical, administrative procedures tend to be ranked lowest as conflict sources. Cost, somewhat surprisingly, was not a major determinant of conflict. Discussions with project personnel suggest that while cost control can be troublesome in this phase, intense conflicts usually do not develop. Most problems in this area develop gradually and provide little ground for arguments.[16] The reader should be cautioned, however, that the low level of

---

16. Depending on the work environment and particular business there might be various reasons why conflicts over cost are low. First, some of the project components may be purchased externally on a fixed-fee basis. In such cases the contractor would bear the burden of costs. Second, costs are one of the most difficult project variables to control throughout the life cycle of a project and budgets are frequently adjusted for increase in material and manpower costs over the life of the project. These incremental cost adjustments frequently eliminate some of the "sting" in cost when they exceed the original estimates of the project manager. Moreover, some projects in the high technology area are managed on a cost-plus basis. In some of these projects precise cost estimates cannot always be rigidly adhered to.

conflict is by not means indicative of the importance of cost performance to over-all rating of a project manager. During discussions with top management, it was repeatedly emphasized that cost performance is one of the key evaluation measures in judging the performance of project managers.

Technical and administrative procedures ranked lowest in project phase-out. When a project reaches this stage, most of the technical issues are usually resolved. A similar argument holds for administrative procedures.

A graphical summary of the relative conflict intensity over the four conflict stages is provided in Figure 7-3. The diagram, an abstract of Figures 7-1 and 7-2, shows the change of relative conflict intensity over the project life for each of the seven conflict sources.

It is important to note that while a determinant conflict may be ranked rela-tively low in a specific life-cycle stage, it can, nevertheless, cause severe problems. A project manager, for example, may have serious ongoing problems with sched-ules throughout his project, but a single conflict over a technical issue can be equally detrimental and could jeopardize his performance to the same extent as schedule slippages. This point should be kept in mind in any discussion on project management conflict. Moreover, problems may develop which are virtually "con-flict-free" (i.e., technological anomalies or problems with suppliers) but may be just as troublesome to the project manager as any of the conflict issues discussed.

The problem which now should be addressed is how these various conflict sources and the situations they create are managed.

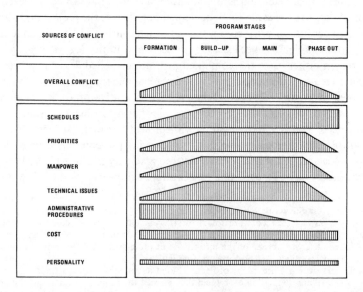

Figure 7-3. Trend of Conflict Intensity Over the Four Project Life-Cycle Stages. (Source: Hans J. Thamhain and David L. Wilemon, "Conflict Management in Project Life Cycles," *Sloan Management Review,* Spring, 1975 pp. 31-50 Reprinted by permission.)

Conflict-handling Modes

The investigation into the conflict-handling modes of project managers developed a number of interesting patterns. The actual style of project managers was determined from their scores on the aphorisms. As indicated in Figure 7-4, confrontation was most frequently utilized as a problem-solving mode. This mode was favored by approximately 70 percent of the project managers.[17] The compromise approach which is characterized by trade-offs and a give-and-take attitude ranked second, followed by smoothing. Forcing and withdrawal ranked as the fourth and fifth most favored resolution modes, respectively.

In terms of the most and least favored conflict resolution modes, the project managers had similar rankings for the conflict-handling method used between him and his personnel, his superior, and his functional support departments except in the cases of confrontation and compromise. While confrontation was the most favored mode for dealing with superiors, compromise was more favored in handling disagreements with functional support departments. The various modes of conflict resolution used by project managers are summarized in the profile of Figure 7-4.

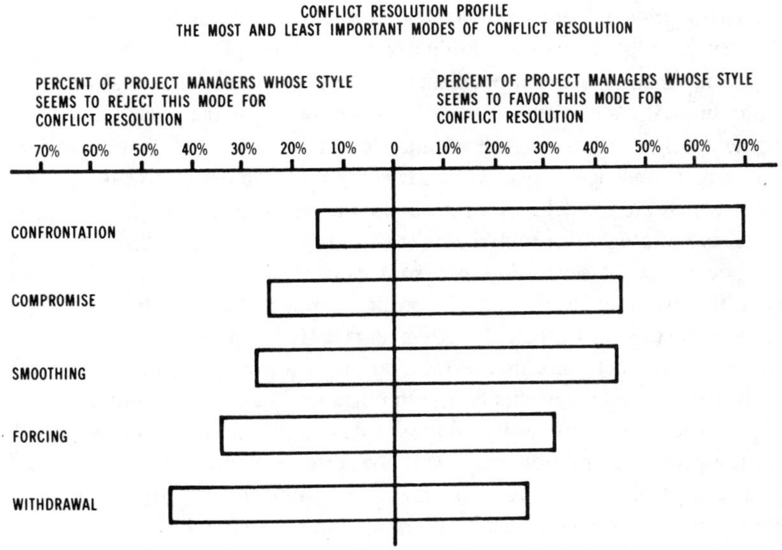

CONFLICT RESOLUTION PROFILE
THE MOST AND LEAST IMPORTANT MODES OF CONFLICT RESOLUTION

Figure 7-4. Conflict Resolution Profile. The Various Modes of Conflict Resolution Actually used to Manage Conflict in Project-Oriented Work Environments. (Source: Hans J. Thamhain, and David L. Wilemon, "Conflict in Project Life Cycles," *Sloan Management Review,* Summer 1975, pp. 31-50 Reprinted by Permission.)

17. Quantitatively, this means that 70 percent of the project managers in the sample indicated that the proverbs which are representative of this mode (i.e., confrontation) describe the actual way the manager is resolving conflict "accurately" or "very accurately" as related to his project situations.

Implications

A number of ideas evolved for improving conflict management effectiveness in project-oriented environments from this research. As the data on the mean conflict intensities indicate, the three areas most likely to cause problems for the project manager over the entire project cycle are disagreements over schedules, project priorities, and manpower resources. One reason these areas are apt to produce more intense disagreements is that the project manager may have limited control over other areas that have an important impact on these areas particularly the functional support departments. These three areas (schedules, project priorities, and manpower resources) require careful surveillance throughout the life cycle of a project. To minimize detrimental conflict, intensive planning prior to actually launching the project is recommended. Planning can help the project manager anticipate many potential sources of conflict before they occur. Scheduling, priority setting, and resource allocation require effective planning to avoid problems later in the project. In our discussions with project managers who have experienced problems in these areas, almost all maintain that these problems frequently originate from lack of effective pre-project planning.

Managing projects involves managing change. It is not our intention to suggest that all such problems can be eliminated by effective planning. A more realistic view is that many potential problems can be minimized. There always will be random, unpredictable situations which defy forecasting in project environments.

Some specific suggestions are summarized in Table 7-1. The table provides an aid to project managers in recognizing some of the most important sources of conflict which are most likely to occur in various phases of projects. The table also suggests strategies for minimizing their detrimental consequences.

As one views the seven potential sources of disagreements over the life of a project, the dynamic nature of each conflict source is revealed. Frequently, areas which are most likely to foster disagreements early in a project, become less likely to induce severe conflicts in the maturation of a project. Administrative procedures, for example, continually lose importance as an intense source of conflict during project maturation. By contrast, personality conflict, which ranks lowest in the project formation stage, is the second most important source of conflict in project phase-out. In summary, it is posited that if project managers are aware of the importance of each potential conflict source by project life cycle, then more effective conflict minimization strategies can be developed.

In terms of the means by which project managers handle conflicts and disagreements, the data revealed that the confrontation or problem-solving mode was the most frequent method utilized. While our study did not attempt to explore the effectiveness of each mode separately, an earlier research project Burke[18] sug-

---

18. R.J. Burke, "Methods of Resolving Interpersonal Conflict," *Personnel Administration,* July-August, 48-55, 1969.

Table 7-1. Major Conflict Source and Recommendations for Minimizing Dysfunctional Consequences.

PROJECT LIFE CYCLE PHASE	CONFLICT SOURCE	RECOMMENDATIONS
Project formation	Priorities	Clearly defined plans. Joint decision-making and/or consultation with affected parties.
	Procedures	Develop detailed administrative operating procedures to be followed in conduct of project. Secure approval from key administrators. Develop statement of understanding or charter.
	Schedules	Develop schedule commitments in advance of actual project commencement.
		Forecast other departmental priorities and possible impact on project.
Buildup phase	Priorities	Provide effective feedback to support areas on forecasted project plans and needs via status review sessions.
	Schedules	Schedule work breakdown packages (project subunits) in cooperation with functional groups.
	Procedures	Contingency planning on key administrative issues.
Main program	Schedules	Continually monitor work in progress. Communicate results to affected parties.
		Forecast problems and consider alternatives.
		Identify potential "trouble spots" needing closer surveillance.
	Technical	Early resolution of technical problems.
		Communication of schedule and budget restraints to technical personnel.
		Emphasize adequate, early technical testing.
		Facilitate early agreement on final designs.
	Manpower	Forecast and communicate manpower requirements early.
	Manpower	Establish manpower requirements and priorities with functional and staff groups.
Phaseout	Schedules	Close schedule monitoring in project life cycle.
		Consider reallocation of available manpower to critical project areas prone to schedule slippages.
		Attain prompt resolution of technical issues which may impact schedules.
	Personality and Manpower	Develop plans for reallocation of manpower upon project completion.
		Maintain harmonious working relationships with project team and support groups. Try to loosen up "high-stress" environment.

Source: Hans J. Thamhain, and Wilemon, David L. "Conflict Management in Project Life Cycles," *Sloan Management Review,* Summer, 1975. pp. 31-50. Reprinted by permission.

gests that the confrontation approach is the most effective conflict-handling mode.[19]

In some contrast to studies of general management, the findings of our research in project-oriented environments suggest that it is less important to search for a best mode of effective conflict management. It appears to be more significant that project managers, in their capacity as integrators of diverse organizational resources, employ the full range of conflict-resolution modes. While confrontation was found as the ideal approach under most circumstances, other approaches may be equally effective depending upon the situational content of the disagreement. Withdrawal, for example, may be used effectively as a temporary measure until new information can be sought or to "cool off" a hostile reaction from a colleague. As a basic long-term strategy, however, withdrawal may actually escalate a disagreement if no resolution is eventually sought.[20]

In other cases, compromise and smoothing might be considered an effective strategy by the project manager, if it does not severely affect the overall project objectives. Forcing, on the other hand, often proves to be a win/lose mode. Even though the project manager may win over a specific issue, effective working arrangements with the "forced" party may be jeopardized in future relationships. Nevertheless, some project managers find that forcing is the only viable mode in some situations. Confrontation or the problem-solving mode may actually encompass all conflict-handling modes to some extent. A project manager, for example, in solving a conflict may use withdrawal, compromise, forcing, and smoothing to eventually get an effective resolution. The objective of confrontation, however, is to find a solution to the issue in question whereby all affected parties can live with the eventual outcome.

In summary, conflict is fundamental to complex task management. It is not only important for project managers to be cognizant of the potential sources of conflict, but also to know when in the life cycle of a project they are most likely to occur. Such knowledge can help the project manager avoid the detrimental aspects of conflict and maximize its beneficial aspects. Conflict can be beneficial when disagreements result in the development of new information which can enhance the decision-making process. Finally, when conflicts do develop, the project manager needs to know the advantages and disadvantages of each resolution mode for conflict resolution effectiveness.

---

19. Although Burke's study was conducted on general management personnel, it offers an interesting comparison to our research. Burke's paper notes that "Compromising" and "Forcing" were effective in 11.3 percent and 24.5 percent of the cases while "Withdrawal" or "Smoothing" approaches were found mostly ineffective in the environment under investigation.

20. H.J. Thamhain, and D.L. Wilemon, "Conflict Management in Project Oriented Work Environments." *Proceedings of the Sixth International Meeting of the Project Management Institute,* Washington, D.C., September, 18-21, 1974.

7.4 CONFLICT RESOLUTION

Although each project within the company may be inherently different, the company may wish to have the resulting conflicts resolved in the same manner. The four most common methods are:

1. The development of company-wide conflict resolution policies and procedures.
2. The establishment of project conflict resolutions procedures during the early planning activities.
3. The use of hierarchical referral.
4. The requirement of direct contact.

With each of the above methods, the project manager may still select any of the conflict resolution modes discussed in the previous section.

Many companies have attempted to develop company-wide policies and procedures for conflict resolution. Results have shown that this method is doomed to failure because each project is different and not all conflicts can be handled the same way. Furthermore, project managers, by virtue of their individuality, and sometimes differing amounts of authority and responsibility, prefer to resolve conflicts in their own fashion.

A second method for resolving conflicts, and one which is often very effective, is to "plan" for conflicts during the planning activities. This can be accomplished through the use of linear responsibility charts. Planning for conflict resolution is similar to the first method except that each project manager can develop his own policies, rules and procedures.

Hierarchical referral for conflict resolution, in theory, appears as the best method because neither the project manager nor functional manager will dominate. Under this arrangement, the project and functional managers agree that in order for a proper balance to exist, their common superior must resolve the conflict in order to protect the company's best interest. Unfortunately, this is not a realistic course of action because the common superior cannot be expected to continually resolve lower-level conflicts. Going to the "well" too often gives the impression that the functional and project managers cannot resolve their own problems.

The last method is direct contact and is an outgrowth of the policies and procedures methods where established guidelines dictate that conflicting parties meet face-to-face and resolve their disagreement. Unfortunately, this method does not always work and, if continually stressed, can result in conditions where individuals will either suppress the identification of problems or develop new ones during confrontation.

Many conflicts can be either reduced or eliminated by constantly communicating the project objectives to the team members. Many times this continual repetition will prevent individuals from going too far into the "wrong" and thus avoid the creation of a conflict situation.

7.5 UNDERSTANDING SUPERIOR, SUBORDINATE, AND FUNCTIONAL CONFLICTS[21]

In order for the project manager to be effective, an understanding of how to work with the various employees who must interface with the project is necessary. These various employees include upper-level management, subordinate project team members, and functional personnel. Quite often, especially when conflicts are possible, the project manager must demonstrate an ability for continuous adaptability by creating a different working environment with each group of employees. The need for this was shown in the previous section by the fact that the relative intensity of conflicts can vary in the life cycle of a project.

The type and intensity of conflicts can also vary with the type of employee that the project manager must interface with, as shown in Figure 7-5. Both con-

| CONFLICT CAUSES | SOURCES: CONFLICTS OCCURRED MOSTLY WITH | | | | | |
	FUNCTIONAL MANAGERS	FUNCTIONAL PERSONNEL	BETWEEN PROJECT PERSONNEL	SUPERIORS	SUBORDINATES	RELATIVE CONFLICT INTENSITY (HIGH→LOW)
SCHEDULES	■	■				HIGH
PRIORITIES	■	■	■			
MANPOWER	■	■				
TECHNICAL	■	■	■			
PROCEDURES	■	■		■	■	
PERSONALITY	■	■	■	■	■	
COSTS	■	■		■		LOW

HIGH ◀——— RELATIVE CONFLICT INTENSITY ———▶ LOW

Figure 7-5. Relationship Between Conflict Causes And Sources.

21. The majority of this section, including the figures has been adapted from *Seminar in Project Management Workbook*, © 1977 by Hans J. Thamhain. Reproduced by permission of Dr. Hans J. Thamhain.

flict causes and sources are rated according to relative conflict intensity. Any conflict that the project manager has with a functional manager can also occur with the functional employee, and *vice versa*. The data in Figure 7-5 was obtained for a 75 percent confidence level.

In the previous section we discussed the five basic resolution modes for handling conflicts. The specific type of resolution mode that a project manager will use might easily depend upon the conflict is with, as shown in Figure 7-6. The data in Figure 7-6 does not necessarily show the modes that project managers would prefer, but rather identifies the modes that will increase or decrease the potential conflict intensity. For example, although project managers consider, in general, that withdrawal is their least favorite mode, it can be used quite effectively with functional managers. In dealing with superiors, project managers would rather be ready for an immediate compromise than for face-to-face confrontation which could easily result in having the resolution forced in the favor of upper-level management.

Figure 7-7 identifies the various influence styles that project managers find effective in helping to reduce potential conflicts. Penalty power, authority, and expertise are considered as strongly unfavorable associations with respect to low conflicts. As expected, work challenge and promotions (if the project manager has the authority) are strongly favorable associations with his personnel.

Therefore, for the project manager to be truly effective, he or she should understand not only what types of conflicts are possible in the various stages of the life cycle, but with whom these conflicts can occur and how to effectively deal with them.

(The figure shows only those associations which are statistically significant at the 95 percent level)

INTENSITY OF CONFLICT PERCEIVED BY PROJECT MANAGERS (P.M.)	ACTUAL CONFLICT RESOLUTION STYLE				
	FORCING	CONFRONTA- TION	COMPROMISE	SMOOTHING	WITHDRAWAL
BETWEEN P.M. AND HIS PERSONNEL	■	▲	▲	▲	■
BETWEEN P.M. AND HIS SUPERIOR		■	▲		
BETWEEN P.M. AND FUNCTIONAL SUPPORT DEPARTMENTS	■	■			▲

▲ STRONGLY FAVORABLE ASSOCIATION WITH REGARD TO LOW CONFLICT ($-\tau$)

■ STRONGLY UNFAVORABLE ASSOCIATION WITH REGARD TO LOW CONFLICT ($+\tau$)

*KENDALL τ CORRELATION

Figure 7-6. Association Between Perceived Intensity Of Conflict And Mode Of Conflict Resolution.*

(The figure shows only those associations which are statistically significant at the 95 percent level)

INTENSITY OF CONFLICT PERCEIVED BY PROJECT MANAGER (P.M.)	INFLUENCE METHODS AS PERCEIVED BY PROJECT MANAGERS						
	EXPERTISE	AUTHORITY	WORK CHALLENGE	FRIENDSHIP	PROMOTION	SALARY	PENALTY
BETWEEN P.M. AND HIS PERSONNEL	■	■	▲		▲		■
BETWEEN P.M. AND HIS SUPERIOR			▲				■
BETWEEN P.M. AND FUNCTIONAL SUPPORT DEPARTMENTS		■					■

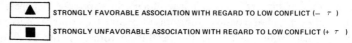

▲ STRONGLY FAVORABLE ASSOCIATION WITH REGARD TO LOW CONFLICT (− τ)

■ STRONGLY UNFAVORABLE ASSOCIATION WITH REGARD TO LOW CONFLICT (+ τ)

*KENDALL τ CORRELATION

Figure 7-7. Association Between Influence Methods Of Project Manager And Their Perceived Conflict Intensity.*

7.6 THE MANAGEMENT OF CONFLICTS[22]

Good project managers realize that conflicts are inevitable and that procedures or techniques must be developed for their resolution. If the project manager is not careful, he or she could easily worsen the conflict by not knowing how to manage it. Once a conflict occurs, the project manager must do certain preliminaries. This includes:

- Studying the problem and collecting all available information
- Developing a situational approach or methodology
- Setting the appropriate atmosphere or climate

In setting the appropriate atmosphere, the project manager must establish a willingness to participate for himself as well the other participants. The manager must clearly state the objectives of the forthcoming meeting, establish the credibility of the meeting and sanction the meeting.

If a confrontation meeting is necessary between conflicting parties, then the project manager should be aware of the logical steps and sequence of events which should be taken. These include:

- Setting the climate: Establishing a willingness to participate.
- Analyzing the images: How do you see yourself and others, and how do they see you?

22. See Ref. 21.

- Collecting the information: Getting feelings out in the open.
- Defining the problem: Defining and clarifying all positions.
- Sharing the information: Making the information available to all.
- Setting the appropriate priorities: Develop working sessions for setting priorities and time tables.
- Organizing the group: Form cross-functional problem-solving groups.
- Problem solving: Obtaining cross-functional involvement, securing commitments and setting the priorities and time table.
- Developing the action plan: Getting commitment.
- Implementing the work: Taking action on the plan.
- Following up: Obtaining feedback on the implementation for the action plan.

Once the conflict has been defined and a meeting is necessary, the project manager or team leader should understand the conflict minimization procedures. These include:

- Pausing and thinking before reacting
- Building trust
- Trying to understand the conflict motives
- Keeping the meeting under control
- Listening to all involved parties
- Maintaining a give and take attitude
- Educating others tactfully on your views
- Be willing to say when you were wrong
- Not acting as a superman and level the discussion only once in a while.

We can now sum up these actions by defining the role of the effective manager in conflict problem solving. The effective manager:

- Knows the organization
- Listens with understanding rather than evaluation
- Clarifies the nature of the conflict
- Understands the feelings of others
- Suggests the procedures for resolving differences
- Maintains relationships with disputing parties
- Facilitates the communications process
- Seeks resolutions

7.7 FORCE FIELD ANALYSIS

Project managers must live in a dynamic environment in which continuous and rapid change becomes a way of life. To operate effectively under these circumstances, the project manager must be able to diagnose the situation, design alternatives which will remedy the situation, provide the necessary leadership such that these changes can be implemented, and develop an atmosphere conducive for the employees to readily adapt to these changes.

One of the early pioneers in developing theories for managing change was Kurt Lewin.[23] Lewin advocated that at any given point in time during the life cycle of a project there will exist driving forces which will push the project toward success and restraining forces which may induce failure. In a steady-state environment, the driving and restraining forces are in balance. If, however, the driving forces increase or the restraining forces decrease, whether they act independently or together, change is likely to take place. The formal analysis of these forces is commonly referred to as Force Field Analysis. This type of analysis can be used to:[24]

- Monitor the project team and measure potential deficiencies
- Audit the project on an ongoing basis
- Involve project personnel which can be conducive to team-building
- Measure the sensitivity of proposed change

Current studies in Force Field Analysis have been conducted by Dugan *et al.*[24] The research involved 125 project managers in approximately 70 different technology-oriented companies. The research study and questionnaire were personally explained to the participating project managers so as to minimize potential communications problems.

The researchers obtained information in several areas, including:

- Personal drive, motivation, and leadership
- Team motivation
- Management support
- Functional support
- Technical expertise
- Project objectives

The research study catagorized each of the above areas according to project life-cycle phase. However, for simplicity's sake, only a brief synopsis of each of these areas will be presented. The reader is directed to the reference article for a more detailed description.

Personal drive, motivation, and leadership were found to be the strongest driving forces, an important attribute to the project manager and team members, and important in all project life-cycle phases. The lack of these qualities was found to result in a strong restraining force. The following results were found:

- Driving Forces
  - Desire for accomplishment

---

23. Kurt Lewin "Fontiers in Group Dynamics," *Human Relations,* 1, 1, 1947, also, *Field Theory in Social Science,* New York, 1951.
24. See Ref. 2.

- Interest in project
- Work challenge
- Group acceptance
- Common objectives

- Restraining Forces
  - Inexperienced project leader
  - Uncertain roles
  - Lack of technical knowledge
  - Personality problems

Team motivation was identified as having the strongest overall influence on project success and an important factor in all phases of the project. Team motivation was a powerful driver and, if lacking, became a strong restraint. The following results for team motivation were found:

- Driving Forces
  - Good interpersonal relations
  - Desire to achieve
  - Expertise
  - Common goal
- Restraining Forces
  - Poor team organization
  - Communication barriers
  - Poor leadership
  - Uncertain rewards
  - Uncertain objectives

Management support was identified as being both an important driving and restraining force, and associated with all project phases. The following results were obtained:

- Driving Forces
  - Sufficient resources
  - Proper priorities
  - Authority delegation
  - Management interest
- Restraining Forces
  - Unclear objectives
  - Insufficient resources
  - Changing priorities
  - Insufficient authority/charter
  - Management indifference

Functional support was identified as important during project build-up, main phase, and project phase-out, as well as being a must for successful project completion. Functional support was impacted by top management support, funding, and organizational structure. The forces behind functional support were found to be:

- Driving Forces
  - Clear goals and priorities
  - Proper planning
  - Adequate task integrators

- Restraining Forces
  - Priority conflicts
  - Funding restraints
  - Poor project organization

Technical expertise was particularly important during project formation and build-up. The forces identified were:

- Driving Forces
  - Ability to manage technology
  - Prior track record
  - Low risk project
- Restraining Forces
  - Lack of technical information
  - Unexpected technical problems
  - Inability to cope with change

Project objectives were most important during project formation and start-up. The forces identified were:

- Driving Forces
  - Clear goals
  - Clear expectations/responsibilities
  - Clear interface relationships
  - Clear specifications
- Restraining Forces
  - Conflict over objectives
  - Customer uncertainties

The authors then summarized their results as follows:

- Implications for project managers
  - Understand interaction of organizational and behavioral elements to build an effective team
  - Show concern for team members — know their needs
  - Provide work challenge
  - Communicate objectives clearly

- Plan effectively and early in the project cycle
- Establish contingency plan
- Implications for top management
  - Poor organizational climate has a negative effect on project performance
  - Project leader abilities are crucial to effective project management. Program management selection should be carefully considered. Formal training and development may be necessary.
  - Senior management support is important
  - Clearly defined decision channels and priorities may improve operating effectiveness with functional departments
  - Smooth project start-up and phase-out procedures help to ease personnel problems and power plays

CASE STUDY: GREYSON CORPORATION

Greyson Corporation was formed in 1940 by three scientists from the University of California. The major purpose of the company was research and development for advanced military weaponry. Following World War II, Greyson became a leader in the field of Research and Development. By the mid 1950s, Greyson employed over 200 scientists and engineers.

The fact that Greyson handled only R & D contracts was advantageous. First, all of the scientists and engineers were dedicated to R & D activities, not having to share their loyalties with production programs. Second, a strong functional organization was established. The project management function was the responsibility of the functional manager whose department would perform the majority of the work. Working relationships between departments were excellent.

By the late 1950s, Greyson was under new management. Almost all R & D programs called for establishment of qualification and production planning as well. As a result, Greyson decided to enter into the production of military weapons as well, and capture some of the windfall profits of the production market. This required a major reorganization from a functional to a matrix structure. Personnal problems occurred, but none that proved major catastrophies.

In 1964, Greyson entered into the aerospace market with the acquisition of a subcontract for the propulsion unit of the Hercules Missile. The contract was projected at $200 million over a five year period, with excellent possibilities for follow-on work. Between 1964 and 1968 Greyson developed a competent technical staff composed mainly of young, untested college graduates. The majority of the original employees who were still there were in managerial positions. Greyson never had any layoffs. In addition, Greyson had excellent career development programs for almost all employees.

Between 1967 and 1971 the Department of Defense procurement for new Weapon Systems was on the decline. Greyson relied heavily on their two major production programs, Hercules and Condor II both of which gave great promise for continued procurement. Greyson also had some thirty smaller R & D contracts as well as two smaller production contracts for hand weapons.

Because R & D money was becoming scarce, Greyson's management decided to phase out much of the R & D activities and replace them with lucrative production contracts. Greyson believed that they could compete with anyone in regard to low-cost production. Under this philosophy, the R & D community was reduced to minimum levels necessary to support in-house activities. The Director of Engineering froze all hiring except for job-shoppers with special talents. All nonessential engineering personnel were transferred to production units.

In 1972, Greyson entered into competition with Cameron Aerospace Corporation for development, qualification and testing of the Navy's new Neptune Missile. The competition was an eight-motor shoot-off during the last ten months of 1973. Cameron Corporation won the contract due to technical merit. Greyson Corporation, however, had gained valuable technical information in rocket motor development and testing. The loss of the Neptune Program made it clear to Greyson's management that aerospace technology was changing too fast for Greyson to maintain a passive position. Even though funding was limited, Greyson increased the technical staff and sound found great success in winning research and development contracts.

By 1975, Greyson had developed a solid aerospace business base. Profits had increased by 30 percent. Greyson Corporation expanded from a company with 200 employees in 1964 to 1800 employees in 1975. The Hercules Program which began in 1964 was providing yearly follow-on contracts. All indications projected a continuation of the Hercules Program through 1982.

Cameron Corporation, on the other hand, had found 1975 a difficult year. The Neptune Program was the only major contract which Cameron Corporation maintained. The current production buy for the Neptune Missile was scheduled for completion in August 1975 with no follow-on work earlier than January, 1976. Cameron Corporation anticipated that overhead rates would increase sharply prior to next buy. The cost per motor would increase from $55,000 to $75,000 for a January procurement, $85,000 for a March procurement and $125,000 for an August procurement.

In February, 1975, the Air Force asked Greyson Corporation if they would be interested in submitting a sole-source bid for production and qualification of the Neptune Missile. The Air Force considered Cameron's position as uncertain, and wanted to maintain a qualified vendor should Cameron Corporation decide to get out of the aerospace business.

Greyson submitted a bid of $30 million for qualification and testing of 30 Neptune motors over a 30-month period beginning in January 1976. Current testing of the Neptune Missile indicated that the minimum motor age life would extend through January 1979. This meant that production funds over the next 30 months could be diverted toward requalification of a new vendor and still meet production requirements for 1979.

In August of 1975, upon delivery of the last Neptune Rocket to the Air Force, Cameron Corporation announced that without an immediate production contract for Neptune follow-on work it would close its door and get out of the aerospace business. Cameron Corporation invited Greyson Corporation to interview all of their key employees for possible work on the Neptune Requalification Program.

Greyson hired 35 of Cameron's key people to begin work in October, 1975. The key people would be assigned to ongoing Greyson programs so as to become familiar with Greyson methods. Greyson's lower-level management was very unhappy about bringing in their 35 employees for fear that they would be placed into slots which could have resulted in promotions for some of Greyson's people. Management then decreed that these 35 people would work solely on the Neptune Program and other vacancies would be filled, as required, from the Hercules and Condor 11 Programs. Greyson estimated that the cost of employing these 35 people was approximately $150,000 per month, almost all of which was being absorbed through overhead. Without these 35 people, Greyson did not believe that they would have won the contract as sole-source procurement. Other competitors could have "grabbed" these key people and forced an open bidding situation.

Because of the increased overhead rate, Greyson maintained a minimum staff to prepare for contract negotiations and document preparation. So as to minimize costs, the Directors of Engineering and Program Management gave the Neptune Program Office the authority to make decisions for departments and divisions which were without representation in the program office. Top management had complete confidence in the program office personnel because of their past performance on other programs and years of experience.

In December 1975, the Department of Defense announced that spending was being curtailed sharply and that funding limitations made it impossible to begin the qualification program before July, 1976. To make matters worse, consideration was being made for a compression of the requalification program to 25 motors in a 20 month period. However, long-lead funding for raw materials would be available.

After lengthy consideration, Greyson decided to maintain its present position and retain the thirty-five Cameron employees by assigning them to in-house programs. The Neptune Program Office was still maintained for preparations to support contract negotiations, rescheduling of activities for a shorter program, and long-lead procurement.

In May of 1976, contract negotiations began between the Navy and Greyson. At the beginning of contract negotiations, the Navy stated the three key elements for negotiations:

1. Maximum funding was limited to the 1975 quote for a 30 motor/30 month program.
2. The amount of money available for the last six months of 1976 was limited to $3.7 million
3. The contract would be cost plus incentive fee (CPIF)

After three weeks of negotiations there appeared a stalemate. The Navy contended that the production man-hours in the proposal were at the wrong level on the learning curves. It was further argued that Greyson should be a lot "smarter" now because of the 35 Cameron employees and because of experience learned during the 1971 shoot-off with Cameron Corporation during the initial stages of the Neptune Program.

Since the negotiation teams could not agree, top level management of the Navy and Greyson Corporation met to iron out the differences. An agreement was finally reached on a figure of $28.5 million. This was $1.5 million below Greyson's original estimate to do the work. Management, however, felt that, by "tightening our belts," the work could be accomplished within budget.

The program began on July 1, 1976 with the distribution of the department budgets by the program office. Almost all of the department managers were furious. Not only were the budgets below their original estimates, but the 35 Cameron employees were earning salaries above the department mean salary, thus reducing total man-hours even further. Almost all department managers asserted that cost overruns would be the responsibility of the program office and not the individual departments.

By November, 1976 Greyson was in trouble. The Neptune Program was on target for cost but 35 percent behind for work completion. Department managers refused to take responsibility for certain tasks that were usually considered to be joint department responsibilities. Poor communication between program office and department managers provided additional discouragement. Department managers refused to have their employees work on Sunday.

Even with all this being considered, program management felt that catch-up was still possible. The 35 former Cameron employees were performing commendable work equal to their counterparts on other programs. Management considered that the potential cost overrun situation was not in the critical stage and that more time should be permitted before corporate funding is considered.

In December, 1976 the Department of Defense announced that there would be no further buys of the Hercules Missile. This announcement was a severe blow to Greyson's management. Not only were they in danger of having to lay off 500 employees, but overhead rates would rise considerably. There was an indication last year that there would be no further buys, but management did not consider the indications as being positive enough to require corporate strategy changes.

Although Greyson was not unionized, there was a possibility of a massive strike if Greyson career employees were not given seniority over the 35 former Cameron employees in case of layoffs.

1. The higher overhead rates threatened to increase total program costs by $1 million on the Neptune Program.
2. Because the activities were behind schedule, the catch-up phases would have to be made in a higher salary and overhead rate quarter, thus increasing total costs further.
3. Inventory costs were increasing. Items purchased during long-lead funding were approaching shelf-life limits. Cost impact may be as high as $1 million.

The vice-president and general manager considered the Neptune Program critical to the success and survival of Greyson Corporation. The directors and division heads were ordered to take charge of the program. The following options were considered:

1. Perform overtime work to get back on schedule.
2. Delay program activities in hope that the Navy can come up additional funding.

3. Review current material specifications in order to increase material shelf-life, thus lowering inventory and procurement costs.
4. Begin laying off noncritical employees
5. Purchase additional tooling and equipment (at corporate expense) so that schedule requirements can be met on target

March 1, 1977 Greyson gave merit salary increases to the key employees on all in-house programs. At the same time, Greyson laid off 700 employees, some of whom were seasoned veterans. By March 15, Greyson employees formed a union and went out on strike.

CASE STUDY: THE PROBLEM WITH PRIORITIES

For the past several years, Kent Corporation had achieved remarkable success in winning R & D contracts. The customers were pleased with the analytical capabilities of the R & D staff at Kent Corporation. Theoretical and experimental results were usually within 95 percent agreement. But many customers still felt that 95 percent was too low. They wanted 98-99 percent.

In 1973, Kent updated their computer facility by renting an IBM-370 computer. The increased performance with the new computer encouraged the R & D group to attempt to convert from two-dimensional to three-dimensional solutions to their theoretical problems. Almost everyone except the Director of R & D thought that this would give better comparison between experimental and theoretical data.

Kent Corporation had tried to develop the computer program for three-dimensional solutions with their own internal R & D programs, but the cost was too great. Finally, after a year of writing proposals, Kent Corporation convinced the federal government to sponsor the project. The project was estimated at $750,000, to begin January 2, 1975 and to be completed by December 20, 1975. Dan McCord was selected as project manager. Dan had worked with the EDP Department on other projects and knew the people and the man-hour standards.

Kent Corporation was big enough to support one hundred simultaneous projects. With so many projects in existence at one time, continual reshuffling of resources was necesssary. The corporation directors met every Monday morning to establish project priorities. Priorities were not enforced unless project and functional managers could not agree upon the allocation and distribution of resources.

Because of the R & D Director's persistence, the computer was given a low priority. This posed a problem for Dan McCord. The computer department manager refused to staff the project with his best people. As a result, Dan had severe scepticism about the success of the project.

In July, two other project managers held a meeting with Dan to discuss the availability of the new computer model.

"We have two proposals which we're favored to win, providing that we can state in our proposal that we have this new computer model available for use," remarked one of the project managers.

"We have a low priority and, even if we finish the job on time, I'm not sure of the quality of work because of the people we have assigned," said Dan.

"How do you propose we improve our position?" asked a project manager.

"Let's try to get in to see the Director of R & D," asserted Dan.

"And what are we going to say in our defense?" asked one of the project managers.

CASE STUDY: L.P. MANNING CORPORATION

In March, 1977 the Marketing Division of the L.P. Manning Corporation performed a national survey to test the public's reaction to a new type of toaster. Manning had achieved success in the past and established themselves as a leader in the home appliance industry.

Although the new toaster was just an idea, the public responded favorably. In April of the same year, the vice-presidents for planning, marketing, engineering, and manufacturing all met to formulate plans for the development and ultimately the production of the new toaster. Marketing asserted that the manufacturing cost must remain below $30 per unit or else Manning Corporation would not be competitive. Based upon the specifications drawn up in the meeting, manufacturing assured marketing that this cost could be met.

The engineering division was given six months to develop the product. Manning's executives were eager to introduce the product for the Christmas rush. This might give them an early foothold on a strong market share.

During the R & D phase, marketing continually "pestered" engineering with new designs and changes in specifications such that the new product would be easier to market. The ultimate result was a one-month slip in the schedule.

Pushing the schedule to the right greatly displeased manufacturing personnel. According to the vice-president for manufacturing, speaking to the marketing manager,

"I've just received the final specifications and designs from engineering. This is not what we had agreed upon last March. These changes will cost us to lose at least one additional month to change our manufacturing planning. And because we're already one month behind, I don't see any way that we could reschedule our Christmas production facilities to accommodate this new product. Our established lines must come first. Furthermore, our estimating department says that these changes will increase the cost of the product by at least 25 to 35 percent. And, of course, we must include the quality control section which has some question as to whether or not we can actually live with these specifications. Why don't we just cancel this project or at least postpone it until next year?"

CASE STUDY: SCHEDULING THE SAFETY LAB

"Now see here, Tom, I understand your problem well," remarked Dr. Polly, Director of the Research Laboratories. "I pay you a good salary to run the Safety Labs. That salary also includes doing the necessary scheduling to match our priorities. Now, if you can't handle the job, I'll get someone who can."

Tom: Every Friday morning your secretary hands me a sheet with the listing of priorities for the following week. Once, just once, I'd like to sit in on the director's meeting and tell you people what you do to us in the Safety Lab when you continually shuffle around the priorities from week to week.

On Friday afternoons, my people and I meet with representatives from each project to establish the following week's schedules.

Dr. Polly: Can't you people come to an agreement?

Tom: I don't think you appreciate my problem. Two months ago, we all sat down to work out the lab schedule. Project X-13 had signed up to use the lab last week. Now, mind you, they had been scheduled for the past two months. But the Friday before they were to use it, your new priority list forced them to reschedule the lab at a later date, so that we could give the use of the lab to a higher priority project. We're paying an awful lot of money for idle time and the redoing of network schedules. Only the project managers on the top priority projects end up smiling after our Friday meetings.

Dr. Polly: As I see your problem, you can't match long-range planning with the current priority list. I agree that it does create conflicts for you. But you have to remember that we, upstairs, have many other conflicts to resolve. I want that one solved at your level, not mine.

Tom: Every project we have requires use of the Safety Lab. This is the basis for our problem. Would you consider letting us modify your priority list with regard to the Safety Lab?

Dr. Polly: Yes, but you had better have the agreement of all of the project managers. I don't want them coming to see me about your scheduling problems.

Tom: How about if I let people do long-range scheduling for the lab, say for three out of the four weeks each month? The fourth week will be for the priority projects.

Dr. Polly: That might work. You had better make sure that each project manager informs you immediately of any schedule slippages so that you can reschedule accordingly. From what I've heard, some of the project managers don't let you know until the last minute.

Tom: That has been part of the problem. Just to give you an example, Project VX-161 was a top priority effort and had the lab scheduled for the first week in March. I was never informed that they had accelerated their schedule by two weeks. They walked into my office and demanded use of the lab for the third week in February. Since they had the top priority, I had to grant them their request. However, Project BP-3 was planning on using the lab during that week and was bumped back three weeks. That cost them a pile of bucks in idle time pay and, of course, they're blaming me.

Dr. Polly: Well Tom, I'm sure you'll find a solution to your problem.

CASE STUDY: ROBERT L. FRANK & COMPANY*

It was Friday afternoon, a late November day in 1978, and Ron Katz, a project purchasing agent for Robert L. Frank, poured over the latest man-hour figures. The results kept pointing out the same fact — the Lewis Project was seriously over budget. Man-hours expended to date were running 30% over the projection and, despite this fact, the project was not progressing sufficiently to satisfy the customer. Material deliveries had experienced several slippages and the unofficial indication from the project scheduler was that, due to delivery delays on several of the project's key items, the completion date of the coal liquifaction pilot plant was no longer possible.

Katz was completely baffled. Each day for the past few months as he reviewed the daily printout of project time charges, he would note that almost the entire purchasing and expediting departments were working on the Lewis project, which was not an unusually large project, dollar-wise, for Frank. Two years before, Frank was working on a $300 million dollar contract, a $100 million dollar contract, and a $50 million dollar contract concurrently with the Frank Chicago Purchasing Department responsible for all the purchasing, inspection, and expediting on all three contracts. The Lewis project was the largest project in house and was only valued at $90 million. What made this project so different from previous contracts and cause such problems? There was little Katz could do to correct the situation. All that could be done was to understand what had occurred in an effort to prevent a reccurrence. He began to write his man-hour report for submission to the project manager the next day.

Company Background

Robert L. Frank and Company is an engineering and construction firm serving the petroleum, petrochemical, chemical, iron and steel, mining, pharmaceutical, and food processing industries from its corporate headquarters in Chicago, Illinois and its world-wide offices. Its services include engineering, purchasing, inspection, expediting, construction, and consultation.

Frank's history began in 1947 when Robert L. Frank opened his office. In 1955, a corporation was formed and by 1960 the company had completed contracts for the majority of the American producers of iron and steel. In 1962, an event which was to have a large impact on Frank's future occurred. This was the merger of Wilson Engineering Company, a successful refinery concern, with Robert L. Frank, now a highly successful iron and steel concern. This merger greatly expanded Frank's scope of operations and brought with it a strong period of growth. Several offices were opened in the United States in an effort to better handle the increase in business. Future expansions and mergers enlarged the Frank organization to the point where today it has fifteen offices or subsidiaries located in

---

*This case is partially fictitious and was prepared by Robert J. Hamill under the direction of the author as a basis for discussion rather than to illustrate either the effective or ineffective handling of an administrative situation.

the United States and twenty offices worldwide. Through its first twenty years of operations, Frank had over 2,500 contracts for projects having an erected value of over one billion dollars.

Frank's organizational structure has been well suited to the type of work undertaken. The projects Frank contracted for typically have a time constraint, a budget constraint, and a performance constraint. They all involved an outside customer such as a major petroleum company or a steel manufacturer. Upon acceptance of a project, a project manager is chosen (usually contained in the proposal). The project manager heads up the project office. Typically consisting of the project manager, one to three project engineers, project control manager, and the project secretaries. The project team then includes the necessary functional personnel from the engineering, purchasing, estimating, cost control, and scheduling areas. Exhibit 1 is a simplified graphical depiction. Of the functional areas, one is somewhat unique in its organization. The purchasing department is organized on a project management basis much as the project as a whole is organized. Within the purchasing department, each project has a project office which includes a project purchasing agent, one or more project expeditors and a project purchasing secretary. Within the purchasing department the project purchasing agent has line authority over only the project expeditor(s) and project secretary. However, for the project purchasing agent to accomplish his goals, the various functions within the purchasing department have to commit sufficient resources to that end. Exhibit 2 illustrates the organization within the purchasing department.

History of the Lewis Project

Since 1976, the work backlog at Frank has been steadily declining. The Rovery project, valued at $300 million, had increased company employment sharply since its inception in 1973. In fact, the engineering on the Rovery Project was such a large undertaking that in addition to the Chicago office's participation,

Exhibit 1. Frank Organization.

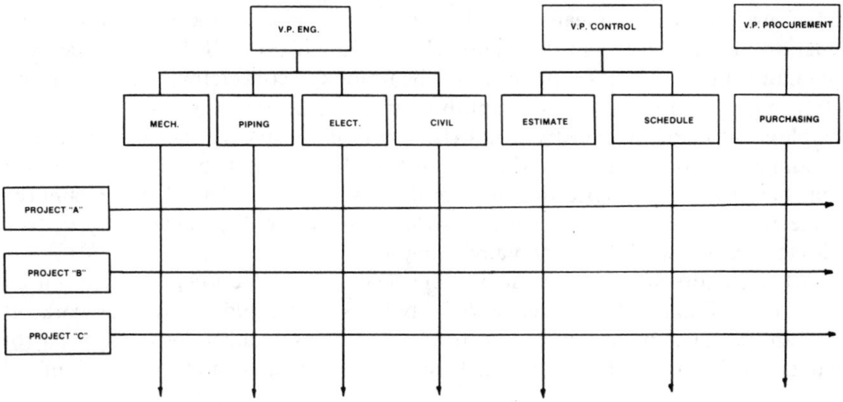

Exhibit 2. Frank Purchasing Organization.

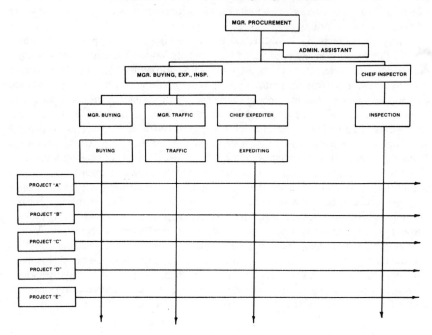

two other U.S. offices, the Canadian office and the Italian subsidiary were heavily involved. However, since the Rovery project completion in 1976, not enough new work was received to support the work force thus necessitating recent lay-offs of engineers and even a few project engineers.

Company officials were very disturbed with the situation. Point 1 of Frank's company policy was to "maintain an efficient organization of sufficient size and resources, and staffed by people with the necessary qualifications, to execute projects in any location for the industries served by Frank." However, the recent downturn in business meant that there was not enough work even with the re-duction in employees. Further cutbacks would jeopardize Frank's prospects of obtaining future projects as prospective clients look to contractors with a sufficient staff of qualified people to accomplish their work. On the other hand, supporting employees out of overhead was not the way to do business either. It became in-creasingly important to "cut the fat out" of the proposals being submitted for possible projects. Despite this, new projects were few and far between and the projects that were received were small in scope and dollar value and therefore did not provide work for very many employees.

When rumors of a possible facility for a new coal liquifaction pilot plant started circulating, Frank officials were extremely interested in bidding for the work. It was an excellent prospect for two reasons. Besides Frank's desperate need for work, the Lewis process being used for the pilot plant would benefit Frank in the long run. If the pilot plant project could be successfully executed, when it came time to construct the full-scale facility, Frank would have the inside track as they had already worked with the technology. The full-scale facility offered prospects exceeding the Rovery project, Frank's largest project to date. Top priority was therefore put on obtaining the Lewis project. It was felt that Frank had a slight edge due to successful completion of a Lewis project six years ago. The proposal submitted to Lewis contained estimates for material costs, man-hours, and the fee. Any changes in scope after contract award would be handled by change order to the contract. The functional department affected would submit an estimate of extra man-hours involved to the project manager who would review the request and submit it to the client for approval. Frank's preference is for cost plus fixed fee contracts.

One of the unique aspects about the Lewis proposal was the requirement for participation by both of Frank Chicago's operating divisions. Previous Frank contracts were well suited to either Frank's Petroleum and Chemical Division (P & C) or the Iron and Steel Division (I & S). However, due to the unusual process, one that starts with coal and ends up with a liquid energy form, one of the plant's three units was well suited to the P & C Division and one was well suited to the I & S Division. The third unit was an off-site unit and was not of particular engineering significance.

The acceptance of the proposal six weeks later led to expectations by most Frank personnel that the company's future was back on track again.

The Lewis Project

The project began inauspiciously. The project manager was a well liked, easy going sort who had been manager of several Frank projects. The project office included three of Frank's most qualified Project Engineers.

In the Purchasing Department, the project purchasing agent (PPA) assigned to the project was Frank's most experienced PPA. Bill Hall had just completed his assignment on the Rovery Project and had done well considering the magnitude of the job. The project had its problems but they were small in comparison to the achievements. He had alienated some of the departments slightly but that was to be expected. Purchasing upper management was somewhat dissatisfied with him in that, due to the size of the project, he didn't always use the normal Frank purchasing methods; rather, he used whatever method he felt was in the best interest of the project. Also, after the Rovery Project, a purchasing upper management reshuffling left him in the same position but with less power rather than receiving a promotion as he had felt he had earned. As a result, he began to subtly criticize the purchasing management. This action caused upper management to hold him in less than high regard but, at the time of the Lewis Project, Hall was the best man available.

Due to the lack of float in the schedule and the early field start date, it was necessary to "fast start" the Lewis Project. All major equipment was to be purchased within the first three months. This, except for a few exceptions, was accomplished. The usual problems occurred such as late receipt of requisition from Engineering and late receipt of bids.

One of the unique aspects of the Lewis project was the requirement for purchase order award meetings with vendors. Typically, Frank would hold award meetings with vendors of major equipment such as reactors, compressors, large process towers, or large pumps. However, almost each time Lewis approved purchase of a mechanical item or vessel they requested that the vendor come in for a meeting. Even if the order was for a fairly stock pump or small drum or tank, a meeting was held. Initially, the purchasing department attendees included the project purchasing agent, the buyer, the manager of the traffic department, the chief Expeditor, and the chief Inspector. Engineering representatives included the responsible engineer and one or two of the project engineers. Other Frank attendees were the project control manager and the scheduler. Quite often these meetings would accomplish nothing except the reiteration of what had been included in the proposal or what could have been resolved with a phone call. The project purchasing agent was responsible for issuing meeting notes after each meeting.

One day at the end of the first three month period the top ranking Lewis representative met with Larry Broyles, the Frank project manager.

Lewis Rep: Larry, the project is progressing but I'm a little concerned. We don't feel like we have our finger on the pulse of the project. The information we are getting is sketchy and untimely. What we would like to do is meet with Frank every Wednesday to review progress and resolve problems.

Larry: I'd be more than happy to meet with any of the Lewis people because I think your request has a lot of merit.

Lewis Rep: Well, Larry, what I had in mind was a meeting between all the Lewis people, yourself, your project office, the project purchasing agent, his assistant, and your scheduling and cost control people.

Larry: This sounds like a pretty involved meeting. We're going to tie up a lot of our people for one full day a week. I'd like to scale this thing down. Our proposal took into consideration meetings, but not to the magnitude we're talking about.

Lewis Rep: Larry, I'm sorry but we're footing the bill on this project and we've got to know what's going on.

Larry: I'll set it up for this coming Wednesday.

Lewis Rep: Good.

The required personnel were informed by the project manager that effective immediately, meetings with the client would be held weekly. The meetings were held and due to Lewis's dissatisfaction with the results of the meetings, the Frank project manager informed his people that a pre-meeting would be held each Tuesday to prepare the Frank portion of the Wednesday meeting. All of the Wednesday participants attended the Tuesday pre-meetings.

Lewis requests for additional special reports from the Purchasing Department were given into without comment. The Project Purchasing Agent and his assistants (project started with one and expanded to four) were devoting the great majority of their time to special reports and "putting out fires" instead of being able to track progress and prevent problems.

For example, recommended spare parts lists are normally required from vendors on all Frank projects. Lewis was no exception. However, after the project began, Lewis decided they wanted the spare parts recommendations early in the job. Usually spare parts lists are left for the end of an order. For example, on a pump with 15 week delivery, normally Frank would pursue the recommended spare parts list three to four weeks prior to shipment as it will tend to be more accurate. This improved accuracy is due to the fact that at this point in the order all changes probably have been made. In the case of the Lewis project, spare parts recommendations had to be expedited from the day the material was released for fabrication. Changes could still be made which could dramatically affect the design of the pump. Thus, a change in the pump after receipt of the spare parts list would necessitate a new spare parts list. The time involved in this method of expediting the spare parts list was much greater than the time involved in the normal Frank method. Added to this situation was Lewis's request for a fairly involved bi-weekly report on the status of spare parts lists on all the orders. In addition, a full-time spare parts coordinator was assigned to the project.

The initial lines of communication between Frank and Lewis were initially well defined. The seven in-house Lewis representatives occupied the area adjacent to the Frank project office (see Exhibit 3). Initially all communications from

Exhibit 3. Floor Plan — Lewis Project Teams.

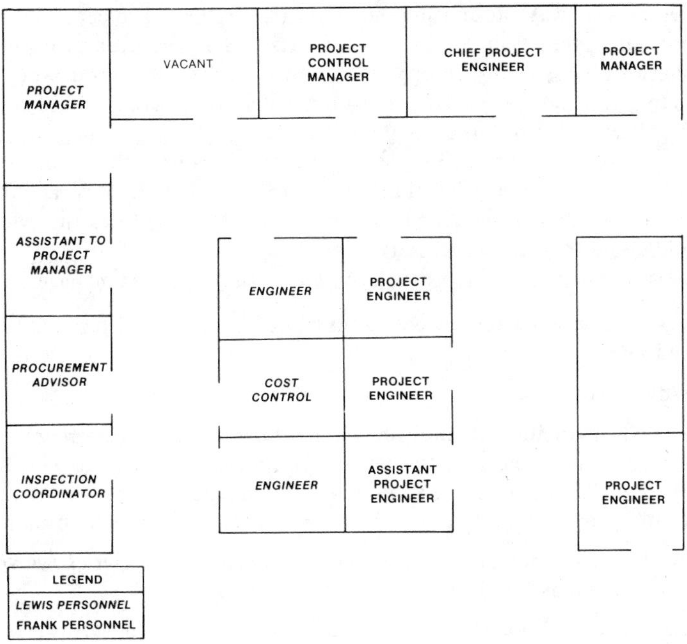

Lewis were channeled through the Frank project office to the applicable functional employee. In the case of the purchasing department, the Frank project office would channel Lewis requests through the Purchasing project office. Responses or return communications followed the reverse route. Soon the volume of communications increased to the point where response time was becoming unacceptable. In several special cases, in an effort to cut this response time. Larry Broyles told the Lewis people to call or go see the functional person (i.e., buyer or engineer) for the answer. However, this practice soon became the rule rather than the exception. Initially, the project office was kept informed of these conversations but this soon stopped. The Lewis personnel had integrated themselves into the Frank organization to the point where they became part of the organization.

The project went on and numerous problems cropped up. Vendor's material delays occurred, companies with Frank purchase orders went bankrupt, and progress was not to Lewis's satisfaction. Upper management became aware of the problems on this project due to its sensitive nature and soon the Lewis project was receiving much more intense an effort than it had been previously. Upper management sat in on the weekly meetings in an attempt to pacify Lewis. Further problems plagued the project. Purchasing management, in an attempt to placate Lewis, replaced the project purchasing agent. Ron Katz, a promising young MBA graduate, had five years experience as an assistant to several of the project purchasing agents. He was most recently a project purchasing agent on a fairly small project which had been very successful. It was thought by purchasing upper management that this move was a good one for two reasons. First, it would remove Bill Hall from the project as PPA. Second, by appointing Ron Katz, Lewis would be pacified as Katz was a promising talent with a successful project under his belt.

However, the project under direction of Katz still experienced problems in the purchasing area. Revisions by engineering to material already on order caused serious delivery delays. Recently requisitioned material could not be located with an acceptable delivery promise. Katz and Purchasing upper management, in an attempt to improve the situation, assigned more personnel to the project, personnel that were more qualified than the positions dictated. Buyers and upper level purchasing officials were sent on trips to vendors' facilities that were normally handled by traveling expediters.

In the last week the Lewis representative met with the project manager, Broyles:

Lewis Rep: Larry, I've been reviewing these man-hour expenditures and I'm disturbed by them.

Larry: Why's that?

Lewis Rep: The man-hour expenditures are far outrunning project progress. Three months ago, you reported that the project completion percentage was 30% but according to my calculations, we've used 47% of the man-hours. Last month you reported 40% project completion and I show a 60% expenditure of man-hours.

Larry: Well, as you know, due to problems with vendors' deliveries, we've really had to expedite intensively to try to bring them back in line.

Lewis Rep: Larry, I'm being closely watched by my people on this project and a cost or schedule overrun not only makes Frank look bad, it makes me look bad.

Larry: Where do we go from here?

Lewis Rep: What I want is an estimate from your people on what is left, man-hour wise. Then I can sit down with my people and see where we are.

Larry: I'll have something for you the day after tomorrow.

Lewis Rep: Good.

The functional areas were requested to provide this information which was reviewed and combined by the project manager and submitted to Lewis for approval. Lewis's reaction was unpleasant to say the least. The estimated man-hours in the proposal were now insufficient. The revised estimate was for almost 40% over the proposal. The Lewis representative immediately demanded an extensive report on the requested increase. In response to this the project manager requested man-hour breakdowns from the functional areas. Purchasing was told to do a Purchase Order by Purchase Order breakdown of expediting and inspection man-hours. The buying section had to breakdown the estimate of the man-hours needed to purchase each requisition, many of which were not even issued.

CASE STUDY: THE LYLE PROJECT*

At 6:00 P.M. on Thursday in late November of 1978, Don Jung, an Atlay company Project Manager (assigned to the Lyle contract) sat in his office thinking about the comments brought up during a meeting with his immediate superior earlier that afternoon. During that meeting Fred Franks, the Supervisor of Project Managers, criticized Don for not promoting a cooperative attitude between himself and the functional managers. It seems that Fred Franks had a high level meeting with the vice-presidents in charge of the various functional departments (i.e., engineering, construction, cost control, scheduling, and purchasing) earlier that day. One of these vice-presidents, John Mabby (head of the purchasing department) had indicated that his department, according to his latest projections, would overrun their man-hour allocation by 6000 hours. This fact had been relayed to Don by Bob Stewart (the project purchasing agent assigned to the Lyle project) twice in the past, but Don had not seriously considered the request since some of the purchasing was now going to be done by the subcontractor at the job site (who had enough man-hours to cover this additional work.) John Mabby, during this meeting, complained that even though the subcontractor was doing some of the purchasing in the field his department still will overrun their man-hour allocation. He also indicated to Fred Franks that Don Jung had better do something about this man-hour problem now. At this point in the meeting, the vice-president of Engineering, Harold Mont, stated that he was experiencing the same problem in that Don Jung seemed to ignore their requests for additional man-hours.

Also at this meeting the various vice-presidents indicated that Don Jung had not been operating within the established standard company procedures. In an

---

*This case is partially fictitious and was prepared by R.A. Popelmayer under the direction of the author as a basis for discussion rather than to illustrate either the effective or ineffective handling of an administrative situation.

effort to make up for time lost due to initial delays that occurred in the process development stage of this project, Don and his project team had been getting the various functional people working on the contract to "cut corners" and in many cases to "buck" the standard operating procedures of their respective functional departments in an effort to save time. His actions and the actions of his project team were alienating the vice-presidents in charge of the functional departments. During this meeting, Fred Franks received a good deal of criticism due to this fact. He was also told that Don Jung had better shape up because it was the joint opinion of these vice-presidents that his method of operating might seriously hamper the project's ability to finish on time and within budget. It was very important that this job be completed in accordance with the Lyle requirements since they will be building two more similar plants within the next ten years. A good effort on this job could further enhance Atlay's chances for being awarded the next two jobs as well.

Fred Franks related these comments and a few of his own to Don Jung. Fred seriously questioned Don's ability to manage the project effectively and told him. However, Fred was willing to allow Don to remain on the job if he would begin to operate in accordance with the various functional departments' standard operating procedures and if he would "listen" and be more attentive to the comments from the various functional departments and do his best to cooperate with them in the best interests of the company and the project itself.

Inception of the Lyle Project

In April of 1978, Bob Briggs, Atlay's vice-president of Sales was notified by Lyle's vice-president of operations (Fred Wilson) that Atlay had been awarded the 60 million dollar contract to design, engineer, and construct a polypropylene plant in Louisiana. Bob Briggs immediately notified Atlay's president and other high level officials in the organization (see Exhibit 1). He then contacted Fred Franks in order to finalize the members of the project team. Briggs wanted George Fitz who was involved in developing the initial proposal to be the project manager. However, Fitz was in the hospital and would be essentially "out of action" for another three months. Atlay then had to scramble to choose a project manager since Lyle wanted to conduct a "kickoff meeting" with all the principals present in a week. One of the persons most available for the position of project manager was Don Jung. Don had been with the company for about 15 years. He had started with the company as a project engineer, and then was promoted to the position of manager of computer services. He was in charge of computer services for six months until he had a confrontation with Atlay's upper management regarding the policies under which the computer department was operating. He had served the company in two other functions since — the most recent position, that of being a senior project engineer on a small project that was handled out of the Chicago office. One big plus was the fact that Don knew Lyle's Fred Wilson personally since they belonged to the same community organization. It was decided that Don Jung would be the project manager and John Neber (an experienced project engineer) would be assigned as the senior project engineer. The next week was

Exhibit 1. Atlay And Company Organizational Chart.

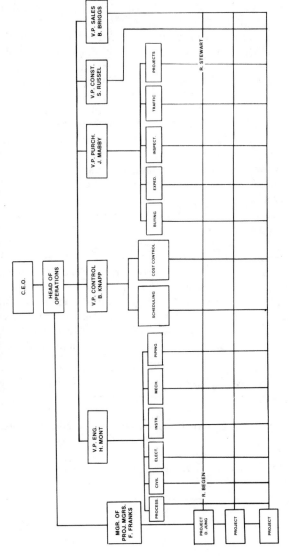

spent advising Don Jung regarding the contents of the proposal and determining the rest of the members of the project team.

A week later Lyle's contingent arrived at Atlay's headquarters (see Exhibit 2). Atlay was informed that Steve Zorn would be the assistant project manager on this job for Lyle. The position of project manager would be left vacant for the time being. They then introduced the rest of Lyle's project team. Lyle's project team consisted of individuals from various Lyle sections around the country — Texas, West Virginia, and Philadelphia. Many of the Lyle project team members had only met each other for the first time two weeks ago.

During this initial meeting, Fred Wilson emphasized the point that it was essential that this plant be completed on time since their competitor was also in the process of preparing to build a similar facility in the same general location. The first plant finished would most likely be the one that would establish control over the southwestern United States market for polypropylene material. Mr. Wilson felt that Lyle had a six week head start over their competitor at the moment and would like to increase that difference if at all possible. He then introduced Lyle's assistant project manager who completed the rest of the presentation.

At this initial meeting the design package was handed over to Atlay's Don Jung so that the process engineering stage of this project could begin. This package was, according to their inquiry letter, so complete that all material requirements for this job could be placed within three months after project award (since very little additional design work was required by Atlay on this project). Two weeks later, Don contacted the lead process engineer on the project — Raphael Begen. He wanted to get Raphael's opinion regarding the condition of the design package.

Begen: Don, I think you have been sold a bill of goods. This package is in bad shape.

Exhibit 2. Lyle Project Team Organizational Chart.

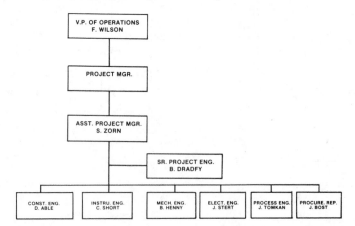

Jung: What do you mean this package is in bad shape? We were told by Lyle that we would be able to have all the material on order within three months since this package was in such good shape.

Begen: Well in my opinion, it will take at least six weeks to straighten out the design package. Then within three months from that point you will be able to have all the material on order.

Jung: What you are telling me then is that I am faced with a six week schedule delay right off the bat due to the condition of the package.

Begen: Exactly.

Don Jung went back to his office after his conversation with the lead process engineer. He thought about the status of his project. He felt that Begen was being overly pessimistic and that the package wasn't really all that bad. Besides, a month shouldn't be too hard to make up if the engineering section would do its work quicker than normal and if purchasing would cut down on the amount of time it takes to purchase materials and equipment needed for this plant.

Conduct of the Project

Thus, the project began. Two months after contract award, Lyle sent in a contingent of their representatives. These representatives would be located at Atlay's headquarters for the next eight to ten months. Don Jung had arranged to have the Lyle offices set up on the other side of the building from his project team. At first there were complaints from Lyle's assistant project manager regarding the physical distance that separated Lyle's project team and Atlay's project team. However, Don Jung assured him that there just wasn't any available space that was closer to the Atlay project team than the one they were now occupying.

The Atlay project team operating within a matrix organizational structure plunged right into the project (see Exhibit 3). They were made aware of the delay that was incurred at the onset of the job (due to the poor design package) by Don Jung. His instructions to them were to cut corners whenever doing so might result in a time savings. They were also to suggest to members of the functional departments that were working on this project methods that could possibly result in quicker turnaround of the work required of them. The project team coerced the various engineering departments into operating outside of their normal procedures due to the special circumstances surrounding this job. For example, the civil engineering section prepared a special preliminary structural steel package and the piping engineering section prepared preliminary piping packages so that the purchasing department could go out on inquiry immediately. Normally, the purchasing department would have to wait for formal take-offs from both of these departments before they could send out inquiries to potential vendors. Operating in this manner could result in some problems, however. For example, the purchasing department might arrange for discounts from the vendors based on the quantity of structural steel estimated during the preliminary take-off.

Exhibit 3. Atlay Company
Procurement Department Organizational Chart.

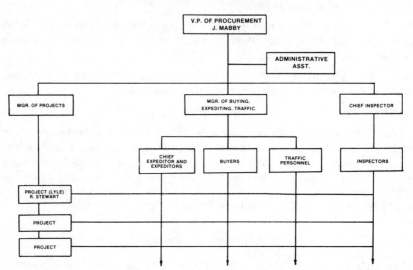

However, after the formal take-off has been done by the civil engineering section (which would take about a month) they might find out that they underestimated the quantity of structural steel required on the project by 50 tons. Knowing that there was an additional 50 tons of structural steel might have aided the purchasing department in securing an additional discount of $.20 per pound (or $160,000 discount for 400 tons of steel).

Also, in an effort to make up for lost time the project team convinced the functional engineering departments to use catalogue drawings or quotation information whenever they lacked engineering data on a particular piece of equipment. The engineering section leaders pointed out that this procedure could be very dangerous and could result in additional work and further delays to the project. If, for example, you base the dimensions for the scale model being built on this project on preliminary information without the benefit of having certified vendor drawings in house you run the risk of building an inaccurate scale for that section of the model. When the certified data prints are later received and it is apparent that the dimensions are incorrect you may have to disassemble that portion of the model and rebuild it correctly. This would further delay the project. However, if the information does not change substantially, you could save approximately a month in engineering time. Lyle was advised in regards to the risks and potential benefits involved when Atlay operates outside of their normal operating procedure. Steve Zorn informed Don Jung that Lyle was willing to take these risks in an effort to make up for lost time. The Atlay project team then proceeded accordingly.

The method that the project team was utilizing appeared to be working. It seemed as if the work was being accomplished at a much quicker rate than what was initially anticipated. The only snag in this operation occurred when Lyle had to review/approve something. Drawings, engineering requisitions, and purchase orders would sit in the Lyle area for about two weeks before they would be reviewed by Lyle personnel. Half of the time these documents were returned two weeks later with a request for additional information or with changes noted by some of Lyle's engineers. Then the Atlay project team would have to review the comments/changes, incorporate them into the documents and resubmit them to Lyle for review/approval. They would then sit for another week in that area before finally being reviewed and eventually returned to Atlay with their final approval. It should be pointed out that the contract procedures stated that Lyle would have only five days to review/approve the various documents being submitted to them. Don Jung felt that part of the reason for this delay had to do with the fact that all the Lyle team members went back to their homes for the weekends. Their routine was to leave around 10:00 a.m. on Friday and return around 3:00 p.m. on the following Monday. Therefore, essentially two days of work by the Lyle project team out of the week were lost. Don reminded Steve Zorn that according to the contract, Lyle was to return documents that needed approval within five days after receiving them. He also suggested that if the Lyle project team would work a full day on Monday and Friday it would probably increase the speed at which documents were being returned. However, neither corrective action was undertaken by Lyle's assistant project manager and the situation failed to improve. All the time the project team had saved by cutting corners was now being wasted and further project delays seemed inevitable.

In addition to the above, there were other problems that were being encountered during the interface process between the Lyle and Atlay project team members. It seems that the Lyle project team members (who were on temporary loan to Steve Zorn from various functional departments within the Lyle organization) were more concerned with producing a perfect end product. They did not seem to realize that their actions as well as the actions of the Atlay project team had a significant impact on this particular project. They did not seem to be aware of the fact that they were also constrained by time and cost as well as performance. Instead, they had a very relaxed and informal operating procedure. Many of the changes made by Lyle were given to Atlay verbally. They explained to the Atlay project team members that written confirmation of the changes were unnecessary since we are all working "on the same team." Many significant changes in the project were made when a Lyle engineer was talking directly to an Atlay engineer. The Atlay engineer would then incorporate the changes into the drawings he was working on and sometimes failed to advise his project engineer about the changes. Because of this informal way of operating, there were instances in which Lyle was dissatisfied with Atlay because changes were not being incorporated or were not made in strict accordance with their requests. Steve Zorn called Don Jung into his office to discuss this problem:

Steve: Don, I've received complaints from my personnel regarding your teams inability to follow through and incorporate Lyle's comments/changes accurately into the P & ID drawings.

Don: Steve, I think my staff has been doing a fairly good job of incorporating your team's comments/changes. You know the whole process would work a lot better, however, if you would send us a letter detailing each change. Sometimes my engineers are given two different instructions regarding the scope of the change by your people. For example, one of your people will tell our process engineer to add a check valve to a specific process line and another would tell him that check valves are not required in that service.

Steve: Don, you know that if we documented everything that was discussed between our two project teams we would be buried in paperwork. Nothing would ever get accomplished. Now, if you get two different instructions from my project team you should advise me accordingly so that I can resolve the discrepancy. I've decided that since we seem to have a communication problem regarding engineering changes, I want to set up a weekly engineering meeting for every Thursday. These meetings should help to cut down on the misunderstandings as well as keeping us advised of your progress in the engineering area of this contract without the need of a formal status report. I would like all members of your project staff present at these meetings.

Don: Will this meeting be in addition to our overall progress meetings that are held on Wednesdays?

Steve: Yes. We will now have two joint Atlay/Lyle meetings a week — one discussing overall progress on the job and one specifically aimed at engineering.

On the way back to his office Don thought about the request for an additional meeting. That meeting will be a waste of time, he thought, just as the Wednesday meeting presently is. It will just take away another day from the Lyle project team's available time for approving drawings, engineering, requisitions and purchase orders. Now there are three days during the week where at least a good part of the day is taken up by meetings. In addition to a meeting with his own project team on Mondays in order to freely discuss the progress and problems of the job without intervention by Lyle personnel. A good part of his project team's time therefore, was now being spent preparing for and attending meetings during the course of the week. Well, Don rationalized, they are the client and if they desire a meeting then I have no alternative but to accommodate them.

Jung's Confrontation

When Don returned to his desk he saw a message stating that John Mabby (vice-president of procurement) had called. Don returned his call and found out that John requested a meeting. A meeting was set up for the following day. At 9:00 a.m. the next day Don was in Mabby's office. Mabby was concerned about the unusual procedures that were being utilized on this project. It seems as though he had a rather lengthy discussion with Bob Stewart the project purchasing agent assigned to the Lyle project. During the course of that conversation it became very apparent that this particular project was not operating within the normal procedures established for the purchasing department. This deviation from normal procedures was the result of instructions given by Don Jung to Bob Stewart. This upset John Mabby since he felt that Don Jung should have discussed these deviations with him prior to his instructing Bob Stewart to proceed in this manner:

Mabby: Don, I understand that you advised my Project Purchasing Agent to work around the procedures that I established for this department so that you could possibly save time on your project.

Jung: That's right John. We ran into a little trouble early in the project and started running behind schedule, but by cutting corners here and there we've been able to make up some of the time.

Mabby: Well I wish you would have contacted me first regarding this situation. I have to tell you, however, that if I had known about some of these actions I would never have allowed Bob Stewart to proceed. I've instructed Stewart that from now on he is to check with me prior to going against our standard operating procedure.

Jung: But John, Stewart has been assigned to me for this project. Therefore, I feel that he should operate in accordance with my requests, whether they are within your procedures or not.

Mabby: That's not true. Stewart is in my department and works for *me*. I am the one who reviews him, approves the size of his raise and decides if and when he gets a promotion. I have made that fact very clear to Stewart and I hope I've made it very clear to you also. In addition, I hear that Stewart has been predicting a 6,000 man-hour overrun for the purchasing department on your project. Why haven't you submitted an extra to the client?

Jung: Well, if what Stewart tells me is true the main reason that your department is short man-hours is because the project manager who was handling the initial proposal (George Fitz) underestimated your requirements by 7,000 man-hours. Therefore, from the very beginning you were short man-hours. Why should I be the one that goes to the client and tell him that we blew our estimate when I wasn't even involved in the proposal stage of this contract? Besides we are taking away some of your duties on this job and I personally feel that you won't even need those additional 6,000 man-hours.

Mabby: Well, I have to attend a meeting with your boss Fred Franks tomorrow and I think I'll talk to him about these matters.

Jung: Go right ahead. I'm sure you'll find out that Fred stands behind me 100 percent.

CASE STUDY: THE JUSTICE CENTER

Eliot Lee had just completed the Justice Center Construction Project at a mere 24% cost overrun. Eliot now had the unfortunate assignment of having to document the reasons for the cost overrun.

The Justice Center was a 23-story building housing the police department and the county jail. Special design features included an elaborate computerized security alarm system that traces the movement of inmates throughout the complex, 16 elevators, and a sophisticated medical unit that includes dental, detoxification, psychiatric, examination, and treatment offices all grouped on one floor.

In 1972, Carter Construction had submitted a bid for construction of the Justic Center. The effort was to be thirty months, beginning in 1972. The cost estimates in the proposal were rather crude, and no attempt was made to determine what could go wrong. Management's philosophy was to develop a base case and add on 10 percent for contingencies. Carter Construction won the contract and Eliot Lee was appointed project manager.

Eliot began his report by outlining the items that were available for control:

The major achievement of objectives lies in program control. The standard controls for the program were integrated PERT/CPM charts, financial schedules and variance reports, time-scheduled network plans, problem analysis and trend charts, progress reports, and design review meetings. Additional program control analysis should have been made in order to anticipate the unexpected. This includes the risks of man-hour reductions (possibly due to a strike), analysis of competitive bidding, the role of political influence and cost overrun possibilities.

Many things went wrong on the day-to-day management of the project.

Four common occurrences are included below:

1. Insensitive owners were very slow in decision making. Since the project manager did not have the latitude to make the decisions himself, he had to obtain decisions from the owners on a timely basis.
2. Architects need to be available in order to interpret the drawings, since it was quite common for various measurements to be omitted.
3. Design itself becomes a problem when certain aspects of the structure appear to be weak or in some other way deficient.
4. Materials became a problem, not simply through inflation, but because the supplier was on strike and source materials were simply not available. In the management of the Justice Center project, two areas appeared to be nuisances. First, the administrative procedures involving work with city government carried with it an unusual amount of red tape. Second, public funds needed to be raised when community action groups wanted to change the appearance of the building. The thought process involved compelled the project manager to first build the new structure mentally. This involved talking with other people and experts and getting opinions. It has been said in project management that you can have quality, timeliness, or economy, but you cannot have all three.

Eliot Lee then went on to describe his operational tools and objectives:

In order to reduce costs, we selected a four-project Work Breakdown Structure as shown in Exhibit 1. The work was not structured adequately enough such that an itemized definition of the budget could be broken down to lower levels. How-

Exhibit 1. Justice Center Work Breakdown Structure Program — Justice Center.

Project No. 1 — Support and Raw Materials
   Task 1 — Testing and Inspection
   Task 2 — Construction Company A
   Task 3 — Raw Material

Project No. 2 — Exterior Work
   Task 1 — Excavation, caissons, sheeting, shoring
   Task 2 — Concrete: foundation; superstructure; precast
   Task 3 — Metals: structural steel, decks, ornamental, roof, wall
   Task 4 — Miscellaneous exterior: fireproof, paving, doors and hardware

Project No. 3 — Interior
   Task 1 — Masonry, plaster, tile
   Task 2 — Carpentry, floors, paint, siding, architectural
   Task 3 — Miscellaneous service equipment, laundry, detection

Project No. 4 — Electrical, Plumbing, Mechanical
   Task 1 — Electrical: Substructure, electrical, dev., site
   Task 2 — Mechanical: Housing units, elevators, substructure
   Task 3 — Plumbing: HVAC, plumbing, automation, vibration

ever, there were charts and schedules which showed the proper sequence of events and which were used to monitor work-in-place and total cost.

Operational objectives must be the first concern of the project manager during construction. Therefore, he must have an adequate staff which can assist him in carrying out contract negotiations and disputes, minimizing program disruption and slack time, and especially in expediting material handling.

It is impossible for a project manager to accurately project the salary structure of the labor unions throughout the duration of the project. The cost data presented in Exhibit 2 was found to be insufficient for analyzing budgets and performing variance analysis. Statistical analysis and forecasting is needed, together with a survey of possible union contract negotiation activities during the period of performance.

Lee then described the major problems that impacted his project:

The energy crisis of 1974 resulted in temporary shortages of gas and diesel fuel. Prices of these fuels increased significantly in a few short months. Shortages produce hardships for contractors and workers alike. The various contractors were faced with the problem of obtaining sufficient fuel supplies necessary to operate the numerous pieces of equipment on the job. The additional cost of those fuels resulted in the cost of the project being higher than anticipated.

A fuel shortage has an effect on the worker in that it increases his cost of working and may make it difficult to get to the job site. Large projects draw labor

Exhibit 2. Justice Center Project Salary Structure.

	Rate*	OH(%)**
Engineering		169%
Project Engineering	$12.07	
Drafting	10.64	
Program Management	11.17	139%
Finance		109%
Contracts	11.56	
Cost Accounting	8.50	
Operations		239%
Labor	8.41	
Carpenter	7.89	
Ironworker	7.89	
On-site Engineering	11.99	

*Initial department average salaries at program go-ahead.
**Constant for case (i.e., not time dependent).

from many miles in all directions. It's not unusual for workers to drive two and three hours to and from work.

The major cost with projects of this type is labor. People problems are difficult to predict and plan for. A strategic planning model can estimate the cost of a strike, a wage increase, plus many other areas that will increase or decrease costs. Unfortunately, however, some labor problems and their effects are almost impossible to quantify in advance.

The carpenters, laborers, iron workers, and masons are all represented by different unions. These unions have different goals and objectives than the management of a project. Project management is interested in completing the task as efficiently as possible by consuming the least amount of the resources of land, labor, capital, and entrepreneurship. The union's goal is to keep its membership employed. Union workers are normally hired by contractors and subcontractors through the various union halls representing them. Members who are not presently employed are assigned by the hall to the various contractors seeking manpower. The assumption is that if the worker belongs to the union, he is qualified for the job. A contractor may hire some workers who are unqualified. Contractors who fire these individuals will normally find that all the members will walk off the job in protest. If you lay those individuals off, you cannot hire someone to take their places unless you give them first chance. The result is a task you expected to take 400 man-hours to complete may take 450 due to featherbedding or unrest among the union members.

The PERT Chart was found to be an excellent method of determining the probability of meeting specific deadlines. The work schedule may call for 25 iron workers and 25 bricklayers to complete a task in the project. Upon nearing completion, the contractor may lay off 5 bricklayers and 10 iron workers. In all probability, the remaining iron workers will walk off the job claiming discrimination because more iron workers were laid off than bricklayers. Two days may be spent solving the problem. The result is the project is off schedule.

Personal interviews were conducted with union men who worked on similar projects. They described it as being a bad job; too many changes, layoffs, scheduling problems, the basic unrest. One worker said he walked off the job 13 times in one month. He said, the major problems with the job were the subcontractors. They were having problems meeting deadlines and were taking it out on the workers.

What effects can weather have on a project? Iron workers will not hang iron when it rains or snows because the iron becomes slippery. Brick cannot be laid when the temperature goes far below freezing. High winds make it impossible to work the upper floors of unfinished buildings. Extreme heat quickly tires those who are physically exerting themselves. The human factors of production are greatly influenced by the conditions under which the worker must endure.

Another problem area is theft and vandalism. Every project is faced with this. The cost in dollars and time lost is hard to estimate and very costly to reduce.

The following cost data information was obtained at project termination:

1. The proposal price was $96.7 million.
2. Inflationary forces and new labor contract negotiations resulted in a 12 percent yearly salary increase. The proposal estimate was 6 percent. This resulted in a net increase of $2.7 million.
3. The overhead rate for engineering, which was estimated at a constant 170 percent over the duration of the project, was found to be 187 percent. This 10 percent increase resulted in a $1 million cost. This increase was attributed to a change in the original building plan and advancements in technology over the course of the project, which called for internal and external structural changes to conform to new specifications and standards.
4. Additional manpower was needed for the project office in order to deal with material acquisition problems. The cost incurred was $395,000.
5. Cost accounting also increased in manpower, at a cost of $488,000.
6. The operations division was forced to hire additional people in order to keep on schedule. According to union contracts, Carter Construction was forced to pay for idle time because of lack of availability of certain raw materials. The resulting cost was $2.5 million. This included the additional manpower to make up for the one-month strike. Since only one trade was involved in the strike, the costs of the strike were insignificant compared to other costs.
7. The release of funds for the start of the Justice Center was eighteen months late. This pushed all man-hours and materials into higher cost periods. The result was a $30 million increase in final costs. The overall effect was a 24 percent increase in costs.

In conclusion, the final cost overrun can be attributed to two factors. First, the building delay was a combination of project problems and inherent conflicts between the principals. Second, no provisions were made in the original proposal for investigation of the cost impact as a result of those variables which could change during the project.

CASE STUDY: PROJECT MANAGEMENT AT FORD MOTOR COMPANY*

Ken Crandall, the plant manager of Ford Motor Company's Cleveland Casting Plant, was distrubed as he returned from the meeting he had attended with casting division staff. As he sat in his office, he knew that the discussion at this meeting would have a very big effect on the future of the plant. He also wondered about his own future and that of his fellow managers. The reason for his concern was the new plan that Division Staff was proposing: the inclusion of aluminum casting facilities at the Cleveland Casting Plant. Crandall thought that it would fail. Gray iron and aluminum had never been cast in the same plant at the same time fefore. Not only was different equipment needed, but aluminum was considered a contaminant in gray iron. The casting of both metals in the same building did not seem feasible. However, Division Staff had assured him that it could be done.

Background of the Plant

The Cleveland Casting Plant, built in 1952, was, at that time, one of the largest foundries in the world. It still was the biggest foundry in the Ford Motor Company, producing about 55 percent of the gray iron castings required by Ford Engine and Parts Divisions. Between the seven cupolas and ten mold lines, the plant had the capacity to produce 3,700 tons of castings in a day. Several metal holding furnaces helped increase efficiency by "holding" molten metal at a constant temperature until a mold line was ready to accept it. A total of 150 core machines produced all the required cores to be used in the molding area. Several of these core machines utilized the isocure process, which did not require heat. The natural gas savings were important, since most of the core machines used natural gas for curing the cores. Ten cleaning lines finish the castings by getting rid of the excess sand and metal that are on the castings when they come from the molding area. Inspection takes place at a variety of places during the production of a casting, from the checking of sand quality and moisture content in the core area to the final inspection of a casting before it is shipped to an Engine Plant. The Cleveland Casting Plant also helped keep the environment as free from pollutants as possible. The use of 89 various dust collectors and scrubbers helped accomplish this goal.

---

*This case is entirely fictitious. It reflects the writer's perceptions of how personnel at Ford Motor Company may have reacted if such a situation presented itself. This case was prepared by Jeffrey Lonjak under the supervision of the author, as the basis for discussion rather than to illustrate either effective or ineffective handling of an administrative situation.

Background of the Project

In 1974, the world was going through many changes. One of these changes was the rising price of petroleum products due to the Arab oil embargo. For the first time the words "energy crisis" or "energy shortage" were heard and energy, especially that derived from petroleum, became a prime topic of conversation. The crisis was especially felt in the United States, which depended heavily on foreign oil for its energy needs. For years, the American public had been used to driving big, luxurious cars, which comsumed gasoline at an alarming rate. But, prior to 1974, there had been little concern. The price of gasoline hovered around thirty cents a gallon and fluctuations of a penny or two went almost unnoticed. The situation changed drastically, however, and American automobile companies knew that their glory years of high style and horsepower were at an end. Overall, a search began on two fronts: to find alternate sources of energy and to produce vehicles that would use less of the gasoline than was available.

Smaller cars and smaller engines seemed to be the answer, but the problem of public acceptance created a situation of uncertainty. Would the American public accept this new breed of automobile after so many years of luxury? The problem was an immense one and an acceptable solution to the problem could mean survival for the automotive industry in America.

Planning of the Project

It became apparent to the Ford Motor Company that they would have to radically change some aspects of their production philosophies. Lighter cars would have to be made and sold to the public. Many ideas were discussed. Plastic, thinner steel, fiberglass, aluminum and even graphite were considered as substitute materials which would help reduce the weight of the vehicle. Plastic was an excellent substitute for interior parts, but for engine parts, aluminum seemed to be the answer. It was relatively cheap and rather plentiful in its raw form, bauxite, and from recycled material.

Ford had been using aluminum parts on their vehicles for many years, but only for certain parts. Certain intake manifolds, cylinder heads, transmission cases and extensions, pistons and other miscellaneous parts were the ones produced. The main production plant for aluminum parts was located in Gordon, Alabama. It had been in operation since 1957.

In early 1975, a plan was being formulated at the casting division offices in Dearborn, Michigan. The objective was to make aluminum castings much more accessible. It was felt that the Gordon plant, although one of the largest aluminum foundries in the country, could not supply the expected increase in demand for the aluminum products. The decision was made to incorporate aluminum facilities at the Cleveland Casting Plant and to change the smaller Windsor Casting Plant completely to aluminum. The other two foundries, the Michigan Casting Center and Dearborn Specialty Foundry, would remain as full time iron foundries, because several parts had to be iron castings. Exhaust manifolds, crankshafts, camshafts and engine blocks were a few of these parts.

The idea had been discussed for many months. Many meetings between engineers, technicians, research scientists, financial experts and management had produced many alternative plans to implement this project at the two casting plants. Technical specifications, cost analyses and scheduling were examined. The idea itself had the approval of the vice president of North American Automotive Operations, the president and even Henry Ford II. It was a matter of determining the optimal method.

During these many discussions, several younger members of the Casting Division Management team suggested an alternative method of handling the situation: project management. These managers presented their views to John Trenton, the casting division general manager. David Bonds, division engineering manager, acted as spokesman for the group.

Bonds: Mr. Trenton, we believe we have the solution for handling the situations at the Cleveland and Windsor Plants. We feel that these two situations are ideal for using project management. The timing and budget constraints that are required as part of this plan would probably be best handled with this type of management.

Trenton: I've read about project management, but I don't know if it is really necessary in this case. We have never had problems in allocating the funds to a particular plant and allowing them to implement the project as they see fit. We do have capable people in Cleveland and Windsor that have always come through for us. What makes this situation so special, Dave?

Bonds: Well, Mr. Trenton, Windsor may not require it since it involves a complete shutdown of the facility, but Cleveland is another story. We are going to be attempting to add aluminum handling facilities while regular production of iron is in process. I don't think we should bother Cleveland's management with something like this. They have enough problems in running the plant.

Trenton: What happens after the project is complete? Cleveland's management is eventually going to have to handle the aluminum facilities as well as the iron facilities.

Bonds: That is true, Mr. Trenton. However, I think that once the system is installed it will be much easier for their management to control.

Trenton: I don't know. I'll think about what you have said.

Trenton appointed a committee to study the advantages and disadvantages of adopting such a management format for this situation. The committee reported back to Trenton that under the unique circumstances, it would probably be the best method to handle the situation. The overriding reason in their decision was the point that Bonds made concerning the implementation of a new system while an older one was still in operation. After reading the committee's report and talking to a friend in another industry which utilized project management, Trenton decided to use this management style even though it had never been used before at the Ford Motor Company. Trenton called Bonds into his office.

Trenton: Dave, I've decided to adopt your idea of using project management in this situation. Let's hope it works out. You are in charge. I would like to see the usual monthly progress reports as is the requirement on any of our programs.

Bonds: I'm sure it will work out, sir. I know the man to appoint as the project manager; Tim White. He knows aluminum facilities and he works well with people. I know he is an excellent engineer. He and I will coordinate the entire project.

As Bonds walked out of the office, Trenton wondered how the management at the Cleveland Casting Plant would accept this new style. Recently, they had become increasingly reluctant to accept many of the production changes that division staff had suggested. Trenton thought that much of their reluctance may have stemmed from the fact that the new Michigan Casting Center was responsible for many of these changes that division staff was suggesting. He knew that the management at the Cleveland plant probably was irritated by the acceptance of the suggestions without asking for Cleveland's opinion.

Dave Bonds called Tim White into his office and told him of the decision to use project management on the Cleveland portion of the project. He also told White of his decision on the project manager for the project. Tim White was very happy that he was chosen and was eager to get started. He had previous project management experience with another organization, but had never handled any project of this size. White chose Russ Cambell, who had purchasing and inventory experience, as one of his assistants. Larry Owens, an engineer, was chosen as the other assistant. White was told to report to Bonds directly, so that Cleveland management would not have to concern itself with the daily problems of implementing the project (see Exhibit 1).

Exhibit 1. The Cleveland Casting Plant Organization Chart.

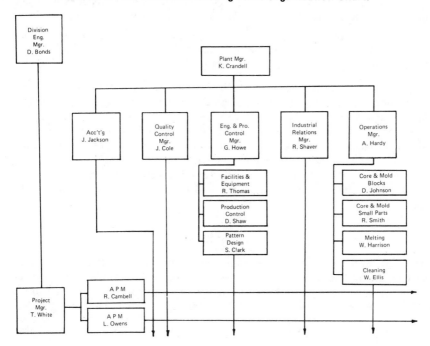

Bonds arranged an introductory meeting with the Cleveland management in early December, 1975. Bonds, White, the two assistant project managers, and other engineers met with the management at Cleveland. They presented a very detailed schedule for the implementation of the aluminum facilities in the Cleveland plant. They also informed management of their decision to use project management.

Bonds: Gentlemen, as you can see, this will be a very involved project. Five of your ten mold lines will be modified for the production of aluminum castings. However, you will still be able to produce gray iron on the other mold lines for almost the entire period during which the new facilities are being installed. We believe that choosing mold lines 6 through 10 will lessen the material handling problem.

Crandall: I still do not understand why we must let divison handle this project. We have capable people here and have handled very big projects like this one before without the use of your project management.

Bonds: We feel that this is the best way to handle the situation, Ken. I'm not saying that your people aren't capable. I'm saying that this is the way that Trenton wants it.

Crandall: I think this is going to create more of a problem. As any of the managers here will tell you, our people are used to working with one supervisor, strict line-function. I don't know if you will get the cooperation you need to get the job done. We will give you full cooperation, of course, but I don't think our people will be able to work this way.

Hardy: I agree with Ken. I don't know if our people are ready for this type of management style. I don't know if I'm ready for it either.

Jackson: How are we going to identify and control costs on this type of project using this type of management? Who is going to be responsible for any overruns? I see too many questions to be answered before we can begin on this project.

Various other managers voiced their opinions. Most of them had expressed uncertainty about project management. Some were not even sure what project management was.

Dave Bonds and Tim White tried to calm the fears and uncertainties of the plant management. They knew that cooperation from the plant was very important, but like all decisions at Ford, they knew plant personnel would eventually have to cooperate with them, willingly or unwillingly. However, they did not want to force the issue and destroy any spirit of commitment or cooperation that was there.

The Project Begins

After the meeting, Crandall called all the managers into his office. He told them that he did not like the situation any better than they did, but that they really had no choice but to comply. Although Crandall had the utmost respect for Trenton, he wondered why he was taking such a radical step for such an important project, especially when the influence the project could have on the future of the plant was tremendous.

The next few months saw the formation of the project team. There were many jobs that had to be done before the actual project got started. A project office was set up in a centrally located area in the foundry. Functional people were interviewed and chosen from the various departments to become full time employees under the project management team. Authorization for additional personnel to take the place of those chosen for the project was granted by Division.

White had planned the project well. He reviewed each area in both productive and nonproductive functions. He determined what was needed in addition to or instead of the facilities that were already in use. He planned procedures so as to minimize interference with production.

White determined that the core area would require the least change, since aluminum could be cast with sand cores. The use of sand cores with resin binders was one of the current methods utilized at the plant. Slight variations in the dimensions of the core would be made to allow for the greater shrinkage of aluminum.

The molding area would require some changes. Aluminum castings can be made with either sand molds or permanent molds. Modifications on the mold lines would be necessary so that the permanent molds could be used. Again, patterns would have to be redesigned slightly in order to allow for shrinkage. White assigned several pattern designers to work on both the mold and core area modifications.

The melting area would require several changes. The cupolas, used in the melting of iron, were not necessary for the melting of aluminum since aluminum had a much lower melting point. Crucible, reverberatory, and induction furnaces were the three most common methods used to melt aluminum. All three were being considered for use on the project. White thought that the use of induction furnaces would be better, since these type of furnaces were now being used in the duplexing of iron and several were available. Melting personnel knew the technical aspects of these furnaces and would therefore know more about their performance and their capabilities. Provisions would also have to be made for the inoculants, or additives, for the aluminum. Materials such as copper, tin, magnesium, zinc, titanium, and others would be added since aluminum itself is a very poor material for casting. This was important, since the typical aluminum alloy contained about seven additives in varying concentrations. The percentages of each had to be carefully controlled.

The cleaning would also need modifications. Gray iron castings are generally cleaned by the use of a shot blast machine or rotary tumbler. Aluminum castings require heat treating to develop a uniform structure, remove internal stress and improve mechanical properties and dimensional stability. Two methods were generally used: solution treatment with aging and artificial aging, a faster method. White felt that, due to the expected demand for the aluminum castings, the artificial aging method would be the better one to use.

Quality control was another important area which White considered. White wanted to be sure that Cleveland's equipment was operating efficiently. He also wanted to know if all the necessary tests, such as hardness determination, spectrographic analysis and dye testing, would be able to be performed.

White was confident that he had foreseen most of the problems that would probably occur. He assigned people to study the modifications he thought were necessary and invited suggestions or criticisms from those who were working on the problems. He also instituted a weekly meeting between the project management team and the functional managers. Any problems could be discussed at that time and a review of project progress would also be reviewed. White was later disappointed in the lack of concern or interest that the functional managers showed for these meetings.

Ford employees assigned to the project on a full time basis responded very favorably to the challenge that was presented to them. They felt that they were special for being chosen. The chances for recognition in an organization like Ford Motor were rather small, especially at a plant level. The cooperation that these employees gave to White was amazing. The fact that they still had to report to their functional supervisors and White did not seem to bother the majority of them.

White kept both the local functional managers and Division personnel well informed on the status of the project. Weekly reports were sent to all parties and monthly meetings became a standard practice.

The lack of response from the local managers again was very evident. White felt that he had done everything that he could to get their interest. He knew that he had stayed out of their way as far as production was concerned. He called Owens and Cambell into his office.

White: I would like to know your feelings on the attitudes of the managers around here. It seems that they don't bother us, but it seems to be from a lack of interest.

Owens: You would think that they would be interested in this project. After all, it is their plant. I don't care as long as I get my job done on time and with no overruns.

Cambell: It certainly makes our jobs easier. I don't care either. They have to live with this new system, not us. We will all be out of here in another couple of months.

White: I understand how you feel, but I think it is very important to get the managers involved. We don't know everything about this plant and there might have been something big that we missed in our plans. Let's try to at least ask for their thoughts on problems you might have. I think it is important.

The project progressed through the first half of 1976 without any major problems or setbacks. During the summer, however, many of the managers in the production area were complaining of excessive downtime. This problem was magnified by the normal high downtime that occurs in foundry operations during the hot summer months. Dan Shaw, the Production Control Manager, was trying to figure out a way to cut this downtime when he noticed several of the employees assigned to the project team back at their desks in the office. Thinking back, he realized that he had seen this episode repeated several times in the past few weeks. Investigating further, he discovered functional employees doing the work for their friends on the project team. Work was being delayed causing several problems. He decided to discuss the subject at one of the meetings with the project managers.

Shaw: Tim, it has come to my attention that several of the employees that were assigned to you are interfering with the normal work in our office. Now I've told them to stop the interference, but I think that you should also impress upon them the importance of not bothering functional employees. I know that I'm still their supervisor, but what they do outside of work I can't control.

White: I was unaware of that problem, Dan. Russ, did you know this was going on?

Cambell: No, I didn't, Tim. I certainly will talk to everyone under my control and I'm sure that Larry will too.

Crandall: I think that is an excellent idea. Our normal production problems are enough. We don't need any additional problems. We have several mold lines and a few cupolas down because of this project. We can not afford to have any further delays or we may not make our quota.

The project continued to cause some delays and interference with regular production. This further alienated the project team from the production managers. Overtime was increased to get jobs done on time, which further increased costs. Dan Shaw suggested charging the overtime to division's budget, since the whole problem was due to their insistence on handling the project.

In several cases, the interference by the project personnel was justified. Office equipment, typewriters, calculators, and telephones were in short supply. Additional equipment was on order, but as was typical at Ford, division approval was needed. The purchase order was traced to a screening office in Detroit, where they were attempting to find suitable used equipment to fill the order. White blamed local management for not following up on the purchase order. Local management said that it was his problem, not theirs.

Several other incidents occurred to further widen the gap between the project management team and the functional managers. Communication was almost non-existant and White was concerned only with completing the project as quickly as possible. Local management, on the other hand, wanted to get their operations back to normal. Responsibility for errors and problems were passed back and forth between the functional managers and the project managers. Tim White called his two assistants into his office to discuss this problem.

White: I don't know what is going on. It seems that all communication has stopped. The people we have working on this project don't even talk to us anymore. I think the initial enthusiasm that was expressed is gone and they realize that this is just another job to be done.

Cambell: I would have to agree with that. What really makes me angry is the fact that this was our big chance and it is not going well at all.

Owens: I think the only thing we can do is to finish up the project the best we can and get out. We have cost overruns in almost every facet of this project. I think that local management has to accept some of the responsibility for these overruns. I don't think that we will ever solve the problem of the two metals contaminating each other. I am surprised that was not thought about before this project was started.

White: I know the project is overrun in almost every area, but you know what happens if division really wants something done. The money seems to come out of nowhere. I think all we can do is finish up and get out. I'm sure both of you noticed how much help we got from Bonds after we started having problems. We're in trouble.

Tim White was especially disappointed in the manner in which the project had been handled. He had hoped, as did the other two assistant project managers, that this would be his chance for success in the company. He tried to pinpoint the major problems, but other than the communication problem with the local management, he found many small problems. He also wondered about the decision to use project management in this situation. He felt it was not necessary and probably did much to actually prevent the completion of the project within the budget allowed. White was also very upset with the lack of cooperation he had received from Dave Bonds.

The project was completed with a very large overrun. A large amount of additional funding was required to finish. Division managers reviewed the use of project management and considered it to be a failure. They decided, on the basis of this project, not to use this type of management form again.

CASE STUDY: FACILITIES SCHEDULING AT MAYER MANUFACTURING

Eddie Turner was elated with the good news that he was being promoted to section supervisor in charge of scheduling all activities in the new engineering research laboratory. The new laboratory was a necessity for Mayer Manufacturing. The engineering, manufacturing and quality control directorates were all in desperate need of a new testing facility. Upper-level management felt that this new facility would alleviate many of the problems that previously existed.

The new organizational structure (as shown in Exhibit 1) required a change in policy over use of the laboratory. The new section supervisor, upon approval from his department manager, would have full authority for establishing priorities for

Exhibit 1. Mayer Manufacturing Organizational Structure.

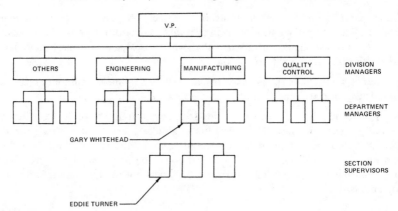

the use of the new facility. The new policy change was a necessity because upper-level management felt that there would be inevitable conflict between manufacturing, engineering, and quality control.

After one month of operations, Eddie Turner was finding his job impossible. Eddie had a meeting with Gary Whitehead, his department manager.

Eddie: I'm having a hell of a time trying to satisfy all of the department managers. If I give engineering prime time use of the facility, then quality control and manufacturing say that I'm playing favorites. Imagine that! Even my own people say that I'm playing favorites with other directorates. I just can't satisfy everyone.

Gary: Well, Eddie, you know that this problem comes with the job. You'll get the job done.

Eddie: The problem is that I'm a section supervisor and have to work with department managers. These department managers look down on me like I'm their servant. If I were a department manager, then they'd show me some respect. What I'm really trying to say is that I would like you to send out the weekly memos to these department managers telling them of the new priorities. They wouldn't argue with you like they do with me. I can supply you with all the necessary information. All you'll have to do is to sign your name.

Gary: Determining the priorities and scheduling the facilities is your job, not mine. This is a new position and I want you to handle it. I know you can because I selected you. I do not intend to interfere.

During the next two weeks, the conflicts got progressively worse. Eddie felt that he was unable to cope with the situation by himself. The department managers did not respect his authority delegated to him by his superiors. For the next two weeks, Eddie sent memos to Gary in the early part of the week asking whether or not Gary agreed with the priority list. There was no response to the two memos. Eddie then met with Gary to discuss the deteriorating situation.

Eddie: Gary, I've sent you two memos to see if I'm doing anything wrong in establishing the weekly priorities and schedules. Did you get my memos?

Gary: Yes, I received your memos. But as I told you before, I have enough problems to worry about without doing your job for you. If you can't handle the work let me know and I'll find someone who can.

Eddie returned to his desk and contemplated his situation. Finally, he made a decision. Next week he was going to put a signature block under his for Gary to sign, with carbon copies for all division managers. "Now, let's see what happens," remarked Eddie.

CASE STUDY: J. A. CONSTRUCTION COMPANY

John Adams asked himself:

Did I make the right decision? Should I have accepted the position as senior project engineer? Would they be splitting my old department if I had stayed on as manager? Was I purposely moved out? Will the engineers in the department feel that I abandoned them? Will I still be effective in getting my project work done by the sections when they find out I'm no longer their boss? Should I accept the position as manager of the newly formed Management Systems and Administration Section, or stay on as a senior project engineer?

History

John Adams was hired by J. A. Construction Company as a compressor specialist. Prior to joining J. A. Construction Company, John was an application engineer for a leading compressor manufacturer. Although he was fairly young (25 years old), John was well known throughout the industry.

John accepted the position as senior mechanical engineer with J. A. Construction Company some 10 years ago mainly to get experience in equipment other than compressors. However, shortly after John came on board, J. A. Construction Company experienced a rapid growth period. J. A. Construction Company grew from a company of about 2000 people to one of about 4000 people worldwide. The metropolitan office John was in grew from about 700 people to about 1500 people. With this rapid growth, new positions were made available. John was promoted to supervisor of the rotating equipment group in the mechanical section just two years after he joined the company. The engineering department organization chart is shown in Exhibit 1.

John did much to organize and build the rotating equipment group into a well organized professional group. The group grew from about three engineers to ten highly qualified specialists. Two years later John was rewarded for his efforts. J. A. Construction Company again experienced a growth and this time John was named manager of the Mechanical Equipment section. Not knowing much about the vessel and exchanger areas, John's management assigned Pete Hunt as his assistant. (Mechanical section's organization chart is in Exhibit 2.) Since John was still affiliated with machinery for the petroleum and chemical industry, he kept active in the industry organizations.

Exhibit 1. Engineering Group Organizational Chart.

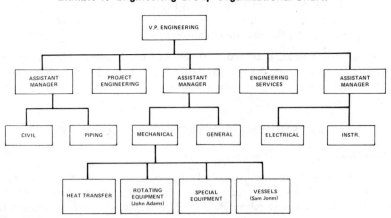

Exhibit 2. Mechanical Group Organizational Chart.

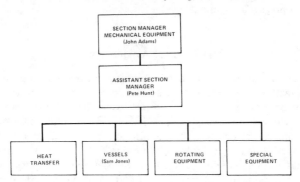

The arrangement of having an Assistant Manager who was strong in the areas where John was weak, was working fine. However, John saw a need to show some of the younger engineers upward mobility. So, he promoted a long standing vessel supervisor, Sam Jones, to an Assistant Section Manager and reorganized the department as shown in Exhibit 3.

John also instituted the concept that the assistant managers would be job leaders for all contracts that involved the mechanical section. This system, as well as some of the scheduling, planning and controlling systems that John authored or co-authored, was widely received and accepted. His department maintained a high degree of accuracy in estimating the man-hours required for each contract. The mechanical estimates were about 99% accurate when compared to the actual time spent. The department also maintained a high degree of professionalism and pride in their work.

John had held this position for about three years when he began to look at where his next move would be. He noticed that all levels higher than his were filled with engineers that had project experience. He also noticed that a number of engineers in his age bracket or younger were presently getting or already had an M.B.A. John decided to enroll in an M.B.A. program at a local college and wait

Exhibit 3. Reorganized Mechanical Equipment Group.

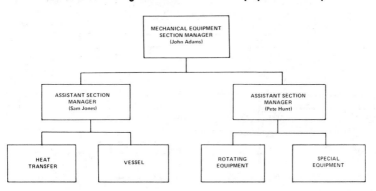

until the opportunity would come to advise the V.P. of Engineering that he was interested in a project assignment.

The Project Assignment

John was Section Manager of Mechanical Equipment for four years now and was getting a bit restless. He had, on several occasions, mentioned to the V.P. of Engineering that he was interested in a project assignment. But to date he had not received one. He was, however, being utilized for more and more proposal work. John's department was basically functioning under the guidance of Sam Jones, the assistant section manager. John became very restless when the announcement came out that the engineering department for the division he was in would be merged with the engineering department of another division in the same location. That wasn't too bad, but the announcement also said the existing V.P. of Engineering was being replaced by a V.P. from another office. John thought, "I'll never get a project assignment now. I'll have to start at the bottom again." The new V.P. took over and set up an interim organization as shown in Exhibit 4.

It was only four months later when John was called into Joe Doe's (his boss) office.

John: What did I do now? (laughing)

Joe: Nothing, that's the problem! (laughing) How about closing the door. You know we have been having problems with the equipment vendors on the XYZ contract, and since I have been formally released from the job, we need some one to step into the number two position. Dave Smith is moving into the number one slot.

John: Do you want someone from my department?

Joe: No, I am asking you if you would accept a five to six month assignment on the project to mainly spearhead the collecting of the equipment information.

John: Couldn't I do that from my present position?

Exhibit 4. Interim Organizational Chart.

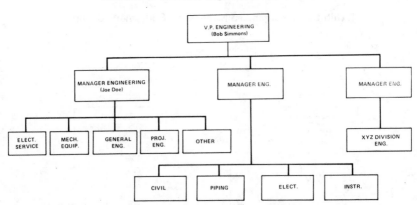

Joe: Yes, but the client is looking for a top notch, highly qualified person to lead the activities from the project team. They want a management-type individual.

John: Would I be coming back to my same position?

Joe: You know we are looking at a reorganization of the engineering department.

John: Yes, I do. When do you need an answer?

Joe: Tomorrow. You know, this will be good experience for you. It will give you the project experience you lack.

John Adams can remember thinking about what he should do. He talked to his wife Lynn.

John: I was asked to accept a project assignment today.

Lynn: That's great. That's what you've been waiting for.

John: Yes, but I wanted to be on a new project as the lead project engineer.

Lynn: Well, how do you feel about the person who's in the number one slot?

John: Oh, Dave is a good engineer and a hell of a nice guy. I like Dave.

Lynn: Well, you have to work on your decision.

The next day John went into the office still not knowing what he was going to do. It was 8:00 a.m. and he needed to make a decision by 9:00 a.m. He talked to his assistant manager, Sam Jones.

John: Hi Sam.

Sam: Hi John. How's it going today?

John: Not too good. I want to talk to you. Sam, Joe asked if I would take a temporary assignment on the XYZ contract. You have been following that for mechanical. Is there a problem or is the client blowing smoke?

Sam: There is a problem and it is basically with the pump and compressor people The vendors won't give use the information we need to do our detail design engineering.

John: Do you think you can hold the fort down for five to six months, keeping in mind I am still responsible for the section, and must be consulted on all major decisions or changes in operation procedures?

Sam: Yes, I can run the department.

John: Fine, thanks Sam. See you later.

John went back to his office and thought about the conversations surrounding the assignment. If I accept, I give up a comfortable position. The section's performance is good. Project engineers and managers are all willing to cooperate and go along with my guidelines because they know I'll get the job done. I'll be giving up a well greased machine for the unknown. At that point his secretary advised him it was two minutes till 9:00. He went to Joe Doe's office.

Joe: Good morning, John. Have you made a decision?

John: Yes, I have. I have decided to accept the assignment. You did say it was for five to six months, right?

Joe: That's right.

John: When do I start?

Joe: Let's plan the move for Monday. I'll advise the client and the project team.

A Project Engineer's Role

That following Monday John joined the project team. His assignment was to follow all the equipment for the main process area as well as to coordinate the civil, piping, and modeling efforts of that area. He didn't mind the additional responsibility, because he wanted the experience. John's problems came when he tried to get the work done. Being manager of a section, he was accustomed to giving assignments to engineers and getting the results without anyone questioning his request. Now, as a project engineer, he had no authority over the people in the sections. He had to change his approach and style of managing if he intended to get the cooperation of the sections to resolve the problems. The client was another problem. The prime responsibility of John was to get the required vendor data to the sections and resolve the problem of specification interpretation. In addition to lack of vendor information, John found unresolved problems dealing with vendor exceptions to specifications which needed client resolution.

In an effort to get some of the problems off dead center, John called a meeting with the client, the mechanical specialist and himself. These meetings were by equipment type because of the different specialities involved. The meetings were a great help in getting John acquainted with the details and to assign the action to the appropriate individual (i.e., client, specialist, or John).

After being on the project for about two weeks, John felt good about the progress that was being made. He had set schedules with the specialist and the client for getting the information and problems resolved. In order to keep control of progress he issued a punch list of the items to the client.

John was following up on the assignments to the specialist areas to see what progress was being made. He found that very little, if any, progress had been made at all. John immediately went to Sam Jones, the acting section manager.

John: Sam, what's going on?

Sam: What do you mean?

John: Two weeks ago I requested your specialist to get busy on my project and they haven't even started yet.

Sam: Well, you know how it is John. We are understaffed in some areas and just haven't got to your job yet.

John: What do you mean you haven't gotten to my job yet. I expect to have my work done on a priority basis. I don't want to hear any excuses like being understaffed!

Sam: Boy! Has your tune changed. I can remember just three weeks ago when you told a project engineer that his work would be done when we could schedule it in.

John: That was three weeks ago, and besides that wasn't my project. I'm still administratively responsible for this section and I expect my work to be done on a priority basis, at least until after this initial thrust is complete. Okay?

Sam: Okay, we'll try! If we can't we'll let you know in plenty of time.

John: That's what I like to hear.

John continued to expedite information from the section, the vendor and the client. He personally made visits to the vendor shops to get the information and/or resolve problems. It was toward the end of the fourth month and things were looking good. The punch list was dwindling and the flow of information was back on track. In reviewing what needed to be done to keep it there, John felt he had to exert his authority over the mechanical group for at least three to four more weeks. This would get him completely over the hump and on the downhill side. John was planning his next status meeting with the client when Joe Doe called and asked him to come to his office.

Joe: Hi, John. How's the project going?

John: Fine, but that's not why you called me up here.

Joe: You're right. As you know we have been working on the reorganization. Well, we have finally finished. I would like your opinions and aid in selecting some of the staff. But first, you should know that your section is being split and general engineering dissolved.

John: Being Split?!

Joe: Yes, we are forming a Vessel Systems Group which will consist of vessels, heat transfer equipment, and some of the general engineering group. We are also going to have a section called mechanical equipment. This section will consist of rotating equipment, special equipment, and noise analysis. We are also forming a new section called Management Systems and Administration. I feel Sam Jones is the best qualified for Vessel Systems, but I need your help on the mechanical section.

John: What about me? Is it your intent that I stay in projects?

Joe: No, not exactly. You have three choices: To be the mechanical section manager; to stay in projects; or to be the manager of the newly formed section, Management Systems and Administration.

John: What are the responsibilities of the new section?

Joe: For that you should talk to Bob Simmons (v.p. of engineering). That's his baby.

John: When can I talk to him?

Joe: Bob is out of town and won't be back for a couple of days. The only thing I can tell you is that the section will include the computerized drafting group and all the secretaries for the engineering department.

John: What about my project assignment? Will I be released in two months?

Joe: From what I can see there should be no problem.

John: Fine. See you later.

A New Challenge

A couple of days later John went to Bob Simmons' office to discuss the responsibilities of the Management Systems and Administration Section.

Bob: Come on in John and close the door.

John: I was talking to Joe and he advised me of the changes that are going to be made and said you could give me more information about the responsibilities of the Management Systems and Administration Section.

Bob: I see. The section manager position of this new group is a training ground for future project managers. This group will be responsible for the interface of the engineering department with all other departments in the company. All proposal work and all estimates will flow through this group. This group will also be responsible for preparing all engineering schedules. In other words it will be the nerve center of the engineering department. It will be the section manager's responsibility to review existing systems and develop new ones. He should always be looking for new and better ways to do our work. If I had a choice of all the sections to be manager of, it would be this one. It offers the most challenge. I have three candidates in mind for the position, but I would like you to take the job.

John: Could I have some time to think it over.

Bob: I can only give you a couple of days.

John: Okay. See you in a couple of days.

CASE STUDY: HANDLING CONFLICT IN PROJECT MANAGEMENT

The next several pages contain a six-part case study in conflict management. Read the instructions carefully on how to keep score and use the boxes below as the worksheet for recording your choice and the group's choice, after the case study has been completed, your instructor will provide you with the proper grading system for recording your scores.

Part 1: Facing The Conflict

As part of his first official duties, the new department manager informs you by memo that he has changed his input and output requirements for the MIS project (on which you are the project manager) because of several complaints by his departmental employees. This is contradictory to the project plan which you developed with the previous manager and are currently working toward. The department manager states that he has already discussed this with the vice-president and general manager, a man to whom both of you report, and feels that the former

LINE	PART	PERSONAL		GROUP	
		CHOICE	SCORE	CHOICE	SCORE
1	1. Facing the Conflict				
2	2. Understanding Emotions	///////		///////	
3	3. Establishing Communications				
4	4. Conflict Resolution	///////		///////	
5	5. Understanding your choices				
6	6. Interpersonal Influences				
	TOTAL	///////		///////	

department manager made a poor decision and did not get sufficient input from the employees who would be using the system as to the best system specifications. You telephone him and try to convince him to hold off on his request for change until a later time, but he refuses.

Changing the input/output requirements at this point in time will require a major revision and will set back total system implementation by three weeks. This will also impact other department managers who expect to see this system operational according to the original schedule. You can explain this to your superiors but the increased project costs will be hard to absorb. The potential cost overrun might be difficult to explain at a later date.

At this point you are somewhat unhappy with yourself at having been on the search committee that found this department manager and especially at having recommended him for this position. You know that something must be done, and the following are your alternatives:

A. You can remind the department manager that you were on the search committee that recommended him and then ask him to return the favor since he "owes you one."

B. You can tell him that you will form a new search committee to replace him if he doesn't change his position.

C. You can take a tranquilizer and then ask your people to try to perform the additional work within the original time and cost constraints.

D. You can go to the vice-president and general manager and request that the former requirements be adhered to, at least temporarily.

E. You can send a memo to the department manager explaining your problem and asking him to help you find a solution.

F. You can tell the department manager that your people cannot handle the request and his people will have to find alternate ways of solving their problems.

G. You can send a memo to the department manager requesting an appoint-ment, at his earliest convenience, to help you resolve your problem.
H. You can go to the department manager's office later that afternoon and continue the discussion further.
I. You can send him a memo telling him that you have decided to use the old requirements but will honor his request at a later time.

Although other alternatives exist, assume that these are the only ones open to you at the moment. Without discussing the answer with your group, record the letter representing your choice in the appropriate space on line 1 of the worksheet under personal choice.

As soon as all of your group have finished, discuss the problem as a group and determine that alternative which the group considers to be best. Record this an-swer on line 1 of the worksheet under group choice. Allow ten minutes for this part.

Part 2: Understanding Emotions

Never having worked with this department manager before, you try to predict what his reactions will be when confronted with the problem. Obviously, he can react in a variety of ways:

a. He can *accept* your solution in its entirety without asking any questions.
b. He can discuss some sort of justification in order to *defend* his position.
c. He can become extremely annoyed with having to discuss the problem again and demonstrate *hostility*.
d. He can demonstrate a willingness to *cooperate* with you in resolving the problem.
e. He can avoid making any decision at this time by *withdrawing* from the discussion.

In the table below are several possible statements that could be made by the department manager when confronted with the problem. Without discussion with your group, place a checkmark beside the appropriate emotion which could de-scribe this statement. When each member of the group has completed his choice. Numerical values will be assigned to your choices in the discussion which will follow. Do not mark the worksheet at this time. Allow ten minutes for this part.

	YOUR CHOICE					GROUP CHOICE				
	ACC	DEF	HOST	COOP	WITH	ACC	DEF	HOST	COOP	WITH
A. I've given you my answer. See the general manager if you're not happy.										
B. I understand your problem. Let's do it your way.										
C. I understand your problem, but I'm doing what is best for my department.										
D. Let's discuss the problem. Perhaps there are alternatives.										
E. Let me explain to you why we need the new requirements.										
F. See my section supervisors. It was their recommendation.										
G. New managers are supposed to come up with new and better ways, aren't they?										

Part 3: Establishing Communications

Unhappy over the department manager's memo and the resulting follow-up phone conversation, you decide to walk in on the department manager. You tell him that you will have a problem trying to honor his request. He tells you that he is too busy with his own problems of restructuring his department and that your schedule and cost problems are of no concern to him at this time. You storm out of his office leaving him with the impression that his actions and remarks are not in the best interest of either the project or the company.

The department manager's actions do not, of course, appear to be those of a dedicated manager. He should be concerned more about what's in the best interest of the company. As you contemplate the situation, you wonder if you could have received a better response from him had you approached him differently. In other words, what is your best approach to opening up communications

632 Project Management for Executives

between you and the department manager? From the list of alternatives shown below, and working alone, select the alternative which best represents how you would handle this situation. When all members of the group have selected their personal choices, repeat the process and make a group choice. Record your personal and group choices on line three of the worksheet.

A. Comply with the request and document all results so that you will be able to defend yourself at a later date in order to show that the department manager should be held accountable.

B. Immediately send him a memo reiterating your position and tell him that at a later time you will reconsider his new requirements. Tell him that time is of the utmost and you need an immediate response if he is displeased.

C. Send him a memo stating that you are holding him accountable for all cost overruns and schedule delays.

D. Send him a memo stating you are considering his request and that you plan to see him again at a later date to discuss changing the requirements.

E. See him as soon as possible. Tell him that he need not apologize for his remarks and actions, and that you have reconsidered your position and wish to discuss it with him.

F. Delay talking to him for a few days in hopes that he will cool off sufficiently and then see him in hopes that you can reopen the discussions.

G. Wait a day or so for everyone to cool off and then try to see him through an appointment; apologize for losing your temper and ask him if he would like to help you resolve the problem.

Allow ten minutes for this part.

Part 4: Conflict Resolution Modes

Having never worked with this manager before, you are unsure about which conflict resolution mode would work best. You decide to wait a few days and then set up an appointment with the department manager without stating what subject matter will be discussed. You then try to determine what conflict resolution mode appears to be dominant based upon the opening remarks of the department manager. Neglecting the fact that your conversation with the department manager might already be considered as confrontation, for each statement shown below, select the conflict resolution mode that the DEPARTMENT MANAGER appears to prefer. After each member of the group has recorded his personal choices, determine the group choices. Numerical values will be attached to your answers at a later time.

Allow ten minutes for this part.

a. *Withdrawal* is retreating from a potential conflict.

b. *Smoothing* is emphasizing areas of agreement and de-emphasizing areas of disagreement.

c. *Compromising* is the willingness to give and take.
d. *Forcing* is directing the resolution in one direction or another; a win or lose position.
e. *Confrontation* is a face-to-face meeting to resolve the conflict.

	PERSONAL CHOICE					GROUP CHOICE				
	WITH	SMOOTH	COMP	FORC	CONF	WITH	SMOOTH	COMP	FORC	CONF
A. The requirements are my decision, and we're doing it my way.										
B. I've thought about it and you're right. We'll do it your way.										
C. Let's discuss the problem. Perhaps there are alternatives.										
D. Let me again explain why we need the new requirements.										
E. See my section supervisors; they're handling it now.										
F. I've looked over the problem and I might be able to ease up on some of the requirements.										

Part 5: Understanding Your Choices

Assume that the department manager has refused to see you again to discuss the new requirements. Time is running out and you would like to make a decision before the costs and schedules get out of hand. From the list below, select your personal choice and then after each group member is finished, find a group choice.

A. Disregard the new requirements since they weren't part of the original project plan.
B. Adhere to the new requirements and absorb the increased costs and delays.
C. Ask the vice-president and general manager to step in and make the final decision.
D. Ask the other department managers who may realize a schedule delay to try to convince this department manager to ease his request or even delay it.

Record your answer on line 5 of the worksheet. Allow five minutes for this part.

Part 6: Interpersonal Influences

Assume that upper-level management resolves the conflict in your favor. In order to complete the original work requirements you will need support from this department manager's organization. Unfortunately, you are not sure as to which type of interpersonal influence to use. Although you are considered as an expert in your field, you fear that this manager's functional employees may have a strong allegiance to the department manager and not want to adhere to your requests. Which of the following interpersonal influence styles would be best under the given set of conditions?

A. You threaten the employees with penalty power by telling them that you will turn in a bad performance report to their department manager.

B. You can use reward power and promise the employees a good evaluation, possible promotion and increased responsibilities on your next project.

C. You can continue your technique of trying to convince the functional personnel to do your bidding because you are the expert in the field.

D. You can try to motivate the employees to do a good job by convincing them that the work is challenging.

E. You can make sure that they understand that your authority has been delegated to you by the vice-president and general manager and that they must do what you say.

F. You can try to build up friendships and off-work relationships with these people and rely on referent power.

G. You can threaten the department manager by asserting that you will tell his wife that you have a picture of him with his mistress.

Allow ten minutes for completion of this part.

The solution to this exercise appears in Appendix C.

8
Problem Identification Checklist

8.0 INTRODUCTION

Quite often project problems are kept well hidden and never come to the surface. How should executives and managers get their people to escalate the problems to the surface instead of hiding them? Therapy sessions, group discussions or individual counseling appears to be the best method. Many times employees are more open with outside consultants than with internal management. In the following 17 sections are checklist questions which the author has used during interviewing sessions.

8.1 INTERPERSONAL SKILLS

- Are interpersonal and management relations courses offered by your company?
- How strongly do you agree or disagree with the following statement about the project/functional environment in your organization?
  "There is not enough opportunity to let management know how we feel about our work."
    - a. strongly agree
    - b. somewhat agree
    - c. hard to decide
    - d. somewhat disagree
    - e. strongly disagree
- For a "job well done" are pats on the back given by project/functional managers?
- Is project/functional management theory X or theory Y?
- Are project or functional managers more people-oriented?
- Is time given off by project/functional management to take care of personal problems?

- Do project/functional managers make an attempt to help solve personal problems of employees?
- Do you receive more counseling from project or functional managers?
- Are project or functional managers more concerned with tardiness and absenteeism?
- How does the project/functional manager handle private rap sessions?
- When discussing personal matters do you feel that the project/functional manager is sincerely interested?
- Does the project/functional manager show an interest in your work other than whether or not you are wasting time?
- Does your project/functional manager have the necessary skills to be able to relate to you personally?
- If not, which ones do you feel he is missing?
- Does your project/functional manager take an interest in your outside activities?
- Does your project/functional manager have a hard time talking to you?

8.2 HORIZONTAL/VERTICAL INTEGRATION OF PROJECT WORK

- Project Manager: Given that you have to integrate your project work over several independent functional areas, what problems do you run into?
- Functional Manager: Given that you have to integrate (schedule) your department's work for several independent projects, what problems do you run into?
- Employee: Given that your work schedule is the result of the integration of functionally-related (vertical) activities, as well as project-related (horizontal) activities, what problems do you run into when "serving two masters"?
- Why do these problems exist?
- What is being done to solve them?
- What should be done to solve them?
- Does upper management know of these problems?
- What scheduling inputs do project managers supply to the functional scheduling process?
- What scheduling inputs do the functional managers supply to the project scheduling process?
- What scheduling inputs do the employees supply?
- Are stated/requested resource requirements usually accurate?
- Are quantitative scheduling techniques used?
- Are schedules rigidly adhered to?
- Are notifications of project/schedule changes provided in a timely fashion?

- Do project managers attempt to expedite their work at the expense of other projects?
- When push comes to shove, which work schedule, horizontal or vertical, has more clout?

8.3 AUTHORITY/RESPONSIBILITY/FREEDOM

- How many people do you supervise?
- What are their responsibilities?
- Do you have any authority over the functional employees?
- Does the functional manager undermine you or give you proper authority.
- Does your authority/responsibility/freedom differ from project to project? Should it?
- Do project managers spell out your individual responsibilities?
- What are some common examples of a functional employees basic responsibilities/freedom on a given project?
- Are lines of authority/responsibility/freedom clearly established at the start of a project?
- What are common problems that result from lack of understanding authority/responsibility/freedom roles in a project environment?
- How should project authority interface problems be solved?
- How does a project manager's authority differ from a functional manager's?
- What do you consider as key factors in the delegation of authority and responsibility on a project?
- Does a project manager frequently negotiate with a functional manager when the pm does not have unilateral authority?
- How elaborate should documented authority be at the start of a project? Why is it necessary?
- How does project authority/responsibility/freedom relate to customer's contracts?
- Do you work on more than one project at the same time?
- Do you prefer to have your authority documented or is it easily understood?

8.4 TECHNICAL KNOWLEDGE

- How do you compare the technological expertise needed in your firm to highly technical industries like the computer and nuclear energy industries?
- Do you believe your company is keeping up with technological advances or is it gradually falling behind other competitors?
- Does your particular job call for a great deal of technical knowledge or are you more of a generalist?

- Do you have a college degree? How much did it provide you with needed technical training? How much did you have to learn in addition to college?
- Describe how your own technical expertise has developed over the past year.
- Is technical training mandatory or optional to employees?
- Is technical learning considered your's or the company's responsibility?
- Does a formal company training program exist for technical training?
- How many outside seminars have you attended? In house seminars?
- Are you willing to personally pay for seminars or training sessions?
- Rank the following technical learning tools in terms of effectiveness and utilization:
  a. on-the-job training
  b. seminars — in house
  c. seminars — outside the company
  d. trade journals
- Do standards exist for measuring technical competency?
- How many hours are spent in an average 40 hour week on learning about technological developments and advances?
- Does the project participation environment help to increase your technological knowledge or is the functional department environment more suitable for personal learning and growth?
- Do you believe technical expertise is utilized more fully in the project or functional department environments?

8.5 EVALUATION OF PROJECT MANAGERS AND TEAM MEMBERS

- Indicate your current position in the organization.
  ——— Functional Employee only
  ——— Project Manager
  ——— Project Office
  ——— Team Member
- The objective of the following questions is to determine the knowledge level of employees regarding job/performance evaluation.
  - What is the frequency or schedule for evaluation?
  - When was your last evaluation?
  - Are both functional managers and project managers involved in the evaluation?
  - Is the same evaluation used to address performance and to determine monetary increases?
  - Do you see all forms prepared and used in your evaluation?

- The objective of the following questions is to solicit employee reaction to performance rating issues.
  - Should project managers participate in the evaluation of employees or is it the functional managers responsibility to keep aware of an individual's performance?
  - Should the project manager comment on performance at the time of the scheduled review or when a project is completed?
  - Should job descriptions include both project team and functional responsibilities?
  - Should job descriptions be changed as project team responsibilities change?
  - Should the project team classification always equal the functional classification (rating, grade, GS level)?
  - Should project team performance appraisal forms be quantitative or narrative comments?
  - Who should have access to performance evaluations completed for employees? Functional manager only? Project managers seeking team members?
  - What happens if 100% of an employee's time is spent on a project team instead of in functional groups?
  - Should evaluation forms be the same for:
    - a. exempt, non-exempt?
    - b. technical, non-technical?
    - c. management, non-management?
    - d. professional, non-professional?
  - How is conflict between functional and team performance resolved?
  - Should performance evaluation be made by comparing the performance of individuals in the same pay grade or by comparing individuals to set performance standards?
  - How should a project manager's performance be rated? By completing project within budget? Within time frames? Level of success?
  - Who should have input when a project manager is rated?

8.6 CONFLICT

- Of the following, which is the major conflict area regarding your project: manpower resources, equipment and facilities, capital expenditures, costs, technical opinions and tradeoffs, administrative procedures, priorities, scheduling, personality clashes, or responsibilities?
- There are five basic ways to resolve a conflict: withdrawal, smoothing, compromising, forcing, and confrontation. Which of these does your supervisor rely heavily upon? Which would be the best method?

- Does your supervisor have the ability to foresee conflict and then act quickly to avoid it?
- After a conflict has been resolved, is there a surveillance method used to prevent future problems?
- If a conflict arises, is it used as an example to avoid future conflicts?
- What are the team leaders' attitudes toward conflict?
- Are there personality clashes within your project team? How are they resolved?
- Do the members of your project work as a team?
- If no, what could be improved?
- Is there a general pattern being established in the types of conflicts that arise and the method in which they are resolved?
- Do you understand your exact responsibilities regarding your project team?
- Can you balance your functional responsibilities with your project team responsibilities?
- Who determines the priorities of a project?
- Whom do you think should determine the priorities?
- How many supervisors do you have?
- Whom do you consider as your immediate supervisor?
- Who considers him/herself as your immediate supervisor?
- Do you believe your team members are well-qualified technically?

8.7 ADAPTABILITY

- Are most individuals aware of the recent organizational changes?
- Is there a chain of communication to effectively relay the changes?
- Do you understand the reason for change in your company?
- Is there a proper introduction/orientation to organizational changes?
- Is there a follow-up session?
- Have there been many changes in the organizational structure in the last five years?
- What is the organization's response time to change?
- Is there a visual model of the organizational chart readily available to you?
- Has the organizational chart been formally explained to you?
- Are there informal responsibility changes once a formal change has taken place?
- Do you understand how the project teams interface with the traditional management structure?
- What level of management do you feel has been initiating the recent organizational changes?
- How do you feel about the most recent changes?
- Do you know what the long-range objectives of your company are?

- Do you know what the short-range objectives of your company are?
- Do you know what the long-range objectives of your project team are?
- Do you know what the short-range objectives of your project team are?
- If given a choice, would you continue to work with the present system of project management or would you go back to the traditional style of management?

8.8 NEGOTIATIONS FOR PROJECT RESOURCES

- Do project office personnel negotiate with functional managers for the personnel they desire.
- Do project office personnel interview perspective project members.
- What is the most frequent method used to recruit personnel.
- Can project office personnel offer incentives to perspective project members.
- Can project office personnel go "higher" up the organization for a particular individual.
- Can project office personnel approve or veto an individual selected by the functional manager.
- Does project importance (priority) have a bearing on personnel selection.
- Can individuals refuse to work for a project (personal differences, no interest, etc.)
- Can individuals request work on a particular projects.
- Whose responsibility (project office or functional manager) is it to provide on-going support for a project during vacations, sickness, educational absences, etc.).
- After project completion, does project office expect on-going support from project personnel or is this support assigned to another group.
- Is there a "pool" of individuals available from which the project manager may choose.
- Can project office be forced to accept an individual.
- Can project office go outside the company (consultants, new hires) for personnel.

8.9 PROJECT DECISION MAKING AND PROBLEM SOLVING

Problem Identification

- Are controls in place to identify problems early to allow sufficient time to address them?
- Is adequate time allotted for decision making and planning?
- Are decisions usually made as a result of crises?
- Are problems thought out and documented before they are brought to you?

- Are problems addressed directly or are they side-stepped or ignored?
- Are the objectives and values of top management known throughout the organization so decisions can be made taking these into account?
- Are alternatives identified and evaluated?
- Are contingency plans developed and maintained?
- Are decisions approached in an orderly manner using decision-making tools (break-even analysis, simulation, models, and decision making under risk and uncertainty)?
- Are all the impacted departments involved in the decision-making process?
  - How are they involved?
  - Are meetings used to involve impacted departments?
  - Who is responsible for involving them?
- Are decisions tracked (followed up) after they are made?
- Is progress and status reported on a regular basis, and in a timely, useable, and reliable manner?
- Do you think you have the proper authority to make the decisions you should be making?
  - Does your manager have the proper authority?
  - Is your manager willing to make decisions on his own?

8.10 WRITING ACTION VS. PROTECTION MEMOS

Memos and Reports Received by You

- Do you get too many memos?
- Do you get too many reports?
- Is the information valuable (useful)?
  - Is it received in a timely manner (in time to use it effectively)?
  - Is it in a useable format?
  - Is it worth what it costs to produce?
- Are routing slips used to assure proper people see memo and initial or stamp it?

Memos and Reports Prepared by You

- Do you write too many memos?
- Do you prepare too many reports?
- Is the information valuable (is it useful)?
  - Could someone else prepare this material?
  - Is it worth what it costs to produce?
  - Is it produced in time for someone to use it?
  - Do you know who is using the information and why?
  - Do the proper people get the information?

Memos and Reports in General

- Are the memos and reports primarily to document past events or are they diagnostic of future problems?
- Are any of your memos diagnostic?
- Would you term your memos primarily informative or are they action memos or protection memos?
- Are memos acted on in a timely manner – do they consistently require follow up? Do you receive feedback on the memo/report?
- Are the memos maintained in a file? Is it updated consistently?
- What problems in written communications have not been addressed by us that you feel are important?

8.11 COMMUNICATIONS

- When communicating with project/functional management do you receive a quick response?
- Would you get a faster response from project or functional managers?
- Do people in different departments share information necessary to coordinate work?
- If the answer to the above is no then how do you get the needed information?
- When project/functional management gives orders are they issued in a manner which will generate immediate compliance?
- When project/functional managers give orders do they have more than one objective?
- As a subordinate are you asked for your solutions to problems by project/ functional managers?
- Does your project/functional manager make it easy for you to talk to him?
- Do you feel that project/functional managers censor bad information?
- When instructions are given by project/functional managers, are you told the whys or do you have to ask? If you ask are you told?
- Would you feel resentful if your project manager lacked the command of technology necessary to successfully run the project?
- Are more memos received in the project or the functional environment?
- Are these memos clear, concise, and easy to read and understand?
- When meetings are held in the project/functional environment do they start on time, are members allowed to contribute, and are opinions sought and are the meetings necessary?
- Is project/functional management interested in receiving your thoughts, opinions, and ideas?
- Does project/functional management consider the impact on employees when making decisions?

8.12 UPPER-LEVEL MANAGEMENT SUPPORT

- How does management communicate or exhibit support or interest in a project?
- Does management share business plans as well as the effect of a given project on those plans?
- Does management insure that appropriate resources are assigned to a project?
- Does management communicate (formally or informally) project priorities?
- Does management regularly (and independently) communicate with the client?
- How does management track the progress of a project?
- Does management want to be informed of project problems?
- Does management participate in problem solving?
- Does management ever become so involved in a project that they override the project manager's or functional manager's authority?
- Should management be closer to projects? Why?
- Does upper, project, and functional management regularly meet? Should they? Why?
- Does upper management usually favor either project management or functional management when conflicts arise? Results?

8.13 COST CONTROL

(Identify the individual toward whom the following questions should be directed — program manager, program office, functional manager, functional employee)

- At what level are you responsible for cost control? (Work center, branch, division)
- What direct control do you personally have over costs?
- How frequently is cost data provided to you?
- Who determines what cost data is provided? (You or a higher level)
- How do you control costs in your area?
- Do other functional elements directly affect your ability to control costs in your area?
- How do you resolve cost conflicts with other elements?
- In a project management environment in your company, who controls costs?
- Does a project manager in your company determine cost limitations for your functional area and for others?
- Do you discuss costs with project managers?
- Do you make detailed input to plans under various projects relative to what costs will be in your area to meet stated objectives and target dates?

- Is your input considered or ignored? Are you told why your cost estimates or analyses are ignored.
- Does your company give you any cost control training?
- Are decisions that adversely affect your costs explained to you? If so, by whom?
- Do you feel that cost is measured properly or that the correct costs are monitored and controlled?
- When you give estimates of costs, are you forced to "pad" your figures to insure you will get what you really need?
- Are you familiar with the term "management reserve" as it relates to cost?
- Do you personally conduct cost variance analysis?
- Do you use standard costs when providing program estimates?
- Who establishes standard costs in your area, you or another element, perhaps the staff?
- Who determines what action, if any, will be taken to correct a cost problem?
- In most instances, are standards available to aid in developing these estimates?
- On a very large project, is there a person in the project office who is responsible for monitoring costs?
- What usually occurs when budgeted costs are materially exceeded by actual costs in a functional area? In a project environment?
- When conflicts arise between functional and project management over costs, how are they normally resolved?
- How accurate have you found project cost estimates to be?
- What mechanisms are utilized to control and/or monitor costs?
- Who is responsible for revising cost estimates or budgets?
- Who is responsible for determing relevant costs?
- To what extent do you believe that you can actually control costs?

8.14 TIME MANAGEMENT

(Identify the individual toward whom the following questions should be directed — program manager, program office, functional manager, functional employee)

- What do you see as your most important activity, based on your current position?
- Do you feel that you spend enough time on this activity?
- Is this activity shared by others?
- How do you insure that this activity will be accomplished?
- Do you have formal or informal priorities?
- Do you inform subordinates of priorities? How?
- Do you like to arrive early or work later in the day? Why? If not, can you see any advantage to doing this?

- How do you schedule your days work?
- How are incoming phone calls handled?
- How are visiters handled?
- On what parameters of your functional area do you focus your time? Why?
- What things normally make demands on you that you feel are a real waste of time? Why?
- Does your boss require an appointment or does he or she accept calls and informal visits?
- How do you think your time could be better spent?
- In your opinion, does project management improve effective use of your time? Why or why not?
- If you could have complete authority to schedule your own time, how would you do it?
- Normally, do you prefer to have a meeting to solve a problem or to make a decision on your own?
- Does the old adage, "Not enough time to do it right, but always enough time to do it over" apply very often in your functional area? In your company?
- How long does it take to get action on important decisions in your functional area? In your company?
- Do you spend a lot of time "stamping out fires?" If so, why do you think this situation exists?
- Do you concentrate on one problem until it is resolved or work on several at the same time?
- Do you believe in management by exception? Why?
- Do you ever consider the gain or value of doing one thing versus the loss or cost of not doing something else?
- Do you often work Saturdays (assuming this is the exception at your company and not the rule)?
- Do you often take work home?
- On the average, what percent of your day is usually spent in meetings? How many of these meetings are self imposed?
- Who develops the project master schedule?
- What types of scheduling systems are used, e.g., Gantt, CPM/PERT, etc.? Is the system always the same?
- Who is responsible for changes to the master schedule?
- Is there an integrated cost/schedule system in use?
- Who develops project milestones?
- How is project progress monitored? Who is responsible?
- How are schedule problems (slippages) identified and reviewed?
- Are standards available for estimating how long a project will take?
- At what point does top management become involved in project scheduling?

8.15 ON-THE-JOB TRAINING (OJT) FOR PROJECT MANAGEMENT

- How long have you been employed here?
- What is your educational background?
- How many projects have you managed?
- Who do you report to as the project manager?
- How many people do you supervise in the project office?
- Do you think your organization has an efficient OJT program for project management?
- Is OJT more or less important than formal training? Should both OJT and formal training be used in your organization?
- What would you consider ideal training for a project manager?
- Who should evaluate the effectiveness of OJT programs in your company and how?
- What kind of preparation did the company give to you as project manager?
- Should functional employees be recruited for project management from within the company or should recruitment be specifically directed toward outsiders?
- How do you teach interpersonal skills to a potential project manager?
- Which has helped you more — OJT or previous experience?
- Has your position in the organization provided personal growth?
- Do you attend company sponsored seminars?

8.16 CUSTOMER RELATIONS

- Do functional employees interface with customers.
- Do customers have direct access (communication, review, etc.) with functional employees.
- Can customers negotiate for project resources (based on past experience).
- Does the customer dictate or negotiate for project schedules (completion dates, test result dates, etc.).
- Does (or can) customer request special (non-contractual) projects — reports, computer programs, meetings, etc.
- If problems occur, are customers advised (about problems and solutions).
- Do customers want to know problem causes (personnel, equipment).
- Do customers deal with functional managers concerning employee performance (or lack of).
- Do customers influence project performance (test results, reports).
- Can customers deal with functional personnel or must they always deal through the project management group.
- Who controls customer relations with other company departments (law, finance, security, etc.)

- Do customers have different levels of support (development, production, maintenance) during project life.
- After project completion (after project personnel have been reassigned) if problems occur, can (or does) customer request (demand) original project personnel.
- Can customers alter company specifications (with regards to documentation standards, testing procedures written reports).
- Do project personnel (functional) negotiate with customers (about schedules, procedures, etc.).

8.17 UNDERSTANDING THE COMPANY

- Is individuality expressed here? Does the company encourage or discourage it?
- Does the company seem to lure the right kind of people? People compatible with the other employees?
- Is there an openness between employees?
- Do you feel you know and trust your supervisor? Your fellow employees? Your subordinates?
- Are policies and procedures stretched for the benefit of the employee?
- Do employees feel free to partake in healthy discussions with their supervisors?
- Do people seem to accomplish a lot more than people you have known in other jobs?
- Do you feel a sense of responsibility toward your job?
- Do you feel you are under stress?
- Does working here give you a sense of personal identity?
- Do you feel you have made a specific accomplishment?
- Are the top managers knowledgeable? Do you think the company is on the right course?
- Do you feel that the review procedures are fair?
- Are you permitted to provide your side of the story when you are reviewed? In what ways?
- Does your company ever rate the supervision? Do employees ever rate their supervisors? Has this caused changes?
- Would you relish the idea of having some fellow employees into your home? Your supervisor?
- Do you enjoy meeting your supervisors and peers at social functions outside of the company?
- Have your years here gradually improved your outlook towards the company? Decreased your opinion of it? No difference?
- If you could change one thing in the company, what would it be?

- Does the company look for innovative ideas in bad economic times or does it usually lay off?
- Would you recommend this company to your friends and relatives as a good place to work?
- Do you intend to stay with the company for a long time? Until you retire?
- Would you choose this company again if you were just entering the job market?
- Do you understand the company's cost saving policies? Do you agree with them?
- Diversification usually stabilizes jobs. Have you offered suggestions to the company for other products?
- Do you feel that this company is run better than most other companies? Worse than other companies? The best you have seen?

9

Detail Scheduling for In-House Control and Customer Presentations

9.0 INTRODUCTION

In Chapter five, we defined the steps involved in establishing a formal program plan with detailed schedules such that the total program can be effectively managed. Once the need has arisen to commit the plan to paper via the master program plan, suitable notations must be adapted. Any plan, schedule, drawing, or specification which will be read by more than one person must be regarded as a vehicle for the communication of information. If effective communication is to be established and maintained in compliance with the requirements, this information must be expressed in a language which is understood by all recipients.

The ideal situation is to construct charts and schedules in suitable notation that can be used for both in-house control and out-of-house customer status reporting. Unfortunately, this is easier said than done. Whenever a project has to be accomplished according to a time or date deadline, then both the customer and contractor must have an accurate picture of the relations between the time allowed and the time needed. Both the customer and contractor are interested mainly in the three vital control parameters:

- time
- cost
- performance

All schedules and charts should consider these three parameters and their relationship to corporate resources.

Information must be available such that proper project evaluation can be made. There are four methods for project evaluation:

- First-hand observation
- Oral and written reports

- Review and technical interchange meetings
- Graphical displays

First-hand observations are an excellent tool for obtaining non-filtered information. Many times, functional managers get a deep sense of pride when they see key project personnel observing work, provided that these personnel are, in fact, observing and not providing direction. First-hand observation may not be possible on large projects.

Although oral and written reports are a way of life, they often contain either too much or not enough detail. Significant information may be disguised. Most organizations do not have standardized reporting procedures, which further complicates the situation.

Review and technical interchange meetings provide face-to-face communications between all concerned parties, a situation which can often result in immediate agreement on problem definitions or solutions, such as changing a schedule. The difficult problem is in the selection of attendees from the customer's and the contractor's organizations.

Graphical displays are the prime means for tracking cost, schedule, and performance. Good graphics usually makes the information easy to identify. Unfortunately, not all information can be displayed, and quite often any additional information requests require additional cost and effort. Proper graphical displays can result in:

- Cutting project costs and reducing the time scale
- Coordinating and expediting planning
- Eliminating idle time
- Obtaining better scheduling and control of subcontractor activities
- Developing better trouble-shooting procedures
- Cutting time for routine decisions, but allowing more time for decision-making

9.1 CUSTOMER REPORTING

There exist between thirty and forty different visual methods for the representation of activities. The exact method chosen should depend upon the intended audience. For example, upper-level management may be interested in costs and integration of activities, with very little detail. Summary-type charts normally suffice for this purpose. Daily practitioners, on the other hand, may require that as much detail as possible be included in activity schedules. If the schedule is to be presented to the customer, then the representation should include cost and performance data.

The presentation of cost and performance data must be considered as both a science and an art. As a science, the figures and graphs should be describable in terms of symbols and expressions that are easily understandable. As an art, the diagram should rapidly bring across the intended message or objective. In many organizations, each department or division may have its own method of showing scheduling activities. Research and Development organizations prefer to show the logic of activities rather than the integration of activities that would normally be representative of a manufacturing plant.

The ability to communicate is a definite prerequisite for successful management of a program. Program review meetings, technical interchange meetings, customer summary meetings and in-house management control meetings all require different representative forms of current program performance status. The final form of the schedule may be bar charts, graphs, tables, bubble charts, or logic diagrams. In the sections which follow, a variety of charting techniques, together with the associated limitations, will be described for various types of a program. The reader should be able to realize the advantages and disadvantages of each chart in relation to his own program activities.

9.2 BAR (GANTT) CHART

The most common type of display is the bar or Gantt chart named for Henry Gantt who first utilized this procedure in the early 1900s. The bar chart is a means of displaying simple activities or events plotted against time or dollars. An activity represents the amount of work required to proceed from one point in time to another. Events are described as either the starting or ending point for either one or several activities.

Bar charts are most commonly used for exhibiting program progress or defining specific work required to accomplish an objective. Bar charts often include such items as listings of activities, activity durations, schedule dates, and progress-to-date. Figure 9-1 shows nine activities required to start up a production line for a new product. Each bar in the figure represents a single activity. Figure 9-1 is a typical bar chart which would be developed by the program office at program inception.

Bar charts are advantageous in that they are simple to understand and easy to change. They are the simplest and least complex means of portraying progress (or the lack of it) and can easily be expanded to identify those specific elements which may be either behind or ahead of schedule.

Bar charts provide only a vague description of how the entire program or project reacts as a system. There are three major discrepancies in the use of a bar chart. First, bar charts do not show the interdependencies of the activities, and therefore do not represent a "network" of activities. This relationship between activities is crucial for controlling program costs. Without this relationship, Bar charts have little predictive value. For example, does the long-lead procurement activity in Figure 9-1 require that the contract be signed before procurement can begin? Can the manufacturing plans be written without the material specifica-

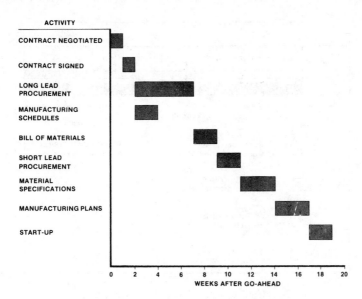

Figure 9-1. Bar Chart for Single Activities.

tions activity being completed? The second major discrepancy is that the bar chart cannot show the results of either an early or a late start in activities. How will a slippage of the manufacturing schedules activity in Figure 9-1 affect the completion date of the program? Can the manufacturing schedules activity begin two weeks later than shown and still serve as an input to the bill of materials activity? What will be the result of a crash program to complete activities in sixteen weeks after go-ahead instead of the originally planned nineteen weeks? Bar charts do not reflect true project status because elements behind schedule do not mean that the program or project is behind schedule. The third limitation is that the bar chart does not show the uncertainty involved in performing the activity and, therefore, does not readily admit itself to sensitivity analysis. For instance, what is the shortest time that an activity might take? What is the longest time? What is the average or expected time to activity completion?

Even with these limitations, bar charts do, in fact, serve as a useful tool for program analysis. Even the earliest form of bar chart, as developed by Henry Gantt, still has merit under certain circumstances. Figure 9-2 shows the conventional usage for work scheduled in a production facility for twelve days in January. On Thursday of the first week, the production facility was idle due to lack of materials. By the end of the work day on Friday of the first week, only 280 out of the planned 300 units were produced. The production line was not available on either Saturday or Sunday, and operations resumed Monday. On Tuesday, the production line was down for repairs and did not resume operations until Thursday. Operations were sporadic on Thursday and Friday, and by the end of the day, only 340 out

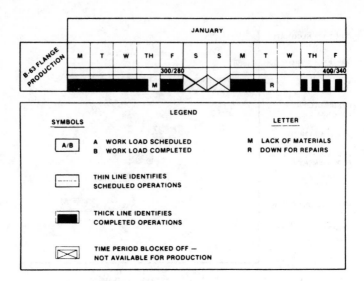

Figure 9-2. Manufacturing Schedule for Model B-63 Flanges.

of a scheduled 400 units were completed. These types of applications are commonly used for equipment layout and usage, department loading and progress tracking.[1]

Some of the limitations of bar charts can be overcome by combining single activities as shown in Figure 9-3. The weakness in this method is that the numbers

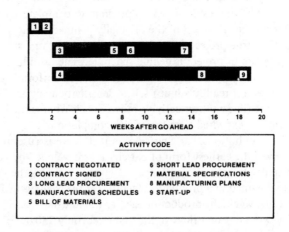

Figure 9-3. Bar Chart for Combined Activities.

---

1. A.C. Laufer, *Operations Management,* Cincinnati, SouthWestern Publishing Co., 1975, see pp. 106-108 for examples of Gantt charts and nomenclature.

representing each of the activities do not indicate whether or not this is the beginning or the end of the activity. Therefore, the numbers should represent events
rather than activities, together with proper identification. As before, no distinction is made as to whether event 2 must be completed prior to the start of event
3 or event 4. The chart also fails to clearly define the relationship between the
multiple activities on a single bar. For example, must event 3 be completed prior
to event 5? Often, combined activity bar charts can be converted to milestone
bar charts by placing small triangles at strategic location in the bars to indicate
completion of certain milestones within each activity or grouping of activities as
shown in Figure 9-4. The exact definition of a milestone differs from company
to company, but usually implies some point where major activity either begins
or ends, or cost data becomes critical.

Bar charts can be converted to partial interrelationship charts by indicating
(with arrows) the order in which activities must be performed. Figure 9-5 represents the partial interrelationship of the activities shown in Figures 9-1 and 9-3.

The most common method of presenting data to both in-house management
and the customer is through the use of bar charts. Care must be taken so as not
to make the figures overly complex such that more than one interpretation can
exist. A great deal of information and color can be included in bar charts. Figure
9-6 shows a grouped bar chart for comparison of three projects performed during
different years. Care must be taken when using different shading techniques that
each area is easily definable and that no major contrast between shaded areas
exists except for possibly the current project. When grouped bars appear on one
chart, non-shaded bars should be avoided. Each bar should have some sort of
shading, whether it be cross-hatched or color-coded.

Contrasting shaded to non-shaded areas is normally used for comparing projected progress to actual progress as shown in Figure 9-7. The tracking date line
indicates the time when the cost data/performance data was analyzed. Project 1
is behind schedule, project 2 is ahead of schedule and project 3 is on target. Unfortunately, the upper portion of Figure 9-7 does not indicate the costs attributed
to the status of the three projects. By plotting the total program costs against

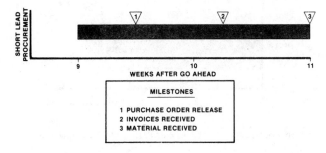

Figure 9-4. Bar/Milestone Chart.

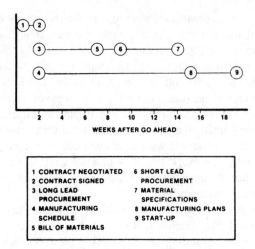

Figure 9-5. Partial Inter-relationship Chart.

the same time axis (as shown in Figure 9-7) a comparison between cost and performance can be made. From the upper section of Figure 9-7 it is impossible to tell the current program cost position. From the lower section, however, it becomes evident that the program is heading for a cost overrun, possibly due to project 1. It is generally acceptable to have the same shading technique represent different situations provided that clear separation between the shaded regions appears, as in Figure 9-7.

Another common means for comparing activities or projects is through the use of step arrangement bar charts. Figure 9-8 shows a step arrangement bar chart for a cost percentage breakdown of the five projects included within a program.

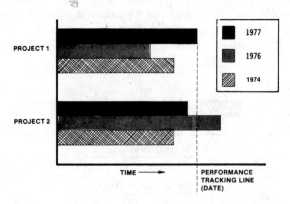

Figure 9-6. Grouped Bar Chart For Performance Comparison.

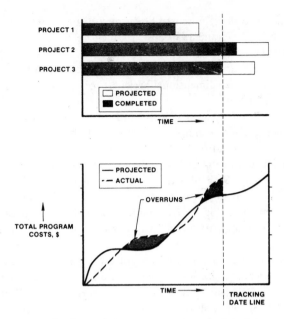

Figure 9-7. Cost And Performance Tracking Schedule.

Figure 9-8 can also be used for tracking, by shading in certain portions of the steps which identify each project. This is not normally done, however, since this type of step arrangement tends to indicate that each step must be completed before the next step can begin.

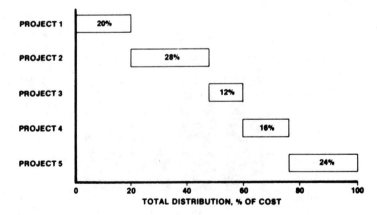

Figure 9-8. Step Arrangement Bar Chart For Total Cost As A Percentage Of The Five Program Projects.

Bar charts need not be represented horizontally. Figure 9-9 indicates the comparison between the 1975 and 1977 costs for the total program and raw materials. Again, care must be taken so as to make proper use of shading techniques. Three-dimensional vertical bar charts are often the most beautiful to behold. Figure 9-10 shows a typical three-dimensional bar chart for direct and indirect labor and material cost breakdowns.

Bar charts can be made quite colorful and appealing to the eye by combining them with other graphic techniques. Figure 9-11 shows a qualitative-pictorial Bar chart for the distribution of total program costs. Figure 9-12 shows the same cost distribution in Figure 9-11, but represented with the commonly used pie technique. Figure 9-13 illustrates how two quantitative bar charts can be used side by side to create a quick comparison. The right-hand side shows the labor hour percentages. Figure 9-13 works best if the scale of each axis is the same, otherwise the comparisons may appear distorted when, in fact, they are not.

The figures shown in this section are some of those previously used by the author for customer interchange meetings and do not, by any means, represent the only method of presenting data in bar chart format. Several other methods exist, some of which will be shown in the sections which follow.

9.3 OTHER CONVENTIONAL PRESENTATION TECHNIQUES

Bar charts serve as a useful tool for presenting data at technical meetings. Unfortunately, programs must be won competitively or organized in-house before

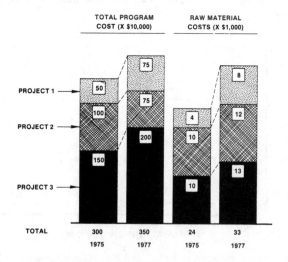

Figure 9-9. 1975 Vs 1977 Cost Comparison.

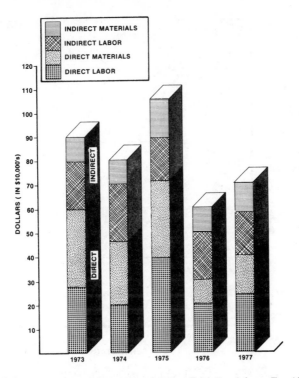

Figure 9-10. Direct and Indirect Material and Labor Costs Breakdown For All Programs Per Year.

technical meeting presentations can be made. Competitive proposals or in-house project requests should contain descriptive figures and charts, not necessarily representing activities, but showing either planning, organizing, tracking or technical procedures designed for the current program or used previously on other programs. Proposals generally contain figures which require either some interpolation or extrapolation. Figure 9-14 shows the breakdown of total program costs. Although this figure would also normally require interpretation, a monthly cost table accompanies it. If the table is not too extensive, then the table can be included with the figure. This is shown in Figure 9-15. During proposal activities, the actual and cumulative delivery columns, as well as the dotted line in Figure 9-15, would be omitted, but would be included after updating for use in technical interchange meetings. It is normally a good practice to use previous figures and tables whenever possible because management becomes accustomed to the manner in which data is presented.

Another commonly used technique is schematic models. Organizational charts are schematic models which depict the interrelationships between individuals,

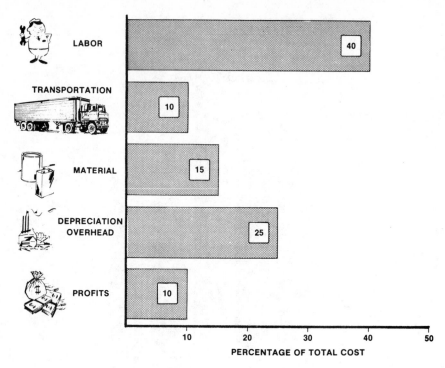

Figure 9-11. Total Program Cost Distribution (Quantitative-Pictorial Bar Chart).

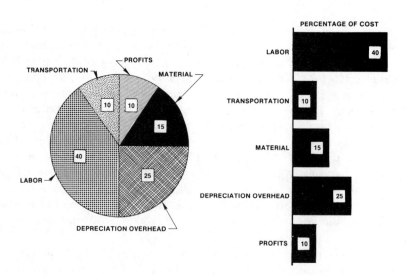

Figure 9-12. Distribution Of The Program Dollar.

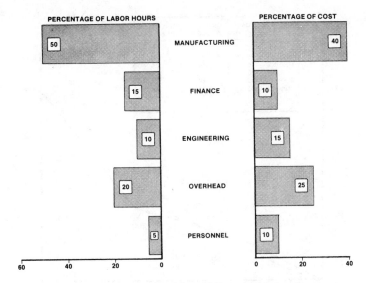

Figure 9-13. Divisional Breakdown Of Costs And Labor Hours.

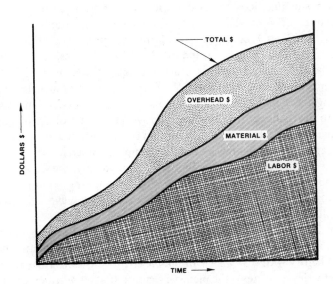

Figure 9-14. Total Program Cost Breakdown.

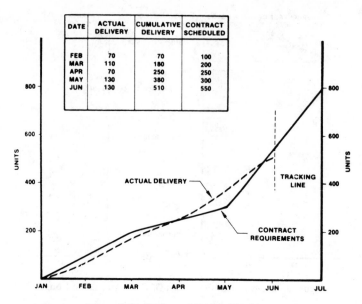

DATE	ACTUAL DELIVERY	CUMULATIVE DELIVERY	CONTRACT SCHEDULED
FEB	70	70	100
MAR	110	180	200
APR	70	250	250
MAY	130	380	300
JUN	130	510	550

Figure 9-15. Delivery Schedule Tracking.

organizations or functions within an organization. One organizational chart normally cannot suffice for describing total program interrelationships. Figure 4-1 identified the Midas Program in relation to other programs within Dalton Corporation. The Midas Program is indicated by the bold lines. The program manager for the Midas Program was placed at the top of the column, even though his program may have the lowest priority. Each major unit of management for the Midas Program should be placed as close as possible to top-level management to indicate to the customer the "implied" relative importance of the program.

Another type of schematic representation is the work flow chart, synonymous with the applications of flowcharting for computer programming. Flow charts are designed to describe, either symbolically or pictorially, the sequence of events required to complete an activity. Figure 9-16 shows the logic flow for production of molding VZ-3. The symbols shown in Figure 9-16 are universally accepted by several industries.

Pictorial representation, although often a costly procedure, can add color and quality to any proposal. Pictorial sketches provide the customer with a document easier to identify with than a logic or bubble chart. Customers may request tours during activities to relate to the pictorial figures. If at all possible, program management should avoid pictorial representation of activities which may be closed off to customer viewing, possibly due to security or safety.

Block diagrams can also be used to describe the flow of activities. Figures 4-2 and 4-3 are examples of block diagrams. Block diagrams can be used to show

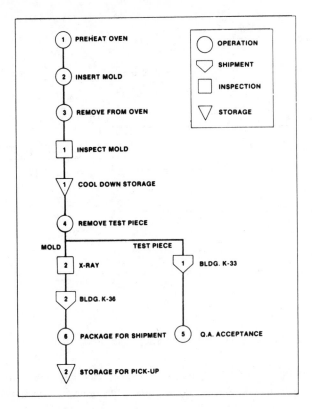

Figure 9-16. Logic Flow For Production of Molding VZ-3.

how information is distributed throughout an organization or how a process or activity is assembled. Figure 9-17 shows the testing matrix for propellant samples. Figures similar to this are developed when tours are scheduled during the production or testing phase of a program. Figure 9-17 shows the customer, not only where the testing will take place, but what tests will be conducted.

Block diagrams, schematics, pictorials, and logic flows all fulfill a necessary need for describing the wide variety of activities within a company. The figures and charts are more than descriptive techniques. They can also provide management with the necessary tools for decision making.

9.4 LOGIC DIAGRAMS/NETWORKS

Probably the most difficult figure to construct is the logic diagram. Logic diagrams are developed to illustrate the inductive and deductive reasoning necessary to achieve some objective within a given time frame. The major difficulty in de-

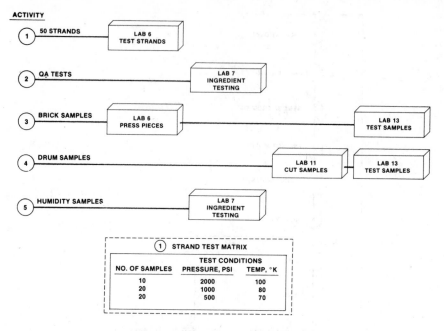

Figure 9-17. Propellant Samples Testing Matrix.

veloping logic diagrams is the inability to answer such key questions as: What happens if something goes wrong? Can I quantify any part of the diagram's major elements?

Logic diagrams are constructed similar to bar charts on the supposition that nothing will go wrong, and are usually accompanied by detailed questions, possibly in a checklist format, which require answering. The following questions would be representative of those which might accompany a logic diagram for a research and development project:

- What documentation is released to start the described activity and possibly the elements within each activity?
- What information is required before this documentation can be released? (i.e., What prior activities must be completed, work designed, studies finalized, etc.?)
- What are the completion or success criteria for the activity?
- What are the alternatives for each phase of the program if success is not achieved?
- What other activities are directly dependent on the result of this activity?
- What other activities or inputs are required to perform this activity?

- What are the key decision points, if any, during the activity?
- What documentation signifies completion of the activity? (i.e., report, drawing, etc.)
- What management approval is required for final documentation?

These types of questions are applicable to many other forms of data presentation, not necessarily logic diagrams.

Appendix A
A Project Management/
Systems Management
Bibliography

1. Abt Associates Inc., *Applications of Systems Analysis Models: A Survey.* Washington, D.C.: Technology Utilization Division, Office of Technology Utilization, National Aeronautics and Space Administration, 1968.
2. Ackoff, Russell Lincoln, and Emery, Fred E., *On Purposeful Systems.* Chicago: Aldine /Atherton, 1972.
3. Ackoff, Russell Lincoln, *Redesigning the Future: A Systems Approach to Societal Problems.* New York: John Wiley, 1974.
4. Alderfer, Clayton P., *Change Processes in Organizations.* New Haven, Connecticut, Department of Administrative Sciences, Yale University, 1971.
5. Allen, Louis A., *The Professional Manager's Guide,* (USA: Louis A. Allen Associates, 1969).
6. Anthony, Robert N. Planning and Control Systems: *A Framework for Analysis.* Boston: Division of Research, Graduate School of Business Administration, Harvard University, 1965.
7. Archibald, Russell D. *Managing High-Technology Programs and Projects.* New York: John Wiley, 1976. pp. 55, 82, 176, 191.
8. Argyris, Chris, "How Tomorrow's Executives Will Make Decisions," *Think,* 33, 18-23, (November-December, 1967).
9. Argyris, Chris, "Resistance to Rational Management Systems," *Innovation,* issue 10: (1969), pp. 28-42.
10. Argyris, Chris, "Today's Problems with Tomorrow's Organizations," *Journal of Management Studies* 4: (February, 1967), pp. 31-55.
11. ARINC Research Corporation. *Guidebook for Systems Analysis/Cost Effectiveness.* Washington, D.C.: U.S. Department of Commerce, National Bureau of Standards; distributed by Clearinghouse for Federal Scientific and Technical Information, 1969.
12. Association for Systems Management. *An Annotated Bibliography for the Systems Professional.* 2nd ed. Cleveland: Association for Systems Management, 1970.
13. Avots, Ivars, "Why Does Project Management Fail?" *California Management Review* 12 (Fall, 1969), pp. 77-82.
14. Avots, Ivars, "Making Project Management Work: The Right Tools For the Wrong Project Manager," *S.A.M. Advanced Management Journal,* 40, 20-26, (Autumn, 1975).

15. Bachman, J., *et al.,* "Bases of Supervisory Power: A Comparative Study in Five Organizational Settings," in *Control in Organizations,* A. Tannenbaum, ed. New York, McGraw-Hill, 1968, pp. 229-238.
16. Baker, Frank, ed. *Organizational Systems; General Systems Approaches to Complex Organizations* Homewood, Illinois, R.D. Irwin Series in Management and the Behavioral Sciences, 1973.
17. Barnes, Lewis B., "Project Management and the Use of Authority: A Study of Structure, Role, and Influence Relationships in Public and Private Organizations," Ph.D. Dissertation, University of Southern California, 1971.
18. Baumgartner, John Stanley, *Project Management,* Homewood, Illinois, R.D. Irwin series, 1963.
19. Beckett, John A., *Management Dynamics: The New Synthesis.* New York: McGraw-Hill, 1971.
20. Benne, K.D. and Birnbaum, M., "Principles of Changing" in *The Planning of Change,* New York, Holt, Rinehart, and Winston, 1969.
21. Bennigson, Lawrence, "The Team Approach to Project Management," *Management Review* 61, (January 1972), pp. 48-52.
22. Benningson, Lawrence, *Project Management,* New York: McGraw-Hill, 1970.
23. Bennis Warren G., "The Coming Death of Bureaucracy." *Think* 32: 30-35, (November-December 1966).
24. Benton, John Breen, *Managing the Organizational Decision Process,* Lexington, Mass, Lexington Books, 1973.
25. Berlinski, David J., "On Systems Analysis: An Essay Concerning the Limitations of some Mathematical Methods in the Social, Political, and Biological Sciences," Cambridge, Mass., M.I.T. Press, 1976.
26. Berrien, F. Kenneth, *General and Social Systems,* New Brunswick, N.J., Rutgers University Press, 1968.
27. Bertalanffy, Ludwig von, *General Systems Theory; Foundations, Development, Applications,* New York, G. Braziller, 1972.
28. ——,*General Systems Theory,* New York, G. Braziller, 1968.
29. Bingham, John E., and Davies, G.W.P. *A Handbook of Systems Analysis.* London, Macmillan, © 1972, 1974. Distributed in North America by Halsted Press, a division of John Wiley, New York and Toronto.
30. Blake, R.R. and Mouton, J.S., *The Managerial Grid,* Houston: Gulf Publishing, 1964.
31. Blankstein, Charles Sidney, "The Base Level Development Assistance Project: A Managerial Perspective," 1972. Cambridge, Mass: M.I.T., Thesis, M.S.
32. Block, Ellery B. "Accomplishment/Cost: Better Project Control." *Harvard Business Review* 49: (May 1971), pp. 110-24.
33. Bobrowski, T.M., "A Basic Philosophy of Project Management," *Journal of Systems Management,* May-June 1974.
34. Boulding, Kenneth, "General Systems Theory—The Skeleton of Science," *Management Science,* (April 1956), pp. 197-208.
35. Bowman, R.R., "An Analysis of Project Management Concepts in the Missile/Space Industry," MBA Thesis, Utah State University, 1967.
36. Boyatzis, R.E., "Building Efficacy: An Effective Use of Managerial Power," *Industrial Management Review,* 11, 1: 65-75, 1969.
37. ——, "Leadership: The Effective Use of Power", *Management of Personnel Quarterly,* Graduate School of Business Administration, University of Michigan (Fall, 1971), pp. 21-25. Reprinted in Richards, Max D., and William A. Nielander, *Readings in Management,* fourth edition, (Cincinnati, Southwestern Publishing Co., 1974), pp. 623-629.

38. Brandon, Dick H., and Gray, Max, *Project Control Standards,* Princeton, Brandon/Systems Press, 1970.
39. Burke, R.J., "Methods of Resolving Interpersonal Conflict," *Personnel Administration,* July-August, 1969, pp. 48-55.
40. ——, "Methods of Managing Superior-Subordinate Conflict," *Canadian Journal of Behavioral Science,* 2, 2: 124-135, 1970.
41. Burke, W.W. and Hornstein, H.A., *The Social Technology of Organization Development.* Fairfax, Virginia, NTL Learning Resources Corporation, 1972.
42. Burt, David N., "Getting the Right Price With the Right Contract," *Management Review* 24-34, (May, 1976).
43. Butler, Arthur G., Jr., "Project Management: A Study in Organizational Conflict," *Academy of Management Journal* 16, 84-101, (March, 1973).
44. ——, "Behavioral Implications for Professional Employees of Structural Conflict Associated with Project Management in Functional Organizations." Ph.D. Dissertation, University of Florida, 1969.
45. Butler, D., and Miller, N, "Power to Reward and Punish in Social Interaction," *Journal of Experimental Social Psychology,* 1, 4: 311-322, 1965.
46. Cicero, John P., and Wilemon, David L, "Project Authority: A Multidimensional View," *IEEE Transactions on Engineering Management,* EM-17: 52-57, (May 1970).
47. Chapman, Richard L. *Project Management in NASA; the System and the Men,* Washinton: Scientific and Technical Information Office, National Aeronautics and Space Administration; for sale by the Superintendent of Documents, U.S. Government Printing Office, 1973.
48. Chen, Gordon K., and Kaczka, Eugene E, *Operations and Systems Analysis; A Simulation Approach,* Boston, Allyn and Bacon, 1974.
49. Churchman, Charles West, *The Systems Approach,* New York, Dell Publishing Company, 1968.
50. Cleland, David I, "Organizational Dynamics of Project Management," *IEEE Transactions on Engineering Management,* EM-13: 201-5, (December, 1966).
51. ——, "The Deliberate Conflict," *Business Horizon,* 11, 1: 78-80, (1968).
52. ——, "Project Management in Industry: An Assessment," *Project Management Quarterly,* 5, 2, 3: 19-21, (1974).
53. ——, "Defining A Project Management System," *Project Management Quarterly,* 8, 4: 37-40, (1977).
54. ——, "Why Project Management?" *Business Horizons,* 7: 81-88, (Winter, 1964),
55. Cleland, David I., and King, William R. *Management: A Systems Approach.* New York, McGraw-Hill, 1972.
56. ——, *Systems Analysis and Project Management,* New York, McGraw-Hill, 1968.
57. ——, *Systems Analysis and Project Management,* New York, McGraw-Hill, 1975. pp. 271, 371-380.
58. ——, *Systems, Organizations, Analysis, Management: A Book of Readings,* New York, McGraw-Hill, 1969.
59. Couger, J. Daniel, and Knapp, Robert W., (eds.) *System Analysis Techniques.* New York, John Wiley, 1974.
60. Crowston, Wallace B., "Models for Project Management," *Sloan Management Review,* 12: pp. 25-42, (Spring, 1971).
61. Cullingford, G. and Prideaux, J.D.C.A., "A Variational Study of Optimal Resource Profiles," *Management Science* 19: 1067-81, (May, 1973).
62. Dahl, R., "The Concept of Power," *Behavioral Science,* 2: 201-215, (July, 1957).

63. Datz, Marvin A. and Wilby, L.R., "What Is Good Project Management?" *Project Management Quarterly, 8,* 1: (March 1977).

64. Davis, Keith, "The Role of Project Management In Scientific Manufacturing,"*Arizona Business Bulletin* 9: (May 1962), pp. 1-8.

65. ——, "The Role of Project Management in Scientific Manufacturing." *IRE Transactions on Engineering Management, 9,* 3, (1962).

66. Davis, S., "An Organic Problem-Solving Method of Organizational Change," *Jouranl of Applied Behavioral Science,* 3-21, (January, 1967).

67. Davis, Stanley, "Two Models of Organization: Unity of Command Versus Balance of Power," *Sloan Management Review,* (Fall, 1974), pp. 29-40.

68. Davis, S.M., and Lawrence, P.R., *Matrix,* Reading, Mass, Addison-Wesley, 1977.

69. De Greene, Kenyon Brenton, *Sociotechnical Systems: Factors in Analysis, Design, and Management.* Englewood Cliffs, N.J., Prentice-Hall, 1973.

70. ——, (ed.) *Systems Psychology,* New York: McGraw-Hill, 1970.

71. Delbecq, André L., Schull, Fremont A., Filley, Alan C., and Grimes, Andrew J.,*Matrix Organization: A Conceptual Guide to Organizational Variation,* Wisconsin Business Papers No. 2. Madison, University of Wisconsin, Bureau of Business Research and Service, 1969.

72. Delbecq, André L., and Filley, Alan C. *Program and Project Management in a Matrix Organization: A Case Study,* Madison, University of Wisconsin, Bureau of Business Research and Service, 1974.

73. Dibble, E.T. and Suojanen, Waino, "Project Management in a Crisis Economy," *Infosystems-Spectrum,* 23: 44-46, (January, 1976).

74. Doering, Robert D., "An Approach Toward Improving the Creative Output of Scientific Task Teams," *IEEE Transactions on Engineering Management,* EM-20: 29-31, (February, 1973).

75. Earle, V.H., "Once Upon a Matrix: A Hindsight on Participation,"*Optimum* 4, 28-36, 1973.

76. Eirich, Peter Lee, "An Information System Design Analysis for a Research Organization." Cambridge, Mass., M.I.T. M.S. Thesis, 1974.

77. Emery, F.E., *Systems Thinking: Selected Readings.* New York, Penguin Eduction, 1974.

78. Emery, J.C., *Organizational Planning and Control Systems,* New York, Macmillan, 1969.

79. Emshoff, James R., *Analysis of Behavioral Systems,* New York, Macmillan, 1971.

80. *European Conference on the Management of Large Space Programs,* (Paris, 1970), New York, Gordon and Breach Science Publishers, 1971.

81. Evan, W.M., "Conflict and Performance in R & D Organization," *Industrial Management Review, 7:* 37-45, (1965).

82. Evan, W.M., "Superior-Subordinate Conflict in Research Organizations," *Administrative Science Quarterly,* 52-64, (July, 1965).

83. Exton, William, *The Age of Systems: The Human Dilemma.* New York, American Management Association, 1972.

84. Fiore, Michael V., "Out of the Frying Pan into the Matrix," *Personnel Administration* 33, 3: 4-7, (1970).

85. Fisher, Gene Harvey, *Cost Considerations in Systems Analysis,* New York, American Elsevier, 1971.

86. Fitzgerald, John M. and Ardra F., *Fundamentals of Systems Analysis,* New York, Wiley, 1973.

87. Flaks, Marvin, and Archibald, Russell D., "The EE's Guide to Project Management," *Electronic Engineer* 27: 28+ (April, 1968); 20+ (May); 27-32 (June); 33-34+ (July); 33+ (August).

88. Forrester, Jay W., "A New Corporate Design," *Industrial Management Review* 7 5-17 (Fall, 1965).

89. Frankwicz, Michael J., "A Study of Project Management Techniques," *Journal of Systems Management* 24: 18-22, (October, 1973).

90. French, J.R., Jr., and Raven, B. "The Bases of Social Power," in *Studies in Social Power*, D. Cartwright, (ed.), Ann Arbor, Mich.: Research Center for Group Dynamics, 1959, pp. 150-165.

91. Fried, Louis. "Don't Smother Your Project in People," *Management Advisor* 9: 46-49, (March, 1972).

92. Friend, Fred L., "Be A More Effective Program Manager," *Journal of Systems Management*, 27: 6-9, (February, 1976).

93. Fuller, R. Buckminster, *Synergetics: Explorations in the Geometry of Thinking.* New York, Macmillan, 1975.

94. Gaddis, P.O., "The Project Manager," *Harvard Business Review*, May-June, 89-97, (1959).

95. Galbraith, Jay R., "Matrix Organization Designs—How to Combine Functional and Project Forms," *Business Horizons*, February, 1971.

96. Geisler, M.A., "How to Plan for Management in New Systems," *Harvard Business Review*, September-October, 1962.

97. Gemmill, G., "Managerial Role Mapping," *The Management Personnel Quarterly*, 8, 3: 13-19, (Fall, 1969).

98. Gemmill, G., and H. Thamhain, "The Power Styles of Project Managers: Some Efficiency Correlates," *20th Annual JEMC, Managing for Improved Engineering Effectiveness* (Atlanta, Ga., Oct. 30-31, 1972), pp. 89-96.

99. Gemmill, G.R. and Thamhain, H.J., "Project Performance as a Function of the Leadership Styles of Project Managers: Results of a Field Study," *Convention Digest, 4th Annual Meeting of the Project Management Institute*, Philadelphia, October 18-21, 1972.

100. ——, "Influence Styles of Project Managers: Some Project Performance Correlates," *Academy of Management Journal*, 17, 2: pp. 216-224, (June, 1974).

101. Gemmill, Gary, and Thamhain, Hans J., "The Effectiveness of Different Power Styles of Project Managers in Gaining Project Support," *IEEE Transactions on Engineering Management* EM-20, 38-44, (May, 1973).

102. ——, "Interpersonal Power in Temporary Management Systems," *Journal of Management Studies*, (October, 1971).

103. ——, and Wilemon, David L., "The Power Spectrum in Project Management," *Sloan Management Review* 12: pp. 15-25, (Fall, 1970).

104. Gemmill, Gary and David Wilemon, "The Product Manager as an Influence Agent," *Journal of Marketing*, 36: 26-31, (January, 1972).

105. Gibson, James L., (ed.) *Readings in Organizations: Structure, Processes, Behavior*, Dallas, Business Publication, 1973.

106. Gildersleeve, Thomas R., *Data Processing Project Management*, New York, Van Nostrand Reinhold, 1974.

107. Gill, P.G., *Systems Management Techniques for Builders and Contractors*, New York, McGraw-Hill, 1968.

108. Goggin, William C., "How the Multidimensional Structure Works at Dow Corning," *Harvard Business Review*, pp. 54-65, (January-February 1974).

109. Goodman, Richard A. "Ambiguous Authority Definitions in Project Management," *Academy of Management Journal* 10: 395-408, (December, 1967).

110. Goodman, Richard A., "Organizational Preference in Research and Development," *Human Relations* 23: 279-298, 1970.

111. Goodman, R., "Ambiguous Authority Definition in Project Management," *Academy of Management Journal,* 10 395-407, (1967).

112. Grinnell, S.K., and Apple, H.P., "When Two Bosses are Better than One," *Machine Design,* 9: 84-87, (January, 1975).

113. Grimes, A., S. Klein, and F. Shull, "Matrix Model: A Selective Empirical Test," *Academy of Management Journal,* 15, 1: 9-31, (March, 1972).

114. Gross, Paul F., *Systems Analysis and Design for Management,* New York, Dun-Donnelley, 1976.

115. Gullet, C. Ray, "Personnel Management in the Project Organization," *Personnel Administration and Public Personnel Review* 1 17-22, (November, 1972).

116. Hall, D.M., *Management of Human Systems,* Cleveland, Ohio: Association for Systems Management, 1971.

117. Hall, H. Lawrence, "Management: A Continuum of Styles," *S.A.M. Advanced Management Journal* 33: pp. 68-74, (January, 1968).

118. Hansen, J.J., "The Case of the Precarious Program," *Harvard Business Review,* (January-February, 1968).

119. Center For, Health Research, "Health Research: The Systems Approach," New York, Springer, 1976.

120. Hellriegel, Don and John W. Slocum, Jr., "Organizational Design: A Contingency Approach," *Business Horizons,* 16, 2: pp. 59-68, (April 1, 1973). Reprinted in Richards, Max. D., and William A. Nielander, *Readings in Management,* fourth edition, (Cincinnati, Southwestern, 1974), pp. 516-527.

121. Hersey, Paul, and Blanchard, K.H., "The Management of Change," *Training and Development Journal,* 26, 1: (January, 1972); 26, 2: (February, 1972); and 26, 3: (March, 1972).

122. Hlavacik, James D., and Thompson, Victor A. "Bureaucracy and New Product Innovation," *Academy of Management Journal* 16: 361-72, (September, 1973).

123. Hodgetts, Richard M. "An Interindustry Analysis of Certain Aspects of Project Management," Ph.D. dissertation, University of Oklahoma, 1968.

124. ——, "Leadership Techniques in the Project Organization," *Academy of Management Journal* 11: 211-19, (June, 1968).

125. Hoge, R.R. "Research and Development Project Management: Techniques for Guiding Technical Programmes Towards Corporate Objectives," *Radio and Electronic Engineer* 39: pp. 33-48, (January, 1970).

126. Holland, Ted, "What Makes a Project Manager?" *Engineering* 207 262, (February 14, 1969).

127. Hoos, Ida Russakoff, *Systems Analysis in Public Policy; A Critique,* Berkeley, University of California Press, 1972.

128. Hopeman, Richard J., *Systems Analysis and Operations Management,* Columbus, Ohio, Merrill, 1969.

129. Hopeman, R.J. and D.L. Wilemon, *Project Management/Systems Management-Concepts and Applications,* Syracuse, Syracuse University/NASA, 1973.

130. Horowitz, J., *Critical Path Scheduling—Management Control Through CPM and PERT,* New York, Roland Press, 1967.

131. Houre, Henry Ronald, *Project Management Using Network Analysis,* New York, McGraw-Hill, 1973.

132. Hynes, Cecil V., "Taking a Look at the Request For Proposal," *Defense Management Journal,* (October, 1977), pp. 26-31.

133. International Congress for Project Planning by Network Analysis, *Project Planning by Network Analysis,* Amsterdam, North-Holland Publishing Company, 1969.

134. Ivancevich, J., and J. Donnelly, "Leader Influence and Performance," *Personal Psychology,* 23: 539-549, (1970).

135. Jacobs, Richard A., "Project Management—A New Style For Success," *S.A.M. Advanced Management Journal,* 41: (Autumn 1976), pp. 4-14.

136. ——, "Putting Management Into Project Management," Paper presented at A.S.M. Workshops in Detroit, Tulsa, Oakland and Las Vegas (1976).

137. Janger, Allen R., "Anatomy of the Project Organization," *Business Management Record,* 12-18, (November, 1963).

138. Jantsh, Erich, *Design for Evolution; Self-Organization and Planning in the Life of Human Systems.* New York, G. Braziller, 1975.

139. Jenett, E., "Guidelines for Successful Project Management," *Chemical Engineering,* 70-82, (July 9, 1973).

140. Johnson, James R., "Advanced Project Control," *Journal of Systems Management,* 24-27, (May, 1977).

141. Johnson, Marvin M., (ed.) *Simulation Systems for Manufacturing Industries,* La Jolla, California: The Society for Simulation, Simulation Councils Inc., 1973.

142. Johnson, Richard Arvid, Newell, William T., and Vergin, Roger C., *Operations Management; A Systems Concept,* Boston, Houghton-Mifflin, 1972.

143. Johnson, R.A., Kast, F.E., and Rosenzweig, J.E., *The Theory and Management of Systems,* New York, McGraw-Hill, 1973.

144. Jonason, Per, "Project Management, Swedish Style," *Harvard Business Review,* 104-109, (Nov/December, 1971).

145. Kahn, R.L., Wolfe, D.M., Quinn, R.P., Snock, J.D., and Rosenthal, R.A., *Organizational Stress: Studies in Role Conflict and Ambiguity,* New York, John Wiley, 1964.

146. Kast, Fremont E., and Rosenzweig, James E. "Organization and management of Space Programs," in *On Advances in Space Science and Technology,* edited by Frederick I. Ordway III, New York, Academic Press, 1965.

147. ——, *Organization and Management; A Systems Approach.* 2nd ed. New York, McGraw-Hill, 1974.

148. Kast, F.E. and Rosenzweig, J.E. *Contingency Views of Organization and Management,* Science Research Associates, 1973.

149. Kast, D. "The Motivational Basis of Organizational Behavior," *Behavioral Science,* 9, 2: 131-143, (1964).

150. Kelleher, Grace J., (ed.) *The Challenge to Systems Analysis: Public Policy and Change,* New York, Wiley-Interscience, 1970.

151. Kelley, William F., *Management Through Systems and Procedures: A Systems Concept,* New York, 1969.

152. Kerzner, Harold, "Systems Management and the Engineer," *Journal of Systems Management,* 18-21, (October, 1977).

153. Killian, William P., "Project Management—Future Organizational Concepts," *Marquette Business Review* 2: 90-107, (1971).

154. Kindred, Alton R., *Data Systems and Management: An Introduction to Systems Analysis and Design,* Englewood Cliffs, N.J., Prentice-Hall, 1973.

155. Kingdon, Donald R., "The Management of Complexity in a Matrix Organization: A Socio-Technical Approach to Changing Organizational Behavior," Los Angeles, University of California, M.S. thesis, 1969.

156. ——, *Matrix Organization: Managing Information Technologies,* London, Tavistock Publications, 1973.

157. Kirchner, Englebert, "The Project Manager." *Space Aeronautics,* 43: 56-64, (February, 1965).

158. Klir, George J., *Trends in General Systems Theory,* New York: John Wiley, 1972.

159. Koplow, Richard A., "From Engineer to Manager—And Back Again," *IEEE Transactions on Engineering Management,* EM-14: 88-92, (June, 1967).

160. Larsen, Niels Ove, "An Evaluation of Managerial Strategies for Dealing with Work Pressure in a Project Oriented Environment," Ph.D. dissertation, M.I.T., Alfred P. Sloan School of Management, 1969.

161. Laszlo, Ervin, *A Strategy for the Future: The Systems Approach to World Order,* New York, G. Braziller, 1974.

162. Lawrence, Paul R. and Lorsch, Jay W., "New Management Job: The Integrator," *Harvard Business Review,* 142, (November/December, 1967).

163. Lawrence, P.R. and Lorsch, J.W., *Organization and Environment,* Boston, Division of Research, Harvard Business School, 1967.

164. Lazer R. G., and A.G. Kellner, "Personnel and Organizational Development in an R and D Matrix-Overlay Operation," *IEEE Transactions on Engineering Management,* EM-11: 78-82, (June, 1964).

165. Ler, Alec M., *Systems Analysis Frameworks,* New York, Wiley, 1970.

166. Lewin, K., "Frontiers in Group Dynamics," *Human Relations,* 1. 1, (1947).

167. Lewin, K., "Group Decision and Social Change," in Maccoby, E.E., *et al., Readings in Social Psychology,* New York: Holt, Rinehart, and Winston, 1958, pp. 197-211.

168. Livingstone, G.S. "Weapon System Contracting," *Harvard Business Review,* (July-August, 1959).

169. Lock, D., *Project Management,* London, Gower Press, 1969.

170. Logistics Management Institute, *Introduction to Military Program Management,* Washington, D.C.: Superintendent of Documents, U.S. Government Printing Office, 1971.

171. London, Keith R., *The People Side of Systems: The Human Aspects of Computer Systems,* New York, McGraw-Hill, 1976.

172. Ludwig, Ernest E., *Applied Project Management for the Process Industries,* Houston, Texas, Gulf Publishing Company, 1974.

173. Lutes, Gerald Scott, "Project Selection and Scheduling in the Massachusetts Department of Public Works," M.S. Thesis M.I.T. Alfred P. Sloan School of Management, 1974.

174. McGregor, D., *The Professional Manager,* New York, McGraw-Hill, 1967.

175. McMillan, Claude, and Gonzalez, Richard F., *Systems Analysis: A Computer Approach to Decision Models,* Irwin, Homewood, Ill., 1973.

176. Maieli, Vincent, "Management by Hindsight: Diary of a Project Manager," *Management Review,* 60: 4-14, (June, 1971).

177. ——, "Sowing the Seeds of Project Cost Overruns," *Management Review,* 61: 7-14, (August, 1972).

178. Maier, N.R., and Hoffman, L.R., "Acceptance and Quality of Solutions as Related to Leader's Attitudes Toward Disagreement in Group Problem Solving," *Journal of Applied Behavioral Science,* 373-386, (1965).

179. Marquis, D.G., and Straight, Jr., D.M., "Organizational Factors in Project Performance," Working Paper pp. 133-65, Cambridge, M.I.T., School of Management, 1965.

180. Martin, Charles C., *Project Management: How to Make It Work,* New York, Amacom, 1976, pp. 41, 137.

181. Martin, James Thomas, *Systems Analysis for Data Transmission,* Englewood Cliffs, Prentice-Hall, 1972.
182. Martino, R.L., *Project Management,* Wayne, Pa., MDI Publications, Management Development Institute, 1968.
183. ——, *Resources Management.* Wayne, Pa., MDI Publications, Management Development Institute, 1968.
184. Matthies, Leslie H., *The Management Systems: Systems are People,* New York, Wiley, 1976.
185. Mechanic, D., "Sources of Power of Lower Participants in Complex Organizations," *Administrative Science Quarterly,* 7: 349-364, (December, 1962).
186. Mee, John F., "Project Management," *Business Horizons* 6: 53-55, (Fall, 1963).
187. ——, "Matrix Organization," *Business Horizons,* 70, (Summer, 1964).
188. Melchner, Arlyn J., (ed.), *General Systems and Organization Theory: Methodological Aspects,* Kent, Ohio, Kent University Press, 1975.
189. Melchner, Arlyn J., and Kayser, Thomas A., "Leadership without Formal Authority: The Project Department," *California Management Review.* 13, 2: 57-64, (1970).
190. Meinhart, W.A., and Delionback, Leon M., "Project Management: An Incentive Contracting Decision Model," *Academy of Management Journal,* 11: 427-34, (December, 1968).
191. Metz, William W., "Identification and Analysis of Research and Development Project Management Problems Based on Nonnuclear Munitions Development in the Air Force," Ph.D. dissertation, George Washington University, 1970.
192. Middleton, C.J., "How to Set Up a Project Organization," *Harvard Business Review* 45: 73-82, (March-April, 1967).
193. Miller, E.J., *Systems of Organization,* New York, Barnes and Noble Book Company, 1967.
194. Moder, Joseph J., and Phillips, Cecil R., *Project Management with CPM and PERT,* 2nd ed., New York, Van Nostrand Reinhold, 1970.
195. Mordlea, Irwin, "A Comparison of a Research and Development Laboratory's Organization Structures," *IEEE Transactions on Engineering Management,* EM-14, 170-76, (December, 1967).
196. Morgan, John, "Coping with Resistance to Change," *Ideas for Management,* Cleveland, Ohio, Association for Systems Management, 1971.
197. Morton, D.H., "The Project Manager, Catalyst to Constant Change: A Behavioral Analysis," *Project Management Quarterly,* 6, 1: 22-3, (1975).
198. Mungo, B.B. "Management Studies in the Field of Aeronautics: Management of Projects," *Journal of the Royal Aeronautical Society* 71, 334-36; 336-38, (May, 1967).
199. Myers, S.M., Conditions for Manager Motivation, *Harvard Business Review,* 58-71, (Jan-Feb. 1966).
200. NATO Institute on Decomposition as a Tool for Solving Large-Scale Problems, Cambridge, England, *Decomposition of Large-Scale Problems,* Amsterdam, North-Holland Publishing Company, 1973.
201. Neuschel, Richard F., *Management Systems for Profit and Growth,* New York, McGraw-Hill, 1976.
202. O'Brien, James B., "The Project Manager: Not Just a Firefighter," *S.A.M. Advanced Management Journal,* 39: 52-56, (January, 1974).
203. Optner, Stanford L., *Systems Analysis for Business and Industrial Problem Solving,* Englewood Cliffs, N.J., Prentice-Hall, 1965.
204. ——, *Systems Analysis for Business Management,* Englewood Cliffs, N.J., Prentice-Hall, 1968.

205. ——, *Systems Analysis for Business Management,* Englewood Cliffs, N.J., Prentice-Hall, 1975.

206. ——, "Organizational Preference in Research and Development," *Human Relations,* 23: 279-98, (August, 1970).

207. Oyer, David William, "The Use of Automated Project Management Systems to Improve Information Systems Development, Cambridge, Mass.: M.S. Thesis, Alfred P. Sloan School of Management, M.I.T. 1975.

208. Pastore, Joseph M. "Organizational Metamorphosis: A Dynamic Model," *Marquette Business Review 15:* 17-31, (Spring, 1971).

209. Patchen, M., *Some Questionnaire Measures of Employee Motivation and Morale: A Report on their Reliability and Validity,* Ann Arbor, Michigan: Institute for Social Research, 1965.

210. Paul, W.J., K. Robertson, and F. Herzberg "Job Enrichment Pays Off," *Harvard Business Review,* 47, 2: 61-78, (1969).

211. Peart, Alan Thomas, *Design of Project Management Systems and Records,* London, Gower Press, 1971.

212. ——, *Design of Project Management Systems and Records.* Boston, Cahners Books, 1971.

213. Pegels, C. Carl, *Systems Analysis for Production Operations,* New York, Gordon and Science Publishers, 1976.

214. Pondy, L.R., "Organizational Conflict: Concepts and Models," *Administrative Science Quarterly,* 298-307, (September, 1967).

215. Potter, William J., "Management in the Ad-hocracy," *S.A.M. Advanced Management Journal,* 39: 19-23, (July, 1974).

216. Reeser, Clayton, "Some Potential Human Problems of the Project Form of Organization," *Academy of Management Journal,* 12: 459-68, (December, 1969).

217. Rogers, L.A., "Guidelines for Project Management Teams," *Industrial Engineering,* 12, (December, 1974).

218. Rudwick, Bernard H., *Systems Analysis for Effective Planning: Principles and Cases,* New York, Wiley, 1969.

219. Rubin, Irwin M., and Seilig, Wychlam, "Experience as a Factor in the Selection and Performance of Project Managers," *IEEE Transactions on Engineering Management* EM 131-35, (September, 1967).

220. Sadler, Philip, "Designing an Organization Structure," (publication source unknown).

221. Sapolsky, Harvey M., *The Polaris System Development: Bureaucratic and Programmatic Success in Government,* Cambridge, Mass., Harvard University Press, 1972.

222. Sayels, Leonard R., and Chandler, Margaret K., *Managing Large Systems: Organizations for the Future,* New York, Harper and Row, 1971.

223. Schaller, L.E., *The Change Agent,* New York, Abington Press, 1972.

224. Schoderbek, Peter P., Kefalas, A.G., and Schoderbek, Charles G., *Management Systems: Conceptual Considerations,* Dallas, Business Publications, 1975.

225. Schmidt, Joseph William, *Mathematical Foundations for Management Science and Systems Analysis,* New York, Academic Press, 1974.

226. Schroder, Harold J., "Making Project Management Work," *Management Review,* 54: 24-28, (December, 1970).

227. ——, "Project Management: Controlling Uncertainty," *Journal of Systems Management,* 24: 28-29, (February, 1975).

228. Seiler, J.A., "Diagnosing Interdepartmental Conflict," *Harvard Business Review,* 121-132, (September-October 1963).

229. Shah, Ramesh P., "Project Management: Cross Your Bridges Before You Come to Them," *Management Review,* 60 21-27, (December, 1971).

230. Sharad, D., "About Delays, Overruns and Corrective Actions," *Project Management Quarterly,* 21-25, (December, 1976).

231. Shannon, Robert E., "Matrix Management Structures," *Industrial Engineering* 4, 26-29, (March, 1972).

232. Sheriff, M., "Superordinate Goals in the Reduction of Intergroup Conflict," *American Journal of Sociology,* 63: 349-358, (1958).

233. Shrode, William A., and Voich, Dan Jr., *Organization and Management: Basic Systems Concepts,* Homewood, Illinois, R.D. Irwin, 1974.

234. Shull, Fremont, and Judd, R.J., "Matrix Organizations and Control Systems," *Management International Review* 11, 6: 65-72, (1971).

235. Shull, Fremont A., *Matrix Structure and Project Authority for Optimizing Organizational Capacity,* Business Science Monograph No. 1. Carbondale, Business Research Bureau, Southern Illinois University, 1965.

236. Simmons, John R., *Management of Change: The Role of Information,* (based on a research project sponsored by the Institute of Office Management), London, Gee & Company, 1970.

237. Sivazlian, B.D., and Stanfeld, L.E., *Analysis of Systems in Operations Research,* Englewood Cliffs, N.J., Prentice-Hall, 1973.

238. Smith, G.A., "Program Management—Art or Science?" *Mechanical Engineering* 96, 18-22, (September, 1974).

239. Smith, Michael Gary, *PCS: A Project Control System,* Ph.D. thesis, M.I.T., Cambridge, Mass., 1973.

240. Smith, William N., "Problem-Solving and Bargaining as Modes of Constructive Conflict Resolution in Aerospace Matrix Organizations," Ph.D. thesis, University of California, Los Angeles, 1972.

241. Smyster, Craig H., "A Comparison of the Needs of Program and Functional Management" (unpublished masters thesis), School of Engineering, Wright-Patterson Air Force Base, Air Force Institue of Technology, 1965.

242. Starr, Martin Kenenth, *Production Management: Systems and Synthesis,* 2nd ed. Englewood, N.J., Prentice-Hall, 1972.

243. Stasch, Stanley F., *Systems Analysis for Marketing Planning and Control,* Glenview, Illinois, Scott, Foresman, 1972.

244. Steger, W.A., "How to Plan for Management in New Systems," *Harvard Business Review,* (September-October), 1962.

245. Steiner, George A., "Project Managers' Problems with the Development of High Performance Aerospace Systems," *Astronautics and Aeronautics,* 75-76, (June, 1966).

246. ——, and Ryan, William G., *Industrial Project Management.* New York, Macmillan, 1968, p. 24.

247. Stewart, John M., "Making Project Management Work," *Business Horizons* 8: 54-68, (Fall, 1965).

248. Stopher, Peter R., and Meyburg, Arnim H., *Transportation Systems Evaluation,* Lexington, Massachusetts, Lexington Books, 1976.

249. Tannenbaum, Robert and Warren H. Schmidt, "How to Choose a Leadership Pattern," *HBR Classic,* 162-180, (May-June, 1973).

250. Taylor, W.J., and Watling, T.F., *Successful Project Management,* London, Business Books, 1970, p. 32-; 1972.

251. ——, "Teamwork Through Conflict," *Business Week,* 44-45, (March 20, 1971).

252. Thamhain, Hans J., and Wilemon, David L. "Diagnosing Conflict Determinants in Project Management," *IEEE Transactions on Engineering Management,* EM-22, 35-44, (February, 1975).

253. ——, and Gemmill, Gary R., "Influence Styles of Project Managers: Some Project Performance Correlates," *Academy of Management Journal,* 17, 216-24, (June, 1974).

254. Thamhain, H.J., and Wilemon, D.L., "Conflict Management in Project-Oriented Work Environments," *Proceedings of the Sixth International meeting of the Project Management Institute,* Washington, D.C., September 18-21, 1974.

255. ——, "Conflict Management in Project Life Cycles," *Sloan Management Review,* 31-50, (Summer, 1975).

256. ——, "The Effective Management of Conflict in Project-Oriented Work Environments," *Defense Management Journal* 11, 3: 975, (1978).

257. Thompson, J.D., *Organization in Action,* New York, McGraw-Hill, 1967.

258. Thompson, Victor A., "Bureaucracy and Innovation," *Administrative Science Quarterly* 10: 1-20, (June, 1965).

259. Toellner, John, "Project Estimating," *Journal of Systems Management,* 6-9, (May, 1977).

260. Trower, Michael H., "Fast Track to Project Delivery: Systems Approach to Project Management," *Management Review* 62 19-23, (April, 1973).

261. Tsai, Martin Chia-Ping, "Contingent Conditions for the Creation of Temporary Management Organizations," M.S. thesis, Alfred P. Sloan School of Management, M.I.T., Cambridge, Mass., 1976.

262. Vaughn, Dennis Henry, "Key Variables of a Management Information System for a Department of Defense Project Manager," M.S. thesis, Alfred P. Sloan School of Management, M.I.T., Cambridge, Mass., 1976.

263. ——, "Understanding Project Management," *Manage* 19, 9: 52-58, (1967).

264. Wadsworth, M., *EDP Project Management Controls,* Englewood Cliffs, N.J., Prentice-Hall, 1972.

265. Walton, R.E., and Dutton, J.M., "The Management of Interdepartmental Conflict: A Model and Review," *Administrative Science Quarterly,* 14, 1: 73-84, (March, 1969).

266. Walton, R.E., Dutton, J.M., and Cafferty, T.P., "Organizational Contest and Interdepartmental Conflict," *Administrative Science Quarterly,* 14, 4: 522-542, (December, 1969).

267. Webb, James E. "NASA as an Adaptive Organization," in *On Technological Change and Management,* ed. by David W. Ewing. Cambridge, Massachusetts, Harvard University Press, 1970.

268. Weinberg, Gerald M., *An Introduction to General Systems Thinking,* New York, Wiley, 1975.

269. Wetzel, John Jay, "Project Control at the Managerial Level in the Automotive Engineering Environment," M.S. thesis, Alfred P. Sloan School of Management, M.I.T. Cambridge, Mass., 1973.

270. Whitehouse, Gary E., "Project Management Techniques," *Industrial Engineering* 5: 24-29, (March, 1973).

271. ——, *Systems Analysis and Design Using Network Techniques.* Englewood Cliffs, N.J., Prentice-Hall, 1973.

272. Whiting, Richard J., "In Defense of Functional Organization," *Management Review, 58,* 7: 49-52, (July, 1969).

273. Wilemon, David L., "Managing Conflict in Temporary Management Systems," *Journal of Management Studies 10:* 282-96, (October, 1973).

274. Wilemon, D.L., "Project Management Conflict. A View from Apollo," *Third Annual Symposium of the Project Management Institute*, Houston, Texas, (October, 1971).
275. ——, "Managing Conflict on Project Teams," *Management Journal*, 28-34, (Summer, 1974).
276. Wilemon, D.L., "Project Management and its Conflicts: A View from Apollo," *Chemical Technology*, 2, 9: 527-534, (September, 1972).
277. ——, and Gary R. Gemmill, "Interpersonal Power in Temporary Management Systems," *Journal of Management Studies*, 8: 315-28, (October, 1971).
278. ——, and Cicero, John P., "The Project Manager: Anomalies and Ambiguities," *Academy of Management Journal* 13: 269-82, (September, 1970).
279. Willoughby, Theodore C. *Business Systems*, Cleveland, Association for Systems Management, 1975.
280. ——, and Senn, J.A., *Business Systems*, The Association for Systems Management, 1975.
281. Wilson, Ira Gaulbert, *Management Innovation and System Design*, Princeton, Auerbach, 1971.
282. Woodgate, Harry Samuel, *Planning by Network: Project Planning and Control Using Network Techniques*, London, Business Publications, 1967.
283. Wooldridge, Susan, *Project Management in Data Processing*, 1st ed. New York, Petrocelli/Charter, 1976.
284. Wrong, D., "Some Problems in Defining Social Power," *American Journal of Sociology*, 73, 6: 673-681, (May, 1968).

Competitive Bidding Bibliography

1. Anderson, R.M., "Handling Risk in Defense Contracting," *Harvard Business Review* (1969), pp. 90-98.
2. Arps, J.J., "A Strategy for Sealed Bidding," *Journal Petroleum Technology,* 1033, (September, 1965).
3. Baumgarten, R.M., "Discussion for Opbid-Competitive Bidding Strategy Model" by Morin and Clough, *Journal of the Construction Division of ASCE 96,* 88, (1970).
4. Benjamin, N.B.H., "Competitive Bidding for Building Construction Contracts," Technical Report No. 106, Department of Civil Engineering, Stanford University, June 1969.
5. Bell, L.B., "A System for Competitive Bidding," *Journal of Systems Management 20,* 26-29, (1969).
6. Bristor, J.D., "Discussion for Bidding Strategies and Probabilities, by Gates" (March, 1967), *Proceedings of the American Society of Civil Engineers Journal,* Construction Division 94, 109, (1968).
7. Bristor, J.D., "Discussion for 'Bidding-Work Loading Game' by Torgersen, *et al.*" (October, 1968), *Proceedings of the American Society of Civil Engineers Journal,* Construction Division 95, 139-140, (1969).
8. Broemser, G.M., "Competitive Bidding in the Construction Industry," Ph.D. dissertation, Stanford University, California, 1968.
9. Brown, K.C., "A Theoretical and Statistical Study of Decision-Making under Uncertainty—Competitive Bidding for Leases on Offshore Petroleum Lands," Ph.D dissertation, Southern Methodist University, Dallas, Texas, 1966.
10. Casey, B.J. and L.R. Shaffer, "An Evaluation of Some Competitive Bid Strategy Models for Contractors," Report No. 4, Department of Civil Engineering, University of Illinois, Urbana, Illinois.
11. Christenson, C., *Strategic Aspects of Competive Bidding for Corporate Securities,* Boston, Mass., Division of Research, Harvard, University School of Business.
12. Clough, R.H., *Construction Contracting,* Appendix L, 2nd Ed., New York, John Wiley, 1969.
13. Cook, Paul W., Jr., "Fact and Fancy on Identical Bids," *Harvard Business Review, 41,* 67-72 (January-February, 1963).
14. Crawford, P.B., "Pattern of Offshore Bidding," Society of Petroleum Engineers of AIME, Paper No. 2613, Dallas, Texas, 1969.
15. Crosby, A.R., "The Client/Contractor Syndrome," *Chemical Engineering Program 61,* 11, 44-48, (1965).

16. Edelman, F., "Art and Science of Competitive Bidding," *Harvard Business Review 43,* 53-66, (July-August, 1965).

17. Emerick, R.H., "How to Find the Unforeseen in Competitive Bidding," *Power Engineering 69,* 45-46, (August, 1965).

18. Flueck, J.A., "A Statistical Decision Theory Approach to a Seller's Bid Pricing Problem under Uncertainty," Ph.D. thesis, University of Chicago, School of Business, 1967.

19. Frey, J.B., "Competitive Bidding on General Construction Contracts," Ph.D. thesis, University of Delaware, 1962.

20. Friedman, L., "A Competitive Bidding Strategy," *Operations Research 4,* 104-112, (1956).

21. Gates, M., "Aspects on Competitive Bidding," Connecticut Society of Civil Engineers, 1959.

22. Gates, M., "Statistical and Economic Analysis of a Bidding Trend," *Journal of the Construction Division,* ASCE, Paper 2651, 13-35 (November, 1960).

23. Gates, M., "Bidding Strategies and Probabilities," *Journal of the Construction Division,* ASCE, Paper 5159, *93,* 75-107, (1967); and subsequent closure, p. *96,* 77-78 and 93, (1970).

24. Green, P., "Bayesian Decision Theory in Pricing Strategy," *Journal of Marketing 27,* 5-14, (1963).

25. Griesmer, J.H. and M. Shubik, "The Theory of Bidding," IBM Research Report, RC-629, IBM Research Center, Yorktown Heights, N.Y., (March 1, 1962).

26. Griesmer, J.H. and M. Shubik, "The Theory of Bidding II," IBM Research Report, RC-688, IBM Research Center, Yorktown Heights, N.Y., (May 25, 1962).

27. Griesmer, J.H. and M. Shubik, "The Theory of Bidding III," IBM Research Report, RC-874, IBM Research Center, Yorktown Heights, N.Y., (January 29, 1963).

28. Griesmer, J.H., R.E. Levitan, and M. Shubik, "Towards a Study of Bidding Processes, Part Four, Unknown Competitive Costs—," IBM Research Paper RC-1532, IBM Research Center, Yorktown Heights, N.Y., (January, 1966).

29. Hanssman, F. and Rivett, B.H.P., "Competitive Bidding," *Operations Research, Quarterly 10,* 49-55, (1959).

30. Harsanyi, J.C., "Games with Incomplete Information Played by Bayesian Players, Parts I-III," *Management Science 14,* 159-182, 320-334, 486-502, (1967-68).

31. Hugo, G.R., "How to Prepare Bids for Crown Lease Sales," *Oil Week 16,* 56-60, (1965).

32. Lavalle, I.H., "A Bayesian Approach to an Individual Player's Choice of Bid in Competitive Sealed Auctions," *Management Science 13,* A584-597, (1967).

33. Moriguti, S. and S. Suganami, "Notes on Auction Bidding," *J. Opns, Res. Soc. (Japan),* 2, 43-59, (1959).

34. Morin, T.L., and R. H. Clough, "Opbid—Competitive Bidding Strategy Model," *Journal of Construction Division,* ASCE, Paper 6690; (June, 1970) and subsequent discussion, pp. *96,* 88-97.

35. Ortega-Reichert, A., "Models for Competitive Bidding under Uncertainty," Technical Report No. 103, Department of Operations Research, Stanford University, Stanford, California, January, 1968.

36. Park, W.R., "How Low to Bid to Get Both Job and Profit," *Engineering News-Record 168,* 38-40, (April 19, 1962).

37. Park, W.R., "Less Bidding for Bigger Profits," *Engineering News-Record 170,* 41 (February 14, 1963).

38. Park, W.R., "Bidders and Job Size Determine Your Optimum Markup, *Engineering News-Record 170,* 122-123, (June 13, 1963).

39. Park, W.R., "Bidding: When to Raise and When to Fold," *The Modern Builder,* Kansas City, Mo., (July, 1963).

40. Park, W.R., "The Problem of Breaking Even," *The Modern Builder,* Kansas City, Mo. (September, 1963).

41. Park, W.R., "The Strategy of Bidding for Profit," *The Modern Builder,* Kansas City, Mo. (September, 1963).

42. Park, W.R., "Better Bidding Will Beget Bigger Profits," *The Modern Builder,* Kansas City, Mo. (October, 1963).

43. Park, W.R., "How Much to Make to Cover Costs," *Engineering News-Record 171,* 168-170, (December 19, 1963).

44. Park, W.R., "It Takes a Profit to Make a Profit," *Mid-West Contractor,* Kansas City, Mo. (March 11, 1964).

45. Park, W.R., "Profit Optimization Through Strategic Bidding," *AACE Bulletin, 6,* 5 (December, 1964).

46. Park, W.R. *The Strategy of Contracting for Profit.* Englewood Cliffs, N.J., Prentice-Hall, 1966.

47. Rothkopf, M.H., "A Model of Rational Competitive Bidding," *Management Science 15,* 362-373, (1969).

48. Sakaguchi, M. "Mathematical Solutions to Some Problems of Competitive Bidding," *Proceedings of the Third International Conference on Operational Res.* (Oslo, 1963), 1964, pp. 179-191, Dunod (Paris) and English University Press (London).

49. Schlaifer, R. *Probability and Statistics for Business Decisions.* New York, McGraw-Hill, 1959.

50. Simmonds, K., "Adjusting Bias in Cost Estimates," *Opnal. Res. Quart., 19,* 325-327, (1968).

51. Simmonds, K., "Competitive Bidding–Deciding the Best Combination of Non-Price Features," *Operational Research Quarterly 19,* 5-15, (1968).

52. Stark, Robert M., "Competitive Bidding: A Comprehensive Bibliography," *Opns. Res. 19,* 484-490, (1971).

53. Symonds, G.H., "A Study of Management Behavior by Use of Competitive Business Games," *Management Science 11,* 135-153, (1964).

54. Vickrey, W., "Counterspeculation, Auctions, and Competitive Sealed Tenders," *Journal of Finance 16,* 8-37, (1961).

55. Wasson, C.R., *Understanding Qualitative Analysis,* New York, Appleton-Century-Crofts, 1969.

56. Wilson, R.B., "Competitive Bidding with Disparate Information," Working Paper No. 114, Graduate School of Business, Stanford University, October 1966.

57. Wilson, R.B., "Competitive Bidding with Asymmetrical Information," *Management Science 13,* A816-820, (1967).

58. Wilson, R.B., "Competitive Bidding with Disparate Options," *Management Science 15,* 46-48, (1969).

Appendix B
Solution to the
Case Study on
Planning Priorities

ACTIVITY	PRIORITY
1	14
2	13
3	2
4	20
5	26
6	22
7	5
8	25
9	1
10	3
11	18
12	17
13	15
14	16
15	12
16	23
17	11
18	24
19	8
20	9
21	7
22	21
23	19
24	6
25	4
26	10

Appendix C
Solutions to the
Project Management
Conflict Exercise

PART ONE: FACING THE CONFLICT

After reading the answers which follow, record your score on line 1 of the worksheet.

    A.   Although many project managers and functional managers negotiate by "returning" favors, this custom is not highly recommended. The department manager might feel some degree of indebtedness at first, but will surely become defensive in follow-on projects in which you are involved, and might even get the idea that this will be the only way that he will be able to deal with you in the future. If this was your choice, allow one point on line 1.

    B.   Threats can only lead to disaster. This is a sure-fire way of ending a potentially good arrangement before it starts. Allow no points if you selected this as your solution.

    C.   If you say nothing, then you accept full responsibility and accountability for the schedule delay and increased costs. You have done nothing to open communications with the department manager. This could lead into additional conflicts on future projects. Enter two points on line 1 if this was your choice.

    D.   Requesting upper-level management to step in at this point can only complicate the situation. Executives prefer to step in only as a last resort. Upper-level management will probably ask to talk to the department manager first. Allow two points on line 1 if this was your choice.

    E.   Although he might become defensive upon receiving your memo, it will become difficult for him to avoid your request for help. The question, of course, is when he will give you this help. Allow eight points on line 1 if you made this choice.

    F.   Trying to force your solution upon the department manager will severely threaten him and provide the basis for additional conflict. Good project managers will always try to predict emotional reactions to whatever decisions they might be forced to make. For this choice, allow two points on line 1 of the worksheet.

G. Making an appointment for a later point in time will give both parties a chance to cool off and think out the situation further. You will probably find it difficult to refuse your request for help and will be forced to think about it between now and the appointment. Allow ten points for this choice.

H. An immediate discussion will tend to open communications or keep communication open. This will be advantageous. However, it can also be a disadvantage if emotions are running high and sufficient time has not been given to the selection of alternatives. Allow six points on line 1 if this was your choice.

I. Forcing the solution your way will obviously alienate the department manager. The fact that you do intend to honor his request at a later time might give him some relief especially if he understands your problem and the potential impact of his decision upon other departments. Allow three points on line 1 for this choice.

PART TWO: UNDERSTANDING EMOTIONS

Using the scoring table shown below, determine your total score. Record your total in the appropriate box on line 2 of the worksheet. There are no "absolutely" correct answers to this problem, merely what appears to be the "most" right.

PART THREE: ESTABLISHING COMMUNICATIONS

A. Although your explanations may be acceptable and accountability for excess costs may be blamed upon the department manager, you have not made any attempt to open communications with the department manager. Further conflicts appear inevitable. If this was your choice, allow a score of zero on line 3 of the worksheet.

B. You are offering the department manager no choice but to elevate the conflict. He probably has not had any time to think about changing his requirements and it is extremely doubtful that he will give in to you since you have now backed him into a corner. Allow zero points on line 3 of the worksheet.

C. Threatening him may get him to change his mind, but will certainly create deteriorating working relationships both on this project as well as any others which will require that you interface with his department. Allow no points if this was your choice.

D. Sending him a memo requesting a meeting at a later date will give him and you a chance to cool down but might not improve your bargaining position. The department manager might now have plenty of time to reassure himself that he was right because you probably aren't under such a terrible time constraint as you led him to believe if you can wait several days to

	REACTION	PERSONAL OR GROUP SCORE
A. I've given you my answer. See the general manager if you're not happy.	Hostile or Withdrawing	4
B. I understand your problem. Let's do it your way.	Accepting	4
C. I understand your problem, but I'm doing what is best for my department.	Defensive or Hostile	4
D. Let's discuss the problem. Perhaps there are alternatives.	Cooperative	4
E. Let me explain to you why we need the new requirements.	Cooperating or Defensive	4
F. See my section supervisors. It was their recommendation.	Withdrawing	4
G. New Managers are supposed to come up with new and better ways, aren't they?	Hostile or Defensive	4
	TOTAL: PERSONAL	
	TOTAL: GROUP	

see him again. Allow four points on line 3 of the worksheet if this was your choice.

E. You're heading in the right direction trying to open communications. Unfortunately, you may further aggravate him by telling him that he lost his cool and should have apologized to you when all along you may have been the one that lost your cool. Expressing regret as part of your opening remarks would benefit the situation. Allow six points on line 3 of the worksheet.

F. Postponing the problem cannot help you. The department manager might consider the problem resolved because he hasn't heard from you. The confrontation should not be postponed. Your choice has merit in that you are attempting to open up a channel for communications. Allow four points on line 3 if this was your choice.

G. Expressing regret and seeking immediate resolution is the best approach. Hopefully, the department manager will now understand the importance of this conflict and the need for urgency. Allow ten points on line 3 of the worksheet.

PART FOUR: CONFLICT RESOLUTION

Use the table shown below to determine your total points. Enter this total on line 4 of the worksheet.

PART FIVE: UNDERSTANDING YOUR CHOICES

A. Although you may have "legal" justification to force the solution your way, you should consider the emotional impact on the organization as a result of alienating the department manager. Allow two points on line 5 of the worksheet.

B. Accepting the new requirements would be an easy way out if you are willing to explain the increased costs and schedule delays to the other participants. This would certainly please the department manager and might even give him the impression that he has a power position and can always resolve problems in this fashion. Allow four points on line 5 of the worksheet.

C. If this situation cannot be resolved at your level, you have no choice but to request upper-level management to step in. At this point you must be pretty sure that a compromise is all but impossible and are willing to accept

		MODE	PERSONAL OR GROUP SCORE
A.	The requirements are my decision and we're doing it my way.	Forcing	4
B.	I've thought about it and you're right. We'll do it your way.	Withdrawal or Smoothing	4
C.	Let's discuss the problem. Perhaps there are alternatives.	Compromise or Confrontation	4
D.	Let me explain why we need the new requirements.	Smoothing, Confrontation, or forcing	4
E.	See my section supervisors; they're handling it now.	Withdrawal	4
F.	I've looked over the problem and I might be able to ease up on some of the requirements.	Smoothing or Compromise	4
		TOTAL: PERSONAL	
		TOTAL: GROUP	

a go-for-broke position. Enter ten points on line 5 of the worksheet if this was your choice.

D. Asking other managers to plead your case for you is not a good situation. Hopefully upper-level management will solicit their opinions when deciding upon how to resolve the conflict. Enter six points on line 5 if this was your choice, and hope that the functional managers do not threaten him by ganging up on him.

PART SIX: INTERPERSONAL INFLUENCES

A. Threatening the employees with penalty power will probably have no effect at all because your conflict is with the department manager who at this time probably could care less about your evaluation of his people. Allow zero points on line 6 of the worksheet if you selected this choice.

B. Offering rewards will probably induce people toward your way of thinking provided that they feel that you can keep your promises. Promotions and increased responsibilities are functional responsibilities, not those of a project manager. Performance evaluation might be effective if the department manager values your judgement. In this situation it is doubtful that he will. Allow no points for this answer and record the results on line 6 of the worksheet.

C. Expert power, once established, is an effective means of obtaining functional respect provided that it is used for a relatively short period of time. For long-term efforts, expert power can easily create conflicts between project and functional managers. In this situation, although relatively short-term, the department manager probably will not consider you as an expert, and this might carry on down to his functional subordinates. Allow six points on line 6 of the worksheet if this was your choice.

D. Work challenge is the best means of obtaining support and in many situations can overcome personality clashes and disagreements. Unfortunately, the problem occurred because of complaints by the functional personnel and it is therefore unlikely that work challenge would be effective here. Allow eight points on line 6 of the worksheet if this was your choice.

E. People who work in a project environment should respect the project manager because of the authority delegated to him from the upper levels of management. But this does not mean that they will follow his directions. When in doubt, employees tend to follow the direction of the person that signs their evaluation form, namely the department manager. However, the project manager has the formal authority to "force" the line manager to adhere to the original project plan. This should be done only as a last resort and here, it looks as though it may be the only alternative. Allow ten points if this was your answer and record the result on line 6 of the worksheet.

F. Referent power cannot be achieved overnight. Furthermore, if the department manager feels that you are trying to compete with him for the friendship of his subordinates, additional conflicts can result. Allow two points on line 6 of the worksheet if this was your choice.

Appendix D
Project Management
Final Exam (A)

For each question, there is one, and only one satisfactory answer.

1. Which of the following is not characteristic of a project?

   a. A finite lifetime
   b. Must have both a formal and informal reporting system
   c. Designed to accomplish a single objective
   d. Designed usually for unique, one-of-a-kind activities

2. The best definition for an ongoing project would be

   a. A project
   b. A program
   c. A system
   d. A continuous stream of unrelated tasks

3. Another name for aggregate projects would be

   a. Individual
   b. Line/staff
   c. Special
   d. Matrix

4. John has been assigned a project which requires communications between two departments within the same division. Which of the following forms would be the *least* appropriate?

   a. Individual
   b. Line/staff
   c. Special
   d. Matrix

5. The conflict resolution procedure works best if the project manager and resource managers report to the same person.

   a. True
   b. False

6. An employee refuses to dress appropriately when interfacing with the customer. The responsibility rests with the

   a. Project manager
   b. Functional manager

7. The inability for functional members to keep current in their respective disciplines is characteristic of which organizational form?

   a. Line/staff
   b. Product
   c. Matrix
   d. none of the above

8. The time required to change over from a traditional structure to a matrix structure can be expected to take (for large companies)

   a. six months or less
   b. six months to one year
   c. two years
   d. three years

9. Who determines which member of a functional department will present technical data to the customer? (Assume that more than one functional team member is assigned to this project.)

   a. The project manager
   b. The functional manager
   c. The Director of Project Management
   d. The Director of Engineering

10. The highest ranking individual in the company, who would have as his/her responsibility the resolution of project conflicts, would be the

   a. Vice-President and General Manager
   b. Functional manager
   c. Project manager
   d. Director of Project Management

11. In general, which of the following would not pertain to the functions of a project manager

   a. Planning
   b. Staffing
   c. Controlling
   d. Directing

12. Master production schedules are prepared by the

   a. Functional managers or functional team members
   b. Project manager
   c. Project office team members

13. Departmental PERT Charts are prepared by the project office team members for the functional departments to follow.
    a. True
    b. False

14. Adhering to the milestones established by the customer is the responsibility of
    a. The project manager
    b. The functional manager
    c. Both the project and functional manager

15. The project plan is a document designed to tell _____ exactly what should be happening in a given period of time.
    a. Anyone associated with the project
    b. The project manager
    c. The functional manager

16. Adhering to contractual requirements is the responsibility of
    a. The project manager
    b. The functional manager
    c. The Director of Project Management
    d. The contracts team member

17. The decision to increase resources on the project is the responsibility of the
    a. The functional manager
    b. The project manager
    c. The Director of Project Management
    d. The customer

18. Which of the following is *not* considered as a role for top management?
    a. Setting the selection criteria for projects
    b. Selecting functional team members for project assignments
    c. Establishing priorities among projects

19. A functional manager would most likely consider project management as a
    a. Threat to establish authority
    b. Challenge
    c. Research area
    d. Means to an end

    Answer Questions 20-23 using the choices given below:
    a. Conceptual Phase
    b. Definition Phase
    c. Production Phase
    d. Operational Phase
    e. Divestment Phase

20. In which phase do we identify human and non-human resources?

21. In which phase do we perform a feasibility study?

22. In which phase do we examine alternative ways of accomplishing the objectives?

23. In which phase do we transfer resources to other systems?

24. Which of the following is not a characteristic of a dynamic system?

    a. Subsystem integration
    b. System effectiveness
    c. System efficiency
    d. System life cycles
    e. None of the above

25. One of the major causes for the failure of the line/staff form of project management was that upper-level management was reluctant to relinquish any of their power and authority to project managers.

    a. True
    b. False

26. Which of the following are characteristics of a project manager?

    a. Honesty and integrity
    b. Decision-making ability
    c. Understanding of personnel problems
    d. Versatility
    e. All of the above

27. A project manager is far more likely to succeed if it is obvious that general management has appointed him.

    a. True
    b. False

28. Which of the following is not a prime responsibility of a project manager?

    a. In-house communications
    b. Evaluating interface employee for promotion
    c. Customer communications
    d. Negotiation with functional management

29. Insuring that all work performed is both authorized and funded by contractual documentation is the responsibility of the

    a. Functional manager
    b. Project manager
    c. Director of Project Management

30. Which of the following factors would have the least effect on project office membership?

    a. Customer support requirements
    b. Project size
    c. Employee pay grade and level
    d. Type of project
    e. Level of technical competency required

31. The project manager may have the authority to make commitments in which of the following areas?

    a. Salary
    b. Grade
    c. Bonus and overtime pay
    d. An individual's assignment after project termination
    e. None of the above

32. In many project organizational forms, project office team members worry more about setbacks in their careers than do functional personnel.

    a. True
    b. False

33. Planning is

    a. Selecting policies and procedures in order to achieve objectives
    b. Decision making
    c. A means for monitoring and controlling work
    d. All of the above

34. Which of the following is *not* one of the major reasons why plans fail?

    a. Plan requires too much in too little time
    b. Planning performed by a planning group
    c. Management assumes that all activities will not be completed on schedule
    d. Poor financial estimates
    e. None of the above

35. The project manager must be given sufficient authority to organize activities across functional lines.

    a. True
    b. False

36. Which of the following is *not* a major result of poor authority relations being established?

    a. Poor communications channels
    b. Misleading information
    c. Good employee working relations
    d. Surprises for the customer

37. Which individual or group would normally not be shown on a linear responsibility chart?

    a. Functional members
    b. Functional managers
    c. Directors
    d. Vice-presidents and general managers
    e. They can all be shown on an LRC

Answer Questions 38-40 using the alternatives shown below:

    a. Formal authority
    b. Reward power
    c. Penalty power
    d. Expert power
    e. Referent power

38. Which interpersonal influence results from having a project manager reporting to someone high in the organization?

39. Which interpersonal influence would be most common if a functional manager were promoted to project manager for a high-technology effort?

40. Which interpersonal influence would be impacted by the relationships that exist in the informal organization?

41. The relative influence in decision making that a functional manager possesses depends upon the organization form of project management.

    a. True
    b. False

42. Which of the following is the responsibility of functional manager?

    a. What is to be done?
    b. When will the task be done?
    c. Where will the task be done?
    d. Why will the task be done?
    e. How much money is available to do it?

43. In the inevitable conflict between project and functional managers, the project manager blames cost overruns on the functional manager with the argument that there were too many changes.

    a. True
    b. False

44. Which of the following reasons for project management failure is the one most often overlooked?

    a. The wrong man as project manager
    b. Poorly defined tasks
    c. Project termination not planned
    d. Company management unsupportive
    e. Management techniques misused

45. The major obstacle in using MBO in project management is

    a. Evaluating how people spend their time
    b. Giving employees clearly defined objectives
    c. Letting employees have a part in setting their own objectives

46. A resource manager would best be defined as a

    a. Department manager
    b. Project manager
    c. Division manager
    d. Director

47. If a project office has a diversity of disciplinary expertise, then

    a. The project will be a success
    b. There will be no overlap of activities
    c. Conflicts will probably occur
    d. All of the above

    Answer Questions 48-52 using the following alternatives

    a. Withdrawal
    b. Smoothing
    c. Compromising
    d. Forcing
    e. Confrontation

48. Most project managers would prefer to resolve conflicts by _____ .

49. Hierarchical referral is suggestive of which mode for handling conflicts? (Two answers are possible.)

50. Which mode gives a win or lose position?

51. Which mode usually ends up with a give and take position?

52. Which mode does the least to resolve a conflict?

53. If project management is to be successful, functional employees must be willing to be treated as both theory X and theory Y.

    a. True
    b. False

54. Communications can best be defined as

    a. Providing written or oral directions
    b. An exchange of information
    c. Eliminating the filters and barriers that stand between people
    d. None of the above

55. Which of the following cannot be tracked using the Work Breakdown Structure?
    a. Time
    b. Cost
    c. Performance
    d. None of the above

56. The fourth level in the Work Breakdown Structure is the
    a. Project
    b. Subtask
    c. Level of effort
    d. Work package
    e. Task

57. For effective project management to exist, there should be flexibility built into the Work Breakdown Structure.
    a. True
    b. False

58. Which is considered to be a part of the planning cycle?
    a. Work authorization
    b. Data collection
    c. Variance analysis
    d. Cost accounting
    e. Information reporting
    f. None of the above

59. Most organizations prepare multiple schedules in order to satisfy
    a. Upper-level reporting
    b. Customer reporting
    c. Functional reporting
    d. All of the above

60. Reviewing schedules with the customer during the planning cycle shows him that you welcome his help and input.
    a. True
    b. False

61. The program plan can be used to eliminate conflict between functional managers.
    a. True
    b. False

62. Which of the following is not one of the primary needs for good charting and scheduling?
    a. Cutting costs and reducing time
    b. Increase the time required for routine decisions
    c. Eliminating idle time
    d. Develop better troubleshooting procedures

Answer Questions 63-68 based upon the PERT network shown below:

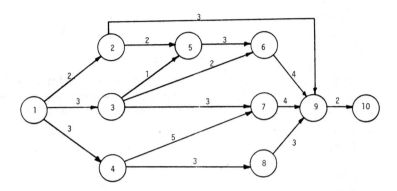

63. The critical path contains events
    a. 1-2-9-10
    b. 1-2-5-6-9-10
    c. 1-3-5-6-9-10
    d. 1-3-6-9-10
    e. 1-4-8-9-10
    f. 1-4-7-9-10

64. For Event 8, the early time will be
    a. 3 days
    b. 4 days
    c. 6 days
    d. 8 days
    e. 9 days
    f. 12 days
    g. none of the above

65. For Event 8, the late time will be
    a. 3 days
    b. 6 days
    c. 9 days
    d. 12 days
    e. 15 days
    f. none of the above

66. The total slack time for event 8 is

    a. 2 days
    b. 3 days
    c. 5 days
    d. 6 days
    e. 9 days
    f. none of the above

67. If activities 1-2, 1-3, and 1-4 use the same manpower, and if a one day decrease in one activity causes a one day increase in one of the other two activities, then replanning will reduce the length of the critical path by

    a. 0 days
    b. 1 day
    c. 2 days
    d. 3 days
    e. none of the above

68. If the most likely time for activity 4-7 is the same as the estimated time, and if the pessimistic time is 8 days, then the optimistic time is

    a. 0 days
    b. 2 days
    c. 3 days
    d. 4 days
    e. none of the above

69. The environmental factors (legal, social, political, technological, and economical):

    a. Are always monitored by the project manager, especially during project execution.
    b. Are the responsibility of the functional manager
    c. Are the responsibility of top-level management
    d. None of the above

70. If material expenditures are $1000 per month, commitments are six months and termination liability is 80%, what is the termination liability for the second month?

    a. $4800
    b. $6000
    c. $5600
    d. $7000
    e. none of the above

71. The time necessary to complete a project is referred to as

    a. Implementation time
    b. Life cycle
    c. Operations cycle
    d. none of the above

72. The most important paperwork to help a project manager control the project is the

    a. Work Breakdown Structure
    b. Specifications
    c. Statement of Work
    d. Schedule

73. The successful project managers spend most of their time

    a. Planning with top management
    b. Planning with their personnel
    c. Studying project results
    d. Talking with personnel

74. The term interface refers to

    a. The relationship between various parts of a project
    b. How a project looks to the outsiders
    c. How a project looks to its personnel
    d. The beginning and end of a project

75. Good project managers:

    a. Have at least one heart attack a year
    b. Drive people into the ground until success is at hand
    c. Love power and title
    d. Make X-rated movies in their spare time
    e. All of the above
    f. none of the above

Appendix E
Project Management
Final Exam (B)

PROJECT MANAGEMENT EXAM (B)*

1. The primary responsibility of the Project Management Department is:

   A. to maintain the necessary good working relationships with functional departments to complete the project.
   B. to ensure the functional groups conform to the cost, schedule, and technical requirements of the project.
   C. the development and implementation of plans for assigned projects.
   D. conformance to project cost and schedule constraints.

2. Projects assigned to Project Management:

   A. encompass the planning, design, construction, start-up, and associated activities required for the completion and operation of any new effort.
   B. include any task assigned by management.
   C. include responsibility for new projects and planning.
   D. A and C but not B.

3. The Project Management Department is dependent upon the functional departments to provide qualified personnel for assignment to projects and:

   A. to perform project supporting work.
   B. to prepare analysis of project variance reports for the functional area.
   C. to maintain a commitment system for the functional area.
   D. to communicate decisions regarding the project to upper management in a timely manner.

---

*Adapted from *Project Management Workshop,* developed by Project Control Services Department, Florida Power & Light Company. Reproduced by permission of Florida Power & Light Company.

4. For some project decisions, Project Management and other departments act in concurrence. This is:

   A. because when it is mutually agreed, the decision is the best one for the project.
   B. not relevant since concurrence is a term used in Mission Statements.
   C. part of a "checks and balance" system.
   D. what happens when upper management makes the decision.

5. Which of the following is *not* an objective of the Project Management Department:

   A. timely, good quality planning for assigned projects with realistic schedules and accurate cost forecasts.
   B. timely, decisive response to project needs based upon objective analysis of available information.
   C. completion of original projects within approved budget and schedule constraints and in compliance with technical specifications, regulations and agreements made with outside agencies or organizations.
   D. to provide project information identifying deviations and trends from approved plans, schedules, cash flows or budgets.

6. "Success" targets for the Project General Manager (PGM) are:

   A. cost, schedule, and technical performance objectives and other specifications of the project defined by the approved project plan.
   B. cost, schedule, and technical performance objectives and other specifications of the project set when the PGM was assigned.
   C. under-budget and ahead of schedule targets.
   D. There are no "success" targets. Response to a dynamic environment precludes meeting fixed targets.

7. In order to successfully develop and implement an approved plan for a project, the PGM:

   A. must be technically competent in all disciplines.
   B. must be able to select the functional personnel.
   C. has the responsibility for managing, directing and controlling project activities.
   D. has the authority to override functional department heads.

8. The basic performance indices for the Project General Manager are:

   A. actual milestone dates met vs. planned milestone dates met.
   B. actual project costs vs. planned project costs.
   C. actual plant reliability vs. planned plant reliability.
   D. actual performance vs. planned performance to targets in approved project plan.

9. Using a football team as an analogy, the PGM performs the role of:

   A. Coach
   B. Quarterback
   C. Owner
   D. Trainer

10. Project Management:

    A. is not needed if all functional managers would carry out their assigned responsibilities.
    B. is needed because the functional organization and its methods of planning and control cannot otherwise assure that complex projects will be completed on schedule and within budget.
    C. is not needed unless the project is in serious trouble.
    D. is needed only on projects which have high visibility.

11. Project Management uses a matrix organization because:

    A. with functional organizations, the burden of managing projects falls on upper management.
    B. project needs overlap functional boundaries.
    C. it prevents problems within functional departments.
    D. A and B but not C.

12. The key concepts of Project Management are:

    A. appointment of a Project General Manager with total authority and responsibility for the project, and with direct control of all contributing specialists.
    B. formation of a separate division or other self-supporting organization specifically for the project, with the Project General Manager in charge.
    C. identification of a single point of integrative responsibility for the project in addition to existing responsibilities of contributing functional managers, and establishment of integrated planning and control of all aspects of the project.
    D. establishment of integrated planning and control of all phases of and all functional contributions to the project, and appointment of a Project Engineer for its technical aspects.

13. The Project General Manager assignment should ideally be rotated during each project.

    A. True, because it is the best way to fill the Project General Manager role, since the assigned person in each phase is very knowledgeable of that phase.
    B. False, because it breaks the continuity of responsibility and allows unsolved problems to be swept forward to the end of the project.
    C. True, because it is the only practical approach, since no one person will have the required expertise to manage the project in all its phases.
    D. False, because it combines functional and project management responsibilities, thereby creating organizational conflicts.

14. The task of providing necessary expertise to solve project related technical problems is:

    A. a role of the functional departments.
    B. a role of the Project General Manager.
    C. a task of the consultants hired by the project team.
    D. the role of upper-level management.

15. The Project General Manager's basic responsibility is:

    A. to provide the functional departments with budget and to schedule constraints for completing the project.
    B. to act as the interface with top management.
    C. to complete the project within established budget, schedule and project specifications.
    D. to act as the central collection point for budget and schedule information.

16. The Project General Manager is designated a line manager

    A. and has decision making authority on all project matters.
    B. and has decision making authority on all project matters, but his decisions may be disputed by functional department heads with PGM having the last word.
    C. and has decision making authority on all project matters, but his decisions may be disputed by functional department heads with mutual agreement necessary prior to implementation.
    D. and has decision making authority on all project matters, but his decision may be disputed by functional department heads with conflict being resolved by a common boss.

17. In dealing with functional managers and their functional project leaders, the Project General Manager should:

    A. maintain a formal and official relationship with each, in order to ensure respect and acceptance of his authority.
    B. avoid too much personal contact, which tends to generate unnecessary interpersonal conflict, and rely mainly on the formal organization communications structure.
    C. develop a personal rapport with each manager through frequent face-to-face contact, and provide each with pertinent available information on the project.
    D. restrict information to what a manager absolutely has to know about his part of the project.

18. The Project General Manager should use an organization development (team-building) program. Organization Development is:

    A. a process by which the overall effectiveness of the project team is maximized in achieving its objectives.
    B. a process by which the functional departments are reorganized to more effectively support project management.
    C. a process by which the Project General Manager can make the project team as large as he believes necessary to support the project.
    D. a process by which project correspondence can be classified to improve team communications.

19. The Project General Manager should seek speedy resolution of conflict between the project and functional departments primarily because

    A. conflict impedes the decision-making necessary to stay within schedule and budget constraints.
    B. conflict represents a challenge to authority.
    C. conflict indicates that the Project Management concept is not well understood.
    D. None of the above. The resolution of conflict is a problem to be resolved by the Director of Projects.

20. Project General Managers:

    A. must approve all project expenditures.
    B. may delegate the approval of expenditures to Team Members in an amount selected by the PGM.
    C. have corporate defined limits of approval and delegation of approval.
    D. can approve only customer-specified expenditures.

21. Timely decisions directly and dramatically affect the ability of the project team to meet commitments to cost and schedule constraints. Therefore:

    A. the project team must be able to make decisions or obtain decisions from upper management.
    B. functional departments should make their decisions as quickly as possible.
    C. upper management should communicate decisions to the project team at least weekly.
    D. since consensus decision making is time consuming, provisions have been made for budget and schedule revisions.

22. Project Team Members:

    A. are in a "line" reporting relationship to the PGM and are extensions of his authority.
    B. have relatively little authority and responsibility and usually can only recommend courses of action.
    C. primary allegiance should be to their functional department.
    D. receive technical and administrative direction from the PGM.

23. Careful and early planning for a project provides an integrated, comprehensive approach to successfully meeting project schedule and budgetary constraints. Such planning means:

    A. that a comprehensive approach to project objectives (including alternative approaches) is developed early, when the ability to influence costs is greatest.
    B. development of achievable schedules to control design, procurement, and construction activities.
    C. development of sound cost estimates, budget items, and cash flow estimates.
    D. sound and comprehensive plans, supported by schedules, yield control points, or definitive decision points for the project.
    E. All of the above

24. The project plan is developed by:

    A. the PGM
    B. the Director of Projects
    C. the Project Team
    D. top management

25. For the comprehensively planned project, the schedule is:

    A. the agenda for carrying out the plan or a portion of it.
    B. not important, as each team member acts according to plan.
    C. used to generate a time table of major commitments for the project.
    D. provides opportunities for upper-management to significantly alter the course of the project.

26. The primary objective of Project Control Services is to identify deviations and trends from approved plans and to:

    A. request the functional managers to take steps to correct the deviations.
    B. evaluate the impact of suggested, forced or actual deviations from the approved plan.
    C. monitor project cash flow.
    D. prepare budget items and revisions for projects.

27. For projects assigned to Project Management, Project Control Services is responsible for:

    A. revising project plans and schedules when deviations occur.
    B. obtaining Budget Committee approval for project budget revisions.
    C. collecting, analyzing and reporting the cost, budget and schedule data.
    D. the team members compliance to budget and schedule constraints.

28. Planning and Scheduling are:

    A. separate and distinct tasks and have little relationship with each other.
    B. distinct but inseparable aspects of the successful project.
    C. the only means for assuring project success.

29. The control of Project Cost is through the Project Schedule.

    A. True
    B. False

30. Projected cost tied to schedule equals cash flow.

    A. True
    B. False

31. Cash flow is monitored by relating project cost to physical progress.

    A. True
    B. False

32. Earned value versus actual cots ties cost to progress.

    A. True
    B. False

33. Ordinarily the analyst seeks to correct identified deviations from planned targets by:

    A. making recommendations to the PGM or appropriate Team Member.
    B. working with counterparts in other organizations to adjust targets.
    C. reporting the deviation so that the appropriate persons know action is required.
    D. working with the Supervisor of the Planning, Scheduling and Cost Group to effect correction to the deviation.

34. The purpose of project reporting is to:

    A. keep company management informed and to check progress by reporting pertinent facts.
    B. allow for communication of plans, performance, and problems to the proper decision making level of management.
    C. apprise company management of project status.
    D. All of the above.

35. The primary purpose of the reporting system is:

    A. to inform the PGM of project progress.
    B. to apprise management of the status of each project.
    C. to apprise management of costs and cost trends of each project.
    D. provide management with the information necessary to make project decisions.

36. You start developing the logic diagram from:

    A. The beginning.
    B. The middle.
    C. The tail end.
    D. Any place.

37. The next step after development of the logic is:

   A. Make a "forward pass."
   B. Develop the duration of each activity.
   C. Make a "backward pass."
   D. Determine the critical path.

38. The critical path is calculated by:

   A. Making a forward pass.
   B. Making a backward pass.
   C. Making a forward and a backward pass.
   D. Adding up the durations of all the important activities.

39. The range of time (i.e., the time between early finish and late finish date) to complete an activity is called:

   A. Expected time.
   B. Float (or slack).
   C. Planned start date.
   D. Allowable time.

40. Five weeks negative float for an activity means the activity is scheduled to start, or did start, five weeks after the late start date.

   A. True
   B. False

41. A man-loaded schedule means that:

   A. Manpower requirements, by craft, are assigned to each activity.
   B. Extra men are required to "load" the schedule in to the computer.
   C. We have loaded more men into the schedule than required.
   D. Manpower availability was superimposed on the schedule.

42. Resource (manpower) allocation is a process whereby activities are scheduled within the constraints imposed by labor availability or self-set limits of desired or affordable manpower.

   A. True
   B. False

43. Manpower levels can be constrained to less than the amount required but this will:

   A. Require more manpower in the long run.
   B. Push out the end date.
   C. Reduce total manpower costs for the project.
   D. Have no effect on the schedule.

44. A report listing only those activities with four weeks negative float cannot be obtained.

   A. True
   B. False

45. A report listing only those activities scheduled to start next month can be produced.

    A. True
    B. False

46. Why do we need good estimates?

    A. to correct poor estimating history.
    B. to give management confidence in estimates.
    C. to determine budget costs.
    D. to provide work for good estimators.

47. What are estimating objectives? (Answer one or more.)

    A. to determine the time sequence of expenditures.
    B. to keep project costs from increasing.
    C. to provide input to the scheduling process.
    D. to give management confidence in estimates.

48. What does the estimate control?

    A. costs
    B. schedule
    C. productivity
    D. quantities
    E. all of the above
    F. none of the above

49. What are the functions of the Project Estimating Group? (Answer one or more.)

    A. to do all estimating.
    B. to review and analyze contractor estimates.
    C. to provide technical direction and coordination of estimating activities.
    D. to provide estimating support to all departments, as required.

50. What are Project Estimating prerequisites for doing a detailed project estimate?

    A. contractual requirements to do the estimate.
    B. detailed written scope document agreed to by top management.
    C. milestone summary schedule.
    D. availability of estimating personnel.
    E. all of the above.

51. Which of the following items must be evaluated in developing an estimate work plan with the contractor? (Answer one or more.)

    A. in-house requirements for information
    B. results of quantity take-offs
    C. scope of estimate
    D. productivity assumptions

52. Which portions of an estimate are usually developed internally rather than by the contractor? (Answer one or more.)

    A. major equipment pricing
    B. builders risk insurance
    C. cost of money
    D. temporary construction facilities
    E. labor costs

53. Management considers the most important output of an estimate to be:

    A. total cost.
    B. bid comparison estimates.
    C. defined scope base.
    D. control base for field.

54. Which of the following are characteristics of Estimated Value of Uncertainty?

    A. the magnitude and timing of costs are unknown.
    B. the overall risk is low.
    C. sufficient scope definition is available.
    D. occurrence is probable.
    E. all of the above.

55. What is required to determine the Estimated Value of Uncertainty?

    A. crystal ball
    B. knowledge
    C. experience
    D. judgement
    E. details of estimate

56. In general, why does any management lack confidence in estimates?

    A. lack of good estimators
    B. lack of understanding
    C. bad estimates by contractors

57. Which of the following are types of estimates that Project Estimating will be involved in?

    A. definitive estimates
    B. conceptual estimates
    C. budget estimates
    D. order of magnitude estimates
    E. A, B and D, but not C

58. Key factors that govern *how* an estimate will be prepared are:

    A. end use of the estimate.
    B. tools available.
    C. time available.
    D. information available.
    E. all of the above.

59. What is contingency?

    A. money to cover costs which, based on past experience, are likely to be encountered but difficult or impossible to qualify at the time the estimate is prepared.
    B. money to cover uncertainties in the estimate within the defined scope and schedule.
    C. money to cover changes in scope.
    D. the Project Manager's fund.

60. Which of the following are elements of cost control?

    A. estimates, commitments, and corrective action.
    B. budgets, performance analysis, and corrective action.
    C. forecasts, performance analysis, and follow-up.
    D. performance analysis, corrective action, and follow-up.

61. Which of the following are *not* major judgement areas in a contractor's estimate? (Answer one or more.)

    A. quantities
    B. productivity
    C. escalation
    D. contingency
    E. none of the above

62. Which of the following are essential to a successful estimating department?

    A. the availability of computer estimating systems
    B. detail definition of project scope
    C. management recognition/support
    D. all of the above

63. "Work Sampling" is a technique that provides estimators with the following information: (Answer one or more.)

    A. a measure of actual productivity.
    B. a measure of labor effectiveness.
    C. a measure of schedule performance.
    D. a measure of time spent working vs. time spent not working.
    E. a measure of actual work vs. planned work.

64. Although "time lapse photograph" is primarily intended as a tool for management to view job progress, it also has several specific applications in regard to estimates. (Answer one or more.)

    A. it can show actual productivity for specific tasks.
    B. it can be used to evaluate material handling effectiveness.
    C. it can be used to evaluate schedule performance.
    D. it can show safety hazards.
    E. it can be used to identify poor supervision.

65. Unit rates for work performed on past jobs are commonly:

    A. averaged and used as a basis for current estimates.
    B. not useful since they contain all the errors of the previous work.
    C. disregarded since each job is different.
    D. adjusted by specific factors for use on current estimates.
    E. none of the above.

66. A power plant project is estimated to cost one billion dollars and take twelve million labor man-hours to construct. Ten percent allowance for contingency has been included in the estimate of cost. *Total* project man-hours are likely to be:

    A. less than twelve million
    B. between twelve and fifteen million
    C. between fifteen and twenty million
    D. over twenty million

67. Three 800 MW power plants in different parts of the country went into service in December, 1976. Plant A cost $200 million, Plant B cost $400 million and Plant C cost $600 million. What are the most likely reasons for the differences.

    A. labor productivity, wages, and supervision.
    B. quantities, schedule, and wages.
    C. scope, schedule, and labor productivity.
    D. owner imposed requirements, management, and equipment cost.

Author Index

Subject Index